Lecture Notes in Computer Science 4134

Commenced Publication in 1973
Founding and Former Series Editors:
Gerhard Goos, Juris Hartmanis, and Jan van Leeuwen

Kwangkeun Yi (Ed.)

Static Analysis

13th International Symposium, SAS 2006
Seoul, Korea, August 29-31, 2006
Proceedings

 Springer

Volume Editor

Kwangkeun Yi
Seoul National University
School of Computer Science and Engineering
Seoul 151-744, Korea
E-mail: kwang@ropas.snu.ac.kr

Library of Congress Control Number: 2006931004

CR Subject Classification (1998): D.3.2-3, F.3.1-2, D.2.8, F.4.2, D.1

LNCS Sublibrary: SL 2 – Programming and Software Engineering

ISSN   0302-9743
ISBN-10   3-540-37756-5 Springer Berlin Heidelberg New York
ISBN-13   978-3-540-37756-6 Springer Berlin Heidelberg New York

Springer is a part of Springer Science+Business Media

springer.com

© Springer-Verlag Berlin Heidelberg 2006

Typesetting: Camera-ready by author, data conversion by Scientific Publishing Services, Chennai, India
Printed on acid-free paper   SPIN: 11823230   06/3142   5 4 3 2 1 0

Preface

Static Analysis is increasingly recognized as a fundamental tool for program verification, bug detection, compiler optimization, program understanding, and software maintenance. The series of Static Analysis Symposia has served as the primary venue for presentation of theoretical, practical, and applicational advances in the area.

This volume contains the proceedings of the 13th International Static Analysis Symposium (SAS 2006), which was held 29-31 August 2006 at Seoul National University, Seoul, Korea. A total of 80 papers were submitted; the Program Committee held a 6-day long online discussion, during which they selected 23 papers. The selection was based on scientific quality, originality and relevance to the scope of SAS. Almost all submissions were reviewed by three (or more) PC members with the help of external reviewers.

In addition to the 23 accepted papers, this volume also contains abstracts of talks given by three invited speakers: Manuvir Das (Microsoft), Peter O'Hearn (Queen Mary, University of London), and Hongseok Yang (Seoul National University).

On behalf of the Program Committee, I would like to thank all of the authors who submitted papers. I would also like to thank the members of the Program Committee for their thorough reviews and dedicated involvement during the paper selection process, and all the external reviewers for their invaluable contributions. I would also like to thank the Steering Committee for their help and advice. Last but not least, I would like to thank Deokhwan Kim for his help in preparing this volume and in maintaining the on-line conference system, and Hyunjun Eo for the local arrangements.

June 2006   Kwangkeun Yi

Organization

Program Chair

Kwangkeun Yi   Seoul National University, Korea

Program Committee

Anindya Banerjee	Kansas State Univ., USA
Wei-Ngan Chin	National Univ. of Singapore, Singapore
Patrick Cousot	École Normale Supérieure, France
Roberto Giacobazzi	Univ. of Verona, Italy
Chris Hankin	Imperial College, UK)
Luddy Harrison	Univ. of Illinois at Urbana-Champaign, USA
Naoki Kobayashi	Tohoku Univ., Japan
Oukseh Lee	Hanyang Univ., Korea
Alan Mycroft	Univ. of Cambridge, UK
Kedar Namjoshi	Bell Labs., USA
Jens Palsberg	Univ. of California L.A., USA
Andreas Podelski	Max-Planck-Institut, Germany
Ganesan Ramalingam	IBM T.J.Watson Research, USA
Radu Rugina	Cornell Univ., USA
Harald Søndergaard	Univ. of Melbourne, Australia
Zhendong Su	Univ. of California Davis, USA
Reinhard Wilhelm	Univ. des Saarlandes, Germany

Steering Committee

Patrick Cousot	École Normale Supérieure, Paris, France
Giberto Filé	Univ. of Padova, Italy
David Schmidt	Kansas State Univ., USA

External Referees

Stefan Andrei	Julien Bertrane	Philppe Clauss
Roberto Bagnara	Silvia Breu	Christopher L. Conway
Joerg Bauer	Satish Chandra	Florin Craciun
Josh Berdine	Taehyoung Choi	Dennis Dams

Sponsoring Institutions

Seoul National University
Korea Information Science Society (KISS)
KISS Special Interest Group on Programming Languages (SIGPL)

In Memoriam: Alain Deutsch (1965-2006)

It is with great sadness that we must note the untimely death of Alain Deutsch, one of the foremost researchers in static analysis.

From 1988 to 1992, Alain conducted his PhD research at Ecole Polytechnique, under the direction of Christian Queinnec and Patrick Cousot. His thesis, entitled *Modèles Opérationnels de Langage de Programmation et Représentations de Relations sur des Langages Rationnnels avec Application à la Détermination Statique de Propriétés de Partages Dynamiques de Données*, was a landmark work, employing abstract interpretation, temporal logic, and formal-language theory to produce powerful aliasing and lifetime analyses for data structures of programs in higher-order languages. Alain's development of "storeless semantics," where rational trees and right-regular equivalence relations are used in place of environments and stores to give access-path semantics to data structures, initiated a line of research that continues to this day.

Following post-doctoral studies at Carnegie-Mellon University, Alain joined INRIA Rocquencourt in 1993, where he continued his research in static analysis and published seminal papers in the Principles of Programming Languages (POPL) and Programming Language Design and Implementation (PLDI) conferences. With Patrick Cousot, he jointly supervised the PhD research of Bruno Blanchet.

Alain is perhaps best known for his efforts at Polyspace Technologies Company; at the time of his death, he was Polyspace's Chief Technical Officer. The company was an outgrowth of a project conducted by Alain and his colleagues at INRIA in 1996, where Alain's techniques were applied to a post-mortem analysis of the software of the Ariane 501 rocket. Their successes at error detection for the 501 and validation of the software of its successor, the Ariane 502, inspired Alain and Daniel Pilaud in 1999 to co-found Polyspace, a company dedicated to development of verification and validation tools for on-board, real-time software. At Polyspace, Alain helped produce a family of sophisticated tools that analyze annotation-free software to validate correct behavior in variable initialization, array indexing, arithmetic, type casts, and pointer deferencing — all the classic problems addressed by static analysis researchers, handled all together. Polyspace's tool set has been used with great success by companies in the aerospace, automotive, medical instrument, and defense industries, and the company has grown from a group of ten to a multi-national corporation with offices in France and the United States.

Above all, Alain was a brilliant, incredibly hard working, friendly, sympathetic individual. He will not be forgotten.

Table of Contents

Invited Talk

Session 1

Session 2

Session 3

Invited Talk

Session 4

Invited Talk

Session 5

Session 6

Session 7

Unleashing the Power of Static Analysis

Manuvir Das

Program Analysis Group
Center for Software Excellence
Microsoft Corporation
manuvir@microsoft.com

The last few years have seen a surge of activity in the static analysis community on the application of static analysis to program verification and defect detection. Researchers have long believed in the benefit of exposing and fixing potential defects in a program before it is ever run, especially when the program can be made correct by construction, as in the case of compiler-enforced type systems. But every static analysis tool (other than a compiler's type checker) ever built, no matter how precise, suffers from the same fatal flaw in the eyes of the programmer: Defect reports do not come with known user scenarios that expose the defects. Therefore, programmers have been loathe to examine and fix defect reports produced by static analysis tools as a routine part of the software development process. In spite of recent advancements in analysis techniques, there are no papers we are aware of that report programmers fixing more than a few dozen defects.

Like many others, we at the Program Analysis group at Microsoft have spent the last few years building defect detection tools based on static analysis. For the last two years, we have focused our efforts on pushing these tools into the regular software development process of the largest products groups at Microsoft, involving thousands of developers working on tens of millions of lines of code against strict deadlines. Our goal was to answer the following question: If we do enough engineering on the tools, will a large group of programmers who build software for money adopt the tools? In other words, will programmers recognize the inherent preventive value of static analysis?

We are now in a position to answer this question. Programmers have fixed over 25,000 defects reported by our tools in the last 12 months, and they have added over 500,000 formal specifications of function pre-conditions and post-conditions to their programs. Today, many of our tools are enabled by default on the desktop machines of every programmer in the organization. Programmers only enter properly specified, defect-free code into the source code repository. Some of our tools are based on heavyweight global static analysis; these tools are run periodically in a centralized manner, and the defects identified by the tools are filed automatically into the defect database of the product.

In order to achieve this result, we have leaned heavily on advancements from the static analysis community, including but not limited to abstract interpretation [1], inter-procedural dataflow analysis [2], linear constraint solving, memory alias analysis [3], and modular analysis with formal specifications [4,5].

K. Yi (Ed.): SAS 2006, LNCS 4134, pp. 1–2, 2006.

We have used these ideas to build a suite of static analysis tools that includes: A global inter-procedural symbolic evaluator (PREfix [6]) for detecting memory usage errors; a global inter-procedural path-sensitive dataflow analysis (ESP [7,8]) for detecting security vulnerabilities and concurrency defects; a local intra-procedural abstract interpretation with widening and linear constraint solving (espX [9]) for detecting buffer overruns; a global inter-procedural dataflow analysis (SALinfer [9]) for inferring function pre-conditions and post-conditions; and a formal language of function specifications (SAL [9]) that is understood and enforced by all of our tools. SAL is now available to programmers at large via the Visual Studio compiler and various developer kits that are released periodically by Microsoft.

Along the way, we have learnt important lessons about what it takes to convince programmers to adopt static analysis tools, and which areas of static analysis research would be of the most benefit to software developers.

References

1. P. Cousot and R. Cousot. Abstract interpretation: A unified lattice model for static analysis of programs by construction or approximation of fixpoints. In *Proceedings of the ACM Symposium on Principles of Programming Languages (POPL)*, 1977.
2. Thomas Reps, Susan Horwitz, and Mooly Sagiv. Precise interprocedural data flow analysis via graph reachability. In *Proceedings of the ACM Symposium on Principles of Programming Languages (POPL)*, 1995.
3. Manuvir Das. Unification-based pointer analysis with directional assignments. In *ACM SIGPLAN 2000 Conference on Programming Language Design and Implementation (PLDI)*, 2000.
4. C. Flanagan, K. R. M. Leino, M. Lillibridge, G. Nelson, J. B. Saxe, and R. Stata. Extended Static Checking for Java. In *Proceedings of the ACM SIGPLAN 2002 Conference on Programming Language Design and Implementation*, 2002.
5. Nurit Dor, Michael Rodeh, and Mooly Sagiv. CSSV: Towards a realistic tool for statically detecting all buffer overflows in C. In *Proceedings of the SIGPLAN 2003 Conference on Programming Language Design and Implementation*, 2003.
6. William R. Bush, Jonathan D. Pincus, and David J. Sielaff. A static analyzer for finding dynamic programming errors. *Software - Practice and Experience*, 30(7):775–802, 2000.
7. Manuvir Das, Sorin Lerner, and Mark Seigle. ESP: Path-sensitive program verification in polynomial time. In *ACM SIGPLAN 2002 Conference on Programming Language Design and Implementation (PLDI)*, 2002.
8. Nurit Dor, Stephen Adams, Manuvir Das, and Zhe Yang. Software validation via scalable path-sensitive value flow analysis. In *Proceedings of the International Symposium on Software Testing and Analysis (ISSTA)*, 2004.
9. Brian Hackett, Manuvir Das, Daniel Wang, and Zhe Yang. Modular checking of buffer overflows in the large. In *28th International Conference on Software Engineering*, 2006.

Static Analysis in Disjunctive Numerical Domains

Sriram Sankaranarayanan, Franjo Ivančić, Ilya Shlyakhter, and Aarti Gupta

NEC Laboratories America,
4 Independence Way, Princeton, NJ

Abstract. The convexity of numerical domains such as polyhedra, octagons, intervals and linear equalities enables tractable analysis of software for buffer overflows, null pointer dereferences and floating point errors. However, convexity also causes the analysis to fail in many common cases. Powerset extensions can remedy this shortcoming by considering disjunctions of predicates. Unfortunately, analysis using powerset domains can be exponentially more expensive as compared to analysis on the base domain. In this paper, we prove structural properties of fixed points computed in commonly used powerset extensions. We show that a fixed point computed on a powerset extension is also a fixed point in the base domain computed on an "elaboration" of the program's CFG structure. Using this insight, we build analysis algorithms that approach path sensitive static analysis algorithms by performing the fixed point computation on the base domain while discovering an "elaboration" on the fly. Using restrictions on the nature of the elaborations, we design algorithms that scale polynomially in terms of the number of disjuncts. We have implemented a light-weight static analyzer for C programs with encouraging initial results.

1 Introduction

Static analysis over numerical domains has been used to check programs for buffer overflows, null pointer references and other violations such as division by zero and floating point errors [26,4,12]. Numerical domains such as intervals, octagons and polyhedra maintain information about the set of possible values of integer and real-valued program variables along with their inter-relationships. The *convexity* of these domains makes the analysis tractable. On the other hand, fundamental limitations arising out of convexity leads to imprecision in the analysis, ultimately yielding many false alarms. Elimination of these false alarms is achieved through *path-sensitive analysis* by means of disjunctive domains obtained through powerset extensions. Such extensions can be constructed systematically from the base domain using standard techniques [14,8].

Powerset extensions of numerical domains consider a disjunction of predicates at each program location. While the presence of these disjuncts helps surmount convexity limitations, the complexity of the analysis can be exponentially higher due to more complex domain operations and also due to the large number of

K. Yi (Ed.): SAS 2006, LNCS 4134, pp. 3–17, 2006.

disjuncts that can be produced during the course of the analysis. Furthermore, the presence of disjuncts requires special techniques to lift the widening from the base domain up to the disjunctive domain [2].

Controlling the production of disjuncts during the course of the analysis is one of the key aspects of managing the complexity of the analysis. The design of such strategies can be performed by techniques that annotate data flow objects by partial trace information such as *trace partitioning* [21,16], and other path-sensitive data-flow analysis techniques that implicitly manage complexity by joining predicates only when the property to be proved remains unchanged as a result [11], or "semantically" by careful domain construction [20,2].

In this paper, we first show that fixed points computed over powerset extensions correspond to fixed points over the base domain computed on an "elaboration" of the CFG. As a result, the complexity of flow-sensitive analysis can also be controlled by means of a strategy for producing elaborations of the CFG being analyzed. We consider analysis techniques that perform the fixed point iteration hand in hand with the construction of the elaboration that characterizes the fixed point. As an application, we consider *bounded elaborations*, that correspond to power-set extensions wherein the number of disjuncts in each abstract object is bounded by a fixed number K. We discuss the implementation our ideas in a light weight static analyzer for the C language as a part of the F-Soft project [18] and demonstrate promising results.

This paper is organized as follows: Section 2 presents preliminary concepts of abstract interpretation and presents numerical domains along with their limitations. Powerset extensions are presented in Section 3. Section 4 presents the notion of an elaboration and techniques for constructing an elaboration while performing the analysis. Section 5 describes our implementation and results over some benchmark programs.

2   Preliminaries

We present basic notions of abstract interpretation and numerical domains.

Programs and Invariants

Since the paper focuses on static analysis over numerical domains, we may regard programs as purely ranging over integer or real-valued variables. Let $V = \{x_1, \ldots, x_n\}$ denote integer-valued program variables, collectively referred to as $\boldsymbol{x}$. The program operations over these variables include numerical operations such as addition and multiplication. We shall assume first-order predicates over the program state belonging to an appropriate language. Given such a predicate ψ, the set of valuations to $\boldsymbol{x}$ satisfying ψ is denoted $[\![\psi]\!]$. A program is represented by its *Control-flow graph*(CFG).

Definition 1 (Control-flow Graphs (CFGs)). *Formally, a CFG is a tuple* $\Pi : \langle V, L, \mathcal{T}, \ell_0, \Theta \rangle$:

- *L: a set of locations (cutpoints);*
- *T: a set of transitions (edges), where each transition $\tau : \ell_i \to \ell_j$ is an edge between the pre-location ℓ_i and a post-location ℓ_j. Each transition models the changes in the values of program variables using a transition relation.*
- *$\ell_0 \in L$: the initial location; Θ is an assertion over $\boldsymbol{x}$ representing the initial condition.*

A state s of the program maps each variable x_i to an integer value $s(x_i)$. Let Σ denote the set of program states. The relational semantics of a transition can be modeled using the notion of a (concrete) post condition:

Definition 2 (Post Condition). *Let $S \subseteq \Sigma$ be a set of states. The (concrete) post condition $S' : post_\Sigma(S, \tau)$ across a transition τ is a set of states $S' \subseteq \Sigma$. The post condition models the effect(s) of executing τ on each state satisfying S.*

An assertion ψ over $\boldsymbol{x}$ is an *invariant* of a CFG at a location ℓ iff it is satisfied by every state reachable at ℓ. An *assertion map* associates each location of a CFG with a predicate. An assertion map η is *invariant* if $\eta(\ell)$ is an invariant, for each $\ell \in L$. Invariants are established using the *inductive assertions method* due to Floyd and Hoare [13,17].

Definition 3 (Inductive Assertion Maps). *An assertion map η is inductive iff it satisfies the following conditions:*

Initiation: $[\![\Theta]\!] \subseteq [\![\eta(\ell_0)]\!]$,
Consecution: *For each transition $\tau : \ell_i \to \ell_j$,*

$$post_\Sigma([\![\eta(\ell_i)]\!], \tau) \subseteq [\![\eta(\ell_j)]\!] .$$

It is well known that any inductive assertion map is invariant. However, the converse need not be true. The standard technique for proving an assertion invariant is to find an inductive assertion that strengthens it.

Abstract Interpretation

Abstract interpretation [7] is a generic technique for computing inductive assertions of CFGs using an iterative process. In order to compute an inductive map, we start from an initial map and repeatedly weaken the predicates mapped at each location to converge to a *fixed point*. The assertions labeling each location can be shown to be inductive when the fixed point is reached.

Abstract Domain. In order to carry out an abstract interpretation, we define an *abstract domain* along with some operations on the elements of the abstract domain known as the *domain operations*. Informally, an abstract domain is a lattice of predicates Γ over the program state including the assertions $\top$ and $\bot$ representing *true* and *false* respectively. The domain is defined by the abstract lattice $\langle \Gamma, \models \rangle$ and the concrete lattice of sets of program states ordered by inclusion $\langle 2^\Sigma, \subseteq \rangle$ along with the abstraction function $\alpha : 2^\Sigma \mapsto \Gamma$ and the concretization (or the meaning) function $\gamma : \Gamma \mapsto 2^\Sigma$. A key requirement is that α, γ form a *Galois connection* (see [7,9] for comprehensive surveys). The abstract domain operations include:

Join. Given $d_1, \ldots, d_m \in \Gamma$, their join $d : d_1 \sqcup \ldots \sqcup d_m \in \Gamma$ satisfies $d_i \models d$.

Meet (Intersection). Given $d_1, \ldots, d_m \in \Gamma$, their meet $d : d_1 \sqcap \ldots \sqcap d_m$ satisfies $d \models d_i$.

Post-Condition. Given $d \in \Gamma$ and a transition τ, its abstract post condition $d' : post_\Gamma(d, \tau)$ satisfies

$$post_\Sigma(\gamma(d), \tau) \subseteq \gamma(post_\Gamma(d, \tau)).$$

Note that if the abstract domain is clear from context, we may drop the subscript from the abstract post condition.

Inclusion Test. Given objects d_1 and d_2, decide if $d_1 \models d_2$.

Widening. Given $d_1, d_2 \in \Gamma$ such that $d_1 \models d_2$, their widening $d : d_1 \nabla d_2$ over-approximates the join, i.e., $d_1 \sqcup d_2 \models d$. Repeated applications of widening on an increasing sequence of abstract objects, guarantees convergence to a fixed point in a finite number of iterations.

Other operations of interest include *projection*, which is commonly used to eliminate variables that are out of scope in inter-procedural analysis and the *weakest precondition*, which may be used to refine the abstraction in case of failure to prove a property.

Forward Propagation. An abstract assertion map $\eta : L \mapsto \Gamma$ labels each CFG location ℓ with an abstract object $\eta(\ell) \in \Gamma$. An abstract assertion map η is inductive iff the map $\gamma \circ \eta$ is an inductive assertion map. Given a CFG Π along with an abstract domain Γ, *forward propagation* seeks to construct an inductive abstract assertion map, iteratively as follows:

Initial Step. The initial map $\eta^{(0)}$ is defined as follows:

$$\eta^{(0)}(\ell_0) = \begin{cases} \Theta, & \ell = \ell_0, \\ \bot, & \text{otherwise.} \end{cases}$$

Iterative Step. The iterative step computes the join of the current assertion at a location ℓ with the post-condition of all its incoming transitions

$$\eta^{(i+1)}(\ell) = \eta^{(i)}(\ell) \sqcup \bigsqcup_{\tau_j : \ell_j \to \ell} post_\Gamma(\eta^{(i)}(\ell_j), \tau_j).$$

For convenience, we denote this as $\eta^{(i+1)} = \mathfrak{F}(\eta^{(i)})$. Note that $\mathfrak{F}$ is *monotonic* w.r.t $\models$, i.e., $\eta^{(i)}(\ell) \models \eta^{(i+1)}(\ell)$ for all $\ell \in L$.

Convergence. Convergence occurs if $\eta^{(i+1)}(\ell) \models \eta^{(i)}(\ell)$ for each $\ell \in L$.

For the sake of simplicity, we do not consider the use of narrowing to improve the fixed point in this discussion. Given an initial map $\eta^{(0)}$, forward propagation computes $\eta^{(i+1)}$ iteratively as $\mathfrak{F}(\eta^{(i)})$ until convergence $\eta^{(i+1)}(\ell) \models \eta^{(i)}(\ell)$. Such a map is a *fixed point* w.r.t $\mathfrak{F}$. It can be shown that a fixed point map is also inductive. Hence, if the forward propagation converges, it results in an inductive assertion at each cutpoint. Convergence is guaranteed in finitely many iterative steps if the domain satisfies the *ascending chain condition*. Examples of such domains include finite domains and notably the domain of linear equalities [19]. On the other hand, domains such as intervals and polyhedra do not satisfy this condition. Hence, the widening operation ∇ is used repeatedly to force convergence in finitely many steps.

Numerical Domains. Numerical domains such as intervals, octagons and polyhedra reason about the values of integer or real-valued program variables. These domains are widely used to check programs for buffer-overflows, null pointer dereferences, division-by-zero, floating point instabilities [4].

The *interval domain* consists of interval predicates of the form $\bigwedge_i x_i \in [l_i, u_i]$ with the possibility of open intervals. The complexity of the domain operations is linear in the number of variables. Analysis techniques for this domain have been widely studied [6,22]. The *octagon domain* due to Miné consists of assertions of the form $\bigwedge \pm x_i \pm x_j \leq c$ along with interval constraints over the variables. The nature of the constraints in this domain permits a graphical representation and the computation of many domain operations using the shortest path algorithm as a primitive. The operations in this domain are at most cubic in the number of variables. The polyhedral domain consists of convex polyhedra over the program variables represented by constraints of the form $\bigwedge a_0 + a_1 x_1 + \cdots + a_n x_n \geq 0$ [10,15]. Domain operations over this domain are expensive (exponential space in the size of the polyhedra). However, relaxations of the operations and the structure of the constraints in the domain can yield polynomial time approximations to these operations [25,24,23,5].

One of the key properties of these domains is that of *convexity*. Convexity makes the domain operations tractable. However, it also limits the ability of these domains to represent sets of states. For instance, consider a convex predicate including states A and B represented as points x_1, x_2 in $\mathcal{R}^n$. Such a predicate necessarily includes states that lie on the line joining these two points. In many cases, the reachable states of a program form a non convex set in $\mathcal{R}^n$. Therefore, convex abstract domains cannot represent such sets without the addition of spurious states. Such a drawback leads to cases wherein the domain is fundamentally unable to compute an invariant that proves the property of interest.

Example 1. Figure 1 shows a program that stores the result of a condition $0 \leq i \leq 9$ in a variable x. The table to the right shows the invariants computed after each labeled location. Note that the invariant $i \leq 9$, required at L4 to prove the absence of overflows, cannot be established. Although the program is free from overflows, convex numerical domains will not be able to establish correctness.

Powerset extensions are used to remedy the problem of convexity.

3   Powerset Extensions

Given a base abstract domain of predicates, a *powerset extension* of the domain consists of disjunctions of the base domain predicates.

```
int a[10]
if  (i ≥ 0 ∧ i ≤ 9)  then
    L1: x := 1
else
    L2: x := 0
end if
L3: · · ·
if  x = 1 then
    L4: a[i] := · · ·
end if
```

Location	Invariant
L1	$i \geq 0 \wedge i \leq 9 \wedge x = 1$
L2	$x = 0$
L3	$0 \leq x \wedge x \leq 1$
L4	$x = 1$

Fig. 1. Example program (left) and the polyhedral invariants (right)

Definition 4 (Powerset extension). *A powerset extension of an abstract domain* $\langle \Gamma, \models \rangle$ *is given by the domain* $\langle \hat{\Gamma}, \widehat{\models} \rangle$ *such that*

$$\hat{\Gamma} = \{S : \langle d_1, \ldots, d_m \rangle \mid d_i \in \Gamma, \ m \geq 0\} \ .$$

The concretization function $\hat{\gamma}$ for a powerset extension is defined as $\hat{\gamma}(S) = \bigcup_{d \in S} \gamma(d)$. The abstraction function $\hat{\alpha}(X)$ can be defined in many ways, for instance $\hat{\alpha}(X) = \{\alpha(X)\}$. The ordering relation $\widehat{\models}$ may be defined in many ways to derive different extensions. However, any such definition needs to be faithful to the semantics induced by $\hat{\gamma}$, i.e. if $S_1 \widehat{\models} S_2$ then $\hat{\gamma}(S_1) \subseteq \hat{\gamma}(S_2)$.

Extending Partial Orders. The *natural powerset extension* is obtained by considering $\langle \hat{\Gamma}, \models_N \rangle$ such that $S_1 \models_N S_2$ iff $\hat{\gamma}(S_1) \subseteq \hat{\gamma}(S_2)$. This is the partial order induced by the concrete domain on the abstract domain through $\hat{\gamma}$. The *Hoare powerset extension* $\models_P$ is a partial order defined as follows:

$$S_1 \models_P S_2 \iff (\forall d_1 \in S_1) \, (\exists d_2 \in S_2) \, d_1 \models d_2 \ .$$

Informally, we require that every object in S_1 be "covered" by some object in S_2. This can be refined to yield a *Egli-Milner type* partial order $\models_{EM}$ [1,2]

$$S_1 \models_{EM} S_2 \iff S_1 = \emptyset \text{ or } (S_1 \models_P S_2 \text{ and } (\forall \, d_2 \in S_2) \, (\exists \, d_1 \in S_1) \, d_1 \models d_2) \ .$$

In addition to $S_1 \models_P S_2$, each element in S_2 must cover some element in S_1.

Example 2. Consider the interval domain $\langle I, \sqsubseteq \rangle$ over variable x_1. Let $S_1 = \{\varphi_1 : x_1 \in [0, 1]\}$ and $S_2 = \{x_1 \in [\frac{1}{2}, 2], x_1 \in [-1, \frac{1}{2}]\}$. It is easily seen that $S_1 \sqsubseteq_N S_2$, however $S_1 \not\sqsubseteq_P S_2$ since each element of S_2 is incomparable with φ_1.

On the other hand let $S_3 = \{\xi_1 : x_1 \in [0, 2], \xi_2 : x_1 \in [-1, 0]\}$. Note that $S_1 \sqsubseteq_P S_3$ since $\varphi_1 \sqsubseteq \xi_1$. On the other hand ξ_2 does not cover any object in S_1, hence $S_1 \not\sqsubseteq_{EM} S_3$.

Consider the interval domain $\langle I, \sqsubseteq \rangle$ of conjunctions of closed, open and half-open intervals over the program variables and its natural powerset extension $\langle \hat{I}, \sqsubseteq_N \rangle$. It is well-known that deciding the $\sqsubseteq_N$ relation is computationally hard.

Theorem 1. *Given $S_1, S_2 \in \hat{I}$, deciding if $S_1 \sqsubseteq_N S_2$ is co-NP-hard.*

The proof is essentially a direct translation from the universality checking problem for DNF propositional formulas and holds on many abstract domains (including many finite domains). Specifically, $\models_N$ is hard for numerical domains such as intervals, octagons and polyhedra. Other partial orders $\models_P$ and $\models_{EM}$ are easier to compute using $O(|S_1| + |S_2|)^2$ base domain ($\models$) comparisons.

The domain operations in a powerset domain can be defined by suitably lifting the base domain operations. Notably, set union defines a valid join operator. The meet operation $S_1 \hat{\sqcap} S_2$ is given by the pairwise meet of elements from S_1, S_2. Post condition is computed element-wise; i.e., if $S = \{d_1, \ldots, d_k\} \in \hat{I}$, $\widehat{post}(S, \tau) = \{post(d_1, \tau), \ldots, post(d_k, \tau)\}$.

Widening operations can be obtained as extensions of the widening on the base domain using carefully crafted strategies [2]. The use of such widening operators frequently results in fixed points which satisfy inclusion using the $\models_P$ or even the $\models_{EM}$ ordering. Thus, even if a domain were designed to use joins over a stronger partial order, the final fixed point obtained may be over $\models_P$ or the $\models_{EM}$ ordering.

Example 3. Consider the program below:

$s := -1$
while $\cdots$ **do**
$\quad s := -s$ { Invariant: $(s = 1 \lor s = -1)$ }
end while

The invariant $s = 1 \lor s = -1$ is a fixed point in the powerset extension of the interval domain using the $\sqsubseteq_P$ ordering.

CFG Elaboration

We now prove a simple connection between the fixed point obtained on a domain $\langle \hat{I}, \models_P \rangle$ using forward propagation on a CFG Π and the fixed point in the base domain using the notion of an *"elaboration"*. Intuitively, an elaboration of a CFG replicates each location of the CFG multiple times. Each such replication preserves all the outgoing transitions from the original location.

Definition 5. *Consider CFGs $\Pi_e : \langle L_e, \mathcal{T}_e, \ell'_0, \Theta \rangle$ and $\Pi : \langle L, \mathcal{T}, \ell_0, \Theta \rangle$ over the same set of variables V. The CFG Π_e is an* elaboration *of Π iff there exists a map $\rho : L_e \mapsto L$ such that*

- *The initial location in Π_e maps to the initial location of Π: $\rho(\ell'_0) = \ell_0$.*
- *Consider locations $\ell \in \Pi$ and $\ell_e \in \Pi_e$ such that $\rho(\ell_e) = \ell$. For each outgoing transition $\tau : \ell \to m \in \mathcal{T}$, there is an outgoing transition $\tau_e : \ell_e \to m_e \in \mathcal{T}_e$ such that $\rho(m_e) = m$. Furthermore every outgoing transition $\tau_e : \ell_e \to m_e \in \mathcal{T}_e$ is a replication of some transition $\tau : \rho(\ell_e) \to \rho(m_e) \in \mathcal{T}$.*

Each $\ell_e \in L_e$ is said to be a replication *of $\rho(\ell_e) \in L$. Note that every outgoing transition of $\rho(\ell_e)$ is replicated in ℓ_e. We denote the replication of the transition $\tau : \ell \to m$ starting from ℓ_e as $\tau(\ell_e) : \ell_e \to m_e$. An elaboration resembles a (structural) simulation relation between Π_e and Π.*

Example 4. The figure below shows a CFG Π from Example 3 along with an elaboration. The dashed line shows the relation ρ.

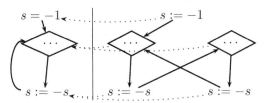

We shall now prove that every fixed point assertion map on a powerset domain $\langle \hat{\Gamma}, \models_P \rangle$ on a CFG Π corresponds to a fixed point in the base domain $\langle \Gamma, \models \rangle$ on some elaboration Π_e and vice-versa.

Definition 6 (Collapsing). *Let $\eta_e : L_e \mapsto \Gamma$ be an assertion map on the elaboration Π_e in the base domain. Its collapse $C(\eta_e)$ is a map on the original CFG Π, $L \mapsto \hat{\Gamma}$ such that for each $\ell \in L$,*

$$C(\eta_e)(\ell) = \{\eta(\ell_e) \mid \rho(\ell_e) = \ell\}.$$

The collapsing operator computes the disjunction of the domain objects at each replicated location.

Lemma 1. *If η_e is a fixed point map for Π_e in the domain $\langle \Gamma, \models \rangle$ then $C(\eta_e)$ is a fixed point map for Π in the domain $\langle \hat{\Gamma}, \models_P \rangle$.*

Proof. (Sketch) For convenience we denote $\eta_c = C(\eta_e)$. It suffices to show initiation $\Theta \models_P \eta_c(\ell_0)$ and consecution for each transition $\tau : \ell_i \to \ell_j$, we require $\widehat{post}(\eta_c(\ell_i), \tau) \models_P \eta_c(\ell_j)$. Initiation is obtained by noting that initial states must be replicated in an elaboration. Expanding the definition for LHS,

$$\widehat{post}(\eta_c(\ell_i), \tau) = \widehat{post}(\{\eta_e(\ell_e)|\rho(\ell_e) = \ell_i\}, \tau)$$
$$= \{post(\eta_e(\ell_e), \tau)|\rho(\ell_e) = \ell_i\}$$

Similarly the RHS is expanded $\eta_c(\ell_j) = \{\eta_e(\ell_e') \mid \rho(\ell_e') = \ell_e\}$. In order to show the containment, note that an elaboration requires that $\tau(\ell_{ie}) : \ell_{ie} \to \ell_{je}$ should be an outgoing transition for each replication ℓ_{ie} with $\rho(\ell_{ie}) = \ell_i$ and $\rho(\ell_{je}) = \ell_j$.

Using the fact that η_e is a fixed point map, we note that each element $post(\eta_e(\ell_{ie}), \tau)$ on the LHS is contained in the element $\eta_e(\ell_{je})$ from the RHS. □

Conversely, the fixed point in $\langle \hat{\Gamma}, \models_P \rangle$ induces an elaboration of the CFG.

Definition 7 (Induced Elaboration). *Let $\hat{\eta}$ be a fixed point map for Π in the domain $\langle \hat{\Gamma}, \models_P \rangle$. Such a fixed point induces an elaboration Π_e and a induced map η_e defined as follows:*

- *Locations: Let $\hat{\eta}(\ell) = \{d_1, \ldots, d_m\}$. The elaboration contains replicated locations $\langle \ell, 1 \rangle, \ldots, \langle \ell, m \rangle \in L_e$, one per disjunct such that $\rho(\langle \ell, j \rangle) = \ell$. Also, $\eta_e(\langle \ell, j \rangle) = d_j$.*

– *Transitions: For each transition $\tau : \ell_i \rightarrow \ell_j$ we require an outgoing transition $\tau(\ell_i, k) : \langle \ell_i, k \rangle \rightarrow \langle \ell_j, l \rangle$ for some l. The target index l is defined using the proof of consecution of $\hat{\eta}$ under τ: $\widehat{post}(\hat{\eta}(\ell_i), \tau) \models_P \hat{\eta}(\ell_j)$.*
Let $\hat{\eta}(\ell_i) = \{d_1, \ldots, d_m\}$ and $\eta(\ell_j) = \{e_1, \ldots, e_n\}$ (Note that we may represent the empty set equivalently by the singleton $\{\perp\}$). We require

$$\widehat{post}(\{d_1, \ldots, d_m\}, \tau) \models_P \{e_1, \ldots, e_n\}.$$

However, $\widehat{post}(\{d_1, \ldots, d_m\}, \tau) = \{post(d_1, \tau), \ldots, post(d_m, \tau)\}$. By definition of $\models_P$ order, we require for each k,

$$(\forall\, k \in [1, m])(\exists\, l \in [1, n])\ post(d_k, \tau) \models e_l.$$

Therefore, we set $\tau(\ell_i, k) : \langle \ell_i, k \rangle \rightarrow \langle \ell_j, l \rangle$. It immediately follows that η_e satisfies consecution for this transition in the base domain $\langle \Gamma, \models \rangle$. Note that since the choice of a target index l is not unique, there may be many induced elaborations for a given assertion map.

Example 5. The elaboration shown in Example 4 is induced by the fixed point shown in Example 3.

Lemma 2. *Given a fixed point map η_c for Π in the domain $\left\langle \hat{\Gamma}, \models_P \right\rangle$, its induced map η_e is a fixed point for the induced elaboration Π_e in the base domain $\langle \Gamma, \models \rangle$.*

Proof. The proof follows from the definition above.

Thus, elaborations are structural connections among the disjuncts of the final fixed point made explicit using a syntactic representation. In fact, interesting structural connections can be defined for powerset domains with other partial orders such as $\models_{EM}$, and even the $\models_N$ order for certain domains. Making these connections explicit enables us to get around the hardness of checking $\models_N$ in these domains. We defer the details to an extended version of this paper.

4   On-the-Fly Elaborations

In the previous section, we have demonstrated a close connection between fixed points in a class of powerset domains and the fixed point in the base domain computed on a structural elaboration of the original CFG. As a result, analysis in powerset domains can be reduced to the process of an analysis on the base domain carried out on some CFG elaboration. As a caveat, we observe that even though it is possible to find some elaboration that produces the same fixed point as in the powerset extension with some widening operator, an *a priori* fixed elaboration scheme may not be able to produce the same fixed point.

In order to realize the full potential of a powerset extension, the process of producing an elaboration of the CFG needs to be dynamic, by considering *partial elaborations* of the CFG as the analysis progresses. Such a scheme can also be seen as a powerset extension wherein the containment relations between the individual disjuncts in a predicate are explicitly depicted.

Partial Elaboration. A partial elaboration $\langle \Pi_e, U \rangle$ of a CFG $\Pi : \langle L, \mathcal{T}, \ell_0 \rangle$ is a tuple consisting of a CFG $\Pi_e : \langle L_e, \mathcal{T}_e, \ell_{0e} \rangle$ and an *unresolved* set $U \subseteq L_e \times \mathcal{T}$ of pairs, each consisting of a location from Π_e and a transition from Π.

As with a CFG elaboration, each location $\ell_e \in \Pi_e$ is a replication of some location $\rho(\ell_e) \in \Pi$. Furthermore, for each transition $\tau : \ell_i \rightarrow \ell_j \in \Pi$ and each $\ell_{ie} \in L_e$ replicating ℓ_i, exactly one of the following holds:

- There exists a replicated transition $\tau(\ell_{ie}) : \ell_{ie} \rightarrow \ell_{je} \in \mathcal{T}_e$, or else,
- $\langle \ell_{ie}, \tau \rangle \in U$.

In other words, U contains all the outgoing transitions of Π which have not been replicated in a given location of Π_e. A partial elaboration is a (complete) elaboration iff $U = \emptyset$. Given a CFG Π, an *initial* partial elaboration Π_e^0 is given by $L_e^0 = \{\ell_0\}$, $\mathcal{T}_e = \emptyset$ and $U = \{\langle \ell_0, \tau \rangle \mid \tau : \ell_0 \rightarrow \ell_i\}$; in other words, the initial location of Π is replicated exactly once and all its outgoing transitions are unresolved. Two basic transformations are permitted on a partial elaboration:

Location Addition: We add a new location ℓ_{ie} to L_e replicating some node $\rho(\ell_{ie}) \in L$, i.e., $L_e' = L_e \cup \{\ell_{ie}\}$. Furthermore, all transitions in $\mathcal{T}$ outgoing from ℓ_i are treated as unresolved, i.e., $U' = U \cup \{\langle \ell_{ie}, \tau \rangle \mid \tau : \rho(\ell_{ie}) \rightarrow \ell_j\}$.

Transition Resolution: Given a pair $\langle \ell_{ie}, \tau : \ell_i \rightarrow \ell_j \rangle \in U$, we replicate τ in Π_e as $\tau(\ell_{ie}) : \ell_{ie} \rightarrow \ell_{je}$ for some replication ℓ_{je} of the target location ℓ_j.

Our analysis at each stage consists of a partial elaboration $\left\langle \Pi_e^{(i)}, U^{(i)} \right\rangle$ along with an abstract assertion map $\eta^{(i)} : L_e \mapsto \Gamma$. Each iteration involves an update to the map $\eta^{(i)}$ followed by an update to the partial elaboration.

Consider an unresolved entry $\langle \ell_e, \tau : \ell_i \rightarrow \ell_j \rangle \in U^{(i)}$. Its resolution involves the choice of a target node ℓ_{je} replicating ℓ_j. Let $d : post(\eta^{(i)}(\ell_{ie}), \tau)$ denote the result of the post condition of the unresolved transition. Furthermore, let $\ell_{(j,1)}, \ldots, \ell_{(j,m)} \in L_e$ denote the existing replications of the target location ℓ_j and $d_k = \eta^{(i)}(\ell_{(j,k)})$ denote the kth disjunct. The choice of a target location for the transition $\tau(\ell_{ie})$ depends on the post condition d and the assertions $d_1, \ldots, d_m$. The target can either be chosen from the existing target replications $\ell_{(j,1)}, \ldots, \ell_{(j,m)}$, or a new node $\ell_{(j,m+1)}$ can be added as a new replication of the target. We shall assume a *merging heuristic* $\mathsf{MergeHeuristic}(d, \langle d_1, \ldots, d_m \rangle)$ to compute the index i s.t. $1 \leq i \leq m+1$ for the target location of the transition.

Formally, at each step we first update the map $\eta^{(i)} = \mathfrak{F}(\eta^{(i-1)})$ as described in Section 2. The partial elaboration $\left\langle \Pi_e^{(i)}, U^{(i)} \right\rangle$ is then refined by first choosing an unresolved pair $\langle \ell_{ie}, \tau : \ell_i \rightarrow \ell_j \rangle \in U$, and then applying a merging heuristic

$$\ell_{j,*} = \mathsf{MergeHeuristic}\left(post(\eta^{(i)}(\ell_{ie}), \tau), \left\langle \eta^{(i)}(\ell_{je}) \mid \ell_{je} \text{ replicates } \ell_j \right\rangle \right).$$

The transition $\tau(\ell_{ie})$ is resolved as a result, and the entry $\langle \ell_{ie}, \tau \rangle$ is removed from $U^{(i)}$. If the merging heuristic results in a new location $\ell_{j,*}$, then new entries are added to $U^{(i)}$ to reflect unresolved outgoing transitions from the newly added location. If there are no more unresolved pairs in $U^{(i+1)}$, the partial elaboration is also a full elaboration. Thenceforth, the map η is simply propagated on this elaboration until fixed point is reached.

Upon termination, we guarantee that $U^{(i)} = \emptyset$, i.e., the partial elaboration is a full elaboration and the map $\eta^{(i)}$ is a fixed point map on this elaboration. Termination of the scheme depends mainly on the nature of the merging heuristic chosen. Since a transition from U is resolved at each step, termination is guaranteed as long as the creation of new locations ceases at some point in the analysis. A simple way to ensure this requirement is to bound the number of replications of each location to a prespecified limit $K > 0$.

Merging Heurstics. Formally a merging heuristic MergeHeuristic $(d, \langle d_1, \ldots, d_m \rangle)$ chooses an index $1 \leq i \leq m+1 \leq K$ in order to compute the join $d_i \sqcup d$ if $i \leq m$ or create a new location in the partial elaboration as described above. The key goal of a merging heuristic is that the resulting join add as few extraneous concrete states as possible. Such extraneous states arise since the join is but an approximation of the disjunction of concrete states: $\gamma(d_1) \cup \gamma(d_2) \subseteq \gamma(d_1 \sqcup d_2)$.

In numerical domains, the states of the program can be viewed as points in $\mathcal{R}^n$. It is possible to correlate the extraneous concrete states with a distance metric on the abstract objects. Let $k(d, d')$ be a distance metric defined on Γ and $\alpha \in \mathcal{R}$ be a *distance cutoff*. Let $d_{\min} = \text{argmin}\{k(d, d_i) | 1 \leq i \leq m\}$ be the "closest" abstract object to d w.r.t k. The merging heuristic induced by k, α is defined as

$$\text{MergeHeuristic}\,(d, \langle d_1, \ldots, d_m \rangle) = \begin{cases} d_{m+1}, & m < K \ \text{ and } k(d, d_{\min}) \geq \alpha \\ d_{\min}, & m = K \ \text{or } k(d, d_{\min}) < \alpha \end{cases}$$

In other words, a new location is spawned whenever it is possible to do so (i.e., $m < K$) and the closest object is farther than α apart in terms of distance. Failing these, the closest object is chosen as the target of the unresolved transition. The cutoff α ensures that newly formed disjuncts are initially well separated from the others in terms of the metric k.

The *Hausdorff distance*, is a commonly used measure of distance between two sets. Given $P, Q \subseteq \mathcal{R}^n$, their Hausdorff distance is defined as

$$\text{Hausdorff}(P, Q) = max_{\boldsymbol{x} \in P}\{min_{\boldsymbol{y} \in Q} \ \{ \ ||\boldsymbol{x} - \boldsymbol{y}|| \}\} \,.$$

While such metrics provide a good measure of the accuracy of the join, they are hard to compute. We shall use a range-based Hausdorff distance metric.

Range Distance Metric. Let $x_1, \ldots, x_n$ be the program variables and d_1, d_2 be abstract objects. For each variable x_i, we shall compute ranges $I_1 : [p_1, q_1]$ and $I_2 : [p_2, q_2]$ of the values of x_i. Such ranges may be efficiently computed for most numerical domains including the polyhedral domain by resorting to linear programming. The ranges are said to be *incompatible* if one of the two intervals is open in a direction where the other interval is closed, i.e., their Hausdorff distance is unbounded (∞). If the ranges are compatible, the Hausdorff distance is computed based on their end points. The overall distance is a lexicographic tuple $\langle m, s \rangle$ where m is the number of dimensions along which d_1, d_2 have incompatible ranges while s is the sum of the distances along the compatible dimensions.

Example 6. Consider the polyhedra $p_1 : 1 \leq x \leq 5 \wedge y \geq 0$ and $p_2 : -1 \leq y \leq 1 \wedge 10 \leq x \leq 20$. The ranges along x, $[1, 5]$ and $[10, 20]$ have a Hausdorff distance of 9. On the other hand the ranges along y are $[0, \infty)$ and $[-1, 1]$ are incompatible. The overall distance between p_1, p_2 is therefore $(1, 9)$.

Widening. Widening is applied to loops formed on the partial elaboration of the CFG by identifying cutpoints, i.e., a set of CFG locations that cut every loop in the CFG. Note that any loop in the partial elaboration results from a loop in the original CFG:

Lemma 3. *If C_e be a loop in a partial elaboration Π_e, then $\rho(C_e)$ is a loop in the original CFG.*

The converse is not true. Therefore, not all loops in a CFG need be replicated as a loop in the partial elaboration. However, once a loop is formed in a partial elaboration, it remains a cycle regardless of the other edges or locations that may be added to the elaboration. These observations can be used to simplify the application of widening on a CFG elaboration. To begin with, we use the widening defined on the base domain as if the (partial) elaboration were a regular CFG. Furthermore, not all back-edges on the original CFG form a cycle in the elaboration. This lets us limit the number of applications of widening only to cycle-forming back-edge replications. This is one of the key advantages of maintaining structural connections among the disjuncts in terms of a partial elaboration. While our current treatment of widening is simplistic, the possibility of improving some of the existing widening operators over powersets [2] using explicit connections between the domain objects, such as those arising from a CFG elaboration, remains open.

5 Applications

We consider an application of our ideas to an intra-procedural static analyzer for checking run time errors of systems programs written in the C language, such as buffer overflows and null pointer dereferences. Our prototype analyzer constructs a CFG representation by parsing while performing memory modeling for arrays and data structures using a flow insensitive pointer analysis. This is followed by model simplification using constant folding and range analysis. A linearization abstraction converts operations such as multiplication, integer division, modulo and bitwise logical operations into non-deterministic choices. Similarly, arrays and pointers are modeled by their allocated sizes while their contents are abstracted away.

Our analyzer is targeted towards proving buffer overflows and string access patterns of systems code. The analyzer is *context insensitive*; all function calls are inlined using caller ID variables to differentiate between calling contexts. All

Table 1. Performance comparison using benchmark programs

Name	KLOC	#Prop	#C	K = 1		K = 2		K = 5		K = 10	
				T	#P	T	#P	T	#P	T	#P
code1	1.5	136	56	143	44	134	76	233	77	370	77
code2	1.5	126	46	51	65	115	67	193	68	343	68
code3	2	189	92	207	84	232	81	367	84	600	83
code4	1.9	142	10	31	44	42	44	101	50	191	52
code5	15	634	22	215	176	270	176	375	182	652	184

variables are assumed to have global scope. Reduction in the number of variables in the model is achieved by tracking live variables during the analysis and by creating small clusters of related variables. Clusters are detected by backward traversal of the CFG, collecting the variables that occur in the same expressions or conditions. The maximum number of variables in each cluster is artificially limited by a user specified parameter. For each cluster, statements involving variables that do not belong to the current cluster are abstracted away. The analysis is performed on each of these clusters. A property is considered proved only if it can be proved on at least one of the abstractions.

The analysis is performed using the polyhedral domain using base domain operations implemented in the PPL library [3] and relaxations described in our previous work [23]. The maximum number of disjuncts K and the maximum cluster sizes are parameters to this analysis. The merging heuristic used is induced by a slight modification of the range Hausdorff distance described previously. Back-edges are tracked dynamically in the partial elaboration thereby avoiding unnecessary widening operations.

We analyzed a variety of benchmark programs using our analysis for different values of K. Table 1 shows the performance comparisons for a selection of benchmark programs. For each program "#Prop" indicates the total number of properties to be checked, "#C" indicates the number of clusters. We employ a clustering strategy wherein the number of variables per cluster is kept uniformly close to 15. For each value of K, we report the time taken (T) and the number of proofs("#P"). Timings were measured on an Intel Pentium 3GHz processor with 4GB RAM. The gains produced by the use of disjunctive invariants are tangible and pronounced in some cases. The lack of monotonicity of our scheme, evident in "code3", can be remedied by performing the analysis for smaller values of K before attempting a large value. For a small number of disjuncts, the overhead of merging disjuncts seems to be linear in K.

Our results are preliminary; the false positive rate is high, primarily due to our reliance on a fixed K. The heuristics used to produce and merge disjuncts need to be sensitive to the program locations involved. For instance, maintaining a fixed number of disjuncts at function entry nodes produces an effect similar to an inter-procedural analysis with a bounded number of function summaries. However, inter-procedural analyses typically use a much larger number of summaries per function. As a result, for programs with a deep nesting of functions, a bounded disjunctive domain with $K = 10$ does not produce a dramatic improvement over the non disjunctive analysis ($K = 1$). Even though polyhedral analysis is intractable for larger values of K such as $K = 100$, such an analysis should be feasible for a less complex domain such as intervals and octagons. We believe that pronounced improvements are also possible by considering elaborations that are not a priori bounded by a fixed K. However, such a scheme requires sophisticated merging heuristics to prevent an unbounded increase in the number of disjuncts. The coarseness of the abstractions currently employed along with the lack of a clustering strategy that performs uniformly well on all the benchmarks is another bottleneck. Improving the abstraction and scaling up to larger values of K will substantially reduce the number of false positives for our analyzer.

References

1. ABRAMSKY, S., AND JUNG, A. Domain theory. In *Handbook of Logic in Computer Science*, vol. 3. Clarendon Press, UK, 1994, ch. 1, pp. 1–168.

2. BAGNARA, R., HILL, P. M., AND ZAFFANELLA, E. Widening operators for powerset domains. In *Proc. VMCAI* (2004), vol. 2947 of *LNCS*, pp. 135–148.

3. BAGNARA, R., RICCI, E., ZAFFANELLA, E., AND HILL, P. M. Possibly not closed convex polyhedra and the Parma Polyhedra Library. In *SAS* (2002), vol. 2477 of *LNCS*, Springer–Verlag, pp. 213–229.

4. BLANCHET, B., COUSOT, P., COUSOT, R., FERET, J., MAUBORGNE, L., MINÉ, A., MONNIAUX, D., AND RIVAL, X. A static analyzer for large safety-critical software. In *ACM SIGPLAN PLDI'03* (June 2003), vol. 548030, ACM Press, pp. 196–207.

5. CLARISÓ, R., AND CORTADELLA, J. The octahedron abstract domain. In *Static Analysis Symposium* (2004), vol. 3148 of *LNCS*, Springer–Verlag, pp. 312–327.

6. COUSOT, P., AND COUSOT, R. Static determination of dynamic properties of programs. In *Proc. Intl. Symp. on Programming* (1976), Dunod, pp. 106–130.

7. COUSOT, P., AND COUSOT, R. Abstract Interpretation: A unified lattice model for static analysis of programs by construction or approximation of fixpoints. In *ACM Principles of Programming Languages* (1977), pp. 238–252.

8. COUSOT, P., AND COUSOT, R. Systematic design of program analysis frameworks. In *Symposium on Principles of Programming Languages (POPL 1979)* (1979), ACM Press, New York, NY, pp. 269–282.

9. COUSOT, P., AND COUSOT, R. Comparing the Galois connection and widening/narrowing approaches to Abstract interpretation, invited paper. In *PLILP '92* (1992), vol. 631 of *LNCS*, Springer–Verlag, pp. 269–295.

10. COUSOT, P., AND HALBWACHS, N. Automatic discovery of linear restraints among the variables of a program. In *ACM POPL* (Jan. 1978), pp. 84–97.

11. DAS, M., LERNER, S., AND SEIGLE, M. ESP: Path-sensitive program verification in polynomial time. In *Proceedings of Programming Language Design and Implementation (PLDI 2002)* (2002), ACM Press, pp. 57–68.

12. DOR, N., RODEH, M., AND SAGIV, M. CSSV: Towards a realistic tool for statically detecting all buffer overflows in C. In *Proc. PLDI'03* (2003), ACM Press.

13. FLOYD, R. W. Assigning meanings to programs. *Proc. Symposia in Applied Mathematics 19* (1967), 19–32.

14. GIACOBAZZI, R., AND RANZATO, F. Optimal domains for disjunctive abstract intepretation. *Sci. Comput. Program. 32*, 1-3 (1998), 177–210.

15. HALBWACHS, N., PROY, Y., AND ROUMANOFF, P. Verification of real-time systems using linear relation analysis. *Formal Methods in System Design 11* (1997), 157–185.

16. HANDJIEVA, M., AND TZOLOVSKI, S. Refining static analyses by trace-based partitioning using control flow. In *SAS* (1998), vol. 1503 of *LNCS*, Springer–Verlag, pp. 200–214.

17. HOARE, C. A. R. An axiomatic basis for computer programming. *Commun. ACM 12*, 10 (1969), 576–580.

18. IVANČIĆ, F., GUPTA, A., GANAI, M. K., KAHLON, V., WANG, C., AND YANG, Z. Model checking C programs using F-Soft. In *Computer Aided Verification (CAV)* (2005), pp. 301–306.

19. KARR, M. Affine relationships among variables of a program. *Acta Inf. 6* (1976), 133–151.

20. MANEVICH, R., SAGIV, S., RAMALINGAM, G., AND FIELD, J. Partially disjunctive heap abstraction. In *Static Analysis Symposium (SAS)* (2004), vol. 3148 of *LNCS*, Springer–Verlag, pp. 265–279.

21. MAUBORGNE, L., AND RIVAL, X. Trace partitioning in abstract interpretation based static analyzers. In *ESOP* (2005), vol. 3444 of *LNCS*, Springer–Verlag, pp. 5–20.

22. RUGINA, R., AND RINARD, M. Symbolic bounds analysis of pointers, array indices, and accessed memory regions. In *Proc. PLDI* (2000), ACM Press.

23. SANKARANARAYANAN, S., COLÓN, M., SIPMA, H. B., AND MANNA, Z. Efficient strongly relational polyhedral analysis. In *VMCAI* (2006), LNCS, Springer–Verlag, pp. 111–125.

24. SANKARANARAYANAN, S., SIPMA, H. B., AND MANNA, Z. Scalable analysis of linear systems using mathematical programming. In *Verification, Model-Checking and Abstract-Interpretation (VMCAI 2005)* (January 2005), vol. 3385 of *LNCS*.

25. SIMON, A., KING, A., AND HOWE, J. M. Two variables per linear inequality as an abstract domain. In *LOPSTR* (2003), vol. 2664 of *Lecture Notes in Computer Science*, Springer, pp. 71–89.

26. WAGNER, D., FOSTER, J., BREWER, E., , AND AIKEN, A. A first step towards automated detection of buffer overrun vulnerabilities. In *Proc. NDSS* (2000), ACM Press, pp. 3–17.

Static Analysis of Numerical Algorithms

Eric Goubault and Sylvie Putot

CEA Saclay, F91191 Gif-sur-Yvette Cedex, France
{eric.goubault, sylvie.putot}@cea.fr

Abstract. We present a new numerical abstract domain for static analysis of the errors introduced by the approximation by floating-point arithmetic of real numbers computation, by abstract interpretation [3]. This
work extends a former domain [4,8], with an implicitly relational domain
for the approximation of the floating-point values of variables, based on
affine arithmetic [2]. It allows us to analyze non trivial numerical computations, that no other abstract domain we know of can analyze with
such precise results, such as linear recursive filters of different orders,
Newton methods for solving non-linear equations, polynomial iterations,
conjugate gradient algorithms.

1   Introduction

The idea of the domain of [4,8][1] is to provide some information on the source
of numerical errors in the program. The origin of the main losses of precision
is most of the time very localized, so identifying the operations responsible for
these main losses, while bounding the total error, can be very useful. The analysis
follows the floating-point computation, and bounds at each operation the error
committed between the floating-point and the real result. It relies on a model of
the difference between the result x of a computation in real numbers, and the
result f^x of the same computation using floating-point numbers, expressed as

$$x = f^x + \sum_{\ell \in L \cup \{hi\}} \omega_\ell^x \varphi_\ell \, . \tag{1}$$

In this relation, a term $\omega_\ell^x \varphi_\ell$, $\ell \in L$ denotes the contribution to the global
error of the first-order error introduced by the operation labeled ℓ. The value
of the error $\omega_\ell^x \in \mathbb{R}$ expresses the rounding error committed at label ℓ, and its
propagation during further computations on variable x. Variable φ_ℓ is a formal
variable, associated to point ℓ, and with value 1. Errors of order higher than
one, coming from non-affine operations, are grouped in one term associated to
special label hi. We refer the reader to [4,8] for the interpretation of arithmetic
operations on this domain.

   A natural abstraction of the coefficients in expression (1), is obtained using
intervals. The machine number f^x is abstracted by an interval of floating-point

---

[1] Some notations are slightly different from those used in these papers, in order to
avoid confusion with the usual notations of affine arithmetic.

K. Yi (Ed.): SAS 2006, LNCS 4134, pp. 18–34, 2006.

numbers, each bound rounded to the nearest value in the type of variable x. The error terms $\omega_i^x \in \mathbb{R}$ are abstracted by intervals of higher-precision numbers, with outward rounding. However, results with this abstraction suffer from the over-estimation problem of interval methods. If the arguments of an operation are correlated, the interval computed with interval arithmetic may be significantly wider than the actual range of the result.

Resembling forms, though used in a very different way, were introduced in the interval community, under the name of affine arithmetic [2], to overcome the problem of loss of correlation between variables in interval arithmetic. We propose here a new relational domain, relying on affine arithmetic for the computation of the floating-point value f^x. Indeed, we cannot hope for a satisfying computation of the bounds of the error without an accurate computation of the value, even with very accurate domains for the errors. But affine arithmetic is designed for the estimation of the result of a computation in real numbers. We will show that it is tricky to accurately estimate from there the floating-point result, and that the domain for computing f^x had to be carefully designed.

In section 2, we introduce this new domain and establish the definition of arithmetic operations over it. First ideas on these relational semantics were proposed in [12,13]. In section 3, we present a computable abstraction of this domain, including join and meet operations, and a short insight into practical aspects, such as fixed-point computations, cost of the analysis, and comparison to other domains such as polyhedra. For lack of space, we only give hints of proofs of the correctness of the abstract semantics, in sections 2.3 and 3.1. Finally, we present in section 4, results obtained with the implementation of this domain in our static analyzer FLUCTUAT, that demonstrate its interest.

Notations: Let $\mathbb{F}$ be the set of IEEE754 floating-point numbers (with their infinities), $\mathbb{R}$ the set of real numbers with ∞ and $-\infty$. Let $\uparrow_\circ \colon \mathbb{R} \to \mathbb{F}$ be the function that returns the rounded value of a real number x, with respect to the rounding mode $\circ$. The function $\downarrow_\circ \colon \mathbb{R} \to \mathbb{F}$ that returns the roundoff error is defined by

$$\forall x \in \mathbb{R}, \ \downarrow_\circ (x) = x - \uparrow_\circ (x) .$$

We note $\mathbb{IR}$ the set of intervals with bounds in $\mathbb{R}$. In the following, an interval will be noted in bold, $\boldsymbol{a}$, and its lower and upper bounds will be noted respectively $\underline{a}$ and $\overline{a}$. And we identify when necessary, a number with the interval with its two bounds equal to this number. $\wp(X)$ denotes the set of subsets of X.

2 New Domain for the Floating-Point Value f^x

Affine arithmetic was proposed by De Figueiredo and Stolfi [2], as a solution to the overestimation in interval arithmetic. It relies on forms that allow to keep track of affine correlations between quantities. Noise symbols are used to express the uncertainty in the value of a variable, when only a range is known. The sharing of noise symbols between variables expresses dependencies. We present here a domain using affine arithmetic for the floating-point computation.

In section 2.1, we present briefly the principles of affine arithmetic for real numbers computations. Then in section 2.2, we show on an example the challenges of its adaptation to the estimation of floating-point computations. In sections 2.3 and 2.4, we present the solution we propose, and finally in section 2.5 we demonstrate this solution on the example introduced in section 2.2.

2.1   Affine Arithmetic for Computation in Real Numbers

In affine arithmetic, a quantity x is represented by an affine form, which is a polynomial of degree one in a set of noise terms ε_i :

$$\hat{x} = \alpha_0^x + \alpha_1^x \varepsilon_1 + \ldots + \alpha_n^x \varepsilon_n, \quad \text{with } \varepsilon_i \in [-1,1] \text{ and } \alpha_i^x \in \mathbb{R}.$$

Let $\mathbb{AR}$ denote the set of such affine forms. Each noise symbol ε_i stands for an independent component of the total uncertainty on the quantity x, its value is unknown but bounded in [-1,1]; the corresponding coefficient α_i^x is a known real value, which gives the magnitude of that component. The idea is that the same noise symbol can be shared by several quantities, indicating correlations among them. These noise symbols can be used not only for modelling uncertainty in data or parameters, but also uncertainty coming from computation.

Let $\mathcal{E}_0$ be the set of expressions on a given set $\mathcal{V}$ of variables (all possible program variables) and constants (intervals of reals), built with operators $+$, $-$, $*$, $/$ and $\sqrt{\ }$. We note $\hat{\mathcal{C}}_\mathbb{A}$ the set of abstract contexts in $\mathbb{AR}$. We can now define, inductively on the syntax of expressions, the evaluation function $\widehat{eval} : \mathcal{E}_0 \times \hat{\mathcal{C}}_\mathbb{A} \to \mathbb{AR}$. For lack of space, we only deal with a few operations. The assignment of a variable x whose value is given in a range $[a, b]$, introduces a noise symbol ε_i :

$$\hat{x} = (a + b)/2 + (b - a)/2\,\varepsilon_i.$$

The result of linear operations on affine forms, applying polynomial arithmetic, can easily be interpreted as an affine form. For example, for two affine forms $\hat{x}$ and $\hat{y}$, and a real number r, we get

$$\hat{x} + \hat{y} = (\alpha_0^x + \alpha_0^y) + (\alpha_1^x + \alpha_1^y)\varepsilon_1 + \ldots + (\alpha_n^x + \alpha_n^y)\varepsilon_n$$
$$\hat{x} + r = (\alpha_0^x + r) + \alpha_1^x \varepsilon_1 + \ldots + \alpha_n^x \varepsilon_n$$
$$r\hat{x} = r\alpha_0^x + r\alpha_1^x \varepsilon_1 + \ldots + r\alpha_n^x \varepsilon_n$$

For non affine operations, the result applying polynomial arithmetic is not an affine form : we select an approximate linear resulting form, and bounds for the approximation error committed using this approximate form are computed, that create a new noise term added to the linear form. For example, for the multiplication of $\hat{x}$ and $\hat{y}$, defined on the set of noise symbols $\varepsilon_1, \ldots, \varepsilon_n$, a first over-approximation for the result (the one given in [2]), writes

$$\hat{x} \times \hat{y} = \alpha_0^x \alpha_0^y + \sum_{i=1}^{n}(\alpha_i^x \alpha_0^y + \alpha_i^y \alpha_0^x)\varepsilon_i + \left(\sum_{i=1}^{n}|\alpha_i^x|.\sum_{i=1}^{n}|\alpha_i^y|\right)\varepsilon_{n+1}.$$

However, this new noise term can be a large over-estimation of the non-affine part, the additional term is more accurately approximated by

$$\sum_{i=1}^{n} |\alpha_i^x \alpha_i^y|[0,1] + \sum_{1 \le i \ne j \le n} |\alpha_i^x \alpha_j^y|[-1,1].$$

This term is not centered on zero, the corresponding affine form then writes

$$\hat{x} \times \hat{y} = (\alpha_0^x \alpha_0^y + \frac{1}{2} \sum_{i=1}^{n} |\alpha_i^x \alpha_i^y|) + \sum_{i=1}^{n} (\alpha_i^x \alpha_0^y + \alpha_i^y \alpha_0^x)\varepsilon_i + (\frac{1}{2} \sum_{i=1}^{n} |\alpha_i^x \alpha_i^y| + \sum_{i \ne j} |\alpha_i^x \alpha_j^y|)\varepsilon_{n+1}.$$

For example, if $\hat{x} = \varepsilon_1 + \varepsilon_2$ and $\hat{y} = \varepsilon_2$, we get with the first formulation, $\hat{x} \times \hat{y} = 2\varepsilon_3 \in [-2,2]$ and with the second formulation, $\hat{x} \times \hat{y} = \frac{1}{2} + \frac{3}{2}\varepsilon_3 \in [-1,2]$. However, the exact range here is [-0.25,2] : indeed there could be a more accurate computation for the multiplication, using Semi-Definite Programming[2].

2.2 Motivation for the Affine Real Form Plus Error Term Domain

Using affine arithmetic for the estimation of floating-point values needs some adaptation. Indeed, the correlations that are true on real numbers after an arithmetic operation, are not exactly true on floating-point numbers.

Consider for example two independent variables x and y that both take their value in the interval [0,2], and the arithmetic expression $((x+y)-y)-x$. Using affine arithmetic in the classical way, we write $x = 1 + \varepsilon_1$, $y = 1 + \varepsilon_2$, and we get zero as result of the expression. This is the expected result, provided this expression is computed in real numbers. But if we take x as the nearest floating-point value to 0.1, and $y = 2$, then the floating-point result is $-9.685755e - 8$.

In order to model the floating-point computation, a rounding error must thus be added to the affine form resulting from each arithmetic operation. But we show here on an example that the natural extensions of real affine arithmetic are not fully satisfying. We consider an iterated computation $x = x - a * x$, for $0 \le a < 1$ and starting with $x_0 \in [0,2]$.

- With interval arithmetic, $x_1 = x_0 - ax_0 = [-2a, 2]$, and iterating we get an over-approximation (due to the use of floating-point numbers), of the already unsatisfying interval $\boldsymbol{x_n} = [(1-a)^n - (1+a)^n, (1-a)^n + (1+a)^n]$.

- We now consider affine arithmetic with an extra rounding error added for each arithmetic operation. We suppose for simplicity's sake that all coefficients are exactly represented, and we unfold the iterations of the loop. We note u the value $ulp(1)$, which is the absolute value of the difference between 1 and the nearest floating-point number, and $\boldsymbol{u} = [-u, u]$. We note $\hat{f}_n = \hat{x}_n + \boldsymbol{\delta_n}$, where $\hat{x}_n$ is the affine form representing the result of the computation of x_n in real numbers, and $\boldsymbol{\delta_n}$ the interval error term giving the floating-point number. We have $\hat{x}_0 = 1 + \varepsilon_1$ and, using affine arithmetic on real numbers, we get

$$\hat{x}_n = (1-a)^n + (1-a)^n \varepsilon_1, \quad \forall n \ge 0.$$

---

[2] We thank Stéphane Gaubert who pointed out this to us.

The rounding error on x_0 is $\delta_0 = 0$. Using interval arithmetic for the propagation of the error δ_n, and adding the rounding errors corresponding to the product ax_n and to the subtraction $x_n - ax_n$, we get

$$\delta_{n+1} = (1+a)\delta_n + a(1-a)^n u + (1-a)^{n+1} u = (1+a)\delta_n + (1-a)^n u \quad (2)$$

In this computation, u denotes an unknown value in an interval, that can be different at each occurrence of u. Using property $(1-a)^n \geq 1 - an$, $\forall a \in [0,1]$ and $n \geq 1$, we can easily prove that for all n, $nu \subset \delta_n$. The error term increases, and $\hat{f}_n$ is not bounded independently of the iterate n.

- Now, to take into account the dependencies also between the rounding errors, we introduce new noise symbols. For a lighter presentation, these symbols are created after the rounding errors of both multiplication ax and subtraction $x - ax$, and not after each of them. Also, a new symbol is introduced at each iteration, but it agglomerates both new and older errors. In the general case, it will be necessary to keep as many symbols as iterations, each corresponding to a new error introduced at a given iteration. The error term is now computed as an affine form $\hat{\delta}_n = \mu_n \varepsilon_{2,n}$, with $\mu_0 = 0$ and

$$\hat{\delta}_{n+1} = (1-a)\mu_n \varepsilon_{2,n} + a(1-a)^n u + (1-a)^{n+1} u.$$

Introducing a new symbol $\varepsilon_{2,n+1} \in [-1,1]$, it is easy to prove that we can write

$$\hat{\delta}_n = n(1-a)^{n-1} u \varepsilon_{2,n} \quad \forall n \geq 1.$$

The error converges towards zero. However, we still loose the obvious information that x_n is always positive. Also the computation can be costly : in the general case, one symbol per operation and iteration of the loop may be necessary.

We now propose a semantics that avoids the cost of extra noise symbols, and with which we will show in section 2.5, that we can prove that $x_n \geq 0$, $\forall n$.

2.3   Semantics for the Floating-Point Value: Abstract Domain

Linear correlations between variables can be used directly on the errors or on the real values of variables, but not on floating-point values. We thus propose to decompose the floating-point value f^x of a variable x resulting from a trace of operations, in the real value of this trace of operations r^x, plus the sum of errors δ^x accumulated along the computation, $f^x = r^x + \delta^x$. Other proposals have been made to overcome this problem, most notably [10].

We present in this section an abstract domain, in the sense that we model a program for sets of inputs and parameters (given in intervals). However, it is not fully computable, as we still consider coefficients of the affine forms to be real numbers. A more abstract semantics, and lattice operations, will be briefly presented in the implementation section 3.

Real Part r^x: Affine Arithmetic. We now index a noise symbol ε_i by the label $i \in L$ corresponding to the operation that created the symbol. The representation is sparse, as all operations do not create symbols. In this section and for more simplicity, we suppose that at most one operation, executed once, is associated to each label. The generalization will be discussed in the implementation section.

The correctness of the semantics, defined by $\hat{eval}$, is as follows. We note r^x the smallest interval including $\hat{r}^x$ and $\mathcal{C}$, the set of concrete contexts, i.e. functions from the variables to $\mathbb{R}$, seen as a subset of $\hat{\mathcal{C}}_A$. We have an obvious concretisation function $conc_{\mathbb{R}} : \hat{\mathcal{C}}_A \rightarrow \wp(\mathcal{C})$, making all possible choices of values for the noise symbols in the affine forms it is composed of. This also defines γ from affine forms to intervals, which cannot directly define a strong enough correctness criterion. Affine forms define *implicit* relations, we must prove that in whatever expression we are using them, the concretisation as interval of this particular expression contains the concrete values that this expression can take[3]. We have to compare $\hat{eval}$ with the evaluation function $eval : \mathcal{E}_0 \times \mathcal{C} \rightarrow \mathbb{R}$ which computes an arithmetic expression in a given (real number) context. Formally, the semantics of arithmetic expressions in $\mathbb{AR}$, given by $\hat{eval}$, is correct because for all $e \in \mathcal{E}_0$, for all $\hat{C} \in \hat{\mathcal{C}}_A$, we have property:

$$\forall C \in conc_{\mathbb{R}}(\hat{C}), eval(e, C) \in \gamma \circ \hat{eval}(e, \hat{C}) \tag{3}$$

Error Term δ^x : Errors on Bounds Combined with Maximum Error.
The rounding errors associated to the bounds $\underline{r}^x$ and $\overline{r}^x$ is the only information needed to get bounds for the floating-point results. In the general case, our semantics only gives ranges for these errors : we note δ^x_- and δ^x_+ the intervals including the errors due to the successive roundings committed on the bounds $\underline{r}^x$ and $\overline{r}^x$. The set of floating-point numbers taken by variable x after the computation then lies in the interval

$$f^x = [\underline{r}^x + \underline{\delta^x_-}, \overline{r}^x + \overline{\delta^x_+}].$$

Note that $\underline{\delta^x_-}$ can be greater for example than $\overline{\delta^x_+}$, so this is not equivalent to $f^x = r^x + \overline{(\delta^x_- \cup \delta^x_+)}$.

In affine arithmetic, the bounds of the set resulting from an arithmetic operation $x \diamond y$ are not always got from the bounds of the operands x and y as in interval arithmetic : in this case, the error inside the set of values is also needed. We choose to represent it by an interval δ^x_M that bounds all possible errors committed on the real numbers in interval r^x.

This intuition can be formalized again using abstract interpretation [3]. We define $\mathbb{D} = \mathbb{AR} \times \mathbb{IR}^3$ and $\tilde{\gamma} : \mathbb{D} \rightarrow \wp(\mathbb{R} \times \mathbb{F})$ by:

$$\tilde{\gamma}(d, \delta_M, \delta_+, \delta_-) = \begin{cases} \{(r, f) \in \mathbb{R} \times \mathbb{F}/r \in \gamma(d), f - r \in \delta_M\} \\ \cap \left\{(r, f) \in \mathbb{R} \times \mathbb{F}/f \geq inf\ \gamma(d) + \underline{\delta_-}\right\} \\ \cap \left\{(r, f) \in \mathbb{R} \times \mathbb{F}/f \leq sup\ \gamma(d) + \overline{\delta_+}\right\} \end{cases}$$

The correctness criterion for the abstract semantics $\square^\sharp$ of an operator $\square$ ($\square_{\mathbb{R}}$ in the real numbers, $\square_{\mathbb{F}}$ in the floating-point numbers) is then the classical:

---

[3] This is reminiscent to observational congruences dating back to the λ-calculus.

$\forall \tilde{d}, \tilde{e} \in \mathbb{D}, \forall r^x, r^y \in \mathbb{R}, \forall f^x, f^y \in \mathbb{F}$ such that $(r^x, f^x) \in \tilde{\gamma}(d)$ and $(r^y, f^y) \in \tilde{\gamma}(e)$,

$$(r^x \square_\mathbb{R} r^y, f^x \square_\mathbb{F} f^y) \in \tilde{\gamma}(d \square^\sharp e) \tag{4}$$

Now the order[4] on $\mathbb{D}$ is as follows: $(d, \boldsymbol{\delta_M}, \boldsymbol{\delta_+}, \boldsymbol{\delta_-}) \leq_\mathbb{D} (d', \boldsymbol{\delta'_M}, \boldsymbol{\delta'_+}, \boldsymbol{\delta'_-})$ if

$$\begin{cases} d \leq_\mathbb{D} d' \\ \boldsymbol{\delta_M} \subseteq \boldsymbol{\delta'_M} \\ \left[\min\ \gamma(d) + \underline{\boldsymbol{\delta_-}}, \max\ \gamma(d) + \overline{\boldsymbol{\delta_+}}\right] \subseteq \left[\min\ \gamma(d') + \underline{\boldsymbol{\delta'_-}}, \max\ \gamma(d') + \overline{\boldsymbol{\delta'_+}}\right] \end{cases}$$

2.4   Arithmetic Operations on Floating-Point Numbers

The error on the result of a binary arithmetic operation $x \diamond y$, with $\diamond \in \{+, \times\}$, is defined as the sum of two terms :

$$\boldsymbol{\delta^{x \diamond y}_\cdot} = \boldsymbol{\delta^{x \diamond y}_{\cdot,p}} + \boldsymbol{\delta^{x \diamond y}_{\cdot,n}},$$

with $. \in \{-, +, M\}$. The propagated error $\boldsymbol{\delta^{x \diamond y}_{\cdot,p}}$ is computed from the errors on the operands, and $\boldsymbol{\delta^{x \diamond y}_{\cdot,n}}$ expresses the rounding error due to current operation $\diamond$.

Propagation of the Errors on the Operands. The propagation of the maximum error uses the maximum errors on the operands. For computing the errors on the result, we need to compute the values of the noise symbols $r^{\hat{x}}$ and $r^{\hat{y}}$ for which the bounds of $\boldsymbol{r^z}$ are obtained. For that, we compute the values of the ε_i that give the bounds of $\boldsymbol{r^z}$, and check if for these values, we are on bounds of $\boldsymbol{r^x}$ and $\boldsymbol{r^y}$.

Let b^z_i, for $i \in L$ such that $\alpha^z_i \neq 0$, be the value of ε_i that maximizes $r^{\hat{z}}$. We have

$$\underline{r^z} = \alpha^z_0 - \sum_{i \in L,\ \alpha^z_i \neq 0} \alpha^z_i b^z_i = \alpha^z_0 - \sum_{i \in L} |\alpha^z_i|$$

$$\overline{r^z} = \alpha^z_0 + \sum_{i \in L,\ \alpha^z_i \neq 0}^n \alpha^z_i b^z_i = \alpha^z_0 + \sum_{i \in L} |\alpha^z_i|$$

We can then compute the values of x and y that lead to the bounds of $\boldsymbol{r^z}$ (such that $\underline{r^z} = r^{\hat{x}}_-(z) \diamond r^{\hat{y}}_-(z)$ and $\overline{r^z} = r^{\hat{x}}_+(z) \diamond r^{\hat{y}}_+(z)$) :

$$r^{\hat{x}}_-(z) = \alpha^x_0 - \sum_{\{i,\ \alpha^z_i \neq 0\}} \alpha^x_i b^z_i + \sum_{\{i,\ \alpha^z_i = 0\}} \alpha^x_i \varepsilon_i$$

$$r^{\hat{x}}_+(z) = \alpha^x_0 + \sum_{\{i,\ \alpha^z_i \neq 0\}} \alpha^x_i b^z_i + \sum_{\{i,\ \alpha^z_i = 0\}} \alpha^x_i \varepsilon_i$$

We note $e^x_-(z)$ (resp $e^x_+(z)$) the interval of error associated to $r^{\hat{x}}_-(z)$ (resp $r^{\hat{x}}_+(z)$), used to get the lower bound $\underline{r^z}$ (resp the upper bound $\overline{r^z}$) of the result :

---

[4] Depending on the order on $\mathbb{AR}$ to be formally defined in section 3.1.

$$e_-^x(z) = \begin{cases} \delta_-^x & \text{if } r_-^x(z) = \overline{r_-^x}(z) = r_-^x, \\ \delta_+^x & \text{if } \overline{r_-^x}(z) = r_-^x(z) = \overline{r^x}, \\ \delta_M^x & \text{otherwise.} \end{cases} \qquad e_+^x(z) = \begin{cases} \delta_+^x & \text{if } r_+^x(z) = \overline{r_+^x}(z) = \overline{r^x}, \\ \delta_-^x & \text{if } \overline{r_+^x}(z) = r_+^x(z) = r_-^x, \\ \delta_M^x & \text{otherwise.} \end{cases}$$

We deduce the following determination of $e_-^x(z)$ and $e_+^x(z)$:
- if $\forall i \in L$ such that $\alpha_i^x \neq 0$, $\alpha_i^x \alpha_i^z > 0$, then $e_-^x(z) = \delta_-^x$ and $e_+^x(z) = \delta_+^x$
- else if $\forall i \in L$ such that $\alpha_i^x \neq 0$, $\alpha_i^x \alpha_i^z < 0$, then $e_-^x(z) = \delta_+^x$ and $e_+^x(z) = \delta_-^x$
- else $e_-^x(z) = e_+^x(z) = \delta_M^x$.

Then, using these notations, we can state the propagation rules

$$\delta_{-,p}^{x+y} = e_-^x(x+y) + e_-^y(x+y)$$
$$\delta_{+,p}^{x+y} = e_+^x(x+y) + e_+^y(x+y)$$
$$\delta_{M,p}^{x+y} = \delta_M^x + \delta_M^y$$

$$\delta_{-,p}^{x \times y} = e_-^x(x \times y)r^y(x \times y) + e_-^y(x \times y)r^x(x \times y) + e_-^x(x \times y)e_-^y(x \times y)$$
$$\delta_{+,p}^{x \times y} = e_+^x(x \times y)\overline{r^y}(x \times y) + e_+^y(x \times y)\overline{r^x}(x \times y) + e_+^x(x \times y)e_+^y(x \times y)$$
$$\delta_{M,p}^{x \times y} = \delta_M^x r^y + \delta_M^y r^x + \delta_M^x \delta_M^y$$

Addition of the New Rounding Error. Adding the propagation error to the result of the computation in real numbers, we get the real result of the computation of $f^x \diamond f^y$. We then have to add a new error corresponding to the rounding of this quantity to the nearest floating-point number.

We note $\downarrow_\circ (i)$, the possible rounding error on a real number in an interval i. We suppose the rounding mode used for the execution is to the nearest floating-point, and note it "n" as subscript.

$$\downarrow_n (i) = \begin{cases} \downarrow_n (i) & \text{if } i = \overline{i}, \\ \frac{1}{2}\mathrm{ulp}(\max(|\underline{i}|, |\overline{i}|))[-1, 1] & \text{otherwise.} \end{cases}$$

Then, the new rounding error is defined by

$$\delta_{-,n}^{x \diamond y} = -\downarrow_n (\underline{r^{x \diamond y}} + \delta_{-,p}^{x \diamond y})$$
$$\delta_{+,n}^{x \diamond y} = -\downarrow_n (\overline{r^{x \diamond y}} + \delta_{+,p}^{x \diamond y})$$
$$\delta_{M,n}^{x \diamond y} = -\downarrow_n (r^{x \diamond y} + \delta_{M,p}^{x \diamond y})$$

Note that the new rounding errors on the bounds, $\delta_{-,n}^{f \circ g}$ and $\delta_{+,n}^{f \circ g}$, are in fact real numbers, identified to a zero-width interval.

These error computations are correct with respect to (4), section 2.3.

2.5 Example

We consider again the example introduced in section 2.2, and we now use the domain just described. The real part is computed using affine arithmetic, as in section 2.2. We have $\delta_-^{x_0} = \delta_+^{x_0} = \delta_M^{x_0} = 0$, and, for n greater or equal than 1,

$$\delta_-^{ax_n} = a\delta_-^{x_n} + \downarrow_n (a\delta_-^{x_n})$$
$$\delta_+^{ax_n} = a\delta_+^{x_n} + \downarrow_n (2a(1-a)^n + a\delta_-^{x_n})$$

Using $\delta_-^{-ax_n} = -\delta_+^{ax_n}$, we deduce

$$\delta_-^{x_{n+1}} = \delta_-^{x_n} + \delta_+^{-ax_n} + \downarrow_n (\delta_-^{x_n} + \delta_+^{-ax_n})$$
$$= (1-a)\delta_-^{x_n} - \downarrow_n (a\delta_-^{x_n}) + \downarrow_n ((1-a)\delta_-^{x_n} - \downarrow_n (a\delta_-^{x_n}))$$

As $\delta_-^{x_0}$ is zero, the error on the lower bound of x_n stays zero : $\delta_-^{x_n} = 0$ for all n. This means in particular that $f^{x_n} \geq 0$. The same computation for the error on the upper bound leads to

$$\delta_+^{x_{n+1}} = (1-a)\delta_+^{x_n} - \downarrow_n (2a(1-a)^n + a\delta_+^{x_n})$$
$$+ \downarrow_n (2(1-a)^{n+1} + (1-a)\delta_+^{x_n} - \downarrow_n (2a(1-a)^n + a\delta_+^{x_n}))$$

Using real numbers, errors on the lower and upper bounds could be computed exactly. The maximum error on the interval is got by the same computation as in section 2.2 with no extra noise symbols for the errors, that is by (2). Indeed, we could also improve the computation of the maximum error this way, but it will be no longer useful with the (future) relational computation of the errors, to be published elsewhere.

The results got here and in section 2.2, are illustrated in figure 1. In 1 a), the bounds of the computation in real numbers for interval (IA) and affine (AA) arithmetic are compared : the computation by affine arithmetic gives the actual result. In 1 b), we add to the affine arithmetic result the maximum rounding error computed as an interval, and we see that after about 120 iterates, the rounding error prevails and the result diverges. Then in 1 c), we represent the maximum rounding error computed using extra noise symbols. And finally, in 1 d), we represent the rounding error computed on the higher bound of the real interval : it is always negative. Remembering that the error on the lower bound is zero, this proves that the floating-point computation is bounded by the result obtained from the affine computation in real numbers. The fixpoint computation is not presented, as it requires the join operator presented thereafter. However, the analysis does converge to the actual fixpoint.

3   Implementation Within the Static Analyzer FLUCTUAT

We define here a computable abstraction of the domain presented in section 2.3. We now abstract further away from trace semantics : we need control-flow join and meet operators, which must be designed with special care in order to get an efficient analysis of loops. Also, the analyzer does not have access to real numbers, we bound real coefficients by intervals. The semantics for arithmetic operations presented in section 2.3 must thus be extended to interval coefficients. Finally, we insist on the interest of our analysis, in terms of cost and accuracy, compared to existing domains such as polyhedrons.

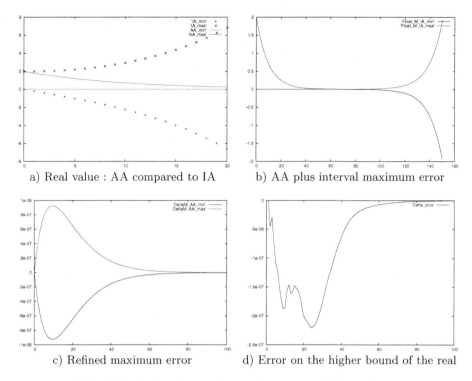

a) Real value : AA compared to IA   b) AA plus interval maximum error

c) Refined maximum error   d) Error on the higher bound of the real

Fig. 1. Evolution of xn and rounding errors with iterations

3.1   Extended Abstract Domain

We note $\mathbb{AI}$ the set of affine forms $\hat{x} = \alpha_0^x + \boldsymbol{\alpha_1^x}\varepsilon_1 + \ldots + \boldsymbol{\alpha_n^x}\varepsilon_n$ with $\alpha_0^x \in \mathbb{R}$ and $\boldsymbol{\alpha_i^x} \in \mathbb{IR}$ ($i > 0$). $\mathbb{AR}$ is seen as a subset of $\mathbb{AI}$. Let now $\mathcal{E}$ be the set of expressions on variables in $\mathcal{V}$, constant sets, and built with operators $+$, $-$, $*$, $/$, $\sqrt{}$, $\cup$ and $\cap$. The semantics we are going to define, through $\hat{eval}$ generalized to expressions in $\mathcal{E}$ and for $\mathbb{AI}$, is correct with respect to criterion as (3), but now with expressions in $\mathcal{E}$. We will only need to define the additional join $\cup$ and meet $\cap$ operations.

The set $\mathbb{AI}$ forms a poset, with the following order: $\hat{f} \leq \hat{g}$ if for all variables x, for all abstract contexts $\hat{C}$, calling $\hat{C}_{\hat{f}}$ (respectively $\hat{C}_{\hat{g}}$) the context which has value $\hat{C}(y)$ for all variables $y \neq x$, and value $\hat{f}$ (respectively $\hat{g}$) for variable x, we have:

$$conc_{\mathbb{R}} \circ \hat{eval}(e, \hat{C}_{\hat{f}}) \subseteq conc_{\mathbb{R}} \circ \hat{eval}(e, \hat{C}_{\hat{g}})$$

Note this implies that the concretization as a subset of $\mathbb{R}$ of $\hat{C}_{\hat{f}}$ is included in the concretization as a subset of $\mathbb{R}$ of $\hat{C}_{\hat{g}}$ (take $e = x$). Note as well that this is coherent with property (3), defining correctness: any bigger affine interval than a correct one remains correct. Unfortunately, this does not define a lattice, and we will only have approximate join and meet operations. Also, an important property is that $conc_\mathbb{R}$ does not always provide with an upper approximation of an environment, i.e. intervals are not always less precise than affine forms, depending on the "continuation". This can be true though, for instance if continuations only contain linear expressions.

3.2 Join and Meet Operations

Affine Forms. Technically, we use a *reduced product* of the domain of affine intervals with the domain of intervals. As we just saw, it is not true that the evaluation of any expression using affine forms is always more accurate than the evaluation of the same expression using intervals (i.e. $\hat{f} \leq \gamma(\hat{f})$).

For any interval i, we note

$$\text{mid}(i) = \uparrow_\circ \left(\frac{\underline{i} + \overline{i}}{2}\right), \quad \text{dev}(i) = max(\uparrow_\circ (\overline{i} - \text{mid}(i)), \uparrow_\circ (\text{mid}(i) - \underline{i}))$$

the center and deviation of the interval, using finite precision numbers. Suppose for instance $\alpha_0^x \leq \alpha_0^y$. A natural join between affine forms $r^{\hat{x}}$ and $r^{\hat{y}}$, associated to a new label k is

$$\hat{r}^{x \cup y} = \text{mid}([\alpha_0^x, \alpha_0^y]) + \sum_{i \in L} (\boldsymbol{\alpha_i^x} \cup \boldsymbol{\alpha_i^y}) \, \varepsilon_i + \text{dev}([\alpha_0^x, \alpha_0^y]) \, \varepsilon_k \tag{5}$$

This join operation is an upper bound of $r^{\hat{x}}$ and $r^{\hat{y}}$ in the order defined in section 3, but might be greater than the union of the corresponding intervals. However, if the over-approximation is not too large, it is still interesting to keep the relational formulation for further computations.

There is no natural intersection on affine forms, except in particular cases. In the general case, a possibility is to define the meet (at a new label k) of the affine forms as the intersection of the corresponding intervals :

$$\hat{r}^{x \cap y} = \text{mid}(\boldsymbol{r^x} \cap \boldsymbol{r^y}) + \text{dev}(\boldsymbol{r^x} \cap \boldsymbol{r^y}) \, \varepsilon_k$$

Another simple possibility is to take for $\hat{r}^{x \cap y}$ the smaller of the two affine forms $\hat{r}^x$ and $\hat{r}^y$, in the sense of the width of the concretized intervals $\boldsymbol{r^x}$ and $\boldsymbol{r^y}$.

Also, a relation can sometimes be established between the noise symbols of the two affine forms, that may be used in further computations.

Error Domain. The union on the intervals of possible errors due to successive roundings is

$$\delta_M^{x \cup y} = \delta_M^x \cup \delta_M^y.$$

For errors on the bounds, a natural and correct union is $\delta_-^{x \cup y} = \delta_-^x \cup \delta_-^y$ and $\delta_+^{x \cup y} = \delta_+^x \cup \delta_+^y$. However, the set of floating-point values coming from this model can be largely overestimated in the cases when the union of affine forms gives a larger set of values than $\boldsymbol{r^x} \cup \boldsymbol{r^y}$ would do. We thus propose to use a more accurate model, still correct with respect to correctness criterion (4), where $\delta_-^{x \cup y}$ is no longer the error on the lower bound due to successive roundings, but the representation error between the minimum value represented by the affine form, and the minimum of the floating-point value (same thing for the error on the maximum bound) :

$$\delta_-^{x \cup y} = \left(\delta_-^x + \underline{r^x} - \underline{r^{x \cup y}}\right) \bigcup \left(\delta_-^y + \underline{r^y} - \underline{r^{x \cup y}}\right)$$

$$\delta_+^{x \cup y} = \left(\delta_+^x + \overline{r^x} - \overline{r^{x \cup y}}\right) \bigcup \left(\delta_+^y + \overline{r^y} - \overline{r^{x \cup y}}\right)$$

A disturbing aspect of this model is that we no longer have for all variable x, $\delta_-^x \subset \delta_M^x$ and $\delta_+^x \subset \delta_M^x$. However, we still have $\underline{\delta_-^x} \geq \underline{\delta_M^x}$ and $\overline{\delta_+^x} \leq \overline{\delta_M^x}$.

For the meet operation on errors, we define the obvious:

$$\delta_M^{x \cap y} = \delta_M^x \cap \delta_M^y$$

$$\delta_-^{x \cap y} = \delta_-^x \text{ if } \underline{r^x} \geq \underline{r^y}, \text{ else } \delta_-^y$$

$$\delta_+^{x \cap y} = \delta_+^x \text{ if } \overline{r^x} \leq \overline{r^y}, \text{ else } \delta_+^y$$

3.3   Loops and Widening

In practice, a label may correspond not to a unique operation, but to sets of operations (for example a line of program or a function). The semantics can be easily extended to this case, creating noise symbols only when a label is met.

Moreover, in loops, different noise symbols will have to be introduced for the same arithmetic operation at different iterations of the loop : a first solution, accurate but costly, is to introduce each time a new symbol, that is $\varepsilon_{i,k}$ for label i in the loop and iteration k of the analyzer on the loop, and to keep all symbols. A fixpoint is got when the error terms are stable, for each label j introduced out of the loop, the interval coefficient $\alpha_j^{x^n}$ is stable, and for each label i introduced in the loop, the sum of contributions $\sum_{k=1}^n \alpha_{i,k}^{x^n}[-1,1]$ is stable[5]. That is, a fixpoint of a loop is got at iteration n for variable x if

$$\delta_-^{x_n} \subset \delta_-^{x_{n-1}}, \quad \delta_+^{x_n} \subset \delta_+^{x_{n-1}}, \quad \delta_M^{x_n} \subset \delta_M^{x_{n-1}}$$
$$\alpha_j^{x_n} \subset \alpha_j^{x_{n-1}} \qquad\qquad \text{for all } j \text{ outside the loop}$$
$$\sum_{k=1}^n \alpha_{i,k}^{x_n}[-1,1] \subset \sum_{k=1}^{n-1} \alpha_{i,k}^{x_{n-1}}[-1,1] \qquad \text{for all } i \text{ in the loop}$$

In the same way, a natural widening consists in applying a standard widening componentwise on errors, on coefficients of the affine forms for labels outside the loop, and on the sum $\sum_{k=1}^n \alpha_{i,k}^{x_n}[-1,1]$ for a label i in the loop. However, in some cases, reducing the affine form, or part of it, to an interval after a number of iterations, allows to get a finite fixpoint while the complete form does not.

Another possible implementation is to keep only dependencies between a limited number of iterations of a loop, and agglomerate older terms introduced in the loop. For example, a first order recurrence will need only dependencies from one iteration to the next to get accurate results, while higher order recur-

---

[5] This is a correct criterion with respect to the order defined in section 3.1, but weaker conditions may be used as well.

rences will need to keep more information. This problem has to be considered again when getting out of the loop, for a good trade-off between efficiency and accuracy.

3.4 Use of Finite Precision Numbers in the Analysis

The analyzer does not have access to real numbers, real coefficients in the affine forms are abstracted using intervals with outward rounding. We use for this the MPFR library [11] that provides arithmetic on arbitrary precision floating-point numbers, with exact rounding. However, the abstract domain defined in 3.1 has a real and not an interval coefficient α_0^x. Technically, this is achieved by creating a new noise symbol whenever coefficient α_0^x can no longer be computed exactly with the precision used. Morally, these additional noise symbols are used to keep the maximum of correlations, even between errors introduced artificially because of the imprecision of the analysis. Also, in some cases, using high precision numbers is useful to get more accurate results.

3.5 Comparison with Related Abstract Domains

There is a concretisation operator from affine intervals to polyhedra, whose image is the set of center-symmetric bounded polyhedra. Calling m the number of variables, n the number of noise symbols, the joint range of the m variables is a polyhedra with at most of the order of $2n$ faces within a n-dimensional linear subspace of R^m (if $m \geq n$). Conversely, there is no optimal way in general to get an affine form containing a given polyhedra.

Zones [9] are particular center-symmetric bounded polyhedra, intersected with hypercubes, so our domain is more general (since we always keep affine forms together with an interval abstraction), even though less general than polyhedra. It is more comparable to templates [7], where new relations are created along the way, when needed through the evaluation of the semantic functional.

We illustrate this with the following simple program (labels are given as comments):

```
x = [0,2]      // 1        z = xy;        // 3
y = x+[0,2]    // 2        t = z-2*x-y;   // 4
```

In the polyhedral approach, we find as invariants the following ones:

line 2	line 3	line 4
$\begin{cases} 0 \leq x \leq 2 \\ 0 \leq y - x \leq 2 \end{cases}$	$\begin{cases} 0 \leq x \leq 2 \\ 0 \leq y - x \leq 2 \\ 0 \leq z \leq 8 \end{cases}$	$\begin{cases} 0 \leq x \leq 2 \\ 0 \leq y - x \leq 2 \\ 0 \leq z \leq 8 \\ -8 \leq t \leq 8 \end{cases}$

At line 3, we used the concretisation of the invariant of line 2 on intervals to get the bounds for z, as is customarily done in zones and polyhedra for non-linear expressions. The particular polyhedra that affine intervals represent make it possible to interpret precisely non-linear expressions, which are badly handled in other linear relational domains:

line 2	line 3	line 4
$\begin{cases} x = 1 + \epsilon_1 \\ y = 2 + \epsilon_1 + \epsilon_2 \end{cases}$	$\begin{cases} x = 1 + \epsilon_1 \\ y = 2 + \epsilon_1 + \epsilon_2 \\ z = \frac{5}{2} + 3\epsilon_1 + \epsilon_2 + \frac{3}{2}\epsilon_3 \in [-3, 8] \end{cases}$	$\begin{cases} x = 1 + \epsilon_1 \\ y = 2 + \epsilon_1 + \epsilon_2 \\ z = \frac{5}{2} + 3\epsilon_1 + \epsilon_2 + \frac{3}{2}\epsilon_3 \\ t = -\frac{3}{2} + \frac{3}{2}\epsilon_3 \in [-3, 0] \end{cases}$

Notice the polyhedral approach is momentarily, at line 3, better than the estimate given by affine arithmetic [6], but the relational form we compute gives much better results in subsequent lines: t has in fact exact range in $[-\frac{9}{4}, 0]$ close to what we found: $[-3, 0]$. This is because the representation of z contains implicit relations that may prove useful in further computations, that one cannot guess easily in the explicit polyhedral format (see the work [7] though).

Another interest of the domain is that the implicit formulation of relations is very economical (in time and memory), with respect to explicit formulations, which need closure operators, or expensive formulations (such as with polyhedra). For instance: addition of two affine forms with n noise symbols costs n elementary operations, independently of the number of variables. Multiplication costs n^2 elementary operations. Moreover, affine operations (addition and subtraction) do not introduce new noise symbols, and existing symbols can be easily agglomerated to reduce this number n. This leads to an analysis whose cost can be fairly well controlled.

It is well known that it is difficult to use polyhedra when dealing with more than a few tens or of the order of one hundred variables. We actually used this domain on programs containing of the order of a thousand variables (see example CG10 where we deal with 189 variables already) with no help from any partitioning technique.

4   Examples

Our static analyzer Fluctuat is used in an industrial context, mostly for validating instrumentation and control code. We refer the reader to [6] for more on our research for industrial applications, but present here some analysis results. They show that the new domain for the values of variables is of course more expensive than interval arithmetic, but comparable to the domain used for the errors. And it allows us to accurately analyze non trivial numerical computations.

Consider the program of figure 2 that computes the inverse of A by a Newton method. The assertion A = __BUILTIN_DAED_DBETWEEN(20.0,30.0) tells the analyzer that the double precision input A takes its value between 20.0 and 30.0. Then the operation PtrA = (signed int *) (&A) casts A into an array of two integers. Its exponent exp is got from the first integer. Thus we have an initial estimate of the inverse, xi, with 2^{-exp}. Then a non linear iteration is computed until the difference temp between two successive iterates is bounded by e-10.

---

[6] However, as pointed out in section 2.1, we could use a more accurate semantics for the multiplication. Note also that in our analyzer, we are maintaining a reduced product between affine forms and intervals, hence we would find here the same enclosure for z as with general polyhedra.

Here, using the relational domain, Fluctuat proves that, for all inputs between 20.0 and 30.0, the algorithm terminates in a number of iterations between 5 and 9, and states that the output `xi` is in the interval [3.33e-2,5.00e-2] with an error due to rounding in [-4.21e-13,4.21e-13]. Executions confirm that respectively 5 iterations for `A = 20.0`, and 9 iterations for `A = 30.0`, are needed. Exact bounds for the number of iterations of this loop for a range of input values is a difficult information to be synthetized by the analyzer : indeed, if we study the same algorithm for simple precision floating-point numbers, instead of double precision, there are cases in which the algorithm does not terminate. Also, the interval for the values indeed is a tight enclosure of the inverse of the inputs. The error is over-estimated, but this will be improved by the future relational domain on the errors. More on this example can be found in [6].

Now, to demontrate the efficiency of our approach, we used it on several typical examples, with performances shown on the table below. Column #1 is the number of lines of C code of the program, #v describes the number of variables known to the main function (local variables are not counted). Column Int shows the floating-point value plus global error result, using an interval abstraction of the floating-point value. On the next line is the time spent by the analyzer, in seconds (laptop PC, Pentium M 800MHz, 512Mb of memory), and the maximal memory it had to use (which is allocated by big chunks, hence the round figures). The same is done in column Aff, with the affine forms plus error domain.

Name	#l	#v (fl/int)	Int (time/mem)	Aff (time/mem)
Poly	8	3 (3/0)	$[-7,8] + [-3.04,3.04]$e-6 ε (0s/4Mb)	$[-2.19, 2.75] + [-2.2,2.2]$e-6 ε (0.01s/4Mb)
Inv	26	9 (4/5)	$[-\infty,\infty] + [-\infty,\infty]\varepsilon$ ($\geq$12000s/4Mb)	$[3.33,5]$e-2 $+ [-4.2,4.2]$e-13 ε (228s/4Mb)
F1a	29	8 (6/2)	$[-\infty,\infty] + [-\infty,\infty]\varepsilon$ (0.1s/4Mb)	$[-10,10] + [-\infty,\infty]\varepsilon$ (0.63s/7Mb)
F1b	11	6 (4/2)	$[-\infty,\infty] + [-\infty,\infty]\varepsilon$ (0.03/4Mb)	$[-0.95,0.95] + [-\infty,\infty]\varepsilon$ (0.26/4Mb)
idem			$[-1.9,1.9]$e2 $+ [-4.8,4.8]$e-3 ε (9.66s/8Mb)	
F2	19	7 (6/1)	$[-2.5,2.5]$e12 $+ [-2.3,2.3]$e-2 ε (0.13s/4Mb)	$[-1.22$e-4,1.01] $+ [-9.4,9.4]$e-4 ε (0.45s/7Mb)
SA	164	32 (24/8)	$[1.06,2.52] + [-4.4,4.4]$e-5ε (24.96s/16Mb)	$[1.39,2.03] + [-4.1,4.1]$e-5 ε (25.2s/16Mb)
SH	162	9 (7/2)	$[-\infty,\infty] + [-\infty,\infty]\varepsilon$ (116.72s/4Mb)	$[4.47,5.48] + [-1.4,1.4]$e-4 ε (54.07s/4Mb)
GC4	105	56 (53/3)	$[-\infty,\infty] + [-\infty,\infty]\varepsilon$ (4.72s/10Mb)	$[9.99,10.0] + [-3.2,3.1]$e-5 ε (1.11s/7Mb)
GC10	105	189 (186/3)	$[-\infty,\infty] + [-\infty,\infty]\varepsilon$ (22.18s/15Mb)	$[54.97,55.03] + [-\infty,\infty]\varepsilon$ (15.6s/23Mb)
A2	576	75 (59/16)	$[6.523,6.524] + [-5.5,5.6]$e-6 ε (1.43s/9Mb)	$[6.523,6.524] + [-5.5,5.6]$e-6 ε (2.4s/13Mb)

```
double xi, xsi, A, temp;
signed int *PtrA, *Ptrxi, cond, exp, i;
A = __BUILTIN_DAED_DBETWEEN(20.0,30.0);
PtrA = (signed int *) (&A); Ptrxi = (signed int *) (&xi);
exp = (signed int) ((PtrA[0] & 0x7FF00000) >> 20) - 1023;
xi = 1; Ptrxi[0] = ((1023-exp) << 20);
cond = 1; i = 0;
while (cond) {
  xsi = 2*xi-A*xi*xi; temp = xsi-xi;
  cond = ((temp > e-10) || (temp < -e-10));
  xi = xsi; i++; }
```

Fig. 2. Newton method for computing $\frac{1}{A}$

Poly is the computation of a polynomial of degree 4, not in Horner form, from an initial interval. Inv is the program we depicted above. F1a and F1b are two linear recursive filters of order 1. F1b is almost ill-conditionned, and needs an enormous amount of virtual unrollings to converge in interval seman- tics (we use 5000 unfoldings of the main loop, in the line below the entry cor- responding to F1b, named idem). The potentially infinite error found by our current implementation of affine forms, in F1a and F1b, is due to the fact we do not have a relational analysis on errors yet. F2 is a linear recursive filter of order 2. SA and SH are two methods for computing the square root of a num- ber, involving iterative computations of polynomials (in SH, of order 5). GC4 and GC10 are gradient conjugate algorithms (iterations on expressions involv- ing division of multivariate polynomials of order 2), for a set of initial matrices "around" the discretisation of a 1-dimensional Laplacian, with a set of initial con- ditions, in dimensions 4x4 and 10x10 respectively in GC4 and GC10. A2 is a sam- ple of an industrial program, involving filters, and mostly simple iterative linear computations.

5   Conclusion

In this paper, we introduced a new domain which gives tight enclosures for both floating-point and real value semantics of programs. This domain has been im- plemented in our static analyzer Fluctuat, which is used in an industrial context.

As we see from the examples of section 4, it always provides much more precise results than the interval based abstract domain of [4], at a small memory expense, and sometimes even faster. Notice that our domain is in no way specialized, and works also well on non-linear iterative schemes. As far as we know, no current static analyzer is able to find as tight enclosures for such computations as we do, not mentionning that we are also analyzing the difference between floating-point and real number semantics. The only comparable work we know of, for bounding the floating-point semantics, is the one of [1]. But the approach in [1] is more specialized, and would probably compare only on first and second order linear recursive filters.

Current work includes relational methods for the error computation, as quickly hinted in [13] (it should be noted that the computation of values will also benefit from the relational computation of errors), and better heuristics for join, meet and fixed point approximations in the domain of affine forms. We are also working on underapproximations relying on the same kind of domains.

References

1. B. Blanchet, P. and R. Cousot, J. Feret, L. Mauborgne, A. Miné, D. Monniaux and X. Rival. A static analyzer for large safety-critical software. PLDI 2003.
2. J. Stolfi and L. H. de Figueiredo. An introduction to affine arithmetic. TEMA Tend. Mat. Apl. Comput., 4, No. 3 (2003), pp 297-312.
3. P. Cousot and R. Cousot. Abstract interpretation frameworks. Journal of Logic and Symbolic Computation, 2(4), 1992, pp 511-547.
4. E. Goubault. Static analyses of the precision of floating-point operations. In Static Analysis Symposium, SAS'01, number 2126 in LNCS, Springer-Verlag, 2001.
5. E. Goubault, M. Martel, and S. Putot. Asserting the precision of floating-point computations : a simple abstract interpreter. In ESOP'02, LNCS, Springer 2002.
6. E. Goubault, M. Martel, and S. Putot. Some future challenges in the validation of control systems. In European Symposium on Real-Time Systems ERTS'06.
7. S. Sankaranarayanan, M. Colon, H. Sipma and Z. Manna. Efficient strongly relational polyhedral analysis. In Proceedings of VMCAI, to appear 2006.
8. M. Martel. Propagation of roundoff errors in finite precision computations : a semantics approach. In ESOP'02, number 2305 in LNCS, Springer-Verlag, 2002.
9. A. Miné. The octagon abstract domain. In Journal of Higher-Order and Symbolic Computation, to appear 2006.
10. A. Miné. Relational abstract domains for the detection of floating-point run-time errors. In ESOP'04, number 2986 in LNCS, Springer-Verlag, 2004.
11. MPFR library Documentation and downloadable library at http://www.mpfr.org.
12. S. Putot, E. Goubault and M. Martel. Static analysis-based validation of floating-point computations. In LNCS 2991, Springer-Verlag, 2004.
13. S. Putot, E. Goubault. Weakly relational domains for floating-point computation analysis. In Proceedings of NSAD, 2005.

Static Analysis of String Manipulations in Critical Embedded C Programs

Xavier Allamigeon, Wenceslas Godard, and Charles Hymans

EADS CCR DCR/STI/C
12, rue Pasteur – BP 76 – 92152 Suresnes, France
firstname.lastname@eads.net

Abstract. This paper describes a new static analysis to show the absence of memory errors, especially string buffer overflows in C programs. The analysis is specifically designed for the subset of C that is found in critical embedded software. It is based on the theory of abstract interpretation and relies on an abstraction of stores that retains the length of string buffers. A *transport structure* allows to change the granularity of the abstraction and to concisely define several inherently complex abstract primitives such as destructive update and string copy. The analysis integrates several features of the C language such as multi-dimensional arrays, structures, pointers and function calls. A prototype implementation produces encouraging results in early experiments.

1 Introduction

Programming in C with strings, and more generally with buffers, is risky business. Before any copy, the programmer should make sure that the destination buffer is large enough to accept the source data in its entirety. When it is not the case, random bytes may end up in unexpected memory locations. This scenario is particularly unpleasant as soon as the source data can somehow be forged by an attacker: he may be able to smash [19] the return address on the stack and run its own code instead of the sequel of the program. Indeed, buffer overflows account for more than half of the vulnerabilities reported by the CERT [13] and are a popular target for viruses [10].

Needless to say defects that may abandon control of the equipment to an intruder are unacceptable in the context of embedded software. Testing being not a proof, we aim at designing a static analysis that shows the absence of memory manipulation errors (buffer, string buffer and pointer overflows) in embedded C software. We expect such a tool to be sound; to yield as few false alarms as possible in practice; to require as less human intervention as possible (manual annotations are unsuitable) and to scale to realistically sized programs. Any software engineer would easily benefit from a tool with all these traits and could rely on its results. Obviously the analysis should be able to handle all the features of the C language that are used in practice in the embedded world. This requires the smooth integration of several analysis techniques together. Simplicity of design is also a crucial point, since the analysis implementation should be bug-free and

K. Yi (Ed.): SAS 2006, LNCS 4134, pp. 35–51, 2006.

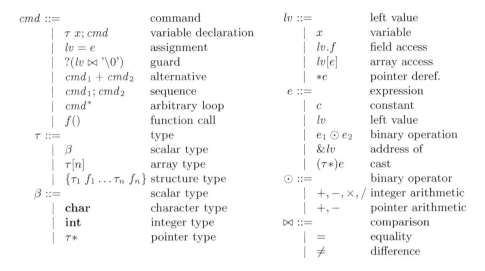

Fig. 1. Syntax

maintainable. This is not an easy task especially for a language as complex as C. To attain these goals we adopt the methodology of abstract interpretation [5]: section 2 presents the subset of C we tackle and its concrete semantics; section 3 describes the abstraction of strings and the sound static analysis algorithm; section 4 shows how string copy operations are handled, and what checks are performed by the tool; sections 5 and 6 address the implementation, experiments and related work.

2   Embedded C Programs

2.1   Syntax

The C programming language is inherently complex, which makes the formal definition of its semantics a difficult task. Hopefully and for obvious safety reasons, programming critical embedded applications is subject to severe constraints. In practice, only a subset of C is allowed. The main limitation results from the obligation to know at compile time the maximum memory usage of any piece of software. To achieve this, the use of dynamic allocation (function *malloc()*) and recursive functions are both forbidden. For the sake of expositional clarity, we set aside some additional features such as numerous C scalar types, union types and goto statements. Dealing with these features brings issues orthogonal to the object of this paper. Some ideas to address these issues may be found in [7,21]. In the end, we consider the relatively small kernel language with the syntax of figure 1. Complex assignments in C are broken down to simpler assignments between scalar types. All variables declared in a given scope of the program have distinct names.

2.2 Store

A memory address is a pair (x, o) of a variable identifier in $\mathcal{V}$ and an offset. It denotes the oth byte from the address at which the content of variable x is stored. Operation $\boxplus$ shifts an address by a given offset:

$$(x, o) \boxplus i = (x, o + i)$$

Programs manipulate three kinds of basic values: integers in $\mathbb{Z}$, characters in $\mathbb{C}$ and pointers in $\mathbb{P}$. For sake of simplicity, integers are unbounded. The nature of characters is left unspecified. It is sufficient to say that there is one null character denoted by '\0'. A pointer is a triple $\langle a, i, n \rangle$ that references the ith byte of a buffer that starts from address a and is n bytes long.

The store maps each allocated address to a basic value. The kind of values stored at a given address never changes. Hence, a store $\sigma = (\sigma_{\mathbb{Z}}, \sigma_{\mathbb{C}}, \sigma_{\mathbb{P}})$ defined on allocated addresses $\mathcal{A} = \mathcal{A}_{\mathbb{Z}} \oplus \mathcal{A}_{\mathbb{C}} \oplus \mathcal{A}_{\mathbb{P}}$ belongs to the set:

$$\Sigma = (\mathcal{A}_{\mathbb{Z}} \to \mathbb{Z}) \times (\mathcal{A}_{\mathbb{C}} \to \mathbb{C}) \times (\mathcal{A}_{\mathbb{P}} \to \mathbb{P})$$

In this model, any operation that alters the interpretation of data too severely leads to an error at runtime. For instance, a cast from {int a; int b}$*$ to int$*$ is valid; whereas a cast from int$*$ to char$*$ is illegitimate.

The layout of memory is given by two functions: $\mathsf{sizeof}(\tau)$ returns the size of a data of type τ and $\mathsf{offset}(f)$ the offset of a field f from the beginning of its enclosing structure.

2.3 Semantics

We assign a denotational semantics [29] to the kernel language. In the following, we use notations $lv : \tau$ and $e : \tau$ to retrieve the type τ of a left value lv or expression e as computed by a standard C typechecker. A left value lv evaluates to a set of addresses $\mathcal{L}\{\!\lvert lv \rvert\!\}$, as formalized in figure 2. Sets allow to encode both non-determinism and halting behaviours. A pointer of type $\tau*$ can be safely dereferenced, as long as there remains enough space to store an element of type τ. Likewise, an expression e of integer type evaluates to a set of integers $\mathcal{R}_{\mathbb{Z}}\{\!\lvert e \rvert\!\}$. Notice how an access to some address not allocated in the store of integer halts program execution. We skip the classical definition of relation $v_1 \odot v_2 \Rightarrow v$ which explicits the meaning of each binary operation. Definitions for expressions of character or pointer type are completely identical. The last four equations in figure 2 define pointer creation and cast.

Three atomic commands operate on the store:

$$\mathcal{C}\{\!\lvert \tau\ x;\ cmd \rvert\!\}\sigma = \{\sigma'_{\lvert \mathsf{dom}(\sigma)} \mid \sigma_x = \mathcal{I}\{\!\lvert \tau \rvert\!\}(x, 0) \wedge \sigma' \in \mathcal{C}\{\!\lvert cmd \rvert\!\}(\sigma \oplus \sigma_x)\}$$
$$\text{where } \mathsf{dom}(\sigma) \cap \mathsf{dom}(\sigma_x) = \emptyset$$

$$\mathcal{C}\{\!\lvert lv = e \rvert\!\}\sigma = \{\sigma[a \mapsto v] \mid a \in \mathcal{L}\{\!\lvert lv \rvert\!\}\sigma \cap \mathsf{dom}(\sigma_{\mathbb{Z}}) \wedge v \in \mathcal{R}_{\mathbb{Z}}\{\!\lvert e \rvert\!\}\sigma\}$$
$$\text{where } lv, e : \mathbb{Z}$$

$$\mathcal{C}\{\!\lvert ?(lv \bowtie \text{'\textbackslash 0'}) \rvert\!\}\sigma = \{\sigma \mid v \in \mathcal{R}_{\mathbb{C}}\{\!\lvert lv \rvert\!\}\sigma \wedge v \bowtie \text{'\textbackslash 0'}\}$$

$$\mathcal{L}\{|x|\}\sigma = \{(x, 0)\}$$
$$\mathcal{L}\{|lv.f|\}\sigma = \{a \boxplus \mathsf{offset}(f) \mid a \in \mathcal{L}\{|lv|\}\sigma\}$$
$$\mathcal{L}\{|lv[e]|\}\sigma = \{a \boxplus i \times \mathsf{sizeof}(\tau) \mid a \in \mathcal{L}\{|lv|\}\sigma \wedge i \in \mathcal{R}_{\mathbb{Z}}\{|e|\}\sigma \wedge 0 \leq i < n\}$$
$$\text{where } lv : \tau[n]$$

$$\mathcal{L}\{|{*}e|\}\sigma = \{a \boxplus i \mid \langle a, i, n \rangle \in \mathcal{R}_{\mathbb{P}}\{|e|\}\sigma \wedge 0 \leq i \leq n - \mathsf{sizeof}(\tau)\} \quad \text{where } e : \tau{*}$$
$$\mathcal{R}_{\mathbb{Z}}\{|c|\}\sigma = \{c\}$$
$$\mathcal{R}_{\mathbb{Z}}\{|lv|\}\sigma = \{\sigma_{\mathbb{Z}}(a) \mid a \in \mathcal{L}\{|lv|\}\sigma \cap \mathsf{dom}(\sigma_{\mathbb{Z}})\}$$
$$\mathcal{R}_{\mathbb{Z}}\{|e_1 \odot e_2|\}\sigma = \{v \mid v_1 \in \mathcal{R}_{\mathbb{Z}}\{|e_1|\}\sigma \wedge v_2 \in \mathcal{R}_{\mathbb{Z}}\{|e_2|\}\sigma \wedge v_1 \odot v_2 \Rightarrow v\}$$
$$\mathcal{R}_{\mathbb{P}}\{|{\&}x|\}\sigma = \{\langle (x, 0), 0, \mathsf{sizeof}(\tau) \rangle\} \quad \text{where } x : \tau$$
$$\mathcal{R}_{\mathbb{P}}\{|{\&}lv.f|\}\sigma = \{\langle a, 0, \mathsf{sizeof}(\tau) \rangle \mid a \in \mathcal{L}\{|lv.f|\}\sigma\} \quad \text{where } lv.f : \tau$$
$$\mathcal{R}_{\mathbb{P}}\{|{\&}lv[e]|\}\sigma = \{\langle a, i \times \mathsf{sizeof}(\tau), \mathsf{sizeof}(\tau[n]) \rangle \mid a \in \mathcal{L}\{|lv|\}\sigma \wedge i \in \mathcal{R}_{\mathbb{Z}}\{|e|\}\sigma\}$$
$$\text{where } lv : \tau[n]$$

$$\mathcal{R}_{\mathbb{P}}\{|(\tau{*})e|\}\sigma = \mathcal{R}_{\mathbb{P}}\{|e|\}\sigma$$

Fig. 2. Semantics of left values and expressions

At variable declaration, a new store fragment σ_x is initialized and concatenated to the existing store, execution then continues until variable x is eventually deleted from the resulting store. The new store fragment is built by induction on the type of the declared variable:

$$\mathcal{I}\{|\beta|\}a = [a \mapsto v]$$
$$\mathcal{I}\{|\tau[n]|\}a = \bigoplus_{0 \leq i < n} \mathcal{I}\{|\tau|\}(a \boxplus i \times \mathsf{sizeof}(\tau))$$
$$\mathcal{I}\{|\{\tau_1 f_1 \dots \tau_n f_n\}|\}a = \bigoplus_{0 < i \leq n} \mathcal{I}\{|\tau_i|\}(a \boxplus \mathsf{offset}(f_i))$$

where v is any value of type β and $\oplus$ joins two disjoint stores. Assignments come in three flavours, one for each basic type: integer, character and pointer. Here, we only describe the integer assignment since the other two are completely similar. Assignment to a non-allocated address brings the program to a halt. Guards let execution continue when the store satisfies the boolean condition. We consider only equality or disequality with the null character even though other kinds of guards may easily be handled. The remaining commands control the flow of execution:

$$\mathcal{C}\{|cmd_1 + cmd_2|\}\sigma = \mathcal{C}\{|cmd_1|\}\sigma \cup \mathcal{C}\{|cmd_2|\}\sigma$$
$$\mathcal{C}\{|cmd_1; cmd_2|\}\sigma = \mathcal{C}\{|cmd_2|\}(\mathcal{C}\{|cmd_1|\}\sigma)$$
$$\mathcal{C}\{|cmd^{*}|\}\sigma = \mathsf{lfp}_{\emptyset}\, \mathbb{F}_{\sigma}$$
$$\mathbb{F}_{\sigma_0}(X) = \{\sigma_0\} \cup \{\sigma' \mid \sigma \in X \wedge \sigma' \in \mathcal{C}\{|cmd|\}\sigma\}$$
$$\mathcal{C}\{|f()|\}\sigma = \mathcal{C}\{|cmd|\}\sigma \quad \text{where } cmd \text{ is the body of function } f$$

A program P consists of a set of functions and a main command which is executed in an initially empty store: $\{|P|\} = \mathcal{C}\{|cmd|\}\varepsilon$.

$$\mathbb{C}^\sharp = \{\bot_\mathbb{C}, \mathbf{0}, \mathbf{1}, \top_\mathbb{C}\} \qquad\qquad \mathbb{Z}^\sharp = (\overline{\mathbb{Z}} \times \overline{\mathbb{Z}})_\bot \qquad\qquad \mathbb{A}^\sharp = (\mathcal{V} \times \mathbb{Z}^\sharp)_\top^\top$$

$$\gamma_\mathbb{C}(\bot_\mathbb{C}) = \emptyset \quad \gamma_\mathbb{C}(\top_\mathbb{C}) = \mathbb{C} \qquad \gamma_\mathbb{Z}(\bot_\mathbb{Z}) = \emptyset \qquad\qquad \gamma_\mathbb{A}(\bot_\mathbb{A}) = \emptyset$$

$$\gamma_\mathbb{C}(\mathbf{0}) = \{\text{'}\backslash 0\text{'}\} \qquad\qquad \gamma_\mathbb{Z}([l; u]) = \{i \mid l \le i \le u\} \quad \gamma_\mathbb{A}(\top_\mathbb{A}) = \mathbb{A}$$

$$\gamma_\mathbb{C}(\mathbf{1}) = \mathbb{C} \setminus \{\text{'}\backslash 0\text{'}\} \qquad\qquad\qquad\qquad\qquad \gamma_\mathbb{A}(x, O) = \{(x, o) \mid o \in \gamma_\mathbb{Z}(O)\}$$

$$\mathbb{P}^\sharp = (\mathbb{A}^\sharp \times \mathbb{Z}^\sharp \times \mathbb{Z}^\sharp)_\bot$$

$$\gamma_\mathbb{P}(\bot_\mathbb{P}) = \emptyset$$

$$\gamma_\mathbb{P}(A, I, N) = \{\langle a, i, n \rangle \mid a \in \gamma_\mathbb{A}(A) \wedge i \in \gamma_\mathbb{Z}(I) \wedge n \in \gamma_\mathbb{Z}(N)\}$$

Fig. 3. Abstract addresses and values

3 Static Analysis

We wish to automatically verify that all string manipulations in a program are innocuous. This is, by nature, an undecidable problem. So, we design a static analysis that computes an approximate but sound representation of all the stores that result from the execution of a program. Following the methodology of abstract interpretation [5], an abstraction of sets of stores is first devised. The analysis algorithm is then systematically derived thanks to this abstraction from the concrete semantics. The results of the analysis are used to check as many potentially dangerous memory operations as possible and to emit warnings in other cases.

3.1 Abstract Values, Integer, and Pointer Stores

Figure 3 lists the abstract domains and concretization functions used for sets of addresses and values. These abstractions are all built from well-known standard domains: integers are represented by ranges [5]; characters thanks to the domain of equality/disequality with the null character; a pair of a variable identifier and a range of possible offsets stands for a set of addresses; and abstract pointers are triples made of an abstract address, followed by two ranges for possible offsets and sizes. We use the standard set notations for all operations on ranges: $(\subseteq, \cap, \min, \max)$. Moreover, $I_1 \curlyvee I_2$ denotes the smallest range that contains both I_1 and I_2; $I \setminus \{n\}$ the smallest range that contains all elements in I except n; $I + n$ $(I - n)$ is the range obtained after the addition (subtraction) of n to all the elements in I.

The abstract domain $(\boldsymbol{D}, \boldsymbol{\gamma})$ of the analysis is built as the product of three domains: one for each type of basic value. An abstract store $\boldsymbol{S}$ is thus a triple $(S_\mathbb{Z}, S_\mathbb{P}, S_\mathbb{C})$. Abstract integer $S_\mathbb{Z}$ and pointer $S_\mathbb{P}$ stores map each allocated address to an abstract value of corresponding type. A fully fledged description of these standard non-relational domains is skipped. On the other hand, the abstract character store $S_\mathbb{C}$, being the object of our study, is discussed at length in the next section.

3.2   Abstract Character Store

A string in C is a sequence of characters stored in memory. The first null character ('\0') signals the end of the string. If no null character is found before the end of the allocated area, then the string is not well-formed. Hence the length of a string stored on a buffer $(a : n)$ of n consecutive bytes starting at address a in a store σ is:

$$strlen_\sigma(a : n) = \min(\{n\} \cup \{l \mid 0 \leq l < n \wedge \sigma(a \boxplus l) = \text{'\0'}\})$$

Now, in order to prove the correctness of string manipulations it is necessary to at least retain some information about the length of the various strings in the store.

Let π be a partition of the set of all allocated addresses, such that each element in the partition is a connected set (a buffer). The abstract store maps each buffer in the partition to a range that approximates the possible lengths of the string stored on that buffer:

$$\Sigma^\sharp = (\pi \rightarrow \mathbb{Z}^\sharp)_\perp$$
$$\gamma(S) = \{\sigma \mid \forall b \in \pi : strlen_\sigma(b) \in \gamma_\mathbb{Z}(S(b))\}$$
$$\gamma(\perp) = \emptyset$$

Several primitives operate on the domain of character store. Each primitive obeys a soundness condition. Normalization returns the empty store as soon as any buffer is associated with an empty range:

$$\eta(S) = \begin{cases} \perp & \text{if } \exists b : S(b) = \perp_\mathbb{Z} \\ S & \text{otherwise} \end{cases}$$

Normalization preserves the meaning of the abstract store, thus: $\gamma(\eta(S)) = \gamma(S)$. From now on, we assume that the store is always in normal form so that no abstract length can ever be the empty range. A new abstract store with no information at all may be created using primitive universe from a partition π. It is such that for any buffer $(a : n)$ in π:

$$\text{universe}(\pi)(a : n) = [0; n]$$

It is straightforward to show that: $(\mathcal{A} \rightarrow \mathbb{C}) \subseteq \gamma(\text{universe}(\pi))$. Abstract stores S_1 and S_2 defined on the same partition π can be compared:

$$S_1 \sqsubseteq S_2 \iff (S_1 = \perp \vee (S_2 \neq \perp \wedge \forall b \in \pi : S_1(b) \subseteq S_2(b)))$$
$$\iff \gamma(S_1) \subseteq \gamma(S_2)$$

Abstract join $\sqcup$ and meet $\sqcap$ operations are performed pointwise. To deal with variable declarations, we need to concatenate stores of disjoint domains and remove all the buffers allocated for a given variable:

$$\perp \oplus S = S \oplus \perp = \perp$$
$$S_1 \oplus S_2 = S_1 S_2$$
$$S \setminus x = S_{\mid \{(a:n) \in \pi \mid a = (y,o) \wedge y \neq x\}}$$

These operations verify the following set inequalities:

$$\gamma(S_1) \cup \gamma(S_2) \subseteq \gamma(S_1 \sqcup S_2)$$
$$\gamma(S_1) \cap \gamma(S_2) \subseteq \gamma(S_1 \sqcap S_2)$$
$$\{\sigma_1\sigma_2 \mid \sigma_1 \in \gamma(S_1) \wedge \sigma_2 \in \gamma(S_2)\} \subseteq \gamma(S_1 \oplus S_2)$$
$$\{\sigma_{\mid\{(y,o)\in A\mid y\neq x\}} \mid \sigma \in \gamma(S)\} \subseteq \gamma(S \setminus x)$$

Boolean conditions present in if statements, switches and loops must be taken into account in order to produce sufficiently precise results. Primitive guard constrains the store according to an equality or disequality comparison with character '\0':

$$\{\sigma \mid \sigma \in \gamma(S) \wedge a \in \gamma(A) \cap \mathcal{A} \wedge \sigma(a) \bowtie \text{'}\backslash 0\text{'}\} \subseteq \gamma(\text{guard}(A \bowtie \text{'}\backslash 0\text{'}, S))$$

Suppose the constraint implies that there is at least one '\0' character in a memory region that spans from address (x, o_1) to address (x, o_2). Suppose further that this region is contained in a unique buffer $(a : n)$ of the partition. Then, the length of a string starting in a is necessarily smaller than the distance δ from a to (x, o_2). Hence:

$$\text{guard}((x, [o_1; o_2]) = \text{'}\backslash 0\text{'}, S) = \eta(S[a : n \mapsto S(a : n) \cap [0; \delta]])$$

Similarly, suppose now that the value stored at address (x, o) is not the '\0' character. If address (x, o) belongs to some buffer $a : n$ of the partition and δ is the distance from a to (x, o), then:

$$\text{guard}((x, [o; o]) \neq \text{'}\backslash 0\text{'}, S) = \eta(S[b \mapsto S(b) \setminus \{\delta\}])$$

In all other cases, guard simply leaves the store unchanged:

$$\text{guard}(A \bowtie \text{'}\backslash 0\text{'}, S) = S$$

Transport structure and store accesses. Operations to read and write in the store are primordial to the analysis. However they are not easily defined mainly because the region in memory that is impacted by the operation does not necessarily coincide with a particular buffer in the partition. In order to alleviate this difficulty, we first devise transformations on the abstract store that allow to change the underlying partition. Transformation cut C_δ splits the buffer b into two consecutive buffers b_1 and b_2 of respective sizes δ and n; the reverse transformation glue G_δ lumps together two buffers that are *contiguous*:

$$C_\delta([b \mapsto L]) = \begin{cases} [b_1 \mapsto [\delta; \delta]; b_2 \mapsto L - \delta] & \text{if } \delta \leq \min(L) \\ [b_1 \mapsto L \cap [0; \delta]; b_2 \mapsto [0; n]] & \text{otherwise} \end{cases}$$

$$G_\delta([b_1 \mapsto K; b_2 \mapsto L]) = \begin{cases} [b \mapsto K \curlyvee (L + \delta)] & \text{if } \delta \in K \\ [b \mapsto K] & \text{otherwise} \end{cases}$$

$$\mathsf{read}(S, A) = \begin{cases} \bot_C & \text{if } S = \bot \vee A = \bot_A \\ \mathsf{eval}_{|b|}(\varPhi S(b)) & \text{if } A = (x, O) \wedge b = \mathsf{tobuff}(A) \wedge b \subseteq \mathcal{A} \\ \top_C & \text{otherwise} \end{cases}$$

$$\mathsf{write}(S, A, V) =$$
$$\begin{cases} \bot & \text{if } S = \bot \vee A = \bot_A \vee V = \bot_Z \\ \varPhi S[b \mapsto \mathsf{update}_{|b|}(S(b), V)] & \text{if } A = (x, O) \wedge b = \mathsf{tobuff}(A) \wedge b \subseteq \mathcal{A} \\ \mathsf{universe}(\pi) & \text{otherwise} \end{cases}$$

$$\mathsf{tobuff}(x, [o_1; o_2]) = ((x, o_1) : (o_2 - o_1 + 1))$$

$$\mathsf{update}_n([l; u], \mathbf{0}) = [0; \min(u, n - 1)]$$

$$\mathsf{eval}_n(L) = \begin{cases} \mathbf{0} & \text{if } n = 1 \wedge L = [0; 0] \\ \mathbf{1} & \text{if } L = [n; n] \\ \top_C & \text{otherwise} \end{cases} \qquad \mathsf{update}_n([l; u], \mathbf{1}) = \begin{cases} [1; 1] & \text{if } n = 1 \\ [l; n] & \text{otherwise} \end{cases}$$

$$\mathsf{update}_n(L, \top) = [0; n]$$

Fig. 4. Abstract memory access

Both operations are sound in that their result includes at least all the concrete stores originally present:

$$\gamma(S \oplus [b \mapsto L]) \subseteq \gamma(S \oplus \mathsf{C}_\delta([b \mapsto L]))$$
$$\gamma(S \oplus [b_1 \mapsto K; b_2 \mapsto L]) \subseteq \gamma(S \oplus \mathsf{G}_\delta([b_1 \mapsto K; b_2 \mapsto L]))$$

Building on glue and cut, there is a simple algorithm to move from any partition π_1 to another π_2 (of course, π_1 and π_2 must be defined on the same set of allocated addresses). Starting from π_1, the first step consists in splitting buffers until we get to the coarsest partition which is finer than both π_1 and π_2. Then, in a second step buffers are glued together to get back to π_2. Let us introduce two very useful shortcut notations built on top of this algorithm. In the following, all addresses in buffer $b = (a : n)$ are allocated (i.e. $b \subseteq \mathcal{A}$):

- $\varPhi S(b)$ minimally modifies the store so as to include buffer b in the resulting partition and then returns the value associated with this buffer. More accurately, let $\pi \oplus \{(a_1 : n_1) \ldots (a_k : n_k)\}$ be the initial partition, where all buffers that overlap b are listed in increasing order as $(a_1 : n_1)$ to $(a_k : n_k)$. Then the destination partition is $\pi \oplus \{(a_1 : \delta), (a : n), (a \boxplus n : \delta')\}$, where δ and δ' are the respective distances from a_1 to a and from $a \boxplus n$ to $a_k \boxplus n_k$,
- $\varPhi S[b \mapsto L]$ transforms the partition to add buffer b as previously explained, updates its value with L and translates back to the initial partition.

Memory accesses can now be described by the equations of figure 4. Let us comment the cases when the abstract address A that is read or written is of the form $(x, [o_1; o_2])$ and all the addresses from (x, o_1) to (x, o_2) are allocated. In this case, the buffer b that corresponds to A starts in (x, o_1) and stretches over

$n = (o_2 - o_1 + 1)$ bytes. Thanks to the previously introduced transformations, we can easily convert the abstract store so that buffer b belongs to the partition. Then, to evaluate the value that is read, we apply function eval_n to the abstract length L associated with b. There are three cases:

- when the buffer contains only one character that is equal to '\0', then **0** is returned,
- when $L = [n; n]$, the first '\0' character is not in the buffer, so the returned value is **1**,
- in all other cases, there is insufficient information to conclude and $\top_{\mathbb{C}}$ is returned.

The intuition that motivates definition of function update goes as follows:

- After a '\0' character is written somewhere in the buffer, we can be sure that the length is strictly less than its size n. Moreover, previous '\0' characters remain so that $\mathsf{update}_n([l; u], \mathbf{0}) = [0; \min(u, n - 1)]$.
- If exactly one non-null character is copied in a buffer of size $n = 1$, then the first '\0' can not be at index 0, so $\mathsf{update}_1(L, \mathbf{0}) = [1; 1]$.
- In the remaining cases when a non-null character is written, it may erase the first '\0' character in the buffer, so that the length of the string may be unbounded. Since non-null characters are untouched, the information about the lower bound on the possible string lengths is kept, thus $\mathsf{update}_n([l; u], \mathbf{0}) = [l; n]$.
- At last, when an unknown value is copied, all information is lost.

These operations are sound with respect to:

$$\{\sigma(a) \mid \sigma \in \gamma(S) \wedge a \in \gamma_{\mathbb{A}}(A) \cap \mathsf{dom}(\sigma)\} \subseteq \gamma_{\mathbb{C}}(\mathsf{read}(S, A))$$
$$\{\sigma[a \mapsto v] \mid \sigma \in \gamma(S) \wedge a \in \gamma_{\mathbb{A}}(A) \cap \mathsf{dom}(\sigma) \wedge v \in \gamma_{\mathbb{C}}(V)\} \subseteq \gamma(\mathsf{write}(S, A, V))$$

3.3 Abstract Semantics

Building on the previous primitives, the static analysis computes abstract stores while mimicking the concrete semantics. Figure 5 presents the definition that are specifically related to the handling of characters and strings. The remaining aspects of the analysis are standard and thus not thoroughly described here.

Let us paraphrase some of the most spicy equations:

- To initialize a zone of memory starting at address a with a single character or with an array of n characters, $\mathcal{I}\{\!\!\{\tau\}\!\!\}a$ creates a store whose partition is reduced to a unique buffer of size 1 or n and that contains no information,
- Non-deterministic choice amounts to abstract join and the sequence to function composition,
- The abstract store after a loop is the result of an abstract fixpoint computation. The constructive version of Tarski's theorem [6] suggests a naive algorithm: starting from $\bot$, the successive iterates of $\mathbb{F}^{\sharp}$ are computed until stabilization. In practice other more complex algorithms [31], the use of widening, and loop unfolding may be safely applied.

$$\mathcal{R}_{\mathbb{C}}[\![c]\!]S = \begin{cases} 0 & \text{if } c = '\backslash 0' \\ 1 & \text{otherwise} \end{cases}$$

$$\mathcal{I}[\![\mathbf{char}]\!]a = (\bot, \bot, \text{universe}(\{(a,1)\}))$$
$$\mathcal{I}[\![\mathbf{char}[n]]\!]a = (\bot, \bot, \text{universe}(\{(a,n)\}))$$
$$\mathcal{I}[\![\tau[n]]\!]a = \bigoplus_{0 \le i < n} \{\mathcal{I}[\![\tau]\!](a \boxplus i \times \text{sizeof}(\tau))\}$$

$$\mathcal{R}_{\mathbb{C}}[\![lv]\!]S = \text{read}(S_{\mathbb{C}}, \mathcal{L}[\![lv]\!]S)$$
$$\mathcal{I}[\![\{\tau_1 f_1 \ldots \tau_n f_n\}]\!]a = \bigoplus_{0 < i \le n} \{\mathcal{I}[\![\tau_i]\!](a \boxplus \text{offset}(f_i))\}$$

$$\mathcal{C}[\![\tau\ x;\ cmd]\!]S = \mathcal{C}[\![cmd]\!](S \oplus \mathcal{I}[\![\tau]\!](x,0)) \setminus x$$
$$\mathcal{C}[\![lv = e]\!](S_{\mathbb{Z}}, S_{\mathbb{P}}, S_{\mathbb{C}}) = (S_{\mathbb{Z}}, S_{\mathbb{P}}, \text{write}(S_{\mathbb{C}}, \mathcal{L}[\![lv]\!]S, \mathcal{R}_{\mathbb{C}}[\![e]\!])) \qquad \text{where } lv, e : \mathbf{char}$$
$$\mathcal{C}[\![?(lv \bowtie '\backslash 0')]\!](S_{\mathbb{Z}}, S_{\mathbb{P}}, S_{\mathbb{C}}) = (S_{\mathbb{Z}}, S_{\mathbb{P}}, \text{guard}(\mathcal{L}[\![lv]\!]S \bowtie '\backslash 0', S_{\mathbb{C}}))$$
$$\mathcal{C}[\![cmd_1 + cmd_2]\!]S = \mathcal{C}[\![cmd_1]\!]S \sqcup \mathcal{C}[\![cmd_2]\!]S$$
$$\mathcal{C}[\![cmd_1; cmd_2]\!]S = \mathcal{C}[\![cmd_2]\!](\mathcal{C}[\![cmd_1]\!]S)$$
$$\mathcal{C}[\![cmd^*]\!]S = \text{lfp}_\bot \ \mathbb{F}^\sharp_S$$
$$\mathbb{F}^\sharp_{S_0}(S) = S_0 \sqcup \mathcal{C}[\![cmd]\!]S$$
$$\mathcal{C}[\![f()]\!]S = \mathcal{C}[\![cmd]\!]S \qquad \text{where } cmd \text{ is the body of function } f$$

Fig. 5. Abstract evaluation, initialization and execution of commands

Theorem 1 (Soundness). *The abstract semantics of a command cmd on an abstract store S includes all stores that are obtained by any run of the command starting from some initial store in $\gamma(S)$:*

$$\{\sigma' \mid \sigma \in \gamma(S) \wedge \sigma' \in \mathcal{C}\{\!|cmd|\!\}\sigma\} \subseteq \gamma(\mathcal{C}[\![cmd]\!]S)$$

Proof. The proof is done by structural induction on the syntax of commands. It reduces to the assembly of the various atomic soundness conditions of each primitive.

Note, that since, our static analysis is built in a modular way, it would be possible to replace some components to improve either precision or efficiency and still retain the overall soundness theorem. In particular any other non-relational numerical domain can be easily used instead of ranges.

Example 1. Here are the invariants collected by the static analysis with the character store for a small example:

10: char buf [10];	$(\mathbf{buf}, 0) : 10 \mapsto [0; 10]$
11: buf [0] = 'a';	$(\mathbf{buf}, 0) : 10 \mapsto [1; 10]$
12: buf [4] = '\0';	$(\mathbf{buf}, 0) : 10 \mapsto [1; 4]$
13: buf [1] = 'b';	$(\mathbf{buf}, 0) : 10 \mapsto [2; 10]$
14: buf [2] = '\0';	$(\mathbf{buf}, 0) : 10 \mapsto [2; 2]$

The partition is reduced to one buffer that starts at $(\mathbf{buf}, 0)$ of 10 bytes. Let us delve into the details of the computation from label 12 to 13. The tool reaches label 12 with the knowledge that the length of buf is greater than 1:

$$(\mathbf{buf}, 0) : 10 \mapsto [1; 10]$$

The partition is split in three around the zone that is being written:

$$(\mathbf{buf}, 0) : 4 \mapsto [1; 4]$$
$$(\mathbf{buf}, 4) : 1 \mapsto [0; 1]$$
$$(\mathbf{buf}, 5) : 5 \mapsto [0; 5]$$

The null character is written in buffer $(\mathbf{buf}, 4) : 1$, using primitive update:

$$(\mathbf{buf}, 0) : 4 \mapsto [1; 4]$$
$$(\mathbf{buf}, 4) : 1 \mapsto [0; 0]$$
$$(\mathbf{buf}, 5) : 5 \mapsto [0; 5]$$

At last, the buffers are glued together to restore the initial partition:

$$(\mathbf{buf}, 0) : 10 \mapsto [1; 4]$$

Note that at instruction 13, after character 'b' is written at index 1 of buf, the upper bound on the length of the string is forgotten. This is indeed necessary. Consider the concrete store where the first '\0' character is exactly at index 1; since it is overwritten by a non-null character and the tool has no information about the position of the remaining '\0' characters after the first one, the new length is unknown.

Imagine now that the previous example were ended by a call to strcpy that copies string buf into a buffer of size strictly larger than 2. Such a call would be correct and the approximation computed by the tool precise enough to prove this. Next section is about the analysis of the strcpy and the checks that are made to show the correctness of possibly dangerous memory manipulation operations.

4   String Copy

4.1   Concrete Semantics

The syntax of commands is enriched with $\mathsf{strcpy}(e_1, e_2)$. This call copies the string pointed to by pointer e_2 into the buffer starting in e_1:

$$\mathcal{C}\{\!|\mathsf{strcpy}(e_1, e_2)|\!\}\sigma =$$

$$\left\{ \sigma[a_1 \boxplus j \mapsto \sigma(a_2 \boxplus j)]_{0 \leq j \leq l} \;\middle|\; \begin{array}{l} a_1 \in \mathcal{L}\{\!|*e_1|\!\}\sigma \wedge n_1 = \mathsf{allocsz}_{\mathcal{A}}(a_1) \\ a_2 \in \mathcal{L}\{\!|*e_2|\!\}\sigma \wedge n_2 = \mathsf{allocsz}_{\mathcal{A}}(a_2) \\ l = strlen_\sigma(a_2 : n_2) \wedge l \neq n_2 \wedge l < n_1 \end{array} \right\}$$

In the previous equation $\mathsf{allocsz}(a)$ denotes the number of bytes that are allocated starting from address a. The source buffer denoted by e_2 should contain a valid string, i.e. there should be some '\0' character before the end of the allocated source memory zone. In other words, the length $l = strlen_\sigma(a_2 : n_2)$ of the string should be different from n_2. Additionally, l should be smaller than the size n_1 of the destination buffer. Otherwise, there is not enough space to copy the entire string and, according to this semantics, the program halts.

$$\mathsf{strlen}(S, A) = \begin{cases} \bot_{\mathbb{Z}} & \text{if } S = \bot \vee A = \bot_{\mathbb{A}} \\ \varPhi S((x,o):m) \setminus \{m\} & A = (x,[o;o]) \wedge m = \mathsf{allocsz}_{\mathcal{A}}(x,o) \\ \mathsf{weakstrlen}(S,b) & \text{if } A = (x,O) \wedge b = \mathsf{tobuff}(A) \\ [0;+\infty] & \text{otherwise} \end{cases}$$

$$\mathsf{strcpy}(S, A, \bot) = \bot$$

$$\mathsf{strcpy}(S, A, [l;u]) =$$

$$\begin{cases} \bot & \text{if } S = \bot \vee A = \bot_{\mathbb{A}} \\ \eta(\varPhi S[(x,o):m \mapsto [l;m-1]]) & \text{if } A = (x,[o;o]) \wedge m = \min(u+1, \mathsf{allocsz}_{\mathcal{A}}(x,o)) \\ \eta(\mathsf{weakstrcpy}(S,b,[l;u])) & \text{if } A = (x,O) \wedge b = \mathsf{tobuff}(A) \wedge b \subseteq A \\ \mathsf{universe}(\pi) & \text{otherwise} \end{cases}$$

$$\mathsf{weakstrlen}(S, X) = \curlyvee \{\varPhi S(a:m) \setminus \{m\} \mid a \in X \wedge m = \mathsf{allocsz}_{\mathcal{A}}(a)\}$$

$$\mathsf{weakstrcpy}(S, a:n, [l;u]) = \varPhi S[a:m \mapsto \varPhi S(a:m) \curlyvee [l;m-1]]$$
$$\text{where } m = \min(u+n, \mathsf{allocsz}_{\mathcal{A}}(a))$$

Fig. 6. Abstract string length and string copy

4.2   Abstract Semantics

In the abstract world, strcpy is performed in two phases:

$$\mathcal{C}[\![\mathtt{strcpy}(e_1, e_2)]\!] S = (S_{\mathbb{Z}}, S_{\mathbb{P}}, \mathsf{strcpy}(S_{\mathbb{C}}, \mathcal{L}[\![*e_1]\!]S, \mathsf{strlen}(S_{\mathbb{C}}, \mathcal{L}[\![*e_2]\!]S)))$$

Both phases are defined in figure 6. First, strlen retrieves the length of the source string. When the address a of the source string is exactly known, it reads the information associated with the buffer that starts from a and goes until the first non-allocated address $a \boxplus m$. The length m represents the case when no null character is found before the end of the buffer. This case would halt the program and is thus eliminated from the result. Then, primitive strcpy updates the destination buffer with the new abstract length. When the destination address a is precisely known, the information is replaced by the new abstract length bounded by the size of the source zone. When the possible destination addresses are contained in a buffer $(a:n)$, weakstrcpy merges the previous length with interval $[l;u+n-1]$ bounded by the size of the destination zone. The lower bound l corresponds to the case when the smallest string is copied to a. The upper bound $u+n-1$ corresponds to the case when the longest string is copied to $a \boxplus (n-1)$. Notice how both primitives make extensive use of the algorithm $\varPhi$ to change partitions. They satisfy conditions:

$$\left\{ l \;\middle|\; \begin{array}{l} \sigma \in \gamma(S) \wedge a \in \gamma_{\mathbb{A}}(A) \wedge n = \mathsf{allocsz}_{\mathcal{A}}(a) \\ l = \mathsf{strlen}_{\sigma}(a:n) \wedge l \neq n \end{array} \right\} \subseteq \gamma_{\mathbb{Z}}(\mathsf{strlen}(S, A))$$

$$\left\{ \sigma[a \boxplus j \mapsto c_j]_{0 \leq j \leq l} \;\middle|\; \begin{array}{l} \sigma \in \gamma(S) \wedge a \in \gamma_{\mathbb{A}}(A) \wedge l \in \gamma_{\mathbb{Z}}(L) \\ n = \mathsf{allocsz}_{\mathcal{A}}(a) \wedge l < n \\ \forall 0 \leq j < l : c_j \neq \text{'\textbackslash 0'} \wedge c_l = \text{'\textbackslash 0'} \end{array} \right\} \subseteq \gamma(\mathsf{strcpy}(S, A, L))$$

This ensures the soundness of the abstract string copy with respect to its concrete counterpart. Theorem 1 still holds.

4.3   Checks

Information gathered by the static analysis is used to check that all potentially dangerous memory manipulations are safe. A predicate is applied to the abstract value computed for the arguments of each operation. If the predicate does not hold, then the tool has insufficient information to conclude the operation is safe and it emits a warning. We present three such predicates[1]:

– *Buffer overflows:* when accessing an array of size n at any index in $\gamma_{\mathbb{Z}}(I)$, the index should be within bounds:

$$\mathsf{check}_{[]}(I, n) = (0 \leq \min(I)) \wedge (\max(I) < n)$$

– *Pointer overflows:* when dereferencing a pointer P to a data of type τ, the pointer should be within the referenced zone:

$$\mathsf{check}_*(\langle A, I, N \rangle, \tau) = (0 \leq \min(I)) \wedge (\max(I) + \mathsf{sizeof}(\tau) \leq \min(N))$$

– *String buffer overflows:* when copying a string of length l in $\gamma_{\mathbb{Z}}(L)$ from a source address a in $\gamma_{\mathbb{A}}(x, O)$ to some destination address a' in $\gamma_{\mathbb{A}}(y, O')$, there should be a null character before the end of the allocated memory starting in a and there should be at least l bytes of allocated memory from a':

$$\mathsf{check}_{`\backslash 0\text{'}}(S, (x, O), (y, O'), L) =$$
$$\mathsf{tobuff}(x, O) \subseteq A \wedge a = (x, \max(O)) \wedge m = \mathsf{allocsz}_A(a) \wedge m \notin \varPhi S(a : m)$$
$$\wedge \, \mathsf{tobuff}(y, O') \subseteq A \wedge \max(L) < \mathsf{allocsz}_A(y, \max(O'))$$

5   Experiments

The static analysis was implemented in OCaml [16]. It uses CIL [18] as front-end. A simplification phase is applied to the CIL output to get to our kernel language. The analysis then propagates the abstract store following the structure of the code. Loops are dealt with simple fixpoint computation algorithms. Some loops are unfolded in order to improve precision. Once computations have stabilized, an ultimate pass checks potentially dangerous operations and emits warnings. Excluding CIL, the whole source code totals approximately 4000 lines of code.

The design of this static analysis was constantly lead by software most similar to what is found on actual aeronautical products. It is interesting to note that, in these case studies, approximately 60% of calls to `strcpy` have a constant string as source argument. Another 25% are called with a source buffer that is initialized with a constant string. Experiments were performed on small benchmarks from this software base. We sometimes had to manually remove union types which

---

[1] All abstract arguments are suppose to be different from $\bot$.

are not handled by this analysis. Among others, all 63 calls to `strcpy` in a 3000 lines of code program were successfully checked. Here is a small example that embodies some of the more difficult cases the tool had to process:

```
typedef struct {                 int main() {
   char* f;                        s a[2][2];
} s;                               s* ptr = (s*) &a[1];
char buf[10];                      init(ptr);
                                   ptr = (s*) &a[0];
void init(s* x) {                  strcpy(a[1][1].f, "strcpy ok");
   x[1].f = buf;                   strcpy(a[1][1].f, "strcpy not ok");
}                                }
```

The tool flags the second call to `strcpy`. Since it knows variable x and &a[1] are aliased, it deduces that a[1][1].f has size 10 and doesn't emit any warning for the first call. This example demonstrates that the integration of several C features in one tool are necessary to obtain sufficient precision.

6   Related Work

The detection of buffer overflows in C programs is an active field of research and various approaches have been proposed.

Fuzzing is a testing technique that consists in hooking a random generator to the inputs of a program. If the program crashes then defects may be uncovered. Smart fuzzing tools take advantage of the network protocols [1,3] or file formats [23] expected by the software in order to exercise the code in more depth. However, testing can usually not be exhaustive. Tools like StackGuard [8], ProPolice [2], CRED [20] and other [28] are C compiler's extension that implement runtime protection mechanisms. For instance, StackGuard uses a canary to detect attacks on the stack. Unfortunately, these techniques incur a non negligible overhead: either by slowing down execution or using up memory. Light static analyzes may remove unnecessary checks and improve performances [17]. In the end, all these techniques just turn buffer overflows into denial-of-service attacks.

Static analyses can detect defects before execution of the code. Several tools [27,25,4,15,11,30,26,12] sacrifice soundness to scalability or efficiency. Unsound tools include fast and imprecise lexical analyzer such as ITS4 [25]. BOON [26] and [12] both translate the verification problem into an integer constraint problem but ignore potential aliasing. Soundness is clearly mandatory in our context. ASTREE [7], Airac [14], CGS [24] are all sound tools based on abstract interpretation that aim at detecting all runtime errors in C code. ASTREE focuses on control command software without pointers, Airac on array out of bounds and CGS on dynamic memory manipulation. These approaches do not have any special treatment for strings, which is a potential source of imprecision in our case. CSSV [9] and the analysis of [22] are most close to our work. Like us, both adopt the abstraction pioneered in [26] of strings by their possible lengths. Unlike us, they use the expensive numerical domain of polyhedra. They handle dynamic allocation. Instead of incorporating value and pointer analysis together, both perform the pointer analysis separately. CSSV then translates the C program into an integer program. It needs function level annotations to produce precise results during a whole program analysis. CSSV can handle union types, albeit in a very imprecise way: each memory location has a size and any assignments of a value of different size sets the location to *unknown*. Interestingly, the abstraction in [22] associates the length of strings to pointers, rather than to the buffer where the string is stored. It seems difficult to extend the formalism in order to deal with more language features. In particular, two pointers are aliased when they have the same base address and length. This condition is clearly too restrictive and prevents the handling of multi-dimensional arrays or cast operations.

7 Conclusion

We have designed and implemented a new static analysis to check the correctness of all memory manipulations in C programs. It integrates several analysis techniques to handle pointers, structures, multi-dimensional arrays, some kinds of casts and strings. The analysis of strings is made as simple as possible thanks to transport operators that let tune the granularity of the abstraction. First experimental results are extremely promising, and the abstraction seems adequate to prove actual case studies correct. Further work will explore the semantics and abstractions necessary to deal with C union types with much precision.

References

1. Dave Aitel. The advantage of block-based protocol analysis for security testing. Technical report, Immunity,Inc., 2002.
2. A. Baratloo, N. Singh, and T. Tsai. Transparent run-time defense against stack smashing attacks. In *Proceedings of the USENIX Annual Technical Conference*, 2000.
3. Philippe Biondi. Scapy. http://www.secdev.org/projects/scapy/.
4. B. Chess. Improving computer security using extended static checking. In *IEEE Symposium on Security and Privacy*, 2002.
5. P. Cousot and R. Cousot. Abstract interpretation: a unified lattice model for static analysis of programs by construction or approximation of fixpoints. In *Conference Record of the 4th ACM Symposium on Principles of Programming Languages*. ACM Press, 1977.
6. P. Cousot and R. Cousot. Constructive versions of Tarski's fixed point theorems. *Pacific Journal of Mathematics*, 81(1), 1979.
7. P. Cousot, R. Cousot, J. Feret, L. Mauborgne, A. Miné, D. Monniaux, and X. Rival. The ASTRÉE Analyser. In *Proceedings of the European Symposium on Programming*, volume 3444 of *Lecture Notes in Computer Science*. Springer, 2005.
8. C. Cowan and al. StackGuard: Automatic adaptive detection and prevention of buffer-overflow attacks. In *Proceedings of the 7th USENIX Security Symposium*. USENIX Association, 1998.
9. Nurit Dor, Michael Rodeh, and Mooly Sagiv. CSSV: towards a realistic tool for statically detecting all buffer overflows in C. In *Proceedings of the ACM SIGPLAN 2003 conference on Programming language design and implementation*. ACM Press, 2003.

10. Mark W. Eichin and Jon A. Rochlis. With microscope and tweezers: An analysis of the internet virus of november 1988. In *Proceedings of the 1989 IEEE Symposium on Security and Privacy*. IEEE Computer Society Press, 1989.

11. David Evans and David Larochelle. Improving security using extensible lightweight static analysis. *IEEE Software*, 19(1), 2002.

12. Vinod Ganapathy, Somesh Jha, David Chandler, David Melski, and David Vitek. Buffer overrun detection using linear programming and static analysis. In *Proceedings of the 10th ACM conference on Computer and communications security*. ACM Press, 2003.

13. Erich Haugh and Matthew Bishop. Testing C programs for buffer overflow vulnerabilities. In *Proceedings of the Network and Distributed System Security Symposium*. The Internet Society, 2003.

14. Yungbum Jung, Jaehwang Kim, Jaeho Shin, and Kwangkeun Yi. Taming false alarms from a domain-unaware C analyzer by a bayesian statistical post analysis. In *Static Analysis, 12th International Symposium*, volume 3672 of *Lecture Notes in Computer Science*. Springer, 2005.

15. D. Larochelle and D. Evans. Statically detecting likely buffer overflow vulnerabilities. In *Proceedings of the 10th USENIX Security Symposium*, 2001.

16. X. Leroy, D. Doliguez, J. Garrigue, D. Rémy, and J. Vouillon. *The Objective Caml system release 3.06, documentation and user's manual*. Institut National de Recherche en Informatique et en Automatique (INRIA), 2002.

17. George C. Necula, Jeremy Condit, Matthew Harren, Scott McPeak, and Westley Weimer. CCured: type-safe retrofitting of legacy software. *ACM Transactions Programming Languages and Systems*, 27(3), 2005.

18. George C. Necula, Scott McPeak, S.P. Rahul, and Westley Weimer. CIL: Intermediate language and tools for analysis and transformation of C programs. In *Proceedings of Conference on Compiler Construction*, 2002.

19. Aleph One. Smashing the stack for fun and profit. *Phrack*, 7(49), 1996.

20. Olatunji Ruwase and Monica S. Lam. A practical dynamic buffer overflow detector. In *Network and Distributed System Security Symposium*. The Internet Society, 2004.

21. Michael Siff, Satish Chandra, Thomas Ball, Krishna Kunchithapadam, and Thomas W. Reps. Coping with type casts in C. In *7th European Software Engineering Conference*, volume 1687 of *Lecture Notes in Computer Science*. Springer, 1999.

22. Axel Simon and Andy King. Analyzing string buffers in C. In *Proceedings of the 9th International Conference on Algebraic Methodology and Software Technology*. Springer-Verlag, 2002.

23. Michael Sutton and Adam Greene. The art of file format fuzzing. In *Black Hat USA 2005*, 2005.

24. Arnaud Venet and Guillaume Brat. Precise and efficient static array bound checking for large embedded C programs. In *Proceedings of the ACM SIGPLAN 2004 conference on Programming language design and implementation*. ACM Press, 2004.

25. John Viega, J. T. Bloch, Y. Kohno, and Gary McGraw. ITS4: A static vulnerability scanner for C and C++ code. In *16th Annual Computer Security Applications Conference*. IEEE Computer Society, 2000.

26. David Wagner, Jeffrey S. Foster, Eric A. Brewer, and Alexander Aiken. A first step towards automated detection of buffer overrun vulnerabilities. In *Proceedings of the Network and Distributed System Security Symposium*. The Internet Society, 2000.

27. John Wilander and Mariam Kamkar. A comparison of publicly available tools for static intrusion prevention. In *7th Nordic Workshop on Secure IT Systems*, 2002.
28. John Wilander and Mariam Kamkar. A comparison of publicly available tools for dynamic buffer overflow prevention. In *Network and Distributed System Security Symposium*. The Internet Society, 2003.
29. Glynn Winskel. *The Formal Semantics of Programming Languages: An Introduction*. The MIT Press, 1993.
30. Yichen Xie, Andy Chou, and Dawson R. Engler. ARCHER: using symbolic, path-sensitive analysis to detect memory access errors. In *Proceedings of the 11th ACM SIGSOFT Symposium on Foundations of Software Engineering*. ACM, 2003.
31. K. Yi. Yet another ensemble of abstract interpreter, higher-order data-flow equations, and model checking. Technical Memorandum 2001-10, Research on Program Analysis System, National Creative Research Center, Korea Advanced Institute of Science and Technology, 2001.

Abstract Regular Tree Model Checking of Complex Dynamic Data Structures

Ahmed Bouajjani[1], Peter Habermehl[1], Adam Rogalewicz[2], and Tomáš Vojnar[2]

[1] LIAFA, University of Paris 7, Case 7014, 2 place Jussieu, F-75251 Paris 5, France
{Ahmed.Bouajjani, Peter.Habermehl}@liafa.jussieu.fr
[2] FIT, Brno University of Technology, Božetěchova 2, CZ-61266, Brno, Czech Republic
{rogalew, vojnar}@fit.vutbr.cz

Abstract. We consider the verification of non-recursive C programs manipulating dynamic linked data structures with possibly *several* next pointer selectors and with finite domain non-pointer data. We aim at checking basic memory consistency properties (no null pointer assignments, etc.) and shape invariants whose violation can be expressed in an existential fragment of a first order logic over graphs. We formalise this fragment as a logic for specifying bad memory patterns whose formulae may be translated to testers written in C that can be attached to the program, thus reducing the verification problem considered to checking reachability of an error control line. We encode configurations of programs, which are essentially shape graphs, in an original way as extended tree automata and we represent program statements by tree transducers. Then, we use the abstract regular tree model checking framework for a fully automated verification. The method has been implemented and successfully applied on several case studies.

1   Introduction

Automated verification of programs manipulating dynamic linked data structures is currently a very live research area. This is partly due to the fact that programs manipulating pointers are often complex and tricky, and so methods for automatically analysing them are quite welcome, and also because automated verification of such programs is not easy. Programs manipulating dynamic linked data structures are typically infinite-state systems, their configurations have in general the form of unrestricted graphs (often referred to as the *shape graphs*), and the shape invariants of these graphs may be temporarily broken by the programs during destructive pointer updates.

In this paper, we propose a new fully-automated method for analysing various important properties of programs manipulating dynamic linked data structures. We consider non-recursive C programs (with variables over finite data domains) manipulating dynamic linked data structures with possibly *several* next pointer selectors. The properties we consider are basic consistency of pointer manipulations (no *null pointer assignments*, no use of *undefined pointers*, no references to *deleted elements*). Further undesirable behaviour of the verified programs (e.g.,

K. Yi (Ed.): SAS 2006, LNCS 4134, pp. 52–70, 2006.
© Springer-Verlag Berlin Heidelberg 2006

breaking of certain *shape invariants* such as an introduction of undesirable sharing, cycles, etc.) may be detected via *testers written in C* and attached to the verified procedures. Moreover, for a more declarative way of specifying undesirable behaviour of the considered programs, we introduce a special-purpose logic LBMP (*logic of bad memory patterns*) and we show that its formulae may be automatically translated into C testers. Then, verification of these properties reduces to reachability of a designated error location.

Our verification method is based on using the approach of *abstract regular tree model checking* (ARTMC) [9]. In regular tree model checking, configurations of the systems being examined are encoded as trees over a suitable ranked alphabet, sets of configurations are described by tree automata, and transitions of the systems are encoded as tree transducers. Subsequently, one computes the set of all configurations reachable from an initial set of configurations by repeatedly applying the tree transducers on the set of the so-far reached configurations (encoded as tree automata). In order to make the method terminate as often as possible and to fight the state explosion problem arising due to increasing sizes of the automata to be handled, various kinds of automatically refinable abstractions over automata are used in ARTMC.

In order to be able to apply ARTMC for verification of programs manipulating dynamic linked data structures, whose configurations (shape graphs) need not be tree-like, we propose an *original encoding of shape graphs based on tree automata*. We use trees to encode the *tree skeleton* of a shape graph. The edges of the shape graph that are not directly encoded in the tree skeleton are then represented by *routing expressions* over the tree skeleton—i.e., regular expressions over directions in a tree (as, e.g., left up, right down, etc.) and the kind of nodes that can be visited on the way. Both the tree skeletons and the routing expressions are automatically discovered by our method. The idea of using routing expressions is inspired by PALE [28] and graph types [24] although there, they have a bit different form (see below) and are defined manually.

Next, we show how all *pointer-manipulating statements* of the C programming language (without pointer arithmetics, recursion, and with finite-domain non-pointer data) may be *automatically translated to tree transducers* over the proposed tree-automata-based representation of sets of shape graphs.

We implemented our method in a prototype tool based on the Mona tree libraries [23]. We have tested it on a number of non-trivial procedures manipulating singly-linked lists (SLL), doubly-linked lists (DLL), trees (including the Deutsch-Schorr-Waite tree traversal), lists of lists, and also trees with linked leaves. To the best of our knowledge, verifying some properties on trees with linked leaves have so-far not been considered in any other fully automated tool. The experimental results obtained from our tool are quite encouraging (and, moreover, we believe that there is still a lot of room for further improvements as we have, e.g., not used the mechanism of Mona's guided tree automata, we have used general-purpose, not specialised abstractions as in [11], etc.).

Related Work. There have been and there are currently being investigated various approaches to verification of programs manipulating dynamic linked data structures that differ in the degree of automation, generality, and/or principles used. Out of these techniques, we mention TVLA based on 3-valued predicate logic with transitive closure [29,26], PALE based on WSkS and tree automata [28], approaches based on predicate abstraction [4,27], memory patterns [32,15], graph grammars [25], separation logic [18], alias logic [14], or various (extended) automata [20,17,7]. Among these approaches, our method belongs to the most automated and at the same time most general ones.

The closest approach to what we propose here is the one of PALE that also uses tree automata (derived from WSkS formulae) as well as the idea of a tree skeleton and routing expressions. However, first, the encoding of PALE is different in that the routing expressions must deterministically choose their target, and also, for a given memory node, selector, and program line, the expression is fixed and cannot dynamically change during the run of the analysed program. Further, program statements are modelled as transformers on the level of WSkS formulae, not as transducers on the level of tree automata. Finally, the approach of PALE is not fully automatic as the user has to manually provide loop invariants and all needed routing expressions, which are automatically synthesised in our approach.

In [8], we proposed a method based on abstract regular *word* model checking for verifying programs with 1-selector dynamic data structures. The concept of regular word model checking was studied in a series of works—including, for instance, [22,12,1,6,11,21,31]. Several different works [30,13,2,3,9] have appeared on the subject of regular tree model checking as well. Our approach of abstract regular (tree) model checking provides efficiency and is the only one that has been so-far applied in the area of verifying programs with dynamic data structures.

Top-down tree automata on infinite trees are used for verification of pointer manipulating programs in [17]. Here, linked data structures are represented with unfolded loops as infinite trees. Unlike our general approach, the work identifies and concentrates on a decidable fragment of pointer manipulating programs and their properties. The allowed programs may be compiled into an automaton on pairs of trees, composed with the given input tree automaton, the undesirable output tree automaton, and emptiness of the product is then checked.

The logic LBMP we use is close to the existential (positive) fragment of the logic of reachable patterns (LRP) in linked data-structures [33] but there the purpose is to have a decidable logic for reasoning about post- and pre-conditions and closure under negation is important. In our work we only need to express negation of invariance properties, and our verification approach is model checking.

2   The Class of Programs and Properties Considered

2.1   The Considered Programs

We consider standard, non-recursive C programs manipulating dynamic linked data structures (with possibly *several* next pointer selectors). We do not consider pointer arithmetics. We suppose all non-pointer data to be abstracted to a finite domain by some of the existing techniques before our method is applied.

In the paper, we concentrate on the following pointer manipulating program statements: x=NULL, x=y, x = y->next, x->next = y, x = malloc(), free(x), and if (x==y) goto L1; else goto L2; for pointer variables x and y and program line labels L1 and L2. We suppose some further, commonly used statements (such as while loops or nested dereferences) to be encoded by the listed statements. For brevity, we do not explicitly discuss manipulation of non-pointer finite-domain data, which is anyway straightforward. An example of a typical program that our method can handle is the reversion of doubly-linked lists (DLL) shown in Fig. 1, which we also use as our running example.

```
// Doubly-Linked Lists
typedef struct {
    DLL *next, *prev;
} DLL;

DLL *DLL_reverse(DLL *x) {
    DLL *y,*z;
    z = NULL;
    y = x->next;
    while (y!=NULL) {
        x->next = z;
        x->prev = y;
        z = x; x = y;
        y = x->next
    }
    return x;
}
```

Fig. 1. Reversing a DLL

2.2 The Considered Properties

First of all, the properties we intend to check include *basic consistency of pointer manipulations*, i.e. absence of null and undefined pointer dereferences and references to already deleted nodes. Further, we would like to check various *shape invariance properties* (such as absence of sharing, acyclicity, or, e.g., the fact that if x->next == y (and y is not null) in a DLL, then also y->prev == x, etc.). To define such properties we propose two approaches described below.

Shape Testers. First, we use the so-called shape testers written in the C language. They can be seen as instrumentation code trying to detect violations of the memory shape properties at selected control locations of the original program. We extend slightly the C language used by the possibility of following next pointers backwards and by non-deterministic branching. For our verification tool, the testers are just a part of the code being verified. An

```
x = aDLLHead;
while (x != NULL && random())
    x = x->next;
if (x != NULL
        && x->next->prev != x)
    error();
```

Fig. 2. Checking the consistency of the next and previous pointers

error is announced when a line denoted by an error label is reached. This way, we can check a whole range of properties (including acyclicity, absence of sharing and other shape invariants as the relation of next and previous pointers in DLLs—cf. Fig 2).

A Logic of Bad Memory Patterns. Second, in order to allow the undesired violations of the memory shape properties to be specified more easily, we propose a logic-based specification language—namely, a *logic of bad memory patterns* (LBMP)—that is a fragment of the existential first order logic on graphs with (regular) reachability predicates (and an implicit existential quantification over paths). When defining the logic, our primary concern is not to obtain a decidable logic but rather to obtain a logic whose formulae may be automatically translated to the above mentioned C testers allowing us to *efficiently* test whether some bad shapes may arise from the given program by testing reachability of a designated error control line of a tester.

Let $\mathcal{V}$ be a finite set of program variables and $\mathcal{S}$ a finite set of selectors. The *formulae of LBMP* have the form $\Phi ::= \exists w_1, ... w_n.\varphi$ where $\mathcal{W} = \{w_1, ..., w_n\}$, $\mathcal{V} \cap \mathcal{W} = \emptyset$, is a set of formulae variables, $\varphi ::= \varphi \vee \varphi \mid \psi$, $\psi ::= \psi \wedge \psi \mid x \varrho y$, $x, y \in \mathcal{V} \cup \mathcal{W}$, and ϱ is a reachability formula defined below. To simplify the formulae, we allow y in $x \varrho y$ to be skipped if it is not referred to anywhere else. We suppose such a missing variable to be implicitly added and existentially quantified. Given a ψ formula, we define its associated graph to be the graph $G_\psi = (\mathcal{V} \cup \mathcal{W}, E)$ where $(x, y) \in E$ iff $x \varrho y$ is a conjunct in ψ. To avoid guessing in the tester corresponding to a formula, we require G_ψ of every top level ψ formula to have all nodes reachable from elements of $\mathcal{V}$.

An LBMP *reachability formula* has the form $\varrho ::= \xrightarrow{s} \mid \xleftarrow{s} \mid \varrho + \varrho \mid \varrho.\varrho \mid \varrho^* \mid [\sigma]$ where $s \in \mathcal{S}$ and σ is a local neighbourhood formula. Finally, an LBMP *local neighbourhood* formula has the form $\exists u_1, ..., u_m.BC(x \xrightarrow{s} y, x = y)$ where $\mathcal{U} = \{u_1, ..., u_m\}$ is a set of local formula variables, $\mathcal{U} \cap (\mathcal{V} \cup \mathcal{W} \cup \{p\}) = \emptyset$, $p \notin \mathcal{V} \cup \mathcal{W}$, $s \in \mathcal{S}$, $x \in \mathcal{V} \cup \mathcal{W} \cup \mathcal{U} \cup \{p\}$, $y \in \mathcal{V} \cup \mathcal{W} \cup \mathcal{U} \cup \{p, \bot, \top\}$, and BC is the Boolean closure. Here, $\bot$ represents NULL, $\top$ an undefined value, and p is a special variable that always represents the *current position* in a shape graph. Moreover, to avoid guessing in the evaluation of the local neighbourhood formulae, we require that if σ is transformed into σ' in DNF, and we construct a graph based on the positive $\xrightarrow{s}$ literals for each disjunct of σ', each node of such a graph is reachable from p.

The semantics of LBMP formulae is relatively straightforward. Therefore we defer its description to the full version of the paper [10]. Instead, we illustrate the semantics of LBMP formulae on several examples expressing undesirable phenomena that we would like to avoid when manipulating *acyclic doubly-linked lists*. In their case, it is undesirable if one of the following happens after some operation (as, for instance, reversion) on a given list—we suppose the resulting list to be pointed via the program variable l:

1. The list does not end with null, which can be tested via $l \xrightarrow{n}{}^* [p = \top]$,

2. The predecessor of the first element is not null, which corresponds to $l[\neg(p \xrightarrow{b} \bot)]$,

3. The predecessor of the successor of a node n is not n, which can be detected via the formula $l \xrightarrow{n}{}^* [\exists x. p \xrightarrow{n} x \wedge x \neq \bot \wedge \neg(x \xrightarrow{p} p)]$, or

4. The list is cyclic, i.e. $\exists x. l \xrightarrow{n}{}^* [p = x] \xrightarrow{n}\xrightarrow{n}{}^* [p = x]$. (Note that this property is in fact implied by items 2 and 3.)

All the given formulae can be joint by disjunction into a single LBMP formula. Due to the space limitations, we do not provide more examples of LBMP formulae, but we note that for all the structures mentioned later in Section 5, we are able to specify all the commonly considered undesirable situations in LBMP (some more examples of LBMP formulae can then be found in the full version of the paper [10]).

Due to a lack of space, the procedure for translating LBMP formulae is described in the full version of the paper [10]. Intuitively, it is quite easy to see that the existentially quantified LBMP formulae with a stress on exploring paths through the examined linked data structures starting from program variables can be encoded in a slightly extended C code, put after the program being verified, and used in an efficient way for checking safety of the given program. We translate disjunctions to non-deterministic branching, conjunctions and series of reachability formulae to series of tests, iteration in the reachability expressions to non-deterministic while loops. The needed extension of C includes non-deterministic branching and the possibility of following next pointers backwards. Both of these features may easily be handled in our verification framework.

2.3   The Verification Problem

Our verification problem is model checking of the described undesirable existential properties against the given program. Above, we explain that for the specification of a violation of shape invariants, we use shape testers or LBMP whose formulae are translated into shape testers. For shape testers, we need to check unreachability of their designated error location. Moreover, we model all program statements such that if some basic memory consistency error (like a null pointer assignment) happens, the control is automatically transferred to a unique error control location. Thus, we are in general interested in *checking unreachability of certain error control locations* in a program.

3   Automata-Based Verification Framework

In this section, we introduce the abstract tree regular model-checking framework based on tree automata and transducers that we use for solving our verification problem.

3.1   Tree Automata and Transducers

Terms and Trees. An *alphabet* Σ is a finite set of symbols. Σ is called *ranked* if there exists a *rank* function $\rho : \Sigma \to \mathbb{N}$. For each $k \in \mathbb{N}$, $\Sigma_k \subseteq \Sigma$ is the set of all symbols with rank k. Symbols of Σ_0 are called *constants*. Let χ be a denumerable set of symbols called *variables*. $T_\Sigma[\chi]$ denotes the set of *terms* over Σ and χ. The set $T_\Sigma[\emptyset]$ is denoted by T_Σ, and its elements are called *ground terms*. A term t from $T_\Sigma[\chi]$ is called *linear* if each variable occurs at most once in t.

A finite ordered *tree* t over a set of labels L is a mapping $t : \mathcal{P}os(t) \to L$ where $\mathcal{P}os(t) \subseteq \mathbb{N}^*$ is a finite, prefix-closed set of *positions* in the tree. A term $t \in T_\Sigma[\chi]$ can naturally also be viewed as a tree whose leaves are labelled by constants and variables, and each node with k sons is labelled by a symbol from Σ_k [16]. Therefore, below, we sometimes exchange terms and trees. We denote $\mathcal{N}l\mathcal{P}os(t) = \{p \in \mathcal{P}os(t) \mid \neg\exists i \in \mathbb{N} : pi \in \mathcal{P}os(t)\}$ the set of *non-leaf* positions.

Tree Automata. A *bottom-up tree automaton* over a ranked alphabet Σ is a tuple $A = (Q, \Sigma, F, \delta)$ where Q is a finite set of states, $F \subseteq Q$ is a set of final states, and δ is a set of transitions of the following types: (i) $f(q_1, \ldots, q_n) \to_\delta q$, (ii) $a \to_\delta q$, and (iii) $q \to_\delta q'$ where $a \in \Sigma_0$, $f \in \Sigma_n$, and $q, q', q_1, \ldots, q_n \in Q$. Below, we call a bottom-up tree automaton simply a tree automaton.

Let t be a ground term. A run of a tree automaton A on t is defined as follows. First, leaves are labelled with states. If a leaf is a symbol $a \in \Sigma_0$ and there is a rule $a \to_\delta q \in \delta$, the leaf is labelled by q. An internal node $f \in \Sigma_k$ is labelled by q if there exists a rule $f(q_1, q_2, \ldots, q_k) \to_\delta q \in \delta$ and the first son of the node has the state label q_1, the second one q_2, ..., and the last one q_k. Rules of the type $q \to_\delta q'$ are called ε-steps and allow us to change a state label from q to q'. If the top symbol is labelled with a state from the set of final states F, the term t is accepted by the automaton A.

A set of ground terms accepted by a tree automaton A is called a *regular tree language* and is denoted by $L(A)$. Let $A = (Q, \Sigma, F, \delta)$ be a tree automaton and $q \in Q$ a state, then we define the *language of the state q—$L(A, q)$—* as the set of ground terms accepted by the tree automaton $A_q = (Q, \Sigma, \{q\}, \delta)$. The language $L^{\leq n}(A, q)$ is defined to be the set $\{t \in L(A, q) \mid height(t) \leq n\}$.

Tree Transducers. A *bottom-up tree transducer* is a tuple $\tau = (Q, \Sigma, \Sigma', F, \delta)$ where Q is a finite set of states, $F \subseteq Q$ a set of final states, Σ an input ranked alphabet, Σ' an output ranked alphabet, and δ a set of transition rules of the following types: (i) $f(q_1(x_1), \ldots, q_n(x_n)) \to_\delta q(u)$, $u \in T_{\Sigma'}[\{x_1, \ldots, x_n\}]$, (ii) $q(x) \to_\delta q'(u)$, $u \in T_{\Sigma'}[\{x\}]$, and (iii) $a \to_\delta q(u)$, $u \in T_{\Sigma'}$ where $a \in \Sigma_0$, $f \in \Sigma_n$, $x, x_1, \ldots, x_n \in \chi$, and $q, q', q_1, \ldots, q_n \in Q$. In the following, we call a bottom-up tree transducer simply a tree transducer. We always use tree transducers with $\Sigma = \Sigma'$.

A run of a tree transducer τ on a ground term t is similar to a run of a tree automaton on this term. First, rules of type *(iii)* are used. If a leaf is labelled by a symbol a and there is a rule $a \to_\delta q(u) \in \delta$, the leaf is replaced by the term u and labelled by the state q. If a node is labelled by a symbol f, there is a rule $f(q_1(x_1), q_2(x_2), \ldots, q_n(x_n)) \to_\delta q(u) \in \delta$, the first subtree of the node has the state label q_1, the second one q_2, ..., and the last one q_n, then the symbol f and all subtrees of the given node are replaced according to the right-hand side of the rule with the variables $x_1, \ldots, x_n$ substituted by the corresponding left-hand-side subtrees. The state label q is assigned to the new tree. Rules of type *(ii)* are called ε-steps. They allow us to replace a q-state-labelled tree by the right hand side of the rule and assign the state label q' to this new tree with the variable x in the rule substituted by the original tree. A run of a transducer is successful if the root of a tree is processed and is labelled by a state from F.

A tree transducer is *linear* if all right-hand sides of its rules are linear (no variable occurs more than once). The class of linear bottom-up tree transducers is closed under composition. A tree transducer is called *structure-preserving* (or a *relabelling*) if it does not modify the structure of input trees and just changes the labels of their nodes. By abuse of notation, we identify a transducer τ with the relation $\{(t, t') \in T_\Sigma \times T_\Sigma \mid t \to_\delta^* q(t')$ for some $q \in F\}$. For a set $L \subseteq T_\Sigma$ and a relation $R \subseteq T_\Sigma \times T_\Sigma$, we denote $R(L)$ the set $\{w \in T_\Sigma \mid \exists w' \in L : (w', w) \in R\}$ and $R^{-1}(L)$ the set $\{w \in T_\Sigma \mid \exists w' \in L : (w, w') \in R\}$. If τ is a linear tree transducer and L is a regular tree language, then the sets $\tau(L)$ and $\tau^{-1}(L)$ are regular and effectively constructible [19,16].

Let $id \subseteq T_\Sigma \times T_\Sigma$ be the identity relation and $\circ$ the composition of relations. We define recursively the relations $\tau^0 = id$, $\tau^{i+1} = \tau \circ \tau^i$ and $\tau^* = \cup_{i=0}^\infty \tau^i$. Below, we suppose $id \subseteq \tau$ meaning that $\tau^i \subseteq \tau^{i+1}$ for all $i \geq 0$.

3.2   Abstract Regular Tree Model Checking

Let us recall the basic principles of abstract regular tree model checking (ARTMC) [9]. Let Σ be a ranked alphabet and $\mathbb{M}_\Sigma$ the set of all tree automata over Σ. Let $Init \in \mathbb{M}_\Sigma$ be a tree automaton describing a set of initial configurations, τ a tree transducer describing the behaviour of a system, and $Bad \in \mathbb{M}_\Sigma$ a tree automaton describing a set of bad configurations. The verification problem is to check whether

$$\tau^*(L(Init)) \cap L(Bad) = \emptyset \tag{1}$$

One of the methods how to check this is ARTMC [9]. Instead of computing the precise set of reachable configurations, it computes an overapproximation.

We define an abstraction function as a mapping $\alpha : \mathbb{M}_\Sigma \to \mathbb{A}_\Sigma$ where $\mathbb{A}_\Sigma \subseteq \mathbb{M}_\Sigma$ and $\forall M \in \mathbb{M}_\Sigma : L(M) \subseteq L(\alpha(M))$. An abstraction α' is called a *refinement* of the abstraction α if $\forall M \in \mathbb{M}_\Sigma : L(\alpha'(M)) \subseteq L(\alpha(M))$. Given a tree transducer τ and an abstraction α, we define a mapping $\tau_\alpha : \mathbb{M}_\Sigma \to \mathbb{M}_\Sigma$ as $\forall M \in \mathbb{M}_\Sigma :$ $\tau_\alpha(M) = \hat\tau(\alpha(M))$ where $\hat\tau(M)$ is the minimal deterministic automaton describing the language $\tau(L(M))$. An abstraction α is *finitary*, if the set $\mathbb{A}_\Sigma$ is finite.

For a given abstraction function α, we can compute iteratively the sequence of automata $(\tau_\alpha^i(Init))_{i\geq0}$. If the abstraction α is finitary, then there exists $k \geq 0$ such that $\tau_\alpha^{k+1}(Init) = \tau_\alpha^k(Init)$. The definition of the abstraction function α implies, that $L(\tau_\alpha^k(Init)) \supseteq \tau^*(L(Init))$.

If $L(\tau_\alpha^k(Init)) \cap L(Bad) = \emptyset$, then the verification problem (1) has a positive answer. If the intersection is non-empty, we must check whether it is a real counterexample, or a spurious one. The spurious counterexample may be caused by the used abstraction (the counterexample is not reachable from the set of initial configurations). Assume that $\tau_\alpha^k(Init) \cap L(Bad) \neq \emptyset$, which means that there is a symbolic path:

$$Init, \tau_\alpha(Init), \tau_\alpha^2(Init), \cdots \tau_\alpha^{n-1}(Init), \tau_\alpha^n(Init) \tag{2}$$

such that $L(\tau_\alpha^n(Init)) \cap L(Bad) \neq \emptyset$.

Let $X_n = L(\tau_\alpha^n(Init)) \cap L(Bad)$. Now, for each l, $0 \leq l < n$, we compute $X_l = L(\tau_\alpha^l(Init)) \cap \tau^{-1}(X_{l+1})$. Two possibilities may occur: (a) $X_0 \neq \emptyset$, which means that the verification problem (1) has a negative answer, and $X_0 \subseteq L(Init)$ is a set of dangerous initial configurations. (b) $\exists m, 0 \leq m < n, X_{m+1} \neq \emptyset \wedge X_m = \emptyset$ meaning that the abstraction function is too rough—we need to refine it and start the verification process again.

In [9], two general-purpose kinds of abstractions are proposed. Both are based on *automata state equivalences*. Tree automata states are split into several equivalence classes, and all states from one class are collapsed into one state. An abstraction becomes finitary if the number of equivalence classes is finite. The refinement is done by refining the equivalence classes. Both of the proposed abstractions allow for an automatic refinement to exclude the encountered spurious counterexample.

The first proposed abstraction is an *abstraction based on languages of trees of a finite height*. It defines two states equivalent if their languages up to the give height n are equivalent. There is just a finite number of languages of height n, therefore this abstraction is finitary. A refinement is done by an increase of the height n. The second proposed abstraction is an *abstraction based on predicate languages*. Let $\mathcal{P} = \{P_1, P_2, \ldots, P_n\}$ be a set of *predicates*. Each predicate $P \in \mathcal{P}$ is a tree language represented by a tree automaton. Let $M = (Q, \Sigma, F, \delta)$ be a tree automaton. Then, two states $q_1, q_2 \in Q$ are equivalent if their languages $L(M, q_1)$ and $L(M, q_2)$ have a nonempty intersection with exactly the same subset of predicates from the set $\mathcal{P}$. Since there is just a finite number of subsets of $\mathcal{P}$, the abstraction is finitary. A refinement is done by adding new predicates, i.e. tree automata corresponding to the languages of all the states in the automaton of X_{m+1} from the analysis of spurious counterexample ($X_m = \emptyset$).

4 Tree Automata Encoding of Pointer Manipulating Programs

4.1 Encoding of Sets of Memory Configurations

Memory configurations of the considered programs with a finite set of pointer variables $\mathcal{V}$, a finite set of selectors $\mathcal{S} = \{1, ..., k\}$, and a finite domain $\mathcal{D}$ of data stored in dynamically allocated memory cells can be described as shape graphs of the following form. A *shape graph* is a tuple $SG = (N, S, V, D)$ where N is a finite set of memory nodes, $N \cap \{\bot, \top\} = \emptyset$ (we use $\bot$ to represent null, and $\top$ to represent an undefined pointer value), $N_{\bot,\top} = N \cup \{\bot, \top\}$, $S : N \times \mathcal{S} \to N_{\bot,\top}$ is a successor function, $V : \mathcal{V} \to N_{\bot,\top}$ is a mapping that defines where the pointer variables are currently pointing to, and $D : N \to \mathcal{D}$ defines what data are stored in the particular memory nodes. We suppose $\top \in \mathcal{D}$—the data value $\top$ is used to denote "zombies" of deleted nodes, which we keep and detect all erroneous attempts to access them.

To be able to describe the way we encode sets of shape graphs using tree automata, we first need a few auxiliary notions. First, to allow for dealing with more general shape graphs than tree-like, we do not simply identify the next pointers with the branches of the trees accepted by tree automata. Instead, we use the tree structure just as a backbone over which links between the allocated nodes are expressed using the so-called *routing expressions*, which are regular expressions over directions in a tree (like move up, move left down, etc.) and over the nodes that can be seen on the way. From nodes of the trees described by tree automata, we refer to the routing expressions via some symbolic names called *pointer descriptors* that we assign to them—we suppose dealing with a finite set of pointer descriptors $\mathcal{R}$. Moreover, we couple each pointer descriptor with a unique *marker* from a set $\mathcal{M}$ (and so $||\mathcal{R}|| = ||\mathcal{M}||$). The routing expressions may identify several target nodes for a single source memory node and a single selector. Markers associated with the target nodes can then be used to decrease the non-determinism of the description (only nodes marked with the right marker are considered as the target).

Let us now fix the sets $\mathcal{V}$, $\mathcal{S}$, $\mathcal{D}$, $\mathcal{R}$, and $\mathcal{M}$. We use a *ranked alphabet* $\Sigma = \Sigma_2 \cup \Sigma_1 \cup \Sigma_0$ consisting of symbols of ranks $k = ||\mathcal{S}||$, 1, and 0. Symbols of rank k represent allocated memory nodes that may be pointed by some pointer variables, may be marked by some markers as targets of some next pointers, they contain some data and have k next pointers specified either as null, undefined, or via some next pointer descriptor. Thus, $\Sigma_2 = 2^{\mathcal{V}} \times 2^{\mathcal{M}} \times \mathcal{D} \times (\mathcal{R} \cup \{\bot, \top\})^k$. Given an element $n \in \Sigma_2$, we use the notation $n.var$, $n.mark$, $n.data$, and $n.s$ (for $s \in \mathcal{S}$) to refer to the pointer variables, markers, data, and descriptors associated with n, respectively. Σ_1 is used for specifying nodes with undefined and null pointer variables, and so $\Sigma_1 = 2^{\mathcal{V}}$. Finally, in our trees, the leaves are all the same (with no special meaning), and so $\Sigma_0 = \{\bullet\}$.

We can now specify the *tree memory backbones* we use to encode memory configurations as the trees that belong to the language of the tree automaton with the following rules[1]: (1) $\bullet \to q_i$, (2) $\Sigma_2(q_i/q_m, ..., q_i/q_m) \to q_m$, (3) $\Sigma_1(q_m/q_i) \to q_n$, and (4) $\Sigma_1(q_n) \to q_u$. Intuitively, q_i, q_m, q_n, and q_u are automata states, where q_i accepts the leaves, q_m accepts the memory nodes, q_n accepts the node encoding null variables, and q_u, which is the accepting state, accepts the node with undefined variables. Note that there is always a single node with undefined variables, a single node with null variables, and then a sub-tree with the memory allocated nodes. Thus, every memory tree t can be written as $t = undef(null(t'))$ for $undef, null \in \Sigma_1$. We say a memory tree $t = undef(null(t'))$ is *well-formed* if the pointer variables are assigned unique meanings, i.e. $undef \cap null = \emptyset \wedge \forall p \in \mathcal{N}lPos(t') : t'(p).var \cap (null \cup undef) = \emptyset \wedge \forall p_1 \neq p_2 \in \mathcal{N}lPos(t') : t'(p_1).var \cap t'(p_2).var = \emptyset$ where $\mathcal{N}lPos$ are non-leaf positions—cf. Section 3.1.

We let $\mathcal{S}^{-1} = \{s^{-1} \mid s \in \mathcal{S}\}$ be a set of "inverted selectors" allowing one to follow the links in a shape graph in a reverse order. A *routing expression* may then be formally defined as a regular expression on pairs $s.p \in (\mathcal{S} \cup \mathcal{S}^{-1}).\Sigma_2$. Intuitively, each pair used as a basic building block of a routing expression describes one step over the tree memory backbone: we follow a certain branch up or down and then we should see a certain node (most often, we will use the node components of routing expressions to check whether a certain marker is set in a particular node).

A *tree memory encoding* is a tuple (t, μ) where t is a tree memory backbone and μ a mapping from the set of pointer descriptors $\mathcal{R}$ to routing expressions over the set of selectors $\mathcal{S}$ and the memory node alphabet Σ_2 of t. An example of a tree memory encoding for a *doubly-linked list* (DLL) is shown in Fig. 3.

Let (t, μ), $t = undef(null(t'))$, be a tree memory encoding with a set of selectors $\mathcal{S}$ and a memory node alphabet Σ_2. We call $\pi = p_1 s_1 ... p_l s_l p_{l+1} \in$

---

[1] If we put a set into the place of the input symbol in a transition rule, we mean we can use any element of the set. Moreover, if we use q_1/q_2 instead of a single state, one can take either q_1 or q_2, and if there is a k-tuple of states, one considers all possible combinations of states.

The original DLL   A tree memory encoding of the DLL   Descriptors

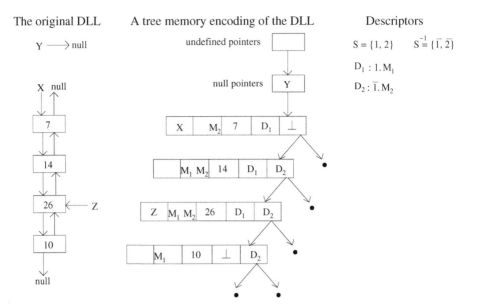

Fig. 3. An example of a tree memory encoding—a doubly linked list (DLL)

$\Sigma_2.((\mathcal{S} \cup \mathcal{S}^{-1}).\Sigma_2)^l$ a *path in* t of length $l \geq 1$ iff $p_1 \in \mathcal{P}os(t')$ and $\forall i \in \{1, ..., l\}$: $(s_i \in \mathcal{S} \wedge p_i.s_i = p_{i+1} \wedge p_{i+1} \in \mathcal{P}os(t')) \vee (s_i \in \mathcal{S}^{-1} \wedge p_{i+1}.s_i = p_i)$. For $p, p' \in \mathcal{N}l\mathcal{P}os(t')$ and a selector $s \in \mathcal{S}$, we write $p \xrightarrow{s} p'$ iff (1) $t'(p).s \in \mathcal{R}$, (2) there is a path $p_1 s_1 ... p_l s_l p_{l+1}$ in t for some $l \geq 0$ such that $p = p_1$, $p_{l+1} = p'$, and (3) $s_1 t'(p_2)...t'(p_l) s_l t'(p_{l+1}) \in \mu(t'(p).s)$.

The *set of shape graphs represented by a tree memory encoding* (t, μ) with $t = undef(null(t'))$ is denoted by $[\![(t, \mu)]\!]$ and given as all the shape graphs $SG = (N, S, V, D)$ for which there is a bijection $\beta : \mathcal{P}os(t') \rightarrow N$ such that:

1. $\forall p, p' \in \mathcal{N}l\mathcal{P}os(t') \; \forall s \in \mathcal{S} : (t'(p).s \notin \{\bot, \top\} \wedge p \xrightarrow{s} p') \Leftrightarrow S(\beta(p), s) = \beta(p')$.
   (The links between memory nodes are respected.)
2. $\forall p \in \mathcal{N}l\mathcal{P}os(t') \; \forall s \in \mathcal{S} \; \forall x \in \{\bot, \top\} : t'(p).s = x \Leftrightarrow S(\beta(p), s) = x$.
   (Null and undefined successors are respected.)
3. $\forall v \in \mathcal{V} \; \forall p \in \mathcal{P}os(t') : v \in t'(p).var \Leftrightarrow V(v) = \beta(p)$.
   (Assignment of memory nodes to variables is respected.)
4. $\forall v \in \mathcal{V} : (v \in null \Leftrightarrow V(v) = \bot) \wedge (v \in undef \Leftrightarrow V(v) = \top)$.
   (Assignment of null and undefinedness of variables are respected.)
5. $\forall p \in \mathcal{N}l\mathcal{P}os(t') \; \forall d \in \mathcal{D} : t'(p).data = d \Leftrightarrow D(\beta(p)) = d$.
   (Data stored in memory nodes is respected.)

A *tree automata memory encoding* is a tuple (A, μ) where A is a tree automaton accepting a regular set of tree memory backbones and μ is a mapping as above. Naturally, A represents the set of shape graphs defined by $[\![(A, \mu)]\!] = \bigcup_{t \in L(A)} [\![(t, \mu)]\!]$.

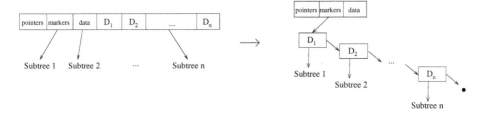

Fig. 4. Splitting memory nodes in Mona into data and next pointer nodes

Remarks. We use ARTMC as our verification method. It syntactically manipulates tree automata A whose languages can be interpreted as shape graphs using
our encoding. Notice, that (A, μ) and $[\![(A, \mu)]\!]$ are two different notions, since the
encoding is not canonical as a given shape graph can be possibly obtained by
several different tree memory encodings. In Section 4.3, we argue that program
statements can, nevertheless, be encoded faithfully as tree transducers. Another
important property of the encoding is that given a tree automata memory encoding (A, μ), the set $[\![(A, \mu)]\!]$ can be empty although $L(A)$ is not empty (since the
routing expressions can be incompatible with the tree automaton). Of course,
if $L(A)$ is empty, then $[\![(A, \mu)]\!]$ is also empty. Therefore, checking emptiness of
$[\![(A, \mu)]\!]$ (which is important for applying the ARTMC framework, see Section
4.4) can be done in a sound way by checking emptiness of $L(A)$.

4.2   Tree Memory Configurations in Mona

In our implementation, we use the tree automata library from the Mona project
[23]. As the library supports binary trees only, and we need n-ary ones, we *split
each memory node* labelled with $\Sigma_2 = 2^{\mathcal{V}} \times 2^{\mathcal{M}} \times \mathcal{D} \times (\mathcal{R} \cup \{\bot, \top\})^k$ in the above
definition of a tree memory encoding into a data node labelled with $2^{\mathcal{V}} \times 2^{\mathcal{M}} \times \mathcal{D}$
and a series of k next pointer nodes, each labelled with $\mathcal{R} \cup \{\bot, \top\}$—cf. Fig. 4.

As for the set of *pointer descriptors* $\mathcal{R}$, we currently fix it by introducing
a unique pointer descriptor for each destructive update x->s = y or x->s =
new that appears in the program. This is because they are the statements that
establish new links among the allocated memory nodes. In addition, we might
have some further descriptors if they are a part of the specification of the input
configurations (see section 4.4).

Further, in our Mona-based framework, we encode *routing expressions* using
tree transducers. A transducer representing a routing expression r simply copies
the input tree memory backbone on which it is applied up to: (1) looking for a data
node n_1 that is labelled with a special token $\blacklozenge \notin \mathcal{V} \cup \mathcal{M} \cup \mathcal{D}$ and (2) moving $\blacklozenge$
to a data node n_2 that is the target of the next pointer described by r and that
is also marked with the appropriate marker. As described in the next section, we
can then implement program statements that follow the next pointers (e.g., x =
y->s) by putting the token $\blacklozenge$ to a node pointed to by x, applying the transducer
implementing the appropriate routing expression, and making y point to the node
to which $\blacklozenge$ was moved. Due to applying abstraction, the target may not always be

unique—in such a case, the transducer implementing the routing expression simply returns a set of trees in which ♦ is put to some target data node such that all possibilities where it can get via the given routing expression are covered.

Note that the use of tree transducers for encoding routing expressions allows us in theory to express more than using just regular expressions. In particular, we can refer to the tree context of the nodes via which the given route is going. In our current implementation, we, however, do not use this fact.

4.3   Encoding Program Statements as Tree Transducers

We encode every of the considered pointer-manipulating statements as a tree transducer. In the transducer, we expect the tree memory encoding to be extended by a new root symbol which corresponds to the *current program line* or to an error indication when an error is found during the analysis. We now briefly describe how the transducers corresponding to the program statements work. Each transducer is constructed in such a way, that it simulates the effect of a program statement on a set of shape graphs represented by a tree automata memory encoding: if a shape SG represented by a tree memory encoding is transformed by the program statement to a shape graph SG', then the transducer transforms the tree memory encoding such that it represents SG'. This makes sure, that although the encoding is non canonical (see end of section 4.1), we simulate faithfully a program statement.

Non-destructive Updates and Tests. The simplest is the case of the x = NULL assignment. The transducer implementing it just goes through the input tree and copies it to the output with the exception that (1) it removes x from the labelling of the node in which it currently is and adds it to the labelling of the *null* node and (2) changes the current line appropriately. The transducer implementing an assignment x = y is similar, it just puts x not to the *null* node, but to the node which is currently labelled by y.

The transducers for the tests of the form if (x == null) goto l1; else goto l2; are very similar to the above—they just do not change the node in which x is, but only change the current program line to either l1 or l2 according to whether or not x is in the *null* node. If x is in *undef*, an error indication is used instead of l1 or l2. The transducers for if (x == y) goto l1; else goto l2; are similar—they just test whether or not x and y appear in the same node (both different from *undef*).

The transducer for an x = y->s statement is a union of several complementary actions. If y is in *null* or *undef*, an error is indicated. If y is in a regular data node and its s-th next pointer node contains either ⊥ or ⊤, the transducer removes x from the node it is currently in and puts it into the *null* or *undef* node, respectively. If y is in a regular data node n and its s-th next pointer node contains some pointer descriptor $r \in \mathcal{R}$, the ♦ token is put to n. Then, the routing expression transducer associated with r is applied. Finally, x is removed from its current node and put into the node to which ♦ was moved by the applied routing expression transducer.

Destructive Updates. The destructive pointer update x->s = y is implemented as follows. If x is in *null* or *undef*, an error is indicated. If x is defined and if y is in *null* or *undef*, the transducer puts $\bot$ or $\top$ into the *s*-th next pointer node below x, respectively. Otherwise, the transducer puts the pointer descriptor r associated with the particular x->s = y statement being fired into the *s*-th next pointer node below x, and it marks the node in which y is by the marker coupled with r. Then, the routing expression transducer associated with r is updated such that it includes the path from the node of x to the node of y.

One could think of various strategies how to *extract the path* going from the node of x to the node of node y. Currently, we use a simple strategy, which is, however, successful in many practical examples as our experiments show: We extract the shortest path between x and y on the tree memory backbone, which consists of going a certain number of steps upwards to the closest common parent of x and y and then going a certain number of steps downwards. (The upward or the downward phase may also be skipped when going just down or up, respectively.) When extracting this path, we project away all information about nodes we see on the way and about nodes not directly lying on the path. Only the directions (left/right up/down) and the number of steps are preserved.

Note that we, in fact, perform the operation of routing expression extraction on a tree automaton, and we extract all possible paths between where x and y may currently be. The result is transformed into a transducer τ_{xy} that moves the token ◆ from the position of x to the position of y, and τ_{xy} is then united with the current routing expression transducer associated with the given pointer descriptor r. The extraction of the routing paths is done partly by rewriting the input tree automaton via a special transducer τ_{π} that in one step identifies all the shortest paths between all x and y positions and projects away the non-necessary information about the nodes on the way. The transducer τ_{π} is simple: it just checks that we are going one branch up from x and one branch down to y while meeting in a single node. The transition relation of the resulting transducer is then post-processed by changing the context of the path to an arbitrary one which cannot be done by transducing in Mona where structure preserving transducers may only be used.

Dynamic Allocation and Deallocation. The x = malloc() statement is implemented by rewriting the right-most ● leaf node to a new data node pointed to by x. Below the node, the procedure also creates all the k next pointer nodes whose contents is set to $\top$.

In order to exploit the regularity that is always present in algorithms allocating new data structures, which typically add new elements at the end/leaves of the structure, we also explicitly support an x.*s* = malloc() statement. We even try to pre-process programs and compact all successive pairs of statements of the form x = malloc(); y->s = x (provided x is not used any further) to y->s= malloc(). Such a statement is then implemented by adding the new element directly under the node pointed to by y (provided it is a leaf) and joining it by a simple routing expression of the form "one level down via a certain branch". This typically allows us to work with much simpler and more precise routing expressions.

Finally, a free(x) statement is implemented by a transducer that moves all variables that are currently in the node pointed to by x to the *undef* node (if x is in *null* or *undef*, an error is indicated). Then, the node is marked by a special marker as a deleted node, but it stays in our tree memory encoding with all its current markers set. In addition to all the other tests mentioned above as done within the transducer implementing an x = y->s assignment, it is also tested whether the target is not deleted—if so, an error is indicated.

4.4   Verification of Programs with Pointers Using ARTMC

Input Structures. We consider two possibilities how to encode the input structures. First, we can directly use the tree automata memory encoding—e.g., a tree automata memory encoding (with two pointer descriptors *next* and *prev* and the corresponding routing expressions) describing all possible doubly-linked lists pointed to by some program variable. Such an encoding can be provided manually or derived automatically from a description of the concerned linked data structure provided, e.g., as a graph type [24]. The main advantage is that the verification process starts

```
aDLLHead = malloc();
aDLLHead->prev = null;
x = aDLLHead;
while (random()) {
    x->next = malloc();
    x->next->prev = x;
    x = x->next;
}
x->next = null;
```

Fig. 5. Generating DLLs

with an exact encoding of the set of all possible instances of the considered data structure.

Another possible approach is to start with the unique "empty" shape graph where all variables are undefined. We can encode such a shape graph using a tree automata encoding where all variables are in *undef*, *null* is empty, there are no other nodes, and all the routing expressions are empty. The set of structures on which the examined procedure should be verified is then supposed to be generated by a *constructor written in C* by the user (as, e.g., in Fig. 5). This constructor is then put before the verified procedure and the whole program is given to the model checker. The advantage is that no further notation is necessary. The disadvantage is that we have more code that is subject to the verification and the set of automatically obtained input structures need not be encoded in the optimal way leading to a slow-down of the verification.

Applying ARTMC. In Section 3.2, we have given an overview of ARTMC. We supposed that one transducer τ is used to describe the behaviour of the whole system. In the application described in this paper, we use a variant of this approach by considering each program statement as one transducer. Then, we compute an overapproximation of the reachable configurations for each program line by starting from an initial set of shape graphs represented by a tree automata memory encoding and iterating the abstract fixpoint computation described in Section 3.2 through the program structure. The fixpoint computation stops if the abstraction α is finitary. In such a case, the number of the abstracted tree automata encoding sets of the memory backbones that can arise in the program being checked is finite. Moreover, the number of the arising routing expressions is also finite as they are extracted from the bounded number of the tree automata describing the encountered sets of memory backbones.[2]

---

[2] The non-canonicity of our encoding does not prevent the computation from stopping. It may just take longer since several encodings for the same graph could be added.

During the computation, we check whether a designated error location in the program is reached or whether a fixpoint is attained. In the latter case, the property is satisfied (the error control location is not reachable). In the former case, we compute backwards to check if the counterexample is spurious as explained in Section 3.2. However, as said in Section 4.1, the check for emptiness is not exact and therefore we might conclude that we have obtained a real counterexample although this is not the case. Such a case does not happen in any of our experiments and could be detected by replaying the path from the initial configurations.

5   Implementation and Experimental Results

An ARTMC Tool for Tree Automata Memory Encodings. We have implemented the above proposed method in a prototype tool based on the Mona tree automata libraries [23]. We use a depth-first strategy when iterating the transducers corresponding to the particular program lines.

We have also refined the basic finite-height and predicate abstractions proposed in [9]. In particular, we do not allow collapsing of data nodes with next pointer nodes, collapsing of next pointer nodes corresponding to different selectors, and we prevent the abstraction of allowing a certain pointer variable to point to several memory nodes at the same time.

We have also proposed one new abstraction schema called the *neighbour abstraction*. Under this schema, only the tree automata states are collapsed that (1) accept equal data memory nodes with equal next pointer nodes associated with them and (2) that directly follow each other (are neighbours). This strategy is very simple, yet it proved useful in some practical cases.

Finally, we allow the abstraction to be applied either at all program lines or only at the loop closing points. In some cases, the latter approach is more advantageous due to some critical destructive pointer updates are done without being interleaved with abstraction. This way, we may avoid having to remove lots of spurious counterexamples that may otherwise arise when the abstraction is applied while some important shape invariant is temporarily broken.

Experimental Results. We have performed several experiments with singly-linked lists (SLL), doubly-linked lists (DLL), trees, lists of lists, and trees with linked leaves. All three mentioned types of automata abstraction—the finite height abstraction (with the initial height being one), predicate abstraction (with no initial predicates), and neighbour abstraction—proved useful (gave the best achieved result) in different examples. All examples were automatically verified for null/undefined/deleted pointer exceptions. Additionally, some further shape properties (such as absence of sharing, acyclicity, preservation of input elements, etc.) were verified in some case studies too. All these properties were specified in the LBMP logic from Sect. 2.2 and translated to C testers. We give a detailed overview of the performed experiments in the full version of the paper [10].

Table 1 contains verification times for the experiments mentioned above (the "+ test" in the name of an experiment means that some shape invariants were

Table 1. Results of experimenting with the prototype implementation of the presented method

Example	Time	Abstraction method	$|Q|$	N_{ref}
SLL-creation + test	0.5s	predicates, restricted	22	0
SLL-reverse + test	6s	predicates	45	1
DLL-delete + test	8s	finite height	100	0
DLL-insert + test	11s	neighbour, restricted	94	0
DLL-reverse + test	13s	predicates	48	1
DLL-insertsort	3s	predicates	38	0
Inserting into trees + test	12s	predicates, restricted	91	0
Linking leaves in trees + test	11min 15s	predicates	217	10
Inserting into a list of lists + test	27s	predicates, restricted	125	1
Deutsch-Schorr-Waite tree traversal	3min 14s	predicates	168	0

checked). We give the best result obtained using the three mentioned abstraction schemas and say for which abstraction schema the result was obtained. The note "restricted" accompanying the abstraction method means that the abstraction was applied at the loop points only. The experiments were performed on a 64bit Xeon 3,2 GHz with 3 GB of memory. The column $|Q|$ gives information about the size of the biggest encountered automaton, and N_{ref} gives the number of refinements.

Despite the prototype nature of the tool, which can still be optimised in multiple ways (some of them are mentioned in the conclusions), the results are quite competitive. For example, for one of the most complex examples—the Deutsch-Schorr-Waite tree traversal, TVLA took 3 minutes on the same machine with manually provided instrumentation predicates and predicate transformers. The verification time for the trees with linked leaves is relatively high, but we are not aware of any other fully automated tool with which experiments with this structure have been performed.

6   Conclusion

We have proposed a new, fully automated method for verification of programs manipulating complex dynamic linked data structures. The method is based on the framework of ARTMC. In order to able to use ARTMC, we proposed a new representation of sets of shape graphs based on tree automata and a representation of the standard C pointer manipulating statements as tree transducers (with some extensions). In particular, we considered verification of the basic memory consistency properties (no null pointer assignments, etc.) and of shape invariants whose corruption may be described in an existential fragment of a first-order logic on graphs. We formalised this fragment as a special-purpose logic called LBMP whose formulae may be translated to C-based testers that may be attached to the verified programs, thus transforming the verification problem to be considered to the control line reachability. We have implemented the technique in a prototype tool and obtained some promising experimental results.

In the future, we would like to optimise the performance of our Mona-based prototype tool, e.g., by exploiting the concept of *guided tree automata* that are suggested as very helpful in many situations by the authors of Mona [5] and that we have not used yet. Further, it is interesting to try come up with some *special purpose automata abstractions* for the considered domain—so-far we have used mostly general purpose tree automata abstractions, and we have an experience from [8] that special purpose abstraction may bring very significant speed-ups (in [8], it was sometimes two orders of magnitude or even more). Further research directions then include, for instance, checking of other kinds of properties (as, e.g., absence of garbage, which we know to be possible—cf. the full version of the paper [10]—but which we have not yet implemented), experimenting with combinations of our technique with techniques of non-pointer data abstraction, or termination checking.

Acknowledgement. This work was supported in part by the French Ministry of Research (ACI project Securité Informatique) and by the Czech Grant Agency within projects 102/05/H050, 102/04/0780, and 102/03/D211.

References

1. P.A. Abdulla, J. d'Orso, B. Jonsson, and M. Nilsson. Regular Model Checking Made Simple and Efficient. In *Proc. of CONCUR'02*, volume 2421 of *LNCS*. Springer, 2002.
2. P.A. Abdulla, B. Jonsson, P. Mahata, and J. d'Orso. Regular Tree Model Checking. In *Proc. of CAV'02*, volume 2404 of *LNCS*. Springer, 2002.
3. P.A. Abdulla, A. Legay, J. d'Orso, and A.Rezine. Simulation-Based Iteration of Tree Transducers. In *Proc. of TACAS'05*, volume 3440 of *LNCS*. Springer, 2005.
4. I. Balaban, A. Pnueli, and L. Zuck. Shape Analysis by Predicate Abstraction. In *Proc. of VMCAI'05*, volume 3385 of *LNCS*. Springer, 2005.
5. M. Biehl, N. Klarlund, and T. Rauhe. Algorithms for Guided Tree Automata. In *Proc. of WIA'96*, volume 1260 of *LNCS*. Springer, 1997.
6. B. Boigelot, A. Legay, and P. Wolper. Iterating Transducers in the Large. In *Proc. of CAV'03*, volume 2725 of *LNCS*. Springer, 2003.
7. A. Bouajjani, M. Bozga, P. Habermehl, R. Iosif, P. Moro, and T. Vojnar. Programs with Lists are Counter Automata. Technical Report TR-2006-3, Verimag, UJF/CNRS/INPG, Grenoble, 2006.
8. A. Bouajjani, P. Habermehl, P. Moro, and T. Vojnar. Verifying Programs with Dynamic 1-Selector-Linked Structures in Regular Model Checking. In *Proc. of TACAS'05*, volume 3440 of *LNCS*. Springer, 2005.
9. A. Bouajjani, P. Habermehl, A. Rogalewicz, and T. Vojnar. Abstract Regular Tree Model Checking. *ENTCS*, 149:37–48, 2006. A preliminary version was presented at Infinity'05.
10. A. Bouajjani, P. Habermehl, A. Rogalewicz, and T. Vojnar. Abstract Regular Tree Model Checking of Complex Dynamic Data Structures, 2006. Full version available on URL: `http://www.fit.vutbr.cz/~vojnar/pubs.php`.
11. A. Bouajjani, P. Habermehl, and T. Vojnar. Abstract Regular Model Checking. In *Proc. of CAV'04*, volume 3114 of *LNCS*. Springer, 2004.
12. A. Bouajjani, B. Jonsson, M. Nilsson, and T. Touili. Regular Model Checking. In *Proc. of CAV'00*, volume 1855 of *LNCS*. Springer, 2000.
13. A. Bouajjani and T. Touili. Extrapolating Tree Transformations. In *Proc. of CAV'02*, volume 2404 of *LNCS*. Springer, 2002.

14. M. Bozga, R. Iosif, and Y. Lakhnech. Storeless Semantics and Alias Logic. In *Proc. of PEPM'03*. ACM Press, 2003.
15. M. Češka, P. Erlebach, and T. Vojnar. Pattern-Based Verification of Programs with Extended Linear Linked Data Structures. *ENTCS*, 145:113–130, 2006. A preliminary version was presented at AVOCS'05.
16. H. Comon, M. Dauchet, R. Gilleron, F. Jacquemard, D. Lugiez, S. Tison, and M. Tommasi. Tree Automata Techniques and Applications, 2005. URL: http://www.grappa.univ-lille3.fr/tata.
17. J.V. Deshmukh, E.A. Emerson, and P. Gupta. Automatic Verification of Parameterized Data Structures. In *Proc. of TACAS'06*, volume 3920 of *LNCS*. Springer, 2006.
18. D. Distefano, P.W. O'Hearn, and H. Yang. A Local Shape Analysis Based on Separation Logic. In *Proc. of TACAS'06*, volume 3920 of *LNCS*. Springer, 2006.
19. J. Engelfriet. Bottom-up and Top-down Tree Transformations—A Comparison. *Mathematical System Theory*, 9:198–231, 1975.
20. P. Habermehl, R. Iosif, and T. Vojnar. Automata-Based Verification of Programs with Tree Updates. In *Proc. of TACAS'06*, volume 3920 of *LNCS*. Springer, 2006.
21. P. Habermehl and T. Vojnar. Regular Model Checking Using Inference of Regular Languages. *ENTCS*, 138:21–36, 2005. A preliminary version was presented at Infinity'04.
22. Y. Kesten, O. Maler, M. Marcus, A. Pnueli, and E. Shahar. Symbolic Model Checking with Rich Assertional Languages. In *Proc. of CAV'97*, volume 1254 of *LNCS*. Springer, 1997.
23. N. Klarlund and A. Møller. MONA Version 1.4 User Manual, 2001. BRICS, Department of Computer Science, University of Aarhus, Denmark.
24. N. Klarlund and M.I. Schwartzbach. Graph Types. In *Proc. of POPL'93*. ACM Press, 1993.
25. O. Lee, H. Yang, and K. Yi. Automatic Verification of Pointer Programs Using Grammar-Based Shape Analysis. In *Proc. of ESOP'05*, volume 3444 of *LNCS*. Springer, 2005.
26. A. Loginov, T. Reps, and M. Sagiv. Abstraction Refinement via Inductive Learning. In *Proc. of CAV'05*, volume 3576 of *LNCS*. Springer, 2005.
27. R. Manevich, E. Yahav, G. Ramalingam, and M. Sagiv. Predicate Abstraction and Canonical Abstraction for Singly-Linked Lists. In *Proc. of VMCAI'05*, volume 3385 of *LNCS*. Springer, 2005.
28. A. Møller and M.I. Schwartzbach. The Pointer Assertion Logic Engine. In *Proc. of PLDI'01*. ACM Press, 2001. Also in SIGPLAN Notices 36(5), 2001.
29. S. Sagiv, T.W. Reps, and R. Wilhelm. Parametric Shape Analysis via 3-valued Logic. *TOPLAS*, 24(3), 2002.
30. E. Shahar and A. Pnueli. Acceleration in Verification of Parameterized Tree Networks. Technical Report MCS02-12, Faculty of Mathematics and Computer Science, The Weizmann Institute of Science, Rehovot, Israel, 2002.
31. A. Vardhan, K. Sen, M. Viswanathan, and G. Agha. Using Language Inference to Verify Omega-regular Properties. In *Proc. of TACAS'05*, volume 3440 of *LNCS*. Springer, 2005.
32. T. Yavuz-Kahveci and T. Bultan. Automated Verification of Concurrent Linked Lists with Counters. In *Proc. of SAS'02*, volume 2477 of *LNCS*. Springer, 2002.
33. G. Yorsh, A. Rabinovich, M. Sagiv, A. Meyer, and A. Bouajjani. A Logic of Reachable Patterns in Linked Data-Structures. In *Proc. of FOSSACS'06*, volume 3921 of *LNCS*. Springer, 2006.

Structural Invariants*

Ranjit Jhala[1], Rupak Majumdar[2], and Ru-Gang Xu[2]

[1] UC San Diego
[2] UC Los Angeles

Abstract. We present *structural invariants* (SI), a new technique for incrementally overapproximating the verification condition of a program in static single assignment form by making a linear pass over the dominator tree of the program. The 1-level SI at a program location is the conjunction of all dominating program statements viewed as constraints. For any k, we define a k-level SI by *recursively strengthening* the dominating join points of the 1-level SI with the $(k-1)$-level SI of the predecessors of the join point, thereby providing a tunable selector to add path-sensitivity incrementally. By ignoring program paths, the size of the SI and correspondingly the time to discharge the validity query remains small, allowing the technique to scale to large programs. We show experimentally that even with $k \leq 2$, for a set of open-source programs totaling 570K lines and properties for which specialized analyses have been previously devised, our method provides an automatic and scalable algorithm with a low false positive rate.

1 Introduction

An invariant at a program location is a (first-order) predicate over the program state that holds whenever the location is visited during execution. Thus to prove that a programmer-specified assertion always holds at a location, it suffices to check if any invariant implies the asserted predicate. Verification-conditions (VC) are a powerful technique for generating invariants, and hence verifying properties of programs [18,13,16]. However, the use of VCs has been hindered by several considerations. First, in order to generate the VC, the fixpoint semantics of every loop in the program must be provided as *loop invariants*. Second, in order to be precise, VC generators encode all execution paths of the program. When applied to large programs, this results in large formulas that cannot be solved efficiently. Thus, while *generic*, in that they are applicable to any user specified assertion, and *precise*, in that they capture all path correlations, the use of VC-based techniques has been limited to proving deep properties of programs, often with substantial manual intervention. For checking properties over large code bases, researchers typically develop specialized analyses based on dataflow analysis or abstract interpretation, which use a fixpoint computation to find the semantics of the program over a fixed abstraction. These techniques often sacrifice genericity and precision to gain automation and scalability: they use

---

* This research was sponsored in part by the NSF grants CCF-0427202 and CNS-0541606.

K. Yi (Ed.): SAS 2006, LNCS 4134, pp. 71–87, 2006.

property-specific abstractions to gain automation and thus are not generic; they gain scalability by merging execution paths at join points, leading to imprecision in the form of false alarms.

In this paper, we consider a middle ground. We present a lightweight VC generation technique that is automatic and scalable enough to prove many useful safety properties over large code bases, without requiring an expert to devise a specialized analysis for each program and each property, and yet is precise enough to capture many structural idioms used by the programmer to ensure correctness, even in the presence of path correlations typically missed by dataflow tools. We achieve this using *structural invariants* (SI), a series of increasingly precise *over-approximations* of the VC, which can be efficiently computed from the *dominator tree* of the program's control-flow graph (CFG) in *static single assignment* (SSA) form. SIs use the dominator tree to capture control flow information and the SSA form to capture data flow information about the program. By using these well-optimized compiler techniques, and by incrementally refining approximate VCs, our algorithm scales to large code bases. By not requiring explicitly provided loop invariants but using simple approximations, our algorithm is automatic. While this restricts the properties we can prove, we provide empirical evidence that shows extremely coarse approximations suffice to prove a large variety of useful properties on many large applications. In particular, we show for a set of different safety properties considered in the software verification literature [19,21,20,7,14], our technique is generic, yet completely automatic and scalable, running in time comparable to specialized dataflow analyses, often with better precision.

The first and coarsest over-approximation (the 1-structural invariant) is obtained as the *conjunction* of the dominating operations' predicates. That this forms an invariant follows from two observations. First, the operations dominating the target location are guaranteed to execute on any path to the target. Second, if the program is in SSA form, then the variables occurring in a dominating operation will not be modified after the last occurrence of that operation on a path to the target. The 1-SI ignores the predecessors of control flow join points dominating the target. Hence, correlated conditional control flow to the target location is not tracked. To regain path-sensitivity that distinguishes between the executions prior to the join point, we *recursively strengthen* the predicate of the join using the *disjunction* of SIs of predecessors of the join. The degree of distinguishing or "branch-sensitivity" is parameterized: for any $k > 1$, the k-SI is obtained by strengthening the join points using the $(k-1)$-SI of the predecessors. By only strengthening join points (and not loop heads), we compute an SI by traversing a subset of the dominator tree in a single pass. For each $k > 0$, the k-SI provides an over-approximation of the VC, becoming more precise with increasing k. In the limit, *i.e.*, when k equals the number of CFG nodes, the SI is equivalent to the standard VC [16,17] obtained by unrolling each loop of the program once and arbitrarily updating the loop-modified variables. The parameter k provides a tunable selector for statements that most influence the assertion. For example, the 1-SI includes only the operations that must happen on *all* CFG paths to the target, and the 2-SI captures one level of branching (required to prove, e.g., conditional locking behavior). Empirically, we have found the 1-SI to be two orders of magnitude smaller than a full VC that sweeps over the entire program, and the resulting validity queries are discharged up to two orders of magnitude faster than the queries for the full VC. Despite dropping the other constraints, we found that the 1-SI is sufficient to prove 70% of the assertions we examined, and for most of the remaining assertions, 2-SI sufficed.

To demonstrate the precision and genericity of our technique, we have implemented a tool psi that generates k-SIs, and used this to successfully analyze a diverse set of open-source programs for three important safety properties with a low false positive rate. psi takes as input a C program annotated with assertions, and a number k, and computes the k-SI for the program at each assertion point, and then uses SIMPLIFY [12] to discharge the validity query, and thus prove the assertion. The first property (studied in [20] using language-level techniques) checks the consistent use of *tag fields* when using unions inside structures in C programs. In the example of Figure 1(a), which is representative of networking code, the header field h corresponds to a TCP packet if the proto field has value TCP and is a UDP packet otherwise, and the property checks that at each cast to TCP * (resp. UDP *), proto==TCP (resp. proto==UDP). The second property (studied in [19,24,14]) checks that Linux drivers acquire and release locks in strict alternation. In most cases, each call to unlock is dominated by a call to lock and vice versa. As seen in Figure 3(a), in the few cases where branch sensitivity is required to capture some idiomatic uses like conditional locks and trylocks, the 2-SI suffices. The third property is for *privilege levels* (studied in [7]): at any point where a suid program calls execv, the effective user-id is non-root. In our experiments, system calls setting the user-id dominate the call to execv so the 1-SI suffices to prove these assertions. We have used psi to check these properties on a total of 570K lines of code containing 759 assertions. With $k \leq 2$, we proved 667 of these, and found 16 bugs and 76 false alarms. The total running time of all experiments was less than one hour. In contrast, the software model checker Blast took at least an order of magnitude more time on all experiments, and did not finish on several runs. We believe this demonstrates that lightweight VC-based techniques can be made as automatic and scalable as a variety of specialized analyses. While our coarse approximations may generate an invariant that is not strong enough to prove the property of interest, our experience is that SIs can be used as an effective pre-pass for any verification effort to "filter out" many assertions, leaving sophisticated program verification tools to focus their resources on more complicated properties.

2   Structural VC Generation

We formalize structural invariants for an imperative language with integer variables. We begin with the intraprocedural case.

Operations. Our programs are built using: (1) *assignment* operations x := e, which correspond to assigning the value of expression e to the variable x. A

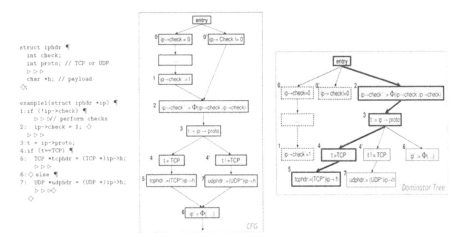

Fig. 1. (a) Example 1 (b) CFG in SSA form (c) Dominator Tree of CFG

basic block is a sequence of assignments. (2) *Assume* operations assume (p), which continue program execution if the boolean expression p evaluates to true, and halt the program otherwise.

Control-Flow Graphs. The control flow of a procedure is given by a *Control-flow Graph* (CFG), a rooted, directed graph $G = \langle N, E, n_e, n_x \rangle$ with:

1. A set of control nodes N, each labeled by a basic block or assume operation;
2. Two distinguished nodes: an *entry* node n_e and an *exit* node n_x;
3. A set of edges $E \subseteq N \times N$ connecting control nodes: $(n_1, n_2) \in E$ if control can transfer from the end of n_1 to the beginning of n_2. We assume that n_e has no incoming edges, and n_x has no outgoing edges.

Let $\mathsf{pred}(n)$ denote the set $\{n' \mid (n', n) \in E\}$ of *predecessors* of n in the CFG. We assume that the set $\mathsf{pred}(n)$ is ordered, and refer to the k-th predecessor of a node n to denote the k-th element in the ordering in $\mathsf{pred}(n)$. We write $\mathsf{vars}(n)$ to denote the set of variables appearing in the operation op labeling n. A *path* π of length m to a node n in the CFG is a sequence $n_1 \ldots n_m$ where $n_1 = n_e$, $n_m = n$, and for each $1 \leq i < m$ the pair $(n_i, n_{i+1}) \in E$. We denote by $\pi(i)$ the ith node n_i along the path. We denote by $\pi[j]$ the prefix of the path, $n_1 \ldots n_j$. A node n is *reachable* in the CFG if there is a path π to n. We assume that all nodes in N are reachable from n_e.

Dominators. For two CFG nodes n, n' we say n *dominates* n' if for every path π to n' of length m, there is some $1 \leq i \leq m$ such that $\pi(i) = n$. We say n *strictly dominates* n', written $n \mathrel{D} n'$, if n dominates n' and n, n' are distinct. We write $\mathsf{D}(n)$ for the set $\{n' \mid n' \mathrel{D} n\}$. We write $\mathsf{D}^{-1}(n)$ for the set $\{n' \mid n \mathrel{D} n'\}$. We say n is the *immediate dominator* of n' if for every $n'' \in \mathsf{D}(n')$, we have n'' dominates n. Each node n of the CFG has a unique immediate dominator which we write as Idom(n). A *dominator tree* is a rooted tree whose nodes are the nodes of the CFG, whose root is the entry node n_e, and where the parent of a node n is Idom(n).

SSA. We assume that programs are represented in *static single assignment* (SSA) form [10], in which each variable in the program is syntactically assigned exactly once. Programs in SSA form have special ϕ-assignment operations of the form $x := \phi(x_1, \ldots, x_n)$ that capture the effect of control flow joins. A ϕ-assignment $x := \phi(x_1, \ldots, x_n)$ for variables x, $x_1, \ldots, x_n$ at a node n implies: (1) n has exactly n predecessors in the CFG, (2) if control arrives at n from its jth predecessor, then x has the value x_j at the beginning of n. Further, we distinguish two kinds of ϕ-assignments: those at the header of natural loops (denoted ϕ^ℓ), and the others (denoted ϕ).

Semantics. For a set of variables X, an X-state is a valuation for the variables X. The set of all X-states is written as $V.X$. Each operation op gives rise to a transition relation $\overset{\text{op}}{\leadsto} \subseteq V.X \times V.X$ as follows. We say $s \overset{\text{op}}{\leadsto} s'$ if either op $\equiv$ assume (p), $s \models p$, and $s' = s$, or op $\equiv x := e$ and $s' = s[x \mapsto s.e]$. The relation $\overset{\text{op}}{\leadsto}$ is extended to basic blocks by sequential composition. We say that a state s *can execute* the operation op if there exists some s' such that $s \overset{\text{op}}{\leadsto} s'$. A formula φ over the variables X represents all X-states where the valuations of the variables satisfy φ. For a formula φ, we write vars(φ) for the set of variables appearing syntactically in φ. We say that φ' is a *postcondition* of φ w.r.t. an operation op if $\{s' \mid \exists s \in \varphi.s \overset{\text{op}}{\leadsto} s'\} \subseteq \varphi'$, *i.e.*, executing op from a state satisfying φ results in a state satisfying φ'. We say that *a path* π *satisfies the formula* φ if φ is a postcondition of *true* w.r.t. the sequence of operations along π. For a CFG node n we say that a formula φ is an n-*invariant* if *every* path π to n satisfies φ.

Operation Predicates. For an operation op, define an *operation predicate* $[\![op]\!]$:

op	$[\![op]\!]$	op	$[\![op]\!]$	op	$[\![op]\!]$
x := e	x = e	assume (p)	p	$op_1; \ldots; op_n$	$\bigwedge_{i=1}^{n} [\![op_i]\!]$
$x := \phi(x_1,, \ldots, x_n)$	$\bigvee_{i=1}^{n} x = x_i$	$x := \phi^\ell(x_1,, \ldots, x_n)$	*true*		

For a node n labeled with operation op, we write $[\![n]\!]$ for $[\![op]\!]$. For a program in SSA form, the operation predicate $[\![op]\!]$ is a postcondition of *true* w.r.t. the operation op. Additionally, for a node n we define $\Phi(n, j)$ to be $x = x_j$ if n is labeled $x := \phi(x_1, \ldots, x_j, \ldots, x_n)$ and $[\![n]\!]$ otherwise. In other words, $\Phi(n, j)$ constrains the variable assigned at a ϕ-node to the value held at the j-th predecessor of n.

2.1 Structural Invariants

Dominator Invariants. We first relate dominator nodes in the CFG to program invariants. This provides an efficient algorithm to compute invariants. Our technique follows from three observations about dominators and programs in SSA form. First, immediately after an operation op is executed, the new state satisfies the operation predicate $[\![op]\!]$. Second, if n$'$ dominates n, then along every execution path to **n**, there is an instant, just after the dominator **n′** is executed, at which ⟦**n′**⟧ is satisfied. Third, if **n′Dn**, then in any execution path, after the *last* occurrence of **n′**, the only nodes visited are those that are dominated by **n′** (this is illustrated in Figure 2(a)), and none of the variables in vars(**n′**) are ever modified. Thus, as ⟦**n′**⟧ held immediately after (the last occurrence of) **n′**, it is preserved until execution reached **n**. Hence ⟦**n′**⟧ is a **n**-invariant. It follows that the conjunction of node predicates for all nodes dominating **n** is an **n**-invariant. We call this the *dominator invariant* of **n**.

Theorem 1. [Dominator Invariants] *For a node* **n** *of a CFG in SSA form, the formula* ⟦**n**⟧ $\land \bigwedge_{n' \in D(n)}$⟦**n′**⟧ *is an* **n**-*invariant.*

Example 1. [**Tagged-Union Verification**] Figure 1(a) shows an example of a C program that deserializes a stream of bytes to extract a packet. The packet is represented by the C structure `iphdr`, with a tag field `int proto` which specifies if the *payload* field `char *h`, a stream of characters, corresponds to a TCP or a UDP payload. Precisely, if `proto` is TCP, then `h` is a TCP payload, else `h` is a UDP payload. Figure 1(b) shows the CFG of the program in SSA form. For simplicity, we treat pointer accesses such as ip→check as unaliased scalars, our implementation handles pointers correctly. Since union types are not tagged explicitly in C, programmers use a tag field to determine the type of the union instance and then cast the data appropriately before access. However, absent or incorrect checks lead to data access bugs which are a common cause of hard to find bugs or crashes. This *data access specification* introduces implicit assertions in the code wherever the field `h` is accessed. For example, in Figure 1(a), there are two implicit assertions: one at line 5 where `h` is cast to a TCP pointer which asserts: ip → proto = TCP and one at line 7 where `h` is cast to UDP pointer which asserts: ip → proto ≠ TCP. To check correct usage of tagged unions, we must find a program invariant at these assertion points that implies the assertions. ∎

Example 2. The CFG in SSA form and the dominator tree for the example of Figure 1(a) are shown in Figures 1(b), 1(c). In Figure 1(c), we see that the nodes dominating n_5 in Figure 1(b) are n_2, n_3, n_4. By conjoining their respective operation predicates we get the dominator invariant:

$$(\text{ip} \rightarrow \text{check}'' = \text{ip} \rightarrow \text{check} \lor \text{ip} \rightarrow \text{check}'' = \text{ip} \rightarrow \text{check}') \land t = \text{ip} \rightarrow \text{proto} \land t = \text{TCP}$$

which implies, and thus proves, the implicit data access assertion ip → proto = TCP at 5. By virtue of the program being in SSA form, the dominator invariant captures the flow of value through the local variable `t`. ∎

φ-**Strengthening.** Dominator invariants ignore conditional control flow merges in the code and, as Example 3 below shows, are often not precise enough to prove properties of interest.

Example 3. In the networking example of Figure 1, suppose that we additionally wish to verify that the payload `h` is only accessed after the checksum has been verified (i.e., `check` field is set to a non-zero value). This yields the additional (implicit) assertions at statements 5: and 7: that $\mathtt{ip} \to \mathtt{check}'' \neq 0$. The conjunction of the operation predicates of the dominators of n_5, namely n_2, n_3, n_4 is insufficient due to the ϕ-node, n_2 where control joins after the branch. At such a node, a variable may get a value from one of several predecessors, neither of which dominates the target node. So, as dominator invariants only conjoin operation predicates for dominating operations, they do not capture branch correlations. ∎

To gain path sensitivity, we recursively compute the invariant of each predecessor of a ϕ-node n (a join point) and take their disjunction to strengthn the node predicate of n. While computing the invariant for the ith predecessor, we additionally conjoin the predicate $\Phi(n, i)$, thus updating the value of each variable assigned at n to the value in the ith predecessor. We call this process *recursive ϕ-strengthening*. We explicitly parameterize the recursive ϕ-strengthening with a bound k. For $k = 1$ we get exactly the dominator invariants (there is no recursive strengthening), while for higher values of k we recursively strengthen using the $(k-1)$-SI of the predecessors of the ϕ-nodes.

Formally, we define k-structural invariants using two recursively defined functions Ψ and Γ. The function Ψ is defined for nodes n_r, n and integer k as:

$$\Psi((n_r, n), k) \equiv [\![n]\!] \wedge \bigwedge_{n' \in D(n) \cap D^{-1}(n_r)} [\![n']\!] \wedge \Gamma(n', k)$$

if $k > 0$ and $n_r \neq n$ and *true* otherwise. Intuitively, the parameter n_r is the ancestor in the dominator tree whose subtree is being used to generate the SI for n, and the parameter k is an explicit bound on the recursion depth. The function Γ is used for the recursive ϕ-strengthening. For node n' and integer k, if $k > 0$, and $\mathsf{pred}(n') \cap D^{-1}(n') = \emptyset$, *i.e.*, n' is a join node (and not a loop header otherwise one of the predecessors would be dominated by n') then:

$$\Gamma(n', k) \equiv \bigvee_{n_j \in \mathsf{pred}(n')} (\Phi(n', j) \wedge \Psi((\mathsf{Idom}(n'), n_j), k - 1))$$

and it is defined as *true* otherwise, *i.e.*, no strengthening is done. Recall that for a join ϕ-node, the formula $\Phi(n', j)$ simply constrains the value of the "merged" variable to be that of the variable at the j-th predecessor of n'. The *k-structural invariant* of a node n of the CFG is $\Psi((n_e, n), k)$. The *structural invariant* of a node n is $\Psi((n_e, n), |N|)$.

A k-SI "unfolds" the *nesting structure* of the program. The parameter k allows us to incrementally tune the precision of the invariant, and use coarser (and faster computed) invariants wherever possible. By raising k, we are increasing the *branch-width* sensitivity of the analysis, and setting k to the number of CFG nodes gives us the exact SI. This provides a dual approximation to the usual "bounded-depth" analyses, where all paths of length less than a certain bound are analyzed.

We use induction on k to prove that k-SI are invariants, Theorem 1 provides the base case.

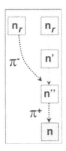 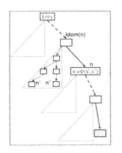 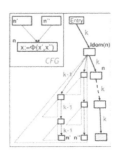

Fig. 2. (a) If a node n'' not dominated by n' appears after the last occurrence of n' on a path to n, then n is not dominated by n'. (b) ϕ-strengthening: For a join ϕ-node n, the strengthening $\Gamma(n)$ is the disjunction of the SIs of the two predecessors n', n'' of n, which are in the tree "hanging off" $\mathsf{Idom}(n)$. (c) To compute the $(k-1)$-SI for n', n'' we strengthen all the join nodes in the path from n', n'' to the root $\mathsf{Idom}(n)$, recursively exploring the trees hanging off the inner paths.

Theorem 2. *[Structural Invariants] For every CFG $G = (N, E, n_e, n_x)$ in SSA form, $n \in N$, and $k \in \mathbb{N}$, (1) the k-Structural Invariant of n is an n-invariant, and (2) $\Psi((n_e, n), k+1) \Rightarrow \Psi((n_e, n), k)$.*

Figure 2 shows how the recursive strengthening works vis-a-vis the dominator tree and the CFG. The 1-SI conjoins the node predicates for each node in the path from the root node to the target node (shaded) in the dominator tree, *i.e.*, the nodes that dominate the target node. The 2-SI strengthens the node predicates *for each join ϕ-node n'* along the path to the root in the dominator tree. To do so, it takes the disjunctions of the 1-SI for the predecessors of the join node. As shown in the figure, for join nodes, the predecessors are guaranteed to be in the subtree "hanging off" the join node's immediate dominator. Hence, the recursive SI for the predecessors is computed using the subtree rooted at the immediate dominator of the join node. The 3-SI would further strengthen each ϕ-node appearing in the recursive strengthening and so on. Thus, by increasing k we pick up more and more of the CFG nodes, but each node only appears once in the SI.

Example 4. Consider the ϕ-node n_2 in the CFG of Figure 1(b). It is a join point and its two predecessors are the nodes n_1 and $n_{0'}$. Notice that in the dominator tree in Figure 1(c), the predecessors belong in the subtree hanging off the immediate dominator of n_2 namely the entry node. We recursively compute the SIs: $\Psi(n_1) = \mathtt{ip} \to \mathtt{check} = 0 \wedge \mathtt{ip} \to \mathtt{check}' = 1$ (from the dominators n_0, n_1), and, $\Psi(n_{0'}) = \mathtt{ip} \to \mathtt{check} \neq 0$, (from the dominating branch condition $n_{0'}$). Thus, the strengthening the ϕ-node n_2 yields the following 2-SI for n_5:

$$
\begin{array}{ll}
(\ \ (\mathtt{ip} \to \mathtt{check}'' = \mathtt{ip} \to \mathtt{check}' & \\
\quad \wedge\ \mathtt{ip} \to \mathtt{check} = 0 & n_0 \\
\quad \wedge\ \mathtt{ip} \to \mathtt{check}' = 1) & n_1 \\
\vee & \Gamma(n_2) \\
\ \ (\mathtt{ip} \to \mathtt{check}'' = \mathtt{ip} \to \mathtt{check} & \\
\quad \wedge\ \mathtt{ip} \to \mathtt{check} \neq 0)) & n_{0'} \\
\wedge\ \mathtt{t} = \mathtt{ip} \to \mathtt{proto} \wedge\ \mathtt{t} = \mathtt{TCP} & n_3\ \text{and}\ n_4
\end{array}
$$

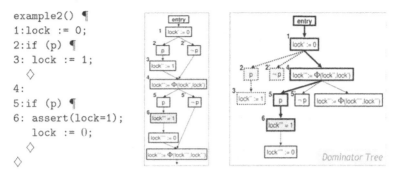

```
example2() ¶
1:lock := 0;
2:if (p) ¶
3:  lock := 1;
    ◇
4:
5:if (p) ¶
6:  assert(lock=1);
    lock := 0;
    ◇
    ◇
```

Fig. 3. (a) Example 2 (b) CFG (c) Dominator Tree

which is strong enough to prove the (implicit) assertion that the **check** field is non-zero, at the access location 5. A similar sufficient SI is obtained for 7. ■

Example 5. [**Conditional Locking**] Figure 3(a) shows conditional locking on an arbitrary predicate p. Consider the ϕ-node n_4 in the CFG of Figure 3(b). It is a join point and its two predecessors are the nodes n_3 and $n_{2'}$. Notice in the dominator tree in Figure 3(c), that the predecessors belong in the subtree "hanging" off the immediate dominator of n_4 namely n_1. We recursively compute the SIs: $\Psi(n_3) = \texttt{lock}' = 0 \wedge p \wedge \texttt{lock}'' = 1$ and $\Psi(n_{2'}) = \texttt{lock}' = 0 \wedge \neg p$. Thus, the strengthening for the ϕ-node 4 is $\Gamma(n_4) \equiv (\texttt{lock}''' = \texttt{lock}'' \wedge \Psi(n_3)) \vee (\texttt{lock}''' = \texttt{lock}' \wedge \Psi(n_2))$. We need not further strengthen the SIs for n_3, n_2' as they have no dominating join nodes. The 2-SI at n_6 is:

$$
\begin{aligned}
&\texttt{lock}' = 0 && \text{from } n_1 \\
&\wedge \,((\texttt{lock}''' = \texttt{lock}'' \wedge \texttt{lock}'' = 1 \wedge p) \vee (\texttt{lock}''' = \texttt{lock}' \wedge \neg p)) && \text{from } \Gamma(n_4) \\
&\wedge \, p && \text{from } n_5
\end{aligned}
$$

This is an invariant strong enough to prove the assertion $\texttt{lock}''' = 1$ at line 6. ■

2.2 Interprocedural Structural Invariants

We now extend programs to include function calls. The set of operations is extended to include *function calls* $\texttt{l} := f(\texttt{e}_1, \ldots, \texttt{e}_n)$ and return statements $\texttt{return(ret)}$, where **ret** is a special variable. A program is now a set of CFG's, one for each function, with a specified function **main** where execution starts. Further, we assume that the only operation on the exit node n_x of each CFG is $\texttt{return(ret)}$, and the operation $\texttt{return}(\cdot)$ does not appear anywhere else. We assume for simplicity there are no global variables, these can be incorporated with additional notation (and are handled by our implementation). We extend k-structural invariants to programs with function calls through two approaches: summarization and abstract summarization.

Summarization. For interprocedural analysis, each function is abstracted into a set of input-output relations, called the *summary*, that captures the observed behavior of the function. For function **foo**, we have to consider both transitive callees of foo (*i.e.,* calls to functions within the body of foo), and transitive callers of foo (*i.e.,* the call chains from main to foo).

To deal with callees, we extend $[\![op]\!]$ to the new operations. First, assume there is no recursion. Let f be a function with formal parameters $x_1, \ldots, x_n$, local variables L, and CFG $G_f = (N^f, E^f, n_e^f, n_x^f)$. We define $[\![1 := f(e_1, \ldots, e_n)]\!]$ as

$$(\exists L.\Psi((n_e^f, n_x^f), k))[1/\mathtt{ret}, e_1/x_1, \ldots, e_n/x_n] \tag{1}$$

and $[\![\mathtt{return}(\mathtt{ret})]\!] = true$. Intuitively, we recursively construct the k-SI for the exit node of f, rename all local variables of f with fresh names (to avoid name clashes), and substitute the formal parameters and return variable in the expression. This k-SI is the summary of f. In the presence of recursion, we additionally pass the stack of function calls in the computation of $[\![\cdot]\!]$, and return $[\![1 := f(e_1, \ldots, e_n), s]\!] = true$ if f appears in the stack s.

To deal with callers, we generalize our definition of dominators to the inter-procedural case, using the call graph of the program. In particular, we add edges from every call site $x := f(\ldots)$ to the entry node n_e of f (but not edges from the exit nodes to the call sites), and compute dominators in this expanded graph. If n' dominates n in this expanded graph, then every return-free path from the entry node of main to n passes through n' (if n' and n are in the same function, we get back the original definition). The algorithm to compute k-SI for the transitive callers is then identical to the intraprocedural algorithm with this new definition.

Abstract Summarization. In abstract summarization, summaries are computed relative to two non-empty sets of *input* and *output* predicates for each function. Fix a function f. Let P and P' be the input and output predicates over variables in scope in f respectively. An abstract summary S is a subset of $P \times P'$ with the property that for every execution of the function starting from a state satisfying p to a state satisfying p', we have $(p, p') \in S$.

To perform abstract summarization, we traverse the call graph of the program bottom up. For any k, function f, and sets P and P' of predicates, our summarization algorithm constructs the k-SI φ of the exit node n_x^f of f with respect to the entry point n_e^f of f. For any function call $1 = g(e_1, \ldots, e_n)$ in the body of f with summary S_g, we use the operation predicate from Equation 1 with $\Psi((n_e^f, n_x^f), k)$ replaced with $\bigvee_{(p,p') \in S_g} (p \wedge p')$. If g has not been summarized, *e.g.* , for recursive calls, we use the constraint *true*. Let φ be the k-SI for f. Finally, the abstract summary S_f of f is computed as the set $\{(p, p') \in P \times P' \mid p \wedge \varphi \wedge p' \text{ is satisfiable}\}$.

If $\bigvee P$ and $\bigvee P'$ are not both equivalent to *true*, abstract summarization can lead to unsoundness. To be sound, we add additional assertions to the program. At each call site $x := f(e_1, \ldots, e_n)$, we add the assertion $\mathtt{assert}(\exists L. \bigvee P)$ $[e_1/x_1, \ldots, e_n/x_n]$ which checks that the precondition of the function holds at the call site. At the exit node of f, we add the assertion $\bigvee P'$ that checks that the postcondition of the function holds at the return point. These assertions are checked in addition to the assertions in the program, and the original assertions are proved soundly if all these assertions also hold. If these assertions do not hold, the summary for the function is replaced with $(true, true)$ when checking other assertions.

Abstract summarization allows our algorithms to scale by keeping the summaries small (just in terms of the abstract predicates), and also acts as a useful fault localization aid in our experiments. However, it requires user-supplied predicates, reducing automation. Instead of requiring user intervention or performing predicate inference [2,21], we adopt the approach of [11,24]. We perform abstract summarization with respect to predicates obtained automatically from the property. For example, to checking correct locking, we add predicates corresponding to each value of lock being taken or freed. This allows our tool to be automatic, though sometimes with less precision.

3   Experiments

We have implemented psi, an assertion checker for C programs using structural invariants. Our tool takes as input a C program annotated with assertions and a number k, statically constructs the k-structural invariant for each assertion, and checks if the k-structural invariant implies the assertion. Our tool is written in Objective Caml and uses the CIL library [22] for manipulating C programs. To prove an assertion, psi checks if the k-SI implies the assertion using the Simplify theorem prover [12]. The implementation is staged in five parts: alias analysis, SSA conversion, dominator tree construction, construction of the k-SI, and assertion verification. Our tool uses a flow-insensitive may alias analysis. After alias analysis, we transform the program so that conditionals on possibly aliased objects are added at each pointer dereference. This accurately reflects state update for the structural invariant. For example, for the code *p = 5, assuming p may point to a or b, we transform the code to *p=5; if(p==&a) a=5; if (p==&b) b=5;. Our alias analysis is field insensitive. We heuristically add field sensitivity based on field types to determine a more precise match. We ran three sets of experiments with psi: checking tagged unions, correct locking, and correct suid privileges. Our experiments were all run on a Dell PowerEdge 1800 with two 3.6Ghz Xeon processors and 5 GB of memory. The running time is dominated by the alias analysis and the generation of the structural invariants. In comparison, the parsing, ssa conversion, dominator tree construction, and theorem prover calls take relatively little time.

1. Tagged Unions. Tagged unions are checked by adding an assertion describing the predicate that must hold when a certain field is accessed or cast before that access or cast. We added these assertions manually. We ran our tool on three programs: icmp (a protocol for error notification on the internet, 7K lines of code), gdk (the GTK+ drawing toolkit, 16K lines of code), and lua (an interpreter, 18K lines of code). We checked 69 assertions and found 14 false positives with $k = 2$ and 18 false positives with $k = 1$. The total run time was 684s with $k = 2$, dominated by lua (682s). Since most programmers check the tag near the data access point, we did not propagate k-SIs to the callers of the function containing the assertion for this set of experiments. This resulted in 8 false pos-

Table 1. Lock experiments. LOC is lines of code. Asserts gives the original number of asserts, and total gives the total asserts to check pre- and post-conditions. ok gives the asserts proved safe. error the number of bugs. False positives are broken into pointers (ptrs), lists, loops, and unclassified errors (unc). t(s) is time in seconds. Cqual shows the false positives from Cqual (N/A indicates we did not run Cqual).

program	LOC	func's	asserts	total	ok	error	ptrs	List	loops	unc	t(s)	cqual
scc	16K	638	36	57	47	2	7	0	0	1	38	60
DAC960	24K	763	46	54	38	0	10	0	4	2	141	N/A
af_netrom	22K	958	23	25	21	0	0	3	1	3	12	20
af_rose	23K	958	15	29	28	0	0	0	0	1	7	9
as-iosched	14K	576	10	17	10	0	4	0	0	3	8	4
elevator	13K	512	2	3	3	0	0	0	0	0	1	0
floppy	18K	696	30	48	43	0	0	0	2	3	35	48
genhd	13K	529	4	6	6	0	0	0	0	0	2	0
ll_rw_blk	15K	625	8	30	25	0	0	0	2	3	8	N/A
nr_route	18K	788	19	34	30	0	0	1	1	2	9	20
wavelan_cs	17K	621	19	35	30	1	4	0	0	0	14	4
rose_route	42K	953	51	73	55	13	0	0	3	2	35	31
Totals	235K	8,617	263	414	336	16	25	4	13	20	310	196

itives that required assumptions about formal parameters. Our theorem prover only models integers so there was 1 false positive that required the modeling of unsigned integers. Four false positives are due to modeling pointer arithmetic and data structures and one due to type-unsafe programmer assumptions about memory layout.

2. Locking. The second set of experiments checked double locking errors in the Linux kernel. Double locking has been extensively studied using dataflow analysis [19] and BMC [24]. Double locking occurs when locking something that already has been locked (causing a deadlock) or unlocking something that already has been unlocked (can cause kernel panic). We model this by adding an assertion that the lock is in a locked (resp. unlocked) state before every call to unlock (resp. lock). We use abstract summarization for locks, similar to Saturn [24]. Predicates for abstract summarization are the lock values. Instead of user provided pre- and post-conditions, we use a simple heuristic to guess predicates and psi automatically checks whether those predicates are correct. For each function, we find the first assertions for each lock and make these the precondition predicates. Similarly, we find the last lock or unlock statements in the function and make the corresponding lock states the postcondition predicates. This is sometimes imprecise, but retains automation. We run psi with a depth $k = 2$. We found increasing $k > 2$ does not reduce the number of false positives in our experiments since a depth $k = 2$ captures all the relevant nesting of conditionals.

Table 1 summarizes our results. We examined 12 device driver files in the Linux kernel, totaling 235K lines of code. Since we consider drivers one file at a time, our current experimentation is unsound in the way we deal with function summaries. In particular, we do a global alias analysis at a per file level, but assume functions in other files do not have any effect on lock values or aliasing. There were a total of 414 asserts. Among these, 151 assertions were due to adding pre- and post-condition assertions for the summaries. We analyzed a total of 8,617 functions in 310 seconds. We found 16 real bugs and 62 false positives. We found errors in wavelan and rose_route not mentioned in the Saturn bug database. The bug in `wavelan_cs`, a wireless card driver, was caused by an obscure case where a packet is recieved when the wireless connection is being handed over from one access point to another. This bug spans 3 functions.

The false positives are in three categories: loss of precision in abstract summarization (25), getting locks from dynamic data structures or external functions (4), and loops (13). There are 20 additional errors we have not classified yet. Loop false positives occur when a lock is acquired and released in a loop. Interestingly, some such examples can be proved using Cqual or dataflow analysis, showing the orthogonality of these methods. Other false positives relate to dynamic data structures (where locks are stored in lists) or pointers returned from external functions.

Imprecise summary predicates are the most significant false positives (25 of them), but could be remedied by better predicate generation heuristics or some editing of the source code. When we heuristically add preconditions and postconditions, it is possible that the predicate we include in our precondition mentions a variable that is not in the formal parameter of our function or a global variable. For example, for the code

```
void lock (dev *ptr) {
  struct receive_queue *q;
  q = ptr -> q; assert (q -> lock == 0); q -> lock = 1; }
```

our heuristics infer that the pre- and post-conditions are (`q->lock == 0`) and (`q->lock == 1`) respectively. This can be solved by correcting the pre- and post-conditions to (`ptr->q->lock == 0`) and (`ptr->q->lock == 1`) respectively. The 25 false positives involving these issues are all removed after these simple modifications. Alternately, we could construct the weakest precondition of these predicates in terms of the formals and used those for abstract summarization.

To compare, we ran Blast [21] on some of the Linux drivers. Table 2 summarizes the results of running Blast on three of the drivers. While the false positive rate is lower (although not zero, since Blast produces false positives when locks are put into lists, and when the driver makes unmodeled assumptions about external pointers), the time taken is significantly higher in all cases.

Table 2. Blast results

Program	FP	Time (s)
af_netrom	4	248
nr_route	1	1755
rose_route	1	1513

Our work in lock analysis is most similar to Saturn. We found all bugs that Saturn found except one that required analysis of two different files. In addition, we find two extra bugs not reported by Saturn. In comparison with Cqual [19], we take more time, but have fewer false positives. Running Cqual on 10 of our 12 device driver examples resulted in 196 type errors, even though Cqual does reduce loop false positives. In contrast to Cqual, we get at most one message per assertion site, making it easier to track down false errors.

Finally, Table 3 summarizes the precision-time trade-off as we increase k over all our lock experiments. Size measures the total size of the Simplify queries written as a text file, time is the time to solve all the queries, and FP the number of false alarms found. In our experiments, $k = 1$ is already enough to prove most assertions, and increasing k beyond to 2 does not help in reducing the false alarms. The size of the formula does not increase appreciably beyond $k = 4$. For our examples, it is rare to find complex control flow, *i.e.*, more than four nested conditionals.

Table 3. Precision

k	Size (KB)	Time	FP
1	259	1.5s	241
2	15764	1m45s	62
3	19996	1m54s	62
4	21091	1m58s	62

Table 4. Suid Programs. Asserts = total number of asserts, Original = original asserts in the code, FP = false positives.

Program	LOC	Asserts	Original	FP	Time (s)
mtr	13K	43	8	0	13s
openssh	61K	37	5	0	51s
gpg	219K	190	3	0	1106s

3. Privilege Levels. Finally, we checked whether a Unix setuid program gives up its owner privileges before executing certain system calls [7]. In unix systems, programs have privileges associated with users. Normally, a program will execute under the permission of the user executing the program. However, *suid programs* run with root privileges when they are started, which are required to access certain system resources. After the privileged action is performed, suid programs give up their root privileges by making a `setuid` or a `seteuid` call. A suid program should give up its root privileges before making further system calls to reduce the chance of an exploit gaining root access. We model the effective user id with an integer which is 0 for root, and 1 for any other user. The id is set to 1 whenever `setuid` or `seteuid` is called. We check that whenever a program calls `system` or `exec`, this id is not zero. We examine three programs: OpenSSH 2.9.9p (the widely used secure shell program), GNU Privacy Guard (open source pgp), and mtr (a network diagnostic tool), for a total of 294K lines of code. All these programs follow good security programming guidelines. After the required privileged action was taken, the effective user id was set to the user executing the program. We used abstract summarization, using the state of the id bit as the predicate. This caused 254 out of 270 assertions to be automatically added, however, summarization made our technique scale well. Further, $k = 1$ was enough to prove all assertions with no false positives. Our results are shown in Table 4, where the time does not include time for alias analysis. Our total running time (excluding alias analysis) was 20 minutes. As the size of the programs increased, CIL's alias analysis became the bottleneck. It took 610s for OpenSSH and did not terminate for gpg within 6 hours. However, since the address of the id bit is not taken and id is only assigned integer constants, and we additionally check that the k-SI is satisfiable, we can conclude in this case that our technique is sound without the alias analysis. In comparison, Blast did not finish the verification of openssh or gpg in two hours.

4 Related Work and Conclusions

Related Work. SIs are similar to bounded model checking (BMC) [4,9,24], which builds VCs capturing all program executions of a certain bounded execution length. Typically BMC is useful for finding bugs, while SI provides a sound verification technique. While BMC unrolls the last (or first) k operations of a program, the "unrolling metric" in k-structural constraints is (roughly) the nesting depth of conditionals. Thus, 1-SI may be strong enough to prove a property even though the relevant code blocks are separated by arbitrarily many lines of irrelevant code. SIs are less precise than VC based program verification tools [16], but we have demonstrated that the loss of precision is not significant for a large class of interesting properties. We have traded off precision for automation and scalability. Algorithms for computing compact weakest preconditions have been studied [17,3], however these did not consider the effects of approximating the VC using the nesting depth, and the results of the loss of precision in property checking.

Counterexample-guided abstraction refinement [8,2,21] automates the discovery of abstractions using spurious counterexamples. While theoretically as efficient as SI and as complete as general VC-generation, in practice, these tools do not scale well for large programs even if there is an "obvious" proof of correctness. This is mainly because these tools strive to be generic, and do not always exploit "simple" control/data flow tricks, reverting to more expensive but more general symbolic processing. In fact, our motivation for this work was the observation that simple algorithms can filter out many assertions quickly before these more sophisticated tools are applied.

SSA and dominators have been used to find program invariants that facilitate certain compiler optimizations [1,6] and to check security properties [25]; our work is a generalization of these algorithms to arbitrary invariants. Independent of our work, dominator invariants have been recognized as a quick way to generate invariants for translation validation [15]. However, that work does not provide a parameter to adjust the precision.

SI vs Dataflow Analysis. Another scalable technique of finding invariants is via fixpoint computations over an abstract domain of dataflow facts tailored to the property being checked. Examples are [5,23], which use sophisticated domains to find complex invariants over data, or [19,14,11] which address more control-oriented properties. Our VC-based method provides a scalable and generic technique to introduce path correlations incrementally to a variety of simple properties without requiring an expert-specified and program dependent abstract domain.

The invariants obtained using k-SI and (flow-sensitive) dataflow analysis that merges information at join points are, in general, incomparable. For $k > 1$, the

k-structural constraints incorporate path correlation information that dataflow analysis merges. For $k = 1$, if the domain of dataflow facts is fixed (as is usual) from the property and not tailored to a particular program, the dominator invariant may be more precise. For example, suppose $p = p_1 \wedge p_2$, and consider the program:

```
if (p1) { if (p2) { L: assert(p); } }
```

where the dataflow domain only tracks p (obtained from the assert).

On the other hand, there are programs where dataflow analysis is more precise. Consider:

```
x := 1; while (*) { if(x=1) x := 1; } L: assert(x=1);
```

When the state of x is tracked, a dataflow analysis produces the invariant $x = 1$ at L. However, for any k, the k-SI at L is *true*, since x within the loop is unconstrained.

Conclusions. SIs form a scalable, lightweight algorithm to prove useful properties of programs. Although our algorithm is simple, we showed it can prove many instances of useful and well-studied properties such as setuid, locking, and tagged unions. These programs and properties are frequently used to test more complex tools such as SLAM or Blast. However, in our experience, for the same properties and programs, Blast is usually an order of magnitude slower than psi. even though the false positive rate is only slightly better than SIs in the programs and properties we checked.

Thus, we advocate a hybrid verification approach where efficient, simple tools that incorporate structural idioms are run first to eliminate most assertions, and more sophisticated but slower tools are focused on the remaining assertions that escape the purview of the simple tools.

References

1. B. Alpern, M.N. Wegman, and F.K. Zadeck. Detecting equality of variables in programs. In *POPL 88*, pages 1–11. ACM, 1988.
2. T. Ball and S.K. Rajamani. The SLAM project: debugging system software via static analysis. In *POPL 02: Principles of Programming Languages*, pages 1–3. ACM, 2002.
3. M. Barnett and K.R.M. Leino. Weakest-precondition of unstructured programs. In *PASTE 2005*, pages 82–87. ACM, 2005.
4. A. Biere, A. Cimatti, E.M. Clarke, and Y. Zhu. Symbolic model checking without BDDs. In *TACAS 99: Tools and Algorithms for the Construction and Analysis of Systems*, LNCS 1579, pages 193–207. Springer, 1999.
5. B. Blanchet, P. Cousot, R. Cousot, J. Feret, L. Mauborgne, A. Miné, D. Monniaux, and X. Rival. A static analyzer for large safety-critical software. In *PLDI 03: Programming Languages Design and Implementation*, pages 196–207. ACM, 2003.
6. R. Bodik, R. Gupta, and V. Sarkar. ABCD: eliminating array bounds checks on demand. In *PLDI 00*, pages 321–333. ACM, 2000.

7. H. Chen, D. Dean, and D. Wagner. Model checking one million lines of c code. In *NDSS 04: Annual Network and Distributed System Security Symposium*, pages 171–185, 2004.

8. E. M. Clarke, O. Grumberg, S. Jha, Y. Lu, and H. Veith. Counterexample-guided abstraction refinement. In *CAV 00: Computer-Aided Verification*, LNCS 1855, pages 154–169. Springer, 2000.

9. E.M. Clarke, D. Kroening, and F. Lerda. A tool for checking ANSI-C programs. In *TACAS 04: Tools and Algorithms for the construction and analysis of systems*, LNCS 2988, pages 168–176. Springer, 2004.

10. R. Cytron, J. Ferrante, B.K. Rosen, M.N. Wegman, and F.K. Zadek. Efficiently computing static single assignment form and the program dependence graph. *ACM Transactions on Programming Languages and Systems*, 13:451–490, 1991.

11. M. Das, S. Lerner, and M. Seigle. ESP: Path-sensitive program verification in polynomial time. In *PLDI 02: Programming Language Design and Implementation*, pages 57–68. ACM, 2002.

12. D. Detlefs, G. Nelson, and J.B. Saxe. Simplify: a theorem prover for program checking. *J. ACM*, 52(3):365–473, 2005.

13. E.W. Dijkstra. *A Discipline of Programming*. Prentice-Hall, 1976.

14. D. Engler, B. Chelf, A. Chou, and S. Hallem. Checking system rules using system-specific, programmer-written compiler extensions. In *OSDI 00: Operating System Design and Implementation*. Usenix Association, 2000.

15. Y. Fang. *Translation validation of optimizing compilers*. PhD thesis, 2005.

16. C. Flanagan, K.R.M. Leino, M. Lillibridge, G. Nelson, J. B. Saxe, and R. Stata. Extended static checking for Java. In *PLDI 02: Programming Language Design and Implementation*, pages 234–245. ACM, 2002.

17. C. Flanagan and J.B. Saxe. Avoiding exponential explosion: generating compact verification conditions. In *POPL 00: Principles of Programming Languages*, pages 193–205. ACM, 2000.

18. R.W. Floyd. Assigning meanings to programs. In *Mathematical Aspects of Computer Science*, pages 19–32. American Mathematical Society, 1967.

19. J.S. Foster, T. Terauchi, and A. Aiken. Flow-sensitive type qualifiers. In *PLDI 02: Programming Language Design and Implementation*, pages 1–12. ACM, 2002.

20. D. Grossman. *Safe Programming at the C Level of Abstraction*. PhD thesis, 2003.

21. T.A. Henzinger, R. Jhala, R. Majumdar, and G. Sutre. Lazy abstraction. In *POPL 02: Principles of Programming Languages*, pages 58–70. ACM, 2002.

22. G. C. Necula, S. McPeak, S. P. Rahul, and W. Weimer. CIL: Intermediate language and tools for analysis and transformation of C programs. In *CC 02: Compiler Construction*, LNCS 2304, pages 213–228. Springer, 2002.

23. S. Sagiv, T.W. Reps, and R. Wilhelm. Parametric shape analysis via 3-valued logic. *ACM Trans. Program. Lang. Syst.*, 24(3):217–298, 2002.

24. Y. Xie and A. Aiken. Scalable error detection using boolean satisfiability. In *POPL 05: Principles of Programming Languages*, pages 351–363. ACM, 2005.

25. X. Zhang, T. Jaeger, and L. Koved. Applying static analysis to verifying security properties, 2004. Grace Hopper Conference.

Existential Label Flow Inference Via CFL Reachability

Polyvios Pratikakis, Jeffrey S. Foster, and Michael Hicks

University of Maryland, College Park
{polyvios, jfoster, mwh}@cs.umd.edu

Abstract. In programming languages, existential quantification is useful for describing relationships among members of a structured type. For example, we may have a list in which there *exists* some mutual exclusion lock l in each list element such that l protects the data stored in that element. With this information, a static analysis can reason about the relationship between locks and locations in the list even when the precise identity of the lock and/or location is unknown. To facilitate the construction of such static analyses, this paper presents a context-sensitive *label flow analysis* algorithm with support for existential quantification. Label flow analysis is a core part of many static analysis systems. Following Rehof et al, we use context-free language (CFL) reachability to develop an efficient $O(n^3)$ label flow inference algorithm. We prove the algorithm sound by reducing its derivations to those in a system based on polymorphically-constrained types, in the style of Mossin. We have implemented a variant of our analysis as part of a data race detection tool for C programs.

1 Introduction

Many modern static program analyses are *context-sensitive*, meaning they can analyze different calls to the same function without conservatively attributing results from one call site to another. While this technique is very useful, it often aids little in the analysis of data structures. In particular, a typical alias analysis, even a context-sensitive one, conflates all elements of the same data structure, resulting in a "blob" of indistinguishable pointers [1] that cannot be precisely analyzed.

One way to solve this problem is to use *existential quantification* [2] to express relations among members of each individual data structure element. For example, an element might contain a buffer and the length of that buffer [3]; a pointer to data and the lock that must be held when accessing it [4,5]; or a closure, consisting of a function and a pointer to its environment [6]. The important idea is that such relations are sound even when the identity of individual data structure elements cannot be discerned.

This paper presents a context-sensitive *label flow analysis* algorithm that supports existential quantification. Label flow analysis attempts to answer queries of the form "During program execution, can a value v flow to some expression e?" Answering such queries is at the core of a variety of static analyses, including points-to analysis [7,8], information flow [9], type qualifier inference [10,11,12], and race detection [4]. Our goal is to provide a formal foundation for augmenting such analyses with support for existential quantification. The core result of this paper is a provably sound and efficient type inference system for label flow that supports existential quantification. This paper makes the following contributions:

K. Yi (Ed.): SAS 2006, LNCS 4134, pp. 88–106, 2006.

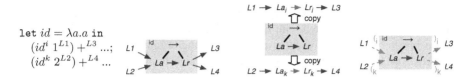

(a) Source program   (b) Monomorphic analysis (c) COPY-based analysis (d) CFL-based analysis

Fig. 1. Universal Types Example

- We present COPY, a subtyping-based label-flow system in the style of Mossin [13]. In COPY, context sensitivity for functions corresponds to universal types (parametric polymorphism). Our contribution is to show how to support existential quantification using existential types [2], applying the duality of $\forall$ and $\exists$. We prove that the resulting system is sound. (Sect. 3)
- We present CFL, an alternative to COPY that supports efficient inference. Following Rehof et al [14,15], determining flow in CFL is reduced to a context-free language (CFL) reachability problem, and the resulting inference system runs in time $O(n^3)$ in the worst case. Our contribution is to show that existentially-quantified flow can also be expressed as a CFL problem, and to prove that CFL is sound by reducing it to COPY. These results are interesting because existential types are *first-class* in our system, as opposed to universal types, which in the style of Hindley-Milner only appear in type environments. To make inference tractable, we require the programmer to indicate where existential types are used, and we restrict the interaction between existentially bound labels and free labels in the program. (Sect. 4)
- We briefly discuss how a variation of CFL is used as part of LOCKSMITH, a race detection tool [4] for C programs that correlates memory locations to mutual exclusion locks protecting them. LOCKSMITH uses existential quantification to precisely relate locks and locations that reside within dynamic data structures, thereby eliminating a source of false alarms. (Sect. 2.3)

2   Polymorphism Via Context-Free Language Reachability

We begin by introducing type-based label flow analysis, presenting the encoding of context sensitivity as universal types, and sketching our new technique for supporting first-class existential types. We also describe our application of these ideas to LOCKSMITH, a race detection tool for C [4]. Sects. 3 and 4 formally develop the label flow systems introduced here.

2.1   Universal Types and Label Flow

The goal of label flow analysis is to determine which values may flow to which operations. In the program in Fig. 1(a), values 1 and 2 are annotated with *flow labels* $L1$ and $L2$, respectively, and the two $+$ operations are labeled with $L3$ and $L4$. Therefore label flow analysis should show that $L1$ flows to $L3$ and $L2$ flows to $L4$. In this program we annotate calls to id with indices i and k, which we will explain shortly.

To compute the flow of labels, we perform a type- and constraint-based analysis in which base types are annotated with labels. For our example, the function id is given the type $int^{La} \to int^{Lr}$, where La and Lr label the argument and return types, respectively. The body of id returns its argument, which is modeled by the *constraint* $La \leq Lr$. The call id^i yields constraints $L1 \leq La$ and $Lr \leq L3$, and the call id^k yields constraints $L2 \leq La$ and $Lr \leq L4$. Pictorially, constraints form the directed edges in a *flow graph*, as shown in Fig. 1(b), and flow is determined by graph reachability. Thus the graph accurately shows that $L1$ flows to $L3$ and $L2$ flows to $L4$. However, the graph conflates the two calls to id—its type is monomorphic—and therefore suggests possible flows from $L1$ to $L4$ and from $L2$ to $L3$, which is sound but imprecise.

The precision of the analysis can be improved by adding *context sensitivity* using Hindley-Milner style universal types. The standard approach [13], shown in Fig. 1(c), is to give id a *polymorphically constrained* universal type $\forall La, Lr[La \leq Lr].int^{La} \to int^{Lr}$, where we have annotated id's type with the flow constraints needed to type its body. Each time id is used, we *instantiate* its type and constraints, effectively "inlining" a fresh copy of id's body. At the call id^i, we instantiate the constraint with the substitution $[La \mapsto La_i, Lr \mapsto Lr_i]$, and then apply the constraints from the call site, yielding $L1 \leq La_i \leq Lr_i \leq L3$, as shown. Similarly, at the call id^k we instantiate again, this time yielding $L2 \leq La_k \leq Lr_k \leq L4$. Thus we see that $L1$ could flow to $L3$, and $L2$ could flow to $L4$, but we avoid the spurious flows from the monomorphic analysis.

While this technique is effective, explicit constraint copying can be difficult to implement, because it requires juggling various sets of constraints as they are duplicated and instantiated, and may require complicated constraint simplification techniques [16,17,18] for efficiency. An alternative approach is to encode the problem in terms of a slightly different graph and use CFL reachability to compute flow, as suggested by Rehof et al [14]. This solution adds call and return edges to the graph and labels them with parentheses indexed by the call site, as shown in Fig. 1(d) with dashed lines. Edges from id^i are labeled with $(_i$ for inputs and $)_i$ for outputs, and similarly for id^k. To compute flow in this graph, we find paths with no mismatched parentheses. In this case the paths from $L1$ to $L3$ and from $L2$ to $L4$ are matched, while the other paths are mismatched and hence not considered. Rehof et al [14] have shown that using CFL reachability with matched paths can be reduced to a type system with polymorphically constrained types.

2.2   Existential Types and Label Flow

The goal of this paper is to show how to use existential quantification during static analysis to efficiently model properties of data structures more precisely. Consider the example shown in Fig. 2(a). In this program, functions f and g add an unspecified value to their argument. As before, we wish to determine which integers flow to which $+$ operations. In the third line of this program we create existentially-quantified pairs using `pack` operations in which f is paired with 1 and g with 2. Using an `if`, we then conflate these two pairs, binding one of them to p. In the last line we use p by applying its first component to its second component. (We use pattern matching in this example for simplicity, while the language in Sect. 3 uses explicit projection.)

```
let f = λa.a +^{L3} ··· in
let g = λb.b +^{L4} ··· in
let p = if ··· then
    pack^i (f, 1^{L1})
else
    pack^k (g, 2^{L2}) in
unpack (p1, p2) = p in
    p1 @ p2
```

(a) Source program   (b) Flow graph

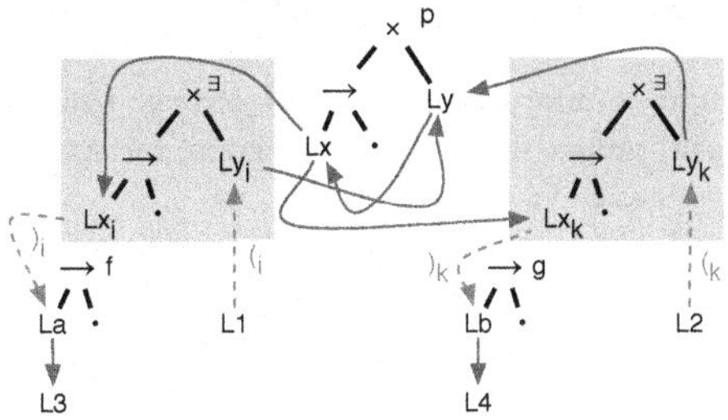

Fig. 2. Existential Types Example

In this example, no matter which pair p is assigned, f is only ever applied to 1, and g is only ever applied to 2. However, an analysis like the one described above would conservatively conflate the types at the two pack sites, generating spurious constraints $L1 \leq L4$ and $L2 \leq L3$. To solve this problem, Sect. 3 presents COPY, a system that can model p precisely by giving it a polymorphically constrained existential type $\exists Lx, Ly[Ly \leq Lx].(int^{Lx} \rightarrow int) \times int^{Ly}$, indicating that p contains a pair whose second element flows to the argument position of its first element. (The uninteresting labels are omitted for clarity.) At $pack^i$, this type is instantiated to yield $L1 \leq La$, and since $La \leq L3$ we have $L1 \leq L3$ transitively. Instantiating at $pack^k$ yields $L2 \leq Lb \leq L4$. Thus we precisely model that 1^{L1} only flows to $+^{L3}$ and 2^{L2} only flows to $+^{L4}$.

To support existential types we have extrapolated on the duality of universal and existential quantification. Intuitively, we give a universal type to id in Fig. 1 because id is polymorphic in the label it is called with—whatever it is called with, it returns. Conversely, in Fig. 2 we give an existential type to p because the *rest of the program* is polymorphic in the pairs—no matter which pair is used, the first element is always applied to the second.

The key contribution of this paper is to show how to perform inference with existential types efficiently using CFL reachability, as presented in Sect. 4. Fig. 2(b) shows the flow graph generated for our example program. When packing the pair $(f, 1^{L1})$, instead of normal flow edges we generate edges labeled by i-parentheses, and we generate edges labeled by k-parentheses when packing $(g, 2^{L2})$. Flow for this graph again corresponds to paths with no mismatched parentheses. For example, in this graph there is a matched path from $L2$ to $L4$, indicating that the value 2^{L2} may flow to $+^{L4}$, and there is similarly a path from $L1$ to $L3$. Notice that restricting flow to matched paths again suppresses spurious flows from $L2$ to $L3$ and from $L1$ to $L4$. Thus, the two existential packages can be conflated without losing the flow relationships of their members.

2.3   Existential Quantification and Race Detection

Our interest in studying existential label flow arose from the development of LOCK-SMITH, a C race detection tool [4]. LOCKSMITH uses label flow analysis to determine what locations ρ may flow to each assignment or dereference in the program, and we use a combination of label flow analysis and linearity checking to determine which locks ℓ

```
struct cache_entry { int refs; pthread_mutex_t refs_mutex; ... };

void cache_entry_addref(cache_entry *entry) { ...
  pthread_mutex_lock(&entry->refs_mutex);
  entry->refs++;
  pthread_mutex_unlock(&entry->refs_mutex);
... }
```

Fig. 3. Example code with a per-element lock

are definitely held at that point. Here ρ and ℓ are just like any other flow labels, and we use different symbols only to emphasize the quantities they label.

Each time a location ρ is accessed with lock ℓ held, LOCKSMITH generates a *correlation constraint* $\rho \triangleright \ell$. After analyzing the whole program, LOCKSMITH ensures that, for each location ρ, there is one lock consistently held for all accesses. Correlation constraints can be easily integrated into flow graphs, and we use a variant of the CFL reachability closure rules to solve for correlations context-sensitively.

During our experiments we found several examples of code similar to Fig. 3, which is taken from the *knot* multithreaded web server [19]. Here cache_entry is a linked list with a per-node lock refs_mutex that guards accesses to the refs field. Without existential quantification, LOCKSMITH conflates all the locks and locations in the data structure. As a result, it does not know exactly which lock is held at the write to entry->refs, and reports that entry->refs may not always be accessed with the same lock held, falsely indicating a potential data race.

With existential quantification, however, LOCKSMITH is able to model this idiom precisely. We add annotations to specify that in type cache_entry, the fields refs and refs_mutex should be given existentially quantified labels. Then we add pack annotations when cache_entry is created and unpack annotations wherever it is used, e.g., within cache_entry_addref. The result is that, in terms of polymorphically constrained types, the entry parameter of cache_entry_addref is given the type $\exists \ell, \rho[\rho \triangleright \ell].\{\texttt{refs} : ref^\rho\ int, \texttt{refs\_mutex} : lock\ \ell, \ldots\}$, and thus LOCKSMITH can verify that the lock refs_mutex always guards the refs field in a given node.

While our prior work sketches the use of existential types, it gives neither type rules nor proofs for them, which are the main contributions of this paper. The remainder of this paper focuses exclusively on existential types for label flow, and we refer the reader to our other paper for details on LOCKSMITH [4].

3   Label Flow with Polymorphically Constrained Types

We begin our formal presentation by studying label flow in the context of a polymorphically-constrained type system COPY, which is essentially Mossin's label flow system [13] extended to include existential types. Note that COPY supports label polymorphism but not polymorphism in the type structure. We use the following source language throughout the paper:

$$e ::= n^L \mid x \mid \lambda^L x.e \mid e_1 @^L e_2 \mid \texttt{if0}^L\ e_0\ \texttt{then}\ e_1\ \texttt{else}\ e_2 \mid (e_1, e_2)^L \mid e.^L j$$
$$\mid\ \texttt{let}\ f = e_1\ \texttt{in}\ e_2 \mid \texttt{fix}\ f.e_1 \mid f^i \mid \texttt{pack}^{L,i}\ e \mid \texttt{unpack}^L\ x = e_1\ \texttt{in}\ e_2$$

$$[\text{Id}]\frac{}{C;\Gamma,x:\tau \vdash_{cp} x:\tau} \qquad\qquad [\text{Int}]\frac{C\vdash L\leq l}{C;\Gamma\vdash_{cp} n^L : int^l}$$

$$[\text{Lam}]\frac{C;\Gamma,x:\tau\vdash_{cp} e:\tau' \quad C\vdash L\leq l}{C;\Gamma\vdash_{cp}\lambda^L x.e:\tau\to^l\tau'} \qquad [\text{App}]\frac{\begin{array}{c}C;\Gamma\vdash_{cp} e_1:\tau\to^l\tau'\\ C;\Gamma\vdash_{cp} e_2:\tau \quad C\vdash l\leq L\end{array}}{C;\Gamma\vdash_{cp} e_1@^L e_2:\tau'}$$

$$[\text{Pair}]\frac{\begin{array}{c}C;\Gamma\vdash_{cp} e_1:\tau_1 \quad C;\Gamma\vdash_{cp} e_2:\tau_2\\ C\vdash L\leq l\end{array}}{C;\Gamma\vdash_{cp}(e_1,e_2)^L:\tau_1\times^l\tau_2} \qquad [\text{Proj}]\frac{\begin{array}{c}C;\Gamma\vdash_{cp} e:\tau_1\times^l\tau_2\\ C\vdash l\leq L \quad j\in\{1,2\}\end{array}}{C;\Gamma\vdash_{cp} e.^L j:\tau_j}$$

$$[\text{Cond}]\frac{\begin{array}{c}C;\Gamma\vdash_{cp} e_0:int^l \quad C\vdash l\leq L\\ C;\Gamma\vdash_{cp} e_1:\tau \quad C;\Gamma\vdash_{cp} e_2:\tau\end{array}}{C;\Gamma\vdash_{cp}\text{if0}^L\ e_0\ \text{then}\ e_1\ \text{else}\ e_2:\tau} \qquad [\text{Sub}]\frac{\begin{array}{c}C;\Gamma\vdash_{cp} e:\tau_1\\ C;\emptyset\vdash\tau_1\leq\tau_2\end{array}}{C;\Gamma\vdash_{cp} e:\tau_2}$$

Fig. 4. COPY Monomorphic Rules

In this language, constructors and destructors are annotated with constant labels L. The goal of our type system is to determine which constructor labels flow to which destructor labels. For example, in the expression $(\lambda^L x.e)@^{L'} e'$, the label L flows to the label L'. Our language includes integers, variables, functions, function application (written with @ to provide a position on which to write a label), conditionals, pairs, and projection, which extracts a component from a pair. Our language also includes binding constructs let and fix, which introduce universal types. Each use of a universally quantified function f^i is indexed by an *instantiation site* i. Expressions also include existential packages, which are created with $\text{pack}^{L,i}$ and consumed with unpack. Here L labels the package itself, since existentials are first-class and can be passed around the program just like any other value, and i identifies this pack as an instantiation site. Instantiation sites are ignored in this section, but are used in Sect. 4.

The types and environments used by COPY are given by the following grammar:

$$\begin{array}{lll}\text{types} & \tau ::= int^l \mid \tau\to^l\tau \mid \tau\times^l\tau \mid \exists^l\vec{\alpha}[C].\tau & \text{schemes} \quad \sigma ::= \forall\vec{\alpha}[C].\tau \mid \tau\\ \text{labels} & l ::= L \mid \alpha & \text{constraints} \quad C ::= \emptyset \mid \{l\leq l\} \mid C\cup C\\ \text{env.} & \Gamma ::= \cdot \mid \Gamma,x:\sigma\end{array}$$

Types include integers, functions, pairs, and existential types. All types are annotated with flow labels l, which may be either constant labels L from the program text or label variables α. Type schemes include normal types and polymorphically-constrained universal types of the form $\forall\vec{\alpha}[C].\tau$. Here C is a set of *flow constraints* each of the form $l\leq l'$. In our type rules, *substitutions* ϕ map label variables to labels. The universal type $\forall\vec{\alpha}[C].\tau$ stands for any type $\phi(\tau)$ where $\phi(C)$ is satisfied, for any substitution ϕ. When $l\leq l'$, we say that label l flows to label l'. The type $\exists^l\vec{\alpha}[C].\tau$ stands for the type $\phi(\tau)$ where constraints $\phi(C)$ are satisfied for *some* substitution ϕ. Universal types may only appear in type environments while existential types may appear arbitrarily. The free labels of types $(fl(\tau))$ and environments $(fl(\Gamma))$ are defined as usual.

The expression typing rules are presented in Figs. 4 and 5. Judgments have the form $C;\Gamma\vdash_{cp} e:\tau$, meaning in type environment Γ with flow constraints C, expression

$$[\text{Let}] \frac{\begin{array}{c} C'; \Gamma \vdash_{cp} e_1 : \tau_1 \quad C; \Gamma, f : \forall \vec{\alpha}[C'].\tau_1 \vdash_{cp} e_2 : \tau_2 \\ \vec{\alpha} \subseteq (fl(\tau_1) \cup fl(C')) \setminus fl(\Gamma) \end{array}}{C; \Gamma \vdash_{cp} \text{let } f = e_1 \text{ in } e_2 : \tau_2}$$

$$[\text{Fix}] \frac{\begin{array}{c} C'; \Gamma, f : \forall \vec{\alpha}[C'].\tau \vdash_{cp} e : \tau \quad C \vdash \phi(C') \\ \vec{\alpha} \subseteq (fl(\tau) \cup fl(C')) \setminus fl(\Gamma) \end{array}}{C; \Gamma \vdash_{cp} \text{fix } f.e : \phi(\tau)}$$

$$[\text{Inst}] \frac{C \vdash \phi(C')}{C; \Gamma, f : \forall \vec{\alpha}[C'].\tau \vdash_{cp} f^i : \phi(\tau)}$$

$$[\text{Pack}] \frac{C; \Gamma \vdash_{cp} e : \phi(\tau) \quad C \vdash \phi(C') \quad C \vdash L \leq l}{C; \Gamma \vdash_{cp} \text{pack}^{L,i} \ e : \exists^l \vec{\alpha}[C'].\tau}$$

$$[\text{Unpack}] \frac{\begin{array}{c} C; \Gamma \vdash_{cp} e_1 : \exists^l \vec{\alpha}[C'].\tau \quad C \cup C'; \Gamma, x : \tau \vdash_{cp} e_2 : \tau' \\ \vec{\alpha} \subseteq (fl(\tau) \cup fl(C')) \setminus (fl(\Gamma) \cup fl(C) \cup fl(\tau')) \quad C \vdash l \leq L \end{array}}{C; \Gamma \vdash_{cp} \text{unpack}^L \ x = e_1 \text{ in } e_2 : \tau'}$$

Fig. 5. COPY Polymorphic Rules

e has type τ. In these type rules $C \vdash l \leq l'$ means that the constraint $l \leq l'$ is in the transitive closure of the constraints in C, and $C \vdash C'$ means that all constraints in C' are in the transitive closure of C.

Fig. 4 contains the monomorphic typing rules, which are as in the standard λ calculus except for the addition of labels and subtyping. The constructor rules ([Int], [Lam] and [Pair]) require $C \vdash L \leq l$, i.e., the constructor label L must flow to the corresponding label of the constructed type. The destructor rules ([Cond], [App] and [Proj]) require the converse. The subtyping rule [Sub] is discussed below.

Fig. 5 contains the polymorphic typing rules. Universal types are introduced by [Let] and [Fix]. As is standard, we allow generalization only of label variables that are not free in the type environment Γ. In both these rules, the constraints C' used to type e_1 become the bound constraints in the polymorphic type. Whenever a variable f with a universal type is used in the program text, written f^i where i identifies this occurrence of f, it is type checked by [Inst]. This rule instantiates the type of f, and the premise $C \vdash \phi(C')$ effectively inlines the constraints of f function into the caller's context.

Existential types are manipulated using pack and unpack. To understand [Pack] and [Unpack], recall that $\forall$ and $\exists$ are dual notions. Notice that $\forall$ introduction ([Let]) restricts what can be universally quantified, and instantiation occurs at $\forall$ elimination ([Inst]). Thus $\exists$ introduction ([Pack]) should perform instantiation, and $\exists$ elimination ([Unpack]) should restrict what can be existentially quantified.

In [Pack], an expression e with a concrete type $\phi(\tau)$ is abstracted to a type $\exists^l \vec{\alpha}[C'].\tau$. Notice that the substitution maps abstract τ and C' to concrete $\phi(\tau)$ and $\phi(C')$—creating an existential corresponds to passing an argument to "the rest of the program," as if that were universally quantified in $\vec{\alpha}$, and the constraints C' are determined by how the existential package is used after it is unpacked. Similarly to [Inst], the [Pack] premise $C \vdash \phi(C')$ inlines the abstract constraints $\phi(C')$ into the current constraints.

$$[\text{Sub-Label-1}] \frac{l, l' \notin D \quad C \vdash l \leq l'}{C; D \vdash l \leq l'} \qquad [\text{Sub-Label-2}] \frac{l \in D}{C; D \vdash l \leq l}$$

$$[\text{Sub-Pair}] \frac{\begin{array}{c} C; D \vdash l \leq l' \\ C; D \vdash \tau_1 \leq \tau_1' \\ C; D \vdash \tau_2 \leq \tau_2' \end{array}}{C; D \vdash \tau_1 \times^l \tau_2 \leq \tau_1' \times^{l'} \tau_2'} \qquad [\text{Sub-Fun}] \frac{\begin{array}{c} C; D \vdash l \leq l' \\ C; D \vdash \tau_1' \leq \tau_1 \\ C; D \vdash \tau_2 \leq \tau_2' \end{array}}{C; D \vdash \tau_1 \to^l \tau_2 \leq \tau_1' \to^{l'} \tau_2'}$$

$$[\text{Sub-Int}] \frac{C; D \vdash l \leq l'}{C; D \vdash int^l \leq int^{l'}} \qquad [\text{Sub-}\exists] \frac{\begin{array}{c} C_1 \vdash C_2 \qquad D' = D \cup \vec{\alpha} \\ C; D' \vdash \tau_1 \leq \tau_2 \qquad C; D \vdash l_1 \leq l_2 \end{array}}{C; D \vdash \exists^{l_1} \vec{\alpha}[C_1].\tau_1 \leq \exists^{l_2} \vec{\alpha}[C_2].\tau_2}$$

Fig. 6. COPY Subtyping

Rule [Unpack] binds the contents of the type to x in the scope of e_2. This rule places two restrictions on the existential package. First, e_2 must type check with the constraints $C \cup C'$.[1] Thus, any constraints among the existentially bound labels $\vec{\alpha}$ needed to check e_2 must be in C'. Second, the labels $\vec{\alpha}$ must not escape the scope of the unpack (as is standard [2]), which is ensured by the subset constraint.

The [Sub] rule in Fig. 4 uses the subtyping relation shown in Fig. 6. These rules are standard structural subtyping rules extended to labeled types. We use a simple approach to decide whether one existential is a subtype of another. Rule [Sub-$\exists$] requires $C_1 \vdash C_2$, since an existential type can be used in any position inducing the same or fewer flows between labels. We allow subtyping among existentials of a "similar shape." That is, they must have exactly the same (alpha-convertible) bound variables, and there must be no constraints between variables bound in one type and free in the other. We use a set D to track the set of bound variables, updated in [Sub-$\exists$].[2] Rule [Sub-Label-2] permits subtyping between identical bound labels ($l \in D$), whereas rule [Sub-Label-1] allows subtyping among non-identical labels only if neither is bound.

These restrictions on existentials forbid some clearly erroneous judgments such as $C \vdash \exists \alpha[\emptyset].int^\alpha \leq \exists \alpha[\emptyset].int^\beta$. The two existential types in this example quantify over the same label; however, the subtyping is invalid because it would create a constraint between a bound label and an unbound label. However, these restrictions also forbid some valid existential subtyping, such as $C \vdash (\exists \alpha, \beta[\alpha \leq \beta].int^\alpha \to int^\beta) \leq (\exists \alpha, \beta[\emptyset].int^\alpha \to int^\alpha)$, which is permissible because β is a bound variable with no other lower bounds except α, hence it can be set to α without losing information. However, our typing rules do not allow this. In our experience with LOCKSMITH we have not found this restriction to be an issue, and we leave it as an open question whether it can be relaxed while still maintaining efficient CFL reachability-based inference.

We prove soundness for COPY using subject reduction. Using a standard small-step operational semantics $e \longrightarrow e'$, we define a *flow-preserving evaluation step* as one

---

[1] Note that we could have chosen this hypothesis to be $C'; \Gamma, x : \tau \vdash_{cp} e_2 : \tau'$ and still had a sound system, but this choice simplifies the reduction from CFL to COPY discussed in Sect. 4.

[2] Our technical report [20] uses an equivalent version of D that makes the reduction proof easier.

whose flow is allowed by some constraint set C. Then we prove that if a program is well-typed according to C then it always preserves flow.

Definition 1 (Flow-preserving Evaluation Step). *Suppose $e \longrightarrow e'$ and in this reduction a destructor* (`if0`, `@`, `.j`, `unpack`) *labeled L' consumes a constructor* (n, λ, $(\cdot, \cdot)$, `pack`, *respectively*) *labeled L. Then we write $C \vdash e \longrightarrow e'$ if $C \vdash L \leq L'$. We also write $C \vdash e \longrightarrow e'$ if no value is consumed during reduction (for `let` or `fix`).*

Theorem 1 (Soundness). *If $C; \Gamma \vdash_{cp} e : \tau$ and $e \longrightarrow^* e'$, then $C \vdash e \longrightarrow^* e'$.*

Here, $\longrightarrow^*$ denotes the reflexive and transitive closure of the $\longrightarrow$ relation. The proof is by induction on $C; \Gamma \vdash_{cp} e : \tau$ and is presented in a companion technical report [20].

4   CFL-Based Label Flow Inference

The COPY type system is relatively easy to understand and convenient for proving soundness, but experience suggests it is awkward to implement directly as an inference system. This section presents a label flow inference system CFL based on CFL reachability, in the style of Rehof et al [14,15]. This system uses a single, global set of constraints, which correspond to flow graphs like those shown in Figs. 1(d) and 2. Given a flow graph, we can answer queries "Does any value labeled l_1 flow to a destructor labeled l_2?", written $l_1 \rightsquigarrow l_2$, by using CFL reachability. We first present type checking rules for CFL and then explain how they are used to interpret the flow graph in Fig. 2. Then we explain how the rules can be interpreted to yield an efficient inference algorithm. Finally, we prove that CFL reduces to COPY and thus is sound.

Types in CFL are as follows:

$$\text{types } \tau ::= int^l \mid \tau \rightarrow^l \tau \mid \tau \times^l \tau \mid \exists^l \vec{\alpha}.\tau \qquad \text{schemes } \sigma ::= (\forall \vec{\alpha}.\tau, \vec{l}) \mid \tau$$

In contrast to COPY, universal types $(\forall \vec{\alpha}.\tau, \vec{l})$ and existential types $\exists^l \vec{\alpha}.\tau$ do not include a constraint set, since we generate a single, global flow graph. Universal types contain a set $\vec{l}$ of labels that are *not* quantified [14,21]. For clarity universal types also include $\vec{\alpha}$, the set of labels that are quantified, but it is always the case that $\vec{\alpha} = fl(\tau) \setminus \vec{l}$. Existential types do not include a set $\vec{l}$, because we assume that the programmer has specified which labels are existentially quantified. We check that the specification is correct when existentials are unpacked (more on this below).

Typing judgments in CFL have the form $I; C; \Gamma \vdash e : \tau$, where I and C describe the edges in the flow graph. C has the same form as in COPY, consisting of subtyping constraints $l \leq l'$ (shown as unlabeled directed edges in Figs. 1 and 2). I contains *instantiation constraints* [14] of the form $l \preceq^i_p l'$. Such a constraint indicates that l is renamed to l' at instantiation site i. (Recall that each instantiation site corresponds to a `pack` or a use of a universally quantified type.) The p indicates a *polarity*, which describes the flow of data. When p is $+$ then l flows to l', and so in our examples we draw the constraint $l \preceq^i_+ l'$ as an edge $l \longrightarrow^{)i} l'$. When p is $-$ the reverse holds, and so we draw the constraint $l \preceq^i_- l'$ as an edge $l' \longrightarrow^{(i} l$. Instantiation constraints correspond to substitutions in COPY, and they enable context-sensitivity without the

$$[\text{Id}]\frac{}{I;C;\Gamma,x:\tau \vdash_{cfl} x:\tau} \qquad [\text{Int}]\frac{C \vdash L \le l}{I;C;\Gamma \vdash_{cfl} n^L : int^l}$$

$$[\text{Lam}]\frac{I;C;\Gamma,x:\tau \vdash_{cfl} e:\tau' \quad C \vdash L \le l}{I;C;\Gamma \vdash_{cfl} \lambda^L x.e : \tau \rightarrow^l \tau'} \qquad [\text{App}]\frac{I;C;\Gamma \vdash_{cfl} e_1 : \tau \rightarrow^l \tau' \quad I;C;\Gamma \vdash_{cfl} e_2 : \tau \quad C \vdash l \le L}{I;C;\Gamma \vdash_{cfl} e_1 @^L e_2 : \tau'}$$

$$[\text{Pair}]\frac{I;C;\Gamma \vdash_{cfl} e_1 : \tau_1 \quad I;C;\Gamma \vdash_{cfl} e_2 : \tau_2 \quad C \vdash L \le l}{I;C;\Gamma \vdash_{cfl} (e_1,e_2)^L : \tau_1 \times^l \tau_2} \qquad [\text{Proj}]\frac{I;C;\Gamma \vdash_{cfl} e : \tau_1 \times^l \tau_2 \quad C \vdash l \le L \quad j \in \{1,2\}}{I;C;\Gamma \vdash_{cfl} e.^L j : \tau_j}$$

$$[\text{Cond}]\frac{I;C;\Gamma \vdash_{cfl} e_0 : int^l \quad C \vdash l \le L \quad I;C;\Gamma \vdash_{cfl} e_1 : \tau \quad I;C;\Gamma \vdash_{cfl} e_2 : \tau}{I;C;\Gamma \vdash_{cfl} \text{if0}^L \ e_0 \text{ then } e_1 \text{ else } e_2 : \tau} \qquad [\text{Sub}]\frac{I;C;\Gamma \vdash_{cfl} e : \tau_1 \quad C;\emptyset;\emptyset \vdash \tau_1 \le \tau_2}{I;C;\Gamma \vdash_{cfl} e : \tau_2}$$

Fig. 7. CFL Monomorphic Rules

need to copy constraint sets. A full discussion of instantiation constraints is beyond the scope of this paper; see Rehof et al [14] for a thorough description.

The monomorphic rules for CFL are presented in Fig. 7. With the exception of [Sub] and the presence of I, these are identical to the rules in Fig. 4. Fig. 8 presents the polymorphic CFL rules. In these type rules $I \vdash l \preceq^i_p l'$ means that the instantiation constraint $l \preceq^i_p l'$ is in I. We define $fl(\tau)$ to be the free labels of a type as usual, except $fl(\forall \vec{\alpha}.\tau, \vec{l}) = (fl(\tau) \setminus \vec{\alpha}) \cup \vec{l}$. Rules [Let] and [Fix] bind f to a universal type. As is standard we cannot quantify label variables that are free in the environment Γ, which we represent by setting $\vec{l} = fl(\Gamma)$ in type $(\forall \vec{\alpha}.\tau_1, \vec{l})$. The [Inst] rule instantiates the type τ of f to τ' using an instantiation constraint $I;\emptyset \vdash \tau \preceq^i_+ \tau' : \phi$. This constraint represents a renaming ϕ, analogous to that in COPY's [Inst] rule, such that $\phi(\tau) = \tau'$. All non-quantifiable labels, i.e., all labels in $\vec{l}$, should not be instantiated, which we model by requiring that any such label instantiate to itself, both positively and negatively.

Rule [Pack] constructs an existential type by abstracting a concrete type τ' to abstract type τ. In COPY's [Pack], there is a substitution such that $\tau' = \phi(\tau)$, and thus CFL's [Pack] has a corresponding instantiation constraint $\tau \preceq^i_- \tau'$. The instantiation constraint has negative polarity because although the substitution is from abstract τ to concrete τ', the direction of flow is the reverse, since the packed expression e flows to the packed value. In [Pack] the choice of $\vec{\alpha}$ is not specified. As in other systems for inferring first-class existential and universal types [22,23,24,25], we expect the programmer to choose this set. In contrast to [Inst], we do not generate any self-instantiations in [Pack], because we enforce a stronger restriction for escaping variables in [Unpack].

Rule [Unpack] treats the abstract existential type as a concrete type within e_2, and thus any uses of the unpacked value place constraints on its existential type. The last premise of [Unpack] ensures that abstract labels do not escape, and moreover abstract labels may not constrain any escaping labels in any way. Specifically, we require that there are no flows (see below) between any labels in $\vec{\alpha}$ and any labels in $\vec{l}$, which is the set of labels that could escape. If this condition is violated, then the existentially

$$[Let]\ \frac{\begin{array}{c} I;C;\Gamma \vdash_{cfl} e_1 : \tau_1 \qquad I;C;\Gamma,f:(\forall\vec{\alpha}.\tau_1,\vec{l}) \vdash_{cfl} e_2:\tau_2 \\ \vec{\alpha} = fl(\tau_1)\setminus\vec{l} \qquad\qquad \vec{l}=fl(\Gamma) \end{array}}{I;C;\Gamma \vdash_{cfl} \texttt{let } f = e_1 \texttt{ in } e_2 : \tau_2}$$

$$[Fix]\ \frac{\begin{array}{c} I;C;\Gamma,f:(\forall\vec{\alpha}.\tau,\vec{l})\vdash_{cfl} e:\tau \qquad \vec{\alpha}=fl(\tau)\setminus fl(\Gamma) \qquad \vec{l}=fl(\Gamma) \\ I;\emptyset \vdash \tau \preceq^i_+ \tau':\phi \qquad I\vdash\vec{l}\preceq^i_+\vec{l} \qquad I\vdash\vec{l}\preceq^i_-\vec{l} \end{array}}{I;C;\Gamma\vdash_{cfl}\texttt{fix } f.e:\tau'}$$

$$[Inst]\ \frac{I;\emptyset\vdash\tau\preceq^i_+\tau':\phi \qquad I\vdash\vec{l}\preceq^i_+\vec{l} \qquad I\vdash\vec{l}\preceq^i_-\vec{l}}{I;C;\Gamma,f:(\forall\vec{\alpha}.\tau,\vec{l})\vdash_{cfl} f^i:\tau'}$$

$$[Pack]\ \frac{I;C;\Gamma\vdash_{cfl} e:\tau' \qquad I;\emptyset\vdash\tau\preceq^i_-\tau':\phi \qquad dom(\phi)=\vec{\alpha} \qquad C\vdash L\leq l}{I;C;\Gamma\vdash_{cfl}\texttt{pack}^{L,i}\ e:\exists^l\vec{\alpha}.\tau}$$

$$[Unpack]\ \frac{\begin{array}{c} I;C;\Gamma\vdash_{cfl} e_1:\exists^l\vec{\alpha}.\tau \qquad\qquad I;C;\Gamma,x:\tau\vdash_{cfl} e_2:\tau' \\ \vec{l}=fl(\Gamma)\cup fl(\exists^l\vec{\alpha}.\tau)\cup fl(\tau')\cup L \qquad \vec{\alpha}\subseteq fl(\tau)\setminus\vec{l} \qquad C\vdash l\leq L \\ \forall l\in\vec{\alpha}, l'\in\vec{l}.(I;C\not\vdash l\leadsto l' \text{ and } I;C\not\vdash l'\leadsto l) \end{array}}{I;C;\Gamma\vdash_{cfl}\texttt{unpack}^L\ x=e_1 \texttt{ in } e_2:\tau'}$$

Fig. 8. CFL Polymorphic Rules

quantified labels $\vec{\alpha}$ chosen by the programmer are invalid and the program is rejected. The [Unpack] rule in COPY does not forbid interaction between free and bound labels, and therefore CFL is strictly weaker than COPY. However, without this restriction we can produce cases where mixing existentials and universals produces flow paths that should be valid but have mismatched parentheses. Sect. 4.3 contains one such example. In practice we believe the restriction is acceptable, as we have not found it to be an issue with LOCKSMITH. We leave it as an open question whether the restriction can be relaxed while still maintaining efficient CFL reachability-based inference.

Fig. 9 defines the subtyping relation used in [Sub]. The only interesting difference with COPY arises because of alpha-conversion. In COPY alpha-conversion is implicit, and only trivial constraints are allowed between bound labels (by [Sub-Label-2] of Fig. 6). We cannot use implicit alpha-conversions in CFL, however, because we are producing a single, global set of constraints. Thus instead of the single D used in COPY's[Sub] rule, CFL uses two Δ_i, which are sequences of ordered vectors of existentially-bound labels, updated in [Sub-∃]. In the rules, the syntax $\Delta \oplus \{l_1,...,l_n\}$ means to append vector $\{l_1,...,l_n\}$ to sequence Δ. Rule [Sub-Ind-2] in Fig. 9, which corresponds to [Sub-Label-2] in Fig. 6, does allow subtyping between bound labels l_j and l'_j—but only if they occur in exactly the same quantification position. Thus these subtyping edges actually correspond to alpha-conversion. We could also allow this in the COPY system, but it adds no expressive power and complicates proving soundness.

Fig. 10 defines instantiation constraints on types in terms of instantiation constraints on labels. Judgments have the form $I;D\vdash\tau\preceq^i_p\tau':\phi$, where ϕ is the renaming defined by the instantiation and D is the same as in Fig. 6—we do not need to allow alpha-conversion here, because we can always apply [Sub] if we wish to alpha-rename. Thus

$$[\text{Sub-Ind-1}]\frac{C \vdash l \leq l'}{C; \emptyset; \emptyset \vdash l \leq l'} \qquad [\text{Sub-Int}]\frac{C; \Delta_1; \Delta_2 \vdash l \leq l'}{C; \Delta_1; \Delta_2 \vdash int^l \leq int^{l'}}$$

$$[\text{Sub-Ind-2}]\frac{C \vdash l_j \leq l'_j}{C; \Delta_1 \oplus \{l_1, \ldots, l_n\}; \Delta_2 \oplus \{l'_1, \ldots, l'_n\} \vdash l_j \leq l'_j}$$

$$[\text{Sub-Ind-3}]\frac{C; \Delta_1; \Delta_2 \vdash l \leq l' \qquad l \neq l_i \qquad l' \neq l'_j \qquad \forall i,j \in [1..n]}{C; \Delta_1 \oplus \{l_1, \ldots, l_n\}; \Delta_2 \oplus \{l'_1, \ldots, l'_n\} \vdash l \leq l'}$$

$$[\text{Sub-Pair}]\frac{C; \Delta_1; \Delta_2 \vdash l \leq l' \qquad C; \Delta_1; \Delta_2 \vdash \tau_1 \leq \tau'_1 \qquad C; \Delta_1; \Delta_2 \vdash \tau_2 \leq \tau'_2}{C; \Delta_1; \Delta_2 \vdash \tau_1 \times^l \tau_2 \leq \tau'_1 \times^{l'} \tau'_2}$$

$$[\text{Sub-Fun}]\frac{C; \Delta_1; \Delta_2 \vdash l \leq l' \qquad C; \Delta_1; \Delta_2 \vdash \tau'_1 \leq \tau_1 \qquad C; \Delta_1; \Delta_2 \vdash \tau_2 \leq \tau'_2}{C; \Delta_1; \Delta_2 \vdash \tau_1 \rightarrow^l \tau_2 \leq \tau'_1 \rightarrow^{l'} \tau'_2}$$

$$[\text{Sub-}\exists]\frac{\Delta'_1 = \Delta_1 \oplus \vec{\alpha_1} \qquad \Delta'_2 = \Delta_2 \oplus \vec{\alpha_2} \qquad \phi(\vec{\alpha_2}) = \vec{\alpha_1} \\ C; \Delta'_1; \Delta'_2 \vdash \tau_1 \leq \tau_2 \qquad C; \Delta_1; \Delta_2 \vdash l_1 \leq l_2}{C; \Delta_1; \Delta_2 \vdash \exists^{l_1}\vec{\alpha_1}.\tau_1 \leq \exists^{l_2}\vec{\alpha_2}.\tau_2}$$

Fig. 9. CFL Subtyping

$$[\text{Inst-Ind-1}]\frac{l, l' \notin D \qquad I \vdash l \preceq^i_p l'}{I; D \vdash l \preceq^i_p l' : \emptyset} \qquad\qquad [\text{Inst-Ind-2}]\frac{l \in D}{I; D \vdash l \preceq^i_p l : \phi}$$

$$[\text{Inst-Pair}]\frac{I; D \vdash l \preceq^i_p l' : \phi \\ I; D \vdash \tau_1 \preceq^i_p \tau'_1 : \phi \\ I; D \vdash \tau_2 \preceq^i_p \tau'_2 : \phi}{I; D \vdash \tau_1 \times^l \tau_2 \preceq^i_p \tau'_1 \times^{l'} \tau'_2 : \phi} \qquad [\text{Inst-Fun}]\frac{I; D \vdash l \preceq^i_p l' : \phi \\ I; D \vdash \tau_1 \preceq^i_{\bar{p}} \tau'_1 : \phi \\ I; D \vdash \tau_2 \preceq^i_p \tau'_2 : \phi}{I; D \vdash \tau_1 \rightarrow^l \tau_2 \preceq^i_p \tau'_1 \rightarrow^{l'} \tau'_2 : \phi}$$

$$[\text{Inst-Int}]\frac{I; D \vdash l \preceq^i_p l' : \phi}{I; D \vdash int^l \preceq^i_p int^{l'} : \phi} \qquad [\text{Inst-}\exists]\frac{D' = D \cup \vec{\alpha} \qquad I; D' \vdash \tau_1 \preceq^i_p \tau_2 : \phi \\ I; D \vdash l_1 \preceq^i_p l_2 : \phi}{I; D \vdash \exists^{l_1}\vec{\alpha}.\tau_1 \preceq^i_p \exists^{l_2}\vec{\alpha}.\tau_2 : \phi}$$

Fig. 10. CFL Instantiation

[Inst-Ind-1] permits instantiation of unbound labels, and [Inst-Ind-2] forbids renaming bound labels. For example, if we have an $\exists$ type nested inside a $\forall$ type, instantiating the $\forall$ type should not rename any of the bound variables of the $\exists$ type. Aside from this the rules in Fig. 10 are standard, and details can be found in Rehof et al [14].

Given a flow graph described by constraints I and C, Fig. 11 gives inference rules to compute the relation $l_1 \rightsquigarrow l_2$, which means label l_1 flows to label l_2. Rule [Level] states that constraints in C correspond to flow (represented as unlabeled edges in the flow graph). Rule [Trans] adds transitive closure. Rule [Match] allows flow on a matched path $l_0 \longrightarrow^{(i} l_1 \rightsquigarrow l_2 \longrightarrow^{)i} l_3$. This rule corresponds to "copying" the constraint $l_1 \rightsquigarrow l_2$ to a constraint $l_0 \rightsquigarrow l_3$ at instantiation site i. Rule [Constant] adds a "self-loop"

$$[\text{Level}]\frac{C \vdash l_1 \leq l_2}{I; C \vdash l_1 \rightsquigarrow l_2} \qquad [\text{Trans}]\frac{I; C \vdash l_0 \rightsquigarrow l_1 \quad I; C \vdash l_1 \rightsquigarrow l_2}{I; C \vdash l_0 \rightsquigarrow l_2}$$

$$[\text{Constant}]\frac{}{I; C \vdash L \preceq_p^i L} \qquad [\text{Match}]\frac{I \vdash l_1 \preceq_-^i l_0 \quad I; C \vdash l_1 \rightsquigarrow l_2 \quad I \vdash l_2 \preceq_+^i l_3}{I; C \vdash l_0 \rightsquigarrow l_3}$$

Fig. 11. Flow

that permits matching flows to or from any constant label. We generate these edges because constants are global names and thus are context-insensitive.

Note that our relation $\rightsquigarrow$ corresponds to the $\rightsquigarrow_m$ relation from Rehof et al [14], where m stands for "matched paths." The Rehof et al system also includes so-called *PN paths*, which allow extra parentheses that are not matched by anything, e.g., extra open parentheses at the beginning of the path, or extra closed parentheses at the end. In our system we concern ourselves only with constants, which by [Constant] have all possible self-loops (this rule is not included in the Rehof et al system). These self-loops mean that any flow from one constant to another via a PN path is also captured by a matched path between the constants. Thus for purposes of showing soundness, matched paths suffice. We could add PN paths to our system with no difficulty to allow queries on intermediate flows, but have not done so for simplicity.

4.1   Example

Consider again the example in Fig. 2. The expression $\text{pack}^i(f, 1^{L1})$ is given the type

$$\exists Lx_i, Ly_i.(int^{Lx_i} \rightarrow int) \times int^{Ly_i}$$

by the [Pack] rule. [Pack] also instantiates the pair's abstract type to its concrete type using the judgment

$$I; C \vdash (int^{Lx_i} \rightarrow int) \times int^{Ly_i} \preceq_-^i (int^{La} \rightarrow int) \times int^{L1}$$

Proving this judgment requires appealing in several places to [Inst-Ind-1], whose premise $I \vdash l \preceq_p^i l'$ requires that I contain constraints $Ly_i \preceq_-^i L1$ and $Lx_i \preceq_+^i La$, among others. These are shown as dashed, labeled edges in the figure. Notice that the direction of the renaming is opposite the direction of flow: The concrete labels flow to the abstract labels, but the abstract type is instantiated to the concrete type. Hence the instantiation has negative polarity. This instantiated existential type flows via subtyping to the type of p shown at the center of the figure. The directed edges between the type components are induced by subtyping (applying [Sub-$\exists$] at the top level).

The unpack of p is typed by the [Unpack] rule. Within the body of the unpack, we apply the second part of the pair ($p2$) to the first part ($p1$). Here, $p2$ has type int^{Ly} while $p1$ has type $int^{Lx} \rightarrow int$, and thus to apply the [App] rule, we must first prove (among other things) that $C; \emptyset; \emptyset \vdash int^{Ly} \leq int^{Lx}$. This requires that $Ly \leq Lx$ be in C according to [Sub-Ind-1], and is shown as an unlabeled edge in the figure. With this edge we have $I; C \vdash L1 \rightsquigarrow L3$ and $I; C \vdash L2 \rightsquigarrow L4$ (but $I; C \nvdash L1 \rightsquigarrow L4$). The final premises of [Unpack] are satisfied because the bound labels Ly and Lx only flow among themselves or to variables bound in existential types, which are not free.

4.2   An Inference Algorithm

CFL has been presented thus far as a checking system in which the flow graph, described by C and I, is assumed to be known. To infer this flow graph automatically requires a simple reinterpretation of the rules. The algorithm has three stages and runs in time $O(n^3)$, where n is the size of the type-annotated program.

First, we type the program according to the rules in Figs. 7-10. As usual the non-syntactic rule [Sub] can be incorporated into the remaining rules to produce a syntax-directed system [26]. During typing, we interpret a premise $C \vdash l \leq l'$ or $I \vdash \vec{l} \preceq_p^i \vec{l}$ as *generating* a constraint; i.e., we add $l \leq l'$ (or $\vec{l} \preceq_p^i \vec{l}$) to the set of global constraints C (or I). Free occurrences of l in the rules are interpreted as fresh label variables. For example, in [Int] we interpret l as a fresh variable α and add $L \leq l$ to C. When choosing types (e.g., τ in [Lam] or τ' in [Inst]) we pick a type τ of the correct shape with fresh label variables in every position. After typing we have a flow graph defined by constraint sets C and I.

Next, we compute all flows according to the rules in Fig. 11. Excluding the final premise of [Unpack] and the D's in [Sub] and [Inst], performing typing and computing all flows takes time $O(n^3)$ [14]. To implement [Sub-Ind-i] efficiently, rather than maintain D sets explicitly and repeatedly traverse them, we temporarily mark each variable with a pair (i, j) indicating its position in D and its position in $\vec{\alpha}$ as we traverse an existential type. We can assume without loss of generality that $|\vec{\alpha}| \leq |fl(\tau)|$ in an existential type, so traversing $\vec{\alpha}$ does not increase the complexity. Then we can select among [Sub-Ind-1] and [Sub-Ind-2] in constant time for each constraint $C; \Delta_1; \Delta_2 \vdash l \leq l'$, so this does not affect the running time, and similarly for [Inst-Ind-i].

Finally, we check the last reachability condition of [Unpack] to ensure the programmer chose a valid specification of existential quantification. Given that we have computed all flows, we can easily traverse the labels in $\vec{\alpha}$ and check for paths to $\vec{l}$ and vice-versa. Since each set is of size $O(n)$, this takes $O(n^2)$ time, and since there are $O(n)$ uses of [Unpack], in total this takes $O(n^3)$ time. Thus the algorithm as a whole is $O(n^3) + O(n^3) = O(n^3)$.

4.3   Differences Between COPY and CFL

As mentioned in Sect. 4, if we weaken CFL's [Unpack] rule to permit existentially bound labels to interact with free labels, then we can construct examples with mismatched flow. Fig. 12(a) shows one such example. Here the function g takes an argument z, packs it, and then returns the result of calling function f with the package. Function f unpacks the existential and returns its contents. Thus g is the identity function, but with complicated data flow. On the last line, the function g is applied to 1^{L1}, and the result is added using $+^{L2}$. Thus $L1$ flows to $L2$. Let us assume that at $\mathtt{pack}^k$, the programmer wishes to quantify the type of the packed integer, and then compare COPY and CFL as applied to the program.

The COPY types rules assign f the type scheme

$$f : \forall Lout[\emptyset]. \left(\exists Lx[Lx \leq Lout].int^{Lx} \right) \rightarrow int^{Lout}$$

```
let g = λz.
    let f = (λx. unpack y = x in y) in
    let p = pack^k z in
    f^i p
in
    (g^m 1^{L1}) +^{L2} ···
```

(a) Source program   (b) Flow graph

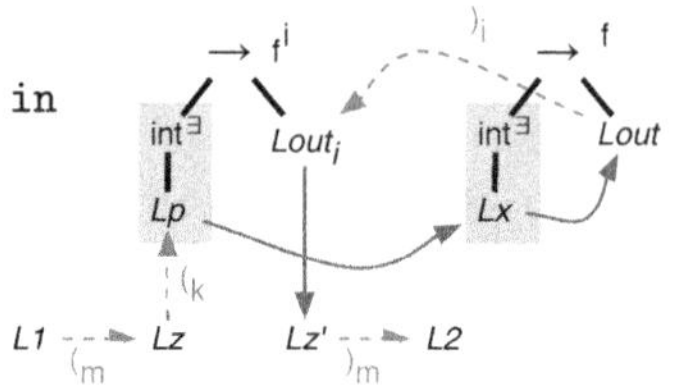

Fig. 12. Example with Mismatched Flow

Notice that since f unpacks its argument and returns the contents, there is a constraint between Lx, the label of the packed integer, and $Lout$, the label on f's result type. The interesting thing here is that Lx is existentially bound and $Lout$ is not, which is acceptable in COPY (technically, we need an application of [Sub] to achieve this), but not allowed in CFL. At the call to f, we instantiate f's type as

$$f^i : \left(\exists Lx[Lx \leq Lout_i].int^{Lx}\right) \rightarrow int^{Lout_i}$$

Let Lz be the label on g's parameter, and let Lz' be the label on g's return type. Then when we pack z and bind the result to p, we instantiate the abstract Lx to concrete Lz and thus generate the constraint $Lz \leq Lout_i$. Then g returns the result of f^i, and hence we have $Lout_i \leq Lz'$. Putting these together and generalizing g's type, we get

$$g : \forall Lz, Lz', Lout_i[Lz \leq Lout_i, Lout_i \leq Lz'].int^{Lz} \rightarrow int^{Lz'}$$

Finally, we instantiate this type at g^m, and we get $L1 \leq Lz_m \leq Lout_{im} \leq Lz'_m \leq L2$, and thus we have flow from $L1$ to $L2$.

Now consider applying CFL to the same program. Fig. 12(b) shows the resulting flow graph. The type of f, shown at the right of the figure, is $(\forall Lout.(\exists Lx.int^{Lx}) \rightarrow int^{Lout}, \emptyset)$ where in the global flow graph there is a constraint $Lx \leq Lout$. As before, this is a constraint between an existentially bound and free variable, which is forbidden by the strong non-escaping condition in CFL's [Unpack] rule. However, assume for the moment that we ignore this condition. Then the type of f^i, shown in the left of the figure, is $(\exists Lp.int^{Lp}) \rightarrow int^{Lout_i}$ where we have an instantiation constraint $Lout \preceq^i_+ Lout_i$, drawn as a dashed edge labeled $)_i$ in the figure. (Note that we have also applied an extra step of subtyping to make the figure easier to read and drawn an edge $Lp \leq Lx$, although we could also set $Lp = Lx$.) Since the result of calling f^i is returned, we have $Lout_i \leq Lz'$, where again Lz' is the label on the return type of g. Moreover, at $pack^k$, we instantiate the abstract type of p to its concrete type, resulting in the constraint $Lp \preceq^k_- Lz$, where Lz is the label on g's parameter. Finally, at the instantiation of g we generate constraints $Lz \preceq^m_- L1$ and $Lz' \preceq^m_+ L2$.

Notice that there is no path from $L1$ to $L2$, because $(_k$ does not match $)_i$. The problem is that instantiation i must not rename Lp, and instantiation k must not rename $Lout_i$. In CFL, we prevent instantiations from renaming labels by adding "self-loops," as in [Inst] in Fig. 8. In this case, we should have $Lp \preceq^i_\pm Lp$ and $Lout_i \preceq^k_\pm Lout_i$. We expended significant effort trying to discover a system that would add exactly these self-loops, but we were unable to find a solution that would work in all cases. For example, adding a self-loop on $Lout_i$ seems particularly problematic, since $Lout_i$ is created only after f^i is instantiated, and not at the pack or the unpack points. Moreover, because we have $(_m$ and $)_m$ at the beginning and end of the mismatched path, the self-loops on $L1$ and $L2$ do not help. Thus in [Unpack] in Fig. 8, we require existentially-quantified labels to not have any flow with escaping labels to forbid this example.

4.4   Soundness

We have proven that programs that check under CFL are reducible to COPY. The first step is to define a translation function $\Psi_{C,I}$ that takes CFL types and transforms them to COPY types. For monomorphic types $\Psi_{C,I}$ is simply the identity. To translate a polymorphic CFL type $(\forall\vec{\alpha}.\tau, \vec{l})$ or $\exists^l\vec{\alpha}.\tau$ into a COPY type $\forall\vec{\alpha}[C'].\tau$ or $\exists^l\vec{\alpha}[C'].\tau$, respectively, $\Psi_{C,I}$ needs to produce a bound constraint set C'. Rehof et al [14,15] were able to choose $C' = C^I = \{l_1 \leq l_2 \mid I; C \vdash l_1 \leadsto l_2\}$, i.e., the closure of C and I. However, the addition of first class existentials causes this approach to fail, because, for example, instantiating a $\forall$ type containing a type $\exists^l\vec{\alpha}[C^I].\tau$ could rename some variables in C^I (since C^I contains all variables used in the program) and thereby violate the inductive hypothesis. Thus we introduce a projection function ψ_S, where we define

$$\psi_S(l) = \begin{cases} l & l \in S \cup L \\ \bigsqcup\{l' \in S \cup L \mid C^I \vdash l' \leq l\} & otherwise \end{cases}$$

where $\sqcup$ represents the union of two labels. Then for a universal type, $\Psi_{C,I}$ sets $C' = \psi_{(\vec{\alpha}\cup\vec{l})}(C^I)$, and for an existential type $\Psi_{C,I}$ sets $C' = \psi_{\vec{\alpha}}(C^I)$. We extend $\Psi_{C,I}$ to type environments in the natural way and define $C_S^I = \psi_S(C^I)$. Now we can show:

Theorem 2 (Reduction from CFL to COPY). *Let $\mathcal{D}$ be a normal CFL derivation of $I; C; \Gamma \vdash_{cfl} e : \tau$. Then $C_{fl(\Gamma)\cup fl(\tau)}^I; \Psi_{C,I}(\Gamma) \vdash_{cp} e : \Psi_{C,I}(\tau)$.*

Proof. The proof is by induction on the derivation $\mathcal{D}$. There are two key parts of the proof. The first is a lemma that shows that the bound constraint sets chosen by $\Psi_{C,I}$ for universal and existential types are closed under substitutions at instantiation sites, so that when we translate an occurrence of [Inst] or [Pack] from CFL to COPY we can prove the hypothesis $C \vdash \phi(C')$. The other key part occurs in translating an occurrence of [Unpack] from CFL to COPY. In this case, by induction on the typing derivation for e_2 we have $C_{fl(\Gamma)\cup fl(\tau)\cup fl(\tau')}^I; \Psi_{C,I}(\Gamma), x : \Psi_{C,I}(\tau) \vdash_{cp} e_2 : \Psi_{C,I}(\tau')$. By the last hypothesis of [Unpack] in CFL, we know that there are no constraints between the quantified labels $\vec{\alpha}$ and any other labels. Thus we can partition the constraints on the left-hand side of the above typing judgment into two disjoint sets: $C_{(fl(\Gamma)\cup fl(\tau)\cup fl(\tau'))\setminus\vec{\alpha}}^I$ and $C_{\vec{\alpha}}^I$. The former are the constraints needed to type check e_1 in COPY, and the latter are those bound in the existential type of e_1 by $\Psi_{C,I}$. These two constraint sets form the sets C and C', respectively, needed for the [Unpack] rule of COPY. A full, detailed proof can be found in our companion technical report [20].

By combining Theorems 1 and 2, we then have soundness for the flow relation $\leadsto$ computed by CFL. Notice that we have shown reduction but not equivalence. Rehof et al [14,15] also only show reduction, but conjecture equivalence of their systems. In our case, equivalence clearly does not hold, because of the extra non-escaping condition on [Unpack] in CFL. We leave it as an open question whether this condition can be relaxed to yield provably equivalent systems.

5   Related Work

Our work builds directly on the CFL reachability-based label flow system of Rehof et al [14]. Their cubic-time algorithm for polymorphic recursive label flow inference improves on the previously best-known $O(n^8)$ algorithm [13]. The idea of using CFL reachability in static analysis is due to Reps et al [27], who applied it to first-order data flow analysis problems. Our contribution is to extend the use of CFL reachability further to include existential types for modeling data structures more precisely.

Existential types can be encoded in System F [28] (p. 377), in which polymorphism is first class and type inference is undecidable [29]. There have been several proposals to support first-class polymorphic type inference using type annotations to avoid the undecidability problem. In ML^F [22], programmers annotate function arguments that have universal types. Laufer and Odersky [23] propose an extension to ML with first-class existential types, and Remy [24] similarly proposes an extension with first-class universal types. In both systems, the programmer explicitly lists which type variables are quantified. Packs and unpacks correspond to data structure construction and pattern matching, and hence are determined by the program text. Our system also requires the programmer to specify packs and unpacks as well as which variables are quantified, but in contrast to these three systems we support subtyping rather than unification, and thus we need polymorphically constrained types. Note that our solution is restricted to label flow, and only existential types are first-class, but we believe adding first-class universals with programmer-specified quantification would be straightforward. We conjecture that full first-class polymorphic type inference for label flow is decidable, and plan to explore such a system in future work.

Simonet [25] extends HM(X) [30], a generic constraint-based type inference framework, to include first-class existential and universal types with subtyping. Simonet requires the programmer to specify the polymorphically constrained type, including the subtyping constraints C, whereas we infer these (we assume we have the whole program). Another key difference is that we use CFL reachability for inference. Once again, however, our system is concerned only with label flow.

In ours and the above systems, both existential quantification as well as pack and unpack must be specified manually. An ideal inference algorithm requires no work from the programmer. For example, we envision a system in which all pairs and their uses are considered as candidate existential types, and the algorithm chooses to quantify only those labels that lead to a minimal flow in the graph. It is an open problem whether such an algorithm exists.

6   Conclusion

Existential quantification can be used to precisely characterize relationships within elements of a dynamic data structure, even when the precise identity of those elements is unknown. This paper aims to set a firm theoretical foundation on which to build efficient program analyses that benefit from existential quantification. Our main contribution is a context-sensitive inference algorithm for label flow analysis that supports existential quantification. Programmers specify where existentials are introduced and eliminated, and our inference algorithm automatically infers the bounds on their flow. Our algorithm is efficient, employing context free language (CFL) reachability in the style of Rehof et al [14], and we prove it sound by reducing it to a system based on polymorphically-constrained types in the style of Mossin [13]. We have adapted our algorithm to improve the precision of LOCKSMITH, a tool that aims to prove the absence of race conditions in C programs [4] by correlating locks with the locations they protect. We plan to explore other applications of existential label flow in future work.

Acknowledgments

We would like to thank Manuel Fähndrich, Mike Furr, Ben Liblit, Nik Swamy, and the anonymous referees for their helpful comments. This research was supported in part by NSF grants CCF-0346982, CCF-0346989, CCF-0430118, and CCF-0524036.

References

1. Das, M.: Unification-based Pointer Analysis with Directional Assignments. In: The 2000 Conference on Programming Language Design and Implementation, Vancouver B.C., Canada (2000) 35–46
2. Mitchell, J.C., Plotkin, G.D.: Abstract types have existential type. ACM Transactions on Programming Languages and Systems **10** (1988) 470–502
3. Xi, H., Pfenning, F.: Dependent Types in Practical Programming. In: The 26th Annual Symposium on Principles of Programming Languages, San Antonio, Texas (1999) 214–227
4. Pratikakis, P., Foster, J.S., Hicks, M.: LOCKSMITH: Context-Sensitive Correlation Analysis for Race Detection. In: The 2006 Conference on Programming Language Design and Implementation, Ottawa, Canada (2006) To appear.
5. Flanagan, C., Abadi, M.: Types for Safe Locking. In Swierstra, D., ed.: 8th European Symposium on Programming. Volume 1576 of Lecture Notes in Computer Science., Amsterdam, The Netherlands, Springer-Verlag (1999) 91–108
6. Minamide, Y., Morrisett, G., Harper, R.: Typed closure conversion. In: The 23rd Annual Symposium on Principles of Programming Languages, St. Petersburg Beach, Florida (1996) 271–283
7. Fähndrich, M., Rehof, J., Das, M.: Scalable Context-Sensitive Flow Analysis using Instantiation Constraints. In: The 2000 Conference on Programming Language Design and Implementation, Vancouver B.C., Canada (2000) 253–263
8. Das, M., Liblit, B., Fähndrich, M., Rehof, J.: Estimating the Impact of Scalable Pointer Analysis on Optimization. In Cousot, P., ed.: Static Analysis, Eighth International Symposium, Paris, France (2001) 260–278
9. Myers, A.C.: Practical Mostly-Static Information Flow Control. In: The 26th Annual Symposium on Principles of Programming Languages, San Antonio, Texas (1999) 228–241
10. Foster, J.S., Johnson, R., Kodumal, J., Aiken, A.: Flow-insensitive type qualifiers. (ACM Transactions on Programming Languages and Systems) To appear.

11. Kodumal, J., Aiken, A.: The Set Constraint/CFL Reachability Connection in Practice. In: The 2004 Conference on Programming Language Design and Implementation, Washington, DC (2004) 207–218
12. Johnson, R., Wagner, D.: Finding User/Kernel Bugs With Type Inference. In: The 13th Usenix Security Symposium, San Diego, CA (2004)
13. Mossin, C.: Flow Analysis of Typed Higher-Order Programs. PhD thesis, DIKU, Department of Computer Science, University of Copenhagen (1996)
14. Rehof, J., Fähndrich, M.: Type-Based Flow Analysis: From Polymorphic Subtyping to CFL-Reachability. In: The 28th Annual Symposium on Principles of Programming Languages, London, United Kingdom (2001) 54–66
15. Fähndrich, M., Rehof, J., Das, M.: From Polymorphic Subtyping to CFL Reachability: Context-Sensitive Flow Analysis Using Instantiation Constraints. Technical Report MS-TR-99-84, Microsoft Research (2000)
16. Flanagan, C., Felleisen, M.: Componential Set-Based Analysis. In: The 1997 Conference on Programming Language Design and Implementation, Las Vegas, Nevada (1997) 235–248
17. Fähndrich, M., Aiken, A.: Making Set-Constraint Based Program Analyses Scale. In: First Workshop on Set Constraints at CP'96. (1996) Available as CSD-TR-96-917, University of California at Berkeley.
18. Fähndrich, M.: BANE: A Library for Scalable Constraint-Based Program Analysis. PhD thesis, University of California, Berkeley (1999)
19. von Behren, R., Condit, J., Zhou, F., Necula, G.C., Brewer, E.: Capriccio: Scalable threads for internet services. In: ACM Symposium on Operating Systems Principles. (2003)
20. Pratikakis, P., Hicks, M., Foster, J.S.: Existential Label Flow Inference via CFL Reachability. Technical Report CS-TR-4700, University of Maryland, Computer Science Department (2005)
21. Henglein, F.: Type Inference with Polymorphic Recursion. ACM Transactions on Programming Languages and Systems **15** (1993) 253–289
22. Botlan, D.L., Rémy, D.: ML^F—Raising ML to the Power of System F. In: The Eighth International Conference on Functional Programming, Uppsala, Sweden (2003) 27–38
23. Läufer, K., Odersky, M.: Polymorphic type inference and abstract data types. ACM Transactions on Programming Languages and Systems **16** (1994) 1411–1430
24. Rémy, D.: Programming objects with MLART: An extension to ML with abstract and record types. In: The International Symposium on Theoretical Aspects of Computer Science, Sendai, Japan (1994) 321–346
25. Simonet, V.: An Extension of HM(X) with Bounded Existential and Universal Data Types. In: The Eighth International Conference on Functional Programming, Uppsala, Sweden (2003) 39–50
26. Mitchell, J.C.: Type inference with simple subtypes. Journal of Functional Programming **1** (1991) 245–285
27. Reps, T., Horwitz, S., Sagiv, M.: Precise Interprocedural Dataflow Analysis via Graph Reachability. In: The 22nd Annual Symposium on Principles of Programming Languages, San Francisco, California (1995) 49–61
28. Pierce, B.C.: Types and Programming Languages. The MIT Press (2002)
29. Wells, J.B.: Typability and type checking in System F are equivalent and undecidable. Ann. Pure Appl. Logic **98** (1999) 111–156
30. Odersky, M., Sulzmann, M., Wehr, M.: Type inference with constrained types. Theory and Practice of Object Systems **5** (1999) 35–55

Abstract Interpretation with Specialized Definitions

Germán Puebla[1], Elvira Albert[2], and Manuel Hermenegildo[1,3]

[1] School of Computer Science, Technical U. of Madrid
{german, herme}@fi.upm.es
[2] School of Computer Science, Complutense U. of Madrid
elvira@sip.ucm.es
[3] Depts. of Comp. Sci. and El. and Comp. Eng., U. of New Mexico
herme@unm.edu

Abstract. The relationship between abstract interpretation and partial evaluation has received considerable attention and (partial) integrations have been proposed starting from both the partial evaluation and abstract interpretation perspectives. In this work we present what we argue is the first generic algorithm for efficient and precise integration of abstract interpretation and partial evaluation from an abstract interpretation perspective. Taking as starting point state-of-the-art algorithms for context-sensitive, polyvariant abstract interpretation and (abstract) partial evaluation of logic programs, we present an algorithm which combines the best of both worlds. Key ingredients include the accurate success propagation inherent to abstract interpretation and the powerful program transformations achievable by partial deduction. In our algorithm, the calls which appear in the analysis graph are not analyzed w.r.t. the original definition of the procedure but w.r.t. *specialized definitions* of these procedures. Such specialized definitions are obtained by applying both unfolding and abstract executability. Also, our framework is parametric w.r.t. different control strategies and abstract domains. Different combinations of these parameters correspond to existing algorithms for program analysis and specialization. Our approach efficiently computes strictly more precise results than those achievable by each of the individual techniques. The algorithm is one of the key components of `CiaoPP`, the analysis and specialization system of the `Ciao` compiler.

1 Introduction and Motivation

The relationship between abstract interpretation [5] and partial evaluation [14] has received considerable attention. See, for instance, the relationship established in a general context in [4,13,6] and the work in the context of partial evaluation of logic programs (also known as *partial deduction* [21,11]) of [8,10,18,15,24,26,9,19,25,16]). In order to motivate our proposal, we use the running "challenge" example of Fig. 1. It is a simple `Ciao` [3] program which uses

K. Yi (Ed.): SAS 2006, LNCS 4134, pp. 107–126, 2006.

```
:- module(_,[main/2],[assertions]).
:- entry main(s(s(s(L))),R) : (ground(L),var(R)).
main₁(X,X2):-formula₁,₁(X,X1), formula₁,₂(X1,X2), ground₁,₃(X2).
formula₂(X,W):-ground₂,₁(X),var₂,₂(W),two₂,₃(T),minus₂,₄(X,T,X2),twice₂,₅(X2,W).
minus₄(X,0,X).
minus₅(s(X),s(Y),R) :- minus₅,₁(X,Y,R).
minus₆(0,s(_Y),_R).
twice₇(X,_Y) :- var₇,₁(X).
twice₈(X,Y) :- ground₈,₁(X), tw₈,₂(X,Y).
tw₉(0,0).
tw₁₀(s(X),s(s(NX))) :- tw₁₀,₁(X,NX).
```

Fig. 1. Running Example

Peano's arithmetic.[1] The `entry` declaration is used to inform that all calls to the exported predicate `main/2` will always be of the form $\leftarrow \mathtt{main}(\mathtt{s}(\mathtt{s}(\mathtt{s}(\mathtt{L}))), \mathtt{R})$ with L ground and R a variable. The predicate `main/2` performs two calls to predicate `formula/2`. A call `formula(X,W)` performs mode tests `ground(X)` and `var(W)` on its input arguments and returns $W = (X - 2) \times 2$. Predicate `two/1` returns `s(s(0))`, i.e., the natural number 2. A call `minus(A,B,C)` returns $C = A - B$. However, if the result becomes a negative number, C is left as a free variable. This indicates that the result is not valid. In turn, a call `twice(A,B)` returns $B = A \times 2$. Prior to computing the result, this predicate checks whether A is valid, i.e., not a variable, and simply returns a variable otherwise. For initial queries satisfying the `entry` declaration, all calls to the tests $\mathtt{ground}_{1,3}(\mathtt{X})$, $\mathtt{ground}_{2,1}(\mathtt{X})$, and $\mathtt{var}_{2,2}(\mathtt{W})$ will definitely succeed. Thus, they can be replaced by *true*, even if we do not know the concrete values of variable L at compile time. Also, the calls to $\mathtt{ground}_{8,1}(\mathtt{X})$ will succeed, while the calls to $\mathtt{var}_{7,1}(\mathtt{X})$ will fail, and can thus be replaced by *fail*. These kinds of optimizations require abstract information from analysis (e.g., groundness and freeness).

The example illustrates four difficulties and challenges. First, the benefits of (1) *exploiting abstract information in order to abstractly execute certain atoms. Furthermore, this may allow unfolding of other atoms.* However, the use of an abstract domain which captures groundness and freeness information will in general not be sufficient to determine that in the second execution of `formula/2` the tests $\mathtt{ground}_{2,1}(\mathtt{X})$ and $\mathtt{var}_{2,2}(\mathtt{W})$ will also succeed. The reason is that on success of $\mathtt{minus}_{2,4}(\mathtt{X,T,X2})$, X2 cannot be guaranteed to be ground since $\mathtt{minus}_6/3$ succeeds with a free variable in its third argument position. It can be observed, however, that for all calls to `minus/3` in executions described by the `entry` declaration the third clause for `minus/3` is useless. It will never contribute to a success of `minus/3` since this predicate is always called with a value greater than zero

---

[1] Rules are written with a unique subscript attached to the head atom (the rule number), and a double subscript (rule number, body position) attached to each body literal for later reference. We sometimes use this notation for denoting calls to atoms as well.

in its first argument. Unfolding can make this explicit by fully unfolding calls to minus/3 since they are sufficiently instantiated (and as a result the "dangerous" third clause is disregarded). This unfolding allows concluding that in our particular context all calls to minus/3 succeed with a ground third argument. This illustrates the importance of (2) *performing unfolding steps in order to prune away useless branches, and that this may result in improved success information.* By the time execution reaches $\mathtt{twice}_{2,5}(\mathtt{X2,W})$, we hopefully know that X2 is ground. In order to determine that upon success of $\mathtt{twice}_{2,5}(\mathtt{X2,W})$ (and thus on success of $\mathtt{formula}_{1,1}(\mathtt{X,W})$) W is ground, we need to perform a fixpoint computation. Since, for example, the success substitution for $\mathtt{formula}_{1,1}(\mathtt{X,X1})$ is indeed the call substitution for $\mathtt{formula}_{1,2}(\mathtt{X1,X2})$, the success of the second test $\mathtt{ground}_{2,1}(\mathtt{X})$ (i.e., the one reachable from $\mathtt{formula}_{1,2}(\mathtt{X1,X2})$) cannot be established unless we propagate success substitutions. This illustrates the importance of (3) *propagating (abstract) success information, and performing fixpoint computations when needed, and that this simultaneously may result in an improved unfolding.* Finally, whenever we call formula(X,W), the argument W is a variable, a property which cannot be captured if we restrict ourselves to downwards-closed domains (i.e., domains capturing properties such that once a property holds, it will keep on holding in every state accessible in forwards execution). This indicates (4) *the usefulness of having information on non* downwards-closed *properties.*

Example 1. CiaoPP, which implements our proposed abstract interpretation with specialized definitions, produces the following specialized code for the example of Fig. 1 (rules are renamed using the prefix sp):

```
sp_main₁(s(s(s(0))),0).
sp_main₂(s(s(s(s(B)))),A) :- sp_tw₂,₁(B,C),sp_formula₂,₂(C,A).
sp_tw₂(0,0).
sp_tw₃(s(A),s(s(B))) :- sp_tw₃,₁(A,B).
sp_formula₄(0,s(s(s(s(0))))).
sp_formula₅(s(A),s(s(s(s(s(s(B)))))))  :- sp_tw₅,₁(A,B).
```

Thus, our proposal can indeed eliminate all calls to mode tests ground/1 and var/1, and fully unfold predicates two/1 and minus/3 so that they no longer appear in the residual code. In addition, the algorithm also produces an accurate analysis for such a program. In particular, the success information for sp_main(X,X2) guarantees that X2 is ground on success. Note that this is equivalent to proving $\forall X \geq 3,\ main(X,X2) \rightarrow X2 \geq 0$. Furthermore, our system is able to get to that conclusion even if the entry only informs about X being any possible ground term and X2 a free variable. This is because, during the computation of the specialized definitions, the branches corresponding to values of X smaller than 3 are detected to be failing and the residual code is indeed equivalent to the one achieved with the more precise entry declaration. This illustrates how our proposal is useful for improving the results of the analysis even in cases where there are no initial constants in the query which can be propagated through the program.

The above results cannot be achieved unless all four points mentioned before are addressed by a program analysis/specialization system. For example, if we use traditional partial deduction (PD) with the corresponding *Generalize* and *Unfold* rules followed by abstract interpretation and *abstract specialization* as described in [24,25] we only obtain a comparable program after four iterations of the: "PD + abstract interpretation + abstract specialization" cycle. This shows the importance of achieving an algorithm which is able to *interleave* PD with abstract interpretation, extended with abstract specialization, in order to communicate the accuracy gains achieved from one to the other as soon as possible. In any case, iterating over "PD + analysis" is not a good idea from the efficiency point of view.

2   Preliminaries

This section introduces some preliminary concepts on abstract interpretation [5] and partial deduction [21]. We assume some basic knowledge on the terminology of logic programming (see for example [20] for details). Very briefly, an *atom* A is a syntactic construction of the form $p(t_1, \ldots, t_n)$, where p/n, with $n \geq 0$, is a predicate symbol and $t_1, \ldots, t_n$ are terms. A *clause* is of the form $H \leftarrow B$ where its head H is an atom and its body B is a conjunction of atoms. A *definite program* is a finite set of clauses. A *goal* (or query) is a conjunction of atoms.

2.1   The Notions of Unfolding and Resultant

Let G be a goal of the form $\leftarrow A_1, \ldots, A_R, \ldots, A_k$, $k \geq 1$. The concept of *computation rule*, denoted by $\mathcal{R}$, is used to select an atom within a goal for its evaluation. If $\mathcal{R}(G) = A_R$ we say that A_R is the *selected* atom in G. The operational semantics of definite programs is based on derivations [20]. Let $C = H \leftarrow B_1, \ldots, B_m$ be a renamed apart clause in P such that $\exists \theta = mgu(A_R, H)$. Then, the goal $\leftarrow \theta(A_1, \ldots, A_{R-1}, B_1, \ldots, B_m, A_{R+1}, \ldots, A_k)$ is *derived* from G and C via $\mathcal{R}$. As customary, given a program P and a goal G, an *SLD derivation* for $P \cup \{G\}$ consists of a possibly infinite sequence $G = G_0, G_1, G_2, \ldots$ of goals, a sequence $C_1, C_2, \ldots$ of properly renamed apart clauses of P, and a sequence $\theta_1, \theta_2, \ldots$ of mgus such that each G_{i+1} is derived from G_i and C_{i+1} using θ_{i+1}. A derivation step can be non-deterministic when A_R unifies with several clauses in P, giving rise to several possible SLD derivations for a given goal. Such SLD derivations can be organized in *SLD trees*. A finite derivation $G = G_0, G_1, G_2, \ldots, G_n$ is called *successful* if G_n is empty. In that case $\theta = \theta_1 \theta_2 \ldots \theta_n$ is called the computed answer for goal G. Such a derivation is called *failed* if G_n is not empty and it is not possible to perform a derivation step from it. We will also allow *incomplete* derivations in which, though possible, no further resolution step is performed.

Given an atom A, an *unfolding rule* [21,11] computes a set of finite SLD derivations $D_1, \ldots, D_n$ (i.e., a possibly incomplete SLD tree) of the form $D_i = A, \ldots, G_i$ with computed answer substitution θ_i for $i = 1, \ldots, n$ whose associated *resultants* (or residual rules) are $\theta_i(A) \leftarrow G_i$. The set of resultants for the computed SLD tree is called a *partial deduction* (PD) for the initial goal.

2.2   Abstract Interpretation

Abstract interpretation [5] provides a general formal framework for computing safe approximations of program behaviour. Programs are interpreted using
abstract values instead of *concrete values*. An abstract value is a finite representation of a, possibly infinite, set of concrete values in the concrete domain
D. The set of all possible abstract values constitutes the *abstract domain*, denoted D_α, which is usually a complete lattice or cpo which is ascending chain
finite. The subset relation $\subseteq$ induces a partial order on sets of concrete values.
The $\subseteq$ relation induces the $\sqsubseteq$ relation on abstract values. Values in the abstract
domain $\langle D_\alpha, \sqsubseteq \rangle$ and sets of values in the concrete domain $\langle 2^D, \subseteq \rangle$ are related
via a pair of monotonic mappings $\langle \alpha, \gamma \rangle$: the *abstraction* function $\alpha : 2^D \rightarrow D_\alpha$
which assigns to each (possibly infinite) set of concrete values an abstract value,
and the *concretization* function $\gamma : D_\alpha \rightarrow 2^D$ which assigns to each abstract
value the (possibly infinite) set of concrete values (e.g., program variable values)
it represents, such that $\forall x \in 2^D : \gamma(\alpha(x)) \supseteq x$ and $\forall y \in D_\alpha : \alpha(\gamma(y)) = y$.
Concrete values denote typically (but not exclusively) which data structures
program variables are bound to in actual executions, i.e., the *substitutions*. Correspondingly, abstract values will be often referred to as *abstract substitutions*.
The following operations on abstract substitutions are domain-dependent and
will be used in our algorithms:

- Arestrict(λ, E) performs the abstract restriction (or projection) of a substi-
  tution λ to the set of variables in the expression E, denoted $vars(E)$;
- Aextend(λ, E) extends the substitution λ to the variables in the set $vars(E)$;
- Aunif(t_1, t_2, λ) obtains the description which results from adding the abstrac-
  tion of the unification $t_1 = t_2$ to the substitution λ;
- Aconj(λ_1, λ_2) performs the abstract conjunction of two substitutions;
- Alub(λ_1, λ_2) performs the abstract disjunction ($\sqcup$) of two substitutions.

An *abstract atom* of the form $A : CP$ is a concrete atom A which comes equipped
with an *abstract substitution* CP which is defined over $vars(A)$ and provides additional information on the context in which the atom will be executed at run-time.
We write $A : CP \sqsubseteq A' : CP'$ to denote that $\{\theta(A)|\theta \in \gamma(CP)\} \subseteq \{\theta'(A')|\theta' \in
\gamma(CP')\}$. In our algorithms, we also use Atranslate$(A : CP, H \leftarrow B)$ which adapts
and projects the information in an abstract atom $A : CP$ to the variables in the
clause $C = H \leftarrow B$. This operation can be defined in terms of the operations above
as: Atranslate$(A : CP, H \leftarrow B) = $ Arestrict$($Aunif$(A, H, $Aextend$(CP, C)), C)$. As
customary, the most general abstract substitution is represented as $\top$, and the least
general (empty) abstract substitution as $\bot$.

The following standard operations are used in order to handle keyed-tables:
Create_Table(T) initializes a table T. Insert$(T, Key, Info)$ adds *Info* associated to
Key to T and deletes previous information associated to *Key*, if any. IsIn(T, Key)
returns true iff *Key* is currently stored in the table T. Finally, Look_up(T, Key)
returns the information associated to *Key* in T. For simplicity, we sometimes
consider tables as sets and we use the notation $(Key \rightsquigarrow Info) \in T$ to denote that
there is an entry in the table T with the corresponding *Key* and associated *Info*.

3   Unfolding with Abstract Substitutions

We now present our notion of *abstract unfolding* —based on an extension of the SLD semantics which exploits abstract information— which is used later to generate specialized definitions. This will pave the way to overcoming difficulties (1) and (2) posed in Section 1.

3.1   SLD with Abstract Substitutions

Our extended semantics handles *abstract goals* of the form $G : CP$, i.e., a concrete goal G equipped with an *abstract substitution* CP. The first definition captures derivation steps.

Definition 1 (Derivation Step). *Let $G : CP$ be an abstract goal where $G =\leftarrow A_1,\ldots, A_R,\ldots, A_k$ and CP is an abstract substitution defined over $vars(G)$. Let $\mathcal{R}$ be a computation rule and let $\mathcal{R}(G) =A_R$. Let $C = H \leftarrow B_1,\ldots, B_m$ be a renamed apart clause in P. Then the abstract goal $G' : CP'$ is derived from $G : CP$ and C via $\mathcal{R}$ if there exist $\theta = mgu(A_R, H)$ and $CP_u \neq \bot$, where:*

$$CP_u = \mathsf{Aunif}(A_R, \theta(H), \mathsf{Aextend}(CP, C\theta))$$
$$G' = \theta(A_1,\ldots, A_{R-1}, B_1,\ldots, B_m, A_{R+1},\ldots, A_k)$$
$$CP' = \mathsf{Arestrict}(CP_u, vars(G'))$$

An important difference between the above definition and the standard derivation step is that the use of abstract (call) substitutions allows imposing further conditions for performing derivation steps, in particular, CP_u cannot be $\bot$. This is because if $CP \neq \bot$ and $CP_u = \bot$ then the head of the clause C is incompatible with CP and the unification $A_R = H$ will definitely fail at run-time. Thus, abstract information allows us to remove useless clauses from the residual program. This produces more efficient resultants and increases the accuracy of analysis for the residual code.

Example 2. Consider the goal: $\mathtt{formula}(\mathtt{s}^4(\mathtt{X}), \mathtt{X2}) : \{\mathtt{X/G}, \mathtt{X2/V}\}$ which appears during the analysis of our running example (c.f. Fig. 2). We abbreviate as $\mathtt{s}^n(\mathtt{X})$ the successive application of n symbols $\mathtt{s}$ to variable $\mathtt{X}$. We have used sharing-freeness as abstract domain in the analysis though, for simplicity, we will represent the results using traditional "modes": the notation $\mathtt{X/G}$ (resp. $\mathtt{X/V}$) indicates that variable $\mathtt{X}$ is ground (resp. free). After applying a derivation step using the only rule for $\mathtt{formula}$, we derive:

$\mathtt{ground}(\mathtt{s}^4(\mathtt{X})), \mathtt{var}(\mathtt{X2}), \mathtt{two}(\mathtt{T}), \mathtt{minus}(\mathtt{T}, \mathtt{s}^4(\mathtt{X}), \mathtt{X2'}), \mathtt{twice}(\mathtt{X2'}, \mathtt{X2}) :$
    $\{\mathtt{X/G}, \mathtt{X2/V}, \mathtt{T/V}, \mathtt{X2'/V}\}$

where the abstract description has been extended with updated information about the freeness of the newly introduced variables, i.e., both $\mathtt{T}$ and $\mathtt{X2'}$ are $\mathtt{V}$.

The second extension we present makes use of the availability of abstract substitutions to perform *abstract executability* [24] during resolution. This allows replacing some atoms with simpler ones, and, in particular, with the predefined atoms *true* and *false*, provided certain conditions hold. We assume the existence of a predefined *abstract executability table* which contains entries of the form $T : CP \rightsquigarrow T'$ which specify the behaviour of external procedures: builtins, libraries, and other user modules. For instance, for predicate **ground** the abstract execution table contains the information $\texttt{ground(X)} : \{\texttt{X/G}\} \rightsquigarrow \texttt{true}$. For **var**, it contains $\texttt{var(X)} : \{\texttt{X/V}\} \rightsquigarrow \texttt{true}$.[2]

Definition 2 (Abstract Execution). *Let $G : CP$ be an abstract goal where $G = \leftarrow^c A_1, \ldots, A_R, \ldots, A_k$. Let $\mathcal{R}$ be a computation rule and let $\mathcal{R}(G) = A_R$. Let $(T : CP_T \rightsquigarrow T')$ be a renamed apart entry in the abstract executability table. Then, the goal $G' : CP'$ is abstractly executed from $G : CP$ and $(T : CP_T \rightsquigarrow T')$ via $\mathcal{R}$ if $A_R = \theta(T)$ and $CP_A \sqsubseteq CP_T$, where*

$$G' = A_1, \ldots, A_{R-1}, \theta(T'), A_{R+1}, \ldots, A_k$$
$$CP' = \mathsf{Arestrict}(CP, G')$$
$$CP_A = \mathsf{Atranslate}(A_R : CP, T \leftarrow true)$$

Example 3. From the derived goal in Ex. 2, we can apply twice the above definition to abstractly execute the calls to **ground** and **var** and obtain:

$$\texttt{two(T), minus(T, s}^4\texttt{(X), X2'), twice(X2', X2)} : \{\texttt{X/G, X2/V, T/V, X2'/V}\}$$

since both calls succeed by using the abstract executability table described above.

3.2   Abstract Unfolding

In our framework, resultants for abstract atoms will be obtained using abstract unfolding in a similar way as it is done in the concrete setting using unfolding (see Sect. 2.1).

Definition 3 (*AUnfold*). *Let $A : CP$ be an abstract atom and P a program. We define $AUnfold(P, A : CP)$ as the set of resultants associated to a finite (possibly incomplete) SLD tree computed by applying definitions 1 and 2 to $A : CP$.*

The so-called *local control* of PD ensures the termination of the above process. For this purpose, the unfolding rule must incorporate some mechanism to stop the construction of SLD derivations (we refer to [17] for details).

Example 4. Consider an unfolding rule *AUnfold* based on homeomorphic embedding [17] to ensure termination and the initial goal in Ex. 2. The derivation continuing from Ex. 3 performs several additional derivation steps and abstract executions and branches (we do not include them due to space limitations and also because it is well understood). The following resultants are obtained from the resulting tree:

```
formula(s(s(s(s(0),s(s(s(s(0)))))).
formula(s(s(s(s(s(A))))),s(s(s(s(s(s(B)))))))) :- tw(A,B).
```

which will later be filtered and renamed as they appear in rules 5 and 6 of Ex. 1.

---

[2] In **CiaoPP** *assertions* express such information in a domain-independent manner.

It is important to note that SLD resolution with abstract substitutions is not restricted to the left-to-right computation rule. For the case of derivation steps (Def. 1), it is well-known that non-leftmost steps can produce incorrect results if the goal contains *impure* atoms to the left of A_R. More details can be found, e.g., in [1] and its references. For the case of abstract execution (Def. 2), the execution of non-leftmost atoms can be incorrect if the abstract domain used captures properties which are not downwards closed. A simple solution in this case is to allow only leftmost abstract execution steps for non-downwards closed domains.

4   Specialized Definitions

Typically, PD is presented as an iterative process in which partial evaluations are computed for the new generated atoms until they *cover* all calls which can appear in the execution of the residual program. This is formally known as the *closedness* condition of PD [21]. In order to ensure termination of this global process, the so-called *global* control defines a *Generalize* operator (see, e.g., [17]) which guarantees that the number of SLD trees computed is kept finite, i.e., it ensures the finiteness of the set of atoms for which partial deduction is produced. However, the residual program is not generated until such iterative process terminates.

We now define an Abstract Partial Deduction (APD) algorithm whose execution can later be *interleaved* in a seamless way with a state-of-the-art abstract interpreter. For this, it is essential that the APD process be able to generate residual code for each call pattern as soon as we finish processing it. This will make it possible for the analysis algorithm to have access to the improved definition. As a consequence, the accuracy of the analyzer may be increased and difficulty (2) described in Sect. 1 overcome.

4.1   Abstract Partial Deduction

Algorithm 1 presents an APD algorithm. The main difference with standard algorithms for APD is that the resultants computed by *AUnfold* (L23) are added to the program during execution of the algorithm (L27) rather than in a later code generation phase. In order to avoid conflicts among the new clauses and the original ones, clauses for specialized definitions are renamed with a fresh predicate name (L26) prior to adding them to the program (L27). The algorithm uses two global data structures. The *specialization table* contains entries of the form $A : CP \rightsquigarrow A'$. The atom A' provides the link with the clauses of the specialized definition for $A : CP$. The *generalization table* stores the results of the *AGeneralize* function and contains entries $A : CP \rightsquigarrow A' : CP'$ where $A' : CP'$ is a generalization of $A : CP$, in the sense that $A = A'\theta$ and $(A : CP) \sqsubseteq (A' : CP')$.

Let us briefly discuss some *AGeneralize* functions which can be used within our algorithms when using it as a specializer. In both of them, the decision on whether to lose information in a call *AGeneralize*$(\mathcal{ST}, A : CP)$ is based on the

---

Algorithm 1. Abstract Partial Deduction with Specialized Definitions

---

```
 1: procedure PARTIAL_EVALUATION_WITH_SPEC_DEFS(P, {A_1 : CP_1, ..., A_n : CP_n})
 2:     Create_Table(GT); Create_Table(ST)
 3:     for j = 1..n do
 4:         PROCESS_CALL_PATTERN(A_j : CP_j)
 5: procedure PROCESS_CALL_PATTERN(A : CP)
 6:     if not IsIn(GT, A : CP) then
 7:         (A_1, A'_1) ← SPECIALIZED_DEFINITION(P, A : CP)
 8:         A_1 : CP_1 ← Look_up(GT, A : CP)
 9:         for all renamed apart clause C_k = H_k ← B_k ∈ P s.t. H_k unifies with A'_1
            do
10:             CP_k ← Atranslate(A'_1 : CP_1, C_k)
11:             PROCESS_CLAUSE(CP_k, B_k)
12: procedure PROCESS_CLAUSE(CP, B)
13:     if B = [L|R] then
14:         CP_L ← Arestrict(CP, L)
15:         PROCESS_CALL_PATTERN(L : CP_L)
16:         PROCESS_CLAUSE(CP, R)
17: function SPECIALIZED_DEFINITION(P, A : CP)
18:     A' : CP' ← AGeneralize(ST, A : CP)
19:     Insert(GT, A : CP, A' : CP')
20:     if IsIn(ST, A' : CP') then
21:         A'' ←Look_up(ST, A' : CP')
22:     else
23:         Def ← AUnfold(P, A' : CP')
24:         A'' ← new_filter(A')
25:         Insert(ST, A' : CP', A'')
26:         Def' ← {(H' ← B) | (H ← B) ∈ Def ∧ H' = ren(H, {A'/A''})}
27:         P ← P ∪ Def'
28:     return (A', A'')
```

---

concrete part of the atom, A. This allows easily defining *AGeneralize* operators in terms of existing *Generalize* operators. Let *Generalize* be a (concrete) generalization function. Then we define $AGeneralize_\alpha(ST, A : CP) = (A', CP')$ where $A' = Generalize(ST, A)$ and $CP' = \mathsf{Atranslate}(A : CP, A' \leftarrow true)$. Function $AGeneralize_\alpha$ only assigns the same specialized definition for different abstract atoms when we know that after adapting the analysis info of both $A_1 : CP_1$ and $A_2 : CP_2$ to the new atom A' the same entry substitution CP' will be obtained in either case. Similarly, we define $AGeneralize_\gamma(ST, A : CP) = (A', CP')$ where $A' = Generalize(ST, A)$ and $CP' = \top$. The function $AGeneralize_\gamma$ assigns generalizations taking into account the concrete part of the abstract atom only, which is the same for all OR-nodes which correspond to a literal k, i. These functions are in fact two extremes. In $AGeneralize_\alpha$ we try to keep as much abstract information as possible, whereas in $AGeneralize_\gamma$ we lose all abstract information. The latter is useful when we do not have an unfolding system which can exploit abstract information or when we do not want the specialized program to have different implemented specialized definitions for atoms with the same concrete part but different abstract substitution.

Procedure PARTIAL_EVALUATION_WITH_SPEC_DEFS (L1-4) initiates the computation. It first initializes the tables and then calls PROCESS_CALL_PATTERN for each abstract atom $A_j : CP_j$ in the initial set to be partially evaluated. The task of PROCESS_CALL_PATTERN is, if the atom has not been processed yet (L6), to compute a specialized definition for it (L7) and then process all clauses in its specialized definition by means of calls to PROCESS_CLAUSE (L9-11). For simplicity of the presentation, we assume that clause bodies returned by SPECIALIZED_DEFINITION are represented as lists rather than conjunctions. Procedure PROCESS_CLAUSE traverses clause bodies, processing their corresponding atoms by means of calls to PROCESS_CALL_PATTERN, in a depth-first, left-to-right fashion. In contrast, the order in which pending call patterns (atoms) are handled is usually not fixed in APD algorithms. They are often all put together in a set. The purpose of the two procedures PROCESS_CLAUSE and PROCESS_CALL_PATTERN is to traverse the clauses in the left-to-right order and add the corresponding call patterns. In principle, this does not have additional advantages w.r.t. existing APD algorithms because success propagation has not been integrated yet. However, the reason for our presentation is to be as close as possible to our analysis algorithm with success propagation, which enforces a depth-first, left-to-right traversal of program clauses. Correctness of Algorithm 1 can be established using the framework for APD in [16].

4.2   Integration with an Abstract Interpreter

For the integration we propose, the most relevant part of the algorithm comprises L17-28, as it is the code fragment which is *directly* executed from our abstract interpreter. The remaining procedures (L1-L16) will be overridden by more accurate ones later on. The procedure of interest is SPECIALIZED_DEFINITION. It performs (L18) a generalization of the call $A : CP$ using the abstract counterpart of the *Generalize* operator, denoted by A*Generalize*, and which is in charge of ensuring termination at the global level. The result of the generalization, $A' : CP'$, is inserted (L19) in the generalization table $\mathcal{GT}$. It is required that $(A : CP) \sqsubseteq (A' : CP')$. If $A' : CP'$ has been previously treated (L20), then its specialized definition A'' is looked up in $\mathcal{ST}$ (L21) and returned. Otherwise, a specialized definition Def is computed by using the A*Unfold* operator (L23).

As already mentioned, the specialized definition Def for the abstract atom $A : CP$ is used to extend the original program P. First, the atom A' is renamed by using new_filter which returns an atom with a fresh predicate name, A'', and optionally filters constants out (L24). Then, function ren is applied to rename the clause heads using atom A' (L26). The function $\mathsf{ren}(A, \{B/B'\})$ returns $\theta(B')$ where $\theta = mgu(A, B)$. Finally, the program P is extended with the new, *renamed* specialized definition, Def'.

Example 5. Three calls to SPECIALIZED_DEFINITION appear (within an oval box) during the analysis of our running example in Fig. 2 from the following abstract atoms, first $\mathtt{main}(\mathtt{s}^3(\mathtt{X}), \mathtt{X2}) : \{\mathtt{X/G}, \mathtt{X2/V}\}$, then $\mathtt{tw}(\mathtt{B}, \mathtt{C}) : \{\mathtt{B/G}, \mathtt{C/V}\}$ and finally $\mathtt{formula}(\mathtt{C}, \mathtt{A}) : \{\mathtt{C/G}, \mathtt{A/V}\}$. The output of such executions is used later (with the proper renaming) to produce the resultants in Ex. 1. For instance, the second clause obtained from the first call to SPECIALIZED_DEFINITION is

$$\texttt{sp\_main}_2(\texttt{s(s(s(s(B)))),A}) \texttt{ :- } \texttt{tw}_{2,1}(\texttt{B,C}),\texttt{formula}_{2,2}(\texttt{C,A}).$$

where only the head is renamed. The renaming of the body literals is done in a later code-generation phase.

It is important to note that Algorithm 1 does not perform success propagation yet (difficulty 3). In L16, it becomes apparent that all atom(s) in R will be analyzed with the same call pattern CP as L, which is to their left in the clause. This may clearly lead to substantial precision loss. In the above example, Alg. 1 is not able to obtain the three abstract atoms above due to the absence of success propagation. For instance, the abstract pattern $\texttt{formula}(\texttt{C}, \texttt{A}) : \{\texttt{C/G}, \texttt{A/V}\}$ which is necessary in order to obtain the last two resultants of Ex. 1 cannot be obtained with this algorithm. In particular, we cannot infer the groundness of C which, in turn, prevents us from abstractly executing the next call to ground and, thus, from obtaining this optimal specialization. In addition, this lack of success propagation makes it difficult or even impossible to work with non downwards closed domains (difficulty 4), since CP may contain information which holds before execution of the leftmost atom L but which can no longer hold after that. In fact, in our example CP contains the info C/V, which becomes false after execution of $\texttt{tw}(\texttt{B}, \texttt{C})$, since now C is ground. This problem is solved in the algorithm we present in the next section, where analysis information flows from left to right, adding more precise information and eliminating information which is no longer safe or even definitely wrong.

5   Abstract Interpretation with Specialized Definitions

The main idea in *abstract interpretation with specialized definitions* is that a generic abstract interpreter is equipped with a generator of specialized definitions. Such generator provides, upon request, the specialized definitions to be analyzed by the interpreter. Certain data structures, which take the form of tables in the algorithms (i.e., the specialization, generalization, answer and dependency arc tables) will be used to communicate between the two processes and achieve a smooth interleaving. The input to the whole process is a program together with a set of calling patterns for it. The output is a specialized program together with the analysis results inferred for it. The scheme can be parameterized with different (abstract) unfolding rules, generalization operators, abstract domains and widenings. The different instances give rise to interesting analysis and specialization methods, some of which are well known and others are novel (see Section 7).

Algorithm 2 presents our final algorithm for abstract interpretation with specialized definitions. This algorithm extends both the APD Algorithm 1 and the abstract interpretation algorithms in [23,12]. The main improvement w.r.t. Algorithm 1 is the addition of success propagation, which requires computing a

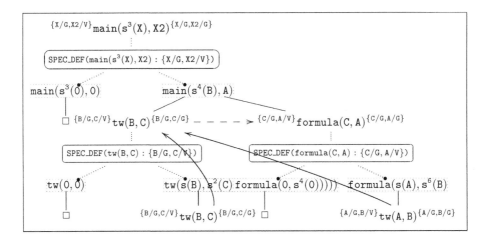

Fig. 2. Analysis Graph computed by ABS_INT_WITH_SPEC_DEF

global fixpoint. It is an important objective for us to be able to compute an accurate fixpoint in an efficient way. The main improvements w.r.t the algorithms in [23,12] are the following. (1) It interleaves program analysis and specialization in a way that is efficient, accurate, and practical. (2) Algorithm 2 deals directly with non-normalized programs. This point, which does not seem very relevant in a pure analysis system, becomes crucial when combined with a specialization system in order to profit from constants propagated by unfolding. (3) It incorporates a hardwired efficient graph traversal strategy which eliminates the need for maintaining priority queues explicitly [12]. (4) The algorithm includes a widening operation for calls, *Widen_Call*, which limits the amount of multi-variance in order to keep the number of call patterns analyzed finite. This is required in order to be able to use abstract domains with an infinite number of elements, such as regular types. (5) It also includes a number of simplifications to facilitate understanding, such as the use of the keyed-table ADT, which we assume encapsulates proper renaming apart of variables and the application of renaming transformations when needed.

5.1   The Program Analysis Graph: Answer and Dependency Tables

In order to compute and propagate success substitutions, Algorithm 2 computes a *program analysis graph* in a similar fashion as state of the art analyzers such as the CiaoPP analyzer [23,12]. For instance, the analysis graph computed by Algorithm 2 for our running example is depicted in Fig. 2. The graph has two sorts of nodes. Those which correspond to atoms are called "OR-nodes". An OR-node of the form $^{CP}A^{AP}$ is interpreted as the answer (success) pattern for the abstract atom $A : CP$ is AP. The OR-node $^{\{X/G,X2/V\}}\mathtt{main}(\mathtt{s}^3(X),X2)^{\{X/G,X2/G\}}$ in the example indicates that when the atom $\mathtt{main}(\mathtt{s}^3(X),X2)$ is called with description $\{X/G,X2/V\}$ the answer (or success) substitution computed is $\{X/G,X2/G\}$.

Those nodes which correspond to rules are called "AND-nodes". In Fig. 2, they appear within a dashed box and contain the head of the corresponding clause. Each AND-node has as children as many OR-nodes as literals there are in its body. If a child OR-node is already in the tree, it is not expanded any further and the currently available answer is used. We show within an oval box the calls to SPECIALIZED_DEFINITION which appear during the execution of the running example (see the details in Sect. 4). The heads of the clauses in the specialized definition are linked to the box with a dotted arc. For instance, the analysis graph in Figure 2 contains three occurrences of the abstract atom $\texttt{tw}(\texttt{B}, \texttt{C}) : \{\texttt{B/G}, \texttt{C/V}\}$ (modulo renaming), but only one of them has been expanded. This is depicted by arrows from the two non-expanded occurrences of $\texttt{tw}(\texttt{B}, \texttt{C}) : \{\texttt{B/G}, \texttt{C/V}\}$ to the expanded one. More information on the efficient construction of the analysis graph can be found in [23,12,2].

The program analysis graph is implicitly represented in the algorithm by means of two data structures, the *answer table* ($\mathcal{AT}$) and the *dependency table* ($\mathcal{DT}$). The answer table contains entries of the form $A : CP \rightsquigarrow AP$ which are interpreted as the answer (success) pattern for $A : CP$ is AP. For instance, there exists an entry of the form $\texttt{main}(\texttt{s}^3(\texttt{X}), \texttt{X2}) : \{\texttt{X/G}, \texttt{X2/V}\} \rightsquigarrow \{\texttt{X/G}, \texttt{X2/G}\}$ associated to the OR-node discussed above.

Dependencies indicate direct relations among OR-nodes. An OR-node $A_F : CP_F$ *depends on* another OR-node $A_T : CP_T$ iff in the body of some clause for $A_F : CP_F$ there appears the OR-node $A_T : CP_T$. The intuition is that in computing the answer for $A_F : CP_F$ we have used the answer pattern for $A_T : CP_T$. In our algorithm we store *backwards* dependencies, i.e., for each OR-node $A_T : CP_T$ we keep track of the set of OR-nodes which depend on it. I. e., the keys in the dependency table are OR-nodes and the information associated to each node is the set of other nodes which depend on it, together with some additional information required to iterate when an answer is modified (updated). Each element of a *dependency set* for an atom $B : CP_2$ is of the form $\langle H : CP \Rightarrow [H_k : CP_1] \, k, i \rangle$. It should be interpreted as follows: the OR-node $H : CP$ through the literal at position k, i depends on the OR-node $B : CP_2$. Also, the remaining information $[H_k : CP_1]$ encodes the fact that the head of this clause is H_k and the substitution (in terms of all variables of clause k) just before the call to $B : CP_2$ is CP_1. Such information avoids having to reprocess atoms in the clause k to the left of position i.

Example 6. For instance, the dependency set for $\texttt{formula}(\texttt{C}, \texttt{A}) : \{\texttt{A/V}, \texttt{C/G}\}$ is $\{\langle \texttt{main}(\texttt{s}^3(\texttt{X}), \texttt{X2}) : \{\texttt{X/G}, \texttt{X2/V}\} \Rightarrow [\, \texttt{main}(\texttt{s}^4(\texttt{B}), \texttt{A}) : \{\texttt{B/G}, \texttt{A/V}, \texttt{C/G}\} \,] \, 2, 2 \rangle\}$ It indicates that the OR-node $\texttt{formula}(\texttt{C}, \texttt{A}) : \{\texttt{A/V}, \texttt{C/G}\}$ is only used in the OR-node $\texttt{main}(\texttt{s}^3(\texttt{X}), \texttt{X2}) : \{\texttt{X/G}, \texttt{X2/V}\}$ via literal 2,2 (see Example 1). Thus, if the answer pattern for $\texttt{formula}(\texttt{C}, \texttt{A}) : \{\texttt{A/V}, \texttt{C/G}\}$ is ever updated, then we must reprocess the OR-node $\texttt{main}(\texttt{s}^3(\texttt{X}), \texttt{X2}) : \{\texttt{X/G}, \texttt{X2/V}\}$ from position 2,2.

5.2   The Algorithm

Algorithm 2 presents our proposed algorithm. Procedure ABS_INT_WITH_SPEC_ DEFS initializes the four tables used by the algorithm and calls PROCESS_CALL_

Algorithm 2. Abstract Interpretation with Specialized Definitions

---

1: **procedure** ABS_INT_WITH_SPEC_DEFS$(P, \{A_1 : CP_1, \ldots, A_n : CP_n\})$
2:     Create_Table$(\mathcal{AT})$; Create_Table$(\mathcal{DT})$; Create_Table$(\mathcal{GT})$; Create_Table$(\mathcal{ST})$;
3:     **for** $j = 1..n$ **do**
4:         PROCESS_CALL_PATTERN$(A_j : CP_j, \langle A_j : CP_j \Rightarrow [A_j : CP_j], j, entry\rangle)$

5: **function** PROCESS_CALL_PATTERN$(A : CP, Parent)$
6:     $CP_1 \leftarrow Widen\_Call(\mathcal{AT}, A : CP)$
7:     **if not** IsIn$(\mathcal{AT}, A : CP_1)$ **then**
8:         Insert$(\mathcal{AT}, A : CP_1, \bot)$; Insert$(\mathcal{DT}, A : CP_1, \emptyset)$
9:         $(A', A_1') \leftarrow$ SPECIALIZED_DEFINITION$(P, A : CP_1)$
10:         $A'' \leftarrow$ ren$(A, \{A'/A_1'\})$
11:         **for all** renamed clause $C_k = H_k \leftarrow B_k \in P$ s.t. H_k unifies with A'' **do**
12:             $CP_k \leftarrow$ Atranslate$(A'' : CP_1, C_k)$
13:             PROCESS_CLAUSE$(A : CP_1 \Rightarrow [H_k : CP_k] B_k, k, 1)$
14:     $Deps \leftarrow$ Look_up$(\mathcal{DT}, A : CP_1) \bigcup \{Parent\}$; Insert$(\mathcal{DT}, A : CP_1, Deps)$
15:     **return** Look_up$(\mathcal{AT}, A : CP_1)$

16: **procedure** PROCESS_CLAUSE$(H : CP \Rightarrow [H_k : CP_1] B, k, i)$
17:     **if** $CP_1 \neq \bot$ **then**
18:         **if** $B = [L|R]$ **then**
19:             $CP_2 \leftarrow$ Arestrict(CP_1, L)
20:             $AP_0 \leftarrow$ PROCESS_CALL_PATTERN$(L : CP_2, \langle H : CP \Rightarrow [H_k : CP_1], k, i\rangle)$
21:             $CP_3 \leftarrow$ Aconj$(CP_1,$ Aextend$(AP_0, CP_1))$
22:             PROCESS_CLAUSE$(H : CP \Rightarrow [H_k : CP_3]R, k, i+1)$
23:         **else**
24:             $AP_1 \leftarrow$ Atranslate$(H_k : CP_3, H \leftarrow true)$; $AP_2 \leftarrow$ Look_up$(\mathcal{AT}, H : CP)$
25:             $AP_3 \leftarrow$ Alub(AP_1, AP_2)
26:             **if** $AP_2 \neq AP_3$ **then**
27:                 Insert$(\mathcal{AT}, H : CP, AP_3)$
28:                 $Deps \leftarrow$ Look_up$(\mathcal{DT}, H : CP)$; PROCESS_UPDATE$(Deps)$

29: **procedure** PROCESS_UPDATE$(Updates)$
30:     **if** $Updates = \{A_1, \ldots, A_n\}$ with $n \geq 0$ **then**
31:         $A_1 = \langle H : CP \Rightarrow [H_k : CP_1], k, i\rangle$
32:         **if** $i \neq entry$ **then**
33:             $B \leftarrow$ get_body(P, k, i)
34:             REMOVE_PREVIOUS_DEPS$(H : CP \Rightarrow [H_k : CP_1] B, k, i)$
35:             PROCESS_CLAUSE$(H : CP \Rightarrow [H_k : CP_1] B, k, i)$
36:         PROCESS_UPDATE$(Updates - \{A_1\})$

PATTERN for each abstract atom in the initial set. PROCESS_CALL_PATTERN applies, first of all (L6), the *Widen_Call* function to $A : CP$ taking into account the set of entries already in $\mathcal{AT}$. This returns a substitution CP_1 s.t. $CP \sqsubseteq CP_1$. The most precise *Widen_Call* function possible is the identity function, but it can only be used with abstract domains with a finite number of abstract values for each set of variables. This is the case with *sharing–freeness* and thus we will use the identity function in our example. If the call pattern $A : CP_1$ has not been processed before, it places (L8) $\bot$ as initial answer in $\mathcal{AT}$ for $A : CP$ and sets to empty the set of OR-nodes in the graph which depend on $A : CP_1$. It then computes (L9) a specialized definition for $A : CP_1$. We do not show in Algorithm 2 the definition of SPECIAL-IZED_DEFINITION, since it is identical to that in Algorithm 1. Then (L11-13) calls to PROCESS_CLAUSE are launched for the clauses in the specialized definition w.r.t.

which $A : CP_1$ is to be analyzed. Then, the *Parent* OR-node is added (L14) to the dependency set for $A : CP_1$.

The function PROCESS_CLAUSE performs the success propagation and constitutes the core of the analysis. First, the current answer (AP_0) for the call to the literal at position k, i of the form $B : CP_2$ is (L21) conjoined (Aconj), after being extended (Aextend) to all variables in the clause, with the description CP_1 from the program point immediately before B in order to obtain the description CP_3 for the program point after B. If B is not the last literal, CP_3 is taken as the (improved) calling pattern to process the next literal in the clause in the recursive call (L22). This corresponds to left-to-right success propagation and is marked in Fig. 2 with a dashed horizontal arrow. If we are actually processing the last literal, CP_3 is (L24) adapted (Atranslate) to the initial call pattern $H : CP$ which started PROCESS_CLAUSE, obtaining AP_1. This value is (L25) disjoined (Alub) with the current answer, AP_2, for $H : CP$ as given by Look_up. If the answer changes, then its dependencies, which are readily available in $\mathcal{DT}$, need to be recomputed (L28) using PROCESS_UPDATE. This procedure restarts the processing of all body postfixes which depend on the calling pattern for which the answer has been updated by launching new calls to PROCESS_CLAUSE. There is no need of recomputing answers in our example. The procedure REMOVE_PREVIOUS_DEPS eliminates (L34) entries in $\mathcal{DT}$ for the clause postfix which is about to be re-computed. We do not present its definition here due to lack of space. Note that the new calls (L35) to PROCESS_CLAUSE may in turn launch calls to PROCESS_UPDATE. On termination of the algorithm a global fixpoint is guaranteed to have been reached. Note that our algorithm also stores in the dependency sets calls from the initial entry points (marked with the value *entry* in L4). These do not need to be reprocessed (L32) but are useful for determining the specialized version to use for the initial queries after code generation.

The next theorem presents the correctness of the results of Algorithm 2 in terms of analysis. We use $\theta|_{\{X_1,\dots,X_n\}}$ to denote the projection of substitution θ onto the set of variables $\{X_1, \dots, X_n\}$. We denote by $success(A : CP, P)$ the set of computed answers for initial queries described by the abstract atom $A : CP$ in a program P.

Theorem 1 (Correctness of Success). *Let P be a program and let $S = \{A_1 : CP_1, \dots, A_n : CP_n\}$ be a set of abstract atoms. For all $A_i : CP_i \in S$, after termination of* ABS_INT_WITH_SPEC_DEFS(P, S)*, there exists $(A_i : CP'_i \rightsquigarrow AP_i) \in \mathcal{AT}$ s.t. $CP_i \sqsubseteq CP'_i \wedge success(A_i : CP_i, P) \subseteq \gamma(AP_i)$.*

Intuitively, correctness holds since Algorithm 2 computes an abstract and–or graph and, thus, we inherit a generic correctness result for success substitutions of [12]. However, now we analyze the call patterns in S w.r.t. specialized definitions rather than their original definition in P. Since the transformation rules in Definitions 1 and 2 are semantics preserving, then analysis of each specialized definition is guaranteed to produce a safe approximation of its success set, which is also a safe approximation of the success of the original definition.

5.3   The Framework as a Specializer

If we compose a terminating analysis strategy (abstract domain plus widening operator) with a terminating PD strategy (local control plus global control), then Algorithm 2 also terminates for such strategies. The set of specialized definitions computed during the execution of the algorithm is a specialization of the program w.r.t. the initial entries.

Theorem 2 (Correctness of Specialization). *Consider the Algorithm 2 parameterized with terminating operators AUnfold, Widen_Call and AGeneralize. Then, for any program P and set of abstract atoms S,* ABS_INT_WITH_SPEC-_DEFS(P, S) *terminates and the set of renamed specialized definitions is a correct specialization of P w.r.t. S.*

Intuitively, if we have a terminating *AUnfold* rule and the abstract domain is ascending chain finite, non-termination can only occur if the set of call patterns handled by the algorithm is infinite. Since the *Widen_Call* function guarantees that a given concrete atom A can only be analyzed w.r.t. a finite number of abstract substitutions CP, non-termination can only occur if the set of atoms has an infinite number of elements with different concrete parts. If the *AGeneralize* function guarantees that an infinite number of different concrete atoms cannot occur, then termination is guaranteed.

6   Experiments

In this section we show some experimental results aimed at studying two crucial points for the practicality of our proposal: the cost associated to computing specialized definitions and the optimization obtained by the process. We have implemented the abstract interpreter with specialized definitions as an extension of the generic abstract interpretation system of `CiaoPP`. The whole system is implemented in Ciao 1.13#5666 [3]. Execution times are given in milliseconds and measure *runtime*. They are computed as the arithmetic mean of five runs. All of our experiments have been performed on a Pentium M at 1.86GHz and 1GB RAM running Ubuntu Breezy Linux. The Linux kernel used is 2.6.12.

A relatively wide range of programs has been used as benchmarks. The program `running_ex` is that in Fig. 1. The rest are the same programs used in [12] as benchmarks for static analysis.[3] Thus, they do not necessarily contain static data which can be exploited by partial evaluation. Interestingly, some (first group of rows in Table 1) contain static data, while others (second and third groups of rows in Table 1) contain little or no static data. In `zebra` all the data is static and it can be potentially fully evaluated at compile-time.

As the analyzers within `CiaoPP` it derives from, our abstract interpreter with specialized definitions is parametric w.r.t. the abstract domain. In these experiments we have used mostly the *sharing+freeness* domain [22] (for the first and

---

[3] More details on such benchmarks can be found in [12].

Table 1. Some implementations of AI with Specialized Definitions. Cost and efficiency

Bench	Abs	Traditional			SD_γ		$SD_{\alpha-}$		SD_α		Exec T
		Ana	PD	Ana PD	SD_γ	SU	$SD_{\alpha-}$	SU	SD_α	SU	SU
running_ex	shfr	5	11	5	13	1.20	14	1.14	14	1.10	1.33
grammar	shfr	24	4	21	24	1.03	27	0.92	34	0.72	1.59
query	shfr	358	160	15	173	1.01	187	0.93	453	0.38	2.69
zebra	shfr	261	1523	1	1522	1.00	1604	0.95	6476	0.24	1148.08
aiakl	shfr	13	25	25	44	1.15	53	0.95	50	1.01	1.00
ann	shfr	432	159	452	558	1.10	625	0.98	604	1.01	1.00
boyer	shfr	154	90	161	232	1.08	271	0.93	241	1.04	1.00
progeom	shfr	9	26	14	37	1.10	39	1.03	41	0.98	0.99
warplan	shfr	318	63	311	410	0.91	607	0.62	553	0.68	1.01
witt	shfr	103	183	118	255	1.18	288	1.04	276	1.09	1.00
browse	eterms	33	18	36	50	1.07	71	0.75	65	0.83	1.00
deriv	eterms	149	5	151	151	1.03	160	0.97	161	0.97	1.00
fib	eterms	13	2	13	15	1.03	17	0.89	17	0.87	1.00
hanoiapp	eterms	61	5	65	73	0.96	101	0.70	97	0.73	1.00
mmatrix	eterms	68	4	69	71	1.04	74	0.99	72	1.03	1.00
occur	eterms	24	7	24	30	1.02	49	0.62	44	0.69	1.00
serialize	eterms	68	13	73	85	1.03	108	0.81	97	0.89	1.03
tak	eterms	5	3	5	7	1.21	9	0.95	9	0.95	1.00
Overall						1.03		0.90		0.41	

second group of rows in Table 1). We have selected this domain because it is on one hand well known and on the other orthogonal w.r.t. partial evaluation, in the sense that it does not contain any concrete information (as, for example, a depth-k or types domain would). We have also conducted experiments with the *eterms* domain [27] which infers regular types (third group of rows in the table).

For each benchmark, the columns under **Traditional** present the analysis (**Ana**) and partial deduction (**PD**) times using the standard algorithms. Column **Ana PD** provides the time taken by analysis of the specialized program (rather than the original one). Each of the following six columns presents the time taken by the abstract interpreter with specialized definitions, as well as the ratio (speedup/slowdown, **SU**) of this time w.r.t. **PD** + **Ana PD**. Columns marked SD_α are for the case where $AGeneralize_\alpha$ (Section 5) is used, whereas SD_γ columns use $AGeneralize_\gamma$, with $SD_{\alpha-}$ representing the case where we only check for useless clauses once a derivation is fully computed, rather than at each derivation step. Finally, the last column represents the *speedup* in the execution time of the program after applying $SD_{\alpha-}$.

The last row summarizes the analysis times for the different benchmarks using a weighted mean, which places more importance on those benchmarks with relatively larger analysis times. We believe that this weighted mean is more informative than the arithmetic mean, as, for example, doubling the speed in which a large and complex program is analyzed (checked) is more relevant than achieving this for small, simple programs.

Overall, we first observe that the time taken by the abstract interpreter with specialized definitions compares well with that taken by a traditional PD phase followed by a traditional analysis phase (**Ana PD**). In the case of SD_γ there is actually some speedup (1.03), presumably because fewer traversals of the program are required, whereas in the case of SD_α we observe a reasonable slowdown (0.41), with $SD_\alpha-$ representing an interesting tradeoff (0.90). The execution times of the resulting programs show significant speedups for the first group (in which concrete information is available for specialization) and (as expected) only very minor variations for the other programs. This shows that our system performs well as a specializer. At the same time, the analysis information obtained (which is of course one of the fundamental objectives of the process) is always at least as accurate as that obtained when performing analysis after a standalone specialization pass (`Ana PD`), and is more accurate for the programs in the first group, which shows that it also performs well as an analyzer.

7   Discussion and Related Work

The versatility of our approach can be seen by recasting well-known specialization and analysis frameworks as instances where the parameters unfolding rule, widen call rule, abstraction operator, and analysis domain, take different values.

From an analysis point of view, our algorithm can behave as the *polyvariant abstract interpretation* algorithm described in [12,23] by defining an *AGeneralize* operator which returns the base form of an expression (i.e., it loses all constants) and an *AUnfold* operator which performs a single derivation step (i.e., it returns the original definition). Also, the specialization power of the *multivariant abstract specialization* framework described in [25,24] can be obtained by using the same *AGeneralize* described in the above point plus an *AUnfold* operator which always performs a derive step followed by zero or more abstract execution steps. However abstract executability is performed now online, during analysis, instead of offline.

From a partial evaluation perspective, our method can be used to perform *classical partial deduction* in the style of [21,11] by using an abstract domain with the single abstract value $\top$ and the identity function as *Widen_Call* rule. This corresponds to the $\mathcal{PD}$ domain of [16] in which an atom with variables represents all its instances. Let us note that, in spite of the fact that the algorithm follows a left-to-right computation flow at the global control level, the process of generating specialized definitions (as discussed in Section 3) can perform *non-leftmost* unfolding steps at the local control level and achieve the same optimizations as in PD. Several approaches for *abstract partial deduction* have been proposed which extend PD with SLDNF-trees by using abstract substitutions [15,9,19,16]. In essence, such approaches are very similar to APD with call propagation shown in Algorithm 1. Though all those proposals identify the need of propagating success substitutions, they either fail to do so or propose means for propagating success information which are not fully integrated within the APD algorithm and, in our opinion, do not fit in as nicely as the use of and–or trees. Also, these proposals are either strongly coupled to a particular (downward closed) abstract domain, i.e., regular types, as in [9,19] or do not provide the exact description of operations on the abstract domain which are needed by the framework, other than general correctness criteria [15,16]. However, the latter allow Conjunctive PD [7], which is not available in our framework yet. It remains as future work to investigate the extension of our framework in order to analyze conjunctions of atoms and in order to achieve optimizations like tupling and deforestation.

Finally, [26] was a very preliminary (and only informally published) step towards our current framework which identified the need for including unfolding in abstract interpretation frameworks in order to increase their power. Then, four different alternatives for doing so (Section 5.3) were discussed. The framework we propose in this work does not correspond to any of those alternatives and is in fact more powerful than any of them.

Acknowledgments

The authors would like to thank John Gallagher and Michael Leuschel for useful discussions. This work was funded in part by the Information Society Technologies program of the European Commission, Future and Emerging Technologies under the IST-15905 *MOBIUS* project, by the MEC project TIN-2005-09207 *MERIT*, and the CAM project S-0505/TIC/0407 *PROMESAS*. Manuel Hermenegildo is also supported by the Prince of Asturias Chair in Information Science and Technology at UNM.

References

1. E. Albert, G. Puebla, and J. Gallagher. Non-Leftmost Unfolding in Partial Evaluation of Logic Programs with Impure Predicates. In *Proc. of LOPSTR'05*. Springer LNCS 3901, April 2006.
2. M. Bruynooghe. A Practical Framework for the Abstract Interpretation of Logic Programs. *Journal of Logic Programming*, 10:91–124, 1991.
3. F. Bueno, D. Cabeza, M. Carro, M. Hermenegildo, P. López-García, and G. Puebla. The Ciao Prolog System. Reference Manual (v1.8). The Ciao System Documentation Series–TR CLIP4/2002.1, School of Computer Science, Technical University of Madrid (UPM), May 2002. System and on-line version of the manual available at http://clip.dia.fi.upm.es/Software/Ciao/.
4. C. Consel and S.C. Koo. Parameterized partial deduction. *ACM Transactions on Programming Languages and Systems*, 15(3):463–493, July 1993.
5. P. Cousot and R. Cousot. Abstract Interpretation: a Unified Lattice Model for Static Analysis of Programs by Construction or Approximation of Fixpoints. In *Proc. of POPL'77*, pages 238–252, 1977.
6. P. Cousot and R. Cousot. Systematic Design of Program Transformation Frameworks by Abstract Interpretation. In *POPL'02*, pages 178–190. ACM, 2002.
7. D. De Schreye, R. Glück, J. Jørgensen, M. Leuschel, B. Martens, and M.H. Sørensen. Conjunctive Partial Deduction: Foundations, Control, Algorihtms, and Experiments. *Journal of Logic Programming*, 41(2&3):231–277, 1999.
8. J. Gallagher, M. Codish, and E. Shapiro. Specialisation of Prolog and FCP Programs Using Abstract Interpretation. *NGC*, 6(2–3):159–186, 1988.
9. J. P. Gallagher and J. C. Peralta. Regular tree languages as an abstract domain in program specialisation. *HOSC*, 14(2,3):143–172, 2001.

10. J.P. Gallagher. Static Analysis for Logic Program Specialization. In *Workshop on Static Analysis WSA'92*, pages 285–294, 1992.
11. J.P. Gallagher. Tutorial on specialisation of logic programs. In *Proc. of PEPM'93*, pages 88–98. ACM Press, 1993.
12. M. Hermenegildo, G. Puebla, K. Marriott, and P. Stuckey. Incremental Analysis of Constraint Logic Programs. *ACM TOPLAS*, 22(2):187–223, March 2000.
13. N. D. Jones. Combining Abstract Interpretation and Partial Evaluation. In *Static Analysis Symposium*, number 1140 in LNCS, pages 396–405. Springer-Verlag, 1997.
14. N.D. Jones, C.K. Gomard, and P. Sestoft. *Partial Evaluation and Automatic Program Generation*. Prentice Hall, New York, 1993.
15. M. Leuschel. Program Specialisation and Abstract Interpretation Reconciled. In *Joint International Conference and Symposium on Logic Programming*, June 1998.
16. M. Leuschel. A framework for the integration of partial evaluation and abstract interpretation of logic programs. *ACM TOPLAS*, 26(3):413 – 463, May 2004.
17. M. Leuschel and M. Bruynooghe. Logic program specialisation through partial deduction: Control issues. *Theory and Practice of Logic Programming*, 2(4 & 5):461–515, July & September 2002.
18. M. Leuschel and D. De Schreye. Logic program specialisation: How to be more specific. In *Proc. of PLILP'96*, LNCS 1140, pages 137–151, 1996.
19. M. Leuschel and S. Gruner. Abstract conjunctive partial deduction using regular types and its application to model checking. In *Proc. of LOPSTR*, number 2372 in LNCS. Springer, 2001.
20. J.W. Lloyd. *Foundations of Logic Programming*. Springer, second, extended edition, 1987.
21. J.W. Lloyd and J.C. Shepherdson. Partial Evaluation in Logic Programming. *Journal of Logic Programming*, 11(3–4):217–242, 1991.
22. K. Muthukumar and M. Hermenegildo. Combined Determination of Sharing and Freeness of Program Variables Through Abstract Interpretation. In *1991 International Conference on Logic Programming*, pages 49–63. MIT Press, June 1991.
23. G. Puebla and M. Hermenegildo. Optimized Algorithms for the Incremental Analysis of Logic Programs. In *SAS'96*, pages 270–284. Springer LNCS 1145, 1996.
24. G. Puebla and M. Hermenegildo. Abstract Multiple Specialization and its Application to Program Parallelization. *JLP*, 41(2&3):279–316, November 1999.
25. G. Puebla and M. Hermenegildo. Abstract Specialization and its Applications. In *Proc. of PEPM'03*, pages 29–43. ACM Press, 2003. Invited talk.
26. G. Puebla, M. Hermenegildo, and J. Gallagher. An Integration of Partial Evaluation in a Generic Abstract Interpretation Framework. In *PEPM'99*, number NS-99-1 in BRISC Series, pages 75–85. Univ. of Aarhus, Denmark, 1999.
27. C. Vaucheret and F. Bueno. More precise yet efficient type inference for logic programs. In *Proc. of SAS'02*, pages 102–116. Springer LNCS 2477, 2002.

Underapproximating Predicate Transformers

David A. Schmidt*

Kansas State University, Manhattan, Kansas, USA
schmidt@cis.ksu.edu

Abstract. We study the underapproximation of the predicate transformers used to give semantics to the modalities in dynamic and temporal logic. Because predicate transformers operate on state sets, we define appropriate powerdomains for sound approximation. We study four such domains — two are based on "set inclusion" approximation, and two are based on "quantification" approximation — and we apply the domains to synthesize the most precise, underapproximating $\widetilde{pre}$ and pre transformers, in the latter case, introducing a *focus* operation. We also show why the expected abstractions of $post$ and $\widetilde{post}$ are unsound, and we use the powerdomains to guide us to correct, sound underapproximations.

1 Introduction

When we prove a property, ϕ, of a program, P, we typically employ an abstraction on P's and ϕ's concrete domain, C, so that we *over*approximate P to $P^\sharp$ and *under*approximate ϕ to $\phi^\flat$, where $P^\sharp$ and $\phi^\flat$ are stated within an abstract domain, A. If we show $P^\sharp$ has property $\phi^\flat$, then we conclude P has ϕ as well.

This approach quickly becomes complicated: Although C might be a set, A is usually partially ordered. For example, when C is *Int* and A is *Sign*, we have orderings like $isPositive \sqsubseteq_{Sign} isNotNegative$, because $\gamma(isPositive) \subseteq \gamma(isNotNegative)$, where $\gamma : Sign \to \mathcal{P}(Int)$ concretizes signs. Even when A is a set, e.g., a set of state partitions, computing least- and greatest fixed points of state-transition functions and recursively defined assertions requires a powerset of the state partitions, partially ordered by subset inclusion [25].

Next, a logical property, ϕ, is interpreted as a set, $\llbracket \phi \rrbracket \in \mathcal{P}(C)$. When the property is abstracted to $\phi^\flat$, which is itself a set, $\llbracket \phi \rrbracket^A \in \mathcal{P}(A)$, A's ordering affects $\mathcal{P}(A)$'s, and denotational semantics indicates there are a variety of powerdomains that one might use [18, 24] to establish soundness, i.e., $\llbracket \phi \rrbracket \supseteq \gamma^* \llbracket \phi \rrbracket^A$.

The situation becomes more complex when program P's concrete transition function is nondeterministic, $f : C \to \mathcal{P}(C)$, meaning its abstraction should be $f^\sharp : A \to \mathcal{P}(A)$. What powerdomain should be used for $f^\sharp$'s codomain? Is it the same one as that used to define $\llbracket \phi \rrbracket^A$?

Yet another complication is that properties, ϕ, can be expressed by the predicate transformers, $\widetilde{pre}$, pre, $post$, and $\widetilde{post}$. The four predicate transformers behave differently with respect to a given $f^\sharp : A \to \mathcal{P}(A)$. Fortunately, for an

---

* Supported by NSF ITR-0086154 and ITR-0326577.

K. Yi (Ed.): SAS 2006, LNCS 4134, pp. 127–143, 2006.

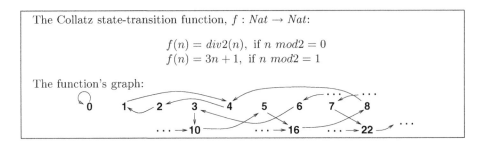

The Collatz state-transition function, $f : Nat \to Nat$:

$$f(n) = div2(n), \text{ if } n \bmod 2 = 0$$
$$f(n) = 3n + 1, \text{ if } n \bmod 2 = 1$$

The function's graph:

Fig. 1. Collatz program and its state-transition graph

overapproximating $f^{\sharp}$, $\widetilde{pre}_{f^{\sharp}}[\![\phi]\!]^{A}$ underapproximates $\widetilde{pre}_{f}[\![\phi]\!]$, meaning we can soundly calculate abstract preconditions like those in ACTL [3, 7].

But $pre_{f^{\sharp}}$ is *not* well behaved for $f^{\sharp}$, and the situations for *post* and $\widetilde{post}$ are even less clear.

This paper's primary contribution is its systematic study of the powerdomains and Galois connections necessary for sound *under*approximation of all four of the classic predicate transformers. The transformers operate on state sets, and we will require four powerdomains for sound approximation: two are based on "set inclusion" approximation, and two are based on "quantification" approximation. The first two are applied to abstract a logic; the latter two are applied to abstract state-transition functions. Our study of *pre*'s abstraction exposes its fundamental incompleteness, which is repaired by means of a *focus*sed abstraction. We also see why the expected abstractions of $post_{f}$ and $\widetilde{post}_{f}$ are *unsound*, and we use the powerdomains to define correct, sound underapproximations (which must be expressed in terms of $pre_{f^{-1}}$ and $\widetilde{pre}_{f^{-1}}$, respectively).

The guiding principle throughout our investigation is that property sets, $[\![\phi]\!]^{A}$, are *downwards-closed subsets* of A. We tailor the abstractions of the four predicate transformers so that their answers are always downwards-closed sets, and in two cases, this requires that the abstract transition function, $f^{\sharp} : A \to \mathcal{P}(A)$, used by the predicate transformer must calculate answer sets that are *upwards closed*. We select the appropriate Galois connection with the appropriate powerdomain to abstract f to the appropriate $f^{\sharp}$.

2   Background

Say that a program's semantics is defined by (the least fixpoint of) a state-transition function, $f : C \to C$. Figure 1 shows a coding of the Collatz function and its state-transition semantics, drawn as a graph. When $f \subseteq C \times C$ is a non-functional state-transition relation, we model it by $f : C \to \mathcal{P}(C)$, and we use this format hereon.

For calculating postconditions, we lift f to $f^{*} : \mathcal{P}(C) \to \mathcal{P}(C)$ in the usual way: $f^{*}(S) = \cup_{c \in S} f(c)$. For example, for $odd = \{2n + 1 \mid n \geq 0\}$, the strongest f-postcondition from Figure 1 is $f^{*}(odd) = \{4, 10, 16, 22, \cdots\}$.

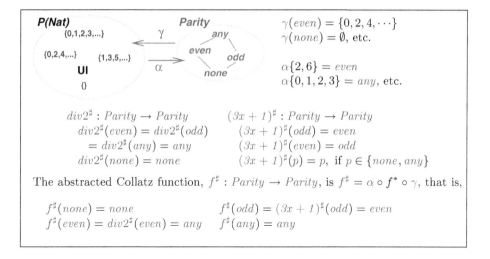

Fig. 2. Parity abstraction of natural numbers and the Collatz function

If a program's state space is "too large," we might abstract it. The abstraction might be a state partitioning [2, 25], but more generally it is a complete lattice, $(A, \sqsubseteq)$, such that there is a Galois connection of the form $(\mathcal{P}(C), \subseteq)\langle\alpha, \gamma\rangle(A, \sqsubseteq)$:[1] Figure 2 abstracts the concrete domain *Nat* in Figure 1 to the complete lattice of parities, *Parity*, which is applied to abstracting the Collatz function.

Each set, $S \subseteq C$, is abstracted by $\alpha(S) \in A$, and each $a \in A$ models the set $\gamma(a) \subseteq C$. The Galois connection *overapproximates* C, because for all $S \subseteq C$, $S \subseteq \gamma(\alpha(S))$.

$f^* : \mathcal{P}(C) \rightarrow \mathcal{P}(C)$ is *soundly abstracted* by a monotone function, $f^\sharp : A \rightarrow A$, iff $\alpha \circ f^* \sqsubseteq_{\mathcal{P}(C)\rightarrow A} f^\sharp \circ \alpha$ iff $f^* \circ \gamma \sqsubseteq_{A\rightarrow\mathcal{P}(C)} \gamma \circ f^\sharp$ [7]. We work only with monotone functions. The most precise, sound, abstraction of f^* is $\alpha \circ f^* \circ \gamma$ — see Figure 2 for an example.

Complete lattice A possesses an "internal logic," where $\gamma(a)$ interprets the "assertion" $a \in A$, and for $c \in C$, write $c \models a$ iff $c \in \gamma(a)$. This makes $f^\sharp : A \rightarrow A$ a sound postcondition transformer for f: if $c \models a$, then $f(c) \models f^\sharp(a)$. Since γ preserves meets in A,[2] $\sqcap_A$ is "logical conjunction": $c \models a_1 \sqcap a_2$ iff $c \models a_1$ and $c \models a_2$. This logic forms the foundation for static analyses based on A.

There is no guarantee that γ preserves joins; see lattice *Sign* in Figure 3 and consider $0 \models neg \sqcup pos$, which holds even though $0 \not\models neg$ and $0 \not\models pos$. We can improve the situation by building the *disjunctive completion* [7] of A, which is

---

[1] A *Galois connection* between two complete lattices, P and Q, written $P\langle\alpha,\gamma\rangle Q$, is a pair of monotonic functions, $\alpha : P \rightarrow Q$ and $\gamma : Q \rightarrow P$, such that $id_{P\rightarrow P} \sqsubseteq \gamma \circ \alpha$ and $\alpha \circ \gamma \sqsubseteq id_{Q\rightarrow Q}$ [7, 13]. Note that γ's inverse, α, is uniquely defined as $\alpha(p) = \sqcap\{q \mid p \sqsubseteq_P \gamma(q)\}$ and α's inverse is $\gamma(q) = \sqcup\{p \mid \alpha(p) \sqsubseteq_Q q\}$.

[2] That is, for every $T \subseteq A$, $\cap_{a\in T}\gamma(a) = \gamma(\sqcap T)$, which is necessary and sufficient for γ to be the upper adjoint of a Galois connection.

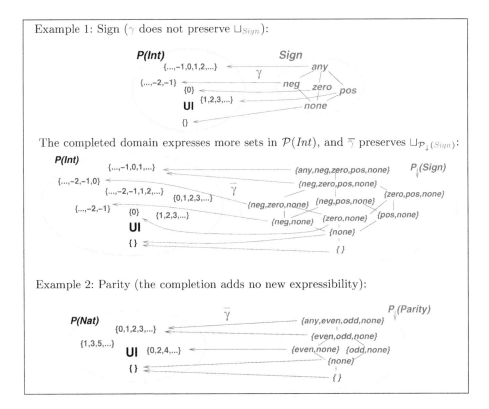

Fig. 3. Two examples of disjunctive completion

$(\mathcal{P}_{\downarrow}(A), \subseteq)$, that is, all downclosed subsets of A, ordered by subset inclusion.[3]
Here is the resulting Galois connection:

$$(\mathcal{P}(C), \subseteq)\langle\overline{\alpha_o}, \overline{\gamma}\rangle(\mathcal{P}_{\downarrow}(A), \subseteq), \text{ where } \begin{array}{l} \overline{\gamma}(T) = \gamma^*(T) = \cup_{a \in A}\gamma(a) \\ \overline{\alpha_o}(S) = \cap\{T \mid S \subseteq \overline{\gamma}(T)\} = \downarrow\{\alpha\{c\} \mid c \in S\} \end{array}$$

See Figure 3. The downclosed sets ensure monotonicity of key functions, like
injection, $\{\!|\cdot|\!\} : A \to \mathcal{P}_{\downarrow}(A)$ (defined $\{\!|a|\!\} = \downarrow\{a\}$ so that $a \sqsubseteq a'$ implies $\{\!|a|\!\} \subseteq \{\!|a'|\!\}$), without changing $\overline{\gamma}$'s image: $\overline{\gamma}(\downarrow S) = \overline{\gamma}(S)$. Because $\overline{\gamma} : \mathcal{P}_{\downarrow}(A) \to \mathcal{P}(C)$
preserves *both* joins and meets, we have this useful internal logic for $\mathcal{P}_{\downarrow}(A)$:

$$\phi ::= a \mid \phi_1 \sqcap \phi_2 \mid \phi_1 \sqcup \phi_2$$

$$c \models a \text{ iff } c \in \gamma(a)$$
$$c \models \phi_1 \sqcap \phi_2 \text{ iff } c \models \phi_1 \text{ and } c \models \phi_2$$
$$c \models \phi_1 \sqcup \phi_2 \text{ iff } c \models \phi_1 \text{ or } c \models \phi_2$$

The Galois connection is overapproximating, and we can define a sound abstraction of $f : C \to \mathcal{P}(C)$ in the form, $f^{\sharp} : A \to \mathcal{P}_{\downarrow}(A)$; the most precise such abstraction is $f^{\sharp}_{best} = \overline{\alpha_o} \circ f^* \circ \gamma$. (E.g., in Figure 3, Example 1,

---

[3] $\mathcal{P}_{\downarrow}(A) = \{\downarrow T \mid T \subseteq A\}$, where $\downarrow T = \{a \in A \mid \text{there exists } a' \in T, a \sqsubseteq_A a'\}$.

$$\mathcal{L} \ni \phi ::= a \mid [f]\phi \mid \langle f \rangle \phi \mid \phi_1 \wedge \phi_2 \mid \phi_1 \vee \phi_2$$

$$[\![\cdot]\!] : \mathcal{L} \to \mathcal{P}(C)$$

$$[\![a]\!] = \gamma(a)$$
$$[\![[f]\phi]\!] = \widetilde{pre}_f[\![\phi]\!] \qquad [\![\phi_1 \wedge \phi_2]\!] = [\![\phi_1]\!] \cap [\![\phi_2]\!]$$
$$[\![\langle f \rangle \phi]\!] = pre_f[\![\phi]\!] \qquad [\![\phi_1 \vee \phi_2]\!] = [\![\phi_1]\!] \cup [\![\phi_2]\!]$$

Fig. 4. Precondition logic

$succ^{\sharp}_{best}(neg) = \{neg, zero, none\}$ (successor), and in Example 2, $div2^{\sharp}_{best}(even)$ $= \{even, odd, none\}$.)

3   Preconditions

For state-transition function, $f : C \to \mathcal{P}(C)$, S's postcondition is $f^*(S)$, but when f is nondeterministic, there are two useful preconditions:

$$\widetilde{pre}_f(S) = \{c \mid \text{for all } c' \in C, \; c' \in f(c) \text{ implies } c' \in S\} = \{c \mid f(c) \subseteq S\}$$
$$pre_f(S) = \{c \mid \text{there exists } c' \in f(c), \; c' \in S\} = \{c \mid f(c) \cap S \neq \emptyset\}.$$

The first computes those states whose f-image lies entirely in S (where the f-image might be empty); the second defines those states whose f-image has at least one state in S. We study the two preconditions in their standard logical representations; Figure 4 gives the syntax and interpretation of the logic. We write $c \models \phi$ iff $c \in [\![\phi]\!]$, e.g., both $12 \models [div2]even$ and $12 \models \langle div2 \rangle even$.

It is important to note that the logic in Figure 4 is *not* an internal logic of $\mathcal{P}_{\downarrow}(A)$ — we have no guarantee that $\overline{\gamma}$ preserves either $\widetilde{pre}_{f^{\sharp}}$ or $pre_{f^{\sharp}}$.[4] To check $c \models \phi$ within $\mathcal{P}_{\downarrow}(A)$, we must abstract each $[\![\phi]\!] \in \mathcal{P}(C)$ to a *sound* $[\![\phi]\!]^A \in \mathcal{P}_{\downarrow}(A)$: that is, for all $\phi \in \mathcal{L}$, $a \in A$, we require

$$a \in [\![\phi]\!]^A \text{ implies } c \in [\![\phi]\!], \text{ for all } c \in \gamma(a)$$

which is equivalent to requiring that $\overline{\gamma}[\![\phi]\!]^A \subseteq [\![\phi]\!]$. We can insert the latter requirement into the following adjunction situation:

$$
\begin{array}{ccc}
\mathcal{P(C)}^{op} & \xleftarrow{\ \overline{\gamma}\ } & \mathcal{P}_{\downarrow}(A)^{op} \\
\overline{\gamma}[\![\varphi]\!]^A & & [\![\varphi]\!]^A \\
\text{In} & & \text{In} \\
[\![\varphi]\!] & \xrightarrow[\ \alpha_u\ ]{} & \overline{\alpha}_u[\![\varphi]\!]
\end{array}
$$

Since $\overline{\gamma} : \mathcal{P}_{\downarrow}(A) \to \mathcal{P}(C)$ preserves joins as well as meets, we realize the adjunction as the Galois connection, $\mathcal{P}(C)^{op}\langle \overline{\alpha_u}, \overline{\gamma} \rangle \mathcal{P}_{\downarrow}(A)^{op}$:[5] where $\overline{\gamma}(T) = \cup_{a \in A} \gamma(a)$, as before, and

---

[4] Giacobazzi, Ranzato, and their colleagues have intensively studied this problem, which is connected to the *backwards completeness* of f [15, 17, 25, 26].

[5] Where $(P, \sqsubseteq_P)^{op}$ is $(P, \sqsupseteq_P)$.

$$\overline{\alpha_u}(S) = \cup\{T \mid S \supseteq \overline{\gamma}(T)\} = \{a \mid \gamma(a) \subseteq S\}.$$

This is an *underapproximating* Galois connection, because $S \supseteq \overline{\gamma}(\overline{\alpha_u}(S))$. We can use it to define this most precise abstraction of $[\![\phi]\!] \in \mathcal{P}(C)$:

$$[\![\phi]\!]^A = \overline{\alpha_u}[\![\phi]\!].$$

But such a definition is not finitely computable, and we desire an inductive definition of $[\![\cdot]\!]^A$. For each logical connective, op_k, interpreted by $g_k : \mathcal{P}(C)^{arity(k)} \to \mathcal{P}(C)$ in the form,

$$[\![op_k(\phi_i)_{i<arity(k)}]\!] = g_k([\![\phi_i]\!])_{i<arity(k)}$$

its most precise, inductively defined underapproximation is

$$[\![op_k(\phi_i)_{i<arity(k)}]\!]^A = g_{k_{best}^\flat}([\![\phi_i]\!]^A)_{i<arity(k)}, \text{ where } g_{k_{best}^\flat} = \overline{\alpha_u} \circ g_k \circ \overline{\gamma}^{arity(k)}$$

Since $g_{k_{best}^\flat}$ as stated is not finitely computable, we search for a sound approximation that is. For example, for logical disjunction we settle for

$$[\![\phi_1 \vee \phi_2]\!]^A = [\![\phi_1]\!]^A \cup [\![\phi_2]\!]^A$$

as a sound underapproximation of

$$\cup_{best}^\flat([\![\phi_1]\!]^A, [\![\phi_2]\!]^A), \text{ where } \cup_{best}^\flat = \overline{\alpha_u} \circ \cup_{\mathcal{P}(C)} \circ (\overline{\gamma} \times \overline{\gamma}).$$

Note that $[\![\phi_1 \vee \phi_2]\!]^A \neq \overline{\alpha_u}[\![\phi_1 \vee \phi_2]\!]$: For example, $any \in \overline{\alpha_u}[\![even \vee odd]\!]$ but $any \notin [\![even \vee odd]\!]^A$, where $[\![even]\!]^A = \overline{\alpha_u}(\gamma(even)) = \{even, none\}$ (and similarly for $[\![odd]\!]^A$).

3.1   Abstracting $\widetilde{pre}_f$

We apply the above-stated techniques to $\widetilde{pre}_f(S) = \{c \mid f(c) \subseteq S\}$ and its logical depiction,

$$[\![[f]\phi]\!] = \widetilde{pre}_f[\![\phi]\!].$$

Using the Galois connections at our disposal, we define $(\widetilde{pre}_f)_{best}^\flat = \overline{\alpha_u} \circ \widetilde{pre}_f \circ \overline{\gamma}$ and compute:

$$\begin{aligned}
[\![[f]\phi]\!]^A &= (\widetilde{pre}_f)_{best}^\flat [\![\phi]\!]^A \\
&= \{a \mid \gamma(a) \subseteq \widetilde{pre}_f(\overline{\gamma}[\![\phi]\!]^A)\} \\
&= \{a \mid f^*[\gamma(a)] \subseteq \overline{\gamma}[\![\phi]\!]^A\}.
\end{aligned}$$

The definition is not finitely computable, so we propose $\widetilde{pre}_{f^\sharp}$ as a sound underapproximation — since $f^\sharp : A \to \mathcal{P}_\downarrow(A)$ overapproximates f's transitions, $f^\sharp$'s preimages will correspond to supersets of f's preimages. This gives the standard result [8]:

Proposition 1. *If* $f^\sharp : A \to \mathcal{P}_\downarrow(A)$ *is overapproximating sound (that is,* $\alpha \circ f \sqsubseteq_{\mathcal{P}(C) \to A} f^\sharp \circ \alpha$*), then* $\widetilde{pre}_{f^\sharp}$ *is underapproximating sound:* $\overline{\alpha_u}(\widetilde{pre}_f(S)) \supseteq \widetilde{pre}_{f^\sharp}(\overline{\alpha_u}(S))$.

We also have this pleasing result, which shows that the preimage of the best overapproximation equals the best underapproximation of the preimage:

Theorem 2. $\widetilde{pre}_{f^\sharp_{best}} = (\widetilde{pre}_f)^\flat_{best}$, *where* $f^\sharp_{best} = \overline{\alpha_o} \circ f^* \circ \gamma$.

Proof. First, $(\widetilde{pre}_f)^\flat_{best}(T) = \{a \mid f^*(\gamma(a)) \subseteq \overline{\gamma}(T)\}$, and next, $\widetilde{pre}_{f^\sharp_{best}}(T) = \{a \mid \overline{\alpha_o} \circ f^* \circ \gamma(a) \subseteq T\}$. Assume $f^*(\gamma(a)) \subseteq \overline{\gamma}(T)$; then $\overline{\alpha_o} \circ f^* \circ \gamma(a) \subseteq \overline{\alpha_o} \circ \overline{\gamma}(T)$. Since $\overline{\alpha_o}(\overline{\gamma}(T)) \subseteq T$, we are finished. $\square$

Function $f^\sharp_{best} : A \to \mathcal{P}_\downarrow(A)$ has been intensively studied:

$$f^\sharp_{best}(a) = (\overline{\alpha_o} \circ f^* \circ \gamma)(a) = \downarrow\{\alpha\{c'\} \mid c \in \gamma(a), c' \in f(c)\}.$$

Cleaveland, Iyer, and Yankelevich [4] and Dams [9] showed that $f^\sharp_{best}$ proves the most $[f]$-properties in the logic in Figure 4.

3.2   Abstracting pre_f

Recall that $pre_f(S) = \{c \mid f(c) \cap S \neq \emptyset\}$. The concrete semantics,

$$[\![\langle f \rangle \phi]\!] = pre_f[\![\phi]\!]$$

defines those states that have a successor state in $[\![\phi]\!]$. We must underapproximate this set, and we define $(pre_f)^\flat_{best} = \overline{\alpha_u} \circ pre_f \circ \overline{\gamma}$. This gives us

$$[\![\langle f \rangle \phi]\!]^A = (pre_f)^\flat_{best}[\![\phi]\!]^A$$
$$= \{a \mid \text{for every } c \in \gamma(a), f(c) \cap \overline{\gamma}(T) \neq \emptyset\}.$$

We search for an approximation of $(pre_f)^\flat_{best}$ expressed in the form, pre_g. Clearly, $pre_{f^\sharp}$, for $f^\sharp : A \to \mathcal{P}_\downarrow(A)$, is unsound, because $f^\sharp(a)$ overestimates a's successors.[6] To underapproximate $f : C \to \mathcal{P}(C)$, we might try $f^\flat_u(a) = (\overline{\alpha_u} \circ f^* \circ \gamma)(a) = \{a' \mid \gamma(a') \subseteq f^*[\gamma(a)]\}$. This looks reasonable, but the consequences are surprising:

Proposition 3. *For* $g : A \to \mathcal{P}_\downarrow(A)$, *for* $T \in \mathcal{P}_\downarrow(T)$, $pre_g(T)$ *is an upwards-closed set and is not necessarily downwards closed.*

Proof. We first show, if $T \neq \emptyset$, then $pre_g(T) = \{a \mid g(a) \neq \emptyset\}$: For $a \in A$, let $g(a) \neq \emptyset$. Then $\perp_A \in g(a)$, because the set is downwards closed. Since T is downwards closed and nonempty, $\perp_A \in T$ as well. This set is upclosed (because g is monotonic) but need not be downclosed (e.g., when $g(\perp_A) = \emptyset$, where $\gamma(\perp_A) = \emptyset$). When $T = \emptyset$, $pre_g(T) = \emptyset$, which is upclosed. $\square$

---

[6] For example, $div2^\sharp_{best}(even) = \downarrow\{even, odd\}$, hence $even \in pre_{div2^\sharp_{best}} \downarrow\{even\}$, yet $6 \in \gamma(even)$ and $div2(6) = \{3\}$.

The result goes against our intuition that propositions are interpreted as down-closed subsets of A. To make $pre_g(T)$ into a downclosed set, it is necessary that $a \sqsubseteq_A a'$ implies $g(a) \supseteq g(a')$, that is, g's codomain must be partially ordered by $\supseteq$. In such a codomain, we must ensure that set injection is monotonic, that is, $a_0 \sqsubseteq_A a_1$ implies $\{|a_0|\} \supseteq \{|a_1|\}$, which forces $\{|a|\} = \uparrow\{a\}$.

For these reasons, we define underapproximating transition functions of arity, $f^\flat : A \to \mathcal{P}_\uparrow(A)$, where $(\mathcal{P}_\uparrow(A), \supseteq)$ is all upclosed subsets of A, ordered by superset inclusion.[7] The following section provides some intuition.

3.3   Interpreting Downclosed and Upclosed Sets

When we use an overapproximating Galois connection, like $\mathcal{P}(Nat)\langle\alpha,\gamma\rangle Parity$, to analyze a program and we compute that the program's output is $even$, we are asserting, "$\forall even$" — all the program's concrete outputs are even-valued. The upper adjoint, $\gamma : Parity \to \mathcal{P}(Nat)$, selects the largest set modelled by $even$,

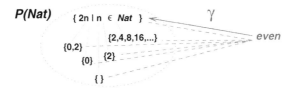

but the program's output set might be any $S \subseteq Nat$ such that $S \subseteq \gamma(even)$.

This reading applies also to the Galois connection, $\mathcal{P}(Nat)\langle\overline{\alpha_o},\overline{\gamma}\rangle\mathcal{P}_\downarrow(Parity)$, where a downclosed set like $\{even, odd, none\}$ asserts $\forall\{even, odd, none\} \equiv \forall(even \lor odd \lor none) \equiv \forall(even \lor odd)$ — all outputs are even- or odd-valued. The program's output might be any $S \subseteq Nat$ such that $S \subseteq \overline{\gamma}\{even, odd, none\}$.

What is the dual of an overapproximating "universal assertion"? In the previous section, we tried using the Galois connection, $\mathcal{P}(Nat)^{op}\langle\overline{\alpha_u},\overline{\gamma}\rangle\mathcal{P}_\downarrow(Parity)^{op}$, to underapproximate a program's outputs, but the results were disappointing[8] and dubious (cf. Proposition 3).

The desired dual is an "existential assertion": If an overapproximating $even \in Parity$ asserts "$\forall even$," then an underapproximating $even$ should assert "$\exists even$" — there exists an even number in the program's outputs. Now, a function like $3x + 1 : Nat \to \mathcal{P}(Nat)$ can be underapproximated such that $(3x + 1)^\flat(odd) = \{even\}$ — there exists an even number in the function's output.

This idea extends to compound "existential assertions": an upclosed set like $\{even, odd, any\}$ asserts $\exists\{even, odd, any\} \equiv \exists even \land \exists odd \land \exists any \equiv \exists even \land \exists odd$ — there exist both even- and odd-valued numbers in the output set.

But there is a problem: How do we concretize an underapproximating set like $\{even\}$ into $\mathcal{P}(Nat)^{op}$? There is no minimal set that contains an even number:

---

[7] $\mathcal{P}_\uparrow(A) = \{\uparrow T \mid T \subseteq A\}$, where $\uparrow T = \{a \in A \mid \text{there exists } a' \in T, a' \sqsubseteq_A a\}$.

[8] For example, $3x + 1 : Nat \to \mathcal{P}(Nat)$ is approximated by $(3x + 1)^\flat_{best} = \overline{\alpha}_u \circ (3x + 1)^* \circ \gamma$. Then, $(3x + 1)^\flat_{best}(odd) = \overline{\alpha}_u((3x + 1)^*\{1, 3, 5, \cdots\} = \overline{\alpha}_u\{4, 10, 16, 22, \cdots\} = \{none\}$ (!)

Universal (over-approximating) interpretation: $\{even, odd\}$ asserts $\forall\{even, odd\} \equiv \forall(even \vee odd)$ — all outputs are even- or odd-valued; use downclosed sets:

$P_{\downarrow}(P(Nat))$ $P_{\downarrow}(Parity)$

{ S | S is a subset of *Nat* }   ←———————————— {any,even,odd,none}

{ S | S has even numbers only }   ←———— $\gamma_{\forall}$ {even,odd,none} = $\forall(even \vee odd)$

                                            {even,none} {odd,none}

{} ←———————————————————— {none}

                                            ———— {}

Existential (under-approximating) interpretation: $\{even, odd\}$ asserts $\exists\{even, odd\} \equiv \exists even \wedge \exists odd$ — there exists an even- valued and an odd-valued output; use upclosed sets:

$P_{\downarrow}(P(Nat)^{op})$ $P_{\uparrow}(Parity)$

{ S | S is a subset of *Nat* } ←———————— {}

{ S | S is nonempty } ←———— $\gamma_{\wedge}$ ————— {any}

{ S | S has an even } ←———— {even,any} {odd,any}

{ S | S has an even and an odd } ←—— {even,odd,any} = $\exists even \wedge \exists odd$

                                            {none,even,odd,any}

{} ←—————————————————

Fig. 5. Powersets for the *Parity* abstraction

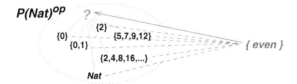

$P(Nat)^{op}$? ←

{0}   {2}   {5,7,9,12}
{0,1}   ————————→ { *even* }
{2,4,8,16,...}
Nat

Indeed, $\{even\}$'s concretization is not a single set — it must be a *set of sets*:

$$\gamma'\{even\} = \{S \in P(Nat) \mid S \cap \gamma(even) \neq \emptyset\}.$$

3.4   Upper and Lower Powerset Constructions

To interpret downclosed sets ("universal assertions") and upclosed sets ("existential assertions") we use concrete domains that are *sets of sets*. Figure 5 displays the universal and existential interpretations of sets of parities.

The universal interpretation is developed as follows: For Galois connection, $P(C)\langle\alpha, \gamma\rangle A$, define $\rho_{\downarrow} \subseteq P(C) \times P_{\downarrow}(A)$ as

$$S \, \rho_{\downarrow} \, T \text{ iff for all } c \in S, \text{ there exists } a \in A \text{ such that } c \in \gamma(a).$$

This is the lower ("Hoare") powerdomain ordering, used in denotational semantics [24]. Note that $S \, \rho_{\downarrow} \, T$ iff $S \subseteq \overline{\gamma}(T)$. Next, define this Galois connection:

$$P_{\downarrow}(P(C))\langle\overline{\alpha_{\downarrow}}, \overline{\gamma_{\downarrow}}\rangle P_{\downarrow}(A) \text{ where } \begin{aligned} \overline{\gamma_{\downarrow}}(T) &= \{S \mid S \, \rho_{\downarrow} \, T\} \\ \overline{\alpha_{\downarrow}}(\overline{S}) &= \cap\{T \mid \text{ for all } S \in \overline{S}, S \, \rho_{\downarrow} \, T\} \end{aligned}$$

$\overline{\gamma_\downarrow}(T)$ concretizes T to all the sets covered by T — It is an *over*approximation of an *over*approximation:

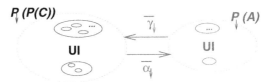

Because $S\,\rho_\downarrow\,T$ iff $S \subseteq \overline{\gamma}(T)$, no new expressibility is gained by using the new Galois connection over $\mathcal{P}(C)\langle\overline{\alpha_o},\overline{\gamma}\rangle\mathcal{P}_\downarrow(A)$: for all $f : C \to \mathcal{P}(C)$, $f^\sharp_{best} : A \to \mathcal{P}_\downarrow(A)$ is $\overline{\alpha_\downarrow} \circ (\{\!|\cdot|\!\} \circ f)^* \circ \gamma = \overline{\alpha_o} \circ f^* \circ \gamma$ [30, 31]. But we might argue nonetheless that this Galois connection "truly defines" the sound overapproximation of f.

On the other hand, the existential interpretation is truly new; it uses the *Smyth-powerdomain ordering* from denotational semantics [24]: Define $\rho_\uparrow \subseteq \mathcal{P}(C) \times \mathcal{P}_\uparrow(A)$ as

$$S\,\rho_\uparrow\,T \text{ iff for all } a \in T, \text{ there exists } c \in S \text{ such that } c \in \gamma(a).$$

That is, every $a \in T$ is a witness to some $c \in S$. Note that $S\,\rho_\uparrow\,T$ iff for all $a \in T$, $\gamma(a) \cap S \neq \emptyset$. Next, define this Galois connection:

$$\mathcal{P}_\downarrow(\mathcal{P}(C)^{op})\langle\overline{\alpha_\uparrow},\overline{\gamma_\uparrow}\rangle\mathcal{P}_\uparrow(A) \text{ where } \begin{aligned}\overline{\gamma_\uparrow}(T) &= \{S \mid S\,\rho_\uparrow\,T\} \\ \overline{\alpha_\uparrow}(\overline{S}) &= \cup\{T \mid \text{ for all } S \in \overline{S}, S\,\rho_\uparrow\,T\}\end{aligned}$$

$\overline{\gamma_\uparrow}(T)$ concretizes T to all sets that T "witnesses" — It is an *over*approximation of an *under*approximation:

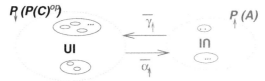

Figure 6 summarizes the Galois connections developed so far.

3.5   Properties of $pre_{f^\flat}$

We underapproximate $f : C \to \mathcal{P}(C)$ by a sound $f^\flat : A \to \mathcal{P}_\uparrow(A)$. We define $f^\flat_{best} : A \to \mathcal{P}_\uparrow(A)$ as

$$\begin{aligned}f^\flat_{best}(a) &= (\overline{\alpha_\uparrow} \circ (\{\!|\cdot|\!\} \circ f)^* \circ \gamma)(a) \\ &= \uparrow\{\alpha(S) \mid \text{ for all } c \in \gamma(a),\ f(c) \cap S \neq \emptyset\} \\ &= \{a' \mid \text{ for all } c \in \gamma(a),\ f(c) \cap \gamma(a') \neq \emptyset\}\end{aligned}$$

We have that $pre_{f^\flat_{best}}(T)$ is downclosed and also that

Proposition 4. $pre_{f^\flat_{best}}$ *is sound:* $pre_{f^\flat_{best}}(T) \subseteq (\overline{\alpha_u} \circ pre_f \circ \overline{\gamma})(T)$.

Figure 7 shows the abstracted precondition logic. Cleaveland, Iyer, and Yankelevich [4], Dams, et al. [10], and Schmidt [30] showed that $pre_{f^\flat_{best}}$ proves the most sound $\langle f \rangle$-properties in the logic of Figure 4.

	overapproximation	underapproximation
set inclusion	$\mathcal{P}(C)\langle\overline{\alpha_o},\overline{\gamma}\rangle\mathcal{P}_{\downarrow}(A)$ where $\overline{\gamma}(T) = \cup_{a \in A}\gamma(a)$ $\overline{\alpha_o}(S) = \downarrow\{\alpha\{c\} \mid c \in S\}$	$\mathcal{P}(C)^{op}\langle\overline{\alpha_u},\overline{\gamma}\rangle\mathcal{P}_{\downarrow}(A)^{op}$ where $\overline{\gamma}(T) = \cup_{a \in A}\gamma(a)$ $\overline{\alpha_u}(S) = \{a \mid \gamma(a) \subseteq S\}$
quantification	$\mathcal{P}_{\downarrow}(\mathcal{P}(C))\langle\overline{\alpha_{\downarrow}},\overline{\gamma_{\downarrow}}\rangle\mathcal{P}_{\downarrow}(A)$ where $\overline{\gamma_{\downarrow}}(T) = \{S \mid S \, \rho_{\downarrow} \, T\}$ $\overline{\alpha_{\downarrow}}(\overline{S}) = \cap\{T \mid \text{for all } S \in \overline{S},$ $S \, \rho_{\downarrow} \, T\}$	$\mathcal{P}_{\downarrow}(\mathcal{P}(C)^{op})\langle\overline{\alpha_{\uparrow}},\overline{\gamma_{\uparrow}}\rangle\mathcal{P}_{\uparrow}(A)$ where $\overline{\gamma_{\uparrow}}(T) = \{S \mid S \, \rho_{\uparrow} \, T\}$ $\overline{\alpha_{\uparrow}}(\overline{S}) = \cup\{T \mid \text{for all } S \in \overline{S},$ $S \, \rho_{\uparrow} \, T\}$

where $\rho_{\downarrow} \subseteq \mathcal{P}(C) \times \mathcal{P}_{\downarrow}(A)$ is defined
   $S \, \rho_{\downarrow} \, T$ iff for all $c \in S$, there exists $a \in A$ such that $c \in \gamma(a)$
and $\rho_{\uparrow} \subseteq \mathcal{P}(C) \times \mathcal{P}_{\uparrow}(A)$ is defined
   $S \, \rho_{\uparrow} \, T$ iff for all $a \in T$, there exists $c \in S$ such that $c \in \gamma(a)$.

Fig. 6. Summary of Galois connections derived from $\mathcal{P}(C)\langle\alpha,\gamma\rangle A$

$$[\![\cdot]\!] : \mathcal{L} \to \mathcal{P}_{\downarrow}(A)$$

$$[\![a]\!]^A = \overline{\alpha_u}(\gamma(a))$$
$$[\![[f]\phi]\!]^A = \widetilde{pre}_{f_{best}^{\sharp}}\,[\![\phi]\!]^A \qquad [\![\phi_1 \wedge \phi_2]\!]^A = [\![\phi_1]\!]^A \cap [\![\phi_2]\!]^A$$
$$[\![\langle f\rangle\phi]\!]^A = pre_{f_{best}^{\flat}}\,[\![\phi]\!]^A \qquad [\![\phi_1 \vee \phi_2]\!]^A = [\![\phi_1]\!]^A \cup [\![\phi_2]\!]^A$$

Fig. 7. The abstracted precondition logic

3.6   Incompleteness and *Focus*

Although $f_{best}^{\flat}$ is the most precise (maximal) sound underapproximation, there
is no guarantee that $pre_{f_{best}^{\flat}}$ equals $(pre_f)_{best}^{\flat} = \overline{\alpha_u} \circ pre_f \circ \overline{\gamma}$.

Here is a counterexample: Consider the *Parity* abstract domain and the as-
sertion, $\langle div2\rangle(even \vee odd)$. This assertion holds for all $c \in \gamma(even)$, and in-
deed, for the downclosed set, $T_0 = \{even, odd, none\}$, we have that $even \in (pre_{div2})_{best}^{\flat}(T_0)$. But $div2_{best}^{\flat}(even) = \{any\}$, and $any \notin T_0$, implying that
$even \notin pre_{div2_{best}^{\flat}}(T_0)$.

The underlying issue is the well-known incompleteness of disjunction in ap-
proximation [8]; here, $any \notin T_0$, even though $\gamma(any) \subseteq \overline{\gamma}(T_0)$. The standard
repair is a *focus* operation, as used in the TVLA system [28], and in disjunc-
tive transition systems [11, 14, 20], and in tree automata [12], to "split" values
like any into more-precise cases that "cover" all of $\gamma(any)$. For the example,
$T_1 = \{even, odd\}$ is a *focus set* that covers any because $\gamma(any) \subseteq \overline{\gamma}(T_1)$. Since
both $even \in T_0$ and $odd \in T_0$, we conclude any "belongs" to T_0 as well.

The domain-theoretic connection is clear: A downclosed set, like $T_0 = \{even,\ odd,\ none\}$ should be read as the quantified disjunction, $\forall(even \vee odd \vee none)$, and a *focus* operation helps validate the disjunction.

Definition 5. *For $a \in A$, define $focus(a) = \{U \subseteq A \mid \gamma(a) \subseteq \overline{\gamma}(U)\}$, and define $pre_{f^{\flat}}^{focus}(T) = \{a \mid there\ exist\ a' \in f^{\flat}(a)\ and\ U \in focus(a')\ such\ that\ U \subseteq T\}$.*

Evidently, $pre_{f^{\flat}}^{focus}(T) = \{a \mid exists\ a' \in f^{\flat}(a),\ T \in focus(a')\}$. Definition 5 yields the expressivity and completeness results immediately below, but of course the selection of a specific focus set is a critical pragmatic decision.[9]

Proposition 6. *For all $T \in \mathcal{P}_{\downarrow}(A)$, $pre_{f^{\flat}_{best}}(T) \subseteq pre_{f^{\flat}_{best}}^{focus}(T) \subseteq (pre_f)^{\flat}_{best}(T)$.*

Proof. The first inclusion follows by choosing $\{a'\} \in focus(a')$. For the second inclusion, assume there exists $a' \in f^{\flat}_{best}(a)$ such that $\gamma(a') \subseteq \overline{\gamma}(T)$. Since $a' \in f^{\flat}_{best}(a)$, this implies for all $c \in \gamma(a)$, $f(c) \cap \gamma(a') \neq \emptyset$. Since $\gamma(a') \subseteq \overline{\gamma}(T)$, we have the result.   □

Theorem 7. *If $\gamma : A \to \mathcal{P}(C)$ preserves joins, then $pre_{f^{\flat}_{best}}^{focus}(T) = (pre_f)^{\flat}_{best}(T)$.*

Proof. We have $\subseteq$; to show $\supseteq$, assume that some $a_0 \in (pre_f)^{\flat}_{best}(T)$, that is, for all $c \in \gamma(a_0)$, $f(c) \cap \overline{\gamma}(T) \neq \emptyset$. We must show that there exists $a' \in f^{\flat}_{best}(a_0)$ such that $T \in focus(a')$.

Define $T_{a_0} = \{a_c \in T \mid exists\ c \in \gamma(a_0), f(c) \cap \gamma(a_c) \neq \emptyset\}$, and define $a' = \sqcup T_{a_0}$. Immediately, we can conclude that $a' \in f^{\flat}_{best}(a_0)$. Now we must show $T \in focus(a')$, that is, $\gamma(a') \subseteq \overline{\gamma}(T)$.

For each $a_c \in T_{a_0}$, we have that $\gamma(a_c) \subseteq \overline{\gamma}(T)$, hence $(\sqcup_{a_c \in T_{a_0}} \gamma(a_c)) \subseteq \overline{\gamma}(T)$. Since γ preserves joins, we have that $\gamma(a') = \gamma(\sqcup T_{a_0}) \subseteq \overline{\gamma}(T)$.   □

Partition domains [25] are the standard example where γ preserves joins: given state set C, partition P, and $\delta : P \to \mathcal{P}(C)$ that maps each partition to its members, the generated partition domain is $(\mathcal{P}(P), \subseteq)$, where $\gamma = \delta^*$.

If γ preserves joins, then we know that the first inclusion in Proposition 6 can be proper (e.g., $T_0 = \{even, odd, none\}$); if γ fails to preserve joins, there can be a T that makes the first inclusion an equality and the second one proper, because there is some $c \in \overline{\gamma}(T)$ that cannot be "isolated" by a focus set [16].

4   Postconditions

Earlier, we noted that $f^* : \mathcal{P}(C) \to \mathcal{P}(C)$, for $f : C \to \mathcal{P}(C)$, defines f's postcondition transformer and $f^{\sharp} : A \to A$ is its sound overapproximation. For example,

---

[9] Focus sets are also known as *must hyper transitions* [32], and there is a dual notion of *may hyper transitions*, which prove useful when $\gamma : A \to C$ is *not* the upper adjoint of a Galois connection [33].

$$[\![\,\cdot\,]\!] : \mathcal{L} \to \mathcal{P}(C)$$

$$[\![a]\!] = \gamma(a)$$
$$[\![[f]\phi]\!] = \widetilde{post}_f[\![\phi]\!] \qquad [\![\phi_1 \wedge \phi_2]\!] = [\![\phi_1]\!] \cap [\![\phi_2]\!]$$
$$[\![\langle f \rangle \phi]\!] = post_f[\![\phi]\!] \qquad [\![\phi_1 \vee \phi_2]\!] = [\![\phi_1]\!] \cup [\![\phi_2]\!]$$

Fig. 8. The postcondition logic

Available Expressions:
$$AE(p) =_{gfp} \bigcap_{p' \in pred\ p}((AE(p') \cap notModified(p')) \cup Gen(p'))$$
$$isAvail(e) = \nu Z.\ \overline{[p]}((Z \wedge \neg isModified(e)) \vee isGen(e))$$

Live Variables:
$$LV(p) =_{lfp} Used(p) \cup (notModified(p) \cap (\bigcup_{p' \in succ\ p} LV(p')))$$
$$isLive(x) = \mu Z.\ isUsed(x) \vee (\neg isModified(x) \wedge (\langle p \rangle Z))$$

Very Busy Expressions:
$$VBE(p) =_{gfp} Used(p) \cup (notModified(p) \cap (\bigcap_{p' \in succ\ p'} VBE(p')))$$
$$isVBE(e) = \nu Z.\ isUsed(e) \vee (\neg isModified(e) \wedge [p]Z)$$

Reaching Definitions:
$$RD(p) =_{lfp} \bigcup_{p' \in pred\ p}((RD(p') \cap notModified(p')) \cup Defined(p'))$$
$$isReaching(d) = \mu Z.\ \langle p \rangle((Z \wedge \neg isModified(d)) \vee isDefined(d))$$

Fig. 9. Data-flow analyses and their encodings in logical form [29]

$succ^*\{1,3,5,\cdots\} = \{2,4,6,\cdots\}$ and $succ^\sharp_{best}(odd) = even$, where $succ^\sharp_{best} = \alpha \circ succ^* \circ \gamma$ is the strongest postcondition transformer for Galois connection, $\mathcal{P}(Nat)\langle\alpha,\gamma\rangle Parity$. Similarly, from $f : C \to \mathcal{P}(C)$ and $\mathcal{P}(C)\langle\overline{\alpha_o},\overline{\gamma}\rangle\mathcal{P}_\downarrow(A)$, we define $f^\sharp_{best} : A \to \mathcal{P}_\downarrow(A)$ as $f^\sharp_{best} = \overline{\alpha_o} \circ f^* \circ \gamma$.

Since $f : C \to \mathcal{P}(C)$ denotes a nondeterministic transition relation, there are two variants of logical postcondition:

$$post_f(S) = \{d \mid \text{there exists } c \in S, d \in f(c)\} = f^*(S)$$
$$\widetilde{post}_f(S) = \{d \mid \text{for all } c \in C, d \in f(c) \text{ implies } c \in S\}.$$

$d \in post_f(S)$ means that *one* of d's immediate f-predecessors belongs to S; $d \in \widetilde{post}_f(S)$ means that *all* of d's immediate f-predecessors belong to S. These transformers have a natural place in a logic; see Figure 8.

Steffen [34] showed how to use the $\overline{[f]}$- and $\langle f \rangle$-modalities to define forwards data-flow analyses, and Schmidt [29] applied Steffen's ideas, as displayed in Figure 9, to write mu-calculus formulas [19] that define the naive but standard forwards and backwards data-flow analyses on annotated control-flow graphs, where $p \in ProgramPoint$.

For the purposes of program validation and code improvement, the abstractions of the two *post*-modalities must be *underapproximating*.[10] Clearly, underapproximating the logical interpretation of the postcondition transformers is different from overapproximating a transition function's postcondition, and the following proposition indicates how careful we must be:

Proposition 8. *Let $f : D \to \mathcal{P}_\delta(D)$, where $\delta \in \{\downarrow, \uparrow\}$. Let $\tilde{\downarrow} = \uparrow$ and $\tilde{\uparrow} = \downarrow$.*

$$\text{Then, for all } S \in \mathcal{P}(D), \quad \begin{array}{ll} - \ \widetilde{pre}_f(S) \in \mathcal{P}_\delta(D) & - \ post_f(S) \in \mathcal{P}_\delta(D) \\ - \ pre_f(S) \in \mathcal{P}_{\tilde{\delta}}(D) & - \ \widetilde{post}_f(S) \in \mathcal{P}_{\tilde{\delta}}(D). \end{array}$$

Proof. Recall that $f : D \to \mathcal{P}_\delta(D)$. When reasoning about f, we use the notation, $\leq_\delta$, to denote $\sqsubseteq_D$, when $\delta = \downarrow$, and $\sqsupseteq_D$, when $\delta = \uparrow$. We have that f is monotonic iff $c \leq_\delta d$ implies $f(c) \subseteq f(d)$. Here are the four proofs:

$\widetilde{pre}_f(S)\{c \mid f(c) \subseteq S\}$: If $f(c) \subseteq S$ and $d \leq_\delta c$, then $f(d) \subseteq f(c)$, by f's monotonicity.

$pre_f S = \{c \mid f(c) \cap S \neq \emptyset\}$: If $f(c) \cap S \neq \emptyset$ and $c \leq_\delta d$ (that is, $d \leq_{\tilde{\delta}} c$), then $f(c) \subseteq f(d)$, implying $f(d) \cap S \neq \emptyset$.

$post_f(S) = \{d \mid \text{exists } c \in S, d \in f(c)\}$: If there exists some $c \in S$ such that $d \in f(c)$, and then $d' \leq_\delta d$, then $d' \in f(c)$, because f's codomain is $\mathcal{P}_\delta(D)$.

$\widetilde{post}_f S = \{d \mid \text{for all } c \in D, d \in f(c) \text{ implies } c \in S\}$: Say that $d \leq_\delta d'$ (that is, $d' \leq_{\tilde{\delta}} d$) and $d \in \widetilde{post}_f S$. For $c' \in D$, say that $d' \in f(c')$ — we must show that $c' \in S$, as well. Since $d \leq_\delta d'$, this means $d \in f(c')$, because f's codomain is $\mathcal{P}_\delta(D)$. This places $c' \in S$. □

The proposition confirms why $\widetilde{pre}_{f^\sharp}$ and $pre_{f^\flat}$ correctly underapproximated $\widetilde{pre}_f$ and pre_f – the abstract transformers generated downclosed sets as answers. The proposition also makes clear that $post_{f^\flat}$ and $\widetilde{post}_{f^\sharp}$ are *unacceptable* as underapproximations, because they generate *upclosed* sets as answers:

$$\text{for } f^\flat : A \to \mathcal{P}_\uparrow(A), \quad post_{f^\flat} : \mathcal{P}_\downarrow(A) \to \mathcal{P}_\uparrow(A)$$
$$\text{for } f^\sharp : A \to \mathcal{P}_\downarrow(A), \quad \widetilde{post}_{f^\sharp} : \mathcal{P}_\downarrow(A) \to \mathcal{P}_\uparrow(A).$$

Unfortunately, starting from $\gamma : A \to \mathcal{P}(C)$ and $f : C \to \mathcal{P}(C)$, there is no nontrivial overapproximating $f^\sharp : A \to \mathcal{P}_\uparrow(A)$ (because, for all $f^\sharp(a) \neq \emptyset$, upclosure implies that $\top_A \in f^\sharp(a)$, implying that $\overline{\gamma}(f^\sharp(a)) = C$). A similar problem arises in the search for a nontrivial underapproximating $f^\flat : A \to \mathcal{P}_\downarrow(A)$.[11] There is a repair, however. If we draw

---

[10] For performing data-flow analysis, one usually abstracts a program, f, to its control-flow graph, $f^\sharp_{cfg}$. A *naive* application of the four analyses in Figure 9 to $f^\sharp_{cfg}$ gives *underapproximating* calculations of available expressions and very-busy expressions and *overapproximating* calculations of reaching definitions and live variables (but see [8] for clarification). The set-complements of the latter two calculations — "not-reaching" and "not-live," respectively — are used in practice.

[11] In contrast, both $post_{f^\sharp}$ and $\widetilde{post}_{f^\flat}$ are well defined *overapproximations* of the two postcondition transformers!

$$f : C \to \mathcal{P}(C) \text{ as } \begin{array}{cccc} \mathbf{a} & \mathbf{b} & \mathbf{c} & \mathbf{d} \\ \downarrow\searrow\downarrow & & \downarrow\nearrow & \\ \mathbf{a} & \mathbf{b} & \mathbf{c} & \mathbf{d} \end{array} \quad , \text{ then } f^{-1} : C \to \mathcal{P}(C) \text{ is } \begin{array}{cccc} \mathbf{a} & \mathbf{b} & \mathbf{c} & \mathbf{d} \\ \uparrow\nwarrow & \uparrow & \uparrow\nearrow & \\ \mathbf{a} & \mathbf{b} & \mathbf{c} & \mathbf{d} \end{array}.$$

That is, $f^{-1}(c) = \{d \mid c \in f(d)\}$.

Proposition 9. *[21]:* $(f^{-1})^{-1} = f$, $post_f = pre_{f^{-1}}$, and $\widetilde{post}_f = \widetilde{pre}_{f^{-1}}$.

Proposition 10. *For* $f : A \to \mathcal{P}_\delta(A)$, $\delta \in \{\downarrow, \uparrow\}$, $f^{-1} : A \to \mathcal{P}_{\bar\delta}(A)$ *is well defined and monotonic.*

Proof. $f^{-1}(a) = \{a' \mid a \in f(a')\}$. We use $\leq_\delta$ to denote $\sqsubseteq_D$, when $\delta = \downarrow$, and to denote $\sqsupseteq_D$, when $\delta = \uparrow$. First, note that $f : A \to \mathcal{P}_\delta(A)$ is monotonic iff $c \leq_\delta d$ implies $f(c) \subseteq f(d)$.

f^{-1}'s *image are $\bar\delta$-closed sets*: Say that $a' \in f^{-1}(a)$, that is, $a \in f(a')$ and say that $a' \leq_\delta b'$. We must show $a \in f(b')$ — this follows from $f(a') \subseteq f(b')$.

f^{-1} *is monotonic*: Assume $a \leq_\delta b$; we must show $f^{-1}(a) \sqsubseteq_{\mathcal{P}_{\bar\delta}(A)} f^{-1}(b)$. First, we show that $f^{-1}(b) \subseteq f^{-1}(a)$: Assume $x \in f^{-1}(b)$, that is, $b \in f(x)$. Then $\delta b \subseteq f(x)$, because $f(x)$ is a δ-closed set. This implies $a \in f(x)$ as well, that is, $x \in f^{-1}(a)$. The monotonicity of f^{-1} follows, because $\mathcal{P}_{\bar\delta}(A)$ uses the inverse ordering used by $\mathcal{P}_\delta(A)$. □

4.1   Abstracting $post_f$ and $\widetilde{post}_f$

With Propositions 8, 9, and 10 in hand, we can define sound underapproximations for the two postcondition transformers. For $post_f$, we have

$$[\![\langle f \rangle \phi]\!] = post_f[\![\phi]\!] = pre_{f^{-1}}[\![\phi]\!]$$

where $f^{-1} : C \to \mathcal{P}(C)$. The inductively defined underapproximation is

$$[\![\langle f \rangle \phi]\!]A = (\overline{\alpha_u} \circ pre_{f^{-1}} \circ \overline{\gamma})[\![\phi]\!]^A.$$

By Proposition 4, this is soundly underapproximated by

$$[\![\langle f \rangle \phi]\!]^A = pre_{(f^{-1})^\flat_{best}}[\![\phi]\!]^A,$$
$$\text{where } (f^{-1})^\flat_{best} : A \to \mathcal{P}_\uparrow(A) \text{ is } (f^{-1})^\flat_{best} = \overline{\alpha_\uparrow} \circ (\{\!\!\} \cdot \}\!\!\} \circ f^{-1})^* \circ \gamma.$$

The same development applied to $\widetilde{post}_f$ yields

$$[\![\overline{[f]}\phi]\!] = \widetilde{post}_f[\![\phi]\!] = \widetilde{pre}_{f^{-1}}[\![\phi]\!].$$

By Theorem 2, the most precise underapproximation is

$$[\![\langle f \rangle \phi]\!]^A = (\overline{\alpha_u} \circ \widetilde{pre}_{f^{-1}} \circ \overline{\gamma})[\![\phi]\!]^A = \widetilde{pre}_{(f^{-1})^\sharp_{best}}[\![\phi]\!]^A,$$
$$\text{where } (f^{-1})^\sharp_{best} : A \to \mathcal{P}_\downarrow(A) \text{ is } (f^{-1})^\sharp_{best} = \overline{\alpha_o} \circ (f^{-1})^* \circ \gamma.$$

This approach of computing postconditions as preconditions of inverted state-transition relations is implemented in Steffen's fixpoint analysis machine [35].

5 Related Work

Abstraction of predicate transformers begin in Cousot's thesis [5]; details were spelled out in a subsequent series of papers by Cousot and Cousot [6–8] and applied by Bourdoncle to *abstract debugging* [1], which was generalized by Massé [22, 23]. Loiseaux, et al. [21] formalized underapproximation of $\widetilde{pre}$.

Cleaveland, Iyer, and Yankelevich [4], Dams [9], and Dams's colleagues [10] were the first to study underapproximations of *pre*. Studies of precision of such approximations were undertaken by Giacobazzi, Ranzato, and Scozzari [17], who developed completeness properties, and by Ranzato and Tapparo [25–27], who studied completeness of *pre* for state-partition abstract domains. The incompleteness of *pre* has been addressed by Larsen and Xinxin [20], Dams and Namjoshi [11, 12], and Shoham and Grumberg [32]. Steffen [34, 35] was the first to connect data-flow analysis to forwards-backwards temporal-logic modalities, and this connection provides the application area for the results in this paper.

Acknowledgments

Allen Emerson and Kedar Namjoshi let me present early thoughts on this work at VMCAI'06, and Kedar asked several key questions. Michael Huth and Dennis Dams provided valuable advice within earlier collaborations. The referees gave many useful comments.

References

1. F. Bourdoncle. Abstract debugging of higher-order imperative languages. In *Proc. ACM Conf. PLDI*, pages 46–55, 2003.
2. E.M. Clarke, O. Grumberg, and D.E. Long. Model checking and abstraction. *ACM Transactions on Programming Languages and Systems*, 16(5):1512–1542, 1994.
3. E.M. Clarke, O. Grumberg, and D.A. Peled. *Model Checking*. MIT Press, 2000.
4. R. Cleaveland, P. Iyer, and D. Yankelevich. Optimality in abstractions of model checking. In *Proc. SAS'95*, LNCS 983. Springer, 1995.
5. P. Cousot. *Méthodes itératives de construction et d'approximation de points fixes d'opérateurs monotones sur un treillis, analyse sémantique de programmes*. PhD thesis, University of Grenoble, 1978.
6. P. Cousot and R. Cousot. Abstract interpretation: a unified lattice model for static analysis of programs. In *Proc. 4th ACM Symp. POPL*, pages 238–252, 1977.
7. P. Cousot and R. Cousot. Systematic design of program analysis frameworks. In *Proc. 6th ACM Symp. POPL*, pages 269–282, 1979.
8. P. Cousot and R. Cousot. Temporal abstract interpretation. In *Proc. 27th ACM Symp. on Principles of Programming Languages*, pages 12–25. ACM Press, 2000.
9. D. Dams. *Abstract interpretation and partition refinement for model checking*. PhD thesis, Technische Universiteit Eindhoven, The Netherlands, 1996.
10. D. Dams, R. Gerth, and O. Grumberg. Abstract interpretation of reactive systems. *ACM Trans. Prog. Lang. Systems*, 19:253–291, 1997.
11. D. Dams and K. Namjoshi. The existence of finite abstractions for branching time model checking. In *Proc. IEEE Symp. LICS'04*, pages 335–344, 2004.

12. D. Dams and K. Namjoshi. Automata as abstractions. In *Proc. VMCAI'05*, LNCS 3385, pages 216–232. Springer-Verlag, 2005.
13. B.A. Davey and H.A Priestly. *Introduction to Lattices and Order, 2d ed.* Cambridge Univ. Press, 2002.
14. H. Fecher and M. Huth. Complete abstractions through extensions of disjunctive modal transition systems. Technical Report 0604, Institut für Informatik und Praktische Mathematik der Christian-Albrechts-Universitaet zu Kiel, 2005.
15. R. Giacobazzi and E. Quintarelli. Incompleteness, counterexamples, and refinements in abstract model checking. In *Static Analysis Symposium*, LNCS 2126, pages 356–373. Springer Verlag, 2001.
16. R. Giacobazzi and F. Ranzato. The reduced relative power operation on abstract domains. *Theoretical Comp. Sci.*, 216:159–211, 1999.
17. R. Giacobazzi, F. Ranzato, and F. Scozzari. Making abstract interpretations complete. *J. ACM*, 47:361–416, 2000.
18. R. Heckmann. *Power domain constructions*. PhD thesis, Univ. Saarbrücken, 1990.
19. K. Larsen. Proof systems for Hennessy-Milner logic with recursion. In *CAAP88*, LNCS 299. Springer-Verlag, 1988.
20. K.G. Larsen and L. Xinxin. Equation solving using modal transition systems. In *LICS'90*, 1990.
21. C. Loiseaux, S. Graf, J. Sifakis, A. Bouajjani, and S. Bensalem. Property preserving abstractions for verification of concurrent systems. *Formal Methods in System Design*, 6:1–36, 1995.
22. D. Massé. Combining backward and forward analyses of temporal properties. In *Proc. PADO'01*, LNCS 2053, pages 155–172. Springer, 2001.
23. D. Massé. Property checking driven abstract interpretation-based static analysis. In *Proc. VMCAI'03*, LNCS 2575, pages 56–69. Springer, 2003.
24. G. Plotkin. Domains. Lecture notes, Univ. Pisa/Edinburgh, 1983.
25. F. Ranzato and F. Tapparo. Strong preservation as completeness in abstract interpretation. In *Proc. ESOP*, LNCS 2986, pages 18–32. Springer, 2004.
26. F. Ranzato and F. Tapparo. An abstract interpretation-based refinement algorithm for strong preservation. In *TACAS'05*, LNCS 3440, pages 140–156. Springer, 2005.
27. F. Ranzato and F. Tapparo. Strong preservation of temporal fixpoint-based operators by abstract interpretation. In *Proc. Conf. VMCAI'06*, LNCS 3855, pages 332–347. Springer Verlag, 2006.
28. M. Sagiv, T. Reps, and R. Wilhelm. Parametric shape analysis via 3-valued logic. *ACM TOPLAS*, 24:217–298, 2002.
29. D.A. Schmidt. Data-flow analysis is model checking of abstract interpretations. In *Proc. 25th ACM Symp. on Principles of Prog. Languages.* ACM Press, 1998.
30. D.A. Schmidt. Closed and logical relations for over- and under-approximation of powersets. In *Proc. SAS'04*, LNCS 3148, pages 22–37. Springer, 2004.
31. D.A. Schmidt. A calculus of logical relations for over- and underapproximating static analyses. *Science of Computer Programming*, in press.
32. S. Shoham and O. Grumberg. Monotonic abstraction refinement for CTL. In *TACAS'04.* Springer LNCS, 2004.
33. S. Shoham and O. Grumberg. 3-valued abstraction: More precision at less cost. In *LICS'06*, 2006.
34. B. Steffen. Generating data-flow analysis algorithms for modal specifications. *Science of Computer Programming*, 21:115–139, 1993.
35. B. Steffen, A. Classen, M. Klein, J. Knoop, and T. Margaria. The fixpoint analysis machine. In *Proc. CONCUR'95*, LNCS 962, pages 72–87. Springer, 1995.

Combining Widening and Acceleration in Linear Relation Analysis*

Laure Gonnord and Nicolas Halbwachs

Vérimag**, Grenoble, France
{Laure.Gonnord, Nicolas.Halbwachs}@imag.fr

Abstract. Linear Relation Analysis [CH78, Hal79] is one of the first, but still one of the most powerful, abstract interpretations working in an infinite lattice. As such, it makes use of a widening operator to enforce the convergence of fixpoint computations. While the approximation due to widening can be arbitrarily refined by delaying the application of widening, the analysis quickly becomes too expensive with the increase of delay. Previous attempts at improving the precision of widening are not completely satisfactory, since none of them is guaranteed to improve the precision of the result, and they can nevertheless increase the cost of the analysis. In this paper, we investigate an improvement of Linear Relation Analysis consisting in computing, when possible, the exact (abstract) effect of a loop. This technique is fully compatible with the use of widening, and whenever it applies, it improves both the precision and the performance of the analysis.

Linear Relation Analysis [CH78, Hal79] (LRA) is one of the very first applications of abstract interpretation [CC77], and aims at computing an upper approximation of the reachable states of a numerical program, as a convex polyhedron (or a set of such polyhedra). It was applied in various domains like compile-time error detection [DRS01], program parallelization [IJT91], automatic verification [HPR97, HHWT97] and formal proof [BBC+00, BBM97].

Like any approximate verification method, LRA is faced with the compromise between precision and cost. Since its relatively high cost restricts its applicability, any situation where the precision can be improved at low cost must be exploited. One source of approximation in LRA is widening, the operator that ensures the termination of iterative computations, by extrapolating an upper approximation of their limit. When the approximation due to widening is the cause of the lack of precision of the result of an analysis, a possible way to improve the precision is to delay widening: instead of applying it at each iteration, one can start with a number of steps without widening, thus providing a more precise basis for subsequent extrapolations. Now, delaying widening is generally very expensive: not only does it increase the number of iterations, but, more importantly, it leads

---

* This work has been partially supported by the APRON project of the "ACI Sécurité Informatique" of the French Ministry of Research.
** Verimag is a joint laboratory of Université Joseph Fourier, CNRS and INPG associated with IMAG.

to the construction of much more complex polyhedra (that would be simplified otherwise thanks to widening). So, if we can find some cheap ways to improve the precision of widening, we may not only improve the overall precision, but also avoid the cost of delaying widening.

The next question then is "what is a better widening?". The fact that one single application of a widening operator gives smaller results [BHRZ03] does not necessarily mean that its repeated application will involve a convergence towards a more precise limit (an example can been seen in [SSM04]). Moreover, the use of such a widening is likely to slow down the convergence, by increasing the number of necessary iterations.

These remarks led us to look at situations where the widening can obviously be improved — in the sense that a faster convergence towards a better limit can be archived — at low cost with respect to the cost of usual polyhedra operators. For that, a source of inspiration are the so-called "acceleration techniques" proposed by several authors [BW94, WB98, CJ98, FS00, BFLP03]. These works consist in identifying categories of loops whose effect can be computed exactly. Roughly speaking, the effect of a simple loop, guarded by a linear condition on integer variables, and consisting of incrementations/decrementations of these variables can be computed exactly as a Presburger formula. These methods have the advantage of giving exact results. Now, because they are exact, they are restricted to some classes of programs (e.g., "flat counter automata", i.e., without nested loops). Moreover, the exact computation with integer variables has a very high complexity (generally double-exp). So the applicability of these methods is somewhat limited.

In this paper, we investigate the use of acceleration methods in LRA, *in complement to widening*. Of course, when the effect of a loop can be computed exactly (and at low cost) there is no need to approximate it. Now, since we want to integrate these results in LRA, only the exact *abstract* effect of the loop is necessary, that is the *convex hull* of the reachable states during or after the loop. This means that we won't use expensive computations in Presburger arithmetic. Moreover, we only look for an improvement of standard LRA: wherever an acceleration is possible, its application will improve the results, but the resulting method will not be restricted to those programs where acceleration applies everywhere.

To illustrate our goal better, let us consider a very simple example, the classical "leaking gas burner" [CHR91]: one wants to model and analyze the assumption that, whenever the "gas burner" leaks, the leakage is fixed within 10 seconds, and that the minimum interval between two leakages is 50 seconds. The standard modelling of this system is by a linear hybrid automaton [ACH+95, HHWT97] (see Fig. 1). The linear relation analysis of this hybrid automaton proceeds as follows (the successive results are projected onto the variables t and ℓ, which represent, respectively, the global time elapsed and the global leaking time, the variable u being a local variable used to count the time elapsed in each location):

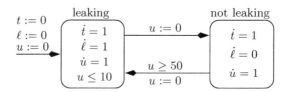

Fig. 1. Hybrid automaton of the gas burner

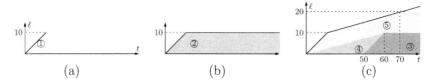

Fig. 2. Analysis of the hybrid gas burner

At first step, the location "leaking" is reached with the single point $\{t = \ell = 0\}$, and the "time elapse" operator[1] gives the polyhedron $\{0 \le t = \ell \le 10\}$ (①, Fig. 2.a). So, the location "not leaking" is reached with $\{0 \le t = \ell \le 10\}$, and the "time elapse" operator provides $\{0 \le \ell \le 10, t \ge \ell\}$ (②, Fig.2.b). At step 2, the location "leaking" is reached back with $\{0 \le \ell \le 10, t \ge \ell + 50\}$, (③, Fig. 2. 2.c) the convex hull with $\{t = \ell = 0\}$, gives $\{0 \le \ell \le 10, t \ge 6\ell\}$ (④, Fig. 2.c), the "time elapse" provides $\{0 \le \ell \le 20, t \ge \ell, t \ge 6\ell - 50\}$, and the (standard) widening provides $\{0 \le \ell \le t, t \ge 6\ell - 50\}$ (⑤, Fig. 2.c), which is also the solution for "not leaking" and terminates the iteration with an optimal result: it is the convex hull of the reachable states in each location.

Now, let us consider a discrete version of the gas burner (Fig. 3). First, since there is a loop around each location, we must apply widening in each of them. Now, if we detail the computations, we get that for the L(eaking) location, initially $t = \ell = 0$, then $t = \ell = 1$ (with no contribution back from N(otleaking)), so the convex hull is $\{0 \le t = \ell \le 1\}$, and widening provides $\{0 \le t = \ell\}$. This is already a less precise result than in the continuous case. Further narrowing does not improve the result. To obtain better results, we should delay widening for at least 10 iterations (because of the constant 10 appearing in the problem). Of course, delaying widening in such a way is expensive; moreover it is rather ad hoc, and it would not work if the constant 10 was replaced by a symbolic parameter, say δ.

This example shows that the analysis of hybrid automata can be much more precise and efficient than the analysis of the corresponding discrete counter automata. The obvious reason is the availability of the "time elapse" operator, which plays the role of a specialized exact widening operation. One goal of the paper is to detect that the effect of the single loops in the counter automaton of

---

[1] Which computes the effect of letting the time pass in the location as long as the location invariant is true.

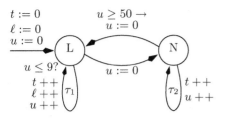

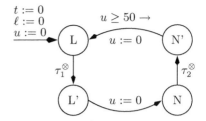

Fig. 3. Automaton of the gas burner   **Fig. 4.** "Accelerated" automaton

Fig. 3 can be computed exactly, so that these loops can be *subsumed by* single transitions, exactly as it is done by using the time elapse operator on hybrid automata. In other words, instead of analyzing the automaton of Fig. 3, we will apply the standard analysis to the automaton of Fig. 4, where $\tau_1^\otimes$, $\tau_2^\otimes$ denote the operations subsuming the effect of the two single loops in the initial automaton. In this standard analysis, the two single loops will be accelerated, but widening is still applied, e.g., in L, because of the remaining global loop.

The paper is organized as follows: after making our notations precise (Section 1), we consider first, in Section 2, the trivial case of a single loop where variables are just incremented with constants. Such a loop is called a *translation loop*. We can then formally define, in Section 3, the *abstract acceleration* we want to compute, which is a convex and dense closure of the exact reachable set. Then, in Section 4, we consider the case of several translation loops, and in Section 5, we deal with combinations of translations and assignments of constants. We conclude the paper with comparisons with related work, and some perspectives.

1   Definitions and Notations

Throughout the paper, n will denote the number of numerical variables, the numerical states will be considered as elements of the affine space $\mathbb{Q}^n$ [2].

Let us recall that a (closed convex) polyhedron in $\mathbb{Q}^n$ can be seen either as the set $\{x \in \mathbb{Q}^n \mid Ax \leq B\}$ of solutions of a system of *linear constraints* $Ax \leq B$ — where A is an $m \times n$ matrix, for some $m \geq 0$, and B is an m-vector — or as the convex hull

$$\{\sum_{v_i \in V} \lambda_i v_i + \sum_{r_j \in R} \mu_j r_j \mid \lambda_i, \mu_j \in \mathbb{Q}^+, \sum \lambda_i = 1\}$$

of a *system of generators* — i.e., a finite set $V \subset \mathbb{Q}^n$ of *vertices*, and a finite set $R \subset \mathbb{Q}^n$ of *rays*.

If $Ax \leq B$ is a system of constraints, we will often note simply $\{Ax \leq B\}$ the polyhedron of its solutions. If P is a polyhedron and $R \subset \mathbb{Q}^n$ is a finite set of vectors, we will note $P \nearrow R$ the polyhedron $\{x + \sum_{r_j \in R} \mu_j r_j \mid x \in P, \mu_j \in \mathbb{Q}^+\}$ obtained by adding to P all vectors in R as new rays.

---

[2] We consider $\mathbb{Q}$ for computational reasons.

2   A Simple Case: Single Translation Loops

We first consider the case of single loops, i.e., single paths in the program control-flow graph looping back to a control point. We consider such a single path as a guarded command $g \rightarrow a$, where g is a condition on numerical variables, and a is a transformation of numerical variables. As usual in LRA, we restrict[3] ourselves to linear conditions $(g(x) \Leftrightarrow Ax \leq B)$ and linear transformations (say $x := Cx + D$, where C is an $n \times n$ matrix, D is an n-vector). Let τ be the corresponding function: $\tau(x) = $ if $Ax \leq B$ then $Cx + D$ else x. We want to build the corresponding polyhedra transformer, i.e., to be able to compute the image P of a polyhedron P_0 by an arbitrary number of applications of τ:

$$x \in P \;\Leftrightarrow\; \exists i \in \mathbb{N}, \; \exists x_0 \in P_0, \; x = \tau^i(x_0)$$

i.e., if we define the sequence (x_k) by $x_k = C^k x_0 + \sum_{j=0}^{k-1} C^j D$:

$$x \in P \;\Leftrightarrow\; \exists i \in \mathbb{N}, \exists x_0 \in P_0, \forall j \in [0, i-1], Ax_j \leq B, \text{ and } x = x_i$$

In general, obtaining a general expression for C^k is too expensive, and the quantification over i and j cannot be computed. So, let us look at some cases where the computation is possible; in such cases, the loop will be said to be *accelerable*:

- [Tiw04] considers the same kind of loops, and shows that their termination is decidable. The method uses algebraic characterisation of the C matrix, but does not provide any loop invariant.
- In [FL02], the linear functions $\lambda x.Cx + D$ such that the cardinal of $\{C^k, k \in \mathbb{N}\}$ is finite is pointed out to be a class that is accelerable. But the upper-bound that is given is too large, and as far as we know, the complexity of the problem of finding whether a monoid generated by a (set of) matrix is finite or not is an open problem (it is known to be decidable [Hal97]).
- The case where $C^2 = C$ is interesting, since it covers the loops which increment or decrement variables by constants, and/or set variables to constants.
- The simplest case is when $C = \mathrm{Id}$, i.e., when all variables are incremented or decremented by constants. We call such loops *translation loops* and we first consider this simple case.

In the case of a translation loop, we get simply $x_k = x_0 + kD$ and

$$x \in P \;\Leftrightarrow\; \exists i \in \mathbb{N}, \exists x_0 \in P_0, \forall j \in [0, i-1], A(x_0 + jD) \leq B, \text{ and } x = x_0 + iD$$

By convexity, the condition $\forall j \in [0, i-1], A(x_0 + jD) \leq B$ reduces to $Ax_0 \leq B \wedge A(x - D) \leq B$. Adding an arbitrary positive number of D is just adding D as a ray. Finally, we get:

$$P = \Big((P_0 \cap \{Ax \leq B\}) \nearrow \{D\}\Big) \cap \{A(x - D) \leq B\}$$

Remark 1. In the last expression, we have lost the points of the initial polyhedron P_0 that don't satisfy g. In the rest of the paper, without loss of generality, we

---

[3] Other cases are over-approximated.

assume that the initial polyhedron verifies the guard of the transition. If it is not the case, we first compute the intersection with the guard, and after all our computations, we make a convex hull with the initial polyhedron.

Example. This allows us to compute the effect of the two simple loops in the gas burner example (Fig. 3). Starting from $P_L^{(0)} = \{t = \ell = 0\}$, we first apply $\tau_1^\otimes$ as in Fig. 4 and get $P'^{(0)}_L = \{0 \le t = \ell \le 10\}$. Then, in location N, we have $P_N^{(0)} = \{0 \le t = \ell \le 10\}$ which is accelerated into $P'^{(0)}_N = \{0 \le \ell \le 10, \ell \le t\}$, and the transition back to L gives $Q = \{0 \le \ell \le 10, \ell + 50 \le t\}$, so[4]

$$P_L^{(1)} = P_L^{(0)} \nabla \left(P_L^{(0)} \sqcup Q \right) = \{t = \ell = 0\} \nabla \{0 \le \ell \le 10, 6\ell \le t\} = \{0 \le 6\ell \le t\}$$

Applying again $\tau_1^\otimes$, we get $P'^{(1)}_N = \{0 \le \ell \le t, 6\ell \le t - 50\}$ which is the correct limit .

3   Abstract Acceleration

We are now able to make our objective more precise: we want to precisely characterize, when possible, the effect of a loop on a polyhedron. Of course, with respect to the exact effect of the loop, we will have to take a convex hull. Moreover, we are faced with a problem of arithmetic, since the effect of a loop is obtained by applying k times its body *where k is an integer*. To avoid the complexity of exact arithmetic, we will perform, as usual, a dense approximation. To summarize, in the case of a simple translation loop, instead of computing the exact effect of the loop:

$$\tau^*(P_0) = \{x \mid \exists i \in \mathbb{N}, \exists x_0 \in P_0, \, g(x_0) \wedge g(x - D), \, x = x_0 + iD\} \cup P_0$$

we compute its *abstract acceleration*:

$$\tau^\otimes(P_0) = \bigsqcup \{x \mid \exists i \in \mathbb{Q}^+, \exists x_0 \in P_0, \, g(x_0) \wedge g(x - D), \, x = x_0 + iD\} \sqcup P_0$$

We now are able to prove the following proposition :

Proposition 1. *Let $\tau : Ax \le B \to x := Cx + D$. Then*

$$\tau^\otimes(P_0 \cap Ax \le B) = \left((P_0 \cap \{Ax \le B\}) \nearrow \{D\} \right) \cap \{A(x - D) \le B\}$$

Sketch of Proof: Let $P = \left((P_0 \cap \{Ax \le B\}) \nearrow \{D\} \right) \cap \{A(x - D) \le B\}$. Then

$$x \in P \Leftrightarrow \left(\exists i \in \mathbb{Q}^+, \exists x_0 \in (P_0 \cap \{Ax \le B\}), x = x_0 + iD \text{ and } A(x - D) \le B \right)$$
$$\Leftrightarrow x \in \tau^\otimes(P_0) \qquad\qquad\qquad \square$$

It is also useful to define the *rational* iteration of a translation loop :

Definition 1. *Let $i \in \mathbb{Q}^+$, then we note :*

$$\tau^i(P_0) = \{x \mid \exists x_0 \in P_0, x = x_0 + iD \wedge g(x_0) \wedge g(x - D)\}$$

---

[4] $\sqcup, \nabla$ respectively denote the convex hull and widening operators.

4 Two Translation Loops

In the presence of several translation loops, the situation becomes more complex. For instance, the control graph is not necessarily flat, and exact acceleration techniques no longer apply.

In order to separate the difficulties, we will first assume, at least conceptually, that the control graph is partitioned according to the combination of guards: in a given location, either both guards are satisfied, or only one or the other is satisfied. Once this partitioning is performed, we are left with the problem of accelerating the loops *as long as both guards are satisfied*.

Let us note $\tau^{\otimes}_{1,2}(P_0)$ the image of an initial polyhedron P_0 by two translation loops $\tau_i : g_i \to x := x + D_i$, $(i = 1, 2)$ as long as $g_1 \wedge g_2$ is satisfied. It is made of all the points x that can be reached from $P_0 \cap g_1 \cap g_2$ by successive rational applications of τ_1 and τ_2 and staying in $g_1 \cap g_2$:

$$x \in \tau^{\otimes}_{1,2}(P_0) \text{ iff } \exists x_0 \in P_0 \cap g_1 \cap g_2,$$
$$\exists x_1, x_2 \ldots, x_\ell \in g_1 \cap g_2, \exists x'_1, x'_2 \ldots, x'_\ell \in g_1 \cap g_2,$$
$$\exists i_1, i_2, \ldots, i_\ell, i'_1, i'_2, \ldots, i'_\ell \in \mathbb{Q}^+,$$
$$\text{such that } x = x'_\ell, \text{ and } x_j = \tau_1^{i_j}(x'_{j-1}), x'_j = \tau_2^{i'_j}(x_j), j = 1..\ell$$

The following proposition gives a way of computing $\tau^{\otimes}_{1,2}(P_0)$:

Proposition 2. *Let τ_i be $g_i \to x := x + D_i$, $(i = 1, 2)$ then,*
- *if $\exists x_0 \in P_0 \cap g_1 \cap g_2$, $\exists \varepsilon > 0$ such that either $x_0 + \varepsilon D_1 \in g_1 \cap g_2$ or $x_0 + \varepsilon D_2 \in g_1 \cap g_2$ (i.e., there is at least one point in P_0 where at least one transition can be "rationally" applied and stay in $g_1 \cap g_2$), then*

$$\tau^{\otimes}_{1,2}(P_0) = ((P_0 \cap g_1 \cap g_2) \nearrow \{D_1, D_2\}) \cap g_1 \cap g_2$$

- *otherwise, $\tau^{\otimes}_{1,2}(P_0) = P_0 \cap g_1 \cap g_2$*

Remark 2. The first condition on $P_0 \cap g_1 \cap g_2$ comes from the fact that the rational application of τ_1 or τ_2 must be initialised. This condition is usually obvious to check (as in the example below), and can anyway be reduced to a Linear Programming problem.

Of course, we don't really partition the control graph, which would involve a combinational explosion in the presence of several loops. But, if we use the combined acceleration computed as in Proposition 2, we compute the (approximate) solution of $P = P_0 \sqcup \tau^{\otimes}_{1,2}(P) \sqcup \tau^{\otimes}_1(P) \sqcup \tau^{\otimes}_2(P)$ using widening if necessary. It often happens that $P_0 \sqcup \tau^{\otimes}_{1,2}(P_0) \sqcup \tau^{\otimes}_1(\tau^{\otimes}_{1,2}(P_0)) \sqcup \tau^{\otimes}_2(\tau^{\otimes}_{1,2}(P_0))$ is a (post-) fixpoint, and that widening does not have to be used. Of course, this is one strategy among others, but it gives good experimental results. We could also compute for example the set $P_0 \sqcup \tau^{\otimes}_{1,2}(P_0) \sqcup \tau^{\otimes}_2(\tau^{\otimes}_1(P_0)) \sqcup \tau^{\otimes}_1(\tau^{\otimes}_2(P_0))$, or other combinations (like, e.g., in Fast [BFLP03]).

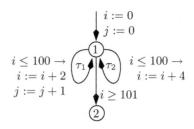

```
i := j := 0;
while (1) i <= 100 do
    if ... then i:=i+2; j:=j+1;
    else i:=i+4;
end
(2)
```

Fig. 5. The program

Fig. 6. The associated CFG

Example. As a very simple application, we can now deal with the old basic example of [Hal79] without using any widening:

In the "program" of Fig 5, we abstract the "if-then-else" statement by the non-deterministic choice of two simple loops around the control point number 1, getting the control graph of figure 6. Applying our result (the two transition can be applied), we first compute $\tau^{\otimes}_{1,2}(\{i = j = 0\}) = \{(0,0)\} \nearrow \{(2,1),(4,0)\} \cap \{i \leq 100\} = \{0 \leq 2j \leq i \leq 100\}$. Then we compute :

- $\tau^{\otimes}_1(\tau^{\otimes}_{1,2}(P_0)) = \{2j \geq 2, 2j \leq i, i \leq 102\}$
- $\tau^{\otimes}_2(\tau^{\otimes}_{1,2}(P_0)) = \{2j \geq 0, 2j < i \leq 104\}$
- The convex hull of the three polyhedra, $\{0 \leq 2j \leq i, i \leq 104, i + 2j \leq 204\}$.

This last set is stable by the application of τ_1 or τ_2, so the convergence is reached and we can propagate the obtained result to location 2, where we get: $\{0 \leq 2j \leq i, 101 \leq i \leq 104, i + 2j \leq 204\}$.

5   Combining Translation and Reset

The next case that we will consider is the combination of translation loops with loops where some variables are set to constants. Without loss of generality, we assume that these variables are simply reset to 0. This situation and the corresponding notations are represented in Fig. 7: we assume $x = (y, z)$; in the first loop, all the variables are translated, while in the second one, only the variables y are translated and the variables z are set to 0. We will consider simple cases first.

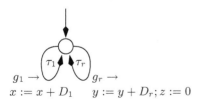

Fig. 7. Transition and reset loops

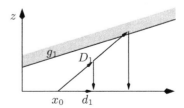

Fig. 8. Complete reset

5.1 Complete Reset

A first simple case is when the second loop performs only resetting, i.e., when $D_r = 0$. Let us note $d_1 = D_1 \downarrow [z = 0]$ the projection of D_1 on the subspace $z = 0$. We assume also that $g_r = true$. Then, the evolution of variables from a point x_0 can be represented in the plane (D_1, d_1) as in Fig. 8 (in this figure, $x_0 \nearrow \{D_1\}$ intersects g_1, but otherwise, the same expression is still valid). In this case, we obviously have:

Proposition 3. *If* $\tau_1 : g_1 \rightarrow x := x + D_1$ *and* $\tau_2 : true \rightarrow z := 0$ *then:*

$$(\tau_1 + \tau_r)^{\otimes}(P_0) = P_0 \nearrow \{D_1, d_1\} \cap g_1(x - D_1)$$

Sketch of Proof : First let us remark that $\tau_r^* = \tau_r$ (τ_r is only a projection).

- $\subseteq$: If $x \in (\tau_1 + \tau_r)^*(x_0)$ (the exact computation), then there has been a succession of τ_1 and τ_r, that can be summarized by the following chain (the i_j are in $\mathbb{N}$) :

$$x_0 \begin{pmatrix} y_0 \\ 0 \end{pmatrix} \rightarrow^{\tau_1^{i_1}} x_0 + i_1 D_1 \rightarrow^{\tau_r} \begin{pmatrix} y_0 + i_1 d_1 \\ 0 \end{pmatrix} \rightarrow^{\tau_1^{i_2}} x_0 + (i_1 + i_2) D_1$$

$$\rightarrow^{\tau_r} \begin{pmatrix} y_0 + (i_1 + i_2) d_1 \\ 0 \end{pmatrix} \rightarrow \ldots$$

So if the chain ends with a τ_r, then there exists $I_1 \in \mathbb{N}$ such that $x = x_0 + I_1 d_1$ and $g_1(x - D_1)$ (it comes from the fact we have $g_1(x_0 + (I_1 - 1)D_1)$). If the chains ends with an iteration of τ_1, then $x = x_0 + I_1 d_1 + I_2 D_1$, with $g(x - D_1)$. As the abstract acceleration is the relaxation of the exact computation, we are done.
- $\supseteq$: If $x = x_0 + I_1 d_1 + I_2 D_1$ and $g_1(x - D_1)$, then we can obtain the point x by applying the following "rational" chain : $x = \tau_1^{I_2}\left((\tau_r(\tau_1(x_0)))^{I_1}\right)$. Indeed, any application of τ_1 followed by an application of τ_r from an initial point $x_0 = (y_0, 0)$ leads to the point $(y_0 + d_1, 0)$, which allows us to define the rational alternation of τ_r and τ_1 as if it were an application of a single translation of vector d_1. So applying I_1 times (possibly 0) this alternation, we obtain the point $(y_0 + I_1 d_1, 0)$. Then we end by applying $\tau_2^{I_2}$.   □

This simple case generalizes naturally:
- for $D_r \neq 0$, if D_r belongs to the plane (D_1, d_1)
- for $g_r \neq true$ if $\{x_0\} \nearrow \{D_1\} \cap g_1$ intersects g_r.

Remark 3. Notice that we can easily produce reachable domains that cannot be described by Presburger formulas, as shown by the figures 9 and 10 (where the exact set is $\exists k \geq 0, (2^{k-1} - 1 \leq x \leq 2^k - 1 \wedge z \geq 0 \wedge x \geq 2z - 1))$, which means that standard exact acceleration techniques cannot work. In this case, the previous proposition leads to the abstract acceleration : $\{x \geq z \geq 0, x \geq 2z - 1\}$.

5.2 Partial Reset

Now, we consider the case when $D_r \neq 0$ does not belong to the plane (D_1, d_1) (i.e., there are variables which are incremented in the second loop, while being unchanged by the first loop). As before, we assume that $g_r = true$, but we also

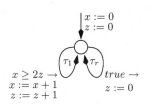

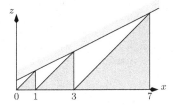

Fig. 9. The CFG   **Fig. 10.** The corresponding behaviour

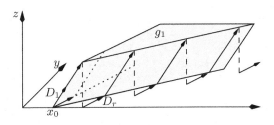

Fig. 11. Partial reset

assume that g_1 is of the form $z \leq K$, i.e., is parallel to the hyperplane $z = 0$ (see Remark 5 about this restriction). Moreover, we consider an initial polyhedron P_0 included in the hyperplane $z = 0$. Now, the variables can evolve from a point x_0 as shown on Fig. 11.

From x_0, τ_1 can be applied at most, say, k_{max} times, where k_{max} is the minimum over all reset variables z_i of the expressions $\lfloor K_{z_i}/D_{1z_i} + 1 \rfloor$, which we denote $k_{max} = \lfloor K/D_{1z} + 1 \rfloor^5$. At any time meanwhile, τ_r can occur, resetting z and translating the result according to D_r in the plane $\{z = 0\}$. So, after some applications of τ_1 followed by one application of τ_r, we have $x = x_0 + kd_1 + D_r$, where $d_1 = D_1 \downarrow [z = 0]$ as before, and $0 \leq k \leq k_{max}$. Then from any such x, the same transformation can occur. One can easily show that the resulting domain is given by the following proposition:

Proposition 4. Let τ_1 be of the form $(z \leq K) \rightarrow x := x + D_1$ and τ_r be true $\rightarrow y := y + D_{ry}; z := 0$. Let $P_0 \subset \{z = 0\}$. Let $u_z = (0, \ldots, 0, 1, \ldots 1)$ where we have $1s$ for the z components, and 0 elsewhere. Let $d_1 = D_1 \downarrow [z = 0]$ and $D_r = \begin{pmatrix} D_{ry} \\ 0 \end{pmatrix}$. Then:

- if $D_1 \cdot u_z < 0$ then $(\tau_1 + \tau_r)^{\otimes}(P_0) = P_0 \nearrow \{D_1, d_1, D_r\}$
- else, let $k_{max} = \lfloor K/D_{1z} + 1 \rfloor$, we have:
$$(\tau_1 + \tau_r)^{\otimes}(P_0) = P_0 \nearrow \{D_1, D_r, k_{max}d_1 + D_r\} \cap g_1(x - D_1)$$

Remark 4. The scalar product $D_1 \cdot u_z$ characterizes whether or not $P_0 \nearrow \{D_1\}$ intersects g_1.

---

[5] Notice that, here, we precisely take arithmetic into account, since it can be done at reasonable cost.

Sketch of Proof : Without loss of generality, we can assume that each time we apply τ_r^i or τ_1^i, we have $i > 0$.

- In the first case, $P_0 \nearrow \{D_1\}$ does not intersect g_1. It means that the guard g_1 is always satisfied :

$$x_0 \xrightarrow{\tau_1^{i_1}} \xrightarrow{\tau_r^{i_1'}} x_0 + i_1 d_1 + i_1' D_r \xrightarrow{\tau_1^{i_2}} \xrightarrow{\tau_r^{i_2'}} x_0 + (i_1 + i_2)d_1 + (i_1' + i_2')D_r \rightarrow \dots$$

Then if the chain ends with some τ_r, $x = x_0 + Id_1 + I'D_r$ (in particular, $z = 0$). If the chain ends with some τ_1, we obtain $x = x_0 + Id_1 + I'D_r + I''D_1$, with no bound for I, I', I''.

- In the second case, the number of iteration of τ_1 following one (or more) application(s) of τ_r is at most k_{max}. We write a similar chain, except that we have the property $\forall j, 0 \le i_j \le k^{max}$. If the chains ends with τ_r^+, we obtain $x = x_0 + (i_1 + i_2 + \dots + i_n)d_1 + (i_1' + \dots + i_n')D_r$. Let $I = i_1 + i_2 + \dots + i_n$. Taking the Euclidean division of I by k_{max}, we get $I = qk_{max} + r$ with $r \le k_{max}$ and $q \le n$. Then $x = x_0 + (q.k_max + r_1)d_1 + (q + r_2)D_r$ with $r_1, r_2 \ge 0$, and finally $x = x_0 + q(k_{max}d_1 + D_r) + r_1 d_1 + r_2 D_r$, which is the good form. x also satisfied $g_1(x - D_1)$ because all the plane $\{z = 0\}$ satisfy g_1, and $-D_1$ moves away x from the guard g_1.

  If the chains ends with τ_1^*, we add some $i_{n+1}D_1$, but we must satisfy g_1 before the last but one application, hence $g_1(x - D_1)$.

These arguments justify the left-to-the right inclusions. The proof of the two other inclusions are very similar to the proof of Proposition 4. □

Example. We consider a very simple reactive program [HPR97], supposed to model a speedometer under the assumption that the speed is less than 4 meters/second: the speedometer perceives either an elapsed second from some clock, in which case the time t is incremented while the instantaneous speed s (which counts the number of meters occurring during each second) is reset to 0, or a

```
t := d := s := 0 ;
while true do
1:  if second then
        t := t+1 ; s:= 0 ;
    else if meter and s<=3 then
        d := d+1 ; s := s+1 ;
end
```

"meter" sensor, in which case both the distance d and the instantaneous speed s are incremented; this "meter" event can only occur when $s \le 3$, because of the assumption on the speed.

With the notations of Fig. 7, we have $x = (t, d, s), y = (t, d), z = (s), u_z = (0, 0, 1)$, $g_1 = (s \le 3)$, $D_1 = (0, 1, 1)$, $D_r = (1, 0, 0)$, and $x_0 = (0, 0, 0)$. We have $u_z \cdot D_1 = 1 \ge 0$ hence we compute $k_{max} = 4$ and $d_1 = (0, 1, 0)$, so $k_{max}d_1 + D_r = (1, 4, 0)$, and finally:

$$(\tau_1 + \tau_r)^\otimes(x_0) = (0, 0, 0) \nearrow \{(0, 1, 1), (1, 0, 0), (1, 4, 0)\} \cap \{s \le 4\}$$
$$= \{t \ge 0, 0 \le s \le 4, 0 \le d \le 4t + s)\}$$

so we get at once the precise result, which is not easy to obtain with widening (in [HPR97], we needed 3 iterations, and a "limited widening").

Remark 5. If the guard is not of the form $z \leq K$, the behaviour can be non linear. In the following example, one border of the reachable domain is a parabola:

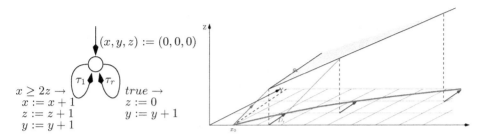

Fig. 12. The CFG	**Fig. 13.** The corresponding behaviour

5.3 Weakening the Assumptions

The previously considered case may appear quite specific. However, we can easily suppress or alleviate some of our assumptions:

- If P_0 is not included in $\{z = 0\}$, first compute $P_0' = \tau_r(\tau_1^{\otimes}(P_0))$, which is included in $\{z = 0\}$ (since it results from an application of τ_r).
- We can extend Proposition 4 in order to take into account a guard of the form $z \bowtie K_r$ ($\bowtie \in \{\leq, =, \geq\}$) for the second loop, using Proposition 5 below.
- Finally, Section 5.4 will give an example of using these results to combine a reset loop with more than one translation loop.

Proposition 5. *Let τ_1, τ_r be respectively of the form:*

$$\tau_1 : (z \leq K_1) \rightarrow x := x + D_1 \text{ and } \tau_r : (z \bowtie K_r) \rightarrow y := y + D_r; z := 0$$

where $\bowtie \in \{\leq, =, \geq\}$. Assume $P_0 \subset \{z = 0\}$ and $K_1 > 0$ and $D_1 \cdot u_z > 0$. Let us note $k_{max1} = \lfloor K_1/D_{1z} + 1 \rfloor$, $d_1 = D_1 \downarrow [z = 0]$, and $k_{maxr} = \lfloor K_r/D_{1z} + 1 \rfloor$. Then:

- *if $\bowtie$ is "$\leq$" then*
  - *if $K_r < 0$ then (τ_r never applies)*
    $$(\tau_1 + \tau_r)^{\otimes}(P_0) = P_0 \nearrow \{D_1\} \cap g_1(x - D_1)$$
  - *if $K_r > K_1$ then*
    $$(\tau_1 + \tau_r)^{\otimes}(P_0) = P_0 \nearrow \{D_1, D_r, D_r + k_{max1}d_1\} \cap g_1(x - D_1)$$
  - *if $K_1 \geq K_r > 0$ then*
    $$(\tau_1 + \tau_r)^{\otimes}(P_0) = P_0 \nearrow \{D_1, D_r, D_r + k_{maxr}d_1\} \cap g_1(x - D_1)$$
- *if $\bowtie$ is "=" then*
  - *if $K_1 \geq K_r > 0$ and $\exists k, K_r = kD_1z$ then*
    $$(\tau_1 + \tau_r)^{\otimes}(P_0) = P_0 \nearrow \{D_1, D_r + kd_1\} \cap g_1(x - D_1)$$

- *else (τ_r never applies)*
$$(\tau_1 + \tau_r)^{\otimes}(P_0) = P_0 \nearrow \{D_1\} \cap g_1(x - D_1)$$
- *if $\bowtie$ is "$\geq$" then*
  - *if $K_r > K_1$ and $K_r > 0$ then (τ_r never applies)*
  $$(\tau_1 + \tau_r)^{\otimes}(P_0) = P_0 \nearrow \{D_1\} \cap g_1(x - D_1)$$
  - *if $K_1 \geq K_r \geq 0$, then*
  $$(\tau_1 + \tau_r)^{\otimes}(P_0) = P_0 \nearrow \{D_1, D_r + k_{max1}d_1, D_r + k_{maxr}d_1\} \cap g_1(x - D_1)$$
  - *if $K_r < 0$ then*
  $$(\tau_1 + \tau_r)^{\otimes}(P_0) = P_0 \nearrow \{D_1, D_r, D_r + k_{max1}d_1\} \cap g_1(x - D_1)$$

Remark 6. If $D_1 \cdot u_z < 0$ under the same assumptions as in Proposition 5, g_1 is always true, and we easily get: $(\tau_1 + \tau_r)^{\otimes}(P_0) = P_0 \nearrow \{D_1, d_1, D_r\}$

Sketch of Proof : The demonstration is mostly like the preceding one, except that we take the second guard into account. In particular, if the second guard is of the form $z = K_2$, then we must check whether or not the *real* set $\{x + iD_1, i \in \mathbb{N}\}$ intersects g_2. □

Remark 7. Because $g_1 = x \leq K_1$ and $P_0 \subset \{z = 0\}$, the successive images of any point $x_0 \in P_0$ are $\{x_0 + kD_1 \mid 0 \leq k \leq k_{max}\}$ with k_{max} independent of x_0. Let us consider the ray $D_r + k_{max}d_1$ of Proposition 4. If we had an algorithm to compute directly $\sqcup \tau_1^*(x_0)$ (the polyhedron representing the convex hull of the exact computation of all $x_0 + kD_1$, with $0 \leq k \leq k_{max1}$), the Proposition 4 ensures that we can use the following algorithm to compute $D_r + k_{max}d_1$ (in this case, the two algorithms are equivalent):

1. Select one point $x_0 \in P_0$.
2. Compute the segment $S = [x_0, x_0^M] = \sqcup \tau_1^*(x_0)$ (exact computation).
3. Compute $D_r + k_{max}d_1 = \tau_r(x_0^M) - x_0$.

Now, in Proposition 5, if we want to compute the rays $D_r + k_{max1}d_1$ and $D_r + k_{maxr}d_1$ (when necessary), we must obtain (if they exist) the "real" points of the set $S \cap g_r$ (i.e., the points that are reachable with τ_1 in i steps where $i \in \mathbb{N}$). Notice that we get an algorithm that does not care about the relative values of K_1 and K_r. Notice also that the extremal points of $S \cap g_r$ can sometimes be computed directly if all the D_{1z_i} belong to $\{-1, 0, 1\}$, because the successive images of x_0 are points with integer coordinates. We will apply this remark in the example below.

5.4   An Example with More Translation Loops and Resets

We saw in the previous paragraph that the key property of τ_1 (the unique translation loop) is that the number of its iterations when $z = 0$ is bounded by a constant k_{max1}. Let us now consider the case of two translation loops τ_1 and τ_2 combined with a reset loop $\tau_r : z \leq K_r \rightarrow y := y + D_r, z := 0$.

If we had a similar bound property for $(\tau_1 + \tau_2)$, we could have a similar expression for $(\tau_1 + \tau_2 + \tau_r)^{\otimes}$. It is the case if both of the two guards g_1 and g_2 only constrain variables in z. This condition guarantees that all points in $\{z = 0\}$ have "parallel futures".

Yet another gas burner example: We consider a modified version of the gas burner example, where it is only assumed that, in each consecutive 60-second interval, the cumulated leaking time is at most 10 seconds. A new variable v must be introduced to count the cumulated leaking time since the last time u has been reset to zero (see Fig 14). Now, we adapt the algorithm of the previous section :

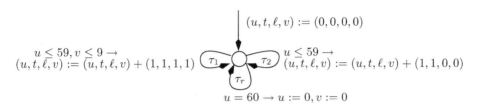

$$(u, t, \ell, v) := (0, 0, 0, 0)$$

$$u \leq 59, v \leq 9 \rightarrow$$
$$(u, t, \ell, v) := (u, t, \ell, v) + (1, 1, 1, 1)$$

$$u \leq 59 \rightarrow$$
$$(u, t, \ell, v) := (u, t, \ell, v) + (1, 1, 0, 0)$$

$$u = 60 \rightarrow u := 0, v := 0$$

Fig. 14. A more complex version of the gas burner

- **Step 1.** At the beginning, the polyhedron associated with the control point is $P^{(0)} = \{u = t = \ell = v = 0\}$. We first compute $(\tau_1 + \tau_2)^{\otimes}(P^{(0)})$, applying the strategy given in Section 4 : $\tau_{12}^{\otimes}(P^{(0)}) = (0, 0, 0, 0) \nearrow \{(1, 1, 1, 1); (1, 1, 0, 0)\} \cap \{u \leq 59; v \leq 9\} = \{0 \leq \ell = v \leq 10; \ell \leq u = t \leq 59\};$ $\tau_1^{\otimes}(\tau_{12}^{\otimes}(P^{(0)})) = \{\ell \leq t, u = t \leq 60, 0 \leq v = \ell \leq 10\}; \tau_2^{\otimes}(\tau_{12}^{\otimes}(P^{(0)})) = \tau_1^{\otimes}(\tau_{12}^{\otimes}(P^{(0)}))$, so finally we get the exact set $(\tau_1 + \tau_2)^{\otimes}(P^{(0)}) = \{\ell \leq t, u = t \leq 60, 0 \leq v = \ell \leq 10\}$.
- Then, we intersect this last set with $g_r = \{u = 60\}^6$, and we get the extremal points $(60, 60, 10, 10)$ and $(60, 60, 0, 0)$, thus $r_1 = \tau_r(60, 60, 10, 10) - (0, 0, 0, 0) = (0, 60, 10, 0)$ and $r_2 = (0, 60, 0, 0)$, Then, $P^{(1)} = (\tau_1 + \tau_2)^{\otimes}(P^{(0)}) \nearrow \{(0, 60, 10, 0), (0, 60, 0, 0)\} \cap \{u \leq 60; v \leq 10\} = \{v \leq \ell, u \leq 60, 0 \leq v \leq 10, v \leq u, u + 6\ell \leq t + 6v\}$.
- **Step 2.** We compute $P^{(2)} = (\tau_1 + \tau_2)^{\otimes}(P^{(1)})$ with the same method, replacing $P^{(0)}$ by $P^{(1)}$. We quickly remark that $(\tau_1 + \tau_2)^{\otimes}(P^{(2)}) \subseteq P^{(2)}, \tau_1^{\otimes}(P^{(2)}) \subseteq P^{(2)}, \tau_2^{\otimes}(P^{(2)}) \subseteq P_2$, hence we get the invariant:[7] $\{v \leq \ell, u \leq 60, 0 \leq v \leq 10, v \leq u, u + 6\ell \leq t + 6v\}$, whose projection on $\{t, \ell\}$ gives $\{0 \leq \ell \leq t, 6\ell \leq t + 50\}$.

6 Related Work and Conclusion

This work is a new attempt at decreasing the imprecision due to the widening in Linear Relation Analysis. The initial widening operator of [CH78] was promptly improved in [Hal79], which proposed the operator often called "standard widening". More recently, [BHRZ03] proposed several ways of improving the standard widening, in the sense that the result of *a single application* of the new operators

---

[6] Here it is not necessary to bother about arithmetic, because our actions are just incrementations, see Remark 7.

[7] We are sure that we have the exact one because we have no loss of precision due to arithmetic.

is guaranteed to be smaller than the one computed with the standard widening. Although these new operators seem to be really better in practice — in the sense that, in many cases they provide more precise limits without significant loss of performance —, there are counterexamples (like the speedometer of Section 5.2) showing that it is not always the case. [GR06] is a nice attempt to improve the precision by carefully alternating increasing widened sequences and descending (possibly narrowed) sequences. The approach has more general applications than Linear Relation Analysis, but could be combined with ours for LRA.

Instead of improving widening, we tried to complement it with some kind of acceleration, whenever possible. The essential difference between acceleration and widening is that widening is only based on the successive results of the abstract semantics of the program (i.e., x_n and $f(x_n)$ are used to compute $x_{n+1} = x_n \nabla f(x_n)$), while acceleration looks at the function f itself to build f^*. Among the techniques that take the abstract function into account, one can mention the "widening with thresholds" [BCC+03] or "widening upto" [HPR97], where the conditions involving a loop exit are used to limit the extrapolation.

Of course, we were strongly inspired by exact acceleration techniques [BW94, WB98, CJ98, FS00, BFLP03]. However, we don't want to pay the price of exact computations, and we want to obtain general analysis techniques. So, we use only an *abstract* acceleration, keeping the polyhedral approximation, and we still combine it with usual widening, to preserve the generality of the method. In [SW04], a class of programs is identified for which the abstract solution of the abstract semantics *in the lattice of intervals* can be computed exactly, without widening. Our goals are similar, but in the richer and more complex lattice of polyhedra. The closest approach to ours is probably the one applied in PIPS [IJT91, Iri05]. First, in this work, the abstract function is naturally taken into account, because PIPS applies a modular relational analysis — i.e., it computes the relation between initial and final values of variables of a program fragment. Then, a kind of abstract acceleration is applied, based on discrete differentiation and integration. However, this technique is not combined with widening, which is not used in PIPS.

When our abstract acceleration applies alone, it is guaranteed to provide better results than widening — in fact, it provides the best possible results in term of polyhedra. Used in combination with widening, it generally improves the precision of the analysis — we don't have any counterexample so far — because it precisely foresees some future behaviors. In spite of apparently strong hypotheses, the abstract acceleration applies quite often in programs with counters, and our first experiments show significant improvements, both in precision and in performance.

A very first implementation of our technique is available. The detection of accelerable loops is not very elaborate, for the time being: the strongly connected subcomponents (SCSC) of the control graph are identified using Bourdoncle's classical extension [Bou92] of Tarjan algorithm [Tar72]. Then the SCSC are considered bottom-up (starting from the deepest ones): in each of them the paths looping around the input node are checked w.r.t. our acceleration criteria, and possibly replaced by meta-transitions [Boi99]. Of course, since the number of such paths can be large, we are not obliged to consider all of them.

Future work include of course further experiments of the proposed techniques, which are also likely to be extended towards more general cases. In particular, loops which may exchange values between variables could be considered.

References

[ACH+95] R. Alur, C. Courcoubetis, N. Halbwachs, T. Henzinger, P. Ho, X. Nicollin, A. Olivero, J. Sifakis, and S. Yovine. The algorithmic analysis of hybrid systems. *Theoretical Computer Science B*, 138:3–34, January 1995.

[BBC+00] N. Bjorner, A. Browne, M. Colon, B. Finkbeiner, Z. Manna, H. Sipma, and T. Uribe. Verifying temporal properties of reactive systems: A STeP tutorial. *Formal Methods in System Design*, 16:227–270, 2000.

[BBM97]   N. Bjorner, I. Anca Browne, and Z. Manna. Automatic generation of invariants and intermediate assertions. *Theoretical Computer Science*, 173(1):49–87, February 1997.

[BCC+03] B. Blanchet, P. Cousot, R. Cousot, J. Feret, L. Mauborgne, A. Miné, D. Monniaux, and X. Rival. A static analyzer for large safety-critical software. In *PLDI 2003, ACM SIGPLAN SIGSOFT Conference on Programming Language Design and Implementation*, pages 196–207, San Diego (Ca.), June 2003.

[BFLP03] S. Bardin, A. Finkel, J. Leroux, and L. Petrucci. Fast: Fast acceleration of symbolic transition systems. In *CAV'03*, pages 118–121, Boulder (Colorado), July 2003. LNCS 2725, Springer-Verlag.

[BHRZ03] R. Bagnara, P. M. Hill, E. Ricci, and E. Zaffanella. Precise widening operators for convex polyhedra. In R. Cousot, editor, *Static Analysis: Proceedings of the 10th International Symposium*, volume 2694 of *Lecture Notes in Computer Science*, pages 337–354, San Diego, California, USA, 2003. Springer-Verlag, Berlin.

[Boi99]   B. Boigelot. Symbolic methods for exploring infinite state spaces. Phd thesis, Université de Liège, 1999.

[Bou92]   F. Bourdoncle. Sémantique des langages impératifs d'ordre supérieur et interprétation abstraite. Thesis Ecole Polytechnique, Paris, 1992.

[BW94]   B. Boigelot and P. Wolper. Symbolic verification with periodic sets. In *CAV'94*, Stanford (Ca.), 1994. LNCS 818, Springer Verlag.

[CC77]   P. Cousot and R. Cousot. Abstract interpretation: a unified lattice model for static analysis of programs by construction or approximation of fixpoints. In *4th ACM Symposium on Principles of Programming Languages, POPL'77*, Los Angeles, January 1977.

[CH78]   P. Cousot and N. Halbwachs. Automatic discovery of linear restraints among variables of a program. In *5th ACM Symposium on Principles of Programming Languages, POPL'78*, Tucson (Arizona), January 1978.

[CHR91]   Z. Chaochen, C.A.R. Hoare, and A.P. Ravn. A calculus of durations. *Information Processing Letters*, 40(5), 1991.

[CJ98]   H. Comon and Y. Jurski. Multiple counters automata, safety analysis and Presburger arithmetic. In *CAV'98*, Vancouver (B.C.), 1998. LNCS 1427, Springer Verlag.

[DRS01]   N. Dor, M. Rodeh, and M. Sagiv. Cleanness checking of string manipu-
          lations in C programs via integer analysis. In P. Cousot, editor, *SAS'01*,
          Paris, July 2001. LNCS 2126.
[FL02]   A. Finkel and J. Leroux. How to compose Presburger-accelerations: Ap-
          plications to broadcast protocols. In *Proceedings of the 22nd Conf. Found.
          of Software Technology and Theor. Comp. Sci. (FSTTCS'2002)*, volume
          2556 of *Lecture Notes in Computer Science*, pages 145–156, Kanpur, In-
          dia, December 2002. Springer.
[FS00]   A. Finkel and G. Sutre. An algorithm constructing the semilinear post* for
          2-dim reset/transfer vass. In *25th Int. Symp. Math. Found. Comp. Sci.
          (MFCS'2000)*, Bratislava, Slovakia, August 2000. LNCS 1893, Springer
          Verlag.
[GR06]   D. Gopan and T. Reps. Lookahead widening. In *CAV'06*, Seattle, 2006.
[Hal79]   N. Halbwachs. Détermination automatique de relations linéaires vérifiées
          par les variables d'un programme. Thèse de troisième cycle, University of
          Grenoble, March 1979.
[Hal97]   Vesa Halava. Decidable and undecidable problems in matrix theory. Tech-
          nical Report TUCS-TR-127, University of Turku, 30, 1997.
[HHWT97] T. A. Henzinger, P.-H. Ho, and H. Wong-Toi. Hytech: A model checker
          for hybrid systems. *Software Tools for Technology Transfer*, 1:110–122,
          1997.
[HPR97]   N. Halbwachs, Y.E. Proy, and P. Roumanoff. Verification of real-time
          systems using linear relation analysis. *Formal Methods in System Design*,
          11(2):157–185, August 1997.
[IJT91]   F. Irigoin, P. Jouvelot, and R. Triolet. Semantical interprocedural par-
          allelization: An overview of the PIPS project. In *ACM Int. Conf. on
          Supercomputing, ICS'91, Köln*, 1991.
[Iri05]   F. Irigoin. Detecting affine loop invariants using modular static analy-
          sis. Technical Report A/367/CRI, Centre de Recherche en Informatique,
          Ecole des Mines de Paris, July 2005.
[SSM04]   Sriram Sankaranarayanan, Henny Sipma, and Zohar Manna. Constraint-
          based linear relations analysis. In *International Symposium on Static
          Analysis, SAS'2004*, pages 53–68. LNCS 3148, Springer Verlag, 2004.
[SW04]   Z. Su and D. Wagner. A class of polynomially solvable range constraints
          for interval analysis without widenings and narrowings. In *TACAS'04*,
          pages 280–295, Barcelona, 2004.
[Tar72]   R. E. Tarjan. Depth-first search and linear graph algorithms. *SIAM
          Journal on Computing*, 1:146–160, 1972.
[Tiw04]   A. Tiwari. Termination of linear programs. In R. Alur and D. Peled,
          editors, *Computer-Aided Verification, CAV*, volume 3114 of *LNCS*, pages
          70–82. Springer, July 2004.
[WB98]   P. Wolper and B. Boigelot. Verifying systems with infinite but regular
          state spaces. In *CAV'98*, pages 88–97, Vancouver, June 1998. LNCS 1427,
          Springer-Verlag.

Beyond Iteration Vectors:
Instancewise Relational Abstract Domains

Pierre Amiranoff, Albert Cohen, and Paul Feautrier

Abstract. We introduce a formalism to reason about program properties at an infinite number of runtime control points, called instances. Infinite sets of instances are represented by rational languages. This framework gives a formal foundation to the well known concept of iteration vectors, extending it to recursive programs with any structured control flow (nested loops and recursive calls). We also extend the concept of induction variables to recursive programs. For a class of monoid-based data structures, including arrays and trees, induction variables capture the exact memory location accessed at every step of the execution. This compile-time characterization is computed in polynomial time as a rational function. Applications include dependence and region analysis for array and tree algorithms, array expansion, and automatic parallelization of recursive programs.

1 Introduction

Most compiler techniques reflect the natural inductive structure of programming languages semantics and machine models. This approach facilitates formal reasoning and proofs, enhances modularity (composition), and leads to fast and simple algorithms.

Yet more and more advanced program analysis and transformation problems benefit from decoupling the construction of static abstractions from the local, inductive semantics of the programs. These abstractions, sometimes called *constraint-based* [31], are custom to a specific class of programs or compilation problem. They are engineered to exhibit statically tractable algebraic properties, e.g., closed mathematical forms amenable to formal (symbolic) computations, typically based on Presburger arithmetic or decidable automata-theoretic classes.

To make this duality more concrete, consider the constant propagation optimization [1] which amounts to computing a property of a variable v at a statement s, asking whether v has some value v before s executes. It is quite natural to formalize constant propagation in an abstract data-flow or interpretation setting. But let us now consider another static analysis problem that may be seen as an extension of constant propagation: *induction variable recognition* [1,22] captures the value of some variable v at a statement s as a function f_v of the number of times s has been executed. In other words, it captures v as a *function of the execution path* itself. Of course, the value of a variable at any stage of the execution is a function of the initial contents of memory and of the execution path leading to this stage. For complexity reasons, the execution path may not

K. Yi (Ed.): SAS 2006, LNCS 4134, pp. 161–180, 2006.

be recoverable from memory. In the case of induction variables, we may assume the number of executions of s is recorded as a genuine loop counter. From such a function f_v for s, we can discover the other induction variables using analyses of linear constraints [9], but such syntactically bound approaches will not easily cope with the calculation of function f_v itself.

*In the following, we will qualify as **instancewise** any compilation method operating on abstract, finitely presented, **relational domains** bewteen the infinite set of **runtime control points** and any semantical domain of interest. Other analyses will be called **statementwise**.*

1.1   Statementwise Analysis

We use the term *statementwise* to refer to the classical type systems, data-flow analysis and abstract interpretation frameworks, that aim for the computation of a *collecting semantics* of a *finite set of collection points*. Few works addressed the attachment of static properties at a finer grain than syntactic program elements. Refinement of this coarse grain abstraction involves a previous *partitioning* [8] of the *control points*: e.g., *polyvariant* analysis distinguishes the context of function calls, and *loop unfolding* virtually unrolls a loop several times. *Dynamic partitioning* [4] integrates partitioning into the analysis itself. Control points can be extended with *call strings* (abstract call stacks) and *timestamps*, but ultimately rely on *k-limiting* [42,26] or *summarization* heuristics [37] to achieve convergence. Although unbounded lattices have long been used to capture abstract properties [9,12]), few works considered the computation of data-flow facts using an *unbounded set of control points*. Even the most advanced non-uniform (a.k.a. elementwise) analyses of arrays or heap structures formalized in abstract interpretation, including the approaches by Deutsch [12,11] and Venet [43,44], although they compute individual properties over an infinite set of heap locations, they do map these properties to a *finite* set of program points only. The seminal paper by Esparza and Knoop [15] is closer to our work since it promises a non-intepretative family of static analysis (semi-)algorithms. Follow-up works building on model-checking of push-down systems or on various path-sensitive abstractions to extend precision and context sensitivity [16,38,25]. Yet all these methods ultimately result in the computation of data-flow properties attached to a *finite number of control points*.

1.2   Instancewise Analysis

On the other hand, ad-hoc approaches to static analysis are able to compute program properties as *functions defined on an infinite (or unbounded) number of runtime control points*. Historically, most works derived from loop-restructuring compiler efforts [45] aiming at a large spectrum of optimizations: vectorization, instruction-level, thread-level or data parallelism, scheduling and mapping for automatic parallelization, locality optimization, and many others [34,45]. In the associated static analyses, the retrieval of abstract properties is often iteration-less [45,46,35] and resort to operation research algorithms thoroughly alien to program interpretation [19]. The work of Creusillet [10] is one of the rare instancewise analyses to resort to abstract interpretation, the reason lying in the interprocedural nature of the analysis. The so-called *polyhedral model* encompasses most works on analysis and transformation of the (Turing-incomplete) class of *static-control programs* [17,34], roughly defined as nested loops with affine loop bounds and array accesses. An *iteration vector* abstracts the runtime control point corresponding to a given iteration of a statement. Program properties are expressed and computed for each vector of values of the surrounding loop counters. In general, the result of the analysis is a mapping from the infinite set of iteration vectors (the run-time control points) to an arbitrary (analysis-specific) vector space (e.g., dependence vector). Instead of iteratively merging data-flow properties, most analyses in the polytope model use algebraic solvers for the direct computation of symbolic relations: e.g., array dependence analysis uses integer linear programming [17]. Iteration vectors are quite different from time-stamps in control point partitioning techniques [4,44]: they are multidimensional, lexicographically ordered, *unbounded*, and constrained by Presburger formula [36].

First Contribution. We introduce a general abstraction of runtime control points that uncompasses most ad-hoc formalisms for the fine grain analysis of loop nests and arrays in sequential procedural languages. Within this framework, one may *define, abstract and compute* program properties as *functions* of an *infinite* set of runtime control points. The concept of *instance* allows to reason about these runtime points across multiple executions of the program; it is the generalization of an iteration vector to general recursion. Rational languages finitely represent infinite set of instances, and instancewise properties may be captured by rational relations [3]. This paper goes far beyond our previous attempts to extend iteration vectors to recursive programs, for the analysis of arrays [6,5,7,2] or recursive data structures [20,7,5].

Second Contribution. Building on the instancewise framework, we extend the concept of *induction variables* to arbitrary recursive programs. This extension demonstrates the ability to characterize properties of programs as functions from an infinite set of runtime control points, beyond the restricted domain of Fortran loop nests. Technically, the valuation of induction variables is analog to parameter passing in a purely functional language: each statement is considered as a function, binding and initializing one or more induction variables. We propose an polynomial algorithm to compute each induction variable as a *binding function* mapping instances to the abstract memory locations they access. It is a *rational function* on the Cartesian product of two monoids and can be efficiently represented as a *rational transducer* [3]. This binding function will give an *exact* result for valid traces.

Organization of the Paper. Section 2 defines the instancewise model. Section 3 extends induction variables to recursive control and data structures. Section 4 states the existence of rational binding functions. Section 5 addresses the computation of binding functions as rational transducers. Section 6 surveys theoretical results that derive from this work.

2   From Traces to Instances

Figure 1 presents our running example. It features a recursive call to the Toy function, nested in the body of a *for* loop, operating on an array A (there is no simple way to remove the recursion).

To focus on the core concepts, we introduce MoGuL, a toy language with high-level constructs for traversing data structures addressed by induction variables in a *finitely presented monoid*. In a general-purpose (imperative or functional) language, our technique would require additional information about the shape of data structures, using dedicated annotations [27,28,21] or shape analyses [23,41].

Figure 3 is a simplified version of the MoGuL C-like syntax, focusing on the control structures. Italic non-terminals are defined elsewhere: *elementary_statement* covers the usual atomic statements, including assignments, input/output statements, void statements, etc.; *predicate* is a boolean expression; *init_list* contains a list of initializations for one or more loop variables, and *translation_list* is the associated list of constant translations

```
int A[100];
void Toy(int n, int k) {
  if (k < n)
  {
    for (int i=k; i<=n;
         i+=2)
    {
      A[i] = A[i] + A[n-i];
      Toy(n, k+1);
    }
  }
}
int main() {
  Toy(99, 0);
}
```

Fig. 1. Program Toy in C

```
   structure Monoid_int A;
A void Toy(Monoid_int n, Monoid_int k) {
B   if (k < n)
C   {
D     for (Monoid_int i=k; i<=n;
d          i=i.2)
E     {
F       A[i] = A[i] + A[n-i] ;
G       Toy(n, k.1);
      }
    }
  }
H int main() {
I   Toy(20, 0);
  }
```

Fig. 2. Program Toy in MoGuL

program	::= function	(S1)
	| function program	(S2)
function	::= 'function' *ident* '(' *formal_parameter_list* ')'	
	block	(S3)
block	::= LABEL ':' '{' *init_list* statement_list '}'	(S4)
	| LABEL ':' '{' statement_list '}'	(S5)
statement_list	::= ε	(S6)
	| LABEL ':' statement statement_list	(S7)
statement	::= *elementary_statement* ';'	(S8)
	| *ident* '(' *actual_parameter_list* ')' ';'	(S9)
	| 'if' *predicate* block 'else' block	(S10)
	| 'for' '(' *init_list* ';' LABEL ':' *predicate* ';'	
	LABEL ':' *translation_list* ')' block	(S11)
	| block	(S12)

Fig. 3. Simplified MoGuL syntax (control structures)

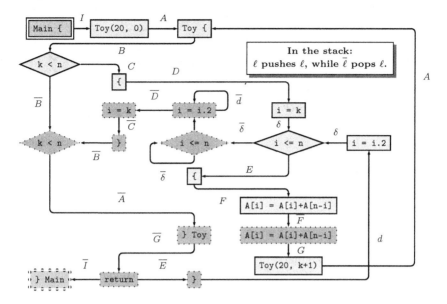

Fig. 4. Pushdown Trace Automaton

for those induction variables; `block` collects a sequence of statements, possibly defining some induction variables. Every statement is labeled.

Figure 2 gives the MOGUL version of `Toy`. It abstracts the shape of array `A` through a monoid type `Monoid_int`. Induction variables `i` and `k` are bound to values in this monoid. Traversals of `A` are expressed through `i`, `k` and the monoid operation ·. Further explanations about MOGUL data structures and induction variables are deferred to Section 3.

Every statement is seen as a function application; therefore the execution stack alphabet holds every statement label. Moreover, each statement is provided with a second *return* label to identify the implicit termination of the statement: if ℓ is a statement label, ℓ corresponds to the beginning of the execution of a statement and $\overline{\ell}$ indicates its completion. Regarding the execution stack, ℓ pushes ℓ while $\overline{\ell}$ pops ℓ. An additional state, called *return state*, is associated to the completion of each statement. The result is called the *pushdown trace automaton* and the recognized words are the *execution traces*. A *trace prefix* is the trace of a partial execution, given by a prefix of a complete trace, it matches the intuitive notion of a runtime control point.

Figure 4 presents the trace pushdown automaton of the `Toy` program. We exhibit here a prefix of a valid trace: $IABCD\delta EF\overline{F}\, GABCD\delta EF\overline{F}\, GAB\overline{B}\, AGE\delta d\delta EF$.

For clarity of exposure and without loss of precision, the following examples will use a simplified representation of the trace pushdown automaton, omitting return states, except for calls to `Toy`, states associated to `block` statements and to loop predicates. Now, the previous trace prefix reduces to: $IBDF\overline{F}\, GBDF\overline{F}\, GB\overline{B}\, GdF$. We will use this simplified representation of traces in the following.

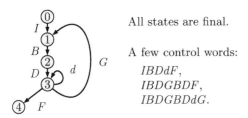

All states are final.

A few control words:

IBDdF,
IBDGBDF,
IBDGBDdG.

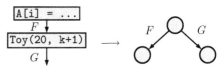

Each statement in a sequence is linked to the enclosing block.

Fig. 5. Example Control Automaton

Fig. 6. Construction of the Control Automaton

The purpose of this paper is to construct a finite-state representation for the (infinite) set of trace prefixes of Toy, *then compute a statically tractable characterization of the precise element of* A *accessed by every given trace prefix(again an infinite relational abstract domain).*

The stack word language of a pushdown automaton $\mathcal{A}$ is the set of stack words u such that there exists a state q for which the configuration (q, u) is both accessible and co-accessible — there is an accepting path traversing q with stack word u.

Definition 1 (Control Word). *The stack word language of the pushdown trace automaton is called the* control word language. *A* control word *is the sequence of labels of all statements that have begun their execution but not yet completed it. Any trace prefix has a corresponding control word.*

Since the stack word language of a pushdown automaton is rational [39], the language of control words is rational. It is easy to build a finite-state automaton accepting the rational language of control words. We call the latter the *control automaton*.

Figure 5 shows the control automaton for Toy; the control word language is $I + IB + IBD(d + GBD)^*(\varepsilon + F + G + GB)$.

The transformation from trace prefixes to control words is a systematic procedure. A similar transformation exists from the pushdown trace automaton to the control automaton; this is important for the design of efficient instancewise analysis algorithms.

- In the pushdown trace automaton, a sequence of successive statements is a chain of arcs, while, in the control automaton, each of these statement is linked by an edge from the common enclosing block, see Figure 6. Thus, the control automaton makes no distinction between the sequence and the conditional.
- As in the pushdown automaton for trace prefixes, all states are final.
- Since a **return** statement closes the corresponding function call and deletes every label relative to it in the control word, **return** nodes are not needed anymore.

The trace language is a Dyck language [3], i.e., a hierarchical parenthesis language. We define the *slimming congruence* generated by $\ell\bar{\ell} \equiv \varepsilon$, for all $\ell \in L_{ab}$.

This definition induces a rewriting rule over L_{ab}^*, obviously confluent. This rule is the direct transposition of the execution stack behavior. Applying it to any trace prefix p we can associate a minimal word w.

Definition 2 (Slimming Function). *The* slimming function *maps each trace prefix to the shortest element in the class of p modulo the slimming congruence.*

Theorem 1. *The set of control words is the quotient set of all prefixes of all traces modulo the restricted Dyck congruence, and the slimming function is the canonical projection of trace prefixes over their control words.*

The following table illustrates the slimming function on a few trace prefixes.

Trace prefix $IBDF\,\overline{F}\,GBDF$
Control word $IBD\quad\ \ GBDF$
Trace prefix $IBDF\,\overline{F}\,GBDF\,\overline{F}\,GB\,\overline{B}\,G\,dF\,\overline{F}\,G$
Control word $IBD\quad\ \ GBD\qquad\quad\ d\ \ \ G$
Trace prefix $IBDF\,\overline{F}\,GBDF\,\overline{F}\,GB\,\overline{B}\,G\,dF\,\overline{F}\,GB\,\overline{B}\,G\,d\,dd\,DBG\,dF$
Control word $IBD\qquad\qquad\qquad\qquad\qquad\quad dF$

The slimming function extends Harrison's NET function; we coined the term control word in favor of *procedure string* [42,26,30] to emphasize the unboundedness of the relation over stack configurations we ought to statically reason about.

Consider any trace t of a MoGuL program and any trace prefix p of t. The slimming function returns a unique control word. Conversely, it is easy to see that a given control word may be the abstraction of many trace prefixes, possibly an infinity. E.g., consider two trace prefixes differing only by the sub-trace of a completed conditional statement:[1] their control words are the same.

The demonstration of the following results and additional relations between trace prefixes and control words are provided in the appendix.

We now come to the formal definition of an instance:

Definition 3 (Instance). *Considering the set of all traces of a MoGuL program, an* instance *is a class of trace prefixes modulo the slimming congruence.*

Thanks to Theorem 1, instances are in bijection with control words. In the following, we will refer to instances or control words interchangeably, without naming a particular trace prefix representative.

From Theorem 1 again, it is fundamental to notice that an instance has a consistent definition across all possible executions; this allows to *collect the semantics* of all trace prefixes congruent to a given control word.

The following results states that an instance is also the finest possible way to collect the semantics over multiple executions.

Theorem 2. *Given one execution trace of a MoGuL program, trace prefixes are in bijection with control words.*

---

[1] I.e., after completing a hammock, the two sub-traces being associated to exclusive branches.

Theorem 2 ensures that control words characterize runtime control points in a more compact way than trace prefixes. It even guarantees that computing a relational domain at each instance is no coarser than dynamically evaluating the concrete property at each runtime control point.

3   Data Structure Model and Induction Variables

This section and the following ones apply instancewise analysis to the *exact characterization of memory locations* accessed by a MoGuL program. For decidability reasons, we will only consider a restricted class of data structures and addressing schemes:

- they do not support destructive updates (deletion of nodes and non-leaf insertions);[2]
- they are addressed through *induction variables* whose only authorized operations are the initialization to a constant and the associative operation of a monoid.

These restrictions are reminiscent of *purely functional data structures* [32].

In this context, we will show that the value of an induction variable at some runtime control point — or the memory location accessed at this point — only depends on the instance. Exact characterization of induction variables will be possible at compile-time by means of so-called *binding functions* from control words to abstract memory locations (monoid elements), independently of the execution.

3.1   Data Model

To simplify the formalism and exposition, MoGuL data structures with side-effects must be *global*. This is not really an issue since any local structure may be "expanded" along the activation tree (e.g., several local lists may be seen as a global stack of lists).

A *finitely-generated monoid* $M = (G, \equiv)$ is specified by a *finite* list of *generators* G and a *congruence* $\equiv$ given by a *finite* list of equations over words in G^*. Elements of M are equivalence classes of words in G^* modulo $\equiv$. When the congruence is empty, M is a *free monoid*. The operation of M is the quotient of the concatenation on the free monoid G^* modulo $\equiv$; it is an associative operation denoted by $\cdot$ with neutral element ε_m.

Definition 4 (Abstract Location). *A data structure is a pair of a data structure name and a finitely-generated monoid $M = (G, \equiv)$. An abstract memory location in this data structure is an element of the monoid. It is represented by an address word in G^*. By definition, two congruent address words represent the same memory location.*

Typical examples are the n-ary tree — the free monoid with n generators (with an empty congruence) — and the n-dimensional array — the free commutative monoid $\mathbb{Z}^n$ (with vector commutation and inversion).

---

[2] Leaf insertions are harmless if data-structures are implicitly expanded when accessed.

Below are listed some practical examples of monoid-based data structures.

Free monoid.
$G = \{\texttt{right}, \texttt{left}\}$, $\equiv$ is the identity relation, $\cdot$ is the concatenation: monoid elements address a binary tree.

Free group.
$G = \{\texttt{right}, \texttt{left}, \texttt{right}^{-1}, \texttt{left}^{-1}\}$, $\equiv$ is the inversion of $\texttt{left}$ and $\texttt{right}$ (without commutation): Cayley graphs [14,24].

Free commutative group.
$G = \{(0,1), (1,0), (0,-1), (-1,0)\}$, $\equiv$ is the vector inversion and commutation, $\cdot$ is vector addition: a two-dimensional array.

Free commutative monoid.
$G = \{(0,1), (1,0)\}$, $\equiv$ is vector commutation: a two-dimensional grid.

Commutative monoid.
$G = \{(0,1), (1,0)\}$, $\equiv$ is vector commutation and $(0,1) \cdot (0,1) \equiv \varepsilon_m$: a two-dimensional grid folded on the torus $\mathbb{Z} \times \frac{\mathbb{Z}}{2\mathbb{Z}}$.

Free partially-commutative monoid.
$G = \{\texttt{next}, 1, -1\}$, $\equiv$ is the inversion and commutation of 1: nested trees, lists and arrays.

Monoid with right-inverse.
$G = \{\texttt{right}, \texttt{left}, \texttt{parent}\}$,
$\texttt{right} \cdot \texttt{parent} \equiv \varepsilon_m$,
$\texttt{left} \cdot \texttt{parent} \equiv \varepsilon_m$: a tree with backward edges.

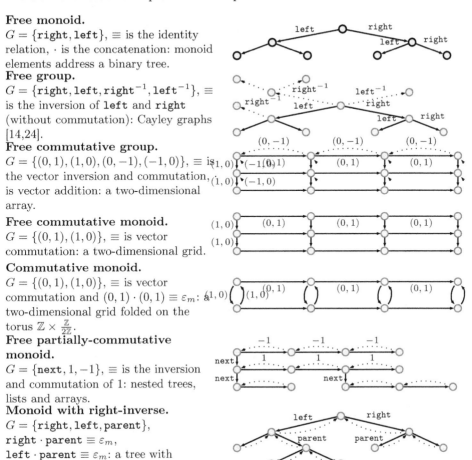

3.2   Induction Variables

Traditionally, induction variables are scalar variables within loop nests with a tight relationship with the surrounding loop counters [1,22]. This relationship, deduced from the regularity of the induction variable updates, is a critical information for many analyses (dependence, array region, array bound checking) and optimizations (strength-reduction, loop transformations, hoisting).

A *basic linear induction variable* x is assigned (once or more) in a loop, each assignment being in the form x = c or x = x + c, where c is a constant known at compile-time. More generally, a variable x is called a *linear induction variable* if on every iteration of the surrounding loop, x is added a constant value. This is the case when assignments to x in the cycle are in the basic form or in the form x = y + c, y being another induction variable. The value of x may then be expressed as *an affine function of the surrounding loop counters*. MoGuL extensions are twofold:

- induction variables can be valued in any monoid;
- their evolution can be captured across loops and recursive calls.

As a consequence, induction variables represent abstract addresses in data structures, and the basic operation over induction variables becomes the monoid operation.

Definition 5 (Induction Variable). *A variable* x *is an induction variable if and only if the three following conditions are satisfied:*

a. x *is defined at a* block *entry, a* for *loop initialization, or* x *is a formal parameter;*

b. x *is constant in the* block, *the* for *loop or the function where it has been defined;*

c. *the definition of* x *(according to* **a***) is in one of the forms:*
  1. x = c, *and c is a constant known at compile-time,*
  2. x = y · c, *and* y *is an induction variable, possibly equal to* x.

A MoGuL induction variable can be used in different address expressions which reference *distinct* data structures, provided these structures are defined over the same monoid. This separation between data structure and shape follows the approach of the declarative language $8_{1/2}$ [24]. It is a convenient way to expose more semantics to the static analyzer, compared with C pointers or variables of product types in ML.

Eventually, the MoGuL syntax is designed such that *every variable of a monoid type is an induction variable*, other variables being ignored. The only valid definitions and operations on MoGuL variables are those satisfying Definition 5. For any monoid shape, data structure accesses follow the C array syntax: D[a] denotes element with address a of structure D, where a is in the form x or x · c, x an induction variable and c a constant.

If A is an array (i.e., A is addressed in a free commutative group), the affine subscript A[i+2j-1] is not a valid MoGuL syntax. This is not a real limitation, however, since affine subscripts may be replaced by new induction variables defined when necessary while i or j are defined. As an illustration, let k be the induction variable equal to i+2j-1, the subscript in the reference above. We have to build, through a backward motion, static chains of induction variables from the program start point to the considered reference. Suppose the last modification of the subscript before the considered program point is given by the statement j= h denoted by s, where h is another induction variable. We have to define a new induction variable g = i+2h-1, living before this statement, and to consider that s initializes k through an additional assignment k= g. This work has to be done recursively for all paths in the control flow graph until reaching the start point.

4   Binding Functions

In MoGuL, the computations on two induction variables in two distinct monoids are completely separate. Thus, without loss of generality, we suppose that all induction variables belong to a single monoid M_{loc}, with operation · and neutral element ε_m, called the *data structure monoid*.

4.1   From Instances to Memory Locations

In a purely functional language, function application is the only way to define a variable. In MoGuL, every statement is handled that way; the scope of a variable is restricted to the statement at the beginning of which it has been declared, and an induction variable is constant in its scope.

Since overloading of variable names occurs at the beginning of each statement, the value of an induction variable depends on the runtime control point of interest. Let x be an induction variable, we define the *binding for* x as the pair (p, v_p), where p is a trace prefix and v_p the value of x after executing p.

Consider two trace prefixes p_1 and p_2 representative of the same instance. The previous rules guarantee that all induction variables living right after p_1 (resp. p_2) have been defined in statements not closed yet. Now, the respective sequences of non-closed statements for p_1 and p_2 are identical and equal to the control word of p_1 and p_2. Thus the bindings of x for p_1 and p_2 are equal. In others words, the function that binds the trace prefix to the value of x is compatible with the slimming congruence.

Theorem 3. *Given an induction variable* x *in a* MoGuL *program, the function mapping a trace prefix p to the value of* x *only depends on the instance associated to p, i.e., on the control word.*

In other words, given an execution trace, the bindings at any trace prefix are identified by the control word (i.e., the instance).

Definition 6 (Binding Function). *A binding for* x *is a pair (w, v), where w is a control word and v the value of* x *at the instance w.*

Λ_{x} *denotes the* binding function for x, *mapping control words to the corresponding value of* x.

4.2   Bilabels

We now describe the mathematical framework to compute binding functions.

Definition 7 (Bilabel). *A bilabel is a pair in the set $L^*_{ab} \times M_{loc}$. The first part of the pair is called the* input label, *the second one is called the* output label.

$B = L^*_{ab} \times M_{\text{loc}}$ denotes the set of bilabels. From the *direct product* of the control word free monoid L^*_{ab} and the data monoid M_{loc}, B is provided with a monoid structure: its operation • is defined componentwise on L^*_{ab} and M_{loc},

$$(\alpha|a) \bullet (\beta|b) \overset{def}{=} (\alpha\beta|a \cdot b). \tag{1}$$

A binding for an induction variable is a bilabel. Every statement updates the binding of induction variables according to their definitions and scope rules, the corresponding equations will be studied in Section 4.3.

Definition 8. *The set of* rational subsets *of a monoid M is the least set that contains the finite subsets of M, closed by union, product and the star operation [3]. A rational relation* over two monoids M and M' *is a rational subset of the monoid $M \times M'$.*

We focus on the family B_{rat} of rational subsets of B.

Definition 9. *A semiring is a monoid for two binary operations, the "addition" $+$, which is commutative, and the "product" $\times$, distributive over $+$; the neutral element for $+$ is the zero for $\times$.*

The powerset of a monoid M is a semiring for union and the operation of M [3]. The set of rational subsets of M is a sub-semiring of the latter [3]; it can be expressed through the set of rational expressions in M. Thus B_{rat} is a semiring.

We overload $\bullet$ to denote the product operation in B_{rat}; $\emptyset$ is the zero element (the empty set of bilabels); and the neutral element for $\bullet$ is $\mathcal{E} = \{(\varepsilon, \varepsilon_m)\}$. From now on, we identify B_{rat} with the set of rational expressions in M, and we also identify a singleton with the bilabel inside it: $\{(s|c)\}$ may be written $(s|c)$.

4.3   Building Recurrence Equations

To compute a finite representation of the binding function for each induction variable, we show that the bindings can be expressed as a finite number of rational sets. First of all, bindings can be grouped according to the last executed statement, i.e., the last label of the control word. Next, we build a system of equations in which unknowns are sets of bindings for induction variable $\mathbf{x}$ at state n of the control automaton. Given $\mathcal{A}_n$ the control automaton modified so that n is the unique final state, let $\mathcal{L}_n$ be the language recognized by $\mathcal{A}_n$. The *binding function for $\mathbf{x}$ at state n, $\Lambda_{\mathbf{x}}^n$*, is the binding function for $\mathbf{x}$ restricted to $\mathcal{L}_n$. We also introduce a new induction variable $\mathbf{z}$, *constant and equal to ε_m*.

The system of equations is a direct translation of the semantics of induction variable definitions; it follows the syntax of a MoGuL program P; we illustrate each rule on the running example.

1. At the initial state 0 and for any induction variable $\mathbf{x}$,

$$\Lambda_{\mathbf{x}}^0 = \mathcal{E} \tag{2}$$

    E.g., the Toy program involves three induction variables, the loop counter $\mathbf{i}$ and the formal parameters $\mathbf{k}$ and $\mathbf{n}$. We will not consider $\mathbf{n}$ since it does not subscript any data structure. The output monoid is $\mathbb{Z}$, its neutral element ε_m is 0.

$$\Lambda_{\mathbf{k}}^0 = \Lambda_{\mathbf{i}}^0 = (\varepsilon|0).$$

2. $\Lambda_{\mathbf{z}}^n$ denotes the set defined by

$$\Lambda_{\mathbf{z}}^n = \bigcup_{w \in \mathcal{L}_n} (w|\varepsilon_m). \tag{3}$$

Λ_z^n is the binding function for the new induction variable z restricted to $\mathcal{L}_n$; it is constant and equal to ε_m.

For each statement s defining an induction variable x to c_{sx} (case **c.1** of Definition 5), and calling d and a the respective departure and arrival states of s in the control automaton,

$$\Lambda_x^a \supseteq \Lambda_z^d \bullet (s|c_{sx}). \tag{4}$$

Since $\Lambda_z^d \bullet (s|c_{sx}) = \bigcup_{w \in \mathcal{L}_d}(ws|c_{sx})$, (4) means: if $w \in \mathcal{L}_d$ is a control word, ws is also a control word and its binding for x is $(ws|c_{sx})$.

The control automaton automaton of **Toy** has 5 states. For the case **c.1** of Definition 5,

statement $I : k = 0$,   and (4) yields $\Lambda_k^1 \supseteq \Lambda_z^0 \bullet (I|0)$.

3. For each statement s defining an induction variable x to $y \cdot c$ (case **c.2** of Definition 5), and d and a the respective departure and arrival states of s,

$$\Lambda_x^a \supseteq \Lambda_x^d \bullet (s|c_{sx}). \tag{5}$$

To complete the system, we add for every induction variable x unchanged by s a set of equations in the form (5), where $c_{sx} = \varepsilon_m$.

E.g., for case **c.2** of Definition 5,

statement $G : k = k \cdot 1$ statement $d : i = i \cdot 2$ statement $D : i = k$

and (5) yields

$\Lambda_i^1 \supseteq \Lambda_i^3 \bullet (G|0)$	$\Lambda_i^3 \supseteq \Lambda_k^2 \bullet (D|0)$	$\Lambda_i^4 \supseteq \Lambda_i^3 \bullet (F|0)$	$\Lambda_z^2 \supseteq \Lambda_z^1 \bullet (B|0)$
$\Lambda_k^1 \supseteq \Lambda_k^3 \bullet (G|1)$	$\Lambda_i^3 \supseteq \Lambda_i^3 \bullet (d|2)$	$\Lambda_k^4 \supseteq \Lambda_k^3 \bullet (F|0)$	$\Lambda_z^3 \supseteq \Lambda_z^2 \bullet (D|0)$
$\Lambda_i^2 \supseteq \Lambda_i^1 \bullet (B|0)$	$\Lambda_k^3 \supseteq \Lambda_k^2 \bullet (D|0)$	$\Lambda_z^3 \supseteq \Lambda_z^2 \bullet (I|0)$	$\Lambda_z^3 \supseteq \Lambda_z^2 \bullet (d|0)$
$\Lambda_k^2 \supseteq \Lambda_k^1 \bullet (B|0)$	$\Lambda_k^3 \supseteq \Lambda_k^2 \bullet (d|0)$	$\Lambda_z^1 \supseteq \Lambda_z^3 \bullet (G|0)$	$\Lambda_z^4 \supseteq \Lambda_z^3 \bullet (F|0)$

Gathering all equations generated from (2), (4) and (5) yields a system $(\mathcal{S})$ of $n_v \times n_s$ equations with $n_v \times n_s$ unknowns, where n_v is the number of induction variables, including z, and n_s the number of statements in the program.[3]

Toy yields the system

$$\Lambda_i^0 = \mathcal{E}$$
$$\Lambda_k^0 = \mathcal{E}$$
$$\Lambda_z^0 = \mathcal{E}$$

$$\Lambda_i^1 = \Lambda_i^3 \bullet (G|0) + (I|0)$$
$$\Lambda_k^1 = \Lambda_k^3 \bullet (G|1) + (I|0)$$
$$\Lambda_i^2 = \Lambda_i^1 \bullet (B|0)$$
$$\Lambda_k^2 = \Lambda_k^1 \bullet (B|0) \qquad \Lambda_i^3 = \Lambda_i^3 \bullet (d|2) + \Lambda_k^2 \bullet (D|0)$$
$$\Lambda_k^3 = \Lambda_k^3 \bullet (d|0) + \Lambda_k^2 \bullet (D|0)$$

$$\Lambda_i^4 = \Lambda_i^3 \bullet (F|0)$$
$$\Lambda_k^4 = \Lambda_k^3 \bullet (F|0)$$
$$\Lambda_z^1 = \Lambda_z^3 \bullet (G|0) + (I|0)$$
$$\Lambda_z^2 = \Lambda_z^1 \bullet (B|0)$$
$$\Lambda_z^3 = \Lambda_z^2 \bullet (D|0) + \Lambda_z^3 \bullet (d|0)$$
$$\Lambda_z^4 = \Lambda_z^3 \bullet (F|0)$$

Let Λ be the set of unknowns for $(\mathcal{S})$, i.e., the set of Λ_x^n for all induction variables x and nodes n in the control automaton. Let C be the set of constant coefficients in the system. $(\mathcal{S})$ is a *left linear system of equations over* (Λ, C) [39]. Let X_i be the unknown in Λ appearing in the left-hand side of the ith equation of $(\mathcal{S})$. If $+$ denotes the union in B_{rat}, we may rewrite the system in the form

---

[3] Some unknown sets correspond to unbound variables at the node of interest, they are useless.

$$\forall i \in \{1, \ldots, m\}, X_i = \sum_{j=1}^{m} X_j \bullet C_{i,j} + R_i, \tag{6}$$

where R_i results from the terms $\Lambda_{\mathbf{x}}^0 = \mathcal{E}$ in right-hand side. Note that $C_{i,j}$ is either $\emptyset$ or a bilabel singleton of B_{rat}. Thus $(\mathcal{S})$ is a *strict* system, and as such, it has a unique solution [39]; moreover, this solution can be characterized by a *rational expression* for each unknown set in Λ.

Definition 10 (Rational Function). *If M and M' are two monoids, a rational function is a function from M to M' whose graph is a rational relation.*

We may conclude that the solution of $(\mathcal{S})$ is a characterization of each unknown set X_i in Λ as a rational function.

Lemma 1. *For any induction variable $\mathbf{x}$ and node n in the control automaton, the binding function for $\mathbf{x}$ restricted to $\mathcal{L}_n \Lambda_{\mathbf{x}}^n$ is a rational function.*

Theorem 4. *For any induction variable $\mathbf{x}$, the binding function $\Lambda_{\mathbf{x}}$ is a rational function.*

This is a corollary of Lemma 1, since the functions $\Lambda_{\mathbf{x}}^n$ are defined on disjoint subsets of control words, partitioned according to the suffix n.

Properties of rational relations and functions are similar to those of rational languages [3]: membership, inclusion, equality, emptiness and finiteness are decidable, projection on the input or output monoid yields a rational sub-monoid, and rational relations are closed for union, star, product and inverse morphism, to cite only the most common properties. The main difference is that they are not closed for complementation and intersection, although a useful sub-class of rational relations has this closure property — independently discovered in [33] and [5]. Since most of these properties are associated with polynomial algorithms, binding functions can be used in many analyses, see [6,20,5,2] for our previous and ongoing applications to the automatic parallelization of recursive programs.

5   Computing Binding Functions

This section investigates the resolution of $(\mathcal{S})$. Starting from (6), one may compute the last unknown in terms of others:

$$X_m = C_{m,m}^* \left(\sum_{i=1}^{m-1} X_j \bullet C_{i,j} + R_m \right). \tag{7}$$

The solution of $(\mathcal{S})$ can be computed by iterating this process analogous to Gaussian elimination. This was the first proposed algorithm [5]; but Gaussian elimination on non-commutative semirings is an exponential process. We present a polynomial algorithm to compute the binding function of each induction variable as a rational transducer.

A *rational transducer* is a finite-state automaton where each transition is labeled by a pair of *input* and *output* symbols (borrowing from Definition 7), a symbol being a letter of the alphabet or the empty word [3].[4]

A pair of words (u, v) is *recognized* by a rational transducer if there is a path from an initial to a final state whose input word is equal to u and output word is equal to v.[5]

A rational transducer recognizes a rational relation, and reciprocally. A transducer offers either a static point of view — as a machine that recognizes pairs of words — or a dynamic point of view — the machine reads an input word and outputs the set of image words.

The representation for the binding function of an induction variable is called the *binding transducer*.

Algorithm 1

Given the control automaton and a monoid with n_v induction variables (including z), the binding transducer is built as follows:

- *For each control automaton state, create a set of n_v states, called a* product-state; *each state of a product-state is dedicated to a specific induction variable.*
- *Initial (resp. final) states correspond to the product-states of all initial (resp. final) states of the control automaton.*
- *For each statement s, i.e., for each transition (d, a) labeled s in the control automaton; call P^d and P^a the corresponding product-states; and create an associated* product-transition t_s. *It is a set of n_v transitions, each one is dedicated to a specific induction variable. We consider again the two cases mentioned in Definition (5.c).*
  - *case c.1: the transition runs from state P_z^d in P^d to the state P_x^a in P^a. The input label is s, the output label is the initialization constant c;*
  - *case c.2: the transition runs from state P_y^d in P^d to state P_x^a in P^a. The input label is s, the output label is the constant c.*

The binding transducer for Toy is shown in Figure 7. Notice that nodes allocated to the virtual induction variable z are not co-accessible except the initial state (there is no path from them to a final state), and initial states dedicated to i and k are not co-accessible either. These states are useless, they are trimmed from the binding transducer.

The binding transducer does not directly describe the binding functions. A binding transducer is *dedicated* to an induction variable x when its final states are restricted to the states dedicated to x in the final product-states.

Theorem 5. *The binding transducer dedicated to an induction variable x recognizes the binding function for x.*

---

[4] Pair of words leads to an equivalent definition.

[5] A transducer is not reducible to an automaton with bilabels as elementary symbols for its alphabet; as an illustration, two paths labeled $(x|\varepsilon)(y|z)$ and $(x|z)(y|\varepsilon)$ recognize the same pair of words $(xy|z)$.

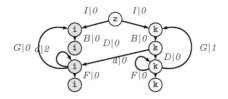

Fig. 7. Binding Transducer for Toy

This result is a corollary of Theorem 4.

From this result, it is possible (yet not mandatory for most analysis purposes) to capture all induction variables and their relations into a single object; this may translate into computing product-states of many transducers, which in the worst case is exponential in the number of induction variables [2].

The construction of the binding transducer is fully implemented in OCaml and has been experimented on a dozen of recursive kernels. Starting from a MoGuL program, the analyzer returns the binding transducer according to the choice of monoid. This analyzer is a part of a more ambitious framework including dependence test algorithms based on the binding transducer [2].

6   Applications of Instancewise Analysis

Instancewise analyses are pervasive when dealing with loop nest programs [45,7]. This section is a short overview of the known applications of instancewise binding functions to the analysis of *recursive* programs. Most applications derive from standard algorithms and decision procedures on rational and push-down transducters [3] which are similar to those of finite-state and push-down automata — with the notable exception of intersection and complementation. In some cases, one must resort to approximation schemes [5] and semi-algorithms [20].

- Instancewise dependence analysis for arrays [6,5]. The relation between dependent instances is computed as a one-counter (context-free) transducer, or by a multi-counter transducer in the case of multi-dimensional arrays. In the multi-counter case, only approximate may/must dependences are available. This technique applies to the Toy example.
- Instancewise reaching-definition analysis for arrays [6,5] (a.k.a. array data-flow analysis [18,29]). Compared to dependence analysis, kills of previous array assignments are taken into account. Due to the conservative assumptions about conditional guards (ignored in this paper), one may only exploit kill information based on structural properties of the program, i.e., exclusive branches and ancestry of control words in the call tree (whether an instance forcibly precedes another in the execution). This limitation seems rather strong, but it already subsumes the loop-nest case [5] and the Toy program.
- Instancewise dependence test for arrays [2]. Amiranoff's thesis proves the decidability and NP-completeness of dependence testing based on binding transducers, in the case of arrays. An extension taking conditional guards

into account is available, provided the guards can be expressed as affine functions of some inductive variables lying in free-commutative monoids (unpublished result). This extension defines conditions for the exactness of the dependence test (i.e., the absence of approximation) that strictly generalize the case of static-control loop nests; e.g., the exact dependence test can be applied to a complex control-flow of the Toy example.

- Instancewise dependence and reaching-definition analysis for trees [5]. The relation between conflicting instances is a rational transducer, from the Elgot and Mezei theorem [13,3]; the dependence relation requires an additional sequentiality constraint, which makes its characterization undecidable in general, but an approximation scheme based on synchronous transducers is available [33,5]. The array and tree cases can be unified: [5] describes a technique to analyze nested trees and arrays in free partially-commutative monoids [40].

- Instancewise dependence test for trees [20]. Instead of a relation between instances, this test leverages on instancewise analysis to compute precise statementwise dependence information with unlimited context-sensitivity (not k-limited). This technique features a semi-algorithm to solve the undecidable dependence problem, and the semi-algorithm is proven to terminate provided the approximation scheme of the previous technique is used (unpublished result).

7   Conclusion and Perspectives

Instancewise compilation decouples the static properties and analyses from the inductive presentation of program semantics, departing from interpretative algorithms to evaluate semantic program properties as relational abstract domains over infinite sets of runtime control points. This paradigm abstracts runtime execution states (or trace prefixes) in a finitely-presented, infinite set of control words. Instancewise analysis is also an extension of the domain-specific iteration-vector approach (the so-called polytope model) to general recursive programs.

As an application of the instancewise framework, we extend the concept of induction variables to recursive programs. For a restricted class of data structures (including arrays and recursive structures), induction variables capture the exact memory location accessed at every step of the execution. This compile-time characterization, called the binding function, is a rational function mapping control words to abstract memory locations. We give a polynomial algorithm for the computation of binding functions.

Our current work focuses on instancewise alias and dependence analysis, for the automatic parallelization and optimization of recursive programs [2]. We also look after new benchmark applications and data-structures to assess the applicability of binding functions; multi-grid and sparse codes are interesting candidates. We would also like to release a few constraints on the data structures and induction variables, aiming for the computation of approximate binding functions through abstract interpretation.

References

1. A. Aho, R. Sethi, and J. Ullman. *Compilers: Principles, Techniques and Tools.* Addison-Wesley, 1986.
2. P. Amiranoff. *An Automata-Theoretic Modelization of Instancewise Program Analysis: Transducers as mappings from Instances to Memory Locations.* PhD thesis, CNAM, Paris, Dec. 2004.
3. J. Berstel. *Transductions and Context-Free Languages.* Teubner, Stuttgart, Germany, 1979.
4. F. Bourdoncle. Abstract interpretation by dynamic partitioning. *J. of Functional Programming*, 2(4):407–423, 1992.
5. A. Cohen. *Program Analysis and Transformation: from the Polytope Model to Formal Languages.* PhD Thesis, Université de Versailles, France, Dec. 1999.
6. A. Cohen and J.-F. Collard. Instancewise reaching definition analysis for recursive programs using context-free transductions. In *Parallel Architectures and Compilation Techniques (PACT'98)*, pages 332–340, Paris, France, Oct. 1998. IEEE Computer Society.
7. J.-F. Collard. *Reasoning About Program Transformations.* Springer-Verlag, 2002.
8. P. Cousot. *Semantic foundations of programs analysis.* Prentice-Hall, 1981.
9. P. Cousot and N. Halbwachs. Automatic discovery of linear restraints among variables of a program. In 5th *ACM Symp. on Principles of Programming Languages*, pages 84–96, Jan. 1978.
10. B. Creusillet. *Array Region Analyses and Applications.* PhD thesis, École Nationale Supérieure des Mines de Paris (ENSMP), France, Dec. 1996.
11. A. Deutsch. *Operational Models of Programming Languages and Representations of Relations on Regular Languages with Application to the Static Determination of Dynamic Aliasing Properties of Data.* PhD thesis, École Polytechnique, France, Apr. 1992.
12. A. Deutsch. Interprocedural may-alias analysis for pointers: beyond k-limiting. In *ACM Symp. on Programming Language Design and Implementation (PLDI'94)*, pages 230–241, Orlando, Florida, June 1994.
13. C. C. Elgot and J. E. Mezei. On relations defined by generalized finite automata. *IBM J. of Research and Development*, pages 45–68, 1965.
14. D. B. A. Epstein, J. W. Cannon, D. F. Holt, S. V. F. Levy, M. Paterson, and W. Thurston. *Word Processing in Groups.* Jones and Bartlett Publishers, Boston, 1992.
15. J. Esparza and J. Knoop. An automata-theoretic approach to interprocedural data-flow analysis. In *FOSSACS'99*, 1999.
16. J. Esparza and A. Podelski. Efficient algorithms for pre* and post* on interprocedural parallel flow graphs. In *ACM Symp. on Principles of Programming Languages (PoPL'00)*, pages 1–11, 2000.
17. P. Feautrier. Array expansion. In *ACM Intl. Conf. on Supercomputing*, pages 429–441, St. Malo, France, July 1988.
18. P. Feautrier. Dataflow analysis of scalar and array references. *Intl. J. of Parallel Programming*, 20(1):23–53, Feb. 1991.
19. P. Feautrier. Some efficient solutions to the affine scheduling problem, part II, multidimensional time. *Intl. J. of Parallel Programming*, 21(6):389–420, Dec. 1992. See also Part I, one dimensional time, 21(5):315–348.
20. P. Feautrier. A parallelization framework for recursive tree programs. In *EuroPar'98*, LNCS, Southampton, UK, Sept. 1998. Springer-Verlag.

21. P. Fradet and D. L. Metayer. Shape types. In *ACM Symp. on Principles of Programming Languages (PoPL'97)*, pages 27–39, Paris, France, Jan. 1997.

22. M. P. Gerlek, E. Stoltz, and M. J. Wolfe. Beyond induction variables: detecting and classifying sequences using a demand-driven ssa form. *ACM Trans. on Programming Languages and Systems*, 17(1):85–122, Jan. 1995.

23. R. Ghiya and L. J. Hendren. Is it a tree, a DAG, or a cyclic graph? A shape analysis for heap-directed pointers in C. In *ACM Symp. on Principles of Programming Languages (PoPL'96)*, pages 1–15, St. Petersburg Beach, Florida, Jan. 1996.

24. J.-L. Giavitto, O. Michel, and J.-P. Sansonnet. Group-based fields. In *Proc. of the Parallel Symbolic Languages and Systems*, Oct. 1995. See also "Design and Implementation of $8_{1/2}$, a Declarative Data-Parallel Language, RR 1012, Laboratoire de Recherche en Informatique, Université Paris Sud 11, France, 1995".

25. H. Hampapuram, Y. Yang, and M. Das. Symbolic path simulation in path-sensitive dataflow analysis. In *Proc. of the ACM Workshop on Program Analysis for Software Tools and Engineering (PASTE'05)*, pages 52–58, Lisbon, Portugal, Sept. 2005.

26. W. L. Harrison. The interprocedural analysis and automatic parallelisation of Scheme programs. *Lisp and Symbolic Computation*, 2(3):176–396, Oct. 1989.

27. L. J. Hendren, J. Hummel, and A. Nicolau. Abstractions for recursive pointer data structures: improving the analysis and transformation of imperative programs. In *ACM Symp. on Programming Language Design and Implementation (PLDI'92)*, pages 249–260, San Francisco, Calfifornia, June 1992.

28. N. Klarlund and M. I. Schwartzbach. Graph types. In *ACM Symp. on Principles of Programming Languages (PoPL'93)*, pages 196–205, Charleston, South Carolina, Jan. 1993.

29. D. E. Maydan, S. P. Amarasinghe, and M. S. Lam. Array dataflow analysis and its use in array privatization. In 20th *ACM Symp. on Principles of Programming Languages*, pages 2–15, Charleston, South Carolina, Jan. 1993.

30. M. Might and O. Shivers. Environment analysis via Delta CFA. In *ACM Symp. on Principles of Programming Languages (PoPL'06)*, pages 127–140, Charleston, South Carolina, Jan. 2006.

31. F. Nielson, H. Nielson, and C. Hankin. *Principles of Program Analysis*. Springer-Verlag, 1999.

32. C. Okasaki. Functional data structures. *Advanced Functional Programming*, pages 131–158, 1996.

33. M. Pelletier and J. Sakarovitch. On the representation of finite deterministic 2-tape automata. *Theoretical Computer Science*, 225(1-2):1–63, 1999.

34. G.-R. Perrin and A. Darte, editors. *The Data Parallel Programming Model*. Number 1132 in LNCS. Springer-Verlag, 1996.

35. S. Pop, A. Cohen, and G.-A. Silber. Induction variable analysis with delayed abstractions. In *Intl. Conf. on High Performance Embedded Architectures and Compilers (HiPEAC'05)*, number 3793 in LNCS, pages 218–232, Barcelona, Spain, Nov. 2005. Springer-Verlag.

36. W. Pugh. A practical algorithm for exact array dependence analysis. *Communications of the ACM*, 35(8):27–47, Aug. 1992.

37. T. Reps, S. Horwitz, and M. Sagiv. Precise interprocedural dataflow analysis via graph reachability. In *ACM Symp. on Principles of Programming Languages (PoPL'95)*, San Francisco, CA, Jan. 1995.

38. T. W. Reps, S. Schwoon, and S. Jha. Weighted pushdown systems and their application to interprocedural dataflow analysis. In *Int. Symp. on Static Analysis (SAS'03)*, pages 189–213, San Diego, CA, June 2003.

39. G. Rozenberg and A. Salomaa, editors. *Handbook of Formal Languages*, volume 1: Word Language Grammar. Springer-Verlag, 1997.
40. G. Rozenberg and A. Salomaa, editors. *Handbook of Formal Languages*, volume 3: Beyond Words. Springer-Verlag, 1997.
41. S. Sagiv, T. W. Reps, and R. Wilhelm. Parametric shape analysis via 3-valued logic. In *ACM Symp. on Principles of Programming Languages (PoPL'99)*, pages 105–118, San Antonio, Texas, Jan. 1999.
42. M. Sharir and A. Pnueli. *Program Flow Analysis: Theory and Applications*, chapter Two Approaches to Interprocedural Data Flow Analysis. Prenticce Hall, 1981.
43. A. Venet. Nonuniform alias analysis of recursive data structures and arrays. In *Int. Symp. on Static Analysis (SAS'02)*, volume 2477 of *LNCS*, pages 36–51. Springer-Verlag, 2002.
44. A. Venet. A scalable nonuniform pointer analysis for embedded programs. In *Int. Symp. on Static Analysis (SAS'04)*, volume 3148 of *LNCS*, pages 149–164, Verona, Italy, 2004. Springer-Verlag.
45. M. J. Wolfe. *High Performance Compilers for Parallel Computing*. Addison-Wesley, 1996.
46. P. Wu, A. Cohen, D. Padua, and J. Hoeflinger. Monotonic evolution: an alternative to induction variable substitution for dependence analysis. In *ACM Intl. Conf. on Supercomputing (ICS'01)*, Sorrento, Italy, June 2001.

Separation Logic and Program Analysis

Peter W. O'Hearn

Queen Mary, University of London, United Kingdom

Abstract. Separation logic is a program logic for reasoning about programs that manipulate pointer data structures. It has a strong form of modularity or locality built in, and has led to simpler by-hand proofs of pointer algorithms than was possible in previous formalisms. It is natural to wonder whether, and in what way, its ideas might be used in program analysis.

In this talk I will begin by describing the basics of separation logic, along the way connecting them to concepts from program analysis. I will then describe some initial, unsuccessful attempts at applying the formalism. This is done in an effort to convey that some of the first ideas at application do not work well, and also to help pin down what some of the central outstanding issues are. This will then lead on to, and partially justify, one way of organizing a program analysis, where the abstract domain is built from formulae in separation logic. Finally, I will survey some recent developments and speculate on further possibilities.

K. Yi (Ed.): SAS 2006, LNCS 4134, p. 181, 2006.
© Springer-Verlag Berlin Heidelberg 2006

Beyond Reachability: Shape Abstraction in the Presence of Pointer Arithmetic

Cristiano Calcagno[1], Dino Distefano[2], Peter W. O'Hearn[2,3],
and Hongseok Yang[4]

[1] Imperial College, London
[2] Queen Mary, University of London
[3] Microsoft Research, Cambridge
[4] Seoul National University

Abstract. Previous shape analysis algorithms use a memory model where the heap is composed of discrete nodes that can be accessed only via access paths built from variables and field names, an assumption that is violated by pointer arithmetic. In this paper we show how this assumption can be removed, and pointer arithmetic embraced, by using an analysis based on separation logic. We describe an abstract domain whose elements are certain separation logic formulae, and an abstraction mechanism that automatically transits between a low-level RAM view of memory and a higher, fictional, view that abstracts from the representation of nodes and multiword linked-lists as certain configurations of the RAM. A widening operator is used to accelerate the analysis. We report experimental results obtained from running our analysis on a number of classic algorithms for dynamic memory management.

1 Introduction

Shape analysis algorithms statically infer deep properties of the runtime heap, such as whether a variable points to a cyclic or acyclic linked list. Previous shape analyses (e.g., [7, 30, 31, 14, 21, 23, 24, 6, 1]) assume a high-level storage model based on records and field access rather than a RAM with arithmetic. This is a significant limitation. They can deliver reasonable results for the usage of pointers or references in high-level languages such as Java or ML, or for programs written in a low-level language that happen to satisfy assumptions not dissimilar to those required by conservative garbage collectors. But, for many important low-level programs they would deliver imprecise results[1].

The crux of the problem is that the assumption of memory as composed of discrete nodes with pointers to one another – essentially as a form of graph – is a fiction that is exposed as such by pointer arithmetic. It is difficult to use the notion of *reachability* to characterize how memory may be accessed, because a memory cell can be accessed by an arithmetic calculation; in a sense, *any* cell is reachable. And yet, most shape analyses rely strongly on reachability

---

[1] Correspondingly, even for high-level languages current analyses are limited in the structures they infer *within* an array.

K. Yi (Ed.): SAS 2006, LNCS 4134, pp. 182–203, 2006.

or, more to the point, what can be inferred from non-reachability (from chosen roots). Several analyses use explicit reachability predicates in their formulation of abstract states [31, 24, 1], where others use graph models [30, 14, 21].

This paper has two main contributions. First, we show that it is possible to define a shape analysis for programs that mutate linked data structures using pointer arithmetic. Our abstract domain uses separation logic [27] formulae to represent abstract states, following on from the work on Space Invader [15] and Smallfoot [3, 4]. We use separation logic because it deals smoothly with pointer arithmetic; crucially, it does not depend in any way on anything about reachability for its soundness. We focus on a particular kind of linked structure that uses arithmetic: linked lists with variable length entries – or more briefly, *multiword lists* [8]. Multiword lists allow for arithmetic operations that split and coalesce blocks, and are one of the kinds of data structure used in memory managers.

We provide experimental results on a series of programs for dynamic memory management, essentially following the development in [20], the classic reference on the subject. Our most involved example is the `malloc` from Section 8.7 of [19].

The second contribution concerns the use of logic in program analysis. We use two techniques to accelerate our analysis: a widening operator and a differential fixpoint algorithm. The way that they are used here makes it difficult to prove soundness by standard means (to do with prefixpoints). However, soundness is easy if we view the analysis algorithm as conducting a proof search in separation logic. The suggestion is that program logic provides a flexible way of exploring non-standard optimizations in program analysis, while maintaining soundness.

2   Basic Ideas

Although pointer arithmetic can potentially lead to an incredible mess, its disciplined use can be very regular. Programmers transit between a RAM-level or even bit-level view and a structured one where, say, a graph structure is laid on top of the sea of bits, even if the structured view is not enforced by the programming language. In this section we describe some of the basic ideas in our analysis in a semi-formal way, highlighting how it negotiates this kind of transit.

The formulae in our analysis take meaning in the standard RAM model of separation logic. The notation $[E]$ is used to dereference address E, where E is an arithmetic expression. We will not repeat the formal definition of the interpretation of formulae in this model, but instead will describe their meanings intuitively as we go along. Familiarity with [27] would be helpful.

We work with linked lists where a node x is a multiword structure storing a pointer y to the next node and an integer z which can be read out of the structure to determine the length of a block of memory associated with it.

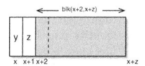

In separation logic we can describe such nodes as follows. First, we consider a basic predicate $\mathsf{blk}(E, F)$, which denotes a (possibly empty) consecutive sequence of cells starting from E and ending in $F-1$. (This could be defined using the iterated separating conjunction [27], but we take blk as primitive.) We also use the usual points-to predicate $E\mapsto F$ which denotes a singleton heap where address E has contents F. Then, the predicate for multiword nodes has the definition

$$\mathsf{nd}(x, y, z) \stackrel{\text{def}}{=} (x\mapsto y) * (x+1\mapsto z) * \mathsf{blk}(x+2, x+z) \tag{1}$$

which corresponds directly to the picture above.

With the node predicate we can define the notion of a multiword linked-list segment from x to y

$$\mathsf{mls}(x, y) \stackrel{\text{def}}{=} (\exists z'.\, \mathsf{nd}(x, y, z')) \vee (\exists y', z'.\mathsf{nd}(x, y', z') * \mathsf{mls}(y', y)). \tag{2}$$

It is understood that this predicate is the least satisfying the recursive equation.

The blk, nd and mls predicates will form the basis for our abstract domain. In several of the memory managers that we have verified (see Section 7) the free list is a circular multiword linked list with header node `free`. Such a circular list, in the case that it is nonempty, can be represented with the formula $\mathsf{mls}(\texttt{free}, \texttt{free})$. In others the free list is acyclic, and we use $\mathsf{mls}(\texttt{free}, 0)$.

If one doesn't look inside the definition of nd, then there is no pointer arithmetic to be seen. The interesting part of the memory management algorithms, though, is how "node-ness" is broken and then re-established at various places.

Dynamic memory management algorithms often coalesce adjacent blocks when memory is freed. If we are given $\mathsf{nd}(x, y, z) * \mathsf{nd}(x+z, a, b)$ then an assignment statement $[x+1]:=[x+1]+[x+z+1]$ effects the coalescence. To reason about this assignment our analysis first breaks the two nodes apart into their constituents by unrolling the definition (1), giving us

$$(x\mapsto y) * (x+1\mapsto z) * \mathsf{blk}(x+2, x+z)$$
$$* (x+z\mapsto a) * (x+z+1\mapsto b) * \mathsf{blk}(x+z+2, x+z+b). \tag{3}$$

This exposes enough $\mapsto$ assertions for the basic forward-reasoning axioms of separation logic to apply to the formula. Even just thinking operationally, it should be clear that the assignment statement above applied to this state yields

$$(x\mapsto y) * (x+1\mapsto z+b) * \mathsf{blk}(x+2, x+z)$$
$$* (x+z\mapsto a) * (x+z+1\mapsto b) * \mathsf{blk}(x+z+2, x+z+b). \tag{4}$$

where the $x+1$ *-conjunct has been updated. At this point, we have lost node-ness of the portion of memory beginning at x and ending at $x+z$, because $z+b$ is stored at position $x+1$.

After transforming an input symbolic state we perform abstraction by applying selected sound implications. First, there is an implication from the rhs to the lhs of (1), which corresponds to rolling up the definition of nd. Applying this to formula (4), with a law of separation logic that lets us use implications within *-conjuncts (modus ponens plus identity plus *-introduction), results in

$$(x\mapsto y) * (x+1\mapsto z+b) * \mathsf{blk}(x+2, x+z) * \mathsf{nd}(x+z, a, b). \tag{5}$$

Next, there is a true implication

$$(x \mapsto y) * (x{+}1 \mapsto z{+}b) * \mathsf{blk}(x{+}2, x{+}z) * \mathsf{nd}(x{+}z, a, b) \Longrightarrow \mathsf{nd}(x, y, z{+}b). \quad (6)$$

When we apply it to (5) we obtain the desired coalesced post-state $\mathsf{nd}(x, y, z{+}b)$. The implication (6) performs abstraction, in the sense that it loses the information that b is held at position $x{+}z{+}1$ and that $x{+}z$ has a pointer to a.

This discussion is intended to illustrate two features of our analysis method.

1. Before a heap access is made, predicate definitions are unrolled enough to reveal $\mapsto$ assertions for the cells being accessed.
2. After a statement is (symbolically) executed, sound implications are used to lose information as well as to establish that "higher-level" predicates hold.

These features were present already in the original Space Invader. The point here is that they give us a way to transit between the unstructured world where memory does not consist of discrete nodes and a higher-level view where memory has been correctly packaged together "as if" the node fiction were valid.

The real difficulty in defining the abstract domain is choosing the implications like (6) that lose enough information to allow fixpoint calculations to converge, without losing so much information that the results are unusably imprecise.

3   Programming Language and Abstract Domain

Programming Language. We consider a sequential programming language that allows arithmetic operations on pointers.

$$
\begin{aligned}
[rclqTlql]e &::= n \mid x \mid e{+}e \mid e{-}e \\
B &::= e{=}e \mid e{\neq}e \mid e{\leq}e \\
S &::= x{:=}\, e \mid x{:=}\, [e] \mid [e]{:=}\, e \mid x{:=}\, \mathsf{sbrk}(e) \\
C &::= S \mid C\,;C \mid \mathtt{if}(B)\,\{C\}\ \mathtt{else}\ \{C\} \mid \mathtt{while}(B)\,\{C\} \mid \mathtt{local}\ x\,;C
\end{aligned}
$$

We use the notation $[e]$ for the contents of the memory cell allocated at address e. Thus, $y{:=}\,[e]$ and $[e]{:=}\,e'$ represent look-up and mutation of the heap respectively. $\mathsf{sbrk}(e)$ corresponds to the UNIX system call which returns a pointer to e contiguous cells of memory. The other commands have standard meaning.

The programs in this language are interpreted in the usual RAM model of separation logic. Concrete states are defined by

$$\mathsf{States} \overset{\text{def}}{=} \mathsf{Stacks} \times \mathsf{Heaps} \qquad \mathsf{Stacks} \overset{\text{def}}{=} \mathsf{Vars} \to \mathsf{Ints} \qquad \mathsf{Heaps} \overset{\text{def}}{=} \mathsf{Nats}^+ \rightharpoonup_{\mathrm{fin}} \mathsf{Ints}$$

where Ints is the set of integers, Nats^+ is the set of positive integers, and Vars is a finite set of variables. The concrete semantics of programs as state transformers can be defined in the standard way (see [15, 27]).

Table 1. Symbolic Heaps

$E, F ::= n \mid x \mid x' \mid E{+}E \mid E{-}E$	$H ::= E{\mapsto}E \mid \mathsf{blk}(E, E) \mid \mathsf{nd}(E, E, E)$
$P \quad ::= E{=}E \mid E{\neq}E \mid E{\leq}E \mid \mathsf{true}$	$\quad\;\mid \mathsf{mls}(E, E) \mid \mathsf{true} \mid \mathsf{emp}$
$\Pi \quad ::= P \mid \Pi \wedge \Pi$	$\Sigma ::= H \mid \Sigma * \Sigma$
	$Q ::= \Pi \wedge \Sigma$

Symbolic Heaps. A symbolic heap Q is a separation-logic formula of a special form, consisting of a *pure part Π* and a *spatial part Σ*. Symbolic heaps are defined in Table 1. Due to pointer arithmetic, we use a richer collection of pure predicates than in [3]. As in [15] the primed variables are a syntactic convenience, which indicates that they are existentially quantified. Note that E is an integer expression, but unlike program expression e, it can contain primed variables. Spatial predicates blk, nd and mls have the meanings alluded to in Section 2.

The concretization $\gamma(Q)$ of Q is the set of the concrete states that satisfy $\exists \vec{y'}$. Q according to the usual semantics of separation logic formulae, where $\vec{y'}$ consists of all the primed variables in Q. We will use the notations $Q * H$ and $P \wedge H$ to express $\Pi \wedge (\Sigma * H)$ and $(P \wedge \Pi) \wedge \Sigma$, respectively. We treat symbolic heaps as equivalent up to commutativity and associativity for $*$ and $\wedge$, identity laws $H * \mathsf{emp} = H$ and $P \wedge \mathsf{true} = P$, and idempotence law $\mathsf{true} * \mathsf{true} = \mathsf{true}$.

Let SH denote the set of all symbolic heaps Q. The abstract domain $\mathcal{D}$ consists of finite sets of symbolic heaps and an extra element $\top$:

$$\mathcal{S} \in \mathcal{D} \stackrel{\mathrm{def}}{=} \mathcal{P}_{\mathrm{fin}}(\mathsf{SH}) \cup \{\top\}$$
$$\gamma(\mathcal{S}) \stackrel{\mathrm{def}}{=} \mathbf{if}\ (\mathcal{S} \neq \top)\ \mathbf{then}\ (\textstyle\bigcup_{Q \in \mathcal{S}} \gamma(Q))\ \mathbf{else}\ (\mathsf{States} \cup \{\mathsf{fault}\}).$$

Intuitively, $\mathcal{S}$ means the disjunction of all symbolic heaps in $\mathcal{S}$. The elements $\mathcal{S}, \mathcal{S}'$ of $\mathcal{D}$ are ordered by the subset relation extended with $\top$:

$$\mathcal{S} \sqsubseteq \mathcal{S}' \iff (\mathcal{S}' = \top \vee (\mathcal{S} \in \mathcal{P}(\mathsf{SH}) \wedge \mathcal{S}' \in \mathcal{P}(\mathsf{SH}) \wedge \mathcal{S} \subseteq \mathcal{S}')).$$

4 Abstraction Rules

The main part of our analysis is the abstraction function $\mathsf{Abs} \colon \mathcal{D} \to \mathcal{D}$, which establishes a fictional view of memory as consisting of nodes and multiword lists (forgetting information, if necessary, to do so). It is applied at the beginning of a loop and after each iteration; in the bodies of loops the fiction can be broken by operations on the RAM level.

The abstraction function has five steps, which successively: synthesize nodes from RAM configurations; simplify arithmetic expressions to control the potential explosion of arithmetic constraints; abstract size fields; reason about multiword lists; and filter out inconsistent symbolic heaps. We will specify the first four steps in terms of rewriting rules on SH. The rules in each step will always be

Table 2. Node Synthesis Rules

Package Rule	Swallow Rule
Precondition: $2 \leq G \leq H$	Precondition: $H+1 \leq G \leq H+K$
$Q * (E \mapsto F, G) * \mathsf{blk}(E+2, E+H)$	$Q * (E \mapsto F, G) * \mathsf{blk}(E+2, E+H) * \mathsf{nd}(E+H, I, K)$
$\Rightarrow Q * \mathsf{nd}(E, F, G) * \mathsf{blk}(E+G, E+H)$	$\Rightarrow Q * \mathsf{nd}(E, F, G) * \mathsf{blk}(E+G, E+H+K)$

Package2 Rule

Precondition: $2 \leq G \leq H$ with x' fresh

$Q * \mathsf{blk}(E, E+1) * (E+1 \mapsto G) * \mathsf{blk}(E+2, E+H) \Rightarrow Q * \mathsf{nd}(E, x', G) * \mathsf{blk}(E+G, E+H)$

normalizing. Thus, a particular strategy for applying the rules induces a function from SH to SH, which will then be lifted to a function on $\mathcal{D}$. For the last step, we will define a partial identity function on SH and lift it to a function on $\mathcal{D}$.

4.1   Node Synthesis

Node synthesis recognizes places where a portion of low-level memory can be packaged into a node. The synthesis rules are in Table 2. The idea of the first, Package, is just to package up a node using the definition of the nd predicate.[2] When we do this, we sometimes have to split off part of the end of a block in order to have the right information to form a node. Figure 1 gives a pictorial view of the Package rule. A node is indicated by a shaded box with a sub-part, G in the diagram, and an outgoing pointer, F there. The picture emphasizes the way in which the abstraction function transfers from the RAM-level view to the structured view where a group of cells becomes a unique entity (a node).

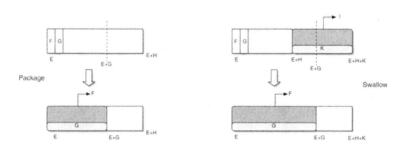

Fig. 1. Package Rule (left) and Swallow Rule (right)

The idea of the second rule, Swallow, is that when we already have a node to the right of a block as well as link and size cells, we might be able to swallow the preceding cells into a node. In doing this we again might have to chop off

---

[2] In these rules $E \mapsto F, G$ is the standard separation logic abbreviation for $E \mapsto F *$ $E+1 \mapsto G$.

the end of the node (see Figure 1 for a depiction of the rule). The special case of this rule where $G = H + K$ corresponds to the discussion in Section 2.

The Package2 rule comes from a situation where a block has been split off to be returned to the user, and the size G of the node has been discovered by the allocation routine.

The technical meaning of these rules is that we can apply a rewriting $Q \Rightarrow Q'$ when Q implies the stated precondition. So, for the Package rule to fire we must establish an entailment

$$Q * (E \mapsto F, G) * \mathsf{blk}(E+2, E+H) \vdash 2 \leq G \leq H.$$

Our analysis does this by calling a theorem prover for entailments $Q \vdash Q'$.

The theorem prover we have implemented builds on the prover used in Smallfoot [3]. It is incomplete, but fast, and it always terminates. The description of the analysis in this paper can be considered as parameterized by a sound prover. The prover is used in the abstraction phase, described in this section, as well as in the widening and rearrangement phases described in Sections 5 and 6.

Finally, there are inference rules which allow us to apply rewriting when the specific quantities in these rules do not match syntactically. For instance, given $E + H = x' \wedge ((E \mapsto F, H) * \mathsf{blk}(E+2, x'))$ we would like to apply the Package rule but we cannot do so literally, because we can only get the formula into the right form after substituting $E + H$ for x' (as mandated by the equality in the formula). For this, we apply the rule

$$\frac{Q[E] \; \Rightarrow \; Q' \qquad Q[F] \vdash E = F}{Q[F] \; \Rightarrow \; Q'} \qquad \mathsf{Match1}$$

Here, $Q[\cdot]$ is a formula with a hole.

4.2 n-Simple Form

The analysis has a non-negative integer n as a parameter. It is used to limit offset arithmetic with a constant. (In our memory manager programs the choice $n = 4$ is sufficient).

When abstraction establishes the fictional view of the heap we must be careful to keep around some arithmetic information in the pure part, for example remembering that a found block packaged into a node was big enough to satisfy a malloc request. Keeping such important arithmetic information but dropping all the other information in the pure part is the purpose of the second abstraction step.

The second abstraction step transforms symbolic heaps to n-simple form, keeping information about only simple numerical relationships among variables and parameters of spatial predicates. The transformation prevents one source of divergence: the generation of increasingly complex arithmetic expressions. This abstraction reflects our intuitive understanding of programs for dynamic memory management: complex numerical relationships only express how heap cells form nodes, but they become unimportant once the nodes are synthesized.

Table 3. Rules for Transforming Symbolic Heaps to n-Simple Form

Substitution1 Rule	Substitution2 Rule
$x{=}E \wedge Q \Rightarrow x{=}E \wedge (Q[E/x])$	$x'{=}E \wedge Q \Rightarrow Q[E/x']$
(if $x{=}E$ is n-simple and $x \in \mathsf{fv}(Q)$)	(if $x'{=}E$ is n-simple and $x' \in \mathsf{fv}(Q)$)

Merge Rule	Simplify Rule
$E{\neq}0 \wedge 0{\leq}E \wedge Q \Rightarrow 0{\leq}E{-}1 \wedge Q$	$Q[E/y'] \Rightarrow Q[x'/y']$
	(if E is not n-simple, $y' \in \mathsf{fv}(Q)$ and $x' \notin \mathsf{fv}(Q, E)$)

Drop Rule

$P \wedge Q \Rightarrow Q$ (if atomic predicate P is not n-simple, or it contains some primed x')

An expression is called *n-simple*, for $n \geq 0$, if it is either a primed variable or an instance of N in the following definition:

$$N, M ::= x_1 + \cdots + x_k - y_1 - \cdots - y_l + m$$

where all x_i, y_j are mutually disjoint nonprimed variables and m is an integer with $|m| \leq n$. For instance, neither $x{+}x{-}y$ nor $x{+}y{-}z{-}5$ is 3-simple, since x appears twice in the first, and $|{-}5| > 3$ in the second. An atomic pure predicate is *n-simple* if it is of the form $x{=}N$ or $0{\leq}N$ where N is n-simple and $x \notin \mathsf{fv}(N)$.

A symbolic heap $Q \equiv \Pi \wedge \Sigma$ is in *n-simple form* iff the following hold:

1. Q contains only n-simple expressions.
2. Π does not contain any primed variables.
3. $\Pi \equiv x_1{=}N_1 \wedge \ldots \wedge x_k{=}N_k \wedge 0{\leq}M_1 \wedge \ldots \wedge 0{\leq}M_l$ where all x_i's are distinct variables that occur in Q only in the left of equation $x_i{=}N_i$.

The third condition ensures that disequalities are dropped from Q, that the equalities define program variables $x_1, \ldots, x_k$ in terms of other program variables, and that these equalities have already been applied in Q. The transformation to n-simple form ensures that the analysis cannot diverge by repeatedly generating symbolic heaps with new pure parts. There are only finitely many pure parts of symbolic heaps in n-simple form, since the number of program variables is finite.

Table 3 shows the rewriting rules for transforming to n-simple form. The first two rules expand a primed or nonprimed variable into its definition. The third rule Merge encodes the $\neq$ relation using the $\leq$ relation. Note that none of these three rules loses information, unlike the last two. The Simplify rule loses some numerical relationships between parameters of spatial predicates in Q, and the Drop rule drops pure conjuncts P which are not in n-simple form. For instance $0{\leq}x{+}x \wedge \mathsf{nd}(x, x{+}x, x{+}x)$ gets transformed first to $0{\leq}x' \wedge \mathsf{nd}(x, x', x')$ by Simplify, then to $\mathsf{nd}(x, x', x')$ by Drop.

The Substitution and Merge rules require that an input symbolic heap should have a specific syntactic form. We have another matching rule to apply them more liberally:

$$\frac{P \wedge Q \; \Rightarrow \; Q' \qquad \vdash P \Leftrightarrow P'}{P' \wedge Q \; \Rightarrow \; Q'} \quad \text{Match2}$$

where P is an atomic pure predicate, such as $E \neq E'$. Our implementation uses Match1 and Match2 in a demand-driven manner, building them into rules in Tables 2 and 3; we omit description of the demand-drivel variants for simplicity.

The reader might be wondering why we didn't use an existing abstract domain for numerical properties, such as [13], in the pure part. The short answer is that it is not obvious how to do so, for example, because of the way that symbolic heaps use existential quantification. An important direction for future work is to find ways to marry symbolic heaps with other abstractions, either directly or, say, through a suitable reduced product construction [10].

4.3   Abstraction at the Structured Level

Abstraction of the Size Field of Nodes. The third step of abstraction renames primed variables that are used to express the size fields of nodes, using the

Size Rule

$$Q * \mathsf{nd}(E, F, x') \; \Rightarrow \; Q * \mathsf{nd}(E, F, y') \quad (\text{if } x' \in \mathsf{fv}(Q, E, F) \text{ but } y' \notin \mathsf{fv}(Q, E, F))$$

This rule loses information about how the size x' of the node E is related to other values in Q. For instance, the rule abstracts $\mathsf{nd}(x, y, v') * \mathsf{nd}(y, 0, v')$ to $\mathsf{nd}(x, y, v') * \mathsf{nd}(y, 0, w')$, thereby losing that the nodes x and y are the same size.

After this step, every primed variable with multiple occurrences in a symbolic heap denotes the address, not the size, of a node. This implicit type information of primed variables is used in the remaining steps of the abstraction.

Multiword-List Abstraction. Next, the analysis applies abstraction rules for multiword-list segments. We use variants of the rewriting rules in [15], which are shown in Table 4[3].

The Append rule merges two smaller list segments, which are expressed by mls or nd. The side condition is for precision, not soundness. The first conjunct in the condition prevents abstraction when x' denotes a shared address: i.e. that two spatial predicates contain x' in their link fields. This case is excluded by the condition $x' \notin \mathsf{fv}(Q, G)$, for the second predicate witnessing the sharing could be in Q or it could be L_1. The second conjunct prevents abstraction when $L_0(E, x')$ is a node predicate which indirectly expresses relationships between variables. For instance, $L_0(E, x') \equiv \mathsf{nd}(y, x', z)$ expresses that z is stored in cell $y+1$.

The three forgetting rules drop atomic predicates. Forget1 removes empty blocks, and Forget2 drops list segments and nodes that cannot be accessed in a "known" way. In the presence of pointer arithmetic we can never conclude that a cell is absolutely inaccessible. Rather, if we cannot be sure of how to safely access it then our analysis decides to forget about it. Forget3 forces abstraction to establish the fictional view of memory: when we have a cell or a block that has not been made into a node in the synthesis phase, we forget it.

---

[3] The rules are slight modifications of the ones in [15], different because of the possible cyclicity of list segments in this paper.

Table 4. Rules for Multiword-List Abstraction

Notation: $L(E, F) ::= \mathsf{mls}(E, F) \mid \mathsf{nd}(E, F, H)$ $U(E, F) ::= \mathsf{blk}(E, F) \mid E \mapsto F$

Append Rule

$Q * L_0(E, x') * L_1(x', G) \Rightarrow Q * \mathsf{mls}(E, G)$

(if $x' \notin \mathsf{fv}(Q, G)$ and $(L_0 \equiv \mathsf{nd}(E, x', F) \Rightarrow E$ or F is a primed variable))

Forget1 Rule	**Forget2 Rule**	**Forget3 Rule**
$Q * \mathsf{blk}(E, E) \Rightarrow Q * \mathsf{emp}$	$Q * L(x', E) \Rightarrow Q * \mathsf{true}$	$Q * U(E, F) \Rightarrow Q * \mathsf{true}$
	(if $x' \notin \mathsf{fv}(Q)$)	

Filtering Inconsistent Symbolic Heaps. Finally, the analysis filters out symbolic heaps that are proved to be inconsistent by our theorem prover[4]. Concretely, given the result $\mathcal{S} \in \mathcal{D}$ of the previous four abstraction steps, the last step returns $\mathcal{S}'$ defined by:

$$\mathcal{S}' \stackrel{\text{def}}{=} \text{if } (\mathcal{S} = \top) \text{ then } \top \text{ else } \{Q \in \mathcal{S} \mid Q \not\vdash \mathsf{false}\}.$$

4.4 n-Canonical Symbolic Heaps

The results of Abs form a subdomain $\mathcal{C}_n$ of $\mathcal{D}$, whose elements we call n-*canonical symbolic heaps*. In this section, we define $\mathcal{C}_n$, and we prove the result that relates canonical symbolic heaps to the termination of the analysis.

Let n be a nonnegative integer. Intuitively, a symbolic heap Q is n-canonical if it is n-simple and uses primed variables in the first position of spatial predicates only for two purposes: to represent shared addresses, or to represent the destination of the link field of a node that is pointed to by a program variable. For instance, the following symbolic heaps are n-canonical:

$$\mathsf{mls}(x, x') * \mathsf{mls}(y, x') * \mathsf{mls}(x', z), \quad \mathsf{nd}(x, x', y) * \mathsf{mls}(x', z).$$

They are both n-simple, and they use the primed variable x' for one of the two allowed purposes. In the first case, x' expresses the first shared address of the two lists x and y, and in the second case, x' means the link field of a node that is pointed to by the program variable x.

To give the formal definition of n-canonical symbolic heap, we introduce some preliminary notions. An expression E *occurs left (resp. right)* in a symbolic heap Q iff there exists a spatial predicate in Q where E occurs as the first (resp. second) parameter. E is *shared* in Q iff it has at least two right occurrences. E is *directly pointed to* in Q iff Q contains $\mathsf{nd}(E_1, E, E_2)$ where both E_1 and E_2 are expressions without primed variables.

---

[4] For Proposition 4 below the prover must at least detect inconsistency when a symbolic heap explicitly defines the same location twice: Q contains $A_1(E) * A_2(E)$ where A_i ranges over $\mathsf{mls}(E, F)$, $E \mapsto F$ and $\mathsf{nd}(E, F, G)$.

Definition 1 (n-Canonical Form). *A symbolic heap Q is n-canonical iff*

1. *it is n-simple and $Q \not\vdash$ false,*
2. *it contains neither* blk *nor* $\mapsto$,
3. *if x' occurs left in Q, it is either shared or directly pointed to, and*
4. *if x' occurs as size of a node predicate in Q, it occurs only once in Q.*

We define CSH_n to be the set of n-canonical symbolic heaps, and write $\mathcal{C}_n$ for the restriction of $\mathcal{D}$ by CSH_n, that is $\mathcal{C}_n = \mathcal{P}(\mathsf{CSH}_n) \cup \{\top\}$.

Proposition 2 (Canonical Characterization). *Let $Q \in \mathsf{SH}$ be n-simple and such that $Q \not\vdash$ false. Q is n-canonical iff $Q \not\twoheadrightarrow$ for rules in Section 4.3.*

Corollary 3. *The range of the abstraction function* Abs *is precisely $\mathcal{C}_n$.*

The main property of n-canonical symbolic heaps is that there are only finitely many of them. This fact is used in Section 6 for the termination of our analysis.

Proposition 4. *The domain $\mathcal{C}_n$ is finite.*

5   Widening Operator

In this section, we define a *widening* operator $\nabla: \mathcal{C}_n \times \mathcal{C}_n \to \mathcal{C}_n$, which is used to accelerate the fixpoint computation of the analysis.

Intuitively, the widening operator ∇ is an optimization of the ($\top$-extended) set union. When ∇ is given two sets $\mathcal{S}, \mathcal{S}'$ of symbolic heaps, it adds to $\mathcal{S}$ only those elements of $\mathcal{S}'$ that add new information. So, $\gamma(\mathcal{S}\nabla\mathcal{S}')$ and $\gamma(\mathcal{S}\cup\mathcal{S}')$ should be equal. For instance, when ∇ is given

$$\mathcal{S} = \{\mathsf{mls}(x,0)\} \quad \text{and} \quad \mathcal{S}' = \{x{=}0 \wedge \mathsf{emp},\ \mathsf{nd}(x,0,y),\ \mathsf{nd}(x,y',y) * \mathsf{nd}(y',0,z)\},$$

it finds out that only the symbolic heap $x{=}0 \wedge \mathsf{emp}$ of $\mathcal{S}'$ adds new information to $\mathcal{S}$. Then, ∇ combines that symbolic heap with $\mathcal{S}$, and returns

$$\{\mathsf{mls}(x,0),\ x{=}0 \wedge \mathsf{emp}\}.$$

The formal definition of ∇ is parameterized by the theorem prover $\vdash$ for showing some (not necessarily all) semantic implications between symbolic heaps. Let rep be a procedure that takes a finite set $\mathcal{S}$ of symbolic heaps and returns a subset of $\mathcal{S}$ such that

$$(\forall Q, Q' \in \mathsf{rep}(\mathcal{S}).\ Q \vdash Q' \Rightarrow Q = Q') \ \wedge \ (\forall Q \in \mathcal{S}.\ \exists Q' \in \mathsf{rep}(\mathcal{S}).\ Q \vdash Q')$$

The first conjunct forces rep to get rid of some redundancies while the second, in conjunction with the assumption $\mathsf{rep}(\mathcal{S}) \subseteq \mathcal{S}$, ensures that $\gamma(\mathsf{rep}(\mathcal{S})) = \gamma(\mathcal{S})$. (Our implementation of rep selects $\vdash$-maximal elements of $\mathcal{S}$; in case two elements are $\vdash$-equivalent a fixed ordering on symbolic heaps is used to select one.)

Using $\vdash$ and rep, we define ∇ as follows:

$$\mathcal{S}\nabla\mathcal{S}' = \begin{cases} \mathcal{S} \cup \{Q' \in \mathsf{rep}(\mathcal{S}') \mid \neg(\exists Q \in \mathcal{S}.\, Q' \vdash Q)\} & \text{if } \mathcal{S}{\neq}\top \text{ and } \mathcal{S}'{\neq}\top \\ \top & \text{otherwise} \end{cases}$$

This definition requires heaps added to $\mathcal{S}$ to, first, not imply any elements in $\mathcal{S}$ (that would be redundant) and, second, to be "maximal" in the sense of rep.

Our operator ∇ satisfies nonstandard axioms [11], which have also been used in the work on the ASTRÉE analyzer [28, 12].

Proposition 5. *The ∇ operator satisfies the following two axioms:*

1. *For all $\mathcal{S}, \mathcal{S}' \in \mathcal{C}_n$, we have that $\gamma(\mathcal{S}) \cup \gamma(\mathcal{S}') \subseteq \gamma(\mathcal{S} \nabla \mathcal{S}')$.*
2. *For every infinite sequence $\{\mathcal{S}'_i\}_{i \geq 0}$ in $\mathcal{C}_n$, the widened sequence $\mathcal{S}_0 = \mathcal{S}'_0$ and $\mathcal{S}_{i+1} = \mathcal{S}_i \nabla \mathcal{S}'_{i+1}$ converges.*

The first axiom means that ∇ overapproximates the concrete union operator, and it ensures that the analysis can use ∇ without losing soundness. The next axiom means that ∇ always turns a sequence into a converging one, and it guarantees that ∇ does not disturb the termination of the analysis.

The first axiom above is not standard. Usually [9], one uses a stronger axiom where ∇ is required to be extensive for both arguments, i.e.,

$$\forall \mathcal{S}, \mathcal{S}' \in \mathcal{C}_n. \, \mathcal{S} \sqsubseteq (\mathcal{S} \nabla \mathcal{S}') \wedge \mathcal{S}' \sqsubseteq (\mathcal{S} \nabla \mathcal{S}').$$

However, we cannot use this usual stronger axiom here, because our widening operator is not extensive for the second argument. For a counterexample, consider $\mathcal{S} = \{\mathsf{mls}(x, y)\}$ and $\mathcal{S}' = \{\mathsf{nd}(x, y, z)\}$. We do not have $\mathcal{S}' \sqsubseteq (\mathcal{S} \nabla \mathcal{S}')$ because the rhs is $\{\mathsf{mls}(x, y)\}$, which does not include $\mathcal{S}'$. Note that although $\mathcal{S}' \not\sqsubseteq (\mathcal{S} \nabla \mathcal{S}')$, we still have that

$$\gamma(\mathcal{S}') = \gamma(\mathsf{nd}(x, y, z)) \subseteq \gamma(\mathsf{mls}(x, y)) = \gamma(\mathcal{S} \nabla \mathcal{S}'),$$

as demanded by our first axiom for the ∇ operator.

Note that $\mathcal{S} \nabla \mathcal{S}'$ is usually smaller than the join of S and S' in $\mathcal{C}_n$. Thus, unlike other typical widening operators, our ∇ does not cause the analysis to lose precision, while making fixpoint computations converge in fewer iterations.

The widening operator is reminiscent of the ideas behind the Hoare power-domain, and one might wonder why we do not use those ideas more directly by changing the abstract domain. For instance, one might propose to use the domain $\mathcal{C}'$ that consists of $\top$ and sets $\mathcal{S}$ of symbolic heaps where no (provably) redundant elements appear (i.e., for all $Q, Q' \in \mathcal{S}$, if $Q \vdash Q'$, then $Q = Q'$). The Hoare order of $\mathcal{C}'$ would be

$$\mathcal{S} \sqsubseteq_H \mathcal{S}' \iff \mathcal{S}' = \top \vee (\mathcal{S}, \mathcal{S}' \in \mathcal{P}(\mathsf{CSH}_n) \wedge \forall Q \in \mathcal{S}. \exists Q' \in \mathcal{S}'. Q \vdash Q').$$

Unfortunately, the proposal relies on the transitivity of the provable order $\vdash$, which is nontrivial for a theorem prover to achieve in practice. If $\vdash$ is not transitive, then $\sqsubseteq_H$ is not transitive. Hence, the fixpoint computation of the analysis might fail to detect that it has already reached a fixpoint, which can cause the analysis to diverge.

On the other hand, our approach based on widening does not require any additional properties of a theorem prover other than its soundness. And neither does it require that the transfer functions be monotone wrt $\vdash$; it only requires that they be sound overapproximations. So, our approach is easier to apply.

Table 5. Abstract Semantics

Let $A[e]$ and A be syntactic subclasses of atomic commands defined by:

$$A[e] ::= [e]:= e \mid x := [e] \qquad A ::= x := e \mid x := \mathsf{sbrk}(e).$$

The abstract semantics $[\![C]\!] : \mathcal{D} \to \mathcal{D}$ is defined as follows:

$$[\![C_0 ; C_1]\!]\mathcal{S} = ([\![C_1]\!] \circ [\![C_0]\!])\mathcal{S}$$

$$[\![\mathtt{if}(B)\ \{C_0\}\ \mathtt{else}\ \{C_1\}]\!]\mathcal{S} = ([\![C_0]\!] \circ \mathsf{filter}(B))\mathcal{S} \sqcup ([\![C_1]\!] \circ \mathsf{filter}(\neg B))\mathcal{S}$$

$$[\![\mathtt{local}\ x ; C]\!]\mathcal{S} = \mathbf{if}\,([\![C]\!](\mathcal{S}[y'/x]) = \top)\ \mathbf{then}\ \top\ \mathbf{else}\ ([\![C]\!](\mathcal{S}[y'/x]))[x'/x]$$

$$[\![\mathtt{while}(B)\{C\}]\!]\mathcal{S} = (\mathsf{filter}(\neg B) \circ \mathit{wfix})(\mathcal{S}_0, F)$$
$$(\text{where } \mathcal{S}_0 = \mathsf{Abs}(\mathcal{S}) \text{ and } F = \mathsf{Abs} \circ [\![C]\!] \circ \mathsf{filter}(B))$$

$$[\![A[e]]\!]\mathcal{S} = \mathbf{if}\ (\mathcal{S} = \top\ \vee\ \exists Q \in \mathcal{S}.\, Q \leadsto_e^* \mathsf{fault})\ \mathbf{then}\ \top$$
$$\mathbf{else}\ \{Q_1 \mid Q \in \mathcal{S}\ \wedge\ Q \leadsto_e^* Q_0\ \wedge\ (Q_0, A[e] \Longrightarrow Q_1)\}$$

$$[\![A]\!]\mathcal{S} = \mathbf{if}\ (\mathcal{S} = \top)\ \mathbf{then}\ \top\ \mathbf{else}\ \{Q_0 \mid Q \in \mathcal{S}\ \wedge\ (Q, A \Longrightarrow Q_0)\}$$

where primed variables are assumed fresh, and $\mathsf{filter} \colon \mathcal{D} \to \mathcal{D}$ and $- \colon \mathcal{C}_n \times \mathcal{C}_n \to \mathcal{C}_n$ and $\mathit{wfix} \colon \mathcal{C}_n \times [\mathcal{C}_n \to \mathcal{C}_n] \to \mathcal{C}_n$ are functions defined below:

$$\mathsf{filter}(B)(\mathcal{S}) = \mathbf{if}\ (\mathcal{S} = \top)\ \mathbf{then}\ \top\ \mathbf{else}\ \{B \wedge Q \mid Q \in \mathcal{S}\ \text{and}\ (B \wedge Q \nvdash \mathsf{false})\}.$$

$$\mathcal{S}_0 - \mathcal{S}_1 = \mathbf{if}\ (\mathcal{S}_0 \neq \top \wedge \mathcal{S}_1 \neq \top)\ \mathbf{then}\ (\mathcal{S}_0 - \mathcal{S}_1)\ \mathbf{else}\ \left(\mathbf{if}\ (\mathcal{S}_1 = \top)\ \mathbf{then}\ \emptyset\ \mathbf{else}\ \top\right)$$

$\mathit{wfix}(\mathcal{S}, F)$ is the first stabilizing element $\mathcal{S}_k$ of the below sequence $\{\mathcal{S}_i\}_{i \geq 0}$:

$$\mathcal{S}_0 = \mathcal{S} \qquad \mathcal{S}_1 = \mathcal{S}_0 \nabla F(\mathcal{S}) \qquad \mathcal{S}_{i+2} = \mathcal{S}_{i+1} \nabla (F(\mathcal{S}_{i+1} - \mathcal{S}_i)).$$

---

6   Abstract Semantics

The abstract semantics of our language follows the standard denotational-style abstract interpretation. It interprets commands as $\top$-preserving functions on $\mathcal{D}$ in a compositional manner. The semantic clauses for commands are given in Table 5. In the table, we use the macro $\neg$ that maps $E = F$, $E \neq F$, $E \leq F$ to $E \neq F$, $E = F$, $F \leq E - 1$, respectively. The semantics of compound commands other than while loops is standard. The interpretation of while loops, however, employs non-standard techniques. First, when the interpretation of the loop does the fixpoint computation, it switches the abstract domain from $\mathcal{D}$ to the finite subdomain $\mathcal{C}_n$, thereby ensuring the termination of the fixpoint computation. Concretely, given a loop $\mathtt{while}(B)\ \{C\}$ and an initial abstract element $\mathcal{S}$, the semantics constructs F and $\mathcal{S}_0$ with types $\mathcal{C}_n \to \mathcal{C}_n$ and $\mathcal{C}_n$, respectively. Then, the semantics uses F and $\mathcal{S}_0$, and does the fixpoint computation in the finite domain $\mathcal{C}_n$. Note the major role of the abstraction function Abs here; Abs abstracts the initial abstract element $\mathcal{S}$, and it is used in F to abstract the analysis results of the loop body, so that the fixpoint computation lives in $\mathcal{C}_n$.

Intuitively, the analysis works at the "RAM level" inside loops and the higher, structured, view of lists and nodes is re-established at every iteration. For the purpose of the analysis described in this paper, this is a necessary choice since very often the precision of the RAM level is needed to meaningfully execute atomic commands; abstracting at every step usually produces imprecise results.

Second, the abstract semantics of while loops uses an optimized fixpoint algorithm called *widened differential fixpoint algorithm*. The main idea of this algorithm is to use two known optimization techniques. The first is to use a widening operator to help the analysis reach a fixpoint in fewer iterations [9].[5] The second is to use the technique of subtraction to prevent the analysis from repeating the same computation in two different iteration steps [17]. Given an abstract element $S \in C_n$ and an abstract transfer function $F: C_n \to C_n$, the widened differential fixpoint algorithm generates a sequence whose $i+2$-th element has the form:

$$S_{i+2} = S_{i+1} \nabla (F(S_{i+1} - S_i)),$$

and returns the first stabilizing element of this sequence.[6] The key to the algorithm is to use the widening operator, instead of the join operator, to add newly generated analysis results to S_{i+1}, and to apply F to the subtracted previous step $S_{i+1} - S_i$, rather than to the whole previous step S_{i+1}.

Usually, these two techniques have been used separately in the denotational-style abstract interpretation. The problem is that the common soundness argument for the subtraction technique does not hold in the presence of widening. The argument relies on at least one of monotonicity, extensiveness or distributivity of F[7] but if the widening operator is used (to define F itself), F does not necessarily have any of these properties. In Section 6.2, we use an alternative approach for showing the soundness of the analysis and prove the correctness of the widened differential fixpoint algorithm.

Finally, the semantic clauses for atomic commands are given following the rules of symbolic execution in [3]. The semantics classifies atomic commands into two groups depending on whether they access existing heap cells. When an atomic command accesses an existing heap cell e, such as $[e] := e_0$ and $x := [e]$, the semantics first checks whether the input S always guarantees that e is allocated. If not, the semantics returns $\top$, indicating the possibility of memory errors. Otherwise, it transforms each symbolic heap in S using the rearrangement rules $\rightsquigarrow^*$ (see Section 6.1) in order to expose cell e. Then, the semantics symbolically runs the command using $\Longrightarrow$ in Table 6. For the atomic commands that do not access heap cells, the semantics skips the rearrangement step.

6.1 Rearrangement Rules

When symbolic execution attempts to access a memory cell e which is not explicitly indicated in the symbolic heap, it appeals to a set of rules (called rearrangement rules) whose purpose is to rewrite the symbolic heap in order to

---

[5] Theoretically, since the analyzer works on the set of canonical heaps which is finite, the use of widening is not necessary for termination. However, widening significantly speeds up the convergence of the fixpoint computation.

[6] S_k is a stabilizing element iff $S_k = S_{k+1}$.

[7] F is distributive iff for all S, S', $F(S \sqcup S') = F(S) \sqcup F(S')$.

Table 6. Rules of Symbolic Execution

$Q,\ x := e$	$\Longrightarrow x = e[x'/x] \wedge Q[x'/x]$
$Q * e \mapsto F,\ x := [e]$	$\Longrightarrow x = F[x'/x] \wedge (Q * e \mapsto F)[x'/x]$
$Q * e_0 \mapsto F,\ [e_0] := e_1$	$\Longrightarrow Q * e_0 \mapsto e_1$
$Q,\ x := \mathsf{sbrk}(e)$	$\Longrightarrow Q[x'/x] * \mathsf{blk}(x, x + (e[x'/x]))$ (when $Q \vdash e > 0$)
$Q,\ x := \mathsf{sbrk}(e)$	$\Longrightarrow x = -1 \wedge Q[x'/x]$

where primed variables are assumed fresh.

Table 7. Rearrangement Rules for Built-in Predicates

Switch Rule	Blk Rule
Precondition: $F = e$	Precondition: $F \le e < G$ with x' fresh
$Q * F \mapsto G \leadsto_e Q * e \mapsto G$	$Q * \mathsf{blk}(F, G) \leadsto_e Q * \mathsf{blk}(F, e) * e \mapsto x' * \mathsf{blk}(e+1, G)$

reveal e. In this paper, we have three sets of rearrangement rules. The first set, in Table 7, handles built-in predicates. The rules in the second set follow the general pattern

$$\frac{\text{Allocated: } e}{\text{Consistency: } Q * Q'[\vec{F}/\vec{x}]}$$
$$\overline{Q * H(\vec{F}) \leadsto_e Q * Q'[\vec{F}/\vec{x}]}$$

Here $H(\vec{F})$ is either nd or mls, and Q' is one of the disjuncts in the definition of H with all the primed variables in Q' renamed fresh. Instead of the precondition requirement as in the abstraction rules in Section 4, the rules generated by this pattern have an *allocatedness* requirement and a *consistency* requirement. Allocatedness guarantees that the heap contains the cell e that we are interested in. This correspond to the check:

$$\Pi_Q \wedge (H(\vec{F}) * e \mapsto x') \vdash \mathsf{false}$$

where Π_Q is the pure part of Q and x' is a fresh primed variable. The consistency requirement of the rule enforces its post-state to be meaningful. This means that in order for the rule to fire the following extra consistency condition should hold:

$$Q * Q'[\vec{F}/\vec{x}] \nvdash \mathsf{false}.$$

The rearrangement rules for nd and mls are reported in Table 8.

The third set consists of a single rule that detects the possibility of memory faults and it is described below:

Fault Rule	$Q \leadsto_e \mathsf{fault}$	(if Q does not contain $e \mapsto F$, but $Q \nleadsto_e$).

Table 8. Rearrangement Rules for Multiword Lists

Mls1 Rule	Mls2 Rule
Allocated: e	Allocated: e
Consistency: $Q * \mathsf{nd}(F, G, z')$	Consistency: $Q * \mathsf{nd}(F, y', z') * \mathsf{mls}(y', G)$
$Q * \mathsf{mls}(F, G) \rightsquigarrow_e Q * \mathsf{nd}(F, G, z')$	$Q * \mathsf{mls}(F, G) \rightsquigarrow_e Q * \mathsf{nd}(F, y', z') * \mathsf{mls}(y', G)$

Node Rule

Allocated: e

Consistency: $-$

$Q * \mathsf{nd}(F, G_0, G_1) \rightsquigarrow_e Q * F \mapsto G_0, G_1 * \mathsf{blk}(F{+}2, F{+}G_1)$

6.2 Soundness

Common soundness arguments in program analysis proceed by showing that the results of an analysis are prefix points of some abstract transfer functions. Then one derives that the analysis results overapproximate program invariants. Unfortunately, we cannot use this strategy, because the fixpoint algorithm described here does not necessarily compute prefix points of abstract transfer functions.

We use an alternative approach that proves soundness by compiling the analysis results into proofs in separation logic. More specifically, we prove:

Proposition 6. *Suppose that* $[\![C]\!]\mathcal{S} = \mathcal{S}'$. *If both* $\mathcal{S}$ *and* $\mathcal{S}'$ *are non-*$\top$ *abstract values, then there is a proof of a Hoare triple* $\{\mathcal{S}\} \, C \, \{\mathcal{S}'\}$ *in separation logic.*

Note that since the proof rules of separation logic are sound, this proposition implies that the results of our analysis overapproximate program invariants.

The proposition can be proved by induction on the structure of C. Most of the cases follow immediately, because the abstract semantics uses sound implications between assertions or proof rules in separation logic. Cases like these have been done in previous work [21, 15, 18], and we will not repeat them here. The treatment of while loops, however, requires a different argument.

Suppose that $[\![\texttt{while}(B)\,\{C\}]\!]\mathcal{S} = \mathcal{S}'$ for some non-$\top$ elements $\mathcal{S}$ and $\mathcal{S}'$. Let $\mathcal{S}''$ and F be the two parameters, $\mathsf{Abs}(\mathcal{S})$ and $\mathsf{Abs} \circ [\![C]\!] \circ \mathsf{filter}(B)$, of *wfix* in the interpretation of this loop. Then, by the definition of *wfix*, the abstract element $wfix(\mathcal{S}'', F)$ is the first stabilizing element $\mathcal{S}_k$ of the sequence $\{\mathcal{S}_i\}_{i \geq 0}$:

$$\mathcal{S}_0 = \mathcal{S}'' \qquad \mathcal{S}_1 = \mathcal{S}_0 \nabla F(\mathcal{S}) \qquad \mathcal{S}_{i+2} = \mathcal{S}_{i+1} \nabla F(\mathcal{S}_{i+1} - \mathcal{S}_i).$$

Moreover, we have that $\mathcal{S}' = \mathsf{filter}(\neg B)(\mathcal{S}_k)$. The following lemma summarizes the relationship among $\mathcal{S}, \mathcal{S}_0, \ldots, \mathcal{S}_{k-1}$ and $\mathcal{S}_k$, which we use to construct the separation-logic proof for the loop.

Lemma 7. *For all* $i \in \{1, \ldots, k\}$, *let* $\mathcal{T}_i$ *be* $\mathcal{S}_i - \mathcal{S}_{i-1}$.

1. *None of* $\mathcal{S}_0, \mathcal{T}_1, \ldots, \mathcal{T}_k$ *and* $\mathcal{S}_k$ *is* $\top$.
2. $\mathcal{S} \Rightarrow \mathcal{S}_k$.

Program	LOC	Max Heap (KB)	States (Loop Inv)	States (Post)	Time (sec)
malloc_firstfit_acyclic	42	240	18	3	0.05
free_acyclic	55	240	6	2	0.09
malloc_besttfit_acyclic	46	480	90	3	1.19
malloc_roving	61	240	33	5	0.13
free_roving	68	720	16	2	0.84
malloc_K&R	179	26880	384	66	502.23
free_K&R	58	3840	89	5	9.69

Fig. 2. Experimental Results

3. $\mathcal{S}_k \Rightarrow \mathcal{S}_0 \vee \mathcal{T}_1 \vee \ldots \vee \mathcal{T}_k$.
4. $F(\mathcal{S}_0) \Rightarrow \mathcal{S}_k$ and $F(\mathcal{T}_i) \Rightarrow \mathcal{S}_k$ for all $i \in \{1, \ldots, k\}$.

We now construct the required proof. Because of the fourth property in Lemma 7 and the induction hypothesis, we can derive the following proof trees:

$$\cfrac{\cfrac{\cfrac{\cfrac{\text{Ind. Hypo.}}{\{\mathsf{filter}(B)(\mathcal{U})\}\, C\, \{([\![C]\!] \circ \mathsf{filter}(B))(\mathcal{U})\}}\quad (B \wedge \mathcal{U} \Leftrightarrow \mathsf{filter}(B)(\mathcal{U}))}{\{B \wedge \mathcal{U}\}\, C\, \{([\![C]\!] \circ \mathsf{filter}(B))(\mathcal{U})\}}\quad \text{Soundness of Abs,}\; F = \mathsf{Abs} \circ [\![C]\!] \circ \mathsf{filter}(B)}{\{B \wedge \mathcal{U}\}\, C\, \{F(\mathcal{U})\}}}{\{B \wedge \mathcal{U}\}\, C\, \{\mathcal{S}_k\}}\text{Prop.4 of Lem.7}$$

twhere $\mathcal{U}$ is $\mathcal{S}_0$ or $\mathcal{T}_i$. We combine those proof trees, and build the required tree for the loop:

$$\cfrac{\cfrac{\cfrac{\cfrac{\{B \wedge \mathcal{S}_0\}\, C\, \{\mathcal{S}_k\}\quad \{B \wedge \mathcal{T}_1\}\, C\, \{\mathcal{S}_k\}\quad \ldots \quad \{B \wedge \mathcal{T}_k\}\, C\, \{\mathcal{S}_k\}}{\{(B \wedge \mathcal{S}_0) \vee (B \wedge \mathcal{T}_1) \vee \ldots (B \wedge \mathcal{T}_k)\}\, C\, \{\mathcal{S}_k\}}\text{Disjunction}}{\{B \wedge \mathcal{S}_k\}\, C\, \{\mathcal{S}_k\}}\text{Prop.3 of Lem.7}}{\{\mathcal{S}_k\}\, \mathtt{while}(B)\, \{C\}\, \{\neg B \wedge \mathcal{S}_k\}}\text{While}}{\{\mathcal{S}\}\, \mathtt{while}(B)\, \{C\}\, \{\mathcal{S}'\}}\text{Prop.2 of Lem.7,}\; \mathcal{S}' = \mathsf{filter}(\neg B)\mathcal{S}_k$$

Note that the proof tree indicates that the subtraction technique of our fixpoint algorithm corresponds to the disjunction rule

$$\frac{\{P_1\}\, C\, \{Q_1\}\quad \{P_2\}\, C\, \{Q_2\}}{\{P_1 \vee P_2\}\, C\, \{Q_1 \vee Q_2\}}$$

of Hoare logic.

7   Experimental Results

We implemented our analysis in OCaml, and conducted experiments on an Intel Pentium 3.2GHz with 4GB RAM; our results are in Figure 2. Our implementation contains a postprocessor that simplifies computed post abstract values using the abstraction Abs and rep in Section 5. malloc_K&R is the only one of the programs with a nested loop; the size of the invariant for it in Figure 2 refers to the outer loop. (The test-programs can be found on the authors' web pages.)

The malloc_firstfit_acyclic and free_acyclic programs are Algorithms A and B from Section 2.5 of [20]. They both manage an acyclic free list maintained in address-sorted order. malloc_firstfit_acyclic walks the free list until a big enough block is found to satisfy a malloc request. That block is returned to the caller if the size is exactly right, and otherwise part of the block is chopped off and returned to the caller, with the leftover resized and kept in the free list. If a correctly-sized block is not found then the algorithm returns 0. The free algorithm inserts a block in the appropriate place in this list, maintaining sorted order and coalescing nodes when possible. malloc_bestfit_acyclic traverses the entire free list to find the best fit for a request, and returns it.

In simplistic first-fit allocators small blocks tend to pile up at the front of the free list. A way to combat this problem is to use a cyclic rather than acyclic free list, with a "roving pointer" that moves around the list [20]. The roving pointer points to where the last allocation was done, and the next allocation starts from it. malloc_roving and free_roving implement this strategy.

The first five programs assume that a fixed amount of memory has been given to the memory manager at the beginning. A common strategy is to extend this by calling a system routine to request additional memory when a request cannot be met. This is the strategy used in the memory manager from Section 8.7 of [19]. When a request cannot be met, sbrk is called for additional memory. In case sbrk succeeds the memory it returns is inserted into the free list by calling free, and then allocation continues. The memory manager there uses the roving pointer strategy. To model this program in the programming language used for our analysis we had to inline the call to free, as what we have described is not an interprocedural analysis. Also, we had to model multiple-dereferences like p→s.ptr→s.size using several statements, as the form in our language has at most one dereference per statement; this is akin to what a compiler front end might do. These points, inline free and basic dereferences, account for the 179 LOC in our program for malloc compared to 66 LOC in the original.

The manager in [19] uses a nonempty circular list with a fixed head node that is never returned to the caller. Its correctness relies on the (unstated) assumption that sbrk will return a block whose address is larger than the head node; otherwise, there are cases in which the header will be coalesced with a block gotten from sbrk, and this can lead to a situation where the same block is allocated twice in a row. Our model of sbrk in Section 6 does not make this assumption explicit, and as a result running the analysis on the original malloc reveals this "problem". By changing our model of sbrk to reflect the assumption we were able to verify the original; the model, though, is not as simple as the one in Section 6. We then altered malloc so that it did not rely on this assumption, and this is the program malloc_K&R reported in Figure 2, for which we used the simple sbrk.

The speedup obtained from the widening operator can be observed in the analysis of malloc_K&R; with widening turned off the analysis took over 20 hours

Prog : `malloc_firstfit_acyclic` and `malloc_bestfit_acyclic`

Pre : $n-2 \geq 0 \wedge \mathsf{mls}(\mathtt{free}, 0)$

Post : $(\mathtt{ans}=0 \wedge n-2 \geq 0 \wedge \mathsf{mls}(\mathtt{free}, 0)) \quad \vee \quad (n-2 \geq 0 \wedge \mathsf{nd}(\mathtt{ans}, p', n) * \mathsf{mls}(\mathtt{free}, 0))$
$\vee \; (n-2 \geq 0 \wedge \mathsf{nd}(\mathtt{ans}, p', n) * \mathsf{mls}(\mathtt{free}, p') * \mathsf{mls}(p', 0))$

Prog : `free_acyclic`

Pre : $\mathsf{mls}(\mathtt{free}, 0) * \mathsf{nd}(\mathtt{ap}-2, p', n')$

Post : $\mathsf{mls}(\mathtt{free}, \mathtt{ap}-2) * \mathsf{mls}(\mathtt{ap}-2, 0) \quad \vee \quad \mathsf{mls}(\mathtt{free}, 0)$

Fig. 3. Sample Computed Post Abstract Values

to terminate. For the other programs the analysis times were similar, except for `free_K&R` where widening resulted in a speedup of a factor of 2.

Memory safety and memory leaks are general properties, in the sense that they can be specified once and for all for all programs. For our analysis if a postcondition is not $\top$ then it follows that the program does not dereference a dangling pointer starting from any concrete state satisfying the precondition. If true does not appear in the post then the program does not have a memory leak. For all seven programs, our analysis was able to prove memory safety and the absence of memory leaks.

But in fact we can infer much more: the postconditions give what might be regarded as full functional specifications.[8] Figure 3 shows sample post abstract values computed by the analysis (with widening enabled). Take the postcondition for `malloc_firstfit_acyclic` and `malloc_bestfit_acyclic`. The first disjunct, when `ans`=0, is the case when the algorithm could not satisfy the malloc request. The second and third correspond to cases when the request has been met. These two cases are different because the analysis distinguishes when the link field of a node happens to point back into the free list. The third disjunct implies the second, so if the user were to write the first two disjuncts as the desired postcondition, which would be intuitive, then a theorem prover could tell us that the computed post in fact established a reasonable specification of partial correctness[9]. Similar remarks apply to the other postcondition for `free_acyclic`.

Finally, it is easy to trick the analysis into reporting a false bug. Our algorithm abstracts to the "fictional level" after each loop iteration. If a program fails to package a portion of RAM into a node before leaving a loop, then the unpackaged RAM will be abstracted to true. If then subsequently, after the loop, the program attempts to package up the node with a heap mutation, then the analysis will return $\top$.

---

[8] The specifications are for *partial* correctness, but using the techniques of [5] we could likely establish termination as well if we were to track lengths of multiword lists.

[9] This specification would not rule out the manager doing things like returning some nodes of the free list to the system, but would be a reasonable spec of the interface to `malloc` nonetheless.

8   Conclusions and Related Work

We believe that the results in this paper may pave the way for improved automatic verification techniques for low-level, "dirty" programs.

As we mentioned earlier, the approach in this paper is a development of the Space Invader shape analysis [15] (also, [22]). Compared to the original, the differences here are the following. First, we use different basic predicates, which are oriented to multiword lists, and different abstraction rules appropriate to the reasoning about multiword lists; this results in a much more complex abstract domain. Some of the abstraction rules, in particular, are perhaps not the first that come to mind, and we settled on them only after some experimentation. Second, in order to accelerate the analysis, we used a particular widening operator. Also, we used much more intricate test-programs in our experiments. These, and the complexity of our abstract domain, are such that the widening had a significant impact on performance.

There have been two previous works on doing mechanical proofs of memory managers in separation logic [33, 25], which both work by embedding separation logic into Coq. They do not consider the exact same algorithms that we do. The most significant difference, though, is degree of automation. They require loop invariants to be provided, and even then the proofs in Coq are not automatic, whereas our proof construction is completely automatic. Or course, working with a proof assistant allows one to say more than is typically done in the lightweight assertions that are used in program analysis. For example, one could say that the free list increases in size on deallocation, where we do not say that here.

Shallow pointer analyses track points-to relationships between fixed-length access paths. They are fast compared to shape analyses, but give imprecise answers on deep heap updates, which occur when linked structures are altered after traversing some distance. There have been a number of shallow pointer analyses that deal with pointer arithmetic before (e.g., [32, 16, 29, 26]), but as far as we are aware not any deep ones.

Between the fast, shallow analyses and the comparatively expensive, deep shape analyses is the recency-abstraction [2]. It is one of the most relevant pieces of related work. The recency-abstraction allows for pointer arithmetic and also connects low-level and high-level, fictional, views of memory. It can distinguish mutations of pointers coming from the same allocation site, but is imprecise on deep heap update. A way to handle deep updates was pioneered in [30], using the method of materialization of summary nodes[10]; recency-abstraction (purposely) avoids materialization, in order to gain efficiency, and experimental results justify the lower precision for its targeted applications. In contrast, here we must handle deep update precisely if we are to obtain reasonable results for the memory management algorithms that we used in our experiments.

An interesting question is whether some other previous shape abstraction might be modified to obtain an effective analysis of multiword lists or similar structures. In any case the problem paper addresses is existence, not uniqueness, of shape abstraction beyond reachability.

---

[10] The rearrangement rules here and in [3, 15] are cousins of materialization.

Acknowledgments. We are grateful to Josh Berdine, Tom Reps and Mooly Sagiv for comments on pointer analysis and pointer arithmetic, and to Xavier Rival and Kwangkeun Yi for advice on widening and non-standard fixpoint operators. Byron Cook's emphasis on the relevance of analyzing memory managers gave us an initial push. We had helpful discussions on memory models and the K&R `malloc` with Richard Bornat. We acknowledge support from the EPSRC. Yang was partially supported by R08-2003-000-10370-0 from the Basic Research Program of Korea Science & Engineering Foundation.

References

1. I. Balaban, A. Pnueli, and L. Zuck. Shape analysis by predicate abstraction. 6th VMCAI, pp164–180, 2005.
2. G. Balakrishnan and T. Reps. Recency-abstraction for heap-allocated storage. 13th SAS (this volume), 2006.
3. J. Berdine, C. Calcagno, and P.W. O'Hearn. Symbolic execution with separation logic. In K. Yi, editor, *APLAS 2005*, volume 3780 of *LNCS*, 2005.
4. J. Berdine, C. Calcagno, and P.W. O'Hearn. Automatic modular assertion checking with separation logic. Proceedings of FMCO'05, to appear, 2006.
5. J. Berdine, B. Cook, D. Distefano, and P. O'Hearn. Automatic termination proofs for programs with shape-shifting heaps. 18th CAV, to appear, 2006.
6. A. Bouajjani, P. Habermehl, P. Moro, and T. Vojnar. Verifying programs with dynamic 1-selector-linked structures in regular model checking. 11th TACAS, pp13–29, 2005.
7. D. Chase, M. Wegman, and F. Zadeck. Analysis of pointers and structures. PLDI, pp296–310, 1990.
8. W.T. Comfort. Multiword list items. CACM 7(6), pp357-362, 1964.
9. P. Cousot and R. Cousot. Abstract interpretation: A unified lattice model for static analysis of programs by construction or approximation of fixpoints. 4th POPL, pp238-252, 1977.
10. P. Cousot and R. Cousot. Systematic design of program analysis frameworks. 6th POPL, pp269-282, 1979.
11. P. Cousot and R. Cousot. Abstract interpretation frameworks. J. Log. Comput. 2(4), pp511-547, 1992.
12. P. Cousot, R. Cousot, J. Feret, L. Mauborgne, A. Miné, D. Monniaux, and X. Rival. The ASTRÉE analyzer. 14th ESOP, pp21-30, 2005.
13. P. Cousot and N. Halbwachs. Automatic discovery of linear restraints among variables of a program. 5th POPL, pp84-96, 1978.
14. D. Distefano, J.-P. Katoen, and A. Rensink. Who is pointing when to whom? On the automated verification of linked list structures. 24th FSTTCS, pp250-262, 2004.
15. D. Distefano, P. O'Hearn, and H. Yang. A local shape analysis based on separation logic. 16th TACAS, pp287–302, 2006.
16. N. Dor, M. Rodeh, and M. Sagiv. Towards a realistic tool for statically detecting all buffer overflows in C. PLDI, pp155-167, 2003.
17. H. Eo, K. Yi, and H. Eom. Differential fixpoint iteration with subtraction for non-distributive program analysis. Sumitted, 2006.
18. A. Gotsman, J. Berdine, and B. Cook. Interprocedural shape analysis with separated heap abstractions. 13th SAS, to appear, 2006.

19. B.W. Kernighan and D.M. Ritchie. *The C Programming Language.* Prentice Hall, New Jersey, 1988. 2nd Edition.
20. D.E. Knuth. *The Art of Computer Programming, Volume I: Fundamental Algorithms.* Addison-Wesley, 1973. 2nd Edition.
21. O. Lee, H. Yang, and K. Yi. Automatic verification of pointer programs using grammar-based shape analysis. 14th ESOP, pp124-140, 2005.
22. S. Magill, A. Nanevski, E. Clarke, and P. Lee. Inferring invariants in Separation Logic for imperative list-processing programs. 3rd SPACE Workshop, 2006.
23. R. Manevich, M. Sagiv, G. Ramalingam, and J. Field. Partially disjunctive heap abstraction. 11th SAS, pp265-279., 2004.
24. R. Manevich, E. Yahav, G. Ramalingam, and M. Sagiv. Predicate abstraction and canonical abstraction for singly-linked lists. 6th VMCAI, pp181-198, 2005.
25. N. Marti, R. Affeldt, and A. Yonezawa. Verification of the heap manager of an operating system using separation logic. 3rd SPACE Workshop, 2006.
26. T. Reps, G. Balakrishnan, and J. Lim. Intermediate-representation recovery from low-level code. *PEPM'06*, pp100-111, 2006.
27. J. C. Reynolds. Separation logic: A logic for shared mutable data structures. In *17th LICS*, pp 55-74, 2002.
28. Xavier Rival. Personal communication. 2005.
29. R. Rugina and M. Rinard. Symbolic bounds analysis of pointers, array indices, and accessed memory regions. *ACM TOPLAS*, 27(2):185–235, 2005.
30. M. Sagiv, T. Reps, and R. Wilhelm. Solving shape-analysis problems in languages with destructive updating. *ACM TOPLAS*, 20(1):1–50, 1998.
31. M. Sagiv, T. Reps, and R. Wilhelm. Parametric shape analysis via 3valued logic. *ACM TOPLAS*, 24(3):217–298, 2002.
32. D. Wagner, J. Foster, E. Brewer, and A. Aiken. A first step towards automated detection of buffer overrun vulnerabilities. Proceedings of NDSS, 2000.
33. D. Yu, N. A. Hamid, and Z. Shao. Building certified libraries for PCC: Dynamic storage allocation. 12th ESOP, pp363–379, 2003.

Specialized 3-Valued Logic Shape Analysis Using Structure-Based Refinement and Loose Embedding

Gilad Arnold

University of California, Berkeley
arnold@cs.berkeley.edu

Abstract. We consider a shape analysis framework based on 3-valued logic, and explore ways for improving its performance and scalability by means of reducing algorithmic overhead and restraining abstract state set inflation. First we propose a new approach to implementing a fast 3-valued logic analyzer, which replaces a general-purpose abstract heap refinement mechanism—accounting for most of the time spent by the reference implementation—with tailored structure-based refinement. We apply our framework to analyze a set of small Java programs manipulating singly- and doubly-linked lists, obtaining results that are comparable to those of the reference implementation, with a process 40-85 times faster and 2-11 times less memory consuming. We then propose a new definition for partial ordering of abstract heap descriptors (embedding), that trims abstract states representing "special cases" in the presence of a state representing a "general case". This extension deflates sets of abstract states by a combinatorial factor, resulting in 45-55% less structures for the same set of benchmarks. Despite its induced algorithmic overhead per operation, this modification further cuts the analysis time by 17-50%. We argue that improving on these two axes together yields a promise for greater applicability of specialized shape analysis to real-life programs.

1 Introduction

The ability to reason about the set of heap configurations that a computer program may exhibit, without actually running the program, has many uses in program analysis and verification. These include whole-program verification tasks, like verifying the absence of null dereferences; proving correctness of heap intensive programs, such as heap sorting algorithms [8]; and checking properties of heap references throughout the program, such as dead objects analysis and its applications to static garbage collection [3]. Nonetheless, shape analysis appears to be among the hardest problems in static program analysis: proving even simple properties of very small programs manipulating dynamically allocated data structures is generally undecidable, and even the compulsory deployment of conservative abstraction methods following Cousot & Cousot [4] implies non-trivial frameworks, in turn inducing considerable complexity issues. Sources for such issues include the size of an abstract domain of this kind, as well as the complexity

K. Yi (Ed.): SAS 2006, LNCS 4134, pp. 204–220, 2006.

of the algorithms used for implementing the abstraction, transformations, and various domain operators.

We consider a shape analysis framework that models heap topology and related properties using logical structures and applies first-order logic formulas to model program semantics [12]. Although analyses instantiated by this framework give precise and meaningful results compared to actual (concrete) heap structures exhibited by a program, it is not widely studied, let alone deployed in actual production-level compilers or analysis tools. Indeed, the 3-Valued Logic Analyzer (TVLA) [9] reference implementation was used to demonstrate the analysis precision and adaptivity to a wide variety of shape-related problems. However, analyzing even tiny programs manipulating linked lists can take as long as seconds. Designed as an extensible analysis generator, TVLA is under-optimized compared to a (presumed) specialized implementation. Still, we can observe at least two aspects which make a reference implementation inherently expensive.

Costly refinement and validation of abstract heaps. A significant portion of the analysis time—namely, up to 90%—is due to particular algorithms that are being used for refining abstract heaps.

State set inflation. The huge abstract domain underlying the analysis—whose induced complexity is doubly-exponential in the number of abstraction predicates (essentially, the number of reference variables in the program)—leads very quickly to a blow-up in the number of heap states being tracked by the analysis, even for mildly complicated programs.

Fig. 1 shows a simple program that constructs and traverses a doubly-linked list. Analyzing an automatically generated dataflow representation of it using the default shape abstraction for linked lists [9] yields a total of 113 abstract heap structures and takes 1.4 seconds to complete with stock TVLA. A slightly

```
x = null;
while (...) {
    y = new DLL();
    ...
    if (x != null) x.p = y;
    y.n = x;
    x = y;
}

y = x;
while (y != null) {
    ...
    t = y.n;
    y = t;
}
```

Fig. 1. A Java program that constructs and traverses a doubly-linked list

more complicated example—a program that manipulates a singly-linked list using three loops, one of which removes an arbitrary element from the list—results in a total of 485 abstract heap descriptors and takes as long as 12 seconds to complete. This demonstrates the steep abstract states inflation and the respective time penalty experienced with programs of increasing complexity.

This paper describes the fresh implementation of a 3-valued logic based shape analysis tool. It is intentionally restricted compared to the fully-parameterized reference implementation, but appears to be better suited for performance and scalability, making the following major contributions.

Specialized structure-based refinement. While using a meet operator for abstraction refinement has already been suggested [3] it was never put into practice with the 3-valued logic framework. We take this concept to the extreme, performing merely all refinement tasks using a sequence of meet and join operations with sets of predefined structures, as explained in Section 3. Consequently, we are able to produce results that are as precise as those achieved using more powerful algorithms, in only a fraction of the time.

Loose embedding. We identify a case for overly elaborate abstract states that neither contribute to precision nor bear a significant descriptive insight as to the represented set of concrete states. Consequently, we propose an alternate definition of embedding of 3-valued logical structures, which allows abstract elements representing one or more concrete heap elements to represent no elements at all, yet still retains connectivity between other elements of the structure in a conservative manner. This extension—explained in Section 4— instantly constrains the abstract domain, and therefore the set of abstract states explored during the analysis. With proper further adjustments to the semantics of abstract transformers, we are able to restate the soundness of the framework.

Implementation and preliminary results. We have implemented the above techniques in our new shape analyzer and applied it to a small set of interesting micro-benchmarks as described in Section 5, showing an overall speed-up of up to 124 and an up to 15 times smaller memory footprint.

2   Basics of 3-Valued Logic Shape Analysis

We explain the heap state abstraction and abstract transformers following Sagiv *et al.* [12], then state the restrictions assumed as the baseline for our specialized analysis.

2.1   Concrete Program States

We represent concrete program states using 2-valued logical structures.

Definition 1 (Concrete state). *A 2-valued logical structure over a vocabulary (set of predicates) $\mathcal{P}$ is a pair $S = (U, \iota)$, where U is the universe of the structure and ι is the interpretation function mapping predicates to their truth-value in the structure: for every predicate $p \in \mathcal{P}$ of arity k, $\iota(p) : U^k \to \{0, 1\}$.*

Table 1. Predicates used in the analysis of programs manipulating doubly-linked lists, with p (f) instantiated over the set of reference variables (fields)

Predicate	Intended meaning
$eq(v_1, v_2)$	v_1 equals v_2
$p(v)$	Variable p points to object v
$f(v_1, v_2)$	The f field of v_1 points to v_2
$r_{p,f}(v)$	v is reachable from variable p along a sequence of f fields
$s_f(v)$	Several f fields point to v
$c_f(v)$	v resides on a directed cycle of f fields references
$b_{f_1,f_2}(v)$	The f_2 field of an object pointed by the f_1 field of v points back at v

Table 1 shows the set of predicates used in the analysis of the program in Fig. 1, with p and f instantiated over $\{x, y, t\}$ and $\{n, p\}$, respectively.[1] We require that the set of predicates includes the binary predicate eq, bearing the semantics of *equality* between individuals. Note the use of *instrumentation predicates*—like transitive reachability, shared referencing, cyclicity, and back-pointing—in addition to core shape predicates, the importance of which in retaining abstraction precision has been widely discussed [9,12].

A concrete state is depicted as a directed graph, where each individual in the universe is a node. The set of unary predicates that hold for each node appear right next to it. A unary predicate representing a reference variable that points to some node v is depicted by an arrow from the variable's name to v. A binary predicate f which holds for a pair of individuals v_1 and v_2 is depicted by an f-labeled directed edge from v_1 to v_2. The predicate eq is not shown, since any two nodes are different and every node is equal to itself.

Fig. 2(a) shows a concrete program state arising after the execution of the statement t = y.n at the second loop of the program in Fig. 1. We denote the set of all 2-valued logical structures over a set of predicates $\mathcal{P}$ by 2-STRUCT$[\mathcal{P}]$, abbreviated to 2-STRUCT under the simplifying assumption that $\mathcal{P}$ is fixed.

2.2   Abstract Program States

We represent abstract program states using Kleene 3-valued logic [12], an extension of Boolean logic which introduces a third value $\frac{1}{2}$ denoting a truth value that may be either 0 or 1. We utilize the partial order defined by $0 \sqsubseteq \frac{1}{2}$ and $1 \sqsubseteq \frac{1}{2}$, with the join operation defined accordingly.

Definition 2 (Abstract state). *A 3-valued logical structure over a set of predicates $\mathcal{P}$ is a pair $S = (U, \iota)$, where U is the universe of the structure and ι is the interpretation function mapping predicates to their truth-value in the structure: for every predicate $p \in \mathcal{P}$ of arity k, $\iota(p) : U^k \to \{0, 1, \frac{1}{2}\}$. A summary node in an abstract state is an individual u for which $eq(u, u) = \frac{1}{2}$, representing one or more concrete nodes.*

---

[1] Note that b_{f_1,f_2} is only instantiated for pairs of *distinct* reference fields.

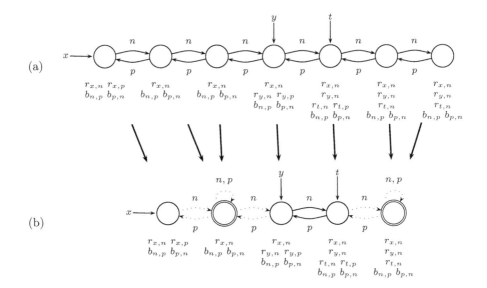

Fig. 2. (a) A concrete program state arising after the execution of the statement t = y.n in Fig. 1; (b) An abstract program state approximating (a)

An abstract state is also depicted as a directed graph, where parenthesized predicates (unaries) and dotted arrows (binaries) denote $\frac{1}{2}$ values, and summary nodes appear as doubly-lined nodes. Fig. 2(b) shows an abstract state with two summary nodes, representing any number of one or more concrete nodes at the infix and suffix of the list, respectively.

We denote the set of all 3-valued logical structures over a set of predicates $\mathcal{P}$ by 3-STRUCT$[\mathcal{P}]$, abbreviated to 3-STRUCT. Note that Definition 2 generalizes Definition 1, therefore 2-STRUCT $\subsetneq$ 3-STRUCT.

We define a partial order on structures based on the concept of *embedding*, and extend it to a preorder on *sets* of structures.

Definition 3 (Embedding). *Let $S = (U, \iota)$ and $S' = (U', \iota')$ be two structures and let $f : U \to U'$ be a surjection. We say that f embeds S in S', denoted $S \sqsubseteq^f S'$, if for every predicate $p \in \mathcal{P}^{(k)}$ and k individuals $u_1, \ldots, u_k \in U$,*

$$p^S(u_1, \ldots, u_k) \sqsubseteq p^{S'}(f(u_1), \ldots, f(u_k)) . \tag{1}$$

S is embedded in S', denoted $S \sqsubseteq S'$, if there exists f such that $S \sqsubseteq^f S'$.

The concrete structure in Fig. 2(a) is embedded in the abstract structure in Fig. 2(b) with respect to the mapping depicted by the bold arrows.

Definition 4 (Powerset embedding). *Given two sets of structures $XS, XS' \subseteq$ 3-STRUCT, $XS \sqsubseteq XS'$ iff for all $S \in XS$ there exists $S' \in XS'$ such that $S \sqsubseteq S'$.*

In the following, we restrict sets of 3-valued structures by disallowing non-maximal structures. This ensures that the above Hoare order is indeed a proper partial order. The set $D_{\text{3-STRUCT}}$, consisting of all finite sets of 3-valued structures that do not contain non-maximal structures, along with the partial order given by Definition 4, form the *abstract domain* underlying our framework. We use the same order to define the concretization of a set of 3-valued structures, given by $\gamma(XS) = \bigcup_{XS' \sqsubseteq XS} XS'$.

2.3   Bounded Program States

Note that the size of a 3-valued structure is potentially unbounded. Therefore, 3-STRUCT contains sets with an infinite number of structures and is in turn infinite. We use a fundamental abstraction method [12] to convert a state descriptor of any size into a bounded (abstract) one.

A 3-valued structure $S = (U, \iota)$ is said to be *bounded* if for every two distinct individuals $u_1, u_2 \in U$, there exists a unary predicate p such that $p^S(u_1)$ and $p^S(u_2)$ evaluate to distinct *definite* truth values (*i.e.*, 0 and 1). The abstract domain $D_{\text{B-STRUCT}}$ is a finite sub-lattice of $D_{\text{3-STRUCT}}$, containing all (finite) sets of bounded structures that do not contain non-maximal structures. The structure abstraction function β—referred to as a *canonical abstraction* [12]—maps a potentially unbounded 2-valued structure into a bounded 3-valued structure. Namely, $\beta((U, \iota)) = (U', \iota')$, where U' consists of the disjoint subsets of U in which no unary predicate evaluates to distinct definite values, and for any pair of individuals in different subsets, there is at least one predicate which evaluates to distinct definite values. The interpretation ι' of each $p \in \mathcal{P}^{(k)}$ and k individuals $c_1, \ldots, c_k \in U'$ is given by

$$p^{S'}(c_1, \ldots, c_k) = \bigsqcup_{u_i \in c_i} p^S(u_1, \ldots, u_k) \ .$$

Fig. 2(b) shows the bounded structure obtained from Fig. 2(a) (note that $S \sqsubseteq \beta(S)$ for all S). Powerset abstraction is given by $\alpha(XS) = \bigsqcup_{S \in XS} \{\beta(S)\}$.[2]

2.4   Abstract Semantics

The abstract interpretation framework of [12] models the semantics of program transformations using first order logic formulas with transitive closure. For example, the update to the value of the unary predicate t through program statement t = y.n from the example in Fig. 1 is modeled by $t(v) \leftarrow \exists v' : y(v') \wedge n(v', v)$. The *embedding theorem* [12] ensures that the result of a transformation on any abstract state is a sound approximation of the best transformer. Yet, as straightforward evaluation of update formulas over bounded abstract states leads to considerable loss of precision, and since a best transformer is generally intractable, we achieve *partial concretization* (*i.e.*, refinement) by means of two auxiliary operations [12].

The *focus* operation applies semantic reduction to a given 3-valued structure such that the evaluation of the first-order logic focus formula on any resulting

---

[2] The operator $\bigsqcup$ is the least upper bound on the lattice $D_{\text{B-STRUCT}}$.

(a)

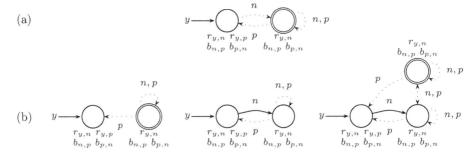

(b)

Fig. 3. Structure refinement using focus: (a) the original inbound structure; (b) structures resulting from focus using the formula $\exists v'.y(v') \wedge n(v', v)$

structures yields a definite truth value (*i.e.*, 0 or 1). Fig. 3(a) shows a canonically bounded doubly-linked list structure that is being focused—prior to an update due to t = y.n—using the formula $\exists v'.y(v') \wedge n(v', v)$. The resulting structures are shown in Fig. 3(b). However, note that focus might lead to structures that do not necessarily satisfy the integrity constraints—such as the leftmost structure in Fig. 3(b)—or are not as precise as could be with respect to the values of instrumentation predicates, such as the middle structure in Fig. 3(b). The functionality of the *coerce* operator in this regard is two-fold: by exhaustively evaluating formulas derived from structure integrity rules, it both dismisses structures for which some constraint is breached and also tightens predicate values where such a tightening is accommodated by the constraints. Thus, a coerce step normally follows a focus operation, so as to complement the weaknesses of the latter.

It should be noted that this refinement method—in particular the coerce step—is by far the most time consuming phase of the analysis in practice, suggesting that an alternate approach may be highly beneficial for efficiency.

2.5   Restricted 3-Valued Logic Shape Analysis

In this work, we assume a restricted instance of the parametric 3-valued logic framework [12] to be the baseline for further proposed improvements. Limiting predicate arity to nullary, unary, and binary predicates only, we further restrict ourselves to the predefined fixed set of instrumentation predicates described in Table 1, which can capture shape properties of any (recursive) data structure. Finally, we support a fixed, universal set of intermediate-level operations—including manipulation of reference and Boolean variables/fields and basic control statements—which allows us to encode a variety of real-world Java programs.[3]

3   Specialized Analysis with Structure-Based Refinement

We describe in [1] the design and implementation of a specialized prototype shape analysis tool, constructed with the long-term goal of exploring techniques

---

[3] Array objects and call/return context-sensitivity are currently not supported.

for faster practical shape analysis. Despite its conformance with the guidelines in Section 2.5, we believe that only one of these restrictions—namely, limited predicate arity—is inherent to the design, bearing the least actual burden to the applicability of derived analyses. Extending the framework beyond the afore-mentioned limitations is considered future work.

One interesting aspect of our implementation is the heavy use it makes of fine-tuned domain operators (*i.e.*, join and meet). Although both are hard problems given the domain of unbounded 3-valued structures,[4] by re-using algorithms developed by Arnold *et al.* [3], we are able to infer certain relationships between 3-valued structures—such as deciding an embedding relation—in a surprisingly effective manner. This feature is heavily relied upon when we introduce structure-based, operator-intensive refinement. Also, we are able to exploit the flexibility of a fundamental graph matching technique as we later loosen the definition of structure embedding. For further details, the interested reader is referred to [1].

The fact that a meet operator can be used to perform abstraction refinement—both focusing an abstract structure prior to an update, as well as filtering structures based on some semantic condition—has already been discussed else-where [2]. Conforming to this approach, a 3-valued structure is used to express the desired semantic condition, and a meet operation is used to extract the sub-set of structures that are both represented by a given abstract state *and* comply with the semantic condition expressed by the refining structure. We have taken this approach to the extreme, essentially doing all abstraction refinements us-ing meet (and join) operations. We demonstrate this approach by describing a simplified structure-based refinement operator for the abstract transformer of t = y.n from Fig. 1. This refinement operator—requiring that the n field of the object pointed by y is focused—is by far the most complicated one, mainly due to the subtle sub-cases that need to be considered for obtaining sufficient precision.

3.1 Sufficiently Tight and Effective Refinement

For simplicity, we assume that any semantically sane input structure is such that its y predicate evaluates to 1 for exactly one individual (*i.e.*, the dereference y.n deterministically succeeds).[5] Therefore, for the purpose of refinement, we can initially use a set of structures consisting of the three distinct cases where y.n is either (a) null, (b) a self-loop, or (c) points to a different node. Note that any of these general cases needs to be split into disjoint sub-cases, indicating whether additional nodes—other than the one pointed to by y and (possibly by) y.n—may exist. Such a refinement set, with the simplification of ignoring x, t, and their induced instrumentation predicates, is shown in Fig. 4.

In this example, the refining structures impose very few constraints on the values of binary predicates between the different nodes—other than focusing the n field of the object pointed to by y—and, consequently, on those of instrumen-tation predicates. Still, for the case of a null y.n, they do require that any node

---

[4] The meet operator was shown particularly hard, even for bounded structures [3].
[5] This condition can be easily enforced using a meet-based precondition filter [2].

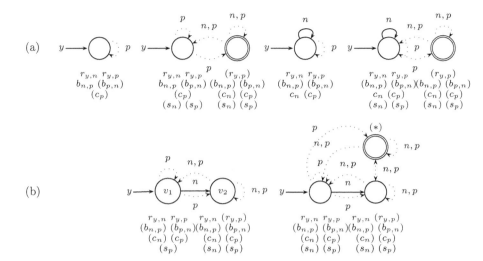

Fig. 4. A simplified structure-based refining set for t = y.n: (a) cases of null or self-loop y.n; (b) cases of y.n pointing to a different node

other than the one pointed to by y has $r_{y,n}$ evaluated to 0. Therefore, in applying the refining set in Fig. 4 to the structure in Fig. 3(a), our operator *does not* yield the leftmost structure of Fig. 3(b) in the first place, as opposed to the traditional focus operation. (This does not guarantee the integrity of structures resulting from refinement in general, though.)

The refining set of Fig. 4 *does* yield the two rightmost structures in Fig. 3(b). While these are conservative and semantically sane refinements of Fig. 3(a), they are evidently not as tight as could be, as explained in Section 2.4. As this over-compromises the precision of our transformer in this case, we first try to further focus the back **p** edge to the node pointed to by **y**. A naive solution to this can be found in the form of further sub-case refinement, namely by semantically reducing the refining structures in Fig. 4(b) down to the point where the back **p** edge is either 0 or 1, corresponding to the value that $b_{n,p}$ takes for the node pointed to by **y**. For example, we can replace the left-hand side structure in Fig. 4(b) by two similar structures, with the difference being that one has both $b_{n,p}(v_1)$ and $p(v_2, v_1)$ evaluating to 1, and the other has their value being 0. This enforces a definite truth value for the back **p** edge from the node pointed to by **y.n** to the node pointed to by **y** in the result of the refinement step.

By applying further reduction in the same style, we can tighten the value of the **n** (**p**) self-loop on the node that **y.n** points to in the middle structure in Fig. 3(b), in correlation with the value of c_n (respectively, c_p) for that node.[6] However, such a level of enumeration will lead to a number of structures that is exponential in the number of tightened instrumentation predicate values—in this case $b_{n,p}(v_1)$, $c_n(v_2)$, and $c_p(v_2)$—resulting in 8 disjoint structures. This

---

[6] For expository reasons, we ignore the case of a two-node cycle, which is also correlated with the value of $c_n(v_2)$ and $c_p(v_2)$.

combinatorial effect gives little hope for scaling a precise enough operator of this kind to cases with even a little more predicate interdependencies. We manage to avoid this explosion in the size of the refining set by exploiting the following properties.

Distributivity of meet over join. As already noted [3], for all sets of structures, $XS \sqcap (XR \sqcup XR') = (XS \sqcap XR) \sqcup (XS \sqcap XR')$. We can therefore split the structures in Fig. 4 such that XR corresponds to Fig. 4(a) and XR' corresponds to Fig. 4(b), with the guarantee that $(\{S\} \sqcap XR) \sqcup (\{S\} \sqcap XR')$ yields the same result as plain meet using the original refining set.

Associativity of meet. As $XS \sqcap (XR'_1 \sqcap XR'_2) = XS \sqcap XR'_1 \sqcap XR'_2$ (the latter being left-associative) for all sets of structures, we can further avoid the combinatorial blow-up in the number of structures needed for the proper reduction, such as the one explained above. Let XR'_1, XR'_2, and XR'_3 be the sets containing a pair of structures which reduces the left-hand side structure of Fig. 4(b) with respect to the value of $b_{n,p}(v_1)$, $c_n(v_2)$, and $c_p(v_2)$, respectively. We observe that the elaborate set of reduced refinement structures described above is obtained by $XR'_1 \sqcap XR'_2 \sqcap XR'_3$, as each of these operands requires that $b_{n,p}(v_1)$, $c_n(v_2)$, or $c_p(v_2)$ has a definite value but keeps the others indefinite ($\frac{1}{2}$), respectively. Therefore, $\{S\} \sqcap XR'_1 \sqcap XR'_2 \sqcap XR'_3$ gives us the desired level of tightness, without needing to store the fully expanded set of structures. Note that each of XR'_i, $1 \leq i \leq 3$, consists of exactly two complementary structures. Hence, the successive application of meet operations is likely to reduce the number of unfocused predicates at each step, down to the point where a single fully-tightened structure is obtained.

We can therefore obtain the desired refinement operation by means of

$$(\{S\} \sqcap XR) \sqcup (\{S\} \sqcap XR'_1 \sqcap XR'_2 \sqcap XR'_3) \ ,$$

for any given structure S. It is important to note that such a formulation in fact shifts the exponential behavior from the size of a single refining structure to the worst case complexity of the additional meet and join operations. Finally, note that the actual refinement operators used in our framework are fairly more complicated, as they enumerate further instrumentation-implied sub-cases, and are well beyond the scope of this paper.

3.2   Enforcing Integrity

As hinted above, a structure resulting from a structure-based refinement operation does not necessarily satisfy the integrity constraints implied by its instrumentation predicates. In one instance of this problem, a refinement operator yields a structure that has a summary node v for which $r_{y,n}(v) = 1$, but $y(v) = 0$ and $n(v', v) = 0$ for all $v' \neq v$. We consider the use of structure-based filtering to dismiss such a structure prior to the transformation update, mimicking the role of coerce in that respect. While arbitrary first-order logic conditions may not necessarily be expressible using 3-valued structures, we can still handle this particular case using our approach. Specifically, it is sufficient here to determine whether a structure has some node that is neither pointed to by y nor has an inbound n field pointing from any other node that may be referenced by y, yet is indicated to be reachable from y by a sequence of n references—namely $\exists v.r_{y,n}(v) \land \neg y(v) \land \forall v'.(y(v') \implies \neg n(v', v))$. Fortunately, a structure S_F consisting of an n-unreachable summary node, which is not pointed to by y but denoted with a definite (1) $r_{y,n}$ value, represents this requirement and makes it evaluate to 1.[7] By the embedding theorem, we have that for any structure that is embedded in S_F, the above formula must evaluate to 1, implying a breached integrity constraint. We therefore apply this test to each structure resulting from a refinement operation, dismissing structures that are embedded in our filter.

4   Loose Embedding

Analyzing the program in Fig. 1 with the framework described so far yields a total of 113 structures, with an average of 3.2 structures per CFG node and a peak of 9 disjoint abstract states for a single node. This large number seems counterintuitive to the actual simple essence of what the program does. In the following, we highlight one source of this inflation and suggest a way to avoid it.

4.1   State-Space Inflation in Loops

Fig. 5 shows three of the abstract structures representing disjoint sets of concrete heap states, arising immediately past the statement t = y.n during the analysis of the program in Fig. 1. The structure in Fig. 5(b) represents the set of concrete doubly-linked lists whose head is pointed to by x, followed by a sequence of (one or more) nodes, followed by a pair of nodes pointed to by y and t, respectively, and finally followed by a sequence of (one or more) nodes forming the list suffix. This structure describes a *general case* that the program exhibits at this program point, providing a conservative approximation of the set of concrete states incurred by the program, and also contributing a general insight regarding the state of computation at this point in the program.

On the contrary, the two other structures in Fig. 5 describe what could be considered a slight variant of the general case. Specifically, Fig. 5(a) represents the set of lists that lack the suffix nodes and Fig. 5(c) represents the set of lists that lack the infix nodes. A fourth structure arising at the same program point—which represents a list with neither infix nor suffix nodes—is not shown.

As is evident from the example, the total number of disjoint abstract states used for representing all possible concrete states is exponential in the number of summary nodes appearing in the general case. The special case descriptors are inevitable by construction of the abstraction framework, given that the loop traverses all nodes of the list. Yet, informally speaking, they seem to contribute very little information compared to what the general case already expresses,

---

[7] In fact, two distinct structures are required to represent all possible configurations corresponding to this case. See [1] for details.

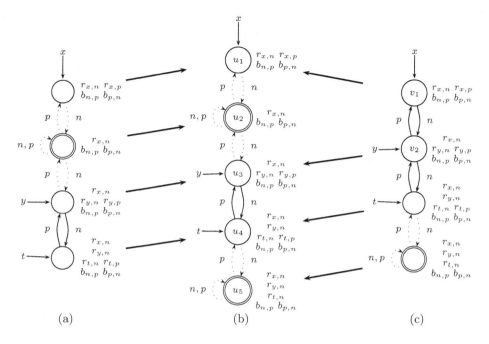

Fig. 5. Abstract heap states arising after the statement t = y.n in Fig. 1

consequently fortifying the analysis with only a little precision, but at a high cost.

4.2 Relaxed Definition of Embedding

Recall that the definition of D_3-STRUCT uses a notion of embedding in order to eliminate non-maximal structures, prohibiting expressive redundancy and ensuring a strict partial order. In attempt to make the special cases of Fig. 5 non-maximal—and therefore disposable—we aim at embedding them into the general case by relaxing the definition of embedding in the following manner.

Allow summaries to represent zero nodes. We allow summary nodes to be excluded from the range of an embedding function, overruling the surjectivity requirement. The individuals of Fig. 5(a) can therefore be mapped to a *subset* of the individuals of Fig. 5(b), as indicated by the bold arrows, excluding only the suffix summary node u_5 from the range of the embedding function. Yet, it is clear that the requirement for predicate interpretation consistency in Definition 3 is satisfied. This allows for the structure in Fig. 5(b) to embed the structure in Fig. 5(a), making the latter disposable.

Retain connectivity via non-mapped summaries. Consider the mapping from individuals of Fig. 5(c) to those of Fig. 5(b), depicted by the bold arrows: the fact that u_2 is excluded from the range of the function breaks the connectivity of the structure in Fig. 5(b) compared to that of the structure in

Fig. 5(c). In particular, while $n(v_1, v_2) = 1$ in the former, $n(f(v_1), f(v_2)) = n(u_1, u_3) = 0$ in the latter, prohibiting embedding by this function. We therefore further permit predicate interpretation consistency of any binary predicate to be checked against the *constrained transitive closure* of that predicate in the target structure, which is only computed via summaries excluded from the range of the function under consideration. Since $n(u_1, u_2) \land n(u_2, u_3) = \frac{1}{2}$, the extended consistency requirement is satisfied, making the mapping in the diagram an admissible embedding function.

We now give the formal definition of the relaxed embedding relation.

Definition 5 (Loose embedding). *Let $S = (U, \iota)$ and $S' = (U', \iota')$ be two structures and let $f : U \rightarrow U'$ be a function, such that $eq(v, v) = \frac{1}{2}$ for all nodes $v \in V = U' \setminus \text{range}(f)$. We say that f loosely embeds S in S', denoted $S \sqsubseteq^{\widetilde{f}} S'$, if Eq. (1) holds for all nullary and unary predicates and all nodes, and for every predicate $p \in \mathcal{P}^{(2)}$ and pair of individuals $u_1, u_2 \in U$,[8]*

$$p^S(u_1, u_2) \sqsubseteq \left(p^{S'}(f(u_1), f(u_2)) \lor \right.$$
$$\left. \bigvee_{v_1, \ldots, v_k \in V} \left(p^{S'}(f(u_1), v_1) \land \left(\bigwedge_{1 \leq i \leq k-1} p^{S'}(v_i, v_{i+1}) \right) \land p^{S'}(v_k, f(u_2)) \right) \right).$$

S is loosely embedded *in S', denoted $S \sqsubseteq^{\widetilde{}} S'$, if there exists f such that $S \sqsubseteq^{\widetilde{f}} S'$.*

Note that the above definition immediately extends to the definition of the abstract domain $D_{3\text{-}\text{STRUCT}}$ and its associated operators (join and meet), as well as its derived bounded state sub-domain. It also extends to the definition of abstraction and concretization accordingly.[9]

4.3   Preserving Soundness

The proposed extensions to the definition of embedding invalidate the foundations of soundness provided by the embedding theorem. We therefore adjust the semantics of logical formula evaluation in accordance with these extensions.

First-order quantification. We interpret each occurrence of the form $\exists u.\phi$ as $\exists u. eq(u, u) \land \phi$, assuring that any predicate that is existentially quantified over a summary node is "lowered" to $\frac{1}{2}$. This accounts for the case where no corresponding node exists in some concrete setting, which could cause the formula to evaluate to a (definite) 0. Similarly, we interpret each occurrence

---

[8] An empty conjunction evaluates to 1 and an empty disjunction evaluates to 0.
[9] Note that for the general case of unbounded 3-valued structures, the loose embedding relation induces a partial *preorder*, in turn inducing a preorder on the powerset domain. We can show it is a strict partial order for the domain of bounded structures, implying that α is still a well-defined function.

of the form $\forall u.P$ as $\forall u.\neg eq(u,u) \vee P$, assuring that any universally quantified predicate is "raised" to $\frac{1}{2}$ for any summary node. This accounts for the
absence of corresponding nodes in some concrete setting, which could cause
the the formula to evaluate to a (definite) 1.

Binary predicate interpretation. We interpret each binary predicate between v_1 and v_2 as the constrained transitive closure of that predicate, namely
considering the conjunction of the predicate's values along any sequence of
(zero or more) summary nodes between v_1 and v_2. As opposed to Definition 5, we cannot consider the set of non-image summaries here, as no
embedding function is due. Instead, we consider any summary node for the
purpose of transitive closure, but also bound the truth value of such a transitive interpretation by $\frac{1}{2}$ in order to ensure that the result is a conservative
approximation with respect to *any* embedding function.[10]

The above extensions suffice to retain the soundness of our local transformers,
consequently implying global soundness. Note, however, that they also imply potential sources of imprecision as well as added computational effort, especially
when transitive binary closure needs to be evaluated. Nonetheless, as binary
edges adjacent to summary nodes are commonly indefinite in the first place,
we do not expect a significant loss of precision due to the contamination of
formula evaluation with $\frac{1}{2}$ values. Also, we expect the excess algorithmic overhead to be absorbed by our highly effective approach for conducting computations over 3-valued structures. Finally, it should be mentioned that loose embedding also deflates some of our structure-based refinement operators, like the two
single-node structures in Fig. 4(a), which are now embedded in their respective
counterparts.

5   Experimental Results

Table 2 presents analysis statistics for a set of five small Java programs that
manipulate singly- or doubly-linked lists, executed on a 1.6GHz Pentium-M,
1GB machine running Linux. This benchmark, along with approximate analysis
statistics using the TVLA reference implementation on similar hardware, were
adopted from [3]. The results suggest several insights regarding the effectiveness
of our framework. First, it is shown to converge significantly faster than the reference implementation, ranging from a factor of 40 (using strict embedding on a
simple singly-linked list traversal) to a factor of 124 (using loose embedding on a
program that deletes an arbitrary element from a singly-linked list). Although an
improvement of this kind was expected—our analyzer is restricted by construction and therefore better tweaked for performance—the actual speed-up factor
is quite encouraging. While our results do not provide sufficient evidence for the
relative effectiveness of structure-based refinement per-se (we implemented neither focus nor coerce in our framework), the fact that the time spent on abstract

---

[10] For the reasoning behind this additional requirement, see [1].

Table 2. Benchmark results for five Java programs processing singly- and doubly-linked lists. Columns denote program statistics (number of CFG locations and loops), running statistics using TVLA (total analysis time and peak memory consumption), and running statistics using the specialized framework in strict and loose embedding mode (total, average, and maximum number of structures for a CFG node, analysis total and refinement times, and peak memory consumption). Time is in milliseconds, and memory is in kilobytes.

	stats		reference		specialized strict					specialized loose				
	loc	loop	tot	mem	tot	ave	top	tot	ref	mem	tot	ave	top	tot	ref	mem
sll-loop	33	2	900	1000	109	3.3	9	20	6	88	59	1.8	4	11	5	72
sll-reverse	52	3	3000	2000	226	4.4	9	34	12	188	104	2.0	4	28	14	129
sll-delete	49	3	12400	3200	485	9.9	48	202	59	379	215	4.4	20	100	44	235
dll-loop	35	2	1400	1300	113	3.2	9	27	18	463	61	1.7	4	19	11	441
dll-pairs	42	2	3000	2000	191	4.6	15	69	50	896	105	2.5	8	43	31	846

heap refinement by our analyzer—ranging between 30-73% of the total analysis time—suggests that our structure-based approach is relatively time effective compared to the remaining operations. However, the fact that refinement takes a larger portion in the doubly-linked list case suggests that it may not scale very well as dependencies among predicates increase. Memory consumption is generally lower than that of TVLA, but then again seems not as low in the heavier abstraction (doubly-linked list) as in the lighter abstraction (singly-linked list). Yet this issue has not been the focus of our performance optimization and could probably be improved significantly in the future.

Second, the case of loose embedding appears quite effective in both deflating the number of structures—45-55% and 46-58% deflation in total and top number of structures, respectively—as well as shortening total analysis time, by 17-50%. The case of sll-delete is particularly notable, as one of its loops may terminate abruptly, allowing a greater number of abstract states to "escape" and propagate to other CFG nodes. Here, the use of loose embedding seems to provide the greatest gain in both state set deflation and analysis performance. Finally, it is worth mentioning that the actual (graphical) results of an analysis using loose embedding are by far more comprehensible—and therefore, more usable—than those of a traditional (strict) analysis. We consider this a nice practical outcome, which supports our view of the problem with strict embedding abstraction.

6   Related Work

This work shares common goals with a few other efforts, all aimed at improving the scalability and applicability of shape analysis to practical uses. In two cases, TVLA powerset heap abstractions were compressed into a single structure [7] or partially disjunctive sets [10] by means of merging (joining) predicate values and allowing individuals to represent zero concrete nodes, or merging structures consisting of isomorphic sets of individuals, respectively. Our loose embedding approach seems to resemble the former to some extent, as both allow certain nodes to represent zero concrete nodes and use a relaxed notion of first-order quantification in formulas. It also shares a similar approach to the latter, as both attempt to reduce the number of structures describing "similar" cases based on some criteria. Nonetheless, by carefully defining the notion of descriptive redundancy, and by extending the definition of the embedding relation—rather than overloading predicates or joining structures—our approach has the advantage of not inducing imprecision on remaining representative abstract states.[11]

Other approaches deviate from 3-valued canonical abstraction and examine the use of predicate abstraction for analyzing shape properties [11,5]. While such approaches were shown to yield precise and descriptive results, their contribution to scalability of shape problems is unclear due to the larger number of predicates required for sufficient precision.

It is well-known that structure-based semantic reduction is expressively inferior to general FOL formula-based refinement (*i.e.*, as obtained by focus and coerce [12]). However, we argue that precision can be improved by further elaboration of refining structures, suggesting a trade-off between sufficient precision and tolerable complexity. As far as we know, our work is the first attempt to deploy practical structure-based abstraction refinement for 3-valued logic shape analysis and may serve as a point of reference for future efforts.

7   Conclusion

We described a new implementation of a 3-valued logic-based shape analysis tool that uses an effective structure-based approach for refining abstract heaps, and deflates abstract state sets using an alternate definition of structure ordering. We applied it to a small set of benchmark programs, with encouraging results, regarding both the effectiveness of the analysis framework as well as the successful restraining of powerset abstract states exhibited by the analysis. We believe that the next step in this direction is to further extend and examine the applicability of our analyzer to different (and more complex) heap structures on the one hand, and to assess the usefulness of loose embedding for programs of higher complexity in attempt to assert its expected advantages on the other. A separate effort, aimed at the automatic derivation of sound and precise structure-based refining operators from logical formulas, should guarantee the correctness and improve the adaptivity of our approach, and is currently a work in progress.

Acknowledgments

I thank Mooly Sagiv and Roman Manevich for their useful feedback and continuous advice. I also thank Ras Bodik for supporting my work on this research.

---

[11] Note that empty summaries have been used by other analyses (*e.g.*, [6]), so the novelty of our approach in this context is restricted to 3-valued logic-based analysis.

References

1. G. Arnold. Lightweight specialized 3-valued logic shape analyzer. Technical Report UCB/EECS-2006-59, EECS Department, University of California, Berkeley, May 2006. Available at http://www.eecs.berkeley.edu/Pubs/TechRpts/2006/EECS-2006-59.html.
2. G. Arnold, R. Manevich, M. Sagiv, and R. Shaham. Intersecting heap abstractions with applications to compile-time memory management. Technical Report TR-2005-04-135520, Tel-Aviv University, Apr. 2005. Available at http://www.cs.tau.ac.il/~rumster/TR-2005-04-135520.pdf.
3. G. Arnold, R. Manevich, M. Sagiv, and R. Shaham. Combining shape analyses by intersecting abstractions. In *Verification, Model Checking and Abstract Interpretation (VMCAI)*, volume 3855, pages 33–48. Springer-Verlag, 2006.
4. P. Cousot and R. Cousot. Systematic design of program analysis frameworks. In *Symposium on Principals of Programming Languages (POPL)*, pages 269–282. ACM Press, 1979.
5. S. K. Lahiri and S. Qadeer. Verifying properties of well-founded linked lists. In *Symposium on Principals of Programming Languages (POPL)*, pages 115–126, 2006.
6. O. Lee, H. Yang, and K. Yi. Automatic verification of pointer programs using grammar-based shape analysis. In *The European Symposium on Programming (ESOP)*, volume 3444, pages 124–140. Springer-Verlag, 2005.
7. T. Lev-Ami. TVLA: A framework for kleene logic based static analysis. Master's thesis, Tel-Aviv University, May 2000.
8. T. Lev-Ami, T. W. Reps, M. Sagiv, and R. Wilhelm. Putting static analysis to work for verification: A case study. In *International Symposium on Software Testing and Analysis (ISSTA)*, pages 26–38, 2000.
9. T. Lev-Ami and M. Sagiv. TVLA: A system for implementing static analyses. In *Static Analysis Symposium (SAS)*, pages 280–301, 2000.
10. R. Manevich, M. Sagiv, G. Ramalingam, and J. Field. Partially disjunctive heap abstraction. In *Static Analysis Symposium (SAS)*, pages 265–279, 2004.
11. R. Manevich, E. Yahav, G. Ramalingam, and M. Sagiv. Predicate abstraction and canonical abstraction for singly-linked lists. In *Verification, Model Checking and Abstract Interpretation (VMCAI)*, pages 181–198, 2005.
12. M. Sagiv, T. W. Reps, and R. Wilhelm. Parametric shape analysis via 3-valued logic. *Transactions on Programming Languages and Systems (TOPLAS)*, 24(3):217–298, 2002.

Recency-Abstraction for Heap-Allocated Storage

Gogul Balakrishnan and Thomas Reps

Comp. Sci. Dept., University of Wisconsin
{bgogul, reps}@cs.wisc.edu

Abstract. In this paper, we present an abstraction for heap-allocated storage, called the *recency-abstraction*, that allows abstract-interpretation algorithms to recover some non-trivial information for heap-allocated data objects. As an application of the recency-abstraction, we show how it can resolve virtual-function calls in stripped executables (i.e., executables from which debugging information has been removed). This approach succeeded in resolving 55% of virtual-function call-sites, whereas previous tools for analyzing executables fail to resolve *any* of the virtual-function call-sites.

1   Introduction

A great deal of work has been done on algorithms for flow-insensitive points-to analysis [1,9,35] (including algorithms that exhibit varying degrees of context-sensitivity [8,12,13,38]), as well as on algorithms for flow-sensitive points-to analysis [18,29]. However, all of the aforementioned work uses a very simple abstraction of heap-allocated storage, which we call the *allocation-site abstraction* [6,24]:

> *All of the nodes allocated at a given allocation site s are folded together into a single summary node n_s.*

In terms of precision, the allocation-site abstraction can often produce poor-quality information because it does not allow strong updates to be performed. A strong update overwrites the contents of an abstract object, and represents a definite change in value to all concrete objects that the abstract object represents [6,33]. Strong updates cannot generally be performed on summary objects because a (concrete) update usually affects only <u>one</u> of the summarized concrete objects. If allocation site s is in a loop, or in a function that is called more than once, then s can allocate multiple nodes with different addresses. A points-to fact "p points to n_s" means that program variable p may point to *one* of the nodes that n_s represents. For an assignment of the form p->selector1 = q, points-to-analysis algorithms are ordinarily forced to perform a weak update: that is, selector edges emanating from the nodes that p points to are *accumulated*; the abstract execution of an assignment to a field of a summary node cannot kill the effects of a previous assignment because, in general, only *one* of the nodes that n_s represents is updated on each concrete execution of the assignment statement. Because imprecisions snowball as additional weak updates are performed (e.g., for assignments of the form r->selector1 = p->selector2), the use of weak

K. Yi (Ed.): SAS 2006, LNCS 4134, pp. 221–239, 2006.

```
void foo() {                          void foo() {
   int **pp, a;                          int **pp, a;
   while(...) {                           while(...) {
      pp =                                   pp =
         (int*)malloc(sizeof(int*));            (int*)malloc(sizeof(int*));
      if(...)                                if(...)
         *pp = &a;                              *pp = &a;
      else {                                 else {
         // No initialization of *pp             *pp = &b;
      }                                      }
      **pp = 10;                             **pp = 10;
   }                                      }
}                                     }
           (a)                                       (b)
```

Fig. 1. Weak-update problem for malloc blocks

updates has adverse effects on what a points-to-analysis algorithm can determine about the properties of heap-allocated data structures.

To mitigate the effects of weak updates, many pointer-analysis algorithms in the literature side-step the issue of soundness. For instance, in a number of pointer-analysis algorithms—both flow-insensitive and flow-sensitive—the initial points-to set for each pointer variable is assumed to be $\emptyset$ (rather than $\top$). For local variables and malloc-site variables, the assumption that the initial value is $\emptyset$ is not a safe one—it does not over-approximate all of the program's behaviors. The program shown in Fig. 1 illustrates this issue. In Fig. 1(a), *pp is <u>not</u> initialized on all paths leading to "**pp = 10", whereas in Fig. 1(b), *pp is initialized on all paths leading to "**pp = 10".

A pointer-analysis algorithm that makes the unsafe assumption mentioned above will not be able to detect that the malloc-block pointed to by pp is possibly uninitialized at the dereference **pp. For Fig. 1(b), the algorithm concludes correctly that "**pp = 10" modifies either a or b, but for Fig. 1(a), the algorithm concludes incorrectly that "**pp = 10" only modifies a, which is not sound.

On the other hand, assuming that the malloc-block can point to any variable or heap-allocated object immediately after the call to malloc (i.e., has the value $\top$) leads to sound but imprecise points-to sets in both versions of the program in Fig. 1. The problem is as follows. When the pointer-analysis algorithm interprets statements "*pp = &a" and "*pp = &b", it performs a weak update. Because *pp is assumed to point to any variable or heap-allocated object, performing a weak update does not improve the points-to sets for the malloc-block (i.e., its value remains $\top$). Therefore, the algorithm concludes that "**pp = 10" may modify any variable or heap-allocated object in the program.[1]

----

[1] Source-code analyses for C and C++ typically use the criterion "any variable whose address has been taken" in place of "any variable". However, this can be unsound for programs that use pointer arithmetic (i.e., perform arithmetic operations on addresses), such as executables.

It might seem possible to overcome the lack of soundness by tracking whether variables and fields of heap-allocated data structures are *uninitialized* (either as a separate analysis or as part of pointer analysis). However, such an approach will also encounter the weak-update problem for fields of heap-allocated data structures. For instance, for the program in Fig. 1(b), the initial state of the malloc-block would be set to *uninitialized*. During dataflow analysis, when processing "*pp = &a" and "*pp = &b" it is not possible to change the state of the malloc-block to *initialized* because *pp points to a summary object. Hence, fields of memory allocated at malloc-sites will still be reported as possibly *uninitialized*.

Even the use of multiple summary nodes per allocation site, where each summary node is qualified by some amount of calling context (as in [16,28]), does not overcome the problem; that is, algorithms such as [16,28] must still perform weak updates.

At the other extreme is a family of heap abstractions that have been introduced to discover information about the possible shapes of the heap-allocated data structures to which a program's pointer variables can point [33]. Those abstractions generally allow strong updates to be performed, and are capable of providing very precise characterizations of programs that manipulate linked data structures; however, the methods are also very costly in space and time.

The inability to perform strong updates not only causes less precise points-to information to be obtained for pointer-valued fields, it also causes less precise numeric information to be obtained for int-valued fields. For instance, with interval analysis (an abstract interpretation that determines an interval for each variable that over-approximates the variable's set of values) when an int-valued field of a heap-allocated data structure is initialized to $\top$ (meaning any possible int value), performing a weak update will leave the field's value as $\top$. Making unsound assumptions (such as an empty interval) for the initial value of int-valued fields nullifies the soundness guarantees of abstract-interpretation. Consequently, the results of the analysis cannot be used to prove absence of bugs.

In this paper, we present an abstraction for heap-allocated storage, referred to as the *recency-abstraction*, that is somewhere in the middle between the extremes of one summary node per malloc site [1,9,35] and complex shape abstractions [33]. In particular, the recency-abstraction enables strong updates to be performed in many cases, and at the same time, ensures that the results are sound.

The recency-abstraction incorporates a number of ideas known from the literature, including

- associating abstract malloc-blocks with allocation sites (*à la* the allocation-site abstraction [6,24])
- isolating a distinguished non-summary node that represents the memory location that will be updated by a statement (as in the k-limiting approach [19,22] and shape analysis based on 3-valued logic [33])
- using a history relation to record information about a node's past state [27]
- attaching numeric information to summary nodes to characterize the number of concrete nodes represented [39]

– for efficiency, associating each program point with a single shape-graph [6,24,25,32,36] and using an independent-attribute abstraction to track information about individual heap locations [17].

The contributions of our work are as follows:

– We propose an inexpensive abstraction for heap-allocated data structures that allows us to obtain some useful results for objects allocated in the heap.
– We apply this abstraction in a particularly challenging context, and study its effectiveness. In particular, we measured how well it resolves virtual-function calls in stripped x86 executables obtained from C++ code. The recency-abstraction permits our tool to recover information about pointers to virtual-function tables assigned to objects when the source code contains a call **new** C, where C is a class that has virtual methods. Using the recency-abstraction, our tool was able to resolve 55% of the virtual-function call-sites, whereas previous tools for analyzing executables—including IDAPro [20] (a commercial disassembler), as well as our own previous work without the recency abstraction [3]—fail to resolve *any* of the virtual-function call-sites.

The recency-abstraction is beneficial when the initialization of objects is between two successive allocations at the same allocation site.

– It is particularly effective for initializing the VFT-field (the field of an object that holds the address of the virtual-function table) because the usual case is that the VFT-field is initialized in the constructor, and remains unchanged thereafter.
– Inside methods that operate on lists, doubly-linked lists, and other linked data structures, an analysis based on the recency-abstraction would typically be forced to perform weak updates. The recency-abstraction does not go as far as methods for shape analysis based on 3-valued logic [33], which can materialize a non-summary node for the memory location that will be updated by a statement and thereby make a strong update possible; however, such analysis methods are considerably more expensive in time and space than the one described here.

The remainder of the paper is organized as follows: §2 provides background on the issues that arise when resolving virtual-function calls in executables. §3 describes our recency-abstraction for heap-allocated data structures. §4 provides experimental results evaluating these techniques. §5 discusses related work.

2   Resolving Virtual-Function Calls in Executables

In recent years, there has been an increasing need for tools to help programmers and security analysts understand executables. For instance, commercial companies and the military increasingly use Commercial Off-The Shelf (COTS) components to reduce the cost of software development. They are interested in ensuring that COTS components do not perform malicious actions (or cannot be forced to perform malicious actions). Therefore, resolving virtual-function calls in executables is important: (1) as a code-understanding aid to analysts who examine executables, and (2) for recovering Intermediate Representations (IRs) so that additional analyses can be performed on the recovered IR (à la Engler et al. [11], Chen and Wagner [7], etc.). Poor information about virtual-function calls typically forces tool builders to treat them either (i) conservatively, e.g., as a call to any function whose address has been taken, which is a source of false positives, (ii) as if the call causes execution to halt, i.e., the analysis does not proceed beyond sites of virtual-function calls, which is a source of false negatives, or (iii) in an unsound fashion, e.g., as if they call a no-op function that returns immediately, which can lead to. both false negatives and false positives.

In this section, we discuss the issues that arise when trying to resolve virtual-function calls in executables. Consider an executable compiled from a C++ program that uses inheritance and virtual functions. The first four bytes of an object contains the address of the virtual-function table. We will refer to these four bytes as the *VFT-field*. In an executable, a call to new results in two operations: (1) a call to malloc to allocate memory, and (2) a call to the constructor to initialize (among other things) the VFT-field. A virtual-function call in source code gets translated to an indirect call through the VFT-field (see Fig. 2).

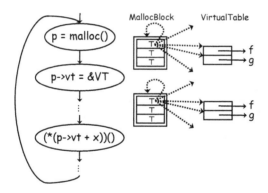

Fig. 2. Resolving virtual-function calls in executables. (A double box denotes a summary node.)

When source code is available, one way of resolving virtual-function calls is to associate type information with the pointer returned by the call to new and then propagate that information to other pointers at assignment statements. However, type information is usually not available in executables. Therefore, to resolve a virtual-function call, information about the contents of the VFT-field needs to be available. For a static-analysis algorithm to determine such information, it has to track the flow of information through the instructions in the constructor. Fig. 2 illustrates the results if the allocation-site abstraction is used. Using the allocation-site abstraction alone, it would not be possible to establish the link between the object and the virtual-function table: because the summary node represents more than one block, the interpretation of the instruction that sets the VFT-field can only perform a weak update, i.e., it can only join the virtual-function table address with the existing addresses, and not overwrite the VFT-field in the object with the address of the virtual-function table. After the call to `malloc`, the fields of the object can have any value (shown as $\top$); computing the join of $\top$ with any value results in $\top$, which means that the VFT-field can point to anywhere in memory (shown as dashed arrows). Therefore, a definite link between the object and the virtual-function table is never established, and (if a conservative algorithm is desired) a client of the analysis can only conclude that the virtual-function call may resolve to any possible function.

The key to resolving virtual-function calls in executables is to be able to establish that the VFT-field definitely points to a certain virtual-function table. §2.1 describes the abstract domain used in Value-Set Analysis (VSA) [3], a combined pointer-analysis and numeric-analysis algorithm that can track the flow of data in an executable. The version of the VSA domain described in §2.1 (the version used in [3]) has the limitations discussed above (i.e., the need to perform weak updates); §3 describes an extension of the VSA domain that uses the recency-abstraction, and shows how it is able to establish a definite link between an object's VFT-field and the appropriate virtual-function table in many circumstances.

2.1 Value-Set Analysis

VSA is a combined numeric-analysis and pointer-analysis algorithm that determines an over-approximation of the set of numeric values or addresses that each variable holds at each program point. A key feature of VSA is that it takes into account pointer arithmetic operations and tracks integer-valued and address-valued quantities simultaneously. This is crucial for analyzing executables because numeric values and addresses are indistinguishable at runtime and pointer arithmetic is used extensively in executables. During VSA, a set of addresses and numeric values is represented by a safe approximation, which we refer to as a *value-set*.

Memory-Regions. In the runtime address space, there is no separation of the activation records of various procedures, the heap, and the memory for global data. However, during the analysis of an executable, we break the address space into a set of disjoint memory areas, which are referred to as *memory-regions*. Each memory-region represents a group of locations that have similar runtime properties. For example, the runtime locations that belong to the activation record of the same procedure belong to a memory-region.

For a given program, there are three kinds of regions: (1) the *global*-region contains information about locations that correspond to global data, (2) the *AR*-regions contain information about locations that corresponds to the activation-record of a particular procedure, and (3) the *malloc*-regions contain information about locations that are allocated at a particular malloc site.

When performing source-code analysis, the programmer-defined variables provide us with convenient compartments for tracking data manipulations involving memory. However, stripped executables do not have information about programmer-defined variables. In our work, we use the variable-recovery mechanism described in [4] to obtain variable-like entities for stripped executables. The variable-recovery algorithm described in [4] identifies the structure of each memory-region based on the data-access patterns in the executable, and treats each field of the structure recovered for the memory region as a variable. For instance, suppose that the structure of the AR-region for a procedure P is

```
struct {
    int a;
    struct {
        int b;
        int c;
    } d;
};
```

Procedure P would be treated as having three int-valued variables a, d.b, and d.c. Similarly, the fields of malloc-regions are treated as variables. In general, if R is a memory-region, Var$_R$ denotes the variables of R. For uniformity, registers are treated as variables.

Value-Sets. A value-set is a safe approximation for a set of addresses and numeric values. Suppose that n is the number of regions in the executable. A value-set is an n-tuple of strided intervals of the form $s[l, u]$, with each component of the tuple representing the set of addresses in the corresponding region. For a 32-bit machine, a strided-interval $s[l, u]$ represents the set of integers $\{i \in [-2^{31}, 2^{31} - 1] | l \leq i \leq u, i \equiv l(\text{mod } s)\}$ [31].

- s is called the *stride*.
- $[l, u]$ is called the *interval*.
- $0[l, l]$ represents the singleton set $\{l\}$.

Call-strings. The call-graph of a program is a labeled graph in which each node represents a procedure, each edge represents a call, and the label on an edge represents the call-site corresponding to the call represented by the edge. A call-string [34] is a sequence of call-sites $(c_1 c_2 \ldots c_n)$ such that call-site c_1 belongs to the entry procedure, and there exists a path in the call-graph consisting of edges with labels $c_1, c_2, \ldots, c_n$. CallString is the set of all call-strings in the program.

A call-string suffix of length k is either $(c_1 c_2 \ldots c_k)$ or $(*c_1 c_2 \ldots c_k)$, where c_1, $c_2, \ldots, c_k$ are call-sites. $(c_1 c_2 \ldots c_k)$ represents the string of call-sites $c_1 c_2 \ldots c_k$. $(*c_1 c_2 \ldots c_k)$, which is referred to as a *saturated* call-string, represents the set $\{cs | cs \in \text{CallString}, cs = \pi c_1 c_2 \ldots c_k, \text{ and } |\pi| \geq 1\}$. CallString$_k$ is the set of call-string suffixes of length k, plus non-saturated call-strings of length $\leq k$. Consider the call-graph shown in Fig. 3(a). The set CallString$_2$ for this call-graph is $\{\epsilon,$ C$_1$, C$_2$, C$_1$C$_3$, C$_2$C$_4$, $*$C$_3$C$_5$, $*$C$_4$C$_5$, $*$C$_5$C$_4\}$.

VSA is a flow-sensitive, context-sensitive, abstract-interpretation algorithm (parameterized by call-string length [34]); it is an independent-attribute method (in the sense of [23]) based on the abstract domain described below. To simplify

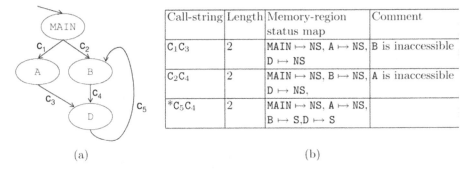

Call-string	Length	Memory-region status map	Comment
C_1C_3	2	MAIN $\mapsto$ NS, A $\mapsto$ NS, D $\mapsto$ NS	B is inaccessible
C_2C_4	2	MAIN $\mapsto$ NS, B $\mapsto$ NS, D $\mapsto$ NS,	A is inaccessible
$*C_5C_4$	2	MAIN $\mapsto$ NS, A $\mapsto$ NS, B $\mapsto$ S,D $\mapsto$ S	

(a)   (b)

Fig. 3. (a) Call-graph; (b) memory-region status map for different call-strings. (Key: NS: non-summary, S: summary; * refers to a saturated call-string.)

the presentation, the discussion in this section uses the allocation-site abstraction for heap-allocated storage.

Let Proc denote the set of memory-regions associated with procedures in the program, AllocMemRgn denotes the set of memory regions associated with heap-allocation sites, and Global denote the memory-region associated with the global data area. We work with the following basic domains:

$$
\begin{aligned}
\text{MemRgn} &= \{\text{Global}\} \cup \text{Proc} \cup \text{AllocMemRgn} \\
\text{ValueSet} &= \text{MemRgn} \rightarrow \text{StridedInterval}_\bot \\
\text{VarEnv}[\text{R}] &= \text{Var}_R \rightarrow \text{ValueSet}
\end{aligned}
$$

AbsEnv maps each region R to its corresponding VarEnv[R] and each register to a ValueSet:

$$
\text{AbsEnv} =
\begin{aligned}
&(\text{register} \rightarrow \text{ValueSet}) \\
\times\ &(\{\text{Global}\} \rightarrow \text{VarEnv}[\text{Global}]) \\
\times\ &(\text{Proc} \rightarrow \text{VarEnv}[\text{Proc}]_\bot) \\
\times\ &(\text{AllocMemRgn} \rightarrow \text{VarEnv}[\text{AllocMemRgn}]_\bot)
\end{aligned}
$$

VSA associates each program point with an AbsMemConfig:

$$\text{AbsMemConfig} = (\text{CallString}_k \rightarrow \text{AbsEnv}_\bot)$$

During VSA, all abstract transformers are passed a *memory-region status map* that indicates which memory-regions, in the context of a given call-string *cs*, are summary memory-regions. Whereas the Global region is always non-summary and all malloc-regions are always summary, to decide whether a procedure P's memory-region is a summary memory-region, first call-string *cs* is traversed, and then the call graph is traversed, to see whether the runtime stack could contain multiple pending activation records for P. Fig. 3(b) shows the memory-region status map for different call-strings of length 2.

The memory-region status map provides one of two pieces of information used to identify when a strong update can be performed. In particular, an abstract

```
struct List {
  int a;
  struct List* next;
};

int main() {
  int i;
  struct List* head = NULL;
  struct List* elem;
  for(i = 0; i < 5; ++i) {
    M1: elem = (struct List*)
               malloc(sizeof(struct List));
    elem->a = i;
    elem->next = head;
    L1: head = elem;
  }
  return 0;
}
```

(a)

```
AR_main ↦ (
    i    ↦ [(Global ↦ 1[0,4])]
    head ↦ [(malloc_M1 ↦ 0[0,0])]
    elem ↦ [(malloc_M1 ↦ 0[0,0])]
)
malloc_M1 ↦ (
    Field_0 ↦ ⊤
    Field_4 ↦ ⊤
)
```
(b)

```
i    ↦ [(Global ↦ 1[0,4])]
head ↦ [(malloc_M1 ↦ 0[0,0])]
elem ↦ [(malloc_M1 ↦ 0[0,0])]
elem->a ↦ ⊤
elem->next ↦ ⊤
```
(c)

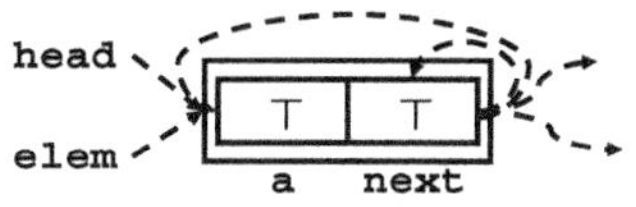

(d)

Fig. 4. Value-Set Analysis (VSA) results (when the allocation-site abstraction is used): (a) C program; (b) value-sets after L1 (registers and global variables are omitted); (c) value-sets in (b) interpreted in terms of the variables in the C program; and (d) graphical depiction of (c). (The double box denotes a summary region. Dashed edges denote may-points-to information.)

transformer can perform a strong update if the operation modifies (a) a register, or (b) a non-array variable in a non-summary memory-region.

Example 1. We will illustrate VSA using the C program[2] shown in Fig. 4(a). For this example, there would be three regions: Global, AR_main, and malloc_M1.

The value-sets that are obtained from VSA at the bottom of the loop body are shown in Fig. 4(b). Fig. 4(c) shows the value-sets in terms of the variables in the C program.

- "i ↦ [(Global ↦ 1[0,4])]" indicates that i has a value (or a global address) in the range $[0, 4]$.
- "elem ↦ [(malloc_M1 ↦ 0[0,0])]" indicates that elem contains offset 0 in the malloc-region associated with malloc-site M1.
- "head ↦ [(malloc_M1 ↦ 0[0,0])]" indicates that head contains offset 0 in the malloc-region associated with malloc-site M1.
- "elem->a ↦ ⊤" and "elem->next ↦ ⊤" indicate that elem->a and elem->next may contain any possible value. VSA could not determine better value-sets for these variables because of the weak-update problem mentioned earlier.

---

[2] In our implementation, VSA is applied to executables. We use C code for ease of understanding.

Because `malloc` does not initialize the block of memory that it returns, VSA assumes (safely) that `elem->a` and `elem->next` may contain any possible value after the call to `malloc`. Because `malloc_M1` is a summary memory-region, only weak updates can be performed at the instructions that initialize the fields of `elem`. Therefore, the value-sets associated with the fields of `elem` remain $\top$.

Fig. 4(d) shows the information pictorially. The double box denotes a summary object. Dashed edges denote may-points-to information. In our example, VSA has recovered the following: (1) `head` and `elem` may point to one of the objects represented by the summary object, (2) "`elem->next`" may point to any possible location, and (3) "`elem->a`" may contain any possible value. $\square$

3   An Abstraction for Heap-Allocated Storage

This section describes the *recency-abstraction*. The recency-abstraction is similar in some respects to the allocation-site abstraction, in that each abstract node is associated with a particular allocation site; however, the recency-abstraction uses two memory-regions per allocation site s:

AllocMemRgn = $\{\text{MRAB}[s], \text{NMRAB}[s] \mid s$ an allocation site$\}$

- MRAB$[s]$ represents the <u>m</u>ost-<u>r</u>ecently-<u>a</u>llocated <u>b</u>lock that was allocated at s. Because there is at most one such block in any concrete configuration, MRAB$[s]$ is *never* a summary memory-region.
- NMRAB$[s]$ represents the <u>n</u>on-<u>m</u>ost-<u>r</u>ecently-<u>a</u>llocated <u>b</u>locks that were allocated at s. Because there can be many such blocks in a given concrete configuration, NMRAB$[s]$ is generally a summary memory-region.

In addition, each MRAB$[s]$, NMRAB$[s] \in$ AllocMemRgn is associated with a "count" value, denoted by MRAB$[s]$.count and NMRAB$[s]$.count, respectively, which is a value of type SmallRange = $\{[0,0], [0,1], [1,1], [0,\infty], [1,\infty], [2,\infty]\}$. The count value records a range for how many concrete blocks the memory-region represents. While NMRAB$[s]$.count can have any SmallRange value, MRAB$[s]$.count will be restricted to take on only values in $\{[0,0], [0,1], [1,1]\}$, which represent counts for non-summary regions. Consequently, an abstract transformer can perform a strong update on a field of MRAB$[s]$.

In addition to the count, each MRAB$[s]$, NMRAB$[s] \in$ AllocMemRgn is also associated with a "size" value, denoted by MRAB$[s]$.size and NMRAB$[s]$.size, respectively, which is a value of type StridedInterval. The size value represents an over-approximation of the set of sizes of the concrete blocks that the memory-region represents. This information can be used to report potential memory-access violations that involve heap-allocated data. For instance, if MRAB$[s]$.size of an allocation site s is $0[12, 12]$, the dereference of a pointer whose value-set is $[(\text{MRAB}[s] \mapsto 0[16, 16])]$ would be reported as a memory-access violation.

Example 2. Fig. 5 shows a trace of the evolution of parts of the AbsEnvs for three instructions in a loop during VSA. It is assumed that there are three fields in the memory-regions MRAB and NMRAB (shown as the three rectangles within

MRAB and NMRAB). Double boxes around NMRAB objects in Fig. 5(c) and (d) are used to indicate that they are summary memory-regions.

For brevity, in Fig. 5 the effect of each instruction is denoted using C syntax; the original source code in the loop body contains a C++ statement "p = new C", where C is a class that has virtual methods f and g. The symbols f and g that appear in Fig. 5 represent the addresses of methods f and g. The symbol p and the two fields of VT represent variables of the Global region. The dotted lines in Fig. 5(b)–(d) indicate how the value of NMRAB after the malloc statement depends on the value of MRAB and NMRAB before the malloc statement.

The AbsEnvs stabilize after four iterations. Note that in each of Fig. 5(a)–(d), it can be established that the instruction "p->vt = &VT" modifies exactly one field in a non-summary memory-region, and hence a strong update can be performed on p->vt. This establishes a definite link—i.e., a *must*-point-to link—between MRAB and VT. The net effect is that the analysis establishes a definite link between NMRAB and VT as well: the vt field of each object represented by NMRAB must point to VT.   □

Example 3. Fig. 6 shows the improved VSA information recovered for the program from Fig. 4 at the end of the loop when the recency-abstraction is used. In particular, we have the following information:

- elem and head definitely point to the beginning of the MRAB region.
- elem->a contains the values (or global addresses) $\{0, 1, 2, 3, 4\}$.
- elem->next may be 0 (NULL) or may point to the beginning of the NMRAB region.
- NMRAB.a contains the values (or global addresses) $\{0, 1, 2, 3, 4\}$.
- NMRAB.next may be 0 (NULL) or may point to the beginning of the NM-RAB region.   □

This idea is formalized with the following basic domains (where underlining indicates differences from the domains given in §2):

$$
\begin{array}{l}
\mathsf{MemRgn} = \{\mathsf{Global}\} \cup \mathsf{Proc} \cup \underline{\mathsf{AllocMemRgn}} \\
\mathsf{ValueSet} = \mathsf{MemRgn} \rightarrow \mathsf{StridedInterval}_{\perp} \\
\mathsf{VarEnv}[\mathsf{R}] = \mathsf{Var}_{\mathsf{R}} \rightarrow \mathsf{ValueSet} \\
\underline{\mathsf{SmallRange}} = \{[0,0], [0,1], [1,1], [0,\infty], [1,\infty], [2,\infty]\} \\
\underline{\mathsf{AllocAbsEnv}[\mathsf{R}]} = \underline{\mathsf{SmallRange} \times \mathsf{StridedInterval} \times \mathsf{VarEnv}[\mathsf{R}]}
\end{array}
$$

The analysis associates each program point with an AbsMemConfig:

$$
\begin{array}{rl}
\mathsf{AbsEnv} = & (\mathsf{register} \rightarrow \mathsf{ValueSet}) \\
& \times (\{\mathsf{Global}\} \rightarrow \mathsf{VarEnv}[\mathsf{Global}]) \\
& \times (\mathsf{Proc} \rightarrow \mathsf{VarEnv}[\mathsf{Proc}]_{\perp}) \\
& \times \underline{(\mathsf{AllocMemRgn} \rightarrow \mathsf{AllocAbsEnv}[\mathsf{AllocMemRgn}])} \\
\mathsf{AbsMemConfig} = & (\mathsf{CallString}_k \rightarrow \mathsf{AbsEnv}_{\perp})
\end{array}
$$

Let count, size, and varEnv, respectively, denote the SmallRange, StridedInterval, and VarEnv[AllocMemRgn] associated with a given AllocMemRgn.

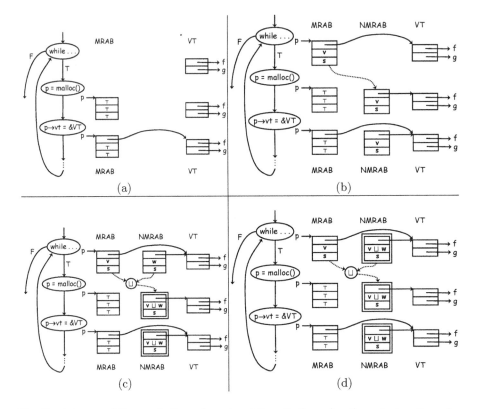

Fig. 5. A trace of the evolution of parts of the AbsEnvs for three instructions in a loop. (Values v and w are unspecified values presented to illustrate that ⊔ is applied on corresponding fields as the previous MRAB value is merged with NMRAB during the abstract interpretation of an allocation site.)

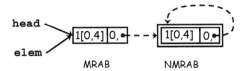

Fig. 6. Improved VSA information for the program from Fig. 4 at the end of the loop (i.e., just after L1) when the recency-abstraction is used. (The double box denotes a summary region. Dashed edges denote may-points-to information.)

A given absEnv ∈ AbsEnv maps allocation memory-regions, such as MRAB[s] or NMRAB[s], to ⟨count, size, varEnv⟩ triples.

The transformers for various operations are defined as follows:

- At the entry point of the program, the AbsMemConfig that describes the initial state records that, for each allocation site s, the AllocAbsEnvs for both MRAB[s] and NMRAB[s] are ⟨[0, 0], ⊥$_{\text{StridedInterval}}$, λvar.⊥$_{\text{ValueSet}}$⟩.
- The transformer for allocation site s transforms absEnv to absEnv', where absEnv' is identical to absEnv, except that all ValueSets of absEnv that contain

$[..., \text{MRAB}[s] \mapsto si_1, \text{NMRAB}[s] \mapsto si_2, ...]$ become $[..., \emptyset, \text{NMRAB}[s] \mapsto si_1 \sqcup si_2, ...]$ in absEnv′. In x86 code, return values are passed back in register eax. Let $size$ denote the size of the block allocated at the allocation site. The value of $size$ is obtained from the value-set associated with the parameter of the allocation method. In addition, absEnv′ is updated on the following arguments:

$$\text{absEnv}'(\text{MRAB}[s]) = \langle [0, 1], size, \lambda\text{var}.\top_{\text{ValueSet}} \rangle$$
$$\text{absEnv}'(\text{NMRAB}[s]).\text{count} = \text{absEnv}(\text{NMRAB}[s]).\text{count} +_{SR} \text{absEnv}(\text{MRAB}[s]).\text{count}$$
$$\text{absEnv}'(\text{NMRAB}[s]).\text{size} = \text{absEnv}(\text{NMRAB}[s]).\text{size} \sqcup \text{absEnv}(\text{MRAB}[s]).\text{size}$$
$$\text{absEnv}'(\text{NMRAB}[s]).\text{varEnv} = \text{absEnv}(\text{NMRAB}[s]).\text{varEnv} \sqcup \text{absEnv}(\text{MRAB}[s]).\text{varEnv}$$
$$\text{absEnv}'(\text{eax}) = [(\text{Global} \mapsto 0[0, 0]), (\text{MRAB}[s] \mapsto 0[0, 0])]$$

where $+_{SR}$ denotes SmallRange addition. In the present implementation, we assume that an allocation always succeeds; hence, in place of the first and last lines above, we use

$$\text{absEnv}'(\text{MRAB}[s]) = \langle [1, 1], size, \lambda\text{var}.\top_{\text{ValueSet}} \rangle$$
$$\text{absEnv}'(\text{eax}) = [(\text{MRAB}[s] \mapsto 0[0, 0])].$$

Consequently, the analysis only explores the behavior of the system on executions in which allocations always succeed.

– The join $\text{absEnv}_1 \sqcup \text{absEnv}_2$ of $\text{absEnv}_1, \text{absEnv}_2 \in \text{AbsEnv}$ is performed pointwise; in particular,

$$\text{absEnv}'(\text{MRAB}[s]) = \text{absEnv}_1(\text{MRAB}[s]) \sqcup \text{absEnv}_2(\text{MRAB}[s])$$
$$\text{absEnv}'(\text{NMRAB}[s]) = \text{absEnv}_1(\text{NMRAB}[s]) \sqcup \text{absEnv}_2(\text{NMRAB}[s])$$

where the join of two AllocMemRgns is also performed pointwise:

$$\langle \text{count}_1, \text{size}_1, \text{varEnv}_1 \rangle \sqcup \langle \text{count}_2, \text{size}_2, \text{varEnv}_2 \rangle$$
$$= \langle \text{count}_1 \sqcup \text{count}_2, \text{size}_1 \sqcup \text{size}_2, \text{varEnv}_1 \sqcup \text{varEnv}_2 \rangle.$$

In all other abstract transformers (e.g., assignments, data movements, interpretation of conditions, etc.), MRAB[s] and NMRAB[s] are treated just like other memory regions—i.e., Global and the AR-regions—with one exception:

– During VSA, all abstract transformers are passed a memory-region status map that indicates which memory-regions, in the context of a given call-string suffix cs, are summary memory-regions. The summary-status information for MRAB[s] and NMRAB[s] is obtained from the values of $\text{AbsMemConfig}(cs)(\text{MRAB}[s]).\text{count}$ and $\text{AbsMemConfig}(cs)(\text{NMRAB}[s]).\text{count}$, respectively.

4   Experiments

This section describes the results of our preliminary experiments. The first three columns of numbers in Tab. 1 show the characteristics of the set of examples

Table 1. Characteristics of the example programs, together with the distribution of the number of callees at indirect call-sites and the running times for VSA. The bold entry indicates that eight call-sites in `deriv1` are identified as definitely unreachable.

	# x86 Instructions	Procs	# Indirect call-sites	⊥	1	2	≥3	⊤	% Reachable call-sites resolved	Time (secs)
NP	252	5	6	0	0	6	0	0	100	1
primes	294	9	2	1	1	0	0	1	50	<1
family	351	9	3	0	3	0	0	0	100	1
vcirc	407	14	5	0	5	0	0	0	100	<1
fsm	502	13	1	0	1	0	0	0	100	5
office	592	22	4	0	4	0	0	0	100	<1
trees	1299	29	3	1	0	0	0	2	0	9
deriv1	1369	38	18	**8**	8	2	0	0	100	4
chess	1662	41	1	0	0	0	0	1	0	16
objects	1739	47	23	18	0	4	0	1	17	2
simul	1920	60	3	2	0	0	0	1	0	6
greed	1945	47	17	6	10	0	0	1	59	10
shapes	1955	39	12	4	4	3	0	1	58	10
ocean	2552	61	5	3	0	0	0	2	0	17
deriv2	2639	41	56	33	22	0	0	1	39	2

that we used in our evaluation. These programs were originally used by Pande and Ryder in [29] to evaluate their algorithm for resolving virtual-function calls in C++ programs. The programs in C++ were compiled without optimization[3] using the Microsoft Visual Studio 6.0 compiler and the .obj files obtained from the compiler were analyzed. We did not make use of debugging information in the experiments.

The final seven columns of Tab. 1 report the performance (both accuracy and time) of the version of VSA that incorporates the recency abstraction to help resolve virtual-function calls.

- In these examples, every indirect call-site in the executable corresponds to a virtual-function call-site in the source code.
- The column labeled ⊥ shows the number of (apparently) unreachable indirect call-sites.
- The column labeled ⊤ shows the number of reachable indirect call-sites at which VSA could not determine the targets. A non-zero value in the ⊤-column means that at some indirect call-sites VSA could not resolve the virtual-function call to a specific subset of the procedures. VSA reports such call-sites to the user, but does not explore any procedures from that call-site. This is a source of false negatives, and occurred for 9 of the 15 programs. On

---

[3] Note that unoptimized programs generally have more memory accesses than optimized programs; optimized programs make more use of registers, which are easier to analyze than memory accesses. Thus, for static analysis of stripped executables, unoptimized programs generally represent a *greater* challenge than optimized programs.

the other hand, for the 6 programs for which the ⊤-column is 0, any call-sites reported in the ⊥-column are definitely unreachable. In particular, the eight call-sites that were identified as unreachable in `deriv1` are definitely unreachable.

– The other columns show the distribution of the number of targets at the indirect call-sites. For example, the column labeled 1 denotes the number of indirect call-sites that had a single target.

It is important to realize that these results are obtained solely by using abstract interpretation to track the flow of data through memory (including the heap). The analysis algorithm does not rely on symbol-table or debugging information; instead it uses the structure-discovery mechanism described in [4]. On average, our method resolved 55% of the virtual-function call-sites, whereas previous tools for analyzing executables—such as IDAPro, as well as our own previous work using VSA without the recency abstraction [3]—fail to resolve *any* of the virtual-function call-sites.

Manual inspection revealed that most of the situations in which VSA could not resolve indirect call-sites were due to VSA not being able to establish that some loop definitely initializes all of the elements of some array. The problem is as follows: In some of the example programs, an array of pointers to objects is initialized via a loop. These pointers are later used to perform a virtual-function call. Even when VSA succeeded in establishing the link between the VFT-field and the virtual-function table, VSA could not establish that all elements of the array are definitely initialized by the instruction in the loop, and hence the abstract value that represents the values of the elements of the array remains ⊤.

Note that this issue is orthogonal to the problem addressed in this paper. That is, even if one were to use other mechanisms (such as the one described in [15]) to establish that all the elements of an array are initialized, the problem of establishing the link between the VFT-field and the virtual-function table still requires mechanisms similar to the recency-abstraction.

This issue makes it difficult for us to give a direct comparison of our approach with that of [29]; in particular, [29] makes the *unsafe* assumption that elements in a array of pointers (say, locally allocated or heap allocated) initially point to nothing (∅), rather than to anything (⊤). Suppose that `p[]` is such an array of pointers and that a loop initializes every other element with `&a`. A sound result would be that p's elements can point to anything. However, because in the algorithm used in [29] the points-to set of p is initially ∅, [29] would determine that p's elements point to a, which is unsound.

5   Related Work

Some of the relationships between our approach and past work on abstractions of heap-allocated storage were already mentioned near the end of §1.

The recency-abstraction is similar in flavor to the allocation-site abstraction [6,24], in that each abstract node is associated with a particular allocation site; however, the recency-abstraction is designed to take advantage of the fact that VSA is a flow-sensitive, context-sensitive algorithm. Note that if the recency-abstraction were used with a flow-insensitive algorithm, it would provide little additional precision over the allocation-site abstraction: because a flow-insensitive algorithm has just one abstract memory configuration that expresses a *program-wide* invariant, the algorithm would have to perform weak updates for assignments to MRAB nodes (as well as for assignments to NMRAB nodes); that is, edges emanating from an MRAB node would also have to be accumulated.

With a flow-sensitive algorithm, the recency-abstraction uses twice as many abstract nodes as the allocation-site abstraction, but under certain conditions it is sound for the algorithm to perform strong updates for assignments to MRAB nodes, which is crucial to being able to establish a definite link between the set of objects allocated at a certain site and a particular virtual-function table.

If one ignores actual addresses of allocated objects and adopts the fiction that each allocation site generates objects that are independent of those produced at any other allocation site, another difference between the recency-abstraction and the allocation-site abstraction comes to light:

- The allocation-site abstraction imposes a *fixed partition* on the set of allocated nodes.
- The recency-abstraction shares the "multiple-partition" property that one sees in the shape-analysis abstractions of [33]. An MRAB node represents a *unique* node in any given concrete memory configuration—namely, the most recently allocated node at the allocation site. In general, however, an abstract memory configuration represents multiple concrete memory configurations, and a given MRAB node generally represents different concrete nodes in the different concrete memory configurations.

Hackett and Rugina [17] describe a method that uses local reasoning about individual heap locations, rather than global reasoning about entire heap abstractions. In essence, they use an independent-attribute abstraction: each "tracked location" is tracked independently of other locations in concrete memory configurations. The recency-abstraction is a different independent-attribute abstraction.

The use of count information on (N)MRAB nodes was inspired by the heap abstraction of Yavuz-Kahveci and Bultan [39], which also attaches numeric information to summary nodes to characterize the number of concrete nodes represented. The information on summary node u of abstract memory configuration S describes the number of concrete nodes that are mapped to u in any concrete memory configuration that S represents. Gopan et al. [14] also attach numeric information to summary nodes; however, such information does not provide a characterization of the number of concrete nodes represented: in both the present paper and [39], each concrete node that is combined into a summary node contributes 1 to a *sum* that labels the summary node; in contrast, when concrete nodes are combined together in the approach presented in [14], the effect is to create a *set* of values (to which an additional numeric abstraction may then be applied).

The size information on (N)MRAB nodes can be thought of as an abstraction of auxiliary size information attached to each concrete node, where the concrete size information is abstracted in the style of [14].

Strictly speaking, the use of counts on abstract heap nodes lies outside the framework of [33] for program analysis using 3-valued logic (unless the framework were to be extended with counting quantifiers [21, Sect. 12.3]). However, the use of counts is also related to the notion of active/inactive individuals in logical structures [30], which has been used in the 3-valued logic framework to give a more compact representation of logical structures [26, Chap. 7]. In general, the use of an independent-attribute method in the heap abstraction described in §3 provides a way to avoid the combinatorial explosion that the 3-valued logic framework suffers from: the 3-valued logic framework retains the use of separate logical structures for different combinations of present/absent nodes, whereas counts permit them to be combined.

Several algorithms [2,5,10,37,29] have been proposed to resolve virtual-function calls in C++ and Java programs. For each pointer p, these algorithms determine an over-approximation of the set of types of objects that p may point to. When p is used in a virtual-function call invocation, the set of types is used to disambiguate the targets of the call. Static information such as the class hierarchy, aliases, the set of instantiated objects, etc. are used to reduce the size of the set of types for each pointer p. Because we work on stripped executables, type information is not available. The method presented in §3 analyzes the code in the constructor that initializes the virtual-function pointer of an object to establish a definite link between the object and the virtual-function table, which is subsequently used to resolve virtual-function calls. Moreover, algorithms such as Rapid Type Analysis (RTA) [2] and Class Hierarchy Analysis (CHA) [10] rely on programs being type-safe. The results of CHA and RTA cannot be relied on in the presence of arithmetic operations on addresses, which is present in executables.

References

1. L. O. Andersen. Binding-time analysis and the taming of C pointers. In *PEPM*, pages 47–58, 1993.
2. D.F. Bacon and P.F. Sweeney. Fast static analysis of C++ virtual function calls. In *Object-Oriented Programming, Systems, Languages, and Applications*, pages 324–341, 1996.
3. G. Balakrishnan and T. Reps. Analyzing memory accesses in x86 executables. In *Comp. Construct.*, pages 5–23, 2004.
4. G. Balakrishnan and T. Reps. Recovery of variables and heap structure in x86 executables. Tech. Rep. 1533, Comp. Sci. Dept., Univ. of Wisconsin, Madison, US., September 2005.
5. B. Calder and D. Grunwald. Reducing indirect function call overhead in C++ programs. In *Princip. of Prog. Lang.*, pages 397–408, 1994.
6. D.R. Chase, M. Wegman, and F. Zadeck. Analysis of pointers and structures. In *Prog. Lang. Design and Impl.*, pages 296–310, 1990.
7. H. Chen and D. Wagner. MOPS: An infrastructure for examining security properties of software. In *Conf. on Comp. and Commun. Sec.*, pages 235–244, November 2002.

8. B.-C. Cheng and W.W. Hwu. Modular interprocedural pointer analysis using access paths: Design, implementation, and evaluation. In *Prog. Lang. Design and Impl.*, pages 57–69, 2000.

9. M. Das. Unification-based pointer analysis with directional assignments. In *Prog. Lang. Design and Impl.*, pages 35–46, 2000.

10. J. Dean, D. Grove, and C. Chambers. Optimization of object-oriented programs using static class hierarchy analysis. In *European Conference on Object-Oriented Programming*, pages 77–101, 1995.

11. D.R. Engler, B. Chelf, A. Chou, and S. Hallem. Checking system rules using system-specific, programmer-written compiler extensions. In *Op. Syst. Design and Impl.*, pages 1–16, 2000.

12. M. Fähndrich, J. Rehof, and M. Das. Scalable context-sensitive flow analysis using instantiation constraints. In *Prog. Lang. Design and Impl.*, 2000.

13. J.S. Foster, M. Fähndrich, and A. Aiken. Polymorphic versus monomorphic flow-insensitive points-to analysis for C. In *SAS*, 2000.

14. D. Gopan, F. DiMaio, N.Dor, T. Reps, and M. Sagiv. Numeric domains with summarized dimensions. In *Tools and Algs. for the Construct. and Anal. of Syst.*, pages 512–529, 2004.

15. D. Gopan, T. Reps, and M. Sagiv. A framework for numeric analysis of array operations. In *Princip. of Prog. Lang.*, pages 338–350, 2005.

16. B. Guo, M.J. Bridges, S. Triantafyllis, G. Ottoni, E. Raman, and D.I. August. Practical and accurate low-level pointer analysis. In *3nd IEEE/ACM Int. Symp. on Code Gen. and Opt.*, pages 291–302, 2005.

17. B. Hackett and R. Rugina. Region-based shape analysis with tracked locations. In *Princip. of Prog. Lang.*, pages 310–323, 2005.

18. M. Hind and A. Pioli. Assessing the effects of flow-sensitivity on pointer alias analyses. In *SAS*, 1998.

19. S. Horwitz, P. Pfeiffer, and T. Reps. Dependence analysis for pointer variables. In *Prog. Lang. Design and Impl.*, pages 28–40, 1989.

20. IDAPro disassembler, http://www.datarescue.com/idabase/.

21. N. Immerman. *Descriptive Complexity*. Springer-Verlag, 1999.

22. N.D. Jones and S.S. Muchnick. Flow analysis and optimization of Lisp-like structures. In S.S. Muchnick and N.D. Jones, editors, *Program Flow Analysis: Theory and Applications*, chapter 4, pages 102–131. Prentice-Hall, Englewood Cliffs, NJ, 1981.

23. N.D. Jones and S.S. Muchnick. Flow analysis and optimization of Lisp-like structures. In S.S. Muchnick and N.D. Jones, editors, *Program Flow Analysis: Theory and Applications*, chapter 12, pages 380–384. Prentice-Hall, Englewood Cliffs, NJ, 1981.

24. N.D. Jones and S.S. Muchnick. A flexible approach to interprocedural data flow analysis and programs with recursive data structures. In *Princip. of Prog. Lang.*, pages 66–74, 1982.

25. J.R. Larus and P.N. Hilfinger. Detecting conflicts between structure accesses. In *Prog. Lang. Design and Impl.*, pages 21–34, 1988.

26. T. Lev-Ami. TVLA: A framework for Kleene based static analysis. Master's thesis, Tel-Aviv University, Tel-Aviv, Israel, 2000.

27. T. Lev-Ami, T. Reps, M. Sagiv, and R. Wilhelm. Putting static analysis to work for verification: A case study. In *Int. Symp. on Softw. Testing and Analysis*, pages 26–38, 2000.

28. A. Milanova, A. Rountev, and B.G. Ryder. Parameterized object sensitivity for points-to analysis for Java. *TOSEM*, 2005.

29. H. Pande and B. Ryder. Data-flow-based virtual function resolution. In *SAS*, pages 238–254, 1996.
30. S. Patnaik and N. Immerman. Dyn-FO: A parallel, dynamic complexity class. In *Symp. on Princ. of Database Syst.*, 1994.
31. T. Reps, G. Balakrishnan, and J. Lim. Intermediate-representation recovery from low-level code. In *PEPM*, 2006.
32. M. Sagiv, T. Reps, and R. Wilhelm. Solving shape-analysis problems in languages with destructive updating. *Trans. on Prog. Lang. and Syst.*, 20(1):1–50, January 1998.
33. M. Sagiv, T. Reps, and R. Wilhelm. Parametric shape analysis via 3-valued logic. *Trans. on Prog. Lang. and Syst.*, 24(3):217–298, 2002.
34. M. Sharir and A. Pnueli. Two approaches to interprocedural data flow analysis. In *Program Flow Analysis: Theory and Applications*, chapter 7, pages 189–234. Prentice-Hall, 1981.
35. B. Steensgaard. Points-to analysis in almost-linear time. In *Princip. of Prog. Lang.*, 1996.
36. J. Stransky. A lattice for abstract interpretation of dynamic (Lisp-like) structures. *Inf. and Comp.*, 101(1):70–102, Nov. 1992.
37. V. Sundaresan, L. Hendren, C. Razafimahefa, R. Vallée-Rai, P. Lam, E. Gagnon, and C. Godin. Practical virtual method call resolution for Java. In *Object-Oriented Programming, Systems, Languages, and Applications*, pages 264–280, 2000.
38. J. Whaley and M. Lam. Cloning-based context-sensitive pointer alias analyses using binary decision diagrams. In *Prog. Lang. Design and Impl.*, 2004.
39. T. Yavuz-Kahveci and T. Bultan. Automated verification of concurrent linked lists with counters. In *SAS*, 2002.

Interprocedural Shape Analysis with Separated Heap Abstractions

Alexey Gotsman[1], Josh Berdine[2], and Byron Cook[2]

[1] University of Cambridge
Alexey.Gotsman@cl.cam.ac.uk
[2] Microsoft Research Cambridge
{jjb, bycook}@microsoft.com

Abstract. We describe an interprocedural shape analysis that makes use of spatial locality (i.e. the fact that most procedures modify only a small subset of the heap) in its representation of abstract states. Instead of tracking reachability information directly and aliasing information indirectly, our representation tracks reachability indirectly and aliasing directly. Computing the effect of procedure calls and returns on an abstract state is easy because the representation exhibits spatial locality mirroring the locality that is present in the concrete semantics. The benefits of this approach include improved speed, support for programs that deallocate memory, the handling of bounded numbers of heap cutpoints, and support for cyclic and shared data structures.

1 Introduction

Interprocedural shape analysis engines infer and prove properties about the shapes of dynamically-allocated linked data structures constructed by imperative programs with (possibly recursive) procedures. We present a local interprocedural shape analysis tool, called SUMMATE, that is efficient and more accurate than previously reported results. The tool's advantage comes from the representation used for abstract program states, which consists of circumscribed portions of a program's heap. The shape of an abstracted portion of heap is determined solely by the representation of *only that* portion of heap. Representing heap portions independently is accomplished by building the shape of the heap into the notion of abstraction, using formulæ in separation logic. That is, abstracted heaps have known shape and are specified using inductive predicates that make positive statements (saying what the shape *is*, rather than what it *is not*) of each circumscribed portion of the abstracted heap.

The benefit of our representation for interprocedural analysis is that, when a procedure is called, the portion of the heap that it will not access can easily be separated from the rest, and easily recombined with the modified heap upon procedure return. Furthermore, spatial locality of code (i.e. the fact that each program statement accesses only a very limited portion of the concrete state) matches the spatial locality *in the representation*, dramatically reducing the amount of reasoning that must be performed when summarizing how procedure

K. Yi (Ed.): SAS 2006, LNCS 4134, pp. 240–260, 2006.

calls and returns change the symbolic representation of a program's state. This is because each instruction can only affect one of the separated heap portions—the transfer functions are parametric with respect to the untouched heap portions.

Our approach provides support for cyclic and shared data structures, procedures that deallocate memory, and a bounded number of *heap cutpoints*[1] [13]— all of which appear commonly in programs. For this reason our analysis is more accurate and applicable: it can be directly applied to, and give precise results for, a larger set of programs than previously reported tools.

Note that our approach also has a limitation: it is specialized to a limited set of data-structures such as linked lists, doubly-linked lists and trees. Our analysis is fortified with inductive axioms from [3]. These axioms accelerate the analysis. However: in order to support new data structures we would need to do additional manual work up-front before fortifying the analysis further. We return to this point in Sect. 6.

2   Fundamentals

SUMMATE implements a fixed-point computation over an abstract domain built from assertions expressed in separation logic. In essence, the analysis performed by SUMMATE can be viewed as a method of constructing proofs in standard separation logic (in fact, our proof of the analysis' soundness is based on this observation). In this section we describe SUMMATE's fundamental operations as proof rules in separation logic. Later, in Sect. 3, we go into more specific detail.

2.1   Abstract Representation of States

SUMMATE's states denote sets of store-heap pairs, and are represented as formulæ of separation logic's assertion language, which include:

$$F, E ::= \mathsf{nil} \mid x \mid x' \qquad\qquad\qquad \text{expressions}$$
$$Q, P ::= \mathsf{emp} \mid E \mapsto F \mid P * Q \mid \mathsf{true} \mid E{=}F \mid P \wedge Q \mid P \vee Q \mid \cdots \quad \text{assertions}$$

Expressions are independent of the heap, while assertions are not. Primed variables are implicitly existentially quantified. The formal semantics of assertions is standard, e.g. as in [12], but informally:

- emp describes states where the heap is empty, with no allocated locations;
- $E{\mapsto}F$ describes states where the heap contains a single allocated location E, with contents F;
- $P{*}Q$ describes states where the heap is the union of two disjoint heaps (with no locations in common), one satisfying P and the other satisfying Q;
- true describes all states;

---

[1] Roughly speaking: a cutpoint is a location in the portion of the heap that the procedure may access distinct from all the actual parameters of the procedure, that the rest of the state knows about in some way, either as the contents of a heap location or value of a variable.

- $E{=}F$ describes states where the store gives E and F equal values;
- $P \wedge Q$ describes states which satisfy both P and Q; and
- $P \vee Q$ describes states which satisfy either P or Q.

Possibly infinite sets of concrete states are finitely represented using inductive predicate assertions. For example, using the predicate $\mathsf{ls}(x, y)$ defined as $x{\neq}y \wedge (x{\mapsto}y \vee \exists x'.\, x{\mapsto}x' * \mathsf{ls}(x', y))$ the symbolic heap $\mathsf{ls}(x, \mathsf{nil})$ represents all of the states in which $x{\neq}\mathsf{nil}$ and the heap has the shape of a linked list starting from location x and ending with nil. There are unboundedly many such states, as the length of the list is unconstrained. Similarly, representations built from formulæ such as $\mathsf{tree}(x)$ or $\mathsf{dlist}(p, f, n, b)$ [12] constitute abstractions of unboundedly many concrete states, shaped like trees or doubly-linked lists. In each case, the abstracted heaps have known shape, specified declaratively by an inductive predicate. The abstraction comes from not tracking the precise number of inductive unfoldings from the base case.

2.2   Local Reasoning for Procedures

Interprocedural analyses commonly compute so-called procedure summaries that approximate the semantics of a procedure by associating representations of the program state at procedure entry to corresponding result states at procedure exit. We represent such computed summaries as a sequence Γ of triples $\{P\}\, f(\vec{x})\, \{Q\}$ in separation logic.[2] In separation logic, a triple $\{P\}\, C\, \{Q\}$ is valid if executing command C from any state satisfying assertion P does not violate memory safety and, if execution terminates, results in a state satisfying assertion Q. Lying behind this is a semantics of commands which results in a memory fault when accessing dangling pointers or other memory locations not guaranteed to be allocated. So validity of $\{P\}\, C\, \{Q\}$ ensures that P describes all the memory (except that which gets freshly allocated) that may be accessed during the execution of C, that is, the *footprint* of C.

The technical foundation of our approach to local interprocedural analysis is the FRAME rule [10]:

$$\text{FRAME} \quad \frac{\{P\}\, C\, \{Q\}}{\{P * R\}\, C\, \{Q * R\}} \quad C \text{ does not modify variables in } R$$

If P ensures C's footprint is allocated, then according to FRAME, executing C in the presence of additional memory R results in the same behavior, and C does not touch the extra memory. Since we represent concrete states with formulæ, FRAME expresses how commands exhibit spatial locality in the abstract representation.

Our aim is to define an analysis which exploits this locality by using FRAME in the case where C is a recursive procedure call $f(\vec{x})$ in order to send only part

---

[2] In this way, each triple in Γ corresponds to an entry in the table computed by tabulation algorithms such as [11], where the set of exit states there is expressed using logical disjunction in the Q's.

of the heap P at the call site to the procedure, while holding the rest of the heap R aside, to be added to the heap Q that results from executing f. This is formalized in the following proof rule for local recursive procedure calls:

$$\text{LOCALPROCCALL}$$
$$\frac{S \vDash P\sigma * R \qquad Q\sigma * R \vDash T}{\Gamma , \{P\}\ f(\vec{x})\ \{Q\} \vdash \{S\}\ f(\vec{x}\sigma)\ \{T\}}$$

This rule is not primitive, but derivable (see Appendix A) from FRAME and Hoare logic rules. Here $\vDash$ means semantic consequence and σ is an injective substitution map from variables, including the formals, to variables, including the actuals. σ adapts the hypothesis (i.e. the procedure summary), which is expressed not in terms of the actual, but formal, parameters (and possibly other variables, as discussed below), to a specification expressed in terms of the actual parameters. The rule LOCALPROCCALL says that to compute the post-heap of a call to procedure f starting from pre-heap S:

1. split S into two disjoint (∗-conjoined) heaps $P\sigma$ (a *local heap*) and R (a *frame*);
2. express the pre-heap $P\sigma$ in terms of the formal parameters, yielding P, which is applicable to the summary of the procedure f;
3. compute the post-heap Q of the procedure call on P;
4. express Q in terms of the actual parameters, yielding $Q\sigma$;
5. ∗-conjoin $Q\sigma$ with the frame axiom R, yielding the post-heap T.

Note that the choice of splitting $P\sigma * R$ of S is not important for soundness: any splitting is sound, but if too small a heap $P\sigma$ is chosen, a false memory fault will be discovered, and no post-heap Q will exist. Here (as in [15]) we choose to split the heap so that we send the procedure all of the heap reachable from the actual parameters.

2.3   Cutpoints

For the procedure call rules above, note that the free variables of the pre- and post-conditions of the procedure summaries in Γ need not contain *only* the formal parameters. For instance, $\{x \mapsto y * y \mapsto \text{nil}\}\ f(x)\ \{x \mapsto y\}$ is a perfectly reasonable procedure summary, whose pre- and post-conditions happen to contain a variable y which does not occur in the command $f(x)$. Such variables, commonly referred to as *ghost* variables, can be instantiated to whatever value is appropriate at a particular call site using Hoare logic's substitution rule (SUBST, see Appendix A), which carries over to our LOCALPROCCALL-based analysis.

For an instance of where this arises in programs, consider the code in Fig. 1, which represents a sequence of operations on a stack s implemented as a linked-list. Imagine that we are trying to summarize the effect that foo can have on the stack passed to it. Notice that, while the stack s is reachable from foo, both i1 and i2 will contain pointers into s but are not reachable from foo. Pointers such

```
Node *s, *i1, *i2;
int x, y, z;
/* ... */
s = push(s, x);
i1 = iterator(s);
s = push(s, y);
i2 = iterator(s);
s = push(s, z);
foo(s);
i2 = next(i2);
assert(i1 == i2);
```

Fig. 1. Simple example code fragment with cutpoints

as i1 and i2 are known as *cutpoints*. It is difficult to make a scalable analysis that will be accurate enough to prove that the **assert** cannot fail.

Without special consideration, cutpoints can be treated just as any other ghost variable. Since we use the standard store-based semantics, and a sepa-rated abstract representation, there are no problems splitting heaps in ways that create pointers that dangle across the split. Hence, if we were not wor-ried about computability and finiteness considerations, the presence of cutpoints would be irrelevant: simply ignoring them and treating them just like any other ghost variable is sound and maximally precise. As a result, our representation enables our analysis to accurately and efficiently handle cutpoints: they cost no more than any other variable which appears in procedure summary pre- or post-conditions.

However, there is a problem in that just ignoring cutpoints potentially leads to unboundedly many of them, which breaks finiteness of the abstract domain. A solution is to abstract cutpoints beyond some bounded number by breaking the connection between them and the pointers to them, that is, by forgetting the destinations of pointers to cutpoints. In this manner, our analysis treats bounded numbers of cutpoints, and is parametric in the bound.

Hoare logic's rule of semantic consequence provides a mechanism for per-forming this abstraction. A cutpoint c in heap splitting $P' * R$ can simply be existentially quantified, since $P' \models \exists c. P'$ is a particular semantic consequence, thereby breaking the connection between pointers in R to c. Quantifying cut-points is productive since quantified variables do not contribute to the size of the abstract domain, in contrast with unquantified variables. So, if a splitting $S \models P' * R$ contains cutpoints $\vec{c}$, then we can abstract them using the derived rule:

$$\text{LocalProcCallCut} \quad \frac{S \models P' * R \qquad \exists \vec{c}. P' \models P\sigma \qquad Q\sigma * R \models T}{\Gamma, \{P\}\, f(\vec{x})\, \{Q\} \vdash \{S\}\, f(\vec{x}\sigma)\, \{T\}}$$

The operational reading of this rule is like that of LocalProcCall except that after splitting the pre-state into $P' * R$, the variables denoting cutpoints in P' should be existentially quantified.

3   Implementation of the Analysis

We consider a simple programming language of while loops and recursive procedures extended with the usual four heap operations for loading from, storing to, allocating, and deallocating heap locations. Note, that although the analysis presented in this section operates on the abstract domain of separation logic formulæ including inductive predicates for lists only, the interprocedural analysis technique can be extended to include inductive predicates for other data structures such as trees and doubly-linked lists.

The syntax of the language is defined as follows:

$$
\begin{array}{lll}
G ::= E{=}F \mid \neg(E{=}F) & \text{branch guards} \\
S ::= \texttt{skip} \mid x{:=}\,E \mid x{:=}\,\texttt{new}() \mid \texttt{assume}(G) & \text{safe commands} \\
A(E) ::= \texttt{dispose}(E) \mid x{:=}\,[E] \mid [E]{:=}\,F & \text{dangerous commands} \\
T ::= S \mid A(E) \mid f(\vec{x}) & \text{atomic commands} \\
C ::= T \mid \texttt{if } (G)\ \{C\}\ \texttt{else}\ \{C\} \mid \texttt{while } (G)\ \{C\} & \text{commands} \\
D ::= f(\vec{x})\ \{\texttt{local } \vec{y}\ \texttt{in } C\} & \text{procedure declarations} \\
M ::= \texttt{letrec } D, \dots, D \texttt{ in main}(\vec{x}) & \text{programs}
\end{array}
$$

Here variables $x, y, \dots$ range over some infinite set Var; existentially quantified variables $x', y', \dots$ range over some disjoint infinite set Var$'$; and, for each program, procedure names f range over some fixed finite set. We also assume given a set of variables Ghost $\subset$ Var used for ghost variables in the analysis to replace cutpoints during the processing of procedure calls. Quantified variables cannot appear in programs, but are included since expressions also appear in formulæ (Sect. 2.1). For convenience of later definitions, commands S are syntactically distinguished from commands $A(E)$. The difference between the two is that for a command S, execution is always safe, while execution of a command $A(E)$ may be unsafe, due to accessing heap location E.

Complications due to reference parameters are orthogonal to our concerns of interprocedurality, so we only consider procedures with value parameters. Additionally, for simplicity of presentation, we treat only programs without global variables or functions returning values (standard treatments such as [8, 5] can be adopted). As a result, for $f(\vec{x})$ $\{\texttt{local } \vec{y} \texttt{ in } C\}$ we require that the list of local variables $\vec{y}$ contain all the free variables $fv(C)$ of C except the formals $\vec{x}$. Finally, we assume programs have been syntactically preprocessed to ensure $\vec{x} \cap \vec{y} = \emptyset$ for each procedure declaration, and actual parameters are distinct variables.

The informal meaning of commands is as follows:

- $\texttt{skip}$ accesses no heap, and has no effect;
- $x{:=}\,E$ does not access the heap, and results in a state where x has the value of E (using the overwritten value of x);
- allocation $x{:=}\,\texttt{new}()$ requires no heap and returns an uninitialized location that is distinct from all other allocated locations (though may be pointed to by a previously dangling pointer);

- `dispose` takes a single location and deallocates it, possibly creating dangling pointers in the process;
- $x := [E]$ accesses heap location E and results in a state where the heap is unmodified and x has value equal to the contents of E;
- $[E] := F$ accesses location E and changes its contents to F;
- `assume`(G) acts as a filter on the state space of programs—G must be true after `assume` is executed;
- and the meaning of the control-flow commands is standard.

We will argue correctness of the analysis by generating proofs in separation logic out of its results, rather than directly in terms of the concrete semantics of the programming language. Therefore we do not present the concrete semantics in any detail here, it is entirely standard and appears elsewhere (such as [12]). Instead, the separation logic axioms for commands [12] together with the rules from the previous section specify the meaning of the programming language in enough detail for our present purpose. We use the following rule (which is derived from standard rules for recursive procedure declarations [8] and variable declarations, see Appendix A) to define the semantics of procedure declarations:

RECPROCDECLLOCALS
$$\frac{\Gamma, \{P\}\, f(\vec{x})\, \{Q\} \vdash \{P\}\, C\, \{T\} \quad \exists \vec{y}.\, T \vDash Q \quad \Gamma, \{P\}\, f(\vec{x})\, \{Q\} \vdash \{R\}\, C'\, \{S\}}{\Gamma \vdash \{R\}\; \texttt{letrec}\; f(\vec{x})\; \{\texttt{local}\; \vec{y}\; \texttt{in}\; C\}\; \texttt{in}\; C'\; \{S\}}$$

where $\vec{x} \cap \vec{y} = \emptyset$, $\vec{y} \cap \mathit{fv}(P) = \emptyset$, $\mathit{fv}(P)$ is the set of all free variables of P. The side condition $\vec{y} \cap \mathit{fv}(P) = \emptyset$ is needed so that variables in P do not clash with local variables of f. Existential quantification of the local variables ensures that they are not visible to a caller after the call returns.

3.1 Symbolic Heaps

SUMMATE's analysis represents sets of concrete program states with sets of symbolic heaps Q of form $\Pi \wedge \Sigma$, where Π and Σ are given by:

$$\Pi ::= \texttt{true} \mid \Pi \wedge \Pi \mid E{=}E \qquad \Sigma ::= \texttt{emp} \mid \Sigma * \Sigma \mid E{\mapsto}E \mid \mathsf{ls}(E, E) \mid \texttt{junk}$$

Symbolic heap formulæ consist of two parts: a Boolean formula Π built from $=$ and $\wedge$ which is insensitive to the heap; and a heap formula Σ which expresses heap shape. The meaning of these formulæ is as in Sect. 2.1, with the addition that junk describes at least one allocated location. Recall also that $\mathsf{ls}(E, F)$ describes non-empty acyclic singly-linked lists. Cyclic lists can be expressed using multiple predicates: e.g. $\mathsf{ls}(x, y') * \mathsf{ls}(y', x)$. Note that $x{\mapsto}x$ is a cycle of length one, while $\mathsf{ls}(x, x)$ is inconsistent.

Formulæ are considered up to symmetry of $=$, permutations across $\wedge$ and $*$ (e.g. $\Pi \wedge B_0 \wedge B_1$ and $\Pi \wedge B_1 \wedge B_0$ are equated), unit laws for true and emp, idempotency of $- *$ junk (e.g. junk $*$ junk and junk are equated), adding or removing consequences of equalities present in the pure part, and interchanging equal (due to the equalities in the pure part) variables in the spatial part. So, $x = y \wedge y = z \wedge \mathsf{ls}(v, x)$ and $x = y \wedge y = z \wedge x = z \wedge \mathsf{ls}(v, y)$ are considered equal. We denote the set of symbolic heaps with $\mathcal{SH}$.

3.2 Intraprocedural Analysis

As a part of its *inter*procedural analysis, SUMMATE must also implement an *intra*procedural analysis. For this SUMMATE implements the analysis from [6, 4]. This analysis is defined in Appendix B. A complete exposition is found in [6].

The intraprocedural analysis defines a set of canonical symbolic heaps $\mathcal{CSH} \subset \mathcal{SH}$ on which the analysis operates, a canonicalization function can: $\mathcal{SH} \to \mathcal{CSH}$, which returns a canonical symbolic heap abstracting a given symbolic heap, and a decision procedure for consistency of canonical symbolic heaps. Note that canonical symbolic heaps are written in the same language as symbolic heaps, i.e. they can have existential quantifiers. A key property of the abstract domain proved in [6] is that although the number of symbolic heaps over a finite number of unquantified variables is infinite, the domain of consistent and canonical symbolic heaps over a finite number of unquantified variables is finite. Hence, due to the presence of canonicalization in the analysis, fixed-point computations over the abstract domain converge in a finite number of steps.

For each atomic command C the intraprocedural analysis defines a transfer function $\mathcal{A}_C \colon \mathcal{SH} \to (2^{\mathcal{CSH}} \cup \{\top\})$ that, given an initial symbolic heap, returns either $\top$ (meaning that a possible memory error has been encountered) or a set of consistent canonical symbolic heaps representing the effect of the command on the initial symbolic heap. If the former case is encountered, our analysis terminates and reports a possible bug.

While performing fixed-point computations both our intraprocedural and interprocedural analyses use subset inclusion as a domain ordering between sets of symbolic heaps. Other, less coarse, approximations of entailment between symbolic heaps (e.g. [3, 2]) would be possible (but note that convergence of fixed-point computation is a question if the entailment prover is not transitive).

3.3 Analyzing Procedure Calls and Returns

In this section we give a detailed explanation of how SUMMATE treats procedure calls and returns. This treatment follows the operational reading of the rules LOCALPROCCALL and RECPROCDECLLOCALS.

According to the proof rule LOCALPROCCALL, to process procedure call $f(\vec{x}\theta)$ we have to determine which part of the symbolic heap at the call-site to send to the procedure. As noted in Sect. 2.2, we send to the procedure the part of the heap reachable from the actual parameters in the formula representing the symbolic heap. Formally, let Σ be the spatial part of a consistent symbolic heap and U be a set of expressions. Let V be the minimal set of expressions such that:

$$U \cup \{F \mid \exists E, \Sigma_1.\, E \in V \text{ and } \Sigma = H(E, F) * \Sigma_1\} \subseteq V$$

Here $H(E, F)$ stands for either $E \mapsto F$ or $\mathsf{ls}(E, F)$. We denote the part of Σ reachable from U with $\mathsf{Reach}(\Sigma, U)$ and define it as the $*$-conjunction of the following set of formulæ:

$$\{\Sigma_1 \mid \exists E, F, \Sigma_2.\, E \in V \text{ and } \Sigma = \Sigma_1 * \Sigma_2 \text{ and } \Sigma_1 = H(E, F)\}$$

Let $\mathsf{Unreach}(\Sigma, U)$ be the formula consisting of all $*$-conjuncts from Σ that are not in $\mathsf{Reach}(\Sigma, U)$.

Consider a procedure call statement $f(\vec{x}\theta)$ with formal parameters $\vec{x}$ and the map from formal parameters to actual parameters θ and let $Q_{\mathrm{call}} = \Pi \wedge \Sigma$ be the heap at the call site. To take the equalities in Π into account while computing the part of Σ reachable from actual parameters we require that the variables in Σ be chosen so that for each equivalence class generated by the equalities in Π at most one variable from this equivalence class is present in Σ (with preference given to unquantified variables over quantified ones, and to actual parameters over other variables). We denote the part of the heap to be sent to the procedure with $\mathsf{local}(\Pi \wedge \Sigma, \vec{x}\theta)$ and define it as:

$$\mathsf{local}(\Pi \wedge \Sigma, \vec{x}\theta) = \mathsf{can}\Big(\exists\big(\mathit{fv}(\Pi \wedge \Sigma)\smallsetminus\mathit{fv}(\mathsf{Reach}(\Sigma, \vec{x}\theta))\big). \ \Pi \wedge \mathsf{Reach}(\Sigma, \vec{x}\theta)\Big)$$

The local heap is obtained by taking the part of the heap reachable in the formula from the actual parameters, projecting it onto those variables appearing in the representation of the reachable heap, and canonicalizing the result. The set of cutpoints in the result is $\mathsf{Cut} = \mathit{fv}(\mathsf{local}(Q_{\mathrm{call}}, \vec{x}\theta))\smallsetminus\vec{x}\theta$. The frame in this case is given by $\mathsf{frame}(\Pi \wedge \Sigma, \vec{x}\theta) = \Pi \wedge \mathsf{Unreach}(\Sigma, \vec{x}\theta)$.

Having obtained a local heap we have to express it in terms of the formal parameters. As follows from the proof rule RECPROCDECLLOCALS, we also have to rename cutpoints so as they do not clash with the local variables of the procedure f. Hence, we rename them to variables in Ghost. Let $\mathsf{ghost}(V)$ be a function that given the set of variables V returns a bijective partial function from variables in Ghost to V and let $\eta = \mathsf{ghost}(\mathsf{Cut})$. Then the heap Q_{entry} at the entry point of the procedure f (expressed in terms of formal parameters and ghost variables) is given by $\mathsf{local}(Q_{\mathrm{call}}, \vec{x}\theta)(\theta \cup \eta)^{-1}$.

Example 1. Suppose that before executing the procedure call $\mathtt{foo}(a)$ (with the formal parameter x) we have a symbolic heap $a{=}d \wedge \mathsf{ls}(a, b) * \mathsf{ls}(b, \mathsf{nil}) * c{\mapsto}b$ so that the tail of the list pointed to by a is shared. Then the part of the heap reachable from actual parameters (in this case just a) is $\mathsf{ls}(a, b) * \mathsf{ls}(b, \mathsf{nil})$ and the local heap is $\mathsf{can}(a{=}d' \wedge \mathsf{ls}(a, b) * \mathsf{ls}(b, \mathsf{nil})) = \mathsf{ls}(a, b) * \mathsf{ls}(b, \mathsf{nil})$. We remind the reader that primed variables are implicitly existentially quantified. Here b is a cutpoint, so we choose a variable $X \in$ Ghost and rename b to X and a to x obtaining $\mathsf{ls}(x, X) * \mathsf{ls}(X, \mathsf{nil})$ as a heap at the entry point of the procedure. ☐

Note that for simplicity of presentation the analysis described above precisely handles only the cutpoints that arise from stack sharing, i.e. in the situation when a location in the local heap is equal to the value of a variable of the caller and distinct from all the actual parameters. Such cutpoints are defined by unquantified variables in the symbolic heap at the call-site. The other kind of cutpoints result from heap sharing, i.e. in the situation when a location in the local heap is equal to the contents of a location in the frame and distinct from all the local variables of the caller. Such cutpoints are defined by quantified variables in the symbolic heap at the call-site (e.g. x' in the local heap $\mathsf{ls}(x, x')$

with frame $\mathsf{ls}(y, x')$ where x is an actual parameter and y is a local variable of the caller). This kind of cutpoints can be handled precisely in a similar fashion (i.e. by replacing them with ghost variables in the local heap).

The way of processing procedure calls described above gives the most precise treatment to cutpoints—no information is lost when the heap at the call site has a cutpoint. However, in the case of recursive procedures the renaming of cutpoints to ghost variables can result in the number of unquantified variables in canonical symbolic heaps growing unboundedly. At the same time, as noted in Sect. 3.1, the abstract domain of canonical symbolic heaps is finite only if the number of unquantified variables is bounded. Hence, as it stands now, the analysis may not terminate. To solve this problem we put a bound m on the maximal number of cutpoints that can appear in a symbolic heap, i.e. on the cardinality of the set Ghost. Our analysis is parametric in this bound. Whenever during a call the number of cutpoints exceeds m, we existentially quantify the *new* cutpoints introduced by this call (i.e. variables in Cut$\setminus$Ghost) using the proof rule LOCALPROCCALLCUT. This guarantees finiteness of the abstract domain, and hence, termination of the analysis. The local heap in the case when we abstract cutpoints is defined as:

$$\mathsf{local}(\Pi \wedge \Sigma, \vec{x}\theta) =$$
$$\mathsf{can}(\exists(\mathsf{Cut}\setminus\mathsf{Ghost} \cup \mathit{fv}(\Pi \wedge \Sigma)\setminus\mathit{fv}(\mathsf{Reach}(\Sigma, \vec{x}\theta))).\ \Pi \wedge \mathsf{Reach}(\Sigma, \vec{x}\theta))$$

Example 2. Consider the previous example and suppose that $m=0$. Then the local heap will be $\mathsf{can}(a{=}d' \wedge \mathsf{ls}(a, b') * \mathsf{ls}(b', \mathsf{nil})) = \mathsf{ls}(a, \mathsf{nil})$. We existentially quantified the cutpoint and this resulted in it being eliminated by the subsequent canonicalization. The heap at the entry point of the procedure is $\mathsf{ls}(x, \mathsf{nil})$. In this case we lost the information about c pointing to a node in the list.   □

We observe that the pathological cases where the number of cutpoints grows unboundedly while analyzing recursive procedures is rarely encountered in practice (especially if some sort of dead variable analysis is used to eliminate unnecessary unquantified variables). Even when the number of cutpoints in a symbolic heap at the call-site exceeds m our analysis is still able to obtain some information (though not the most precise).

According to RECPROCDECLLOCALS, while processing procedure returns we have to existentially quantify the local variables of the procedure in order to obtain a summary (and canonicalize the result so that it is in our abstract domain). To obtain a symbolic heap at the return-site of the caller we just have to rename formal parameters to actual parameters and ghost variables to cutpoints in the resulting heap, and $*$-conjoin it with the frame. The result is guaranteed to be canonicalized.

3.4   Control-Flow Graphs

Before performing the interprocedural analysis we apply a standard translation from the program to its control-flow graph (CFG). A CFG is defined by the set of nodes N and the control-flow relation $F \subseteq N \times L \times N$, where L is the set of edge labels, $L = T \cup \{\mathtt{return}, \mathtt{quantify\_locals}\}$, T is the set of atomic commands.

We translate each procedure f independently, distinguishing its entry node $\mathsf{entry}(f)$ (the node from which the execution of the procedure starts) and exit node $\mathsf{exit}(f)$ (the node from which the procedure returns).

As noted in Sect. 3.3 we have to existentially quantify all the local variables before returning from a procedure. Therefore, as the last statement of each procedure we add a statement (labeled with $\mathtt{quantify\_locals}$) with the transfer function that existentially quantifies the local variables in the given heap and canonicalizes the result. Let $\mathsf{end}(f)$ be the node of the CFG preceding this statement, so that $(\mathsf{end}(f), \mathtt{quantify\_locals}, \mathsf{exit}(f)) \in F$.

For each procedure call statement $f(\vec{x}\theta)$ (where $\vec{x}$ are the formal parameters, θ is the map from the formal parameters to the actual parameters) we introduce two nodes—a call node and a return node—and add two edges to the CFG, one connecting the call node to the entry node of the procedure f (labeled with $f(\vec{x}\theta)$), and the other connecting the exit node of the procedure f to the return node (labeled with $\mathtt{return}$). We connect the statement preceding $f(\vec{x}\theta)$ to the call node and the return node to the statement succeeding $f(\vec{x}\theta)$.

While translating the program to the CFG we translate $\mathtt{while}$ and $\mathtt{if}$ statements in the standard way using $\mathtt{assume}$ statements. Note that although we define our analysis using such a representation, the proof of its soundness relies upon the fact that the resulting CFG is obtained from a well-structured program since it uses Hoare logic's proof rules for $\mathtt{while}$ and $\mathtt{if}$.

3.5   Interprocedural Analysis

To perform the interprocedural analysis using the treatment of procedure calls and returns in our analysis proposed in Sect. 3.3, we adapt the Reps-Horwitz-Sagiv algorithm [11, 14] for using symbolic heaps as the abstract domain and efficiently handling procedure summaries with multiple cutpoints.

The analysis tabulates a function $\varphi \colon N \to 2^{\mathcal{CSH} \times \mathcal{CSH}}$. Intuitively, $\varphi(n)$ represents the set of pairs (Q_1, Q_2) of symbolic heaps at the entry point of a function containing the node n (Q_1) and at the node n (Q_2) such that there exists an execution of a sequence of program statements between these two points transforming Q_1 to Q_2.

The function computed by the analysis is the least function φ satisfying the equations in Fig. 2 under the following order: $\varphi_1 \sqsubseteq \varphi_2 \Leftrightarrow \forall n.\ \varphi_1(n) \subseteq \varphi_2(n)$.

We assume that we are given a symbolic heap I representing the initial state at the start of main expressed purely in terms of the formal parameters of main (the equation for $\varphi(\mathsf{entry}(\mathsf{main}))$). In the equations for $\varphi(n_{\mathrm{entry}})$ and $\varphi(n_{\mathrm{return}})$ the symbolic heap Q_{entry} at the entry point of the procedure is obtained from a heap Q_{call} at the call-site as it is described in Sect. 3.3. Note that in order to effectively treat procedure summaries containing cutpoints (i.e. ghost variables), the procedure is analyzed on this heap only if it has not been analyzed for another heap equal to the current one up to a bijective renaming of ghost variables (this equality can be decided in time polynomial in the length of the symbolic heaps).

$$\varphi(\mathsf{entry}(\mathsf{main})) = \varphi(\mathsf{entry}(\mathsf{main})) \cup (I \times I);$$

$$\varphi(n_{\mathrm{entry}}) = \varphi(n_{\mathrm{entry}}) \cup \{(Q_{\mathrm{entry}}, Q_{\mathrm{entry}}) \mid \exists n_{\mathrm{call}}, Q_0, Q_{\mathrm{call}}, \eta.$$
$$(n_{\mathrm{call}}, f(\vec{x}\theta), n_{\mathrm{entry}}) \in F \wedge (Q_0, Q_{\mathrm{call}}) \in \varphi(n_{\mathrm{call}}) \wedge$$
$$\eta = \mathsf{ghost}(\mathrm{fv}(\mathsf{local}(Q_{\mathrm{call}}, \vec{x}\theta)) \backslash \vec{x}\theta) \wedge Q_{\mathrm{entry}} = \mathsf{local}(Q_{\mathrm{call}}, \vec{x}\theta)(\theta \cup \eta)^{-1} \wedge$$
$$(\neg \exists Q'_{\mathrm{entry}}, \eta'. (Q'_{\mathrm{entry}}, Q'_{\mathrm{entry}}) \in \varphi(n_{\mathrm{entry}}) \wedge Q'_{\mathrm{entry}}(\theta \cup \eta') = Q_{\mathrm{entry}}(\theta \cup \eta))\}$$

for each $n_{\mathrm{entry}} = \mathsf{entry}(f)$ for some procedure f;

$$\varphi(n_{\mathrm{return}}) = \{(Q_0, (Q_{\mathrm{exit}}\sigma) * \mathsf{frame}(Q_{\mathrm{call}}, \vec{x}\theta)) \mid \exists Q_{\mathrm{entry}}, \eta. (Q_0, Q_{\mathrm{call}}) \in \varphi(n_{\mathrm{call}}) \wedge$$
$$\sigma = \theta \cup \eta \wedge \mathsf{local}(Q_{\mathrm{call}}, \vec{x}\theta) = Q_{\mathrm{entry}}\sigma \wedge (Q_{\mathrm{entry}}, Q_{\mathrm{exit}}) \in \varphi(n_{\mathrm{exit}})\}$$

for each pair of a call node n_{call} and a return node n_{return} for a statement $f(\vec{x}\theta)$; here $n_{\mathrm{entry}} = \mathsf{entry}(f)$, $n_{\mathrm{exit}} = \mathsf{exit}(f)$;

$$\varphi(n_2) = \{(Q_0, Q_2) \mid \exists n_1, C, Q_1. (n_1, C, n_2) \in F \wedge (Q_0, Q_1) \in \varphi(n_1) \wedge Q_2 \in \mathcal{A}_C(Q_1)\}$$

for all other nodes n_2.

Fig. 2. The equations defining the analysis. For simplicity we show only the case when cutpoints are not abstracted. All substitutions are injective.

Similarly, in the equation for $\varphi(n_{\mathrm{return}})$ we search for summaries with the initial state equal to Q_{entry} up to a bijective renaming of ghost variables.

Example 3. Consider the following program fragment:

```
append(x, y);
append(u, v);
append(x, z)
```

Here append(a, b) receives as parameters head nodes of two lists and destructively appends the second list to the end of the first one. Suppose the initial state of the program consists of five disjoint lists $\mathsf{ls}(x, \mathrm{nil}) * \mathsf{ls}(y, \mathrm{nil}) * \mathsf{ls}(z, \mathrm{nil}) * \mathsf{ls}(u, \mathrm{nil}) * \mathsf{ls}(v, \mathrm{nil})$. The analysis will process each call to append in turn. The local heap of the first call to append expressed in terms of formal parameters is $\mathsf{ls}(a, \mathrm{nil}) * \mathsf{ls}(b, \mathrm{nil})$. As the analysis has no summaries for append, it will go on analyzing append on the local heap and will discover a post-heap $\mathsf{ls}(a, b) * \mathsf{ls}(b, \mathrm{nil})$. Hence, the heap at the return-site of the call will be $\mathsf{ls}(x, y) * \mathsf{ls}(y, \mathrm{nil}) * \mathsf{ls}(z, \mathrm{nil}) * \mathsf{ls}(u, \mathrm{nil}) * \mathsf{ls}(v, \mathrm{nil})$.

The local heap of the second call is again $\mathsf{ls}(a, \mathrm{nil}) * \mathsf{ls}(b, \mathrm{nil})$. The analysis will reuse the the summary discovered before and the heap at the return-site will be $\mathsf{ls}(u, v) * \mathsf{ls}(v, \mathrm{nil}) * \mathsf{ls}(x, y) * \mathsf{ls}(y, \mathrm{nil}) * \mathsf{ls}(z, \mathrm{nil})$.

The local heap of the third call expressed in terms of actual parameters is $\mathsf{ls}(x, y) * \mathsf{ls}(y, \mathrm{nil}) * \mathsf{ls}(z, \mathrm{nil})$. Here we have a cutpoint y. We replace it with a ghost variable Y, rename actuals to formals and obtain $\mathsf{ls}(a, Y) * \mathsf{ls}(Y, \mathrm{nil}) * \mathsf{ls}(b, \mathrm{nil})$ as a local heap. As there are no summaries for this local heap, the analysis will have to analyze append once again discovering a post-heap $\mathsf{ls}(a, Y) * \mathsf{ls}(Y, b) * \mathsf{ls}(b, \mathrm{nil})$. Hence, the heap at the return-site of the call will be $\mathsf{ls}(u, v) * \mathsf{ls}(v, \mathrm{nil}) * \mathsf{ls}(x, y) * \mathsf{ls}(y, z) * \mathsf{ls}(z, \mathrm{nil})$. □

4   Soundness

Following Lee, Yang, and Yi [9] we show the soundness of our analysis via translation to program proofs in separation logic; each run of the analysis determines
a collection of proofs.

Suppose the analysis has not encountered a possible memory error and φ is
the least function satisfying the equations in Fig. 2. Let $\psi_n(Q) = \{R \mid (Q, R) \in$
$\varphi(n)\}$. Intuitively, for a node $n \in N$ and a symbolic heap $Q \in \mathcal{CSH}$, $\psi_n(Q)$
gives the set of symbolic heaps corresponding to the possible states at the node
n reachable from the state $\{Q\}$ at the entry point to the procedure containing n.

Let s be a set of symbolic heaps. We define the separation logic formula
representing this set as a disjunction of the formulæ representing the heaps in s:
$\mathsf{means}(s) = \bigvee \{Q \mid Q \in s\}$. Note that $\mathsf{means}(\emptyset) = \mathsf{false}$. Throughout this section
Γ denotes the set of specifications of all the procedures obtained as a result of
the analysis: $\Gamma = \{\{Q\}\ f(\vec{x})\ \{\mathsf{means}(\psi_{\mathsf{exit}(f)}(Q))\} \mid \psi_{\mathsf{entry}(f)}(Q) \neq \emptyset\}$.

Theorem 1. *Suppose the analysis succeeded, i.e. a possible memory error has
not been encountered. Let C be a command, n_1 respectively n_2 be the nodes of
the control-flow graph immediately preceding respectively following the command,
and n_0 be the entry node of the procedure containing n_1 and n_2. Then for each
symbolic heap Q such that $\psi_{n_0}(Q) \neq \emptyset$, the following judgment holds in separation logic: $\Gamma \vdash \{\mathsf{means}(\psi_{n_1}(Q))\}\ C\ \{\mathsf{means}(\psi_{n_2}(Q))\}$.*

The proof proceeds by induction on the structure of the command C. The cases
for all the commands except for procedure call are similar to the ones in [9]
and use the usual axioms and inference rules of separation logic [12]. The proof
in the case of procedure call relies upon the proof rule LOCALPROCCALLCUT.
Taking $n_1 = \mathsf{entry}(f)$ and $n_2 = \mathsf{end}(f)$ for each procedure f in the program in
Theorem 1 and using RECPROCDECLLOCALS, we obtain:

Corollary 1. *Let $\vec{D}$ be the list of all procedure declarations in the program, $\vec{v}$
the list of the formal parameters of* main. *Then if the analysis succeeds,*

$$\vdash \{\mathsf{means}(I)\}\ \mathtt{letrec}\ \vec{D}\ \mathtt{in}\ \mathtt{main}(\vec{v})\ \{\mathsf{means}(\psi_{\mathsf{end}(\mathsf{main})}(I))\}.$$

Corollary 1 justifies that the success of our analysis implies that the program is
memory-safe and the computed post-condition is a valid one.

5   Experimental Results

In order to evaluate the performance of our analysis we have applied SUMMATE
to the list processing programs proposed in the literature, including those in
[15] and [14]. The results are displayed in Table 1. The tests were performed on
a 2GHz Pentium 4 Linux PC with 512MB of memory. Each program consists
of a list-processing function and a client calling the function. We consider both
iterative and recursive versions of functions. For each function except `create` we
use three different clients. The first one corresponds to a cutpoint-free call. For

Table 1. Experimental results for iterative and recursive versions of simple list-processing functions with three different clients. The meaning of the programs is straightforward from their names (reverse_via_append reverses a list by appending its head to its reversed tail, reverse8 reverses a list 8 times). Recursive reverse we used is not suitable for reversing a panhandle list. Times are given in seconds. SUM-MATE did not require more than 600KB in any of these cases. reverse_via_append is a recursive function; as in [15] its "iterative" version uses an iterative version of append.

Program	Iterative			Recursive		
	1	2	3	1	2	3
create	0.004	—	—	0.004	—	—
deallocate	0.004	0.005	0.007	0.003	0.005	0.005
traverse	0.004	0.005	0.011	0.004	0.005	0.008
find	0.004	0.008	0.022	0.005	0.010	0.034
insert	0.007	0.019	0.082	0.006	0.014	0.057
remove (element is not in the list)	0.006	0.025	0.115	0.006	0.010	0.022
remove (element is in the list)	0.004	0.006	0.007	0.004	0.005	0.006
reverse (acyclic list)	0.006	0.015	0.066	0.004	0.007	0.015
reverse (panhandle list)	0.030	0.032	0.175	—	—	—
reverse_via_append	0.006	0.020	0.142	0.006	0.013	0.047
append	0.005	0.015	0.066	0.004	0.008	0.021
merge	0.150	0.036	0.884	0.009	0.051	1.138
splice	0.010	0.024	0.041	0.006	0.010	0.019
reverse8	0.011	0.072	0.540	0.008	0.024	0.090

reversing a panhandle list the second client calls the function so that the heap at the call-site is $ls(x, y) * ls(y, z') * ls(z', y)$ (one cutpoint), the third client— $ls(x, y) * ls(y, z) * ls(z, y)$ (two cutpoints). Here (and throughout this section) x, y, and z are local variables of the client. For append, merge, and splice the second client calls the function two times, hence, creating a cutpoint e.g. for append:

```
xy = append(x, y);
xyz = append(xy, z)
```

The third client performs the call three times (thereby creating two cutpoints). For all the other programs the second client calls functions on a list in the case when a part of the list is shared (i.e. the heap at the call-site is $ls(x, y) * ls(y, nil) * ls(z, y)$). In this case one cutpoint is created in each call. The third client calls functions on a list in the case when it has two pointers to the middle of the list thereby modeling the situation shown in the example in Sect. 2.3 (i.e. the heap at the call-site is $ls(x, y) * ls(y, z) * ls(z, nil)$). In this case two cutpoints are created in each call (except for reverse8, which creates an additional cutpoint because the program keeps track of the former head of the list, i.e. the tail of the reversed list).

For each program we were able to prove memory safety, absence of memory leaks, and the fact that the acyclicity of lists is preserved. In the cases when

Table 2. Experimental results for iterative and recursive versions of list sorting programs. `mergesort` and `tailsort` are recursive, `insertionsort`—iterative. As in [15] their "iterative" respectively "recursive" versions are obtained by using these functions with iterative respectively recursive versions of `insert` or `merge`.

Program	Iterative		Recursive	
	Time (sec)	Memory (KB)	Time (sec)	Memory (KB)
`mergesort`	6.159	2288	0.211	368
`quicksort`	—	—	0.300	608
`insertionsort`	0.058	368	0.042	368
`tailsort`	0.008	368	0.007	368

the caller had variables pointing to the middle of a list (i.e. we had calls with cutpoints), we have proved that the elements pointed to by the variables are still present in the resulting list in the order determined by the semantics of the list processing function. Besides, for each particular program the post-condition obtained as the result of the analysis could give some more information. For instance, we were able to prove that after `reverse` or `reverse_via_append` the head of the list moves to its tail, that the result of `append`, `merge`, `splice` still contains the heads of both source lists, and that `insert` actually inserts the element it is given into the list. `remove` was tested two times: in the case when the element being removed is present in the list, and in the case when it is not. In the former case the accurate treatment of cutpoints by our analysis allowed for proving that this element is deleted from the list.

In all these experiments the bound on the number of cutpoints was set to 3. A larger bound would not affect either precision or complexity of the analysis, since 3 is the maximal number of cutpoints created at a time in the programs considered. Setting the bound to a lower number makes the analysis less precise.

We also tested our implementation on list sorting programs. The results for them are shown in Table 2. The client in the programs calls a sorting function on a list once. For each of the programs we proved memory safety and preservation of the list acyclicity. `insertionsort` and `mergesort` have calls with a cutpoint. Accurate processing of this cutpoint by our analysis allowed us to prove that the head of the source list is present in the sorted list.

We have not done a systematic benchmarking of SUMMATE against the other executable shape analysis tools in the same conditions. However, it is fair to say that SUMMATE is at least competitive with the previously reported tools with respect to speed and memory, and clearly better with respect to accuracy:

- We observe a speed-up of up to 3 orders of magnitude in comparison with the numbers reported in [15] and [14]. However: this difference could likely be attributed to differences in machine configuration.
- SUMMATE consumes less memory than previously reported local interprocedural shape analyses.
- Other than SUMMATE, no local shape analysis tool accurately treats calls with multiple cutpoints.

– We have reported experimental results for programs operating on shared and cyclic data structures and programs that deallocate memory.

6   Conclusions

SUMMATE implements an interprocedural shape analysis that makes use of spatial locality. SUMMATE's abstraction simply tracks declarative representations of independent heap portions. Consequently, computing the effect of procedure calls and returns on an abstract state is easy.

SUMMATE is the most accurate interprocedural shape analysis, due to its support of memory disposal, cyclic and shared data structures, and its handling of bounded numbers of cutpoints. To the best of our knowledge, no other tool precisely and efficiently supports these features combined. Furthermore: our interprocedural analysis can be formulated in terms of a handful of proof rules[3] and (unlike in previous efforts [13]) the proof of its soundness follows from them straightforwardly.

Related Work. Hackett & Rugina [7], describe an analysis where transfer function computations benefit from using a form of local reasoning similar to ours. However, procedure summaries are represented in terms of global states and so analysis of procedure calls does not benefit from locality.

Several papers have described TVLA-based interprocedural shape analyses (i.e. [14, 13, 15]) where the procedure summaries operate on local heaps. However: in this work the analysis must dynamically find a way to divide the heap such that the overall shape is preserved. This is delicate with the TVLA reachability-based representation, since the separation significantly alters the represented reachability information. A consequence of this is that accurate treatment of cutpoints is expensive (e.g. in [14] all cutpoints must be abstracted away into a single cutpoint). Furthermore, the transfer function computation in this context is non-local and still expensive, because the analysis must propagate updates throughout the state. SUMMATE's separated representation ensures that the difference between the states in the transfer function computation is limited. This is, in part, because instead of storing reachability information in a quickly queryable form, we only update information from which reachability could be computed. This is possible since the precise structure of abstracted heaps is known.

It is important to note the limitations of SUMMATE's abstraction. SUMMATE is much faster than tools such as TVLA [16], but in some ways can also be less general. Computing a transfer function requires case analysis. Since our representation specifies the precise structure of the abstracted heap, the case analysis phase of the transfer function can rely on it, and so the number of resulting possible cases is significantly lower. However, we use carefully hand-crafted inductive predicates and axioms. These inductive predicates and axioms only needed to be designed once [3], but a similar exercise must be done in order to support additional data types.

---

[3] This is similar in spirit to [1].

Acknowledgments. The authors benefited greatly from discussions of this and related work with Dino Distefano, Peter O'Hearn, Tal Lev-Ami, Roman Manevich, Hongseok Yang, and Greta Yorsh. The authors would also like to thank Noam Rinetzky for providing the test programs used in [15] and the anonymous reviewers for useful suggestions.

References

[1] T. Amtoft and A. Banerjee. Information flow analysis in logical form. In *SAS*, volume 3148 of *LNCS*, pages 100–115, 2004.

[2] J. Berdine, C. Calcagno, and P. O'Hearn. Symbolic execution with separation logic. In *APLAS*, volume 3780 of *LNCS*, pages 52–68, 2005.

[3] J. Berdine, C. Calcagno, and P. W. O'Hearn. A decidable fragment of separation logic. In *FSTTCS*, volume 3328 of *LNCS*, 2004.

[4] J. Berdine, B. Cook, D. Distefano, and P. W. O'Hearn. Automatic termination proofs for programs with shape-shifting heaps. In *CAV*, 2006.

[5] S. A. Cook. Soundness and completeness of an axiomatic system for program verification. *SIAM J. on Computing*, 7:70–90, 1978.

[6] D. Distefano, P. W. O'Hearn, and H. Yang. A local shape analysis based on separation logic. In *TACAS*, volume 3920 of *LNCS*, pages 287–302, 2006.

[7] B. Hackett and R. Rugina. Region-based shape analysis with tracked locations. In *POPL*, pages 310–323, 2005.

[8] C. A. R. Hoare. Procedures and parameters: An axiomatic approach. In *Symposium on the Semantics of Algorithmic Languages*, pages 102–116, 1971.

[9] O. Lee, H. Yang, and K. Yi. Automatic verification of pointer programs using grammar-based shape analysis. In *ESOP*, volume 3444 of *LNCS*, pages 124–140, 2005.

[10] P. O'Hearn, J. Reynolds, and H. Yang. Local reasoning about programs that alter data structures. In *CSL*, volume 2142 of *LNCS*, pages 1–19, 2001.

[11] T. Reps, S. Horwitz, and M. Sagiv. Precise interprocedural dataflow analysis via graph reachability. In *POPL*, pages 49–61, 1995.

[12] J. Reynolds. Separation logic: A logic for shared mutable data structures. In *LICS*, pages 55–74, 2002.

[13] N. Rinetzky, J. Bauer, T. Reps, M. Sagiv, and R. Wilhelm. A semantics for procedure local heaps and its abstractions. In *POPL*, pages 296–309, 2005.

[14] N. Rinetzky, M. Sagiv, and E. Yahav. Interprocedural functional shape analysis using local heaps. Tech. Rep. 26, Tel Aviv Univ., Nov. 2004.

[15] N. Rinetzky, M. Sagiv, and E. Yahav. Interprocedural shape analysis for cutpoint-free programs. In *SAS*, volume 3672 of *LNCS*, pages 284–302, 2005.

[16] M. Sagiv, T. Reps, and R. Wilhelm. Parametric shape analysis via 3-valued logic. *ACM TOPLAS*, 24(3):217–298, 2002.

A   Proof Rules

The proof rules used by our interprocedural analysis can be derived from the FRAME rule and Hoare logic rules, which are listed in Fig. 3. The corresponding derivations, which also involve some predicate calculus, are given in Fig. 4.

ProcCall

$$\overline{\Gamma, \{P\}\, f(\vec{x})\, \{Q\} \vdash \{P\}\, f(\vec{x})\, \{Q\}}$$

Subst
$$\frac{\{P\}\, C\, \{Q\}}{\{P\sigma\}\, C\sigma\, \{Q\sigma\}} \quad \begin{array}{l} C \text{ modifies } x \text{ implies} \\ x\sigma \in \mathrm{Var} \smallsetminus \bigcup_{y \neq x} fv(y\sigma) \end{array}$$

Conseq
$$\frac{P \vDash R \qquad \{R\}\, C\, \{S\} \qquad S \vDash Q}{\{P\}\, C\, \{Q\}}$$

VarDecl
$$\frac{\{P\}\, C\, \{Q\}}{\{P\}\, \mathtt{local}\ \vec{x}\ \mathtt{in}\ C\, \{Q\}} \quad \vec{x} \cap fv(P,Q) = \emptyset$$

RecProcDecl
$$\frac{\Gamma, \{P\}\, f(\vec{x})\, \{Q\} \vdash \{P\}\, C\, \{Q\} \qquad \Gamma, \{P\}\, f(\vec{x})\, \{Q\} \vdash \{R\}\, C'\, \{S\}}{\Gamma \vdash \{R\}\ \mathtt{letrec}\ f(\vec{x})\ \{C\}\ \mathtt{in}\ C'\, \{S\}}$$

Fig. 3. Standard rules of Hoare logic

RecProcDeclLocals

$$\frac{\dfrac{\Gamma' \vdash \{P\}\, C\, \{T\} \qquad T \vDash \exists \vec{y}.\, T}{\Gamma' \vdash \{P\}\, C\, \{\exists \vec{y}.\, T\}}\ \mathrm{Conseq}}{\dfrac{\Gamma' \vdash \{P\}\ \mathtt{local}\ \vec{y}\ \mathtt{in}\ C\, \{\exists \vec{y}.\, T\} \qquad \exists \vec{y}.\, T \vDash Q}{\dfrac{\Gamma' \vdash \{P\}\ \mathtt{local}\ \vec{y}\ \mathtt{in}\ C\, \{Q\} \qquad \Gamma' \vdash \{R\}\, C'\, \{S\}}{\Gamma \vdash \{R\}\ \mathtt{letrec}\ f(\vec{x})\ \{\mathtt{local}\ \vec{y}\ \mathtt{in}\ C\}\ \mathtt{in}\ C'\, \{S\}}}\ \mathrm{Conseq}}\ \mathrm{VarDecl}$$

where $\Gamma' = \Gamma, \{P\}\, f(\vec{x})\, \{Q\}$ and the first rule applied is RecProcDecl;

LocalProcCall

$$\frac{S \vDash P\sigma * R \qquad \dfrac{\dfrac{\dfrac{\Gamma' \vdash \{P\}\, f(\vec{x})\, \{Q\}}{\Gamma' \vdash \{P\sigma\}\, f(\vec{x}\sigma)\, \{Q\sigma\}}\ \mathrm{Subst}}{\Gamma' \vdash \{P\sigma * R\}\, f(\vec{x}\sigma)\, \{Q\sigma * R\}}\ \mathrm{Frame} \qquad Q\sigma * R \vDash T}{\Gamma' \vdash \{S\}\, f(\vec{x}\sigma)\, \{T\}}\ \mathrm{Conseq}}{}$$

where $\Gamma' = \Gamma, \{P\}\, f(\vec{x})\, \{Q\}$;

LocalProcCallCut

$$\frac{S \vDash P' * R \qquad \dfrac{\dfrac{P' \vDash \exists \vec{c}.\, P' \qquad \exists \vec{c}.\, P' \vDash P\sigma}{P' \vDash P\sigma}}{P' * R \vDash P\sigma * R}}{\dfrac{S \vDash P\sigma * R \qquad Q\sigma * R \vDash T}{\Gamma, \{P\}\, f(\vec{x})\, \{Q\} \vdash \{S\}\, f(\vec{x}\sigma)\, \{T\}}}\ \mathrm{LocalProcCall}$$

Fig. 4. Derivations of procedure call and declaration rules

B   Intraprocedural Analysis

In this section we describe SUMMATE's *intra*procedural analysis. This analysis is essentially the same as that of [6, 4].

Transfer functions are defined by this analysis in terms of the symbolic execution relation $\rightsquigarrow$, the rearrangement relation $\rightarrow_E$, and the abstraction relation $\rightarrow^*$. Each individual concrete state can be expressed exactly by a symbolic heap, i.e. there is a subset of symbolic heaps which are simply different syntax for concrete states. In the usual concrete semantics, each command only accesses a small portion of the state: its *footprint*. From this perspective, symbolic execution ($\rightsquigarrow$) expresses the usual concrete semantics of commands[4] in terms of symbolic heaps, where the footprint of the command is expressed as one of the formulæ that is alternate syntax for a concrete state. The task of rearrangement ($\rightarrow_E$) is then to transform an arbitrary symbolic heap, via case analysis, into a set of symbolic heaps where the footprint of the next command is concrete. Abstraction ($\rightarrow$) then takes the symbolic heaps resulting from symbolic execution and maps them into a finite subdomain of symbolic heaps, ensuring that fixed-point computations converge.

The definition of these relations asks several types of questions about symbolic heaps: entailment of an equality ($Q \vdash E{=}F$), or of a disequality ($Q \vdash E{\neq}F$), inconsistency ($Q \vdash \mathsf{false}$), or testing if a location is guaranteed to be allocated ($Q \vdash allocated(E)$). We also sometimes ask the negations of these questions. Decision procedures for these queries are defined in [6].

Symbolic Execution ($\rightsquigarrow$). The symbolic execution relation captures the effect of executing an atomic command from a symbolic heap. That is, $Q_0 \overset{C}{\rightsquigarrow} Q_1$ means that Q_1 over-approximates the concrete states that can result from executing C on states satisfying Q_0. The symbolic execution rules are reported in Fig. 5.

Rearrangement ($\rightarrow_E$). Symbolic execution does not operate on arbitrary pre-states. For instance, LOAD requires that the source heap cell be explicitly known. In order to put symbolic heaps into the form required for symbolic execution of a command, we use the rearrangement relation $\rightarrow_E$, defined by the axioms shown in Fig. 6. When rearrangement fails to reveal the required location E, it indicates a potential memory safety violation and returns $\top$.

Abstraction ($\rightarrow$). Abstraction is accomplished by certain separation logic implications that rewrite a symbolic heap to a logically weaker one. The abstraction relation on symbolic heaps $Q_0 \rightarrow Q_1$ is defined by the axioms shown in Fig .7.

Note that the heap abstraction is defined solely in terms of the representation of heaps, i.e., the dynamic information the analysis knows. The precision of this abstraction immaterializes static information about the program text used by shallow analyses, such as allocation-sites.

We call a symbolic heap Q canonical if it is maximally abstracted, i.e. $Q \not\rightarrow$ and denote the set of all canonical symbolic heaps with $\mathcal{CSH}$. A canonicalization

---

[4] Except that the rule for **dispose** does not quite yield the strongest postcondition.

$$Q \quad \overset{\texttt{skip}}{\leadsto} \quad Q \qquad\qquad\qquad\qquad\qquad\qquad\qquad \text{SKIP}$$

$$Q \quad \overset{x:=E}{\leadsto} \quad x{=}E[x'/x] \wedge Q[x'/x] \qquad\qquad\qquad\qquad \text{ASSIGN}$$

$$Q \quad \overset{x:=\texttt{new()}}{\leadsto} \quad Q[x'/x] * x{\mapsto}y' \qquad\qquad\qquad\qquad \text{NEW}$$

$$Q \quad \overset{\texttt{assume}(E=F)}{\leadsto} \quad Q \wedge E = F \text{ if } Q \nvdash E{\neq}F \qquad\qquad \text{ASSUMET}$$

$$Q \quad \overset{\texttt{assume}(E\neq F)}{\leadsto} \quad Q \text{ if } Q \nvdash E = F \text{ and } Q \nvdash \text{false} \qquad \text{ASSUMEF}$$

$$Q * E{\mapsto}F \quad \overset{\texttt{dispose}(E)}{\leadsto} \quad Q \qquad\qquad\qquad\qquad\qquad \text{DISPOSE}$$

$$Q * E{\mapsto}F \quad \overset{x:=[E]}{\leadsto} \quad x{=}F[x'/x] \wedge (Q * E{\mapsto}F)[x'/x] \qquad \text{LOAD}$$

$$Q * E{\mapsto}F \quad \overset{[E]:=G}{\leadsto} \quad Q * E{\mapsto}G \qquad\qquad\qquad\qquad \text{STORE}$$

Fig. 5. Symbolic Execution ($\leadsto$). Here x', y' are globally fresh ([2] allows more local freshness constraints).

$$Q * F{\mapsto}G \quad \to_E \quad Q * E{\mapsto}G \qquad\quad \text{if } Q \vdash E{=}F \qquad\qquad \text{SWITCH}$$

$$Q * \mathsf{ls}(F,G) \quad \to_E \quad Q * E{\mapsto}G \qquad\quad \text{if } Q \vdash E{=}F \qquad\qquad \text{UNROLL1}$$

$$Q * \mathsf{ls}(F,G) \quad \to_E \quad Q * E{\mapsto}x' * \mathsf{ls}(x',G) \quad \text{if } Q \vdash E{=}F \text{ and } x' \text{ fresh} \quad \text{UNROLL>1}$$

$$Q \quad \to_E \quad \top \qquad\qquad\qquad\qquad \text{if } Q \nvdash \text{allocated}(E) \qquad \text{CRASH}$$

Fig. 6. Rearrangement ($\to_E$)

$$z'{=}E \wedge Q \quad \to \quad Q[E/z'] \qquad\qquad\qquad\qquad\qquad\qquad \text{SUBST}$$

$$Q * H_0(E,x') * H_1(x',F) \quad \to \quad Q * \mathsf{ls}(E,\text{nil}) \qquad\quad \text{if } Q \vdash F{=}\text{nil}$$
$$\text{APPENDLSNIL}$$

$$Q * H_0(E,x') * H_1(x',F_0) * H_2(F_1,G) \quad \to \quad Q * \mathsf{ls}(E,F_0) * H_2(F_1,G) \quad \text{if } Q \vdash F_0{=}F_1$$
$$\text{APPENDLSGUARD}$$

$$Q * H(x',E) \quad \to \quad Q * \text{junk} \qquad\qquad\qquad\qquad\qquad \text{JUNK}$$

$$Q * H_0(x',y') * H_1(y',x') \quad \to \quad Q * \text{junk} \qquad\qquad\qquad \text{JUNKCYCLE}$$

Fig. 7. Abstraction ($\to$). Here $H(E,F)$ stands for either $E{\mapsto}F$ or $\mathsf{ls}(E,F)$; and x', y' do not occur other than where explicitly indicated.

function is defined in [6]. This function, can, is based on a fixed sequence of abstraction axiom applications, and transforms a symbolic heap to a canonical symbolic heap abstracting it, i.e. $Q \to^* \text{can}(Q)$ and $\text{can}(Q) \nrightarrow$.

Transfer Functions. The transfer function $\mathcal{A}_C$ for an atomic command C transforms a given symbolic heap to either $\top$ (indicating a possible crash) or a set of consistent canonical symbolic heaps. Transfer functions are defined separately for safe commands S and unsafe ones $A(E)$ in the following way:

$$\mathcal{A}_S(Q_0) = \{\mathsf{can}(Q_1) \mid Q_0 \overset{S}{\leadsto} Q_1\}$$

$$\mathcal{A}_{A(E)}(Q_0) = \begin{cases} \top, & \text{if } Q \to_E \top \\ \{\mathsf{can}(Q_2) \mid \exists Q_1. \, Q_0 \to_E Q_1 \wedge Q_1 \overset{A(E)}{\leadsto} Q_2\}, & \text{otherwise} \end{cases}$$

Example 4. Suppose we want to compute the value of the transfer function for the command x = [x] on the symbolic heap $\mathsf{ls}(x, \mathsf{nil})$. The rearrangement phase will transform the heap into two symbolic heaps $x \mapsto \mathsf{nil}$ and $x \mapsto x' * \mathsf{ls}(x', \mathsf{nil})$ thereby making the information that x is allocated in the heap explicit. The symbolic execution phase will then symbolically simulate the effect of the command on the heaps producing $x = \mathsf{nil}$ and $x = x' \wedge x'' \mapsto x' * \mathsf{ls}(x', \mathsf{nil})$. Finally, the abstraction phase will leave the first heap unchanged and will canonicalize the second heap to $\mathsf{junk} * \mathsf{ls}(x, \mathsf{nil})$. Hence, the value of the transfer function is $\{x = \mathsf{nil}, \ \mathsf{junk} * \mathsf{ls}(x, \mathsf{nil})\}$. □

Finiteness. A key property of the abstract domain $\mathcal{CSH}$ proved in [6] is that the domain of consistent and canonical symbolic heaps $\{Q \mid Q \nvdash \mathsf{false} \wedge Q \nleadsto\}$ over a finite number of unquantified variables is finite.

Automated Verification of the Deutsch-Schorr-Waite Tree-Traversal Algorithm

Alexey Loginov[1], Thomas Reps[1], and Mooly Sagiv[2]

[1] Comp. Sci. Dept., University of Wisconsin
{alexey, reps}@cs.wisc.edu
[2] School of Comp. Sci., Tel-Aviv University
msagiv@post.tau.ac.il

Abstract. This paper reports on the automated verification of the *total correctness* (partial correctness and termination) of the Deutsch-Schorr-Waite (DSW) algorithm. DSW is an algorithm for traversing a binary tree without the use of a stack by means of destructive pointer manipulation. Prior approaches to the verification of the algorithm involved applications of theorem provers or hand-written proofs. TVLA's abstract-interpretation approach made possible the automatic symbolic exploration of all memory configurations that can arise. With the introduction of a few simple core and instrumentation relations, TVLA was able to establish the partial correctness and termination of DSW.

1 Introduction

The Deutsch-Schorr-Waite (DSW) algorithm provides a way to traverse a tree without the use of a stack by temporarily—but systematically—stealing pointer fields of the tree's nodes to serve in place of the stack that one ordinarily needs during, e.g., an in-order traversal.[1] The benefits of being able to perform a tree traversal without the use of a stack are best seen in the context of garbage collection: such an algorithm can be employed during the *mark* phase of garbage collection, when the scarcity of available memory can preclude the use of either an explicit stack for traversing a tree, or a recursive tree traversal (which would use an implicit stack of activation records).

The subtlety of the algorithm (and the complexity of analyzing it) is due to the fact that, during the traversal, the algorithm visits each node of the tree three times, and performs a kind of pointer rotation on each node visit [10]. By the time the algorithm finishes, it has restored the original values of each node's left-child and right-child pointers, thus restoring the original tree.

Richard Bornat singles out the algorithm as a key test for formal methods: "The [Deutsch-]Schorr-Waite algorithm is the first mountain that any formalism for pointer analysis should climb." [2] Past approaches have involved hand-written proofs of complicated invariants to verify the partial correctness of the algorithm. Even with some automation, these efforts were usually laborious: a proof performed in 2002 with the

---

[1] The variant of the algorithm that we analyzed works correctly when applied to a directed acyclic graph (DAG). While our current analysis applies only when the input is a binary tree, §7 discusses how this limitation can be addressed.

K. Yi (Ed.): SAS 2006, LNCS 4134, pp. 261–279, 2006.

help of the Jape proof editor took 152 pages! [1] The key advantage of TVLA's abstract-interpretation approach over proof-theoretic approaches is that a relatively small number of concepts are involved in defining an abstraction of the structures that can arise on any execution, and verification is then carried out automatically by symbolic exploration of all memory configurations that can arise. In particular, we defined the abstraction using a few simple instrumentation relations—eight key formulas—each containing only two atomic subformulas.

The contributions of this work can be summarized as follows:

– We defined an abstraction (in the canonical-abstraction framework used by TVLA) that captures sufficient invariants of DSW to demonstrate partial correctness and termination.
– We used the fact that each tree node passes through four states (induced by the original state and the three visits to each node) to define a *state-dependent* abstraction, which requires fewer structures to represent the memory configurations that can arise in DSW than would be necessary without state dependence.
– We used the abstraction to establish the partial correctness of DSW via automatic symbolic exploration of all memory configurations.
– We used the *state-dependent* abstraction to establish a bound on the number of iterations of the algorithm's loop, thus establishing that DSW terminates.

2   Program Analysis Using 3-Valued Logic

In this section we give a brief overview of the framework of parametric shape analysis via three-valued logic. For more details, the reader is referred to [17].

Program states are represented using *first-order logical structures*, which consist of a collection of *individuals*, together with an *interpretation* for a finite vocabulary of finite-arity relation symbols, $\mathcal{R}$. An interpretation is a truth-value assignment for each relation symbol for every appropriate-arity tuple of individuals. To ensure termination, the framework puts a bound on the number of distinct logical structures that can arise during analysis by

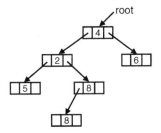

Fig. 1. A possible concrete store for a binary tree

grouping individuals that are indistinguishable according to a special subset of unary relations, $\mathcal{A}$. The grouping of nodes is referred to as *canonical abstraction* and the set $\mathcal{A}$ is referred to as the set of *abstraction relations*.

The application of canonical abstraction typically transforms a logical structure S into a *3-valued logical structure* $S^{\#}$, in which the third value, $1/2$, denotes the possibility of having either 0 (false) or 1 (true) in S. A program state is updated and queried via logical formulas, which are interpreted over the three-valued structure $S^{\#}$ using a straightforward extension of Kleene's 2-valued semantics.

Because of canonical abstraction, individuals in a 3-valued structure can represent more than one individual in a given 2-valued structure; such individuals are referred to as *summary individuals*. In general, a 3-valued logical structure can represent an infinite set of 2-valued structures.

Table 1. (a) Declaration of a binary-tree datatype in C. (b) Core relations used for representing the stores manipulated by programs that use type `Tree`.

```
typedef struct node {
    struct node *left;
    int data;
    struct node *right;
} *Tree;
```

Relation	Intended Meaning
$x(v)$	Does pointer variable x point to heap cell v?
$left(v_1, v_2)$	Does the `left` field of v_1 point to v_2? (Is v_2 the left child of v_1?)
$right(v_1, v_2)$	Does the `right` field of v_1 point to v_2? (Is v_2 the right child of v_1?)

(a)   (b)

Table 2. Defining formulas of instrumentation relations commonly employed in analyses of programs that use type `Tree`. There is a separate relation r_x for every program variable x.

p	Intended Meaning	Defining Formula
$down(v_1, v_2)$	Do the `left` or `right` fields of v_1 point to v_2? (Is v_2 a child of v_1?)	$left(v_1, v_2) \lor right(v_1, v_2)$
$t_{down}(v_1, v_2)$	Is v_2 reachable from v_1 along `left` and `right` fields?	$down^*(v_1, v_2)$
$r_x(v)$	Is v reachable from pointer variable x along `left` and `right` fields?	$\exists v_1 : x(v_1) \land t_{down}(v_1, v)$

Program states are encoded in terms of *core relations*, $\mathcal{C} \subseteq \mathcal{R}$. Core relations are part of the underlying semantics of the language to be analyzed; they record atomic properties of stores. For instance, Tab. 1 gives the definition of a C binary-tree datatype, and lists the core relations that would be used to represent the stores manipulated by programs that use type `Tree`, such as the store in Fig. 1. Unary relations represent pointer variables, and binary relations *left* and *right* represent the `left` and `right` fields of a `Tree` node. Fig. 2(a) shows 2-valued structure S_2, which represents the store of Fig. 1 using the relations of Tab. 1.

The abstraction function on which an analysis is based, and hence the precision of the analysis defined, can be tuned by (i) choosing to equip structures with additional *instrumentation relations* to record derived properties, and (ii) varying which of the unary core and unary instrumentation relations are used as the set of abstraction relations. The set of instrumentation relations is denoted by $\mathcal{I}$. Each arity-k relation symbol is defined by an *instrumentation-relation defining formula* with k free variables. Instrumentation relation symbols may appear in the defining formulas of other instrumentation relations as long as there are no circular dependences.

Tab. 2 lists some instrumentation relations that are important for the analysis of programs that use type `Tree`. Instrumentation relations that involve reachability properties, such as relation $r_x(v)$, often play a crucial role in the definitions of abstractions. These relations have the effect of keeping disjoint subtrees summarized separately. Fig. 2(b) shows 2-valued structure S_2, which represents the store of Fig. 1 using the core relations of Tab. 1, as well as the instrumentation relations of Tab. 2.

If all unary relations are abstraction relations, the canonical abstraction of 2-valued logical structure S_2 is S_3, shown in Fig. 3, with all tree nodes not pointed to by `root` represented by the summary individual at the bottom. In S_2, nodes in the left subtree

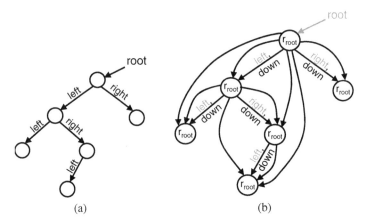

Fig. 2. A logical structure S_2 that represents the store shown in Fig. 1 in graphical form: (a) S_2 with relations of Tab. 1. (b) S_2 with relations of Tabs. 1 and 2 (relations of Tab. 1 appear in grey). Unlabeled (curved) arcs between nodes represent the t_{down} relation. Self-loops of the t_{down} relation (corresponding to the reflexive tuples) have been omitted to reduce clutter.

of root's target are indistinguishable from those in its right subtree according to $\mathcal{A}$ (consisting of relations $x(v)$ and $r_x(v)$ for each program variable x). S_3 represents all trees with two or more elements, with the root node pointed to by program variable root.

The following graphical notation is used for depicting 3-valued logical structures:

- Individuals are represented by circles containing (non-0) values for unary relations. Summary individuals are represented by double circles.
- A unary relation p corresponding to a pointer-valued program variable is represented by a solid arrow from p to the individual u for which $p(u) = 1$, and by the absence of a p-arrow to each node u' for which $p(u') = 0$. (If $p = 0$ for all individuals, the relation name p is not shown.)
- A binary relation q is represented by a solid arrow labeled q between each pair of individuals u_i and u_j for which $q(u_i, u_j) = 1$, and by the absence of a q-arrow between pairs u'_i and u'_j for which $q(u'_i, u'_j) = 0$.
- Relations with value $1/2$ are represented by dotted arrows.

For each kind of statement in the programming language, the concrete semantics is defined by *relation-update formulas* for core relations. The structure transformers for the abstract semantics are defined by the same relation-update formulas for core relations and *relation-maintenance formulas* for instrumentation relations. The latter are generated automatically via *finite differencing* [15]. Abstract interpretation collects a set of 3-valued structures at each program point. It is implemented as an iterative procedure that finds

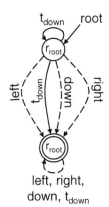

Fig. 3. A 3-valued structure S_3 that is the canonical abstraction of structure S_2. In addition to S_2, S_3 represents any tree of size 2 or more that is pointed to by program variable root.

the least fixed point of a certain set of equations [17]. When the fixed point is reached, the structures that have been collected at a program point describe a superset of all the execution states that can arise there.

Not all logical structures represent admissible stores. To exclude structures that do not, we impose integrity constraints. For instance, relation $x(v)$ of Tab. 1 captures whether pointer variable x points to memory cell v; x would be given the attribute "unique", which imposes the integrity constraint that x can hold for at most one individual in any structure: $\forall v_1, v_2 \colon x(v_1) \wedge x(v_2) \Rightarrow v_1 = v_2$. This formula evaluates to 1 in any 2-valued logical structure that corresponds to an admissible store. Integrity constraints contribute to the concretization function (γ) for our abstraction [23]. Integrity constraints are enforced by *coerce*, a clean-up operation that may "sharpen" a 3-valued logical structure by setting an indefinite value ($1/2$) to a definite value (0 or 1), or discard a structure entirely if an integrity constraint is definitely violated by the structure (e.g., if it cannot represent any admissible store).

2.1 Analyzing Programs That Manipulate (Only) Trees

When analyzing a program in which each data structure at every point is a tree (a property that we will call *treeness*), it is possible to take advantage of this fact to reduce the (abstract) state space that is explored. This is achieved by having the analysis perform a semantic reduction after each step to filter out non-trees that may have crept into the representation. When the analysis relies on the program to maintain treeness, to guarantee that the results are sound, the analysis must check that treeness is preserved at every step. We address the latter obligation first. The techniques described below are applicable whenever one wishes to analyze programs in which all input, output, and intermediate data structures are trees. We call such analyses *tree-specific shape analyses*; our DSW analysis is an example of a particular tree-specific shape analysis. (Other work in which tree-specific shape analyses have been developed include [4, 7, 8].)

Checking That Treeness is Maintained. The analyzer checks that treeness is maintained by asserting certain logical formulas that capture the conditions under which the execution of a program statement could result in a violation of treeness. Before the computation of a transfer function, the logical formulas of corresponding assertions are evaluated. If a formula *possibly fails to hold*, i.e., does not evaluate to 1, then an error report is issued and the analysis is terminated.

For purposes of this paper, a binary tree is a structure containing no cycles and no nodes with multiple incoming left or right pointers. (Our definition disallows the sharing of subtrees, and thus is more restrictive than the traditional definition that merely requires there to be at most one path between any pair of nodes. This is not an inherent limitation of TVLA; if the sharing of subtrees is to be permitted, the restriction on sharing can be relaxed—see footnote 3.)

Given a data structure that satisfies the data-structure invariants for a binary tree, only one type of statement has the potential to transform the data structure into one that violates some of those properties, namely, a statement of the form x->sel = y (where sel can be left or right), which creates a new sel-connection in the data structure. Two logical formulas capture the conditions that guarantee that the application of the transformer for a statement of the form x->sel = y maintains treeness.

The first formula captures the precondition for *down* to remain acyclic:

$$\forall v_1, v_2 \colon x(v_1) \wedge y(v_2) \Rightarrow \neg t_{down}(v_2, v_1) \tag{1}$$

The second formula captures the precondition for the statement to avoid introducing sharing:[2]

$$\forall v_1, v_2 \colon y(v_2) \Rightarrow \neg down(v_1, v_2)^3 \tag{2}$$

Semantic Reduction for Trees. After each application of an abstract transformer, we perform a semantic reduction to filter out non-trees that may have crept into the abstract structures computed by the transformer. The reduction is implemented as an application of *coerce* to enforce integrity constraints that express data-structure invariants.

For instance, relation *down* is given the attributes "acyclic" and "invfunction". The "acyclic" attribute of *down* results in the automatic generation of the following integrity constraint:

$$\forall v_1, v_2 \colon t_{down}(v_1, v_2) \wedge t_{down}(v_2, v_1) \Rightarrow v_1 = v_2 \tag{3}$$

The "invfunction" attribute of *down* results in the automatic generation of the following integrity constraint:

$$\forall v_1, v_2 \colon (\exists v \colon down(v_1, v) \wedge down(v_2, v)) \Rightarrow v_1 = v_2 \tag{4}$$

Operation *coerce* is applied at certain steps of the algorithm, e.g., after the application of an abstract transformer, to enforce Constraints (3) and (4), along with a few others, to help prevent the analysis from admitting non-trees, and thereby possibly losing precision.

3   Deutsch-Schorr-Waite Tree-Traversal Algorithm

The original Deutsch-Schorr-Waite algorithm reverses the direction of `left` and `right` pointers, as it traverses the tree [18]. It attaches two bits, `mark` and `tag`, to each node. The `mark` bit serves to prevent multiple visits to nodes on a cycle or in shared subtrees. The `tag` bit records whether, during the traversal of reversed pointers, a node was reached from its left or right child.

In [10], Lindstrom gave a variant that eliminated the need for both bits, provided the input data structure contains no cycles. His insight was that one could treat the visit step at an internal node as a kind of pointer-rotation operation, and that completion of the tree-traversal could be established having the algorithm watch for a distinguished value that serves as a kind of sentinel. In this paper, we actually consider the Lindstrom

---

[2] As explained in §3, we ensure that `x->sel` is NULL prior an assignment of the form `x->sel = y`, so the assignment indeed creates a new `sel`-connection.

[3] If we relaxed the restriction on the sharing of subtrees, then, in place of Formula (2), we would employ a slightly more complex formula that precludes the possibility of creating two paths between a pair of tree nodes v_1 and v_4 (one path that existed prior to the statement, and the other that was created due to the introduction of the new `sel` edge from x to y):

$$\forall v_1, v_2, v_3, v_4 \colon t_{down}(v_1, v_4) \wedge t_{down}(v_1, v_2) \wedge x(v_2) \wedge y(v_3) \Rightarrow \neg t_{down}(v_3, v_4)$$

```
[1]  void traverse(Tree *root)        void traverse(Tree *root)        [1]
[2]  { Tree *prev, *cur, *next;       { Tree *prev, *cur,              [2]
                                                 *next, *tmp;          [3]
[3]     if (root == NULL)                if (root == NULL)             [4]
[4]        return;                          return;                    [5]
[5]     prev = -1;                       prev = SENTINEL;              [6]
[6]     cur = root;                      cur = root;                   [7]
[7]     while (1) {                      while (1) {                   [8]
           // Save left subtree             // Save the left subtree
[8]        next = cur->left;                next = cur->left;          [9]
                                            // Rotate pointers
                                            tmp = cur->right;          [10]
                                            // Maintain treeness
                                            cur->right = NULL;         [11]
           // Rotate pointers               cur->right = prev;         [12]
[9]        cur->left = cur->right;          cur->left = NULL;          [13]
[10]       cur->right = prev;               cur->left = tmp;           [14]
           // Move forward                  // Move forward
[11]       prev = cur;                      prev = cur;                [15]
[12]       cur = next;                      cur = next;                [16]
[13]       if (cur == -1)                   if (cur == SENTINEL)       [17]
              // Traversal completed           // Traversal completed
[14]          break;                           break;                 [18]
[15]       if (cur == NULL) {               if (cur == NULL) {         [19]
              // Swap prev and cur             // Swap prev and cur
[16]          cur = prev;                      cur = prev;             [20]
[17]          prev = NULL;                     prev = NULL;            [21]
[18]       }                                }                          [22]
[19]  }                                 }                              [23]
[20]}                                 }                                [24]
```

(a)   (b)

Fig. 4. (a) Original version of the Deutsch-Schorr-Waite algorithm (adapted from [10]). (b) Modified version of the Deutsch-Schorr-Waite algorithm that was analyzed using TVLA. (The differences appear in bold.)

variant, but continue to refer to it as Deutsch-Schorr-Waite (DSW). Another connection between our analysis (of the Lindstrom variant) and the original version of DSW is discussed briefly in §7.

Fig. 4 shows two versions of the Deutsch-Schorr-Waite algorithm. The left-hand column shows a version adapted from [10], also known as Lindstrom scanning. The right-hand column shows a slightly modified version of the algorithm that we used in our work. There are two differences between the two versions.

First, the constant –1 on lines [5] and [13] has been replaced with SENTINEL, where SENTINEL is assumed to be a reference to a distinguished node that is not part of the input tree. In TVLA, pointer values can either equal NULL (corresponding to the situation in which the pointer does not point to any heap object) or point to a heap object that was allocated by malloc. In this sense, TVLA follows the semantics of Java, in which new non-NULL pointer values can be generated only via memory-allocation operations.

Second, a purely local transformation (involving the introduction of one temporary variable tmp) has been applied to lines [9]–[10]:

```
                                   [10] tmp = cur->right;
                                   // Maintain treeness
[9]  cur->left = cur->right;   ⟹  [11] cur->right = NULL;
[10] cur->right = prev;            [12] cur->right = prev;
                                   [13] cur->left = NULL;
                                   [14] cur->left = tmp;
```

This really involved three transformations:

1. Assignment statements of the form x->sel1 = y->sel2 have been normalized to statement sequences tmp = y->sel2; x->sel1 = tmp (see lines [10] and [14] of Fig. 4(b)).

2. Assignment statements of the form x->sel = y have been normalized to statement sequences x->sel = NULL; x->sel = y (see lines [11]–[12] and [13]–[14] of Fig. 4(b)). This ensures that statements of the form x->sel = y can never destroy existing sel-paths in the data structure, thus simplifying the task of maintaining information about the reachability of tree nodes from program variables.

3. Assignments cur->right = NULL and cur->right = prev have been moved to lines [11] and [12] (before assignments to cur->left). This change prevents the right child of cur's target from temporarily having two incoming edges after the assignment to cur->left on line [14].[4] The resulting algorithm maintains the invariant that the nodes of the input tree always make up one or two data structures that satisfy the binary-tree properties: after the assignment on line [14] of Fig. 4(b), the nodes of the input tree make up two trees, one rooted at next's target, and the other rooted at cur's target; the original root is a descendant of cur's target.

Transformations 1 and 2 above are simple normalizations that one could expect to find in a translation of programs written in a high-level language into a lower-level intermediate representation. Transformation 3 prevents the temporary sharing of cur's right subtree (it would otherwise briefly become cur's left and cur's right subtree). We could relax our restriction on sharing and analyze the version of the algorithm that does not include transformation 3 (§7 discusses how we would approach this task), but we chose to verify total correctness and preservation of treeness for the slightly modified version of the DSW algorithm shown in Fig. 4(b). Because of transformation 3, the techniques of §2.1 apply in the analysis of this version; we now describe this version in detail.

For each tree node n, the body of the while loop is executed three times with cur pointing to n. Each time that n is considered, its left and right pointers are rotated in a counter-clockwise fashion on lines [10]–[14] of Fig. 4(b) (cf. lines [9] and [10] of Fig. 4(a)). After the third such execution, the original values for the left and right pointers are re-established, as we explain below.

---

[4] Only the assignment cur->right = NULL needs to be moved to achieve the desired effect. We moved both assignments for clarity.

Before the first execution of lines [10]–[14] of Fig. 4(b) with cur pointing to n, no nodes in the subtrees rooted at l or r (n's left and right subtrees in the original tree) have been visited, and no left or right pointers of nodes in the subtrees rooted at l or r have been modified. In this situation, we say that n is in *state 0*. Fig. 5(a) illustrates this situation.

A pointer to node l, the left child of n prior to the rotation of n's left and right pointers, is saved in next on line [9]. After the rotation, the traversal continues by moving into the (sub)tree rooted at next, i.e., l (see lines [15] and [16]). When cur becomes null, the values of cur and prev are swapped on lines [20] and [21]. This causes the traversal to backtrack to the most recently visited node that had a right subtree in the original tree.

When the traversal backtracks to n, the algorithm reaches lines [10]–[14] of Fig. 4(b) for the second time with cur pointing to n. At this point, all nodes in l's subtree and no nodes in r's subtree have been visited. The left and right pointers of nodes in l's subtree have been rotated three times and restored to their original values. No left or right pointers of nodes in r's subtree have been modified. In this situation we say that n is in *state 1*. Fig. 5(b) illustrates this situation.

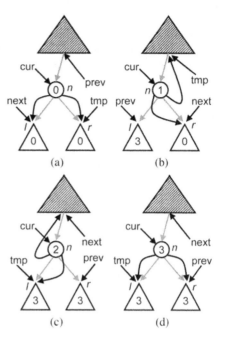

Fig. 5. States of the subtree of n with cur pointing to n: (a) after the first execution of statement on line [10] of Fig. 4(b), n is in state 0; (b) after the second execution of statement on line [10] of Fig. 4(b), n is in state 1; (c) after the third execution of statement on line [10] of Fig. 4(b), n is in state 2; (d) after the third execution of statement on **line [14]** of Fig. 4(b), n is in state 3. Grey edges represent the original values of the left and right fields.

A pointer to node r, the left child of n prior to the second rotation of n's pointers, is saved in next. After the rotation, the traversal continues by moving into the (sub)tree rooted at r (see lines [15] and [16]). Once again, the algorithm backtracks when cur is null. When the traversal backtracks to n, the algorithm reaches lines [10]–[14] of Fig. 4(b) for the third (and final) time with cur pointing to n. At this point, all nodes in l's and r's subtrees have been visited. The left and right pointers of nodes in both subtrees have been rotated three times and restored to their original values. In this situation we say that n is in *state 2*. Fig. 5(c) illustrates this situation.

After the subsequent execution of lines [10]–[14] of Fig. 4(b) with cur pointing to n, n's left and right pointers are restored to their original values. At this point, all nodes in the subtree rooted at n have been visited, and all left and right pointers in the subtree have been rotated three times and restored to their original values. In this situation we say that n is in *state 3*. Fig. 5(d) illustrates this situation.

The algorithm traverses the tree *in order*, visiting each node *n* three times: (1) while following the original `left` pointers from *n*'s parent through *n* into *l*'s subtree, (2) while backtracking from *l*'s subtree to *n* and then traversing *r*'s subtree, and (3) while backtracking from *r*'s subtree through *n* to *n*'s parent in the original tree.

Fig. 6 depicts the states of the tree nodes that are not in the subtree pointed to by `cur`. All ancestors (in the original tree) of `cur`'s target are in state 1 or 2, indicating that the left (1) or right (2), subtree is currently being traversed. If `cur`'s target lies in the left subtree of an ancestor, then that ancestor must be in state 1, otherwise it must be in state 2. The triangular shapes at left represent all nodes that occur earlier than `cur`'s target in an in-order traversal of the tree. For each of these nodes there exists an ancestor of `cur`'s target, such that the node is in the left subtree of the ancestor, and `cur`'s target is in the right subtree of the ancestor. All nodes in that category are in state 3; they have been visited three times, and their `left` and `right` pointers have been reset to their original values. The triangular shapes at right represent all nodes that occur later than `cur`'s target in an in-order traversal of the tree. For each of these nodes there exists an ancestor of `cur`'s target, such that the node is in the right subtree of the ancestor, and `cur`'s target is in the left subtree of the ancestor. All nodes in that category are in state 0; they have not been visited, and their `left` and `right` pointers still have their original values.

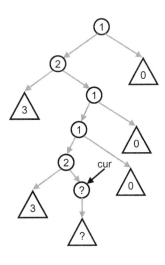

Fig. 6. States of tree nodes that are outside of the subtree pointed to by `cur`. (Grey edges represent the original values of the `left` and `right` fields.)

4   A Shape Abstraction for Verifying DSW

Consider the problem of establishing that the Deutsch-Schorr-Waite algorithm shown in Fig. 4(b) is partially correct. This is an assertion that compares the state of a store at the end of the procedure with its state at the start.

Partial correctness of DSW means (i) the tree produced at exit must be identical to the input tree, and (ii) every node must be visited. We will come back to property (ii) when we discuss the total correctness of DSW in §5. Property (i) can be specified as follows:

$$\forall v_1, v_2 : \textit{left}(v_1, v_2) \Leftrightarrow \textit{left}^0(v_1, v_2) \tag{5}$$

$$\forall v_1, v_2 : \textit{right}(v_1, v_2) \Leftrightarrow \textit{right}^0(v_1, v_2), \tag{6}$$

where $\textit{left}^0$ and $\textit{right}^0$ denote the initial values of relations *left* and *right*, respectively. Additionally, a correct traversal routine must neither lose nodes of the input tree, nor gain new ones. However, this property is implied by properties (5) and (6).

The challenge is that the abstraction has to track the "unintended" use of pointers for stack simulation with sufficient precision to verify that at the end of the algorithm their correct usage has been reestablished. Canonical abstraction with just the properties listed in Tabs. 1 and 2 is an insufficiently precise abstraction to demonstrate that the tree's edges are restored.

The key relations for establishing properties (5) and (6) at the end of the program are those that capture the relationships of pointers that arise between tree nodes during the traversal. The following set of unary relations capture properties of nodes in state 0 (before any changes to the nodes' `left` and `right` pointers) or state 3 (after the nodes' `left` and `right` pointer values have been restored):

$$eq_{l,l^0}(v_1) \stackrel{\text{def}}{=} \forall v_2 : \mathit{left}(v_1, v_2) \Leftrightarrow \mathit{left}^0(v_1, v_2) \tag{7}$$

$$eq_{r,r^0}(v_1) \stackrel{\text{def}}{=} \forall v_2 : \mathit{right}(v_1, v_2) \Leftrightarrow \mathit{right}^0(v_1, v_2) \tag{8}$$

Unary relations $eq_{l,l^0}(v_1)$ and $eq_{r,r^0}(v_1)$ distinguish individuals that represent tree nodes whose `left`, respectively `right`, pointers have their initial values. We can now use $\forall v : eq_{l,l^0}(v)$ in place of Formula (5) and $\forall v : eq_{r,r^0}(v)$ in place of Formula (6) when asserting the partial correctness of DSW.

The following set of unary relations capture properties of nodes in state 1, after one visit to those nodes, i.e., one rotation of the `left` and `right` pointers:

$$eq_{l,r^0}(v_1) \stackrel{\text{def}}{=} \forall v_2 : \mathit{left}(v_1, v_2) \Leftrightarrow \mathit{right}^0(v_1, v_2) \tag{9}$$

$$re_{r,l^0}(v_1) \stackrel{\text{def}}{=} \forall v_2 : \mathit{right}(v_1, v_2) \Leftrightarrow \mathit{left}^0(v_2, v_1) \tag{10}$$

$$re_{r,r^0}(v_1) \stackrel{\text{def}}{=} \forall v_2 : \mathit{right}(v_1, v_2) \Leftrightarrow \mathit{right}^0(v_2, v_1) \tag{11}$$

Unary relation $eq_{l,r^0}(v_1)$ distinguishes individuals that represent tree nodes whose `left` field points to their `right` (in the input tree) subtree. Unary relations $re_{r,l^0}(v_1)$ and $re_{r,r^0}(v_1)$ (*re* is a mnemonic for *reverse*) distinguish individuals that represent tree nodes n whose `right` fields point to their parents in the input tree (assuming that n is the left child in the case of $re_{r,l^0}(v_1)$ and right child, otherwise).

The following set of unary relations capture properties of nodes in state 2, after two visits to those nodes, i.e., two rotations of the `left` and `right` pointers:

$$eq_{r,l^0}(v_1) \stackrel{\text{def}}{=} \forall v_2 : \mathit{right}(v_1, v_2) \Leftrightarrow \mathit{left}^0(v_1, v_2) \tag{12}$$

$$re_{l,l^0}(v_1) \stackrel{\text{def}}{=} \forall v_2 : \mathit{left}(v_1, v_2) \Leftrightarrow \mathit{left}^0(v_2, v_1) \tag{13}$$

$$re_{l,r^0}(v_1) \stackrel{\text{def}}{=} \forall v_2 : \mathit{left}(v_1, v_2) \Leftrightarrow \mathit{right}^0(v_2, v_1) \tag{14}$$

Unary relation $eq_{r,l^0}(v_1)$ distinguishes individuals that represent tree nodes whose `right` field points to their `left` (in the input tree) subtree. Unary relations $re_{l,l^0}(v_1)$ and $re_{l,r^0}(v_1)$ distinguish individuals that represent tree nodes n whose `left` fields point to their parents in the input tree (assuming that n is the left child in the case of $re_{l,l^0}(v_1)$ and right child, otherwise).

Let us give the intuition behind the use of the relations defined by Formulas (7)–(14) for the partial-correctness verification of DSW, which involves establishing that all `left` and `right` pointers have their initial values at the end of DSW.

These relations maintain the relationship between the current and the original values of `left` and `right` pointers. Prior to the first rotation of pointers for node n, n has entries 1 for the state-0 relations (Formulas (7) and (8)), which say that there has been no change from n's starting pointer values. These entries allow the analysis to conclude that after the current iteration's rotation of n's pointers, n should have entry 1 for state-1 relations, Formula (9) and Formulas (10) or (11). Similarly, the 1 entries for the state-1 relations for node n help establish the 1 entries for its state-2 relations (Formula (12) and Formulas (13) or (14)) after the second rotation of n's pointers. Finally, the 1 entries for the state-2 relations for node n help establish the 1 entries for its state-3 relations Formulas (7) and (8) after the third rotation of n's pointers.

In our initial attempt to establish the partial correctness of DSW, we added all relations of Formulas (7)–(14) to the set of abstraction relations, $\mathcal{A}$. This attempt failed (we terminated the analysis after several days of computation) because of the vast abstract state space that needed to be explored. To pare down the abstract state space, we observed that not all node distinctions introduced by the relations of Formulas (7)–(14) were necessary. For instance, note that any leaf node in state 0 or state 3 satisfies (among other relations) Formula (9), which defines eq_{l,r^0}—nominally a state-1 relation—because it has no outgoing `left` or `right` pointers, while an internal tree node in state 0 or state 3 does not satisfy it. As a result, eq_{l,r^0} prevents canonical abstraction from summarizing a leaf node in state 0 or 3 with an internal node in one of those states. The resulting abstraction has a larger-than-necessary state space because we only need to ensure that tree nodes in state 1 have their `left` field pointing to their original right subtree, i.e., have the property defined by the relation eq_{l,r^0}.

To remove such unnecessary distinctions, we introduce the concept of a *state-dependent* abstraction. The first component of such an abstraction is a collection of unary core *state relations*, $state_0(v)$, $state_1(v)$, $state_2(v)$, and $state_3(v)$.[5] Every time the rotation of `left` and `right` pointers of the tree node pointed to by `cur` is completed (after line [14] of Fig. 4(b)), the node's state is changed to the next state. (The state relations carry no semantics with respect to the pointer values of nodes; they simply record the "visit counts" for each node.) As the second component of the abstraction, we introduce state-relation-guarded versions of the relations of Formulas (7)–(14):

$$s_0\_eq_{l,l^0}(v_1) \stackrel{\text{def}}{=} state_0(v_1) \wedge eq_{l,l^0}(v_1) \tag{15}$$

$$s_0\_eq_{r,r^0}(v_1) \stackrel{\text{def}}{=} state_0(v_1) \wedge eq_{r,r^0}(v_1) \tag{16}$$

$$s_1\_eq_{l,r^0}(v_1) \stackrel{\text{def}}{=} state_1(v_1) \wedge eq_{l,r^0}(v_1) \tag{17}$$

$$s_1\_re_{r,l^0}(v_1) \stackrel{\text{def}}{=} state_1(v_1) \wedge re_{r,l^0}(v_1) \tag{18}$$

$$s_1\_re_{r,r^0}(v_1) \stackrel{\text{def}}{=} state_1(v_1) \wedge re_{r,r^0}(v_1) \tag{19}$$

$$s_2\_eq_{r,l^0}(v_1) \stackrel{\text{def}}{=} state_2(v_1) \wedge eq_{r,l^0}(v_1) \tag{20}$$

$$s_2\_re_{l,l^0}(v_1) \stackrel{\text{def}}{=} state_2(v_1) \wedge re_{l,l^0}(v_1) \tag{21}$$

$$s_2\_re_{l,r^0}(v_1) \stackrel{\text{def}}{=} state_2(v_1) \wedge re_{l,r^0}(v_1) \tag{22}$$

---

[5] The state relations are *not* added to the set of abstraction relations, $\mathcal{A}$.

$$s_3\_eq_{l,l^0}(v_1) \overset{\text{def}}{=} state_3(v_1) \wedge eq_{l,l^0}(v_1) \tag{23}$$

$$s_3\_eq_{r,r^0}(v_1) \overset{\text{def}}{=} state_3(v_1) \wedge eq_{r,r^0}(v_1) \tag{24}$$

We replace the relations of Formulas (7)–(14) in the set of abstraction relations, $\mathcal{A}$, with Formulas (15)–(24). The resulting abstraction allows the grouping of nodes that have different values for the relation eq_{l,r^0}, for example, as long as these nodes are not in state 1.

5 Establishing That DSW Terminates

We can establish that DSW terminates using the unary state relations of §4 via a simple progress monitor, which we describe below.

For each state relation s, we create a copy of s, which is used to save the values of relation s at the start of the currently-processed loop iteration (after line [8] of Fig. 4(b)). We give the new relations the superscript lh to indicate that they hold the *loop-head* values. The first abstract operation of each iteration of the loop takes a snapshot of the current states of nodes: $state_i^{lh}(v) \leftarrow state_i(v)$, for each $i \in [0..3]$ and each binding of v to individuals in the abstract structure being processed. Additionally, it asserts that cur does not point to a tree node in state 3 at the head of the loop.

The last operation of every loop iteration performs a progress test by asserting the following formula:

$$\exists v: \left(state_0^{lh}(v) \wedge state_1(v) \vee state_1^{lh}(v) \wedge state_2(v) \vee state_2^{lh}(v) \wedge state_3(v)\right)$$
$$\wedge \forall v_1 \neq v: \left(state_0^{lh}(v_1) \Leftrightarrow state_0(v_1)\right) \wedge \left(state_1^{lh}(v_1) \Leftrightarrow state_1(v_1)\right) \wedge$$
$$\left(state_2^{lh}(v_1) \Leftrightarrow state_2(v_1)\right) \wedge \left(state_3^{lh}(v_1) \Leftrightarrow state_3(v_1)\right)$$

The assertion ensures that one node's state makes forward progress (the first line of the assertion) and that no other node changes state (the second and third lines of the assertion).

Together with the assertion that cur does not point to a tree node in state 3 at the start of the loop, the above progress monitor establishes that each tree node is visited exactly three times, thus establishing that the algorithm terminates, as well as the fact that every node is, in fact, visited by the algorithm (property (ii) of partial correctness).

6 Experimental Evaluation

We applied TVLA to the DSW algorithm shown in Fig. 4(b) and analyzed it using the abstraction defined in §4. As input for the algorithm, we supplied the 3-valued structure S_7 shown in Fig. 7, which is essentially the structure S_3 from Fig. 3 refined with values for relations introduced in §4. Additionally, S_7 contains a special *sentinel* node that is not part of the input tree; it is referenced by program variable SENTINEL. In Fig. 7, as well as Fig. 8, relations $left^0$ and $right^0$ are omitted to reduce clutter. Their values are identical to $left$ and $right$, respectively. We have also omitted the values for state-1 and state-2 relations eq_{l,r^0}, re_{r,l^0}, re_{r,r^0}, eq_{r,l^0}, re_{l,l^0}, and re_{l,r^0}. They have value $1/2$ for the non-sentinel nodes of both figures and value 1 for the sentinel nodes. Because we are performing tree-specific shape analysis, both figures only represent concrete structures that satisfy the treeness integrity constraints (see §2.1).

Fig. 8 shows the unique structure S_8 collected by the analysis at the exit node. The definite 1 values for relations eq_{l,l^0} and eq_{r,r^0} (defined by Formulas (7) and (8)) for each individual of S_8 establish that the outgoing left and right pointers of every tree node are restored, thus establishing partial correctness property (i), i.e., that the tree produced at exit is identical to the input tree. The absence of violations of the progress monitor defined in §5 establishes that DSW terminates, as well as the fact that every node is visited (partial correctness property (ii)).

The analysis took just under nine hours on a 3GHz Linux PC and used 150MB of memory. While the authors have a number of ideas for performance optimizations for the research system, the main goal was to demonstrate the feasibility of automatic symbolic exploration of heap-manipulating programs with vast (abstract) state spaces.

The cost of verifying that DSW terminates is negligible (when compared to the cost that DSW is partially correct) because the progress monitor does not increase the size of the reachable state space. The number of distinct abstract structures that were collected at all program points exceeded 80,000. The number of structures at some program points exceeded 11,000. This number is not surprising, if we consider that some of these structures contained 15 individuals. (At intermediate steps, the analysis explored

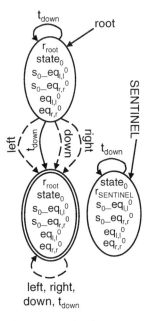

Fig. 7. A 3-valued structure S_7 that represents all trees of size 2 or more

abstracts structures with up to 21 individuals!) However, 80,000 is well below the limit imposed by the number of distinct 3-valued structures, $2^{2^{20}}$, which represents the number of subsets of individuals with every possible vector of unary abstraction-relation values. (There are 20 unary abstraction relations: pointer relations $x(v)$ and reachability relations $r_x(v)$ for each of the five pointer-valued program variables, as well as ten relations of Formulas (15)–(24).) Fig. 9 shows a sample abstract structure S_9 that arises before line [11] of Fig. 4(b). In S_9, as in all other structures that arise at that point, the state relations and state-relation-guarded relations defined by Formulas (15)–(24), have precise values for all individuals.

In summary, our experiment showed that, using the abstraction defined in §4, an automatic analysis can maintain enough precision to identify sufficient invariants to demonstrate both partial correctness and termination of DSW.

7   Discussion and Future Work

The analysis carried out by TVLA performs fully-automatic state-space exploration. However, one has to bring to bear some expertise in specifying TVLA analyses. The concept of tree-specific shape analysis (see §2.1) is of general utility. It can be reused for any analysis in which all input, output, and intermediate data structures are trees. The instrumentation relations defined by Formulas (9)–(14), which capture pointer relationships of tree nodes, and core state relations $state_0(v), \ldots, state_3(v)$, which are used to control the precision of the abstraction, are specific to the problem of verifying the total correctness of DSW.

A key difference between our approach and theorem-prover-based approaches is that we do not need to specify loop invariants. Instead, we need to specify a collection of node distinctions (or node relationships), such as the relations $eq_{l,r^0}(v_1)$ and $re_{r,l^0}(v_1)$ of Formulas (9)–(14); these allow the node distinctions specified to be observable by the analysis. Given the appropriate node distinctions, abstract interpretation automatically infers the invariants satisfied by the program.

Recently, a machine-learning technique has been used to identify key instrumentation relations automatically [11]. In the future, we would like to see if it can be used to identify the key relations for verifying DSW, namely the relations of Formulas (9)–(14).

Although the instrumentation relations introduced in §4 are tailored for establishing the correctness of DSW, the concept of state-dependent abstractions is likely to be of general utility. In fact, simpler versions of state-dependent abstractions have arisen in past work. For example, the unary relation *inOrder* was used to establish the partial correctness of sorting [9]. The state-dependent abstractions defined in this paper are prepared to deal with more than just two states (initial and final, as is the case for the relation *inOrder*), and use the value of the state as a guard to reduce the number of distinct properties recorded for individuals, thereby reducing the size of the (abstract) state space that is explored.

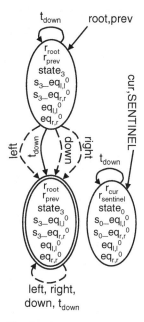

Fig. 8. A 3-valued structure S_8 collected at exit of DSW

There is an interesting analogy between the explicit state-tracking that the original DSW algorithm performs via the mark and tag bits, and the state relations of our abstraction. (In some sense, the state relations introduced for purposes of analysis impose a DSW-like view of the world to track the actions of the Lindstrom variant of the algorithm.)

While we chose to apply a transformation that ensures that the algorithm maintains treeness (transformation 3 of §3), it is possible to verify the unmodified algorithm (Fig. 4(a)) by introducing the following instrumentation relation:

$$isLocallyShared(v) \stackrel{\text{def}}{=} \exists v_1 : \textit{left}(v_1, v) \land \textit{right}(v_1, v)$$

Relation *isLocallyShared* (which has value 0 for all nodes in the input 3-valued structure, indicating that the input is a valid binary tree) allows us to relax the restriction on sharing by tracking where sharing occurs rather than requiring its absence. To be applicable to the version of the algorithm that does not include transformation 3, the tree-specific shape analysis of §2.1 can be generalized to handle the limited class of DAGs that arise in lines [9]–[10] of Fig. 4(a) as follows:

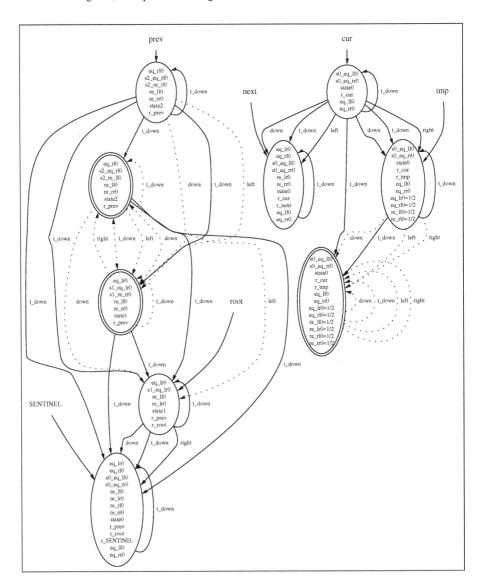

Fig. 9. A 3-valued structure S_9 that arises prior to the first rotation of pointers of the node n pointed to by `cur` (before line [11] of Fig. 4(b)). Relations $left^0$ and $right^0$ are omitted from the figure. Initially, node n was the right child of the node pointed to by `prev`. The latter node is now the root of a tree with leaf `SENTINEL` (the original root is the parent of `SENTINEL`). No nodes in n's subtree have been visited; that subtree has not been modified from its initial state.

1. The precondition for the absence of sharing (Formula (2)) would be removed.
2. The integrity constraints that forbid structures that contain sharing would be modified to include an *isLocallyShared* guard to permit the kind of local sharing that arises in Fig. 4(a). E.g., Constraint (4) becomes:

$$\forall\, v_1, v_2 \colon (\exists\, v \colon \neg isLocallyShared(v) \land down(v_1, v) \land down(v_2, v)) \Rightarrow v_1 = v_2.$$

The DSW algorithm shown in Fig. 4(b) (as well as the algorithm shown in Fig. 4(a)) does not work correctly when applied to a data structure that contains a cycle: the traversal terminates prematurely and not all of the edges are properly restored. However, the algorithm works correctly when applied to a DAG: a node n with k paths from the root to n is visited $3k$ times, rather than 3 times. (Note, however, that k can be exponential in the size of the graph.) Given a bound on k, we may be able to verify the correctness of DSW for DAGs, if we relax the restriction on sharing and introduce $3k$ state relations and the corresponding state-relation-guarded relations. However, unless k is very small it is not likely that the reachable state space can be explored with our computing resources. In the general case, in which the input is a DAG with no bound on k, the partial-correctness result can be obtained by having the state relations of nodes wrap around: a visit to a node in state 3 results in changing the node's state to 1. While this change would be sufficient to establish that the outgoing left and right pointers of every DAG node are restored and that every node is visited, the analysis would no longer be able to establish termination using the simple progress monitor of §5.

In practice, one would rarely be interested in using such an algorithm to traverse a DAG because of the potentially exponential cost. In most applications, one is likely to want to process each node once (e.g., in depth-first order) and visit each node a constant number of times. This can be achieved by equipping the nodes with two bits to record the visit count (a number from 0 to 3). All nodes reachable from a node with visit count 3 must have been visited three times. If cur is set to point to a node with visit count 3, the direction of the traversal can be reversed by swapping the values of cur and prev, thus terminating the exploration of the node's subgraph. By relaxing the restriction on sharing, it should be possible to verify the total correctness of the modified algorithm.

8   Related Work[6]

The general form of the Deutsch-Schorr-Waite algorithm works correctly for arbitrary graphs [18]. (Unlike the algorithm we used in our work, which was taken from [10], the general form is not constant-space because it uses mark and tag bits.) We divide the discussion of related work according to the kind of data structures to which the analyzed algorithm can be applied.

DSW on Arbitrary Graphs. The first formal proofs of the partial correctness of DSW were performed manually by Morris [14] and Topor [20]. In [19], Suzuki automated some steps of the partial-correctness verification of the algorithm by introducing decision procedures that could handle heap-manipulating programs. More recently, Bornat used the Jape proof editor [3] to construct a partial-correctness proof of DSW [2]. The resulting proof used 152 pages [1].

Our automated approach provides the obvious benefit of disposing with the need to provide manual proofs, which require significant investments of time and expertise. However, even in the presence of a powerful theorem prover, proof-based approaches

---

[6] The discussion of [14, 20, 19] relies on what is reported in [22, 13].

rely on the user to provide loop invariants that are sufficient to establish the property being verified. For instance, the properties of nodes and their subtrees that are described in §3 (see Figs. 5 and 6 and the corresponding text) would have to be specified as loop invariants. As discussed in §7, our obligation is simpler: we have to specify instrumentation relations that act as *ingredients* for a loop invariant; the analysis automatically synthesizes a loop invariant—in the form of a collection of 3-valued structures that overapproximate the set of concrete structures that actually arise—by means of state-space exploration.

Yang [21] and Mehta and Nipkow [13] gave manually-constructed, but machine-checkable, proofs of the partial correctness of DSW. The two approaches share the goal of making formal reasoning about heap-manipulating programs more natural. The former approach uses the logic of Bunched Implications [5] (a precursor formalism to Separation Logic [16]), which permits the user to reason with Hoare triples in the presence of complicated aliasing relationships. The latter approach uses Isabelle/HOL to construct formal proofs that are human-readable. These approaches improve the usability of proof-based techniques. However, they still lack the automation of our approach.

DSW on Trees and DAGs. Yelowitz and Duncan were the first to present a termination argument for the Deutsch-Schorr-Waite algorithm [22]. They analyzed Knuth's version of the algorithm [6], which uses tag bits but does not work correctly for graphs that contain a cycle. It does, however, work for DAGs, as does the version we used, taken from [10]. The termination argument involved the use of program invariants to prove bounds on the number of executions of statements in the loop. In §5, we showed how to use the *state relations* defined in §4 in a simple progress monitor for the algorithm's loop to establish that DSW terminates (on trees). As was the case for partial correctness, our task is reduced to establishing appropriate distinctions between nodes. Given the state relations, the complete state-space exploration shows no violation of the progress monitor and establishes a bound (namely, three) on the number of visits to each tree node; consequently, the algorithm must terminate.

Several previous papers reported on automatic verification of weaker properties of the Deutsch-Schorr-Waite algorithm, namely that the algorithm has no unsafe pointer operations or memory leaks, and that the data structure produced at the end is, in fact, a binary tree [15, 12, 7]. The authors first established these properties in [15]. ([12] contains a typo stating that that work establishes partial correctness; however, [12] reused the TVLA specification from [15], and establishes the same properties as [15].) Finally, [7] extended the framework of [17] with grammars, which provide convenient syntactic sugar for expressing shape properties of data structures. That work relied on the use of grammars, instead of instrumentation relations, to express tree properties and the absence of memory leaks.

References

1. R. Bornat. Proofs of pointer programs in Jape. "Available at http://www.dcs.qmul. ac.uk/~richard/pointers/".
2. R. Bornat. Proving pointer programs in Hoare logic. In *Mathematics of Program Construction*, pages 102–126, July 2000.

3. R. Bornat and B. Sufrin. Animating formal proofs at the surface: The Jape proof calculator. *The Computer Journal*, 43:177–192, 1999.

4. L. Hendren. *Parallelizing Programs with Recursive Data Structures*. PhD thesis, Dept. of Computer Science, Cornell University, January 1990.

5. S. Ishtiaq and P. O'Hearn. Bi as an assertion language for mutable data structures. In *Symp. on Principles of Programming Languages*, pages 14–26, January 2001.

6. D. Knuth. *The Art of Computer Programming – Vol. 1, Fundamental Algorithms*. Addison-Wesley, 1973.

7. O. Lee, H. Yang, and K. Yi. Automatic verification of pointer programs using grammar-based shape analysis. In *European Symp. On Programming*, pages 124–140, April 2005.

8. T. Lev-Ami, N. Immerman, and M. Sagiv. Fast and precise abstraction for shape analysis. To appear in *Proc. Computer-Aided Verification*, August 2006.

9. T. Lev-Ami, T. Reps, M. Sagiv, and R. Wilhelm. Putting static analysis to work for verification: A case study. In *Int. Symp. on Software Testing and Analysis*, pages 26–38, August 2000.

10. G. Lindstrom. Scanning list structures without stacks or tag bits. *Information Processing Letters*, 2(2):47–51, June 1973.

11. A. Loginov, T. Reps, and M. Sagiv. Abstraction refinement via inductive learning. In *Proc. Computer-Aided Verification*, pages 519–533, July 2005.

12. R. Manevich, M. Sagiv, G. Ramalingam, and J. Field. Partially disjunctive heap abstraction. In *Static Analysis Symp.*, pages 265–279, August 2004.

13. F. Mehta and T. Nipkow. Proving pointer programs in higher-order logic. In *Automated Deduction — CADE-19*, pages 121–135, July 2003.

14. J. Morris. Verification-oriented language design. Tech. Report TR-7, Computer Science Div., University of California–Berkeley, December 1972.

15. T. Reps, M. Sagiv, and A. Loginov. Finite differencing of logical formulas with applications to program analysis. In *European Symp. On Programming*, pages 380–398, April 2003.

16. J. Reynolds. Separation Logic: A logic for shared mutable data structures. In *Symp. on Logic in Computer Science*, pages 55–74, July 2002.

17. M. Sagiv, T. Reps, and R. Wilhelm. Parametric shape analysis via 3-valued logic. *ACM Trans. on Programming Languages and Systems (TOPLAS)*, 24(3):217–298, 2002.

18. H. Schorr and W. Waite. An efficient machine independent procedure for garbage collection in various list structures. *Communications of the ACM*, 10(8):501–506, August 1967.

19. N. Suzuki. *Automatic Verification of Programs with Complex Data Structures*. PhD thesis, Dept. of Computer Science, Stanford University, February 1976.

20. R. Topor. The correctness of the Schorr-Waite list marking algorithm. Tech. Report MIP-R-104, School of Artificial Intelligence, University of Edinburgh, July 1974.

21. H. Yang. *Local Reasoning for Stateful Programs*. PhD thesis, Dept. of Computer Science, University of Illinois, Urbana-Champaign, June 2001.

22. L. Yelowitz and A. Duncan. Abstractions, instantiations, and proofs of marking algorithms. In *Symp. on Artificial Intelligence and Programming Languages*, pages 13–21, August 1977.

23. G. Yorsh, T. Reps, M. Sagiv, and R. Wilhelm. Logical characterizations of heap abstractions. To appear in *ACM Transactions on Computational Logic (TOCL)*.

Shape Analysis for Low-Level Code

Hongseok Yang

Seoul National University, Korea

Abstract. Shape analysis algorithms statically infer deep properties of the runtime heap, such as whether a variable points to a cyclic or acyclic linked list. Previous shape analyses have tended to avoid features of low-level programming languages, such as memory disposal and pointer arithmetic. Yet, these features are used in many important programs, particularly systems programs.

In this talk I will describe how shape analysis for low-level code can be done with separation logic. A crucial element of the approach is the way it negotiates a transit between a low-level RAM view of memory and a higher, fictional, view that abstracts from the representation of nodes and linked structures as certain configurations of the RAM. The analysis algorithm can be seen as conducting a proof search in separation logic, and I will show how this provides a flexible way of exploring non-standard optimizations, while maintaining soundness.

K. Yi (Ed.): SAS 2006, LNCS 4134, p. 280, 2006.
© Springer-Verlag Berlin Heidelberg 2006

Catching and Identifying Bugs in Register Allocation

Yuqiang Huang[†], Bruce R. Childers[†], and Mary Lou Soffa[‡]

[†] Department of Computer Science
University of Pittsburgh
Pittsburgh, Pennsylvania 15260
{yuqiangh, childers}@cs.pitt.edu
[‡] Department of Computer Science
University of Virginia
Charlottesville, Virginia 22904
soffa@cs.virginia.edu

Abstract. Although there are many register allocation algorithms that work well, it can be difficult to correctly implement these algorithms. As a result, it is common for bugs to remain in the register allocator, even after the compiler is released. The register allocator may run, but bugs can cause it to produce incorrect output code. The output program may even execute properly on some test data, but errors can remain. In this paper, we propose novel data flow analyses to statically check that the output code from the register allocator is correct in terms of its data dependences. The approach is accurate, fast, and can identify and report error locations and types. No false alarms are produced. The paper describes our approach, called SARAC, and a tool, called ra-analyzer, that statically checks a register allocation and reports the errors it finds. The tool has an average compile-time overhead of only 8% and a modest average memory overhead of 85KB.

1 Introduction

One of the most critical compiler transformations is register allocation, as a good allocator can make a dramatic difference in obtaining good performance [4, 11]. One study even reported that careful register allocation makes one order of magnitude difference in performance [26]! Thus, considerable effort has been given to developing new allocation algorithms or variants of existing ones [2-7, 11, 12, 24, 26, 28, 30]. Given the many algorithm variants and the complexity of modern architectures, implementing register allocation is often a complex and error prone task. Particularly, it is difficult to detect and locate bugs in an erroneous output of the allocator if the code runs to completion. Some efforts [13, 18, 21] have proposed techniques to ensure the allocator's implementation is correct. In this paper, we describe a novel technique to check the correctness of register allocation and also to report the bugs. This technique is useful throughout the lifetime of a compiler, particularly during the development period.

Although a compiler undergoes much testing, bugs in the register allocator often slip past regression tests and are reported after release. What is worse is that many of these bugs cause the compiler to fail on some input programs, but not on others. The

K. Yi (Ed.): SAS 2006, LNCS 4134, pp. 281–300, 2006.

generated code may have bugs, although the compiler did not crash. Such latent bugs will not be discovered until a particular test input causes the program to fail. Assuming that a test input catches the bug, the developer is likely to believe that the bug is in the program itself, rather than the compiler. She will spend much time and effort tracking down the bug to only discover that it is in the compiler and cannot be readily fixed. All of this leaves the developer in the unfortunate situation of having little confidence in the correctness of the generated code because bugs may remain even after testing.

The research community has recognized the difficulty of implementing compiler optimizations including register allocation and has proposed techniques to address the situation. Necula et al. [21] proposed a symbolic evaluation approach to check the allocator's output against the input. However, this approach reports false alarms and has four times compile-time overhead. Jaramillo et al. [13] proposed a dynamic checking approach that runs the allocator's input and output code. Then it compares the corresponding values to check that they are the same. However, it does not guarantee the correctness of the allocator's output unless *all* paths are exercised by test inputs.

In this paper, we propose a new approach, called SARAC, that uses *static analysis* to check the correctness of the allocator's output. SARAC reports the location and type of an error in the output due to an incorrect allocation. The analysis checks that the data flow semantics of the output match the semantics of the input. It traverses all program paths, using data flow analysis to gather information about the output. It then checks correctness using the gathered information. A checking step verifies that the data dependences of the input code are preserved in the output code, once the allocator has assigned registers and possibly spilled registers. The information collected during the analysis is used to determine error types and locations. Identifying errors in the dependences is a first step towards a complete tool for checking and reporting bugs.

Our approach does not produce false alarms and gives hints to the compiler engineer to help her diagnose and fix bugs in the allocator. Our analysis does not rely on knowledge about the allocator implementation; it can be used with different register allocation algorithms, including those that perform coalescing and rematerialization. It uses data flow techniques and can be easily implemented. Such independence from the register allocator suggests that a single error analysis tool can be built and employed for different allocators (in different compilers and target machines). Finally, the approach has minimal performance and memory overhead, making it efficient and practical. A prototype tool, called *ra-analyzer*, that implements SARAC has an average compile-time overhead of 8% and an average memory requirement of 85 KB.

This paper makes several contributions:

- A new way (SARAC) to statically check the correctness of a register allocator implementation and to identify and report the location and type of bugs, independently of the register allocator; no false alarms are generated.
- Techniques to support register allocators that perform coalescing, rematerialization and sub-register class allocation.
- The treatment of the register allocator as a black box. SARAC supports many allocator extensions, including live range splitting, interference region spilling, web splitting, spill coalescing, spill propagation and spill coloring.

- A tool (*ra-analyzer*) that implements SARAC in SUIF's back-end optimizer (MachSUIF [29]) for the Intel IA-32.
- An evaluation of *ra-analyzer*'s performance and memory overhead.

The next section describes how allocation preserves the semantics of the input code. The third section presents algorithms for gathering and using data flow information to check for correctness. The fourth section evaluates *ra-analyzer*. The fifth section discusses related work and the final section concludes and describes future work.

2   Register Allocation

This section describes the motivation and background for our static analysis to catch and identify register allocation errors. To provide focus, we make several reasonable assumptions about the allocator. We assume that the allocator is not integrated with other optimizations (e.g. instruction scheduling) [3, 24], and it does not change the control flow graph, as is typical for register allocators. Initially, we assume a register allocator that does only allocation — e.g., it does not do coalescing or rematerialization. We also do not show address calculations. In a later section, we discuss how coalescing, rematerialization, sub-register class allocation and addresses can be incorporated. Lastly, we assume that the input code to the allocator is correct since we address register allocation errors.

When assigning *locations* (registers or memory) to hold *values* (variables or temporaries), a register allocator (e.g., on a RISC-style machine) can make only certain edits to the input code. One edit can change an input statement's operand to a hardware register. Another edit is to insert store/load statements. A copy through a register might also be introduced. The edits take into account the data type and the target machine. For example, a floating point (FP) register should be used to hold a FP value and the appropriate register assignment made to a FP statement. Some target machines may require that specific hardware registers be used for certain operations. In this case, the register allocator has to ensure that its edits (and assignment) conform to the architectural constraints.

Figure 1 provides a running example, which counts the number of integer divisors for some number, n. The allocator's input and output are shown in RTL notation [9]. RTL is a standard low level intermediate code representation used in various compilers (e.g., GNU gcc [10] and VPO [1]). In RTL, r[n] is used to represent register n and M[loc] is used to represent memory location loc. For example, r[1] is register 1 and M[c] is the memory location for variable c. A load is shown as r[n]=M[loc] and a store as M[loc]=r[n]. A register-to-register copy is shown as r[n]=r[m]. Although our technique is not tied to a particular intermediate representation.

In the example, we assume that r[1] is assigned by the allocator to hold variable n, and r[2] is used to hold the other variables as necessary. However, two wrong allocation edits are made as shown in the incorrect output. The first wrong edit occurs at code point 8, where the wrong register has been assigned to the second source operand of the statement. The other incorrect edit is located at code point 12, where the wrong destination operand is used for the spill. The example also shows the locations where the errors are manifested. The location where an error is manifested is not necessarily the location where the wrong edit is made. For example, the erroneous edit at 12 is manifested as error 2 and 3 at code point 11 and 14, respectively.

2.1 Data Flow Semantics and Register Allocation

A semantically correct allocation of registers must preserve the input code's semantics, particularly the data dependences. Thus, variable and temporary definition and use pairs ("du-pairs") in the input should be maintained in the output. We define a "*du-pair*" notationally as (p.x=,q.=x), where the definition of the variable or temporary x at code point p reaches the use of x at q. A code point is a label on a statement in the input or output. For example, in the allocator's input of Figure 1, the variable c is defined at code point 1 and used at code point 6, giving the du-pair (1.c=,6.=c).

Source Code	Input to Allocator

/*count number of divisors
to variable n that is
passed as an argument*/
c=0;
for (d=1; d<=n; d++) {
if (n%d == 0)
c++;
}
	1:c=0;
	2:d=1;
	3:PC=((n<=0)?L3:PC+4);
	L1:
	4:t=n%d;
	5:PC=((t!=0)?L2:PC+4);
	6:c=c+1;
	L2:
	7:d=d+1;
	8:t=d<=n;
	9:PC=((t==1)?L1:PC+4);
	L3:

Correct Output from Allocator	Incorrect Output from Allocator
1:r[1]=M[n]; 2:r[2]=0; 3:M[c]=r[2]; 4:r[2]=1; 5:M[d]=r[2]; 6:PC=((r[1]<=0) ? L3:PC+4); L1: 7:r[2]=M[d]; 8:r[2]=r[1]%**r[2]**; 9:PC=((r[2]!=0)?L2:PC+4); 10:r[2]=M[c]; 11:r[2]=r[2]+1; 12:**M[c]**=r[2]; L2: 13:r[2]=M[d]; 14:r[2]=r[2]+1; 15:M[d]=r[2]; 16:r[2]=r[2]<=r[1]; 17:PC=((r[2]==1)?L1:PC+4); L3:	1:r[1]=M[n]; 2:r[2]=0; 3:M[c]=r[2]; 4:r[2]=1; 5:M[d]=r[2]; 6:PC=((r[1]<=0) ? L3:PC+4); L1: 7:r[2]=M[d]; 8:r[2]=r[1]%**r[1]**; ***err1: wrong reg*** 9:PC=((r[2]!=0) ? L2:PC+4); 10:r[2]=M[c]; 11:r[2]=r[2]+1; ***err2: stale (c)*** 12: **M[d]**=r[2]; ***wrong store(causes err2,3)*** L2: 13:r[2]=M[d]; 14:r[2]=r[2]+1; ***err3: eviction (d)*** 15:M[d]=r[2]; 16:r[2]=r[2]<=r[1]; 17:PC=((r[2]==1) ? L1:PC+4); L3:

Fig. 1. Example source, input to register allocator, correct and incorrect output code

After register allocation, there is not necessarily a one-to-one correspondence between the input du-pairs (involving variables and temporaries) and the output du-pairs (involving registers and memory locations). The allocator can insert loads, stores or copies to move values between the registers and memory. The output correspondence of an input du-pair is termed a "*du-sequence*":

> A *du-sequence* (s.d=, ..., t.=u) *is a chain of du-pairs such that* d *holds the value* v *at* s, u *holds the same value* v *at* t, *and there is a connected chain of du-pairs starting at* s *and ending at* t *that can register copy, load, or store the value* v.

A du-sequence can perform a number of moves; a typical du-sequence has no moves or one store and reload. For example, there is du-sequence (2.r[2]=, 3.M[c]=r[2],10.r[2]=M[c],11.=r[2]) in the correct output of Figure 1. The notation 3.M[c]=r[2] shows a store at code point 3. Similarly, 10.r[2]=M[c] shows a load at 10.

When the allocator correctly maintains the data flow of the input, each input du-pair has a corresponding output du-sequence, where the start of the du-sequence maps to the definition in the du-pair and the end of the du-sequence to the use of the du-pair. Thus, a combination of propagation and substitution is used to recover the du-pair from the du-sequence. For example, in Figure 1 the correct output code points 2 and 11 map to input code points 1 and 6, and 2.r[2]= corresponds to 1.c= and 11.=r[2] to 6.=c. Hence, the input du-pair (1.c=,6.=c) corresponds to the du-sequence (2.r[2]=,3.M[c]=r[2],10.r[2]=M[c],11.=r[2]). The input du-pair can be recovered by propagation and substitution as shown in the steps:

1. (2.r[2]=,3.M[c]=r[2],10.r[2]=M[c],11.=r[2]) // Initial du-sequence
2. (2.r[2]=,10.r[2]=r[2],11.=r[2]) // After propagation of r[2]
3. (2.r[2]=,11.=r[2]) // After propagation of r[2] again
4. (1.c=,6.=c) // Final du-pair after c was substituted for r[2]

When a use has multiple reaching definitions, all defined values need to be in the same register (or memory location) before the use. For example, the use 6.=c has the reaching definitions 6.c= and 2.c= in the allocator's input of Figure 1. These are maintained in the correct output as (11.r[2]=,12.M[c]=r[2],10.r[2]=M[c], 11.=r[2]) and (2.r[2]=,3.M[c]=r[2],10.r[2]=M[c],11.=r[2]).

Thus, the input and output have the equivalent data flow semantics if and only if the input's du-pairs can be recovered from the output's du-sequences. Hence, we use the "recovery" process to check the correctness of an allocation. Because of the "recovery" process, there are no false positive for our techniques.

2.2 Sources of Errors

A bug in the allocator that causes the output program to crash or produce a wrong result (but not the compiler) is manifested through incorrect code edits that can be made by the allocator. For a register allocator, the incorrect edits are:

1. *incorrect register assignment*: the wrong register is used for an operand;
2. *wrong store or load*: a value is stored or loaded incorrectly (the store or load may be redundant or it may use the wrong memory address for a variable or temporary);

3. *missing store or load*: a value is not spilled or reloaded when needed;

4. *wrong register type*: the wrong type is used (e.g., a load-byte statement is used when a load-word statement is needed);

5. *constraint violation*: specific architectural constraints are violated.

These edits can violate the semantics of the input code and affect data dependences. The first three edits can cause the du-sequences in the output code to have no correspondence with the input du-pairs. These incorrect edits can challenge the compiler engineer to detect. We focus on these edits as an important and necessary step to catch and report bugs in an allocation. Both the wrong register type and constraint violation edits usually preserve the correct data dependence. Our algorithms can be extended to automatically check these using a linear inspection of the input and output.

An incorrect edit can lead to errors in the program. An error happens when a du-pair in the input cannot be recovered from the allocator's output. *We define an error as a violation of the input code's data flow.* Note the distinction between an "incorrect edit" and an "error": An incorrect edit is the cause of an error. The incorrect edit defines where something was done wrong to the code, but it is not necessarily the code point where the error is exposed. An incorrect edit may not manifest itself as an error until a value affected by the edit is used. For instance, in Figure 1 the wrong edit at code point 12 is not exposed until code points 11 and 14. In fact, an incorrect edit can be made that does *not* cause an error in the program. For example, when a duplicate load is inserted, it may do no harm in terms of the program's data flow. Our concern is *incorrect edits that cause the program to fail—crashing or computing a wrong value—by disobeying the input code's data flow.*

The incorrect edits can lead to three error types: *stale value error, wrong operand error,* or *eviction error.* Although these errors all involve data flow, we distinguish between them to report causal information about what went wrong. A *stale value error* happens when referring to a register or memory location that holds an old version of the needed value. A wrong or missing store is a common cause. For example, the incorrect output of Figure 1 shows that the wrong store is generated and that $r[2]$ is spilled to $M[d]$, rather than to $M[c]$. Thus, there is no du-sequence for c along the loop back edge that reaches the use at code point 11. Consequently, a stale value for c is used. Equivalently, the input du-pair $(6.c=, 6.=c)$ cannot be recovered. A *wrong operand error* occurs when referring to a register or memory location that does not hold the needed value at all. The value is actually held in some other location(s). This error is usually caused by an incorrect register assignment. An *eviction error* occurs when referring to a value that is not held in any location at all. This error is usually caused by an wrong store. Figure 1 shows examples for both wrong operand and eviction errors.

3   Error Analysis for Register Allocation

To find register allocation errors, we develop a technique, called SARAC (Static and Automatic Register Allocation Checking) that includes mapping generation and data flow analysis. The technique *implicitly* and *efficiently* gathers information about the

```
SARAC(input,output) {
Map map = mapGen(input,output); // Step 1: mapping generation
Dataflow sets = defAnalysis(map,output); //Step 2: dataflow analysis
errAnalysis(output,map,sets); //Step 2: check the allocation
}
```

Fig. 2. SARAC steps

du-pairs and du-sequences to ensure that the du-pairs in the allocator's input code match the du-pairs recovered from the du-sequences in the allocator's output code. As most register allocators operate at the procedural level, SARAC uses the code generated for a procedure. The technique is also applicable to local register allocation and can be extended to interprocedural register allocation [28].

The three steps of SARAC are shown in Figure 2. First, mapping information is generated using the allocator's input and output. Then, iterative forward data flow analysis, called defAnalysis, is performed on the output using mapping information. This analysis collects three types of data flow sets needed to check the correctness of the output and report error locations and types. Finally, a linear scan, called errAnalysis, exposes def-use violations.

3.1 Step 1: Mapping Generation (mapGen)

SARAC needs to know which value (of the original operand) in the input is actually defined/used by the output. Therefore, a mapping or association is determined that relates an operand in the output to its corresponding operand in the input. Intuitively, a location (register or memory) in the output is mapped to the corresponding value(variable or temporary) in the input. A mapping can also relate constants in the

```
mapGen(input,output) {
Map map := ∅;
// get blocks in same order for traversal
Blocks Bin[] := canonicalOrder(input);
Blocks Bout[] := canonicalOrder(output);
Block Bi := Bin.getNextElement();
Block Bo := Bout.getNextElement();
while (Bi≠null) {
  // create maps for stmts in input and output
  foreach Statement Si∈Bi {
    Statement So := find(Si, Bo);
    if (So≠null)
      // map all (*) opers in So to opers in Si
      map := map∪{So.*→Si.*};
  }
  Bi := Bin.getNextElement();
  Bo := Bout.getNextElement();
}
return map;
}
```

Fig. 3. Pseudocode for mapping generation

output and input. Mappings are generated for all necessary statements, including statements in the function prologue and epilogue. For load, store or register copy statements injected by the allocator, there is no corresponding statement in the input. Thus, no mapping is generated for these statements. For each of the other statements in the output code, there is a corresponding statement in the input.

As shown in Figure 3, mapGen generates mappings based on the allocator's input and output, where the allocator is viewed as a black box. First, the basic blocks in the input and output code are put in a canonical order. Next, the input blocks are traversed. For each input statement, the corresponding output statement (if present) is found in a basic block by find. Finally, the operands in the output statement are mapped to operands in the input statement. In the figure, the notation "*" means "any" (e.g., all operands). Although a mapping includes information about statement and operand number, an abbreviation (e.g., *location→value*) is used in the paper. For example, the output code in Figure 1 has statement r[2]=0 corresponding to the input statement c=0. Thus, the mappings are r[2]→c and 0→0.

3.2 Step 2: Data Flow Analysis (defAnalysis)

To check if the register allocation is correct and to determine error locations and types, defAnalysis needs to gather information about the behavior of the register allocator using the output code and the mappings. defAnalysis gathers three types of information at all points in the program: (1) the values that are currently held in locations (registers and memory), (2) the stale values and (3) the evicted values. Note if we only wanted to know if a register allocation is correct, we would not need the eviction information. We develop a data flow algorithm to gather the information by using the mappings to get the values in the input code associated with locations in the output code. For example, when r[2]=1 at output code point 4 in Figure 1 is processed, the original destination operand d is retrieved from the mappings. This gives three pieces of information. First, the current value of d is defined in r[2]. Second, the value c in r[2] is evicted. Finally, any previous values of d in other locations become stale.

These three types of information are collected in three data flow sets — the Location set (L), Stale set (ST) and Eviction set (E). Each set consists of triples $<l, v, c>$, where l is a location (register or memory) from the output code, v is a value (name) from the input code or another location from which the value can be found, and c is a vector consisting of a series of code points where the relationship between l and v occurred. Thus, the semantics of $<l, v, c>$ for L, ST and E are defined as follows.

- L records the fact that location l holds v. The vector c records the du-sequence for v (as a series of code points involved in the sequence).
- ST records that location l holds a stale v due to a series of code points in c, where a value has been killed because of a new defintion at the start of that series.
- E records that v has been evicted from location l at a statement in c. For E, c is always a vector with a single element.

3.2.1 Data Flow Equations

A statement S in the output code can either be a statement passed from the input with registers assigned or a copy statement introduced by the register allocator. We use O to represent original statements and l_d to represent the destination of the statement in the output code. We use C to represent copy statements. A copy statement is either a load, store or register copy inserted by the allocator. Thus, S has the formats:

$$O: l_d = exp \; \{original \; statement\} \quad \text{or} \quad C: l_d = l_s \; \{copy \; statement\}$$

We now describe each set's Gen, Kill, IN and OUT. In a basic block, each set's IN for a statement is its OUT from the immediately preceding statement. The merge points are described separately for each set. The three sets are computed in the same phase.

Our data flow equations extend the traditional data set operations mostly because of the third element of the triple, c, which is an *ordered* set. The elements of c are a set of code points that are used to compute the du-sequence as data flow proceeds. We redefine $\cap$ and $-$ to handle the set c. We also define other operators to propagate the value along du-sequences and to produce a new triple.

Definition of $\cap$:

$$\langle l, v, c\rangle \cap \langle l', v', c'\rangle = \begin{cases} \{\langle l, v, c\rangle, \langle l', v', c'\rangle\} & if \; l==l' \wedge v==v' \wedge c \neq c' \\ \langle l, v, c\rangle & if \; l==l' \wedge v==v' \wedge c==c' \\ \varnothing & otherwise \end{cases}$$

Definition of $-$:

$$\langle l, v, c\rangle - \langle l', v', c'\rangle = \begin{cases} \varnothing & if \; l==l' \wedge v==v' \\ \langle l, v, c\rangle & otherwise \end{cases}$$

These two operators are similar to the normal set operators on the first two elements in the triple. The third element c is handled in a special way.

Computing the Location Set (L)

$$\text{L\_gen[S]} = \begin{cases} \langle l_d, v, \langle S\rangle\rangle & if \; S \in O \wedge l_d \rightarrow v \\ \langle l_d, l_s, \langle S\rangle\rangle & if \; S \in C \end{cases}$$

There are two cases for *L_gen[S]*. The first case occurs when a statement S in O defines a new value in l_d. The location l_d must be mapped to a value v. Therefore, a triple "$<l_d, v, <S>>$" is generated. For example, when $r[2]=1$ at code point 4 in Figure 1 is processed, a triple "$<r[2], d, <4>>$" is generated. The second case happens to a statement S in C, which does not define a new value but copies a value. The value to copy is in l_s. "$<l_d, l_s, <S>>$" is generated to indicate that the value will be found at l_s when applying the value propagation. For example, when $M[d]=r[2]$ at code point 5 in Figure 1 is processed, a triple "$<M[d], r[2], <5>>$" is generated to show that the value in $M[d]$ can be found from $r[2]$.

L_kill[S] considers that the execution of S destroys the value in l_d:

$$\text{L\_kill[S]} = \langle l_d, *, *\rangle$$

This Kill computes the triple indicating any value held in the destination of S.

For the value propagation (i.e., collapsing C statements in a du-sequence), the operator $\oplus$ is defined.

Definition of $\oplus$:

$$\langle l', v', \langle S_1, ..., S_i \rangle \rangle \oplus \langle l, v, \langle S \rangle \rangle = \begin{cases} \langle l, v, \langle S \rangle \rangle & \textit{if } S \in O \\ \langle l, v', \langle S_1, ..., S_i, S \rangle \rangle & \textit{if } S \in C \wedge l' == v \\ \varnothing & \textit{otherwise} \end{cases}$$

This operator just returns the right hand side triple if S is in O. If S is in C, then there are two cases. First, the value propagation along a du-sequence is performed if l' is v and vector $<S_1, ..., S_i>$ appended with S is the third element of the result triple. Second, the value of null is returned if l' is not v.

Given the Gen, Kill and IN sets, $L\_out[S]$ is computed as:

$$L\_out[S] = (L\_in[S] \oplus L\_gen[S]) \cup (L\_in[S] - L\_kill[S])$$

$L\_out[S]$ has all the locations (registers and memory) that hold a value, regardless of whether it is current or stale. When $M[d]=r[2]$ at code point 5 in Figure 1 is processed, $L\_in[5]$ has "$<r[2], d, <4>>$" and $L\_gen[5]$ consists of "$<M[d], r[2], <5>>$". The triple "$<M[d], d, <4, 5>>$" is computed from "$L\_in[5] \oplus L\_gen[5]$". This triple shows that $M[d]$ holds value d after code point 5, which was computed at code point 4 and propagated at code point 5.

At the merge point to block B, L_in is:

$$L\_in[B] = \cap L\_out[Predecessors(B)]$$

L_in is computed by $\cap$ on L_outs of all predecessors to B. A correct register allocation puts the same value in the same location along any preceding path for a later use of that value from that location. Therefore, $\cap$ removes the "inconsistent triples" which have different values in the same location.

Computing the Stale Set (ST)

$$ST\_gen[S] = L\_gen[S]$$

$ST\_gen[S]$ is the same as $L\_gen[S]$ though its two cases have different semantics. First, when S in O defines a new v is into l_d (where $l_d \rightarrow v$), every previous v held in some other locations (not l_d) becomes stale. Which locations holding v will be discovered from $L\_in[S]$ later on. Second, S in C is considered. $ST\_gen[S]$ is computed using a place holder l_s (i.e., the source of S) to represent the actual value. If l_s holds a stale value, l_d also holds a stale value after the value propagation.

$ST\_kill[S]$ is computed similar to $L\_kill[S]$:

$$ST\_kill[S] = \langle l_d, *, * \rangle$$

When a stale value in l_d is destroyed by S, this fact must be reflected in $ST\_kill[S]$.

The operator $\bullet$ is defined for finding stale values.

Definition of ($\square$

r

The first case applies to S in O. Any other location l' (i.e., l'(l) that holds v' (i.e., v' = =v) is discovered and a new triple "<l', v, <S>>" is produced. The second case applies to S in C and the right hand side triple is simply returned. The last case yields null.

ST_out[S] is computed as:

r

For S in O, "L_in[S] (ST_gen[S]" computes the triples where v in any location other than l_d becomes stale because S defines new v in l_d. For example, when r[2]=r[2]+1 at code point 11 in Figure 1 is processed, ST_gen[11] consists of "<r[2], c, <11>>". The triple "<M[c], c, <2,3>>" is retrieved from L_in[11]. "L_in[11] • ST_gen[11]" produces "<M[c], c, <11>>". For S in C, "<l_d, l_s, <S>>" is computed from • operation and "ST_in[S] $\oplus$ (L_in[S] • ST_gen[S])" does the stale value propagation. For example, "ST_in[10] $\oplus$ (L_in[10] • ST_gen[10])" produces "<r[2], c, <11,10>>", which shows that the previous c became stale at code point 11 and propagated to r[2] at code point 10 along the loop back edge.

At the merge point to block B, ST_in is:

$$ST\_in[B] = \cup ST\_out[Predecessors(B)]$$

ST_in is computed by the union on *ST_outs* of all predecessors to B. The union is done because if the value is stale along any path to the block, it is possible that the stale value might be used in the current (or later) block. Hence, the union operation preserves the fact that the value is stale along some path.

Computing the Eviction Set (E)

The equations for E are closely related to the ones for L.

$$E\_gen[S] = \langle l_d, *, \langle S \rangle \rangle, \quad E\_kill[S]= L\_gen[S]$$

E_gen[S] records that any value in l_d will be evicted because of S. But which value is actually evicted must be discovered from *L_in[S]*. *E_kill[S]* is the same as *L_gen[S]*.

To obtain the value currently held in a location (e.g., l_d) and then indicate that it is evicted from there, the operator $\Diamond$ is defined and its semantics is self-explanatory.

Definition of $\Diamond$:

$$\langle l', v', * \rangle \Diamond \langle l, *, \langle S \rangle \rangle = \begin{cases} \langle l', v', \langle S \rangle \rangle & \textit{if } l'==l \\ \varnothing & \text{otherwise} \end{cases}$$

E_out[S] is computed as:

$$E\_out[S] = (E\_in[S] \cup (L\_in[S] \Diamond E\_gen[S])) - (L\_in[S] \oplus E\_kill[S])$$

The operator $\Diamond$ discovers the value evicted by S from l_d with the computation "L_in[S] $\Diamond$ E_gen[S]". "L_in[S] $\oplus$ E_kill[S]" gives the triples that a value is put into l_d by S.

At the merge point to block *B*, *E_in* is computed as:

$$E\_in[B] = \cup\, E\_out[Predecessors(B)]$$

E_in[B] holds any value's history of being most recently evicted from any location along all preceding paths.

3.3 Step 3: Checking and Reporting (errAnalysis)

Once L, ST and E are collected, they are used to check the output code. The error analysis step ensures that the du-pairs from the input are preserved in the output. The algorithm for identifying and reporting errors is shown in errAnalysis in Figure 4.

```
errAnalysis(output,map,sets) {
  L:=sets.L; ST:=sets.ST; E:=sets.E;
  foreach Block B∈output {
    if (B≠Binitial)
      setFinalization(B,map,L,ST,E);
    foreach Statement S∈B {
      typeCheck(S,map);
      constraintCheck(S,map);
      if (S∈O)
        useCheck(S,map,L,ST,E);
    }
  }
}

setFinalization(B,map,L,ST,E) {
  L_union := ∪ L_out[Predecessors(B)];
  L_inconsistent := {<l,v,<B>> |
      ∀<l,v,*>∈ (L_unionL_in[B])};
  ST_in[B] := ST_in[B]L_inconsistent;
  E_in[B] := E_in[B}∪L_inconsistent;
  computeLocalFlow(B,map,L,ST,E);
}
```

```
useCheck(S,map,L,ST,E) {
  foreach l∈uses(S) {
    v := getMap(S,l,map);
    if (<l,v,*>∈L_in[S]) {
      if (<l,v,c>∈ST_in[S]) {
        ε := "S uses stale value,
                 c made v in l stale";
      }else ε := null;
    }elsif (<l',v,c>∈L_in[S])
    {
      ε := "S uses wrong operand,
               but c defined v in l'";
    }else {
      ∀<l",v,c>∈E_in[S];
      ε := "S uses evicted value,
               c evicted v from l"";
    }
  }
}
```

Fig. 4. Pseudocode for checking algorithm

For non-initial blocks, a finalization step is performed on the data flow sets by setFinalization. The finalization is actually done in defAnalysis, but we show it here for clarity. It computes *L_inconsistent* – the "inconsistent triples" where the values in the same location are different for different paths. These triples are not computed into *L_in* because a correct register allocation should put the same value into the same location for any path. To report causes rather than just check errors, we assume that the inconsistent values (in the same location) are "evicted" at the merge. Therefore, *L_inconsistent* is added to *E_in* and removed from *ST_in*. Finally, local data flow sets are updated by the equations discussed in Section 3.2.1.

The next step in errAnalysis iterates over all the statements. First, the operands of the output are verified that they have the correct types as specified by the input.

Second, it verifies that architectural constraints are satisfied with `constraintCheck`, which depends on the target architecture (not shown for brevity). Finally, `useCheck` applies to O statements (C statements are implicitly checked because of the value propagation performed in `defAnalysis`).

`useCheck` checks that all uses in every O statement are correct in terms of the input's data flow. It reports the error location and type for any data flow violation. For each use l (i.e., location), it first consults the mappings to determine which value it should use. When l actually holds v, which is shown as a triple "<l, v, *>" in L_in, it further checks if v in l is stale. Next, it checks if v is in other locations. If this is true, it implies that the wrong operand might be used. Otherwise, an eviction error must have occurred. The history of v being most recently evicted from any location l'' is reported.

3.4 Extensions

Two important extensions to a register allocator are coalescing and rematerialization [4, 5, 6, 11]. This section describes how SARAC can support these extensions. It shows how sub-register class allocation and address expressions are incorporated.

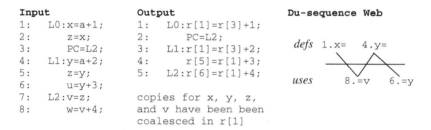

Input	Output	Du-sequence Web
1: L0:x=a+1;	1: L0:r[1]=r[3]+1;	
2: z=x;	2: PC=L2;	
3: PC=L2;	3: L1:r[1]=r[3]+2;	*defs* 1.x= 4.y=
4: L1:y=a+2;	4: r[5]=r[1]+3;	
5: z=y;	5: L2:r[6]=r[1]+4;	
6: u=y+3;		*uses* 8.=v 6.=y
7: L2:v=z;	copies for x, y, z,	
8: w=v+4;	and v have been been	
	coalesced in r[1]	

Fig. 5. Register coalescing example and its du-sequence web

Register Coalescing. Register coalescing removes unnecessary copies from the input code. As shown in Figure 5, the copies at input code points 2, 5, and 7 for z are removed in the output. Thus, r[1] can hold x, y, z or v; a location can correspond to multiple values. The analyses described earlier rely on a one-to-one mapping between locations and values and consequently cannot directly handle coalescing.

To support coalescing, SARAC needs to handle the effect of removing copies. SARAC infers coalescing by examining the du-sequences in the *input code* and updating the mappings to capture all possibly coalesced values. The idea is to use a "*du-sequence web*" to capture the relationship between a definition that begins a du-sequence and a use that ends the sequence. We define a *du-sequence web* as a set of du-sequences sharing a start or end, where the copy statements in each du-sequence are collapsed. There may be many independent webs for the input code, each corresponding to a set of related du-sequences. The most right column of Figure 5 shows a web for the input code. In this web, the du-sequence (1.x=, 2.z=x, 7.v=z, 8.=v) is represented by the edge between 1.x= and 8.=v. The web also captures the relationships among the du-sequences (4.y=, 5.z=y, 7.v=z, 8.=v) and (4.y=, 6.=y).

The webs are used to update the mappings. Once the webs are constructed, each web is assigned a unique name, say n. Then, the name in the mappings for the web's definitions and uses are changed to n. In the example, r[1]→x (where, r[1] is the destination of r[1]=r[3]+1) is changed to r[1]→n. Any input code copy that is actually not coalesced is also considered as C statement besides the copies injected by the register allocator. Thus, the mappings for any copy statement passed from the input to output are removed. With the updated mappings, defAnalysis and errAnalysis are performed normally. In defAnalysis, the value n is propagated along the output du-sequence. In errAnalysis, only the uses in a du-sequence web are analyzed.

Rematerialization. Rematerialization improves spill code by recomputing values rather than reloading them from memory. It usually considers constant expressions in the code, such as integer constants in load-immediate statements and address offsets.

To handle rematerialization, the mappings are extended to bind constants to values and locations. The idea is to bind constants in the input and output code to values and locations in the mappings. The bindings are created by scanning the output code to find uses of constant expressions (i.e., the use is reachable by a constant definition, like a load-immediate). A similar step is performed to bind constants to values in the input code. errAnalysis compares a location that is bound to a constant to the corresponding value's binding. If the constants match, then the output code is correct.

Sub-register Class Allocation. Some architectures allow different registers to overlap. For instance, the IA-32 has the AH and AL registers, which overlap a part of the AX register. Such overlapping registers are a "register alias set" [30] and an allocator has to take into account the overlap when assigning registers. A write to a register will destroy the value in any member of its alias set.

To handle sub-register class allocation, only modest modifications are needed to SARAC's data flow equations at several points. The equations have to be changed to take into account the effect on the full register alias set. For example, when $L\_kill[S]$ is computed, the register alias set of l_d is considered, rather than just l_d.

Address Generation. Some allocators determine an effective address (rather than a variable or temporary name) for spilling a value. In this case, this address is typically computed as an offset from the stack pointer. In SARAC, a "memory location" is the effective address used in a store/load. Assuming that the allocator makes only the edits described earlier, there can be no intervening manipulation of the stack pointer between a store and an associated load. That is, the allowable edits do not permit the insertion of statements that change the stack pointer (except in the function prologue and epilogue). Thus, the effective addresses can be easily determined. When the allocator directly manipulates the stack pointer, SARAC determines an address by evaluating the operations done to the stack pointer and offset.

4 Experiments

We implemented SARAC as a tool (*ra-analyzer*) for SUIF's backend code optimizer (MachSUIF, version 2.02.07.15), on the Intel IA-32 [29]. A global graph coloring register allocator [11] was implemented as a separate pass in MachSUIF. *ra-analyzer* is run after register allocation. Two experiments were conducted. First, faults were injected into the allocator's output to explore how the tool might be used to find bugs. Second, the performance and memory overhead of the tool were measured.

For the experiments, we used benchmarks in SPECint2K [8], MediaBench [15] and MiBench [19] that are compilable by base SUIF. The procedures in the benchmarks span a wide range of code sizes and complexities. All experiments were run on a RedHat Linux computer with a 2.4 GHz Pentium 4 and 1 GB RAM.

4.1 Fault Injection

We checked if MachSUIF's allocator causes errors in the benchmarks and found no errors for two possible reasons. First, MachSUIF's allocator is correct. Second, a very limited number of test suites (many benchmarks cannot be compiled by SUIF) may not expose all latent bugs. Thus, we believe that *ra-analyzer* is particularly useful in a regression testing environment or during the development of a compiler.

To illustrate how *ra-analyzer* might be used by compiler engineers, we injected bugs into the output of MachSUIF's allocator. We then used *ra-analyzer* to find the bugs. The bugs were automatically injected by a "fault injector". The fault injector made incorrect edits to the output code, including incorrect register assignment, wrong store/load, missing store/load. For each edit type, the fault injector randomly selected a basic block to change. An appropriate statement was found to modify, based on the edit type. If an appropriate statement could not be located, the edit was abandoned and a new one was tried. The injector attempted to make 5 changes for each edit type, but it sometimes made fewer edits when it could not find a candidate. Each function in every benchmark had 0 to 25 incorrect edits.

As an example, the fault injector changed one register operand to a different register in the FFT benchmark. In this case, the statement movl $1,%ecx was changed to movl $1,%ebx. The register %ecx holds the virtual register $vr12. When *ra-analyzer* checked the code, it reported the error message:

```
addl %ecx,%eax
//Wrong operand - %ecx,"movl $1,%ebx" defined $vr12 in %ebx
```

From the error message, compiler engineers can identify what went wrong. For example, consistently using the wrong register might suggest that liveness analysis or the interference graph construction has a problem. With the information from *ra-analyzer*, compiler engineers can use a debugger to step through the allocator and find bugs.

In the fault injection experiments, 65 to 10,749 total incorrect edits were made to the benchmarks. The simpler programs (e.g., *FFT*) had the fewest edits, while the more complex ones (e.g., *255.vortex*) had the most. Of the total edits, there were 22–3,198 incorrect register assignment edits, 29–5,104 wrong store/load edits, and 7–2,447 missing store/load edits. The edits made covered the possible changes to the code described in Section 2.2. The edits lead to a total of 108–18,103 errors. There were 18–2,648 stale errors, 49–7,552 wrong operand errors and 35–7,903 eviction errors. When *ra-analyzer* was applied on the code, it correctly caught the errors without generating any false positives or negatives, and reported their locations and types.

4.2 Performance and Memory Overhead

Table 1 shows the performance and memory overhead of *ra-analyzer* for the benchmarks. The major column "# Statements" describes benchmark size. The secondary column "Tot" is the total number of intermediate code statements in a benchmark, "Procs" is the number of procedures, and "Avg" is the average number of statements.

Table 1. Memory and performance overhead

Benchmarks	# Statements			Memory Overhead			Performance Overhead				
	Tot	Procs	Avg	Avg	Max	Min	Analyzer	RA	RA%	MachSuif	Tot%
164.gzip	17,396	106	164	44,338	553,736	200	4.06	3.29	123%	53.30	8%
175.vpr	56,693	300	189	44,481	1,971,892	100	13.02	10.95	119%	169.55	8%
181.mcf	4,844	26	186	40,473	230,884	1,044	1.13	0.95	120%	28.14	4%
197.parser	40,677	324	126	43,675	2,147,404	100	11.64	7.15	163%	112.89	10%
255.vortex	203,810	923	221	80,572	10,027,076	100	53.29	41.78	128%	599.66	9%
256.bzip2	10,680	74	144	48,238	988,144	200	3.21	2.30	139%	32.09	10%
300.twolf	99,780	191	522	454,336	9,881,344	196	87.95	25.29	348%	307.81	29%
FFT	953	7	136	22,057	77,244	1,932	0.23	0.19	122%	6.65	3%
bitcount	816	15	54	7,177	21,000	1,328	0.10	0.13	81%	12.19	1%
dijkstra	434	6	72	10,934	32,792	200	0.07	0.06	122%	1.95	3%
sha	824	8	103	14,381	56,184	5,044	0.15	0.21	71%	4.19	4%
stringsearch	974	10	97	17,967	31,176	552	0.17	0.17	99%	10.25	2%
jpeg	82,923	506	164	38,805	925,564	100	20.90	17.12	122%	279.54	7%
adpcm	710	5	142	27,743	57,408	9,900	0.12	0.13	92%	5.70	2%
epic	11,452	49	234	88,801	1,935,300	956	6.22	4.46	139%	41.49	15%
g721	3,942	28	141	32,769	425,360	3,552	0.79	0.80	98%	13.48	6%
mpeg2	45,995	206	223	67,238	1,919,996	200	13.76	10.26	134%	131.44	10%

In Table 1, the major column "Memory Overhead" gives statistics about the memory overhead. The average (Avg), maximum (Max) and minimum (Min) data in bytes are presented for procedures in each benchmark. As expected, MiBench has the lowest memory requirements. These programs have small procedures (e.g., *bitcount* has an average of 54 statements in a procedure), and as a result, the size of the data flow sets tends to be small. Other programs, namely *255.vortex* and *300.twolf*, have larger memory requirements. In *255.vortex*, Draw701() needs 10 MB because of its large number of intermediate code statements (5,228). However, *255.vortex*'s average memory requirement is consistent with the other benchmarks because it has only a few large procedures and many smaller ones. On the other hand, *300.twolf* has a relatively small number of procedures that are quite large and complex (varying from 3 to 4,462 intermediate statements). As a result, its average memory consumption is the largest among all programs. In this benchmark, uclosepns() has the maximum memory overhead (9.8 MB) because it has a large number of statements (4,001) and basic blocks (417). Although it doesn't have the most statements in *300.twolf*, uclosepns() has the most basic blocks and as a result, it incurs the most memory overhead. The average memory overhead is 85 KB for all benchmarks. This overhead is minimal.

We also investigated how the data flow sets (L, ST, and E) and the mappings contribute to total memory overhead. Because ST is a subset of L (see the data flow equations in Section 3.2), *ra-analyzer* records stale values only in ST for efficiency (i.e., L does not record stale values, which are already in ST). Across all benchmarks, L has the least memory consumption and ST has the most. L tends to be small (e.g., for `uclosepns()`, it is 375KB) because of the relatively small number of locations (operands) that it records. ST, on the other hand, tracks stale values. Thus, it is generally quite large (e.g., in `uclosepns()`, it is 6.26 MB). E is typically moderate in size; in `uclosepns()`, it is 3.2 MB. The mappings also consume memory, which is proportional to the number of intermediate statements and the number of operands. For the benchmarks, the mappings take 88 bytes to 450 KB (average 19 KB).

In Table 1, the major column "Performance Overhead" gives *ra-analyzer*'s run-time performance. The column "Analyzer" is the total run-time in seconds for *ra-analyzer* and the column "RA" is for MachSUIF's allocator. The run-times are totals and account for compilation of all procedures in a benchmark. The column "RA%" is the percentage overhead of *ra-analyzer* over the allocator, which varies from 71% to 348% (average 96%). We expect that the run-time of *ra-analyzer* should be about the same as the run-time for the register allocator since both do somewhat similar analysis steps. In all benchmarks, except *300.twolf* and *197.parser*, the overhead follows this expectation, ranging from 71% to 139%. In *300.twolf* the overhead is 348% and in *197.parser* the overhead is 163%. This higher overhead is due to the use of iterative data flow analysis in *ra-analyzer*. In these two benchmarks, there is at least one complicated procedure where the data flow sets take a while to converge because of multiple, deep loop nests. For example, in *300.twolf*, the procedure `uclosepns()` takes the most time (10.96 Sec). It has 15 loop nests (with a maximum nest depth of 3), and takes up to 5 iterations for the data flow sets to converge.

The last two columns compare *ra-analyzer*'s performance to overall compile-time. The column labeled "MachSuif" is the run-time of the MachSUIF compiler without *ra-analyzer*. The column "Tot%" is the total percentage increase in compile-time when *ra-analyzer* is run. On most benchmarks, *ra-analyzer*'s overhead is less than 10%. In *300.twolf*, the overhead is 29%. Despite this one benchmark, the tool works well: The average overhead relative to total compile-time is 8%. This small cost is worth the benefit of ensuring that the register allocation is correct.

5   Related Work

Several researchers have focused on proving the correctness of compiler optimization algorithms. Lacey et al. [14] used temporal logic to express data flow analysis and prove optimization correctness via reasoning. They did not consider register allocation. Naik and Palsberg [20] presented a proof for the correctness of an ILP register allocation algorithm. Ohori et al. [23] proposed a framework to construct and prove register allocation algorithms. Our work differs in that it addresses the implementation difficulties of register allocation, rather than algorithm correctness. Indeed, our work is complementary to the correctness proof of allocation algorithms.

Lerner et al. [16, 17] proved the soundness of several optimization implementations. Their approach requires the compiler engineer to use a domain-specific language to implement optimizations to automate reasoning about correctness. The verification of the register allocator's implementation is not presented.

Similar to our work, some research efforts suggest automatically checking semantic equivalence between the input and output code [18, 21, 22, 25, 27]. However, the range of optimizations that can be handled in these approaches is typically limited. Among these efforts, only McNerney et al. [18] and Necula et al. [21] have examined how to check the output of the register allocator. The abstract interpretation approach in [18] applies only to a restricted domain of programs and did not present evaluation data. Necula et al. [21] utilize symbolic evaluation in their translation validation infrastructure. However, this approach reports false alarms and has significant compile-time overhead. By focusing on allocation, SARAC can exploit properties of the allocation process (e.g., the property that def-use pairs are preserved in the output). As a result, our technique is accurate and fast. It also reports error casual information.

6   Conclusion and Future Work

This paper describes SARAC, a new approach to catch and identify bugs in register allocation. The approach statically checks that the input def-use pairs are maintained in the output code, given that the register allocator conducts limited edits. It is accurate and fast. The approach can be extended to handle register coalescing, rematerialization and sub-register class allocation. A prototype tool (*ra-analyzer*) shows that our approach has minimal compile-time and memory overhead.

A goal for our future work is to make *ra-analyzer* standalone so that it can be used with other compilers and machine architectures. To achieve this goal, SARAC will need to support more register allocators and register file structures, particularly ones that allow predication or have irregular register types. We also plan to more fully support type and architectural constraint checking. This support is important because the types and architectural constraints can be a common error source in a register allocator. Another issue is how to interface the tool to different compilers and intermediate representations. A final issue in making SARAC standalone is to develop a way to describe machine dependent information about registers to the tool.

References

[1] M. E. Benitez and J. W. Davidson. A portable global optimizer and linker. *ACM SIGPLAN Conf. on Programming Language Design and Implementation*, June 1988.

[2] D. Bernstein, D. Q. Goldin et al. Spill code minimization techniques for optimizing compilers. *ACM SIGPLAN Conf. on Programming Language Design and Implementation*, June 1989.

[3] D. G. Bradlee, S. J. Eggers, and R. R. Henry. Integrating register allocation and instruction scheduling for RISCs. *4th Int'l. Conf. on Architectural Support for Programming Languages and Operating Systems*, April 1991.

[4] P. Briggs, K. D. Cooper and L. Torczon. Improvements to graph coloring register allocation. *ACM Trans. on Programming Languages and Systems*, 3(16): 428-455, May 1994.

[5] P. Briggs, K. D. Cooper and L. Torczon. Rematerialization. *ACM SIGPLAN Conf. on Programming Language Design and Implementation*, June 1992.

[6] G. J. Chaitin. Register allocation & spilling via graph coloring. *Symp. on Compiler Construction*, June 1982.

[7] F. C. Chow and J. L. Hennessy. The priority-based register allocation coloring approach. *ACM Trans. on Programming Languages and Systems*, 4(12):501-536, October 1990.

[8] CPU2000 benchmark. Standard Performance Evaluation Corporation (SPEC), URL: http://www.spec.org.

[9] J. W. Davidson and C. W. Fraser. Register allocation and exhaustive peephole optimization. *Software --- Practice and Experience*, 14 (9): 857-865, September 1984.

[10] GCC. URL: http://gcc.gnu.org/.

[11] L. George and A. W. Appel. Iterated register coalescing. *ACM Trans. on Programming Languages and Systems*, 3(18): 300-324, May 1996.

[12] R. Gupta, M. L. Soffa and T. Steele. Register allocation via clique separators. *ACM SIGPLAN Conf. on Programming Language Design and Implementation*, July 1989.

[13] C. S. Jaramillo, R. Gupta and M. L. Soffa. Verifying optimizers through comparison checking. *Int'l. Workshop on Compiler Optimization Meets Compiler Verification*, April 2002.

[14] D. Lacey, N. D. Jones, E. V. Wyk and C. C. Frederiksen. Proving correctness of compiler optimizations by temporal logic. *Symp. on Principles of Programming Languages*, January 2002.

[15] C. Lee, M. Potkonjak and W. H. Mangione-Smith. MediaBench: a tool for evaluating and synthesizing multimedia and communicatons systems. *ACM/IEEE Int'l. Symp. on Microarchitecture*, 1997.

[16] S. Lerner, T. Millstein and C. Chambers. Automatically proving the correctness of compiler optimizations. *ACM SIGPLAN Conf. on Programming Language Design and Implementation*, June 2003.

[17] S. Lerner, T. Millstein, E. Rice and C. Chambers. Automated soundness proofs for dataflow analyses and transformations via local rules. *Symp. on Principles of Programming Languages*, 2005.

[18] T. M. McNerney. Verifying the correctness of compiler transformations on basic blocks using abstract interpretation. *ACM/SIGPLAN Workshop Partial Evaluation and Semantics-Based Program Manipulation*, 1991.

[19] MiBench. University of Michigan, URL: http://www.eecs.umich.edu/mibench/.

[20] M. Naik and J. Palsberg. Correctness of ILP-based register allocation. Unpublished manuscript. URL: http://theory.stanford.edu/~mhn/pubs/regalloc.pdf.

[21] G. C. Necula. Translation validation for an optimizing compiler. *ACM SIGPLAN Conf. on Programming Language Design and Implementation*, June 2000.

[22] G. C. Necula and P. Lee. The design and implementation of a certifying compiler. *ACM SIGPLAN Conf. on Programming Language Design and Implementation*, June 1998.

[23] A. Ohori. Register allocation by proof transformation. *12th European Symp. on Programming*, April 2003.

[24] S. S. Pinter. Register allocation with instruction scheduling: a new approach. *ACM SIGPLAN Conf. on Programming Language Design and Implementation*, June 1993.

[25] A. Pnueli, M. Siegel and F. Singerman. Translation validation. *4th Tools and Algorithms for Construction and Analysis of Systems*, April 1998.

[26] M. Poletto and V. Sarkar. Linear scan register allocation. *ACM Trans. on Programming Languages and Systems*, 5(21): 895–913, September 1999.

[27] M. C. Rinard. Credible compilation. Technical Report MIT-LCS-TR-776, MIT, March 1999.

[28] V. Santhanam and D. Odnert. Register allocation across procedure and module boundaries. *ACM SIGPLAN Conf. on Programming Language Design and Implementation*, June 1990.

[29] M. D. Smith and G. Holloway. Machine SUIF. URL: http://www.eecs.harvard.edu/hube/ research/machsuif.html.

[30] M. D. Smith, N. Ramsey and G. Holloway. A generalized algorithm for graph-coloring register allocation. *ACM SIGPLAN Conf. on Programming Language Design and Implementation*, June 2004.

Appendices

Mapping Grammar. To define the notation for a mapping, we give a short grammar:

<mapping> := operandposn: <out> → <in>
<out> := codept . location | codept . #constant
<in> := codept . value | codept . #constant
where,
operandposn – operand number in a statement
codept – a statement number in the input or output code
location – a register or memory location
value – a temporary or variable

For example, consider the code from Figure 1. The statement r[2]=0 at output code point 2 corresponds to c=0 at input code point 1; therefore, the mapping for the first operand r[2] at code point 2 is: 1:2.r[2]→1.c, where r[2] is a *location* (memory or register) and c is a *value* (temporary or variable). Similarly, there is a mapping 2:6.#0→3.#0 to give the correspondence between the constants at output code point 6 and input code point 3. The mappings generated for the incorrect output code by mapGen in Figure 3 are:

```
1:2.r[2]→1.c    2:2.#0→1.#0
1:4.r[2]→2.d    2:4.#1→2.#1
1:6.r[1]→3.n    2:6.#0→3.#0     3:6.L3→3.L3
1:8.r[2]→4.t    2:8.r[1]→4.n    3:8.r[1]→4.d
1:9.r[2]→5.t    2:9.#0→5.#0     3:9.L2→5.L2
1:11.r[2]→6.c   2:11.r[2]→6.c   3:11.#1→6.#1
1:14.r[2]→7.d   2:14.r[2]→7.d   3:14.#1→7.#1
1:16.r[2]→8.t   2:16.r[2]→8.d   3:16.r[1]→8.n
1:17.r[2]→9.t   2:17.#1→9.#1    3:17.L1→9.L1
```

The mapping in bold is for error 1 in the incorrect output (code point 8).

Certificate Translation for Optimizing Compilers*

(Extended Abstract)

Gilles Barthe, Benjamin Grégoire, César Kunz, and Tamara Rezk

INRIA Sophia-Antipolis, Project EVEREST
{Gilles.Barthe, Benjamin.Gregoire, Cesar.Kunz,
Tamara.Rezk}@sophia.inria.fr

Abstract. Certifying compilation provides a means to ensure that un-trusted mobile code satisfies its functional specification. A certifying compiler generates code as well as a machine-checkable "certificate", i.e. a formal proof that establishes adherence of the code to specified properties. While certificates for safety properties can be built fully automatically, certificates for more expressive and complex properties often require the use of interactive code verification. We propose a technique to provide code consumers with the benefits of interactive source code verification. Our technique, certificate translation, extends program transformations by offering the means to turn certificates of functional correctness for programs in high-level languages into certificates for executable code. The article outlines the principles of certificate translation, using specifications written in first order logic. This translation is instantiated for standard compiler optimizations in the context of an intermediate RTL Language.

1 Introduction

Program verification environments provide a means to establish that programs meet their specifications, and are increasingly being used to validate safety-critical or security-critical software. Most often, such environments target high-level languages. However it is usually required to achieve correctness guarantees for compiled programs, especially in the context of mobile code—because code consumers may not have access to the source program or, if they do, may not trust the compiler. Yet there is currently no mechanism for bringing the benefits of interactive source code verification to code consumers. The objective of our work is precisely to propose such a mechanism, called *certificate translation*, which allows us to transfer evidence from source programs to compiled programs.

The starting point of our work is Proof Carrying Code (PCC) [9], which provides a means to establish trust in a mobile code infrastructure, by requiring that mobile code is sent along with a formal proof (a.k.a. certificate) showing its adherence to a property agreeable by the code consumer. While PCC does not

---

* This work is partially funded by the IST European Project Mobius.

K. Yi (Ed.): SAS 2006, LNCS 4134, pp. 301–317, 2006.

preclude generating certificates from interactive verification of source programs, the prominent approach to certificate generation is *certifying compilation* [11], which constructs automatically certificates for safety properties such as memory safety or type safety. Certifying compilation is by design restricted to a specific class of properties and programs—a deliberate choice of the authors [11] whose primary goal was to reduce the burden of verification on the code producer side. In contrast, certificate translation is by design very general and can be used to enforce arbitrary properties on arbitrary programs. Of course, generality comes at the cost of automation, so we must assume that programs have been annotated and proved interactively.

Thus the primary goal of certificate translation is to transform certificates of original programs into certificates of compiled programs. Given a compiler $[\![.]\!]$, a function $[\![.]\!]_{\mathrm{spec}}$ to transform specifications, and certificate checkers (expressed as a ternary relation "c is a certificate that P adheres to ϕ", written $c : P \models \phi$), a certificate translator is a function $[\![.]\!]_{\mathrm{cert}}$ such that for all programs p, policies ϕ, and certificates c,

$$c : p \models \phi \quad \Longrightarrow \quad [\![c]\!]_{\mathrm{cert}} : [\![p]\!] \models [\![\phi]\!]_{\mathrm{spec}}$$

The paper outlines the principles of certificate translation, and illustrates its mechanisms in the context of an an optimizing compiler for a Register Transfer Language (RTL). The compiler proceeds in a step by step fashion. For each optimization step, we build an appropriate certificate translator, and combine them to obtain a certificate translator for the complete compilation process.

Building a certificate translator for a non-optimizing compiler is relatively simple to construct since proof obligations are preserved (up to minor differences). Dealing with optimizations is more challenging. The major difficulty arises from the fact that certificate translators for optimizations often take as argument, in addition to the certificate of the original program, a certificate of the results of the analysis that justifies the optimization. In order to enable such an aggregation, one must therefore express the results of the analysis in the logic of the PCC architecture, and enhance the analyzer so that it produces a certificate of the analysis for each program. The overall architecture of a certificate translator is given in Figure 1.

Contents. Sections 2 introduces our programming language RTL and our PCC infrastructure. Section 3 provides a high-level overview of the principles and components that underline certificate translation, whereas Section 4 describe certificate translators for several standard optimizations (at RTL level). In section 5 we compare our work with recent related developments. We conclude in Section 6 with future work.

2   Setting

RTL Language. Our language RTL (Register Transfer Language) is a low-level, side-effect free, language with conditional jumps and function calls, extended with annotations drawn from a suitable assertion language. The choice of the

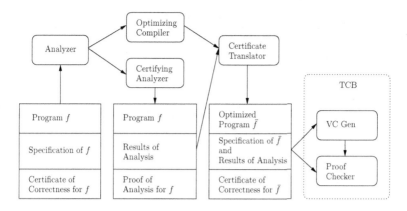

Fig. 1. Overall picture of certificate translation

$$
\begin{array}{lll}
\textbf{comparison} & \lhd & ::= <\mid\leq\mid=\mid\geq\mid> \\
\textbf{expressions} & e & ::= n\mid r\mid -e\mid e+e\mid e*e\mid\dots \\
\textbf{assertions} & \phi & ::= \top\mid e\lhd e\mid\neg\phi\mid\forall r,\ \phi\mid\dots \\
\textbf{comparisons} & \mathsf{cmp} & ::= r\lhd r\mid r\lhd n \\
\textbf{operators} & \mathsf{op} & ::= n\mid r\mid\mathsf{cmp}\mid n+r\mid\dots \\
\textbf{instr. desc.} & \mathsf{ins} & ::= r_d := \mathsf{op},\ L\mid r_d := f(\boldsymbol{r}),\ L\mid\mathsf{cmp}\ ?\ L_t : L_f\mid\mathsf{return}\ r\mid\mathsf{nop},\ L \\
\textbf{instructions} & I & ::= (\phi,\ \mathsf{ins})\mid\mathsf{ins} \\
\textbf{fun. decl} & F & ::= \{\boldsymbol{r};\ \varphi;\ G;\ \psi;\ \lambda;\ \varLambda\} \\
\textbf{program} & p & ::= f\mapsto F
\end{array}
$$

Fig. 2. Syntax of RTL

assertion language does not affect our results, provided assertions are closed under the connectives and operations that are used by the verification condition generator.

The syntax of expressions, formulas and RTL programs (suitably extended to accommodate certificates, see Subsection 2), is shown in Figure 2, where $n \in \mathbb{N}$ and $r \in \mathcal{R}$, with $\mathcal{R}$ an infinite set of register names. We let ϕ and ψ range over assertions.

A program p is defined as a function from RTL function identifiers to function declarations. We assume that every program comes equipped with a special function, namely main, and its declaration. A declaration F for a function f includes its formal parameters $\boldsymbol{r}$, a precondition φ, a (closed) graph code G, a postcondition ψ, a certificate λ, and a function $\varLambda$ from reachable labels to certificates (the notion of reachable label is defined below). For clarity, we often use in the sequel a subscript f for referring to elements in the declaration of a function f, e.g. the graph code of a function f as G_f.

As will be defined below, the VCGen generates one proof obligation for each program point containing an annotation and one proof obligation for the entry point L_{sp}. The component λ certifies the latter proof obligation and $\varLambda$ maps every program point that contains and assertion to the proof of its related proof obligation.

Formal parameters are a list of registers from the set $\mathcal{R}$, which we suppose to be local to f. For specification purposes, we introduce for each register r in $\boldsymbol{r}$ a (pseudo-)register r^*, not appearing in the code of the function, and which represents the initial value of a register declared as formal parameter. We let $\boldsymbol{r}^*$ denote the set $\{r^* \in \mathcal{R} \mid r \in \boldsymbol{r}\}$. We also introduce a (pseudo-)register res, not appearing in the code of the function, and which represents the result or return value of the function. The annotations φ and ψ provide the specification of the function, and are subject to well-formedness constraints. The precondition of a function f, denoted by function $\mathsf{pre}(f)$, is an assertion in which the only registers to occur are the formal parameters $\boldsymbol{r}$; in other words, the precondition of a function can only talk about the initial values of its parameters. The postcondition of a function f, denoted by function $\mathsf{post}(f)$, is an assertion[1] in which the only registers to occur are res and registers from $\boldsymbol{r}^*$; in other words, the postcondition of a function can only talk about its result and the initial values of its parameters.

A graph code of a function is a partial function from labels to instructions. We assume that every graph code includes a special label, namely L_{sp}, corresponding to the starting label of the function, i.e. the first instruction to be executed when the method is called. Given a function f and a label L in the domain of its graph code, we will often use $f[L]$ instead of $G_f(L)$, i.e. application of code graph of f to L.

Instructions are either instruction descriptors or pairs consisting of an annotation and an instruction descriptor. An instruction descriptor can be an assignment, a function call, a conditional jump or a return instruction. Operations on registers are those of standard processors, such as movement of registers or values into registers $r_d := r$, and arithmetic operations between registers or between a register and a value. Furthermore, every instruction descriptor carries explicitly its successor(s) label(s); due to this mechanism, we do not need to include unconditional jumps, i.e. "goto" instructions, in the language. Immediate successors of a label L in the graph of a function f are denoted by the set $\mathsf{succ}_f(L)$. We assume that the graph is closed; in particular, if L is associated with a return instruction, $\mathsf{succ}_f(L) = \emptyset$.

Verification Condition Generator. Verification condition generators (VC-Gens) are partial functions that compute, from a partially but sufficiently annotated program, a fully annotated program in which all labels of the program have an explicit precondition attached to them. Programs in the domain of the VCGen function are called well annotated and can be characterized by an inductive definition. Our definition is decidable and does not impose any specific structure on programs.

Definition 1 (Well Annotated Program)

- *A label L in a function f reaches annotated labels, if its associated instruction contains an assertion, or if its associated instruction is a return (in that case*

---

[1] Notice that a postcondition is not exactly an assertion in the sense that it uses register names from $\boldsymbol{r}^*$, which must not appear in preconditions or annotations of the program.

the annotation is the post condition), or if all its immediate successors reach
annotated labels:

$$f[L] = (\phi, \text{ ins}) \Rightarrow L \in \text{reachAnnot}_f$$
$$f[L] = \text{return } r \Rightarrow L \in \text{reachAnnot}_f$$
$$(\forall L' \in \text{succ}_f(L), L' \in \text{reachAnnot}_f) \Rightarrow L \in \text{reachAnnot}_f$$

– *A function f is well annotated if every reachable point from starting point*
  L_{sp} *reaches annotated labels. A program p is well annotated if all its functions*
  are well annotated.

Given a well-annotated program, one can generate an assertion for each label,
using the assertions that were given or previously computed for its successors.
This assertion represents the precondition that an initial state before the execution of the corresponding label should satisfy for the function to terminate in a
state satisfying its postcondition.

The computation of the assertions for the labels of a function f is performed
by a function vcg_f, and proceeds in a modular way, using annotations from the
function f under consideration, as well as the preconditions and postconditions
of functions called by f. The definition of $\text{vcg}_f(L)$ proceeds by cases: if L points
to an instruction that carries an assertion ϕ, then $\text{vcg}_f(L)$ is set to ϕ; otherwise,
$\text{vcg}_f(L)$ is computed by the function vcg_f^{id}.

$$\text{vcg}_f(L) = \phi \qquad \text{if } G_f(L) = (\phi, \text{ ins})$$
$$\text{vcg}_f(L) = \text{vcg}_f^{\text{id}}(\text{ins}) \quad \text{if } G_f(L) = \text{ins}$$
$$\text{vcg}_f^{\text{id}}(r_d := \text{op}, L) = \text{vcg}_f(L)\{r_d \leftarrow \langle \text{op} \rangle\}$$
$$\text{vcg}_f^{\text{id}}(r_d := g(r), L) = \text{pre}(g)\{r_g \leftarrow r\}$$
$$\wedge(\forall res. \text{ post}(g)\{r_g^* \leftarrow r\} \Rightarrow \text{vcg}_f(L)\{r_d \leftarrow res\})$$
$$\text{vcg}_f^{\text{id}}(\text{cmp } ? L_t : L_f) = (\langle \text{cmp} \rangle \Rightarrow \text{vcg}_f(L_t)) \wedge (\neg \langle \text{cmp} \rangle \Rightarrow \text{vcg}_f(L_f))$$
$$\text{vcg}_f^{\text{id}}(\text{return } r) = \text{post}(f)\{res \leftarrow r\}$$
$$\text{vcg}_f^{\text{id}}(\text{nop}, L) = \text{vcg}_f(f[L])$$

Fig. 3. Verification condition generator

The formal definitions of vcg_f and vcg_f^{id} are given in Figure 3, where $e\{r \leftarrow e'\}$
stands for substitution of all occurrences of register r in expression e by e'. The
definition of vcg_f^{id} is standard for assignment and conditional jumps, where $\langle \text{op} \rangle$
and $\langle \text{cmp} \rangle$ is the obvious interpretation of operators in RTL into expressions in the
language of assertions. For a function invocation, $\text{vcg}_f^{\text{id}}(r_d := g(r), L)$ is defined as
a conjunction of the precondition in the declaration of g where formal parameters
are replaced by actual parameters, and of the assertion $\forall res. \text{ post}(g)\{r_g^* \leftarrow r\} \Rightarrow$
$\text{vcg}_f(L)\{r_d \leftarrow res\}$. The second conjunct permits that information in $\text{vcg}_f(L)$
about registers different from r_d is propagated to other preconditions. In the re-
mainder of the paper, we shall abuse notation and write $\text{vcg}_f^{\text{id}}(\text{ins})$ or $\text{vcg}_f^{\text{id}}(L)$ instead of $\text{vcg}_f^{\text{id}}(\text{ins}, L')$ if $f[L] = \text{ins}, L'$ and neither L' or ins are relevant to the
context.

Certified Programs. Certificates provide a formal representation of proofs, and are used to verify that the proof obligations generated by the VCGen hold. For the purpose of certificate translation, we do not need to commit to a specific format for certificates. Instead, we assume that certificates are closed under specific operations on certificates, which are captured by an abstract notion of proof algebra.

Recall that a judgment is a pair consisting of a list of assertions, called context, and of an assertion, called goal. Then a *proof algebra* is given by a set-valued function $\mathcal{P}$ over judgments, and by a set of operations, all implicitly quantified in the obvious way. The operations are standard (given in Figure 4), to the exception perhaps of the substitution operator that allows to substitute selected instances of equals by equals, and of the operator ring, which establishes all ring equalities that will be used to justify the optimizations.

$$
\begin{array}{lll}
\text{axiom} & : & \mathcal{P}(\Gamma; A; \Delta \vdash A) \\
\text{ring} & : & \mathcal{P}(\Gamma \vdash n_1 = n_2) \qquad \text{if } n_1 = n_2 \text{ is a ring equality} \\
\text{intro}_\Rightarrow & : & \mathcal{P}(\Gamma; A \vdash B) \rightarrow \mathcal{P}(\Gamma \vdash A \Rightarrow B) \\
\text{elim}_\Rightarrow & : & \mathcal{P}(\Gamma \vdash A \Rightarrow B) \rightarrow \mathcal{P}(\Gamma \vdash A) \rightarrow \mathcal{P}(\Gamma \vdash B) \\
\text{elim}_= & : & \mathcal{P}(\Gamma \vdash e_1 = e_2) \rightarrow \mathcal{P}(\Gamma \vdash A\{r \leftarrow e_1\}) \rightarrow \mathcal{P}(\Gamma \vdash A\{r \leftarrow e_2\}) \\
\text{subst} & : & \mathcal{P}(\Gamma \vdash A) \rightarrow \mathcal{P}(\Gamma\{r \leftarrow e\} \vdash A\{r \leftarrow e\})
\end{array}
$$

Fig. 4. Proof Algebra (excerpts)

As a result of working at an abstract level, we do not provide an algorithm for checking certificates. Instead, we take $\mathcal{P}(\Gamma \vdash \phi)$ to be the set of valid certificates of the judgment $\Gamma \vdash \phi$. In the sequel, we write $\lambda : \Gamma \vdash \phi$ to express that λ is a valid certificate for $\Gamma \vdash \phi$, and use proof as a synonym of valid certificate.

Definition 2 (Certified Program)

- *A function f with declaration $\{r; \varphi; G; \psi; \lambda; \Lambda\}$ is certified if:*
  - *λ is a proof of $\vdash \varphi \Rightarrow \text{vcg}_f(L_{\text{sp}})\{r^* \leftarrow r\}$,*
  - *$\Lambda(L)$ is a proof of $\vdash \phi \Rightarrow \text{vcg}_f^{\text{id}}(\text{ins})$ for all reachable labels L in f such that $f[L] = (\phi, \text{ins})$.*
- *A program is certified if all its functions are.*

The verification condition generator is sound, in the sense that if the program p is called with registers set to values that verify the precondition of the function main, and p terminates normally, then the final state will verify the postcondition of main.

3   Principles of Certificate Translation

In a classical compiler, transformations operate on unannotated programs, and are performed in two phases: first, a data flow analysis gathers information about the program. Then, on the basis of this information, (blocks of) instructions are rewritten. In certificate translation, we may also rewrite assertions, and we must also generate certificates for the optimized programs.

Certificate translation is tightly bound to the optimizations considered. According to different optimizations, certificate translators fall in one of the three categories:

- PPO/IPO (Preservation/Instantiation of Proof Obligations): PPO deals with transformations for which the annotations are not rewritten, and where the proof obligations (for the original and transformed programs) coincide. This category covers transformations such as non-optimizing compilation and unreachable code elimination. IPO deals with transformations where the annotations and proof obligations for the transformed program are instances of annotations and proof obligations for the original program, thus certificate translation amounts to instantiating certificates. This category covers dead register elimination and register allocation;
- SCT (Standard Certificate Translation): SCT deals with transformations for which the annotations are not rewritten, but where the verification conditions do not coincide. This category covers transformations such as loop unrolling and in-lining;
- CTCA (Certificate Translation with Certifying Analyzers): CTCA deals with transformations for which the annotations need to be rewritten, and for which certificate translation relies on having certified previously the analysis results used by the transformation. This category covers constant propagation, common subexpression elimination, loop induction, and other optimizations that rely on arithmetic.

For simplicity, assume for a moment that the transformation ¯ does not modify the set of reachable annotated labels. Then certificate translation may be achieved by defining two functions:

$$T_0 : \quad \mathcal{P}(\vdash \mathsf{pre}(f) \Rightarrow \mathsf{vcg}_f^{\mathsf{id}}(L_{\mathsf{sp}})) \rightarrow \mathcal{P}(\vdash \mathsf{pre}(\bar{f}) \Rightarrow \mathsf{vcg}_{\bar{f}}^{\mathsf{id}}(L_{\mathsf{sp}}))$$
$$T_\lambda : \quad \forall L, \ \mathcal{P}(\vdash \phi_L \Rightarrow \mathsf{vcg}_f^{\mathsf{id}}(L)) \rightarrow \mathcal{P}(\vdash \bar{\phi}_L \Rightarrow \mathsf{vcg}_{\bar{f}}^{\mathsf{id}}(L))$$

where $\bar{f}$ is the optimized version of f, and ϕ_L is the original assertion at label L, and $\bar{\phi}_L$ is the rewritten assertion at label L. Here the function T_0 transforms the proof that the function precondition implies the verification condition at program point L_{sp} for f into a proof of the same fact for $\bar{f}$, and likewise, the function T_λ transforms for each reachable annotated label L the proof that its annotation implies the verification condition at program point L for f into a proof of the same fact for $\bar{f}$.

In the remainder of this section, we justify the need for certifying analyzers, and show how they can be used for specific transformations. The following example, which will be used as a running example in the subsequent paragraphs, illustrates the need for certifying analyzers.

Example 1. Let f be a certified function with specification: $\mathsf{pre}(f) \equiv \top$ and $\mathsf{post}(\bar{f}) \equiv res \geq b * n$, where b and n are constants. The graph code of f and its proofs obligations are given by:

$$
\begin{aligned}
&L_1: \quad r_i := 0,\ L_2 \\
&L_2: \xi,\ r_1 := b + r_i,\ L_3 \\
&L_3: \quad r_i := c + r_i,\ L_4 \\
&L_4: \quad r_j := r_1 * r_i,\ L_5 \\
&L_5: \varphi,\ (r_i = n)\ ?\ L_6: L_3 \\
&L_6: \quad \text{return } r_j
\end{aligned}
\qquad
\begin{aligned}
&\vdash \top \Rightarrow 0 \geq 0 \\
&\vdash \xi \Rightarrow \phi \\
&\vdash \varphi \Rightarrow (r_i = n \Rightarrow \phi_t \wedge r_i \neq n \Rightarrow \phi_f)
\end{aligned}
$$

where, $\xi \triangleq 0 \leq r_i$ and $\varphi \triangleq r_j = r_1 * r_i \wedge r_1 \geq b \wedge r_i \geq 0$ and

$$
\begin{aligned}
\phi &\triangleq (b + r_i) * (c + r_i) = (b + r_i) * (c + r_i) \wedge\ b + r_i \geq b \wedge c + r_i \geq 0 \\
\phi_t &\triangleq r_j \geq b * n \\
\phi_f &\triangleq r_1 * (c + r_i) = r_1 * (c + r_i) \wedge r_1 \geq b \wedge c + r_i \geq 0
\end{aligned}
$$

Suppose that constant propagation is applied to the original program, substituting an occurrence of r_1 with b and $b + r_i$ with b, as shown in program (a) in Figure 5. If we do not rewrite assertions, that is we let $\xi_{cp} = \xi$ and $\varphi_{cp} = \varphi$ then the third proof obligation is $\vdash \varphi \Rightarrow (r_i = n \Rightarrow \phi_t \wedge r_i \neq n \Rightarrow \phi'_f)$, where $\phi'_f \triangleq b * (c + r_i) = r_1 * (c + r_i) \wedge r_1 \geq b \wedge c + r_i \geq 0$ cannot be proved since there is no information about the relation between r_1 and b. A fortiori the certificate of the original program cannot be used to obtain a certificate for the optimized program.

Motivated by the example above, optimized programs are defined augmenting annotations by using the results of the analysis expressed as an assertion, and denoted $\mathrm{RES}_A(L)$ below.

Definition 3. *The optimized graph code of a function f is defined as follows:*

$$
G_{\bar{f}}(L) = \begin{cases} (\phi \wedge \mathrm{RES}_A(L),\ \llbracket \mathsf{ins} \rrbracket) & \text{if } G_f(L) = (\phi,\ \mathsf{ins}) \\ \llbracket \mathsf{ins} \rrbracket & \text{if } G_f(L) = \mathsf{ins} \end{cases}
$$

where $\llbracket \mathsf{ins} \rrbracket$ is the optimized version of instruction ins. In the sequel, we write $\bar{\phi}_L$ for $\phi_L \wedge \mathrm{RES}_A(L)$.

In addition, we define the precondition and postcondition of $\bar{f}$ to be those of f. Then one can encode elementary reasoning with the rules of the proof algebra to obtain a valid certificate for the optimized function $\bar{f}$ from a function

$$
T_L^{\mathsf{ins}}\colon\ \forall L,\ \mathcal{P}(\vdash \mathsf{vcg}_f^{\mathsf{id}}(L) \Rightarrow \mathrm{RES}_A(L) \Rightarrow \mathsf{vcg}_{\bar{f}}^{\mathsf{id}}(L))
$$

and a certified program

$$
f_A = \{\boldsymbol{r}_f;\ \top;\ G_A;\ \top;\ \lambda_A;\ \Lambda_A\}
$$

where G_A is a new version of G_f annotated with the results of the analysis, i.e. G_f such that $G_A(L) = (\mathrm{RES}_A(L),\ \mathsf{ins})$ for all label L in f.

Thus, certificate translation is reduced to two tasks: defining the function T_L^{ins}, and producing the certified function f_A. The definition of T_L^{ins} depends upon the program optimization. In the next paragraph we show that T_L^{ins} can be built for many common program optimizations, using the induction principle attached to the definition of reachAnnot$_f$. As to the second task, it is delegated to a procedure, called certifying analyzer, that produces for each function f the certified function f_A. There are two approaches for building certifying analyzers: one can either perform the analysis and build the certificate simultaneously, or use a standard analysis and use a decision procedure to generate the certificate post-analysis. The merits of both approaches will be reported elsewhere; here we have followed the second approach.

As shown in Figure 1, certifying analyzers do not form part of the Trusted Computing Base. In particular, no security threat is caused by applying an erroneous analyzer, or by verifying a program whose assertions are too weak (e.g. taking $\mathrm{RES}_A(L_5) = \top$ in the above example) or too strong (by adding unprovable assertions), or erroneous. In these cases, it will either be impossible to generate the certificate of the analysis, or of the optimized program.

(a) Constant propagation	(b) Loop induction	(c) Dead register
$L_1:\quad r_i := 0,\ L_2$	$L_1:\quad r_i := 0,\ L_2$	$L_1:\quad r_i := 0,\ L_2$
$L_2: \xi_{cp},\ r_1 := b,\ L_3$	$L_2: \xi_{li},\ r_1 := b,\ L_3$	$L_2: \xi_{dr},\ \mathsf{set}\ \hat{r}_1 := b,\ L_3$
$L_3:\quad r_i := c + r_i,\ L_4$	$L_3:\quad r'_j := b * r_i,\ L'_3$	$L_3:\quad r'_j := b * r_i,\ L'_3$
	$L'_3:\quad r_i := c + r_i,\ L''_3$	$L'_3:\quad r_i := c + r_i,\ L''_3$
	$L''_3:\quad r'_j := m + r'_j,\ L_4$	$L''_3:\quad r'_j := m + r'_j,\ L_4$
$L_4:\quad r_j := b * r_i,\ L_5$	$L_4:\quad r_j := r'_j,\ L_5$	$L_4:\quad \mathsf{set}\ \hat{r}_j := r'_j,\ L_5$
$L_5: \varphi_{cp},\ (r_i = n)\ ?\ L_6 : L_3$	$L_5: \varphi_{li},\ (r_i = n)\ ?\ L_6 : L'_3$	$L_5: \varphi_{dr},\ (r_i = n)\ ?\ L_6 : L'_3$
$L_6:\quad \mathsf{return}\ r_j$	$L_6:\quad \mathsf{return}\ r_j$	$L_6:\quad \mathsf{return}\ r'_j$

Fig. 5. Example of different optimizations

4   Instances of Certificate Translation

This section provides instances of certificate translations for common RTL optimizations. The order of optimizations is chosen for the clarity of exposition and does not necessarily reflect the order in which the optimizations are performed by a compiler. Due to space constraints, we only describe certificate translators for constant propagation, loop induction, and dead register elimination. Other transformations (common subexpression elimination, inlining, register allocation, loop unrolling, unreachable code elimination) will be described in the full version of the article.

4.1   Constant Propagation

Goal. Constant propagation aims at minimizing run-time evaluation of expressions and access to registers with constant values.

Description. Constant propagation relies on a data flow analysis that returns a function $A : \mathcal{PP} \times \mathcal{R} \to \mathbb{Z}_\perp$ ($\mathcal{PP}$ denoting the set of program points) such that $A(L, r) = n$ if r holds value n every time execution reaches label L. The optimization consists in replacing instructions by an equivalent one that exploits the information provided by A. For example, if r_1 is known to hold n_1 at label

L, and the instruction is $r := r_1 + r_2$, then the instruction is rewritten into $r := n_1 + r_2$. Likewise, conditionals which can be evaluated are replaced with nop instructions.

Certifying Analyzer. We have implemented a certifying analyzer for constant propagation as an extension of the standard data flow algorithm. First, we attach to each reachable label L the assertion $\mathrm{EQ}_A(L)$ (since the result of the analysis is a conjunction of equations, we now write $\mathrm{EQ}_A(L)$ instead of $\mathrm{RES}_A(L)$):

$$\mathrm{EQ}_A(L) \equiv \bigwedge_{r \in \{r | A(L,r) \neq \perp\}} r = A(L,r)$$

To derive a certificate for the analysis we have to prove that, for each reachable label L,

$$\vdash \mathrm{EQ}_A(L) \Rightarrow \mathsf{vcg}^{\mathrm{id}}_{f,A}(L)$$

After performing all $\Rightarrow$-eliminations (i.e. moving hypotheses to the context), and rewriting all equalities from the context in the goal, one is left to prove closed equalities of the form $n = n'$ (i.e. n, n' are numbers and not arithmetic expressions with variables). If the assertions are correct, then the certificate is obtained by applying reflexivity of equality (an instance of the ring rule). If the assertions are not correct, the program cannot be certified.

Certificate Translation. The function T_L^{ins} is defined by case analysis, using the fact that the transformation of operations is correct relative to the results of the analysis:

$$T_{\mathsf{op}} : \forall L, \forall \mathsf{op}, \mathcal{P}(\vdash \mathrm{EQ}_A(L) \Rightarrow \langle \mathsf{op} \rangle = \langle [\![\mathsf{op}]\!]_L^{\mathsf{op}} \rangle)$$

The expression $\langle [\![\mathsf{op}]\!]_L^{\mathsf{op}} \rangle$ represents the substitution of variables by constants in op. The function T_{op} is built using the ring axiom of the proof algebra; a similar result is required for comparisons and branching instructions.

Example 2. Recall function f, defined in Example 1. Using the compiler and transforming the assertions as explained before, we obtain the optimized program shown in Figure 5 (a), where assertions at L_1 and L_3 have been transformed into $\xi_{cp} \triangleq \xi \wedge r_i = 0$ and $\varphi_{cp} \triangleq \varphi \wedge r_1 = b$. It is left to the reader to check that all proof obligations become provable with the new annotations.

4.2   Loop Induction

Goal. Loop induction register strength reduction aims at reducing the number of multiplication operations inside a loop, which in many processors are more costly than addition operations.

Description. Loop induction depends on two analyzes. The first one is a loop analysis that detects loops and returns for each loop its set of labels $\{L_1, \ldots, L_n\}$, and its header L_H, a distinguished label in the above set such that any jump that goes inside the loop from an instruction outside the loop, is a jump to L_H.

$$\overline{f}[L_H] = r'_d := b * r_i,\ L''_H$$
$$\overline{f}[L''_H] = f[L_H]$$
$$\overline{f}[L_i] = r_i := r_i + c,\ L''_i$$
$$\overline{f}[L''_i] = r'_d := r'_d + b * c,\ L'_i\{L_H \leftarrow L''_H\}$$
$$\overline{f}[L_d] = r_d := r'_d,\ L'_d\{L_H \leftarrow L''_H\}$$
$$\overline{f}[L] = (\phi \wedge r'_d = b * r_i,\ \mathsf{ins}\{L_H \leftarrow L''_H\}) \quad \text{if } f[L] = (\phi,\ \mathsf{ins})$$
$$\overline{f}[L] = f[L]\{L_H \leftarrow L''_H\} \quad \text{in any other case inside the loop}$$

Fig. 6. Loop Induction

The second analysis detects inside a loop an induction register r_i (defined in the loop by an instruction of the form $r_i := r_i + c$) and its derived induction register r_d (defined in the loop by an instruction of the form $r_d := r_i * b$). More precisely, the analysis returns: an induction register r_i and the label L_i in which its definition appears, a derived induction register r_d and the label L_d in which its definition appears, a new register name r'_d not used in the original program, two new labels L''_i and L''_H not in the domain of G_f and two constant values b, c that correspond to the coefficient of r_d and increment of r_i.

The transformation replaces assignments to the derived induction register r_d with less costly assignments to an equivalent induction register r'_d. Then r_d is defined as a copy of r'_d.

Certifying Analyzer. Only the second analysis needs to be certified. First, we define $EQ_A(L) \equiv r'_d = b * r_i$ if $L \in \{L''_H, L_1, \ldots, L_n\} \setminus \{L_H\}$ and $EQ_A(L) \equiv \top$ if L is a label outside the loop or equal to L_H. Then, we need to create a certificate that the analysis is correct. One (minor) novelty w.r.t. constant propagation is that the definition of f_A includes two extra labels L''_H and L''_i, not present in the original function f. The definition of f_A is given by the clauses:

$$f_A[L_H] = (EQ_A(L_H),\ r'_d := b * r_i,\ L''_H)$$
$$f_A[L''_H] = (EQ_A(L''_H),\ \mathsf{ins}_{L_H})$$
$$f_A[L] = (EQ_A(L),\ \mathsf{ins}_L) \qquad \text{if } L \in dom(G_f),\ L \notin \{L_H, L_i\}$$
$$f_A[L_i] = (EQ_A(L_i),\ \mathsf{ins}_{L_i}\{L'_i \leftarrow L''_i\})$$
$$f_A[L''_i] = (\top,\ r'_d := r'_d + b * c,\ L'_i)$$

where ins_L is the instruction descriptor of $f[L]$, and L'_i is the successor label of L_i in f. Interestingly, the certified analyzer must use the fact that the loop analysis is correct in the sense that one can only enter a loop through its header. If the loop analysis is not correct, then the certificate cannot be constructed.

Certificate Translation. Figure 6 shows how instructions for labels $L_1 \ldots L_n$ of a function f are transformed into instructions for the optimized function $\overline{f}$. As expected, the transformation for instructions outside the loop is the identity, i.e. $\overline{f}[L] = f[L]$ for $L \notin \{L_1, \ldots, L_n\}$.

Certificate translation proceeds as with constant propagation, using the induction principle attached to the definition of $\mathsf{reachAnnot}_f$, and the certificate of the analysis, to produce a certificate for $\overline{f}$.

Example 3. Applying loop induction to program (a) in Figure 5, we obtain program (b) where m denotes the result of the product $b * c$ and $\xi_{li} \triangleq \xi_{cp}$ and $\varphi_{li} \triangleq \varphi_{cp} \wedge r'_j = b * r_i$.

4.3   Dead Register Elimination

Goal. Dead register elimination aims at deleting assignments to registers that are not live at the label where the assignment is performed. As mentioned in the introduction, we propose a transformation that performs simultaneously dead variable elimination in instructions and in assertions.

Description. A register r is live at label L if r is read at label L or there is a path from L that reaches a label L' where r is read and does not go through an instruction that defines r (including L, but not L'). A register r is read at label L if it appears in an assignment with a function call, or it appears in a conditional jump, or in a return instruction, or on the right side of an assignment of an assignment operation to a register r' that is live. In the following, we denote $\mathcal{L}(L, r) = \top$ when a register is live at L.

In order to deal with assertions, we extend the definition of liveness to assertions. A register r is live in an assertion at label L, denoted by $\mathcal{L}(L, r) = \top_\phi$, if it is not live at label L and there is a path from L that reaches a label L' such that r appears in assertion at L' or where r is used to define a register which is live in an assertion.

By abuse of notation, we use $\mathcal{L}(L, r) = \bot$ if r is dead in the code and in assertions.

The transformation deletes assignments to registers that are not live. In order to deal with dead registers in assertions, we rely on the introduction of ghost variables. Ghost variables are expressions in our language of assertions (we assume that sets of ghost variables names and $\mathcal{R}$ are disjoint). We introduce as part of RTL, "ghost assignments" of the form set $\hat{v} := \text{op}, L$, where $\hat{v}$ is a ghost variable. Ghost assignments do not affect the semantics of RTL, but they affect the calculus of vcg in the same way as normal assignments.

The transformation is shown below where $\sigma_L = \{r \leftarrow \hat{r} \mid \mathcal{L}(L, r) = \top_\phi\}$ and $\text{dead}_c(L, L') = \{r \mid \mathcal{L}(L, r) = \top \wedge \mathcal{L}(L', r) = \top_\phi\}$.

$$\text{ghost}_L((\phi, \text{ins})) = (\phi\sigma_L, \text{ghost}_L^{\text{id}}(\text{ins}))$$
$$\text{ghost}_L(\text{ins}) \quad = \text{ghost}_L^{\text{id}}(\text{ins})$$

The analysis $\text{ghost}_L^{\text{id}}(\text{ins})$ is defined in Figure 7. We use set $\hat{r} := r$, as syntactic sugar for a sequence of assignments set $\hat{r}_i := r_i$, where for each register r_i in r, $\hat{r}_i$ in $\hat{r}$ is its corresponding ghost variable. The function ghost transforms each instruction of f into a the set of instructions of $\bar{f}$. Intuitively, it introduces for any instruction ins (with successor L') at label L, a ghost assignment set $\hat{r} := r, L'$ immediately after L (at a new label L'') if the register r is live at L but not live at the immediate successor L' of L. In addition, the function ghost_L performs dead register elimination if ins is of the form $r_d := \text{op}$, and the register r_d is not live at L.

$$\begin{aligned}
\mathsf{ghost}_L^{\mathsf{id}}(\mathsf{return}\ r) &= \mathsf{return}\ r \\
\mathsf{ghost}_L^{\mathsf{id}}(r_d := f(r),\ L') &= \left| \begin{array}{l} L\ \ :r_d := f(r),\ L'' \\ L''\ :\mathsf{set}\ \hat{t} := t,\ L'\ \ \text{for each t}\ \in \mathsf{dead}_c(L,L') \end{array} \right. \\
\mathsf{ghost}_L^{\mathsf{id}}(\mathsf{nop},\ L') &= \mathsf{nop},\ L' \\
\mathsf{ghost}_L^{\mathsf{id}}(\mathsf{cmp}\ ?\ L_1 : L_2) &= \left| \begin{array}{l} L\ \ :\mathsf{cmp}\ ?\ L_1' : L_2' \\ L_1' :\mathsf{set}\ \hat{t}_1 := t_1,\ L_1 \quad \text{where}t_1 = \mathsf{dead}_c(L,L_1) \\ L_2' :\mathsf{set}\ \hat{t}_2 := t_2,\ L_2 \quad \text{where}\ t_2 = \mathsf{dead}_c(L,L_2) \end{array} \right. \\
\mathsf{ghost}_L^{\mathsf{id}}(r_d := \mathsf{op},\ L') &= \mathsf{nop},\ L'\ \ \text{if}\ \mathcal{L}(L',r_d) = \bot \\
&= \mathsf{set}\ \hat{r}_d := \mathsf{op}\sigma_L,\ L'\ \ \ \ \text{if}\ \mathcal{L}(L',r_d) = \top_\phi \\
&= \left| \begin{array}{l} L\ \ :r_d := \mathsf{op},\ L'' \quad\quad \text{if}\ \mathcal{L}(L',r_d) = \top \\ L''\ \ \mapsto \mathsf{set}\ \hat{t} := t,\ L' \\ \quad\quad \text{where}\ t = \mathsf{dead}_c(L,L') \end{array} \right.
\end{aligned}$$

Fig. 7. Ghost Variable Introduction-Dead Register Elimination

Instantiation of Proof Obligations. Certificate translation for dead register elimination falls in the IPO category, i.e. the certificate of the optimized program is an instance of the certificate of the source program. This is shown by proving that ghost variable introduction preserves vcg up to substitution.

Lemma 1. $\forall L, \mathsf{vcg}_{\bar{f}}(L) = \mathsf{vcg}_f(L)\sigma_L$

A consequence of this lemma is that if the function f is certified, then it is possible to reuse the certificate of f to certify $\bar{f}$, as from each proof $p :\vdash \phi_L \Rightarrow \mathsf{vcg}_f(L)$ we can obtain a proof $\bar{p} :\vdash \bar{\phi}_L \Rightarrow \mathsf{vcg}_{\bar{f}}(L)$ by applying **subst** rule of Figure 4 to p with substitution σ_L.

After ghost variable introduction has been applied, registers that occur free in $\mathsf{vcg}_{\bar{f}}(L)$, are live at L, i.e. $\mathcal{L}(L,r) = \top$.

Example 4. In Figure 5, applying first copy propagation to program (b), we can then apply ghost variable introduction to obtain program (c), where $\xi_{dr} \triangleq \xi_{li}$ and $\varphi_{dr} \triangleq \hat{r}_j = \hat{r}_1 * r_i \wedge \hat{r}_1 \geq b \wedge r_i \geq 0 \wedge \hat{r}_1 = b \wedge r_j' = b * r_i \wedge r_j' = \hat{r}_j$.

5   Related Work

Certified Compilation. Compiler correctness [6] aims at showing that a compiler preserves the semantics of programs. Because compilers are complex programs, the task of compiler verification can be daunting; in order to tame the complexity of verification and bring stronger guarantees on the validity of compiler correctness proofs, *certified compilation* [8] advocates the use of a proof assistant for machine-checking compiler correctness results. Section 2 of [8] shows that it is theoretically possible to derive certificate translation from certifying compilation. However, we think that the approach is restrictive and unpractical:

- certificates encapsulate the definition of the compiler and its correctness proof on the one hand, and the source code and its certificate on the other hand. Thus certificates are large and costly to check;

- with the above notion of certified compiler, the approach is necessarily confined to properties about the input/output behavior of programs, and rules out interesting properties involving intermediate program points that are expressed with assertions or ghost variables;
- and a further difficulty with this approach is that it requires that the source code is accessible to the code consumer, which is in general not the case.

For similar reasons, it is not appropriate to take as certificates of optimized programs pairs that consist of a certificate for the unoptimized program and of a proof that the optimizations are semantics preserving.

Certifying Compilation. Certifying compilation is concerned with generating automatically safety certificates. The Touchstone compiler [11] is a notable example of certifying compiler, which generates type-safety certificates for a fragment of C. In Chapter 6 of [10], Necula studies the impact of program optimizations on certifying compilation. For most standard optimizations an informal analysis is made, indicating whether the transformation requires reinforcing the program invariants, or whether the transformation does not change proof obligations.

There are many commonalities between his work and ours, but also some notable differences. First, the VCGen used by Necula propagates invariants backwards, whereas ours generates a proof obligation for each invariant. This has subtle implications on the modifications required for the invariant. A main difference is that we not only have to strengthen invariants, but also transform the certificate; further, when he observes that the transformation produces a logically equivalent proof obligation, we have to define a function that maps proofs of the original proof obligation into proofs of the new proof obligation after optimization.

Provable Optimizations through Sound Elementary Rules. Rhodium [7] is a domain-specific language for declaring and proving correct program optimizations. The domain-specific language is used to declare local transformation rules and to combine them into the optimization. Transformations written in Rhodium are given a semantic interpretation that is used to generate sufficient conditions for the correctness of the transformation. The proof obligations are in turn submitted to an automatic prover that attempts to discharge them automatically. The idea also underlies the work of Benton [4], who proposes to use a relational Hoare logic to justify transformation rules from which optimizations can be built. The perspective of decomposing optimizations through sound elementary rules is appealing, but left for future work.

Spec# and BML Project. The Spec# project [2] defines an extension of C# with annotations, and a compiler from annotated programs to annotated .NET files, which can be run using the .NET platform, and checked against their specifications at run-time or verified statically with an automatic prover. The Spec# project implicitly assumes some relation between source and byte-code levels, but does not attempt to formalize this relation. There is no notion of certificate, and thus no need to transform them. A similar line of work for Java was pursued independently by Pavlova and Burdy [5] who define a Byte-code Modeling Language into which annotations of the Java Modeling Language and a VCGen for annotated bytecode programs; the generated proof obligations are sent to an automatic theorem prover. They partially formalize the relation between proof obligations at source code and bytecode level, but they do not consider certificates.

In a similar spirit, Bannwart and Müller [1], provide Hoare-like logics for significant sequential fragments of Java source code and bytecode, and illustrate how derivations of correctness can be mapped from source programs to bytecode programs obtained by non-optimizing compilation.

Certifying Analyzers. Specific instances of certifying analyzers have been studied independently by Wildmoser, Chaieb and Nipkow [13] in the context of a bytecode language and by Seo, Yang and Yi [12] in the context of a simple imperative language. Seo, Yang and Yi propose an algorithm that automatically constructs safety proofs in Hoare logic from abstract interpretation results.

6   Concluding Remarks

Certificate translation provides a means to bring the benefits of source code verification to code consumers using PCC architectures. Certificate translation significantly extends the scope of PCC in that it allows to consider complex security policies and complex programs— at the cost of requiring interactive verification. The primary motivation for certificate translation are mobile code scenarios, possibly involving with several code producers and intermediaries, where security-sensitive applications justify interactive verification. One impor-tant constraint for these scenarios (which originate from mobile phone industry) is that only the code after compilation and optimization is available to the code consumer or a trusted third party: this assumption makes it impossible to use ideas from certified compilation, or to use as certificates for optimized programs a pair consisting of a certificate of the unoptimized program, and a proof of correctness of the optimizations.

There are many directions for future work, including:

– On a side, we would like to build a generic certificate translation, instead of developing a translator per optimization. One natural approach would be to describe standard program optimizations as a combination of more elementary transformations in the style of Rhodium.
– On a practical side, we have developed a prototype certificate translator for our RTL language. This prototype generates proof obligations for the initial program that are sent to the Coq theorem prover. Once the proofs obligations are solved, the proofs are sent to the certificate translator that automatically optimizes the program and transforms the proofs. In the medium term, we intend to extend our prototype to a mainstream programming language such as C or Java to an assembly language.

- On an experimental side, we would like to gather metrics about the size of certificates—which is an important issue, although not always central in the scenarios we have in mind. Preliminary experiments using λ-terms as certificates indicate that their size does not explode during translation, provided we perform after certificate translation a pass of reduction that eliminates all the redexes created by the translation. For example, the size of certificates remains unchanged for dead register elimination. For constant propagation, the size of certificates grows linearly w.r.t. the size of the code. There are other opportunities to reduce certificate size; in particular, not all annotations generated by certifying analyzers are used to build the certificate for the optimized program, so we could use enriched analyses with dependency information to eliminate all annotations that are not used to prove the optimized program, i.e. annotations that are not directly used to justify an optimization, and annotations that are not used (recursively) to justify such annotations;
- On an applicative side, we would like to experiment with certificate translation in realistic settings. E.g. certificate translation could be useful in the component-based development of security-sensitive software, as the software integrator, who will be liable for the resulting product, could reasonably require that components originating from untrusted third parties are certified against their requirements, and use certificate translation to derive a certificate for the overall software from certificates of each component. The benefits of certificate translation seem highest in situations where integration of components involves advanced compilation techniques, e.g. compilation from Domain-Specific Languages to conventional languages.

References

1. F. Bannwart and P. Müller. A program logic for bytecode. In F. Spoto, editor, *Proceedings of Bytecode'05*, Electronic Notes in Theoretical Computer Science. Elsevier Publishing, 2005.
2. M. Barnett, K.R.M. Leino, and W. Schulte. The Spec# Programming System: An Overview. In G. Barthe, L. Burdy, M. Huisman, J.-L. Lanet, and T. Muntean, editors, *Proceedings of CASSIS'04*, volume 3362 of *Lecture Notes in Computer Science*, pages 50–71. Springer-Verlag, 2005.
3. G. Barthe, T.Rezk, and A. Saabas. Proof obligations preserving compilation. In *Proceedings of FAST''05*, volume 3866 of *Lecture Notes in Computer Science*, pages 112–126. Springer-Verlag, 2005.
4. N. Benton. Simple relational correctness proofs for static analyses and program transformations. In *Proceedings of POPL'04*, pages 14–25. ACM Press, 2004.
5. L. Burdy and M. Pavlova. Annotation carrying code. In *Proceedings of SAC'06*. ACM Press, 2006.
6. J. D. Guttman and M. Wand. Special issue on VLISP. *Lisp and Symbolic Computation*, 8(1/2), March 1995.
7. S. Lerner, T. Millstein, E. Rice, and C. Chambers. Automated soundness proofs for dataflow analyses and transformations via local rules. In *Proceedings of POPL'05*, pages 364–377. ACM Press, 2005.

8. X. Leroy. Formal certification of a compiler back-end, or: programming a compiler with a proof assistant. In *Proceedings of POPL'06*, pages 42–54. ACM Press, 2006.
9. G.C. Necula. Proof-Carrying Code. In *Proceedings of POPL'97*, pages 106–119. ACM Press, 1997.
10. G.C. Necula. *Compiling with Proofs*. PhD thesis, Carnegie Mellon University, October 1998. Available as Technical Report CMU-CS-98-154.
11. G.C. Necula and P. Lee. The Design and Implementation of a Certifying Compiler. In *Proceedings of PLDI'98*, pages 333–344. ACM Press, 1998.
12. S. Seo, H. Yang, and K. Yi. Automatic Construction of Hoare Proofs from Abstract Interpretation Results. In A. Ohori, editor, *Proceedings of APLAS'03*, volume 2895 of *Lecture Notes in Computer Science*, pages 230–245. Springer-Verlag, 2003.
13. M. Wildmoser, A. Chaieb, and T. Nipkow. Bytecode analysis for proof carrying code. In F. Spoto, editor, *Proceedings of BYTECODE'05*, Electronic Notes in Theoretical Computer Science. Elsevier Publishing, 2005.

Analysis of Low-Level Code Using Cooperating Decompilers*

Bor-Yuh Evan Chang, Matthew Harren, and George C. Necula

University of California, Berkeley, California, USA
{bec, matth, necula}@cs.berkeley.edu

Abstract. Analysis or verification of low-level code is useful for minimizing the disconnect between what is verified and what is actually
executed and is necessary when source code is unavailable or is, say,
intermingled with inline assembly. We present a modular framework for
building pipelines of cooperating decompilers that gradually lift the level
of the language to something appropriate for source-level tools. Each decompilation stage contains an abstract interpreter that encapsulates its
findings about the program by translating the program into a higher-
level intermediate language. We provide evidence for the modularity of
this framework through the implementation of multiple decompilation
pipelines for both x86 and MIPS assembly produced by `gcc`, `gcj`, and
`coolc` (a compiler for a pedagogical Java-like language) that share several low-level components. Finally, we discuss our experimental results
that apply the BLAST model checker for C and the Cqual analyzer to
decompiled assembly.

1 Introduction

There is a growing interest in applying software-quality tools to low-level representations of programs, such as intermediate or virtual-machine languages, or
even on native machine code. We want to be able to analyze code whose source is
either not available (e.g., libraries) or not easily analyzable (e.g., programs written in languages with complex semantics such as C++, or programs that contain
inline assembly). This allows us to analyze the code that is actually executed and
to ignore possible compilation errors or arbitrary interpretations of underspec-
ified source-language semantics. Many source-level analyses have been ported
to low-level code, including type checkers [23, 22, 8], program analyzers [26, 4],
model checkers [5], and program verifiers [12, 6]. In our experience, these tools
mix the reasoning about high-level notions with the logic for understanding low-
level implementation details that are introduced during compilation, such as
stack frames, calling conventions, exception implementation, and data layout.
We would like to segregate the low-level logic into separate modules to allow for
easier sharing between tools and for a cleaner interface with client analyses. To

---

* This research was supported in part by the National Science Foundation under grants
CCF-0524784, CCR-0234689, CNS-0509544, and CCR-0225610; and an NSF Grad-
uate Research Fellowship.

better understand this issue, consider developing a type checker similar to the Java bytecode verifier but for assembly language. Such a tool has to reason not only about the Java type system, but also the layout of objects, calling conventions, stack frames, with all the low-level invariants that the compiler intends to preserve. We reported earlier [8] on such a tool where all of this reasoning is done simultaneously by one module. But such situations arise not just for type checking but essentially for all analyses on assembly language.

In this paper we propose an architecture that modularizes the reasoning about low-level details into separate components. Such a separation of low-level logic has previously been done to a certain degree in tools such as CodeSurfer/x86 [4] and Soot [28], which expose to client analyses an API for obtaining information about the low-level aspects of the program. In this paper, we adopt a more radical approach in which the low-level logic is packaged as a *decompiler* whose output is an intermediate language that abstracts the low-level implementation details introduced by the compiler. In essence, we propose that an easy way to reuse source-level analysis tools for low-level code is to decompile the low-level code to a level appropriate for the tool. We make the following contributions:

- We propose a decompilation architecture as a way to apply source-level tools to assembly language programs (Sect. 2). The novel aspect of our proposal is that we use decompilation not only to separate the low-level logic from the source-level client analysis, but also as a way to modularize the low-level logic itself. Decompilation is performed by a series of decompilers connected by intermediate languages. We provide a *cooperation* mechanism in order to deal with certain complexities of decompilation.
- We provide evidence for the modularity of this framework through the implementation of multiple decompilation pipelines for both x86 and MIPS assembly produced by `gcc` (for C), `gcj` (for Java), and `coolc` (for Cool [1], a Java-like language used for teaching) that share several low-level components (Sect. 3). We then compare with a monolithic assembly-level analysis.
- We demonstrate that it is possible to apply source-level tools to assembly code using decompilation by applying the BLAST model checker [18] and the Cqual analyzer [17] with our `gcc` decompilation pipeline (Sect. 4).

Note that while ideally we would like to apply analysis tools to machine code binaries, we leave the difficult issue of lifting binaries to assembly to other work (perhaps by using existing tools like IDAPro [19] as in CodeSurfer/x86 [4]).

Challenges. Just like in a compiler, a pipeline architecture improves modularity of the code and allows for easy reuse of modules for different client-analyses. Fig. 1 shows an example of

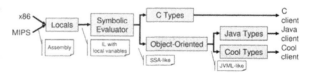

Fig. 1. Cooperating decompilers

using decompilation modules to process code that has been compiled from C, Java, and Cool. Each stage recovers an abstraction that a corresponding

compilation stage has concretized. For example, we have a decompiler that decompiles the notion of the run-time stack of activation records into the abstraction of functions with local variables (Locals). The analogy with compilers is very
useful but not sufficient. Compilation is in many respects a many-to-one mapping and thus not easily invertible. Many source-level variables are mapped to
the same register, many source-level concepts are mapped to the run-time stack,
many source-level operations are mapped to a particular low-level instruction
kind. We address this issue by providing each decompiler with additional information about the instruction being decompiled. Some information is computed
by the decompiler itself using data-flow analysis. For example, the Locals decompiler can keep track of the value of the stack and frame pointer registers
relative to function entry.

The real difficulty is that some information must be provided by higher-level
modules. For example, the Locals module must identify all calls and determine
the number of arguments, but only the object-oriented module (OO) should
understand virtual method invocation. There is a serious circularity here. A
decompiler needs information from higher-level decompilers to produce the input
for the higher-level decompiler. We introduce a couple of mechanisms to address
this problem. First, the entire pipeline of decompilers is executed one instruction
at a time. That is, we produce decompiled programs simultaneously at all levels.
This setup gives each decompiler the opportunity to accumulate data-flow facts
that are necessary for decompiling the subsequent instructions and allows the
control-flow graph to be refined as the analysis proceeds. When faced with an
instruction that can be decompiled in a variety of ways, a decompiler can consult
its own data-flow facts and can also query higher-level decompilers for hints based
on their accumulated data-flow facts. Thus it is better to think of decompilers
not as stages in a pipeline but as cooperating decompilers. The net result is
essentially a reduced product analysis [15] on assembly; we explain the benefits of
this framework compared to prior approaches based on our previous experiences
in Sect. 3 and 5.

2   Cooperating Decompilation Framework

For concreteness, we describe the methodology through an example series of decompiler
modules that together are able to perform Java
type checking on assembly language. We focus
here on the Java pipeline (rather than C), as
the desired decompilation is higher-level and
thus more challenging to obtain. Consider the
example Java program in Fig. 2 and the corresponding assembly code shown in the leftmost
column of Fig. 3. In this figure, we use the stack

```
static int length(List x) {
  int n = 0;
  while (x.hasNext()) {
    x = x.next();
    n++;
  }
  return n;
}
```

Fig. 2. A Java method

and calling conventions from the x86 architecture where the stack pointer r_{sp}
points to the last used word, parameters are passed on the stack, return values

#	length:	length($\mathbf{t}_x$):	length(α_x):	length(α_x : obj):	length(α_x : *List*):
1	length:	length($\mathbf{t}_x$):	length(α_x):	length(α_x : obj):	length(α_x : *List*):
2	...				
3	$\mathbf{m}[\mathbf{r}_{sp}] := 0$	$\mathbf{t}_n := 0$	$\alpha_n = 0$	$\alpha_n = 0$	$\alpha_n = 0$
4	L_{loop}:	L_{loop}:	L_{loop}:	L_{loop}:	L_{loop}:
			$\alpha_n'' = \phi(\alpha_n, \alpha_n')$	$\alpha_n'' = \phi(\alpha_n, \alpha_n')$	$\alpha_n'' = \phi(\alpha_n, \alpha_n')$
			$\alpha_x'' = \phi(\alpha_x, \alpha_x')$	$\alpha_x'' = \phi(\alpha_x, \alpha_x')$	$\alpha_x'' = \phi(\alpha_x, \alpha_x')$
5	$\mathbf{r}_1 := \mathbf{m}[\mathbf{r}_{sp}+12]$	$\mathbf{r}_1 := \mathbf{t}_x$			
6	jzero $\mathbf{r}_1$, L_{exc}	jzero $\mathbf{r}_1$, L_{exc}	if (α_x''=0) L_{exc}	if (α_x''=0) L_{exc}	if (α_x''=0) L_{exc}
7	$\mathbf{r}_2 := \mathbf{m}[\mathbf{r}_1]$	$\mathbf{r}_2 := \mathbf{m}[\mathbf{r}_1]$			
8	$\mathbf{r}_1 := \mathbf{m}[\mathbf{r}_2+32]$	$\mathbf{r}_1 := \mathbf{m}[\mathbf{r}_2+32]$			
9	$\mathbf{r}_{sp} := \mathbf{r}_{sp} - 4$				
10	$\mathbf{m}[\mathbf{r}_{sp}] := \mathbf{m}[\mathbf{r}_{sp}+16]$	$\mathbf{t}_1 := \mathbf{t}_x$			
11	icall [$\mathbf{r}_1$]	$\mathbf{r}_1 :=$ icall [$\mathbf{r}_1$]($\mathbf{t}_1$)	$\alpha_{rv} =$ icall [$\mathbf{m}[\mathbf{m}[\alpha_x'']+32]]$ (α_x'')	$\alpha_{rv} =$ invokevirtual [α_x'', 32]()	$\alpha_{rv} =$ α_x''.hasNext()
12	$\mathbf{r}_{sp} := \mathbf{r}_{sp} + 4$				
13	jzero $\mathbf{r}_1$, L_{end}	jzero $\mathbf{r}_1$, L_{end}	if (α_{rv}=0) L_{end}	if (α_{rv}=0) L_{end}	if (α_{rv}=0) L_{end}
14	$\mathbf{r}_{sp} := \mathbf{r}_{sp} - 4$				
15	$\mathbf{m}[\mathbf{r}_{sp}] := \mathbf{m}[\mathbf{r}_{sp}+16]$	$\mathbf{t}_1 := \mathbf{t}_x$			
16	$\mathbf{r}_1 := \mathbf{m}[\mathbf{r}_2+28]$	$\mathbf{r}_1 := \mathbf{m}[\mathbf{r}_2+28]$			
17	icall [$\mathbf{r}_1$]	$\mathbf{r}_1 :=$ icall [$\mathbf{r}_1$]($\mathbf{t}_1$)	$\alpha_{rv}' =$ icall [$\mathbf{m}[\mathbf{m}[\alpha_x'']+28]]$ (α_x'')	$\alpha_{rv}' =$ invokevirtual [α_x'', 28]()	$\alpha_{rv}' =$ α_x''.next()
18	$\mathbf{r}_{sp} := \mathbf{r}_{sp} + 4$				
19	$\mathbf{m}[\mathbf{r}_{sp}+12] := \mathbf{r}_1$	$\mathbf{t}_x := \mathbf{r}_1$	$\alpha_x' = \alpha_{rv}'$	$\alpha_x' = \alpha_{rv}'$	$\alpha_x' = \alpha_{rv}'$
20	incr $\mathbf{m}[\mathbf{r}_{sp}]$	incr $\mathbf{t}_n$	$\alpha_n' = \alpha_n'' + 1$	$\alpha_n' = \alpha_n'' + 1$	$\alpha_n' = \alpha_n'' + 1$
21	jump L_{loop}	jump L_{loop}	jump L_{loop}	jump L_{loop}	jump L_{loop}
22	L_{end}:	L_{end}:	L_{end}:	L_{end}:	L_{end}:
23	$\mathbf{r}_1 := \mathbf{m}[\mathbf{r}_{sp}]$	$\mathbf{r}_1 := \mathbf{t}_n$			
24	...				
25	return	return $\mathbf{r}_1$	return α_n''	return α_n''	return α_n''
	Assembly	Locals IL	SymEval IL	OO IL	Java IL

Fig. 3. Assembly code for the program in Fig. 2 and the output of successive decompilers. The function's prologue and epilogue have been elided. Jumping to L_{exc} will trigger a Java NullPointerException.

are passed in $\mathbf{r}_1$, and $\mathbf{r}_2$ is a callee-save register. Typically, a virtual method dispatch is translated to several lines of assembly (e.g., lines 6–11): a null-check on the receiver object, looking up the dispatch table, and then the method in the dispatch table, passing the receiver object and any other arguments, and finally an indirect jump-and-link (icall). To ensure that the icall is a correct compilation of a virtual method dispatch, dependencies between assembly instructions must be carefully tracked, such as the requirement that the argument passed as the self pointer is the same as the object from which the dispatch table is obtained (cf., [8]). These difficulties are only exacerbated with instruction reordering and other optimizations. For example, consider the assembly code for the method dispatch to x.next() (lines 14–17). Variable x is kept in a stack slot ($\mathbf{m}[\mathbf{r}_{sp}+16]$ at line 15). A small bit of optimization has eliminated the null-check and the re-fetching of the dispatch table of x, as a null-check was done on line 6 and the dispatch table was kept in a callee-save register r_2, so clearly some analysis is necessary to decompile it into a method call.

The rest of Fig. 3 shows how this assembly code is decompiled by our system. Observe how high-level constructs are recovered incrementally to obtain essentially Java with unstructured control-flow (shown in the rightmost column). Note that our goal is not to necessarily recover the same source code but simply code that is semantically equivalent and amenable to further analysis. To summarize the decompilation steps, the Locals module decompiles stack and calling conventions to provide the abstraction of functions with local variables. The SymEval decompiler performs symbolic evaluation to accumulate and normalize larger expressions to present the program in a source-like SSA form. Object-oriented features, like virtual method dispatch, are identified by the OO module, which must understand implementation details like object layout and dispatch tables. Finally, JavaTypes can do a straightforward type analysis (because its input is already fairly high-level) to recover the Java-like representation.

As can be seen in Fig. 3, one key element of analyzing assembly code is decoding the run-time stack. An assembly analyzer must be able to identify function calls and returns, recognize memory operations as either stack accesses or heap accesses, and must ensure that stack-overflow and calling conventions are handled appropriately. This handling ought to be done in a separate module both because it is not specific to the desired analysis and also to avoid such low-level concerns when thinking about the analysis algorithm (e.g., Java type-checking). In our example decompiler pipeline (Fig. 1), the Locals decompiler handles all of these low-level aspects. On line 17, the Locals decompiler determines that this instruction is a function call with one argument (for now, we elide the details how this is done, see the Bidirectional Communication subsection and Fig. 4). It interprets the calling convention to decompile the assembly-level jump-and-link instruction to a function call instruction with one argument that places its return value in r_{rv}. Also, observe that Locals decompiles reads of and writes to stack slots that are used as local variables into uses of *temporaries* (e.g., t_x) (lines 3, 5, 10, 15, 19, 20, 23). To do these decompilations, the Locals decompiler needs to perform analysis to track, for example, pointers into the stack. For instance, Locals needs this information to identify the reads on both lines 5 and 10 as reading the same stack slot t_x. Section 3 gives more details about how these decompilers are implemented.

Decompiler Interface. Program analyses are almost always necessary to establish the prerequisites for sound decompilations. We build on the traditional notions of data-flow analysis and abstract

```
type abs
    val step : curr × instr_in → instr_out × (succ list)
    val ⊑ : abs × abs → bool
    val ▽ : abs × abs → abs
```

interpretation [14]. Standard ways to combine abstract interpreters typically rely on all interpreters working on the same language. Instead, we propose here an approach in which the communication mechanism consists of successive decompilations. Concretely, a decompiler must define a type of abstract states abs and implement a flow function (i.e., abstract transition relation) step with the type signature given above for some input language $instr_{in}$ and some output language $instr_{out}$. The input type curr represents the abstract state at the given instruction, and succ is an abstract successor state at a particular program location. For simplicity in presentation, we say a decompiler translates one input instruction to one output instruction. Our implementation extends this to allow one-to-many or many-to-one translations. As part of the framework, we provide a standard top-level fixed-point engine that ensures the exploration of all reachable instructions. To implement this fixed-point engine, we require the signature include the standard partial ordering $\sqsubseteq$ and widening $\triangledown$ operators [14] for abstract states.

For simple examples where the necessary communication is unidirectional (that is, from lower-level decompilers to higher-level decompilers via the decompiled instructions), an exceedingly simple composition strategy suffices where we run each decompiler completely to fixed point gathering the entire decompiled program before running the next one (i.e., a strict pipeline architecture). This architecture does not require a product abstract domain and would be more efficient than one. Unfortunately, as we have alluded to earlier, unidirectional communication is insufficient: lower-level decompilers depend on the analyses of higher-level decompilers to perform their decompilations. We give examples of such situations and describe how to resolve this issue in the following subsection.

Bidirectional Communication. In this subsection, we motivate two complimentary mechanisms for communicating information from higher-level decompilers to lower-level ones. In theory, either mechanism is sufficient for all high-to-low communication but at the cost of efficiency or naturalness. As soon as we consider high-to-low communication, clearly the strict pipeline architecture described above is insufficient: higher-level decompilers must start before lower-level decompilers complete. To address this issue, we run the entire pipeline of decompilers one instruction at a time, which allows higher-level decompilers to analyze the preceding instructions before lower-level decompilers produce subsequent instructions. For this purpose, we provide a product decompiler whose abstract state is the product of the abstract states of the decompilers, but in order to generate its successors, it must string together calls to step on the decompilers in the appropriate order and then collect together the abstract states of the decompilers.

Queries. Consider again the dynamic dispatch on line 17 of Fig. 3. In order for the Locals module to (soundly) abstract stack and calling conventions into functions with local variables, it must enforce basic invariants, such as a function can only modify stack slots (used as temporaries) in its own activation record (i.e., stack frame). To determine the extent of the callee's activation record, the Locals module needs to know, among other things, the number of arguments of the called function, but only the higher-level decompiler that knows about the class hierarchy (JavaTypes) can determine the calling convention of the methods that r_1 can possibly point to. We resolve this issue by allowing lower-level decompilers to query higher-level decompilers for hints. In this case, Locals asks:

Locals	SymEval	OO	Java Types
$\boxed{\mathbf{r}_{sp} : \mathsf{sp}(-12)}$	$\boxed{\mathbf{r}_1 = \mathbf{m}[\mathbf{m}[\alpha_x''] + 28]}$	$\boxed{\alpha_x'' : \text{nonnull obj}}$	$\boxed{\alpha_x'' : List}$
isFunc($\mathbf{r}_1$)?	isFunc($\mathbf{m}[\mathbf{m}[\alpha_x''] + 28]$)?	isMethod(α_x'', 28)?	
$\xrightarrow{\hspace{1cm}}$	$\xrightarrow{\hspace{1cm}}$	$\xrightarrow{\hspace{1cm}}$	
Yes, 1 argument	Yes, 1 argument	Yes, 0 arguments	
$\xleftarrow{\hspace{1cm}}$	$\xleftarrow{\hspace{1cm}}$	$\xleftarrow{\hspace{1cm}}$	

17 icall [$\mathbf{r}_1$]   icall [$\mathbf{r}_1$]($\mathbf{t}_1$)   icall [$\mathbf{m}[\mathbf{m}[\alpha_x''] + 28]$]($\alpha_x''$)   invokevirtual [$\alpha_x''$, 28]() α_x''.next()

Assembly	Locals IL	SymEval IL	OO IL	Java IL

Fig. 4. Queries to resolve the dynamic dispatch from line 17 of Fig. 3

"Should icall [$\mathbf{r}_1$] be treated as a standard function call; if so, how many arguments does it take?". If some higher-level decompiler knows the answer, then it can translate the assembly-level jump-and-link (icall [$\mathbf{r}_1$]) to a higher-level call with arguments and a return register and appropriately take into account its possible interprocedural effects.

In Fig. 4, we show this query process in further detail, eliding the return values. Precisely how these decompilers work is not particularly relevant here (see details in Sect. 3). Focus on the original query isFunc($\mathbf{r}_1$) from Locals. To obtain an answer, the query gets decompiled into appropriate variants on the way up to Java Types. The answer is then translated on the way down. For the OO module the method has no arguments, but at the lower-level the implicit this argument becomes explicit. For Java Types to answer the query, it must know the type of the receiver object, which it gets from its abstract state. The abstract states of the intermediate decompilers are necessary in order to translate queries so that Java Types can answer them. We show portions of each decompiler's abstract state in the boxes above the queries; for example, Locals must track the current value of the stack pointer register $\mathbf{r}_{sp}$ (we write $\mathsf{sp}(n)$ for a stack pointer that is equal to $\mathbf{r}_{sp}$ on function entry plus n). By also tracking return addresses, this same query also allows Locals to decompile calls that are implemented in assembly as (indirect) jumps (e.g., tail calls). This canonicalization then enables higher-level decompilers to treat all calls uniformly.

Adjacent decompilers agree upon the queries $\boxed{\textbf{type curr} = \textbf{hints}_{out} \times \textbf{abs}}$ that can be made by defining a type hints in their shared intermediate language. An object of type hints$_{out}$ provides information about the current abstract states of higher-level decompilers, usually in the form of one or more callback functions like isFunc. Such an object is provided as an input to the step function of each decompiler (as part of curr); This architecture with decompilations and callbacks works quite nicely, as long as the decompilers agree on the number of successors and their program locations.

Decompiling Control-Flow. Obtaining a reasonable control-flow graph on which to perform analysis is a well-known problem when dealing with assembly code and is often a source of unsoundness, particularly when handling indirect control-flow. For example, switch tables, function calls, function returns, exception raises may all be implemented as indirect jumps (ijump) in assembly. We approach this problem by integrating the control-flow determination with the decompilation; that is, we make no *a priori* guesses on where an indirect jump goes and rely on the decompiler modules to resolve them to a set of concrete program points. In general, there are two cases where the decompilers may not be able to agree on the same successors: lower-level decompilers *don't know the successors* or higher-level ones have *additional successors*. Sometimes a low-level decompiler does not know the possible concrete successors. For example, if the Locals decompiler cannot resolve an indirect jump, it will produce an *indirect* successor indicating it does not know where the indirect jump will go. However, a higher-level decompiler may be able to refine the indirect successor to a set of concrete successors (that, for soundness, must cover where the indirect jump may actually go). It is then an error if any indirect successors remain unresolved after the entire pipeline. A decompiler may also need to introduce additional successors not known to lower-level modules. In both examples, a high-level decompiler augments the set of successors with respect to those of the low-level decompilers. The problem is that we do not have abstract states for the low-level decompilers at the newly introduced successors. This, in turn, means that it will be impossible to continue the decompilation at one of these successors.

To illustrate the latter situation, consider a static method call C.m() inside the try of a try-catch block and its compilation to assembly (shown to the right). We would like to make use of the run-time stack analysis and expression normalization performed by Locals and SymEval in decompiling exceptions, so the decompiler that handles exceptions should be placed somewhere after them in the pipeline. However, the Locals decompiler, and several decompilers after it, produce one successor abstract state after the call to C.m() (line 2). In order to soundly analyze a possible throw in C.m(), the decompiler that handles exceptions must add one more successor at the method call for the catch block at L_{catch}. The challenge is to generate appropriate low-level abstract states for the successor at L_{catch}. For example, the exceptions decompiler might want to direct all other decompilers to transform their abstract states before the static method call and produce an abstract state for L_{catch} from it by clobbering certain registers and portions of memory.

```
1   ...
2     call C.m
3     ...
4     jump Lexit
5   Lcatch:
6     ...
7   Lexit:
8     ...
```

The mechanism we propose is based on the observation that we already have a pipeline of decompilers that is able to transform

$$\text{type succ} = \text{loc} \times (\text{abs} \times ((\text{instr}_c \text{ list}) \text{ option}))$$

the abstract states at all levels when given a sequence of machine instructions. To take advantage of this we require a decompiler to provide, for each newly introduced successor, a list of machine instructions that will be "run" through the decompilation pipeline (using step) to produce the missing lower-level abstract states. To achieve this, the succ type (used in the return of step) carries an optional list of *machine* instructions (of type instr_c). As a side-condition, the concrete machine instructions returned by step should not include control-flow instructions (e.g., jump). We also extend the concrete machine instruction set with instructions for abstracting effects; for example, there is a way to express that register $\mathbf{r}_x$ gets modified arbitrarily (havoc $\mathbf{r}_x$).

Both queries and these *reinterpretations* introduce a channel of communication from higher-level decompilers to lower-level ones, but they serve complimentary purposes. For one, reinterpretations are initiated by high-level decompilers, while queries are initiated

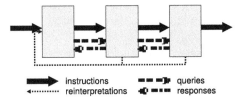

by low-level decompilers. We want to use queries when we want the question to be decompiled, while we prefer to communicate through reinterpretations when we want the answers to be decompiled. The diagram above summarizes these points. In the extended version [9], we give the product decompiler that ties together the pipeline (with queries and reinterpretations), which further clarifies how the decompiler modules interact to advance simultaneously.

Soundness of Decompiler Pipelines. One of the main advantages of the modular architecture we describe in this paper is that we can modularize the soundness argument itself. This modularization increases the trustworthiness of the program analysis and is a first step towards generating machine-checkable proofs of soundness, in the style of Foundational Proof-Carrying Code [3].

Since we build on the framework of abstract interpretation, the proof obligations for demonstrating the soundness of a decompiler are fairly standard local criteria, which we sketch here. Soundness of a decompiler module is shown with respect to the semantics of its *input and output* languages given by concrete transition relations. In particular, leaving the program implicit, we write $I_L \ \colon \ l \leadsto_L l'@\ell$ for the one-step transition relation of the input (lower-level) machine, which says that on instruction I_L and pre-state l, the post-state is l' at program location ℓ (similarly for the output machine $\mathcal{H}$). As usual, we can specify whatever safety policy of interest by disallowing transitions that would violate the policy (i.e., modeling errors as "getting stuck"). Also, we need to define a *soundness relation* $l \precsim a$ between concrete states for the input machine and abstract states, as well as a *simulation relation* $l \sim h$ between concrete states of the input and output machines.

Note that for a given assembly program, we use the same locations for all decompilations since we consider one-to-one decompilations for presentation purposes (otherwise, we would consider a correspondence between locations at different levels). Let $\mathcal{L}_0$ and $\mathcal{H}_0$ denote the initial machine states (as a mapping from starting locations to states) such that they have the same starting locations each with compatible states (i.e., $\mathrm{dom}(\mathcal{L}_0) = \mathrm{dom}(\mathcal{H}_0)$ and $\mathcal{L}_0(\ell) \sim \mathcal{H}_0(\ell)$ for all $\ell \in \mathrm{dom}(\mathcal{L}_0)$). Now consider running the decompiler pipeline to completion (i.e., to fixed point) and let $\mathcal{A}_{\mathrm{INV}}$ be the mapping from locations to abstract states at fixed point. Note that $\mathcal{A}_{\mathrm{INV}}$ must contain initial abstract states compatible with the concrete states in $\mathcal{L}_0$ (i.e., $\mathrm{dom}(\mathcal{L}_0) \subseteq \mathrm{dom}(\mathcal{A}_{\mathrm{INV}})$ and $\mathcal{L}_0(\ell) \precsim \mathcal{A}_{\mathrm{INV}}(\ell)$ for all $\ell \in \mathrm{dom}(\mathcal{L}_0)$).

We can now state the local soundness properties for a decompiler module's step. A decompiler's step need only give sound results when the query object it receives as input yields answers that are sound approximations of the machine state, which we write as $h \gtrsim q$ (and which would be defined and shown separately).

Property 1 (Progress). If $l \sim h$, $l \precsim a$, $h \gtrsim q$, $\mathtt{step}((q, a), I_L) = (I_{\mathcal{H}}, A')$ and $I_{\mathcal{H}} \, \S \, h \leadsto_{\mathcal{H}} h'@\ell$, then $I_L \, \S \, l \leadsto_L l'@\ell$ (for some l').

Progress says that whenever the decompiler can make a step *and* whenever the output machine is not stuck, then the input machine is also not stuck. That is, a decompiler residuates soundness obligations to higher-level decompilers through its output instruction. Thus far, we have not discussed the semantics of the intermediate languages very precisely, but here is where it becomes important. For example, for stack slots to be soundly translated to temporaries by the Locals decompiler, the semantics of the memory write instruction in Locals IL is not the same as a memory write in the assembly in that it must disallow updating such stack regions. In essence, the guarantees provided by and the expectations of a decompiler module for higher-level ones are encoded in the instructions it outputs. If a decompiler module fails to perform sufficient checks for its decompilations, then the proof of this property will fail.

To implement a verifier that enforces a particular safety policy using a decompiler pipeline, we need to have a module at the end that does not output higher-level instructions to close the process (i.e., capping the end). Such a module can be particularly simple; for example, we could have a module that simply checks syntactically that all the "possibly unsafe" instructions have been decompiled away (e.g., for memory safety, all memory read instructions have been decompiled into various safe read instructions).

Property 2 (Preservation). If $l \sim h$, $l \precsim a$, $h \gtrsim q$ and $\mathtt{step}((q, a), I_L) = (I_{\mathcal{H}}, A')$, then for every l' such that $I_L \, \S \, l \leadsto_L l'@\ell$, there exists h', a' such that $I_{\mathcal{H}} \, \S \, h \leadsto_{\mathcal{H}} h'@\ell$ where $l' \sim h'$ and $a' = \mathcal{A}_{\mathrm{INV}}(\ell)$ where $l' \precsim a'$.

Preservation guarantees that for every transition made by the input machine, the output machine simulates it and the concrete successor state matches one of the abstract successors computed by $\mathtt{step}$ (in $\mathcal{A}_{\mathrm{INV}}$).

3   Decompiler Examples

In this section, we describe a few decompilers from Fig. 1. For each decompiler, we give the instructions of the output language, the lattice of abstract values, and a description of the decompilation function $\mathtt{step}$. We use the simplified notation $\mathtt{step}(a_{curr}, I_{in}) = (I_{out}, a_{succ})$ to say that in the abstract state a_{curr} the instruction I_{in} is decompiled to I_{out} and yields a successor state a_{succ}. We write $a_{succ}@\ell$ to indicate the location of the successor, but we elide the location in the common case when it is "fall-through". A missing successor state a_{succ} means that the current analysis path ends. We leave the query object implicit, using q to stand for it when necessary. Since each decompiler has similar structure, we use subscripts with names of decompilers or languages when necessary to clarify to which module something belongs.

Decompiling Calls and Locals. The Locals module deals with stack conventions and introduces the notion of statically-scoped local variables. The two

$$\text{instr} \quad I_L ::= I_C \mid x := \texttt{call } \ell(e_1, ..., e_n)$$
$$\mid x := \texttt{icall } [e](e_1, ..., e_n)$$
$$\mid \texttt{return } e$$
$$\text{abs values} \quad \tau ::= \top \mid n \mid \mathsf{sp}(n) \mid \mathsf{ra} \mid \&\ell \mid \mathsf{cs}(r)$$

major changes from assembly instructions (I_C) are that call and return instructions have actual arguments. The abstract state includes a mapping Γ from variables x to abstract values τ, along with two additional integers, n_{lo} and n_{hi}, that delimit the current activation record (i.e., the extent of the known valid stack addresses for this function) with respect to the value of the stack pointer on entry. The variables mapped by the abstract state include all machine registers and variables $\mathbf{t}_n$ that correspond to stack slots (with the subscript indicating the stack offset of the slot in question). We need only track a few abstract values τ: the value of stack pointers $\mathsf{sp}(n)$, the return address for the function ra, code addresses for function return addresses $\&\ell$, and the value of callee-save registers on function entry $\mathsf{cs}(r)$. These values form a flat lattice, with the usual ordering.

Many of the cases for the step function

$$\frac{\Gamma \vdash e : \mathsf{sp}(n) \quad n_{lo} \leq n \leq n_{hi} \quad n \equiv 0 \ (\mathrm{mod} \ 4)}{\texttt{step}(\langle \Gamma; n_{lo}; n_{hi} \rangle, r := \mathbf{m}[e]) \ = \ (r := \mathbf{t}_n, \langle \Gamma[r \mapsto \Gamma(\mathbf{t}_n)]; n_{lo}; n_{hi} \rangle)}$$

propagate the input instruction unchanged and update the abstract state. We show here the definition of step for the decompilation of a stack memory read to a move from a variable. For simplicity, we assume here that all stack slots are used for locals. This setup can be extended to allow higher-level decompilers to indicate (through some high-to-low communication) which portions of the stack frame it wants to handle separately. We write $\Gamma \vdash e : \tau$ to say that in the abstract state $\langle \Gamma; n_{lo}; n_{hi} \rangle$, the expression e has abstract value τ. For verifying memory safety, a key observation is that Locals proves once and for all that such a read is to a valid memory address; by decompiling to a move instruction, no higher-level decompiler needs to do this reasoning. The analogous translation for stack writes appears on, for example, line 19 in Fig. 3.

The following rule gives the translation of function calls:

$$\frac{\Gamma(x_{ra}) = \&\ell \quad \Gamma(\mathbf{r}_{sp}) = \mathsf{sp}(n) \quad n \equiv 0 \ (\mathrm{mod} \ 4) \quad q.\mathsf{isFunc}(e) = k \quad \Gamma' = scramble(\Gamma, n, k)}{\texttt{step}(\langle \Gamma; n_{lo}; n_{hi} \rangle, \texttt{icall } [e]) \ = \ (x_{rv} := \texttt{icall } [e](x_1, ..., x_k), \langle \Gamma'[\mathbf{r}_{sp} \mapsto \mathsf{sp}(n+4)]; n_{lo}; n_{hi} \rangle @\ell)}$$

It checks that the return address is set, $\mathbf{r}_{sp}$ contains a word-aligned stack pointer, and e is the address of a function according to the query. Based on the calling convention and number of arguments, it constructs the call with arguments and the return register. The successor state Γ' is obtained first by clearing any non-callee-save registers and temporaries corresponding to stack slots in the callee's activation record, which is determined by $scramble$ using the calling convention, n, and k. Then, $\mathbf{r}_{sp}$ is updated, shown here according to the x86 calling convention where the callee pops the return address. In the implementation, we parameterize by a description of the calling convention. Further details, including the verification of stack overflow checking, is given in the extended version [9].

Symbolic Evaluator. The SymEval ($\mathcal{E}$) module does the following analysis and transformations for higher-level decompilers to resolve some particularly pervasive problems when analyzing assembly code.

1. *Simplified and Normalized Expressions.* High-level operations get compiled into long sequences of assembly instructions with intermediate values exposed (as exemplified in Fig. 3). To analyze one instruction at a time, we need to assign types to all intermediate expressions, but this undertaking quickly becomes unwieldy. Additionally, arithmetic equivalences are used extensively by compilers (particularly in optimized code). We want to accumulate larger expression trees and perform arithmetic simplification and normalization before assigning types. Observe how SymEval does this work in the example decompilation of line 17 in Fig. 4.

2. *Static Single Assignment (SSA).* In contrast to source-level variables, flow-sensitivity is generally required to analyze registers because registers are reused for unrelated purposes. To have a set variables suitable for source-level analyses, the symbolic evaluator yields an SSA-like program representation.

3. *Global Value Numbering (GVN).* The same variable may also be placed in multiple locations (yielding an equality on those locations). For example, to check that a reference stored on the stack is non-null, a compiler must emit code that first loads it into a register. On the non-null path, an assembly-level analysis needs to know that the contents of both the register and the stack slot is non-null. So that higher-level decompilers do not have to deal with such low-level details, the symbolic evaluator presents a single *symbolic value* α that abstracts some unknown value but is stored in both the register and the stack slot (implicitly conveying the equality). Combined with the above, the symbolic evaluator can be viewed as implementing an extended form of GVN [2]. Further details are given in the extended version [9].

Decompiling Object-Oriented Features. The OO decompiler ($\mathcal{O}$) recognizes compilations of class-based object-oriented languages, such as Java. The output instruction language for the OO decompiler includes the instructions from the symbolic evaluator, except it is extended for virtual method dispatch, field reads, and field writes. Almost all of the heavy lifting has been done by the symbolic evaluator, so OO is quite simple. The abstract values that we need to track are straightforward: a type for object references, which may be qualified as non-null or possibly null.

$$\text{instr} \quad I_O ::= I_{\mathcal{E}} \mid \alpha = \texttt{putfield}\,[e, n]$$
$$\mid \alpha = \texttt{invokevirtual}\,[e_0, n](e_1, ..., e_n)$$
$$\text{expr} \quad e_O ::= e_{\mathcal{E}} \mid \texttt{getfield}\,[e, n]$$

The decompilation of virtual method dispatch (as on line 17 in Fig. 4) is as follows:

$$\frac{\Gamma(\beta) = \textsf{nonnull obj} \quad \Gamma \vdash e_1 : \tau_1 \quad \cdots \quad \Gamma \vdash e_m : \tau_m \quad q.\textsf{isMethod}(\beta, n) = \tau_1 \times \cdots \times \tau_m \to \tau}{\begin{array}{l}\texttt{step}(\Gamma, \alpha = \texttt{icall}\,[\mathbf{m}[\mathbf{m}[\beta] + n]](\beta, e_1, ..., e_m)) \\ \qquad = (\alpha = \texttt{invokevirtual}\,[\beta, n](e_1, ..., e_m), \Gamma[\alpha \mapsto \tau])\end{array}}$$

It checks that the object reference is non-null and that the dispatch table is obtained from the same object as the object being passed as the receiver object. Observe that since the abstract state is independent of the register and memory state, the successor abstract state is particularly easy to derive. One additional bit of interesting work is that it must recognize null-checks and strengthen a possibly-null object to a non-null one. Because of the symbolic evaluator, OO simply updates the type of a symbolic value α and need not worry about the equivalences between all the registers or temporaries that contain α.

Implementation and Experience. We have implemented and tested the above decompiler modules in multiple decompiler pipelines, including three main ones for assembly generated from Java programs by `gcj`, C programs by `gcc`, and Cool programs by `coolc`. All decompiler pipelines start from a very simple untyped RISC-like assembly language to minimize architecture dependence. We have parsers for x86 and MIPS that translate to this generic assembly. The Locals module is parameterized by the calling convention, so we can easily handle several different calling conventions (e.g., standard x86, standard MIPS, or the non-standard one used by `coolc`). In these pipelines, we use communication in three main ways: queries for identifying function or method calls (as in Fig. 4), queries for pointer types, and reinterpretations for exceptional successors (as in Decompiling Control-Flow of Sect. 2). The responses for the isFunc and isMethod queries contain a bit more information than as shown in Fig. 4, such as the calling convention for the callee and between JavaTypes/CoolTypes and OO, the types of the parameters and the return value (i.e., whether they are object references). The OO decompiler also queries JavaTypes/CoolTypes to determine certain pointer types that may require consulting the class table, such as whether a read field is an object reference.

Each of the decompiler modules described above is actually quite small (at most ∼600 lines of OCaml). Furthermore, each module is approximately the same size providing some evidence for a good division of labor. The overhead (i.e., the definition of the intermediate languages and associated utility functions) seems reasonable, as each language only required 100–150 lines of OCaml. The entire `coolc` pipeline (including the Cool type analysis but not the

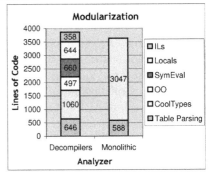

framework code) is 3,865 lines compared to 3,635 lines for a monolithic assembly-level analyzer from our previous work [8], which uses the classic reduced product approach (as shown visually above). Cool is a fairly realistic subset of Java, including features such as exceptions, so the CoolTypes module includes the handling of exceptions as described in Decompiling Control-Flow of Sect. 2. The additional code is essentially in the definition of the intermediate languages, so what we conclude is that our pipeline approach does give us a modular and easier to maintain design without imposing an unreasonable code size penalty with respect to the monolithic version. Additionally, note that 2,159 and 1,515 of the 3,865 lines of the `coolc` decompiler pipeline are reused as-is in the `gcj` and `gcc` pipelines, respectively.

Comparing the implementation experience with our previous assembly-level analyzer, we found that the separation of concerns imposed by this framework made it much easier to reason about and implement such assembly-level analyses. For example, because of the decompilations, Cool/Java type inference is no longer intermingled with the analysis of compiler-specific run-time structures. With this framework, we also obtained comparable stability in a much shorter amount of time. Many of the bugs in the implementation described in our prior work [8] were caused by subtle interactions in the somewhat ad-hoc modularization there, which simply did not materialize here. Concretely, after testing our `coolc` decompiler pipeline on a small suite of regression tests developed with the previous monolithic version, we ran both the decompiler pipeline and the previous monolithic versions on the set of 10,339 test cases generated from Cool compilers developed by students in the Spring 2002, Spring 2003, and Spring 2004 offerings of the compilers course at UC Berkeley (on which we previously reported [8]). Of the 10,339 test cases, they disagreed in 182 instances, which were then examined manually to classify them as either soundness bugs or incompletenesses in either the decompiler or monolithic versions. We found 1 incompleteness in the decompiler version with respect to the monolithic version that was easily fixed (some identification of dead code based on knowing that a pointer is non-null), and we found 0 soundness bugs in the decompiler version. At the same time, we found 5 incompletenesses in the monolithic version; in 2 cases, it appears the SymEval module was the difference. Surprisingly, we found 3 soundness bugs in the monolithic version, which has been used extensively by several classes. We expected to find bugs in the decompiler version to flush out, but in the end, we actually found more bugs in the more well-tested monolithic version. At least 1 soundness bug and 1 incompleteness in the monolithic version were due to mishandling of calls to run-time functions. There seem to be two reasons why the decompiler version does not exhibit these bugs: the updating of effects after a call is implemented in several places in the monolithic version (because of special cases for run-time functions), while in the decompiler version, the Locals decompiler identifies all calls, so they can be treated uniformly in all later modules; and the SSA-like representation produced by SymEval decompiler greatly simplifies the handling of interprocedural effects in higher-level modules.

As another example of the utility of this approach, after the implementation for the class table parser was complete (which are already generated by `gcj` to support reflection), one of the authors was able to implement a basic Java type inference module in 3–4 hours and ∼500 lines of code (without the handling of interfaces and exceptions).

4   Case Studies

To explore the feasibility of applying existing source-level tools to assembly code, we have used BLAST [18] and Cqual [17] on decompilations produced by our

gcc pipeline. To interface with these tools, we have a module that emits C from
SymEval IL. SymEval IL is essentially C, as register reuse with unrelated types
have been eliminated by SSA and expression trees have been recovered. However,
while a straightforward translation from SymEval IL produces a valid C program
that can be (re)compiled and executed, the typing is often too weak for source-
level analysis tools. To avoid this issue for these experiments, we use debugging
information to recover types. When debugging information is not available, we
might be able to obtain typing information using a decompiler module that
implements a type reconstruction algorithm such as Mycroft's [24].

We have taken the
benchmarks shown in the
table, compiled them to
x86 (unoptimized), and
decompiled them back to
C before feeding the de-
compilations to the source-
level tools (B for BLAST

Test Case		Code Size		Decomp.	Verification	
		C	x86		Orig.	Decomp.
		(loc)	(loc)	(sec)	(sec)	(sec)
qpmouse.c	(B)	7994	1851	0.74	0.34	1.26
tlan.c	(B)	10909	10734	8.16	41.20	94.30
gamma_dma.c	(Q)	11239	5235	2.44	0.97	1.05

and Q for Cqual). In all cases, we checked that the tools could verify the presence
(or absence) of bugs just as they had for the original C program. In the table, we
show our decompilation times and the verification times of both the original and
decompiled programs on a 1.7GHz Pentium 4 with 1GB RAM. The BLAST cases
qpmouse.c and tlan.c are previously reported Linux device drivers for which
BLAST checks that lock and unlock are used correctly [18]. For gamma_dma.c,
a file from version 2.4.23 of the Linux kernel, Cqual is able to find in the decompiled program a previously reported bug involving the unsafe dereference of a
user-mode pointer [20]. Both Cqual and BLAST require interprocedural analyses
and some C type information to check their respective properties. We have also
repeated some of these experiments with optimized code. With qpmouse, we were
able to use all the -O2 optimizations in gcc 3.4.4, such as instruction scheduling,
except -fmerge-constants, which yields code that reads a byte directly from
the middle of a word-sized field, and -foptimize-sibling-calls, which introduces tail calls. The latter problem we could probably handle with an improved
Locals module, but the former is more difficult due to limitations with using
the debugging information for recovering C types. In particular, it is challenging
to map complicated pointer offsets back to C struct accesses. Similarly, it is
sometimes difficult to insert casts that do not confuse client analyses based only
on the debugging information because it does not always tell us where casts are
performed. Finally, we do not yet handle all assembly instructions, particularly
kernel instructions.

5   Related Work

In abstract interpretation, the problem of combining abstract domains has also
been considered by many. Cousot and Cousot [15] define the notion of a *reduced product*, which gives a "gold standard" for precise combinations of ab-

stract domains. Unfortunately, obtaining a reduced product implementation is not automatic; they generally require manual definitions of reduction operators, which depend on the specifics of the domains being combined (e.g., [11]). Roughly speaking, we propose a framework for building reduced products based on decompilation, which is particular amiable for modularizing the analysis of assembly code. Cortesi *et al.* [13] describe a framework (called an *open product*) that takes queries as the central (and only) means of communication. They allow arbitrary queries between any pair of domains, whereas our queries are more structured through decompilation. With this structure we impose, modules need only agree upon a communication interface with its neighbors. Combining program analyses for compiler optimization is also a well-known and well-studied problem. Lerner *et al.* [21] propose modular combinations of compiler optimizations also by integrating analysis with program transformation, which then serve as the primary channel of communication between analyses. We, however, use transformation for abstraction rather than optimization. For this reason, we use layers of intermediate languages instead of one common language, which is especially useful to allow residuation of soundness obligations.

Practically all analysis frameworks, particularly for low-level code, perform some decompilation or canonicalization for client analyses. For example, CodeSurfer/x86 [4] seeks to provide a higher-level intermediate representation for analyzing x86 machine code. At the core of CodeSurfer/x86 is a nice combined integer and pointer analysis (*value set analysis*) for abstract locations. The motivation for this analysis is similar to that for the Locals module, except we prefer to handle the heap separately in language-specific ways. Their overall approach is a bit different from ours in that they try to decompile without the assistance of any higher-level language-specific analysis, which leads to complexity and possible unsoundness in the handling of, for example, indirect jumps and stack-allocated arrays. While even they must make the assumption that the code conforms to a "standard compilation model" where a run-time stack of activation records are pushed and popped on function call and return, their approach is more generic out of the box. We instead advocate a clean modularization to enable reuse of decompiler components in order to make customized pipelines more palatable.

Tröger and Cifuentes [27] give a technique to identify virtual method dispatch in machine code binaries based on computing a backward slice from the indirect call. They also try to be generic to any compiler, which necessarily leads to difficulties and imprecision that are not problems for us. Cifuentes *et al.* [10] describe a decompiler from SPARC assembly to C. Driven by the program understanding application, most of their focus is on recovering structured control-flow, which is often unnecessary (if not undesirable) for targeting program analyses.

6   Conclusion and Future Work

We have described a flexible and modular methodology for building assembly code analyses based on a novel notion of cooperating decompilers. We have shown the effectiveness of our framework through three example decompiler pipelines that share low-level components: for the output of `gcc`, `gcj`, and compilers for the Cool object-oriented language.

We are particularly interested in assembly-level analyses for addressing mobile-code safety [25, 23], ideally in a foundational but also practical manner. As such, we have designed our decompilation framework with soundness in mind (e.g., making decompilers work one instruction at a time and working in the framework of abstract interpretation), though we have not yet constructed machine-checkable soundness proofs for our example decompilers. To achieve this, we envision building on our prior work on *certified program analyses* [7], as well as drawing on abstract interpretation-based transformations [16, 26]. Such a modularization of code as we have achieved will likely be critical for feasibly proving the soundness of analysis implementations in a machine-checkable manner. This motivation also partly justifies our use of reflection tables produced by `gcj` or debugging information from `gcc`, as it seems reasonable to trade-off, at least, some annotations for safety checking.

References

[1] A. Aiken. Cool: A portable project for teaching compiler construction. *ACM SIGPLAN Notices*, 31(7):19–24, July 1996.

[2] B. Alpern, M. N. Wegman, and F. K. Zadeck. Detecting equality of variables in programs. In *Principles of Programming Languages (POPL)*, pages 1–11, 1988.

[3] A. W. Appel. Foundational proof-carrying code. In *Logic in Computer Science (LICS)*, pages 247–258, June 2001.

[4] G. Balakrishnan and T. W. Reps. Analyzing memory accesses in x86 executables. In *Compiler Construction (CC)*, pages 5–23, 2004.

[5] G. Balakrishnan, T. W. Reps, N. Kidd, A. Lal, J. Lim, D. Melski, R. Gruian, S. H. Yong, C.-H. Chen, and T. Teitelbaum. Model checking x86 executables with CodeSurfer/x86 and WPDS++. In *Computer-Aided Verification (CAV)*, pages 158–163, 2005.

[6] M. Barnett, B.-Y. E. Chang, R. DeLine, B. Jacobs, and K. R. M. Leino. Boogie: A modular reusable verifier for object-oriented programs. In *Formal Methods for Components and Objects (FMCO)*, 2005.

[7] B.-Y. E. Chang, A. Chlipala, and G. C. Necula. A framework for certified program analysis and its applications to mobile-code safety. In *Verification, Model Checking, and Abstract Interpretation (VMCAI)*, pages 174–189, 2006.

[8] B.-Y. E. Chang, A. Chlipala, G. C. Necula, and R. R. Schneck. Type-based verification of assembly language for compiler debugging. In *Types in Language Design and Implementation (TLDI)*, pages 91–102, 2005.

[9] B.-Y. E. Chang, M. Harren, and G. C. Necula. Analysis of low-level code using cooperating decompilers. Technical Report EECS-2006-86, UC Berkeley, 2006.

[10] C. Cifuentes, D. Simon, and A. Fraboulet. Assembly to high-level language translation. In *Software Maintenance (ICSM)*, pages 228–237, 1998.

[11] M. Codish, A. Mulkers, M. Bruynooghe, M. J. G. de la Banda, and M. V. Hermenegildo. Improving abstract interpretations by combining domains. *ACM Trans. Program. Lang. Syst.*, 17(1):28–44, 1995.

[12] C. Colby, P. Lee, G. C. Necula, F. Blau, M. Plesko, and K. Cline. A certifying compiler for Java. In *Programming Language Design and Implementation (PLDI)*, pages 95–107, 2000.

[13] A. Cortesi, B. L. Charlier, and P. V. Hentenryck. Combinations of abstract domains for logic programming. In *Principles of Programming Languages (POPL)*, pages 227–239, 1994.

[14] P. Cousot and R. Cousot. Abstract interpretation: A unified lattice model for static analysis of programs by construction or approximation of fixpoints. In *Principles of Programming Languages (POPL)*, pages 234–252, 1977.

[15] P. Cousot and R. Cousot. Systematic design of program analysis frameworks. In *Principles of Programming Languages (POPL)*, pages 269–282, 1979.

[16] P. Cousot and R. Cousot. Systematic design of program transformation frameworks by abstract interpretation. In *Principles of Programming Languages (POPL)*, pages 178–190, 2002.

[17] J. Foster, T. Terauchi, and A. Aiken. Flow-sensitive type qualifiers. In *Programming Language Design and Implementation (PLDI)*, pages 1–12, 2002.

[18] T. A. Henzinger, R. Jhala, R. Majumdar, G. C. Necula, G. Sutre, and W. Weimer. Temporal-safety proofs for systems code. In *Computer-Aided Verification (CAV)*, pages 526–538, 2002.

[19] IDA Pro disassembler. http://www.datarescue.com/idabase.

[20] R. Johnson and D. Wagner. Finding user/kernel pointer bugs with type inference. In *USENIX Security Symposium*, pages 119–134, 2004.

[21] S. Lerner, D. Grove, and C. Chambers. Composing dataflow analyses and transformations. In *Principles of Programming Languages (POPL)*, pages 270–282, 2002.

[22] T. Lindholm and F. Yellin. *The Java Virtual Machine Specification*. The Java Series. Addison-Wesley, Reading, MA, USA, Jan. 1997.

[23] J. G. Morrisett, D. Walker, K. Crary, and N. Glew. From system F to typed assembly language. *ACM Trans. Program. Lang. Syst.*, 21(3):527–568, 1999.

[24] A. Mycroft. Type-based decompilation. In *European Symposium on Programming (ESOP)*, pages 208–223, 1999.

[25] G. C. Necula. Proof-carrying code. In *Principles of Programming Languages (POPL)*, pages 106–119, Jan. 1997.

[26] X. Rival. Abstract interpretation-based certification of assembly code. In *Verification, Model Checking, and Abstract Interpretation (VMCAI)*, pages 41–55, 2003.

[27] J. Tröger and C. Cifuentes. Analysis of virtual method invocation for binary translation. In *Reverse Engineering (WCRE)*, pages 65–74, 2002.

[28] R. Vallée-Rai, P. Co, E. Gagnon, L. J. Hendren, P. Lam, and V. Sundaresan. Soot - a Java bytecode optimization framework. In *Centre for Advanced Studies on Collaborative Research (CASCON)*, page 13, 1999.

Static Analysis for Java Servlets and JSP

Christian Kirkegaard and Anders Møller

BRICS*, University of Aarhus, Denmark
{ck, amoeller}@brics.dk

Abstract. We present an approach for statically reasoning about the behavior of Web applications that are developed using Java Servlets and JSP. Specifically, we attack the problems of guaranteeing that all output is well-formed and valid XML and ensuring consistency of XHTML form fields and session state. Our approach builds on a collection of program analysis techniques developed earlier in the JWIG and XACT projects, combined with work on balanced context-free grammars. Together, this provides the necessary foundation concerning reasoning about output streams and application control flow.

1 Introduction

Java Servlets [15] and JSP (JavaServer Pages) [16] constitute a widely used platform for Web application development. Applications that are developed using these or related technologies are typically structured as collections of program fragments (servlets or JSP pages) that receive user input, produce HTML or XML output, and interact with databases. These fragments are connected via forms and links in the generated pages, using deployment descriptors to declaratively map URLs to program fragments. This way of structuring applications causes many challenges to the programmer. In particular, it is difficult to ensure, at compile time, the following desirable properties:

- all output should be well-formed and valid XML (according to, for example, the schema for XHTML 1.0);
- the forms and fields that are produced by one program fragment that generates an XHTML page should always match what is expected by another program fragment that takes care of receiving the user input; and
- session attributes that one program fragment expects to be present should always have been set previously in the session.

Our aim is to develop a program analysis system that can automatically check these properties for a given Web application.

The small example program shown on the following page illustrates some of the many challenges that may arise.

---

* Basic Research in Computer Science (www.brics.dk), funded by the Danish National Research Foundation.

K. Yi (Ed.): SAS 2006, LNCS 4134, pp. 336–352, 2006.

```java
public class Entry extends javax.servlet.http.HttpServlet {
  protected void doGet(HttpServletRequest request,
                       HttpServletResponse response)
      throws ServletException, IOException {
    HttpSession session = request.getSession();
    String url = response.encodeURL(request.getContextPath()+"/show");
    session.setAttribute("timestamp", new Date());
    response.setContentType("application/xhtml+xml");
    PrintWriter out = response.getWriter();
    Wrapper.printHeader(out, "Enter name", session);
    out.print("<form action=\""+url+"\" method=\"POST\">"+
              "<input type=\"text\" name=\"NAME\"/>"+
              "<input type=\"submit\" value=\"lookup\"/>"+
              "</form>");
    Wrapper.printFooter(out);
  }
}

public class Show extends javax.servlet.http.HttpServlet {
  protected void doPost(HttpServletRequest request,
                        HttpServletResponse response)
      throws ServletException, IOException {
    Directory directory = new Directory("ldap://ldap.widgets.org");
    String name = misc.encodeXML(request.getParameter("NAME"));
    response.setContentType("application/xhtml+xml");
    PrintWriter out = response.getWriter();
    Wrapper.printHeader(out, name, request.getSession());
    out.print("<b>Phone:</b> "+directory.phone(name));
    Wrapper.printFooter(out);
  }
}

public class Wrapper {
  static void printHeader(PrintWriter pw, String title,
                          HttpSession session) {
    pw.print("<html xmlns=\"http://www.w3.org/1999/xhtml\">"+
             "<head><title>"+title+"</title></head><body>"+
             "<hr size=\"1\"/>"+
             "<div align=\"right\"><small>"+
             "Session initiated ["+session.getAttribute("timestamp")+"]"+
             "</small></div><hr size=\"1\"/>"+
             "<h3>"+title+"</h3>");
  }

  static void printFooter(PrintWriter pw) {
    pw.print("<hr size=\"1\"/></body></html>");
  }
}
```

This program contains two servlets: one named `Entry` that produces an XHTML page with a form where the user enters a name, and one named `Show` that receives the user input and produces a reply as another XHTML page based on information from an external database. We assume that the deployment descriptor maps the relative URL `enter` to the first servlet and `show` to the second one. Also, `misc.encodeXML` is a method that escapes special XML characters (for example, converting `<` to `&lt;`). At runtime, the pages may look as follows:

Session initiated [Fri Feb 17 13:04:23 CET 2006] **Enter name** [John Doe| Lookup]	Session initiated [Fri Feb 17 13:04:23 CET 2006] **John Doe** **Phone:** (202) 555-1414

In order for the program to work as intended, the programmer must consider many aspects, even for such a tiny program, as the following questions indicate:

- do all open start tags produced by `printHeader` match the end tags produced by `printFooter`?
- does `getAttribute("timestamp")` always return strings that are legal as XML character data? (for example, '`<`' should not appear here)
- does the form action URL that is produced by `Enter` in fact point to the `Show` servlet? (this depends on the value of the `action` and `method` attributes and the deployment descriptor mapping)
- is the parameter `NAME` always present when the `Show` servlet is executed? (checking this requires knowledge of the presence of form fields in the XHTML pages that lead to this servlet)
- is the attribute `timestamp` always present in the session state when the `Show` servlet is executed? (if not, a null reference would appear)

To answer such questions statically, one must have a clear picture of which string fragments are being printed to the output stream and how the servlets are connected in the application. Presently, programmers resort to informal reasoning and incomplete testing in order to obtain confidence of the correctness of the program. A more satisfactory situation would of course be to have *static guarantees* provided by a *fully automatic* analysis tool.

As the desirable properties listed above are clearly undecidable, the analysis we present is necessarily approximative. We design our analysis to be conservative in the sense that it may produce spurious warnings, but a program that passes the analysis is guaranteed to satisfy the properties. Naturally, we aim for an analysis that has sufficient precision and performance to be practically useful.

Application servers handle JSP through a simple translation to servlets [16]. This means that by focusing our analysis efforts on servlets, we become able to handle JSP, and applications that combine servlets and JSP, essentially for free.

Contributions. Our contributions are the following:

- We show how to obtain a context-free grammar that conservatively approximates the possible output of servlet/JSP applications using a variant of the Java string analysis [6].
- On top of the string analysis, we apply theory of balanced grammars by Knuth [12] and grammar approximations by Mohri and Nederhof [14] to check that the output is always well-formed XML.
- On top of the well-formedness checking, we show how a balanced context-free grammar can be converted into an XML graph, which is subsequently validated relative to an XML schema using an existing algorithm [8].
- By analyzing the form and link elements that appear in the XML graph together with the deployment descriptor of the application, we explain how to obtain an inter-servlet control flow graph of the application.
- Based on the knowledge of the control flow, we give examples of derived analyses for checking that form fields and session state are used consistently.

Together, the above components form a coherent analysis system for reasoning about the behavior of Web application that are built using Java Servlets and JSP. The system has a *front-end* that converts from Java code to context-free grammars and a *back-end* that converts context-free grammars to XML graphs and checks well-formedness, validity, and other correctness properties. Our approach can be viewed as combining and extending techniques from the JWIG and XACT projects [5,10,8] and applying them to a mainstream Web application development framework.

Perhaps surprisingly, the analysis of well-formedness and validity can be made both sound and complete relative to the grammar being produced in the front-end. (The completeness, however, relies on an assumption that certain well-defined contrived situations do not occur in the program being analyzed).

The goal of the present paper is to outline our analysis system, with particular focus on the construction of context-free grammars and the translation from context-free grammars to XML graphs. The limited space prevents us from describing the details of each component, so we instead base our presentation on a running example. The system is at the time of writing not yet fully implemented; we return to this issue in Section 6.

Although we here focus on Java-based Web applications, we are not relying on language features that are specific to Java. In particular, the approach we present could also be applied to the .NET or PHP platforms where Web applications are typically also built from loosely connected program fragments that each produce XHTML output and receive form input.

Related Work. We are not aware of previous attempts to statically analyze the aspects mentioned above for Java Servlets and JSP applications. The most closely related work is that of Minamide [13] who combines string analysis with HTML validation for PHP. In [13], a variant of the technique from [6] is used to produce a context-free grammar from a PHP program. HTML validation is performed either by extracting and checking sample documents or by considering only documents with bounded depth, which results in neither sound nor complete analysis results.

There are other related interesting connections between XML data and context-free grammars, in particular, the work by Berstel and Boasson [3] and Brüggemann-Klein and Wood [4]. The paper [3] uses Knuth's results to check some aspects of XML well-formedness for a given context-free grammar, but it does not take the full step to validity. The paper [4] only considers grammars that correspond to well-formed XML documents, whereas our scenario involves arbitrary context-free grammars that need to be checked for well-formedness and validity.

Inter-servlet control flow analysis is closely related to workflow and business protocols for Web services. Much effort is put into designing workflow languages and Web service composition languages to be used for modeling and analyzing properties during the design phase of Web application development (examples are WS-BPEL [2] and YAWL [18]). Our work complements this in the sense that the analysis we present is able to reverse engineer workflows from the source code of existing Web applications (although that is not the focus of the present paper). This is related to process mining [7] but using source code instead of system logs, and thereby obtaining conservative results.

As mentioned, our technique builds on our earlier work on JWIG and XACT. JWIG [5] is a Java-based framework for Web application development where session control-flow is explicit and XHTML pages are built in a structured manner that permits static analysis of validity and form field consistency. XACT [10] is a related language for expressing XML transformations. The notion of *XML graphs*, which is essential to our analysis system, comes from these projects (where they are also called *summary graphs* for historical reasons) – an XML graph is a representation of a potentially infinite set of XML structures that may appear in a running JWIG or XACT program. The paper [8] describes an algorithm for validating an XML graph relative to a schema written in XML Schema.

Overview. We first, in Section 2, describe how to analyze the output stream and produce a context-free grammar that approximates the possible output of a given Web application. Section 3 explains the well-formedness check and the construction of a balanced grammar. In Section 4 we then show how to convert the balanced grammar into an XML graph and check validity relative to an XML schema.

Section 5 describes the construction of the inter-servlet control flow graph, based on the XML graph and the deployment descriptor. We also sketch how to use the XML graph and the control-flow information to check consistency of the use of form fields and session state. Finally, in Section 6 we discuss challenges and considerations for implementing the entire analysis system and expectations for its performance and precision.

More details are given in a technical report [9] where we recapitulate Knuth's algorithm for checking balancing of the language of a context-free grammar, explain our extension of Knuth's algorithm for constructing balanced grammars, and consider the precision of our analysis.

2   Analyzing the Output Stream

A servlet sends data to its clients by writing string values to a special output stream, which is allocated by the Web server for each request. Our analysis must trace these output streams and keep track of all the string values written to them. Given a Web application, the analysis produces for each servlet entry point a context-free grammar whose language is guaranteed to contain all data that can possibly be written to the corresponding output stream at runtime.

To keep track of string values, we first run the Java string analysis as described in [6] with the parameters of each `write`, `print`, and `append` invocation on output streams as hotspots. For each invocation, the result is a regular language containing all the possible string values that may occur at those program points.

The subsequent analysis of output streams is a variant of that of `String-Buffers` in the string analysis [6]. In both cases the basic problem is to keep track of the possible *sequences* of side-effecting operations that may be performed on certain objects. However, there are only append-like operations on output streams, and, since append is an associative operation, this makes the handling of interprocedural data-flow somewhat simpler in our case.

For each method in the Web application, we produce a *flow graph* where edges represent control flow and nodes have the following kinds:

- append: an append operation corresponding to a `write`, `print`, or `append` operation on an output stream, where the argument is given by a regular language of string values as produced by the preliminary string analysis;
- invoke: a method invocation carrying information about its possible targets;
- nop: a join point (for example, for a `while` statement or a method exit).

Constructing such a flow graph, even for a single servlet, is not trivial. The Java language imposes many challenges, such as, virtual method dispatching, exceptions, and data transfer via instance fields and arrays. Additionally, the Java standard library allows stream objects to be nested in different ways (using `BufferedStream`, `PrintWriter`, etc.). Fortunately, most of the hard work can be done using the Soot framework [17], much like in our earlier applications of Soot [6,5,10]. We also need to keep track of the relevant output streams, but that can be done easily with Soot's alias analysis capabilities. The request dispatching mechanism in the Servlet API can be handled similarly.

As an example, we obtain the flow graph shown in Figure 1 for the example program from Section 1.

We use the following terminology about context-free grammars. A *context-free grammar (CFG)* G is a quadruple (V, Σ, S, P) where V is the nonterminal alphabet, Σ is the terminal alphabet (in our grammars, Σ is the Unicode alphabet), $V \cap \Sigma = \emptyset$, $S \subseteq V$ is a set of start nonterminals, and P is a finite set of productions of the form $A \rightarrow \theta$ where $A \in V$ and $\theta \in U^*$, using U to denote the combined alphabet $V \cup \Sigma$. We write $\alpha A \omega \Rightarrow \alpha \theta \omega$ when $A \rightarrow \theta$ is in P and $\alpha, \omega \in U^*$, and $\Rightarrow^+$ and $\Rightarrow^*$ are respectively the transitive closure and the reflexive transitive closure of $\Rightarrow$. The *language* of G is defined as

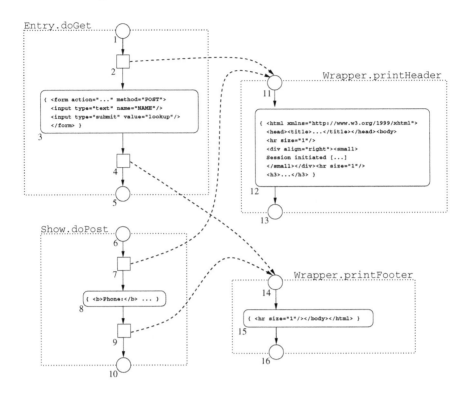

Fig. 1. Flow graph for the example program. (We here depict append nodes as rounded boxes, invoke nodes are squares, nop nodes are circles, and dotted edges represent method boundaries.)

$\mathcal{L}(G) = \{x \in \Sigma^* \mid \exists s \in S : s \Rightarrow^+ x\}$. The language of a nonterminal A is $\mathcal{L}_G(A) = \{x \in \Sigma^* \mid A \Rightarrow^+ x\}$. We sometimes omit the subscript G in $\mathcal{L}_G$ when it can be inferred from the context.

Given a flow graph, we derive a CFG $G = (V, \Sigma, S, P)$ where each flow graph node n is associated with a nonterminal $N_n \in V$ such that $\mathcal{L}(N_n)$ is the set of strings that can be output starting from n:

- for an append node n with an edge to m and whose label is L, we add a production $N_n \rightarrow R_L N_m$ where R_L is the start nonterminal for a linear sub-grammar for L;
- for an invoke node n with a successor m and a possible target method represented by a node t, we add $N_n \rightarrow N_t N_m$; and
- for a nop node n with a successor m we add $N_n \rightarrow N_m$, and for one with no successors we add $N_n \rightarrow \epsilon$.

The start nonterminals are those that correspond to the servlet entry points.

Example. The grammar for the example flow graph has $V = \{N_1, \ldots, N_{16}, R_3, R_8, R_{12}, R_{15}\}$, and P contains the following productions:

$$N_1 \rightarrow N_2 \qquad N_6 \rightarrow N_7 \qquad N_{11} \rightarrow N_{12} \qquad N_{14} \rightarrow N_{15}$$
$$N_2 \rightarrow N_{11}N_3 \qquad N_7 \rightarrow N_{11}N_8 \qquad N_{12} \rightarrow R_{12}N_{13} \qquad N_{15} \rightarrow R_{15}N_{16}$$
$$N_3 \rightarrow R_3N_4 \qquad N_8 \rightarrow R_8N_9 \qquad N_{13} \rightarrow \epsilon \qquad N_{16} \rightarrow \epsilon$$
$$N_4 \rightarrow N_{14}N_5 \qquad N_9 \rightarrow N_{14}N_{10}$$
$$N_5 \rightarrow \epsilon \qquad N_{10} \rightarrow \epsilon$$

$R_3 \rightarrow [\![$ `<form action="..." method="POST">`$\ldots$`</form>` $]\!]$
$R_8 \rightarrow [\![$ `<b>Phone:</b>`$\ldots]\!]$
$R_{12} \rightarrow [\![$ `<html xmlns="http://www.w3.org/1999/xhtml">`
$\qquad$ `<head><title>`$\ldots$`</title></head><body>`$\ldots]\!]$
$R_{15} \rightarrow [\![$ `<hr size="1"/></body></html>`$]\!]$

($[\![\cdot]\!]$ denotes a linear grammar for the given regular language.) For the `Entry` servlet we set $S = \{N_1\}$, and for `Show` we set $S = \{N_6\}$. We may also consider both servlets in combination using $S = \{N_1, N_6\}$.

3   Checking Well-Formedness Using Balanced Grammars

The goal of this phase is to check for a given CFG G whether all strings in $\mathcal{L}(G)$ are well-formed XML documents. We simplify the presentation by ignoring XML comments, processing instructions, entity references, and the compact form of empty elements (for example, that `<br></br>` may be written as `<br/>`), and we assume that all attributes are written on the form $name="value"$.

This phase proceeds in a number of steps that consider different aspects of well-formedness. First, however, we need to be able to easily identify occurrences of the two characters `</` in the language of the grammar. We achieve this by a simple preliminary grammar transformation that – without changing the language of the grammar – eliminates productions on the form $A \rightarrow \alpha$`<`ω where $\omega \in VU^* \wedge$ `/` $\in FIRST(\omega)$ or $\omega \Rightarrow^* \epsilon \wedge$ `/` $\in FOLLOW(A)$. (See, for instance, [1] for a definition of $FIRST$ and $FOLLOW$.) From here on, `</` is treated as a single alphabet symbol.

To be able to identify the XML structure in the grammar, we define six special forms of grammar productions:

$C \rightarrow$ `<` T A `>` C `</` T `>`	(element form)
$C \rightarrow X$	(text form)
$C \rightarrow C\,C$	(content sequence form)
$A \rightarrow W\,T$ `=` `"` V `"`	(attribute form)
$A \rightarrow A\,A$	(attribute sequence form)
$A \rightarrow \epsilon$	(empty form)

Here, C represents nonterminals, called *content nonterminals*, whose productions are all on element form, text form, or content sequence form, and A represents nonterminals, called *attribute nonterminals*, whose productions are all on attribute form, attribute sequence form, or empty form. T represents nonterminals whose languages contain no whitespace and no `<`, `>`, or `=` symbols, W represents nonterminals whose languages consist of nonempty whitespace, X

represents nonterminals whose languages do not contain <, and V means the same as X except that it also excludes ". We say that a CFG is on *tag-form* if every start nonterminal $s \in S$ is a content nonterminal. Our aim is to convert G into an equivalent grammar on tag-form and check various well-formedness requirements on the way.

3.1   Step 1: Obtaining a Balanced Grammar

We now view < (which marks the beginning of a start tag) as a left parenthesis and </ (which marks the beginning of an end tag) as a right parenthesis. A necessary condition for $\mathcal{L}(G)$ to be well-formed is that the language in this view is balanced. (A language L is *balanced* if the parentheses balance in every string $x \in L$.) To check this property, we simply apply Knuth's algorithm [12] (as described in detail in [9]). If the grammar passes this check, Knuth moreover gives us an equivalent *completely qualified* grammar G' (as also explained in [9]).

As the next step towards tag-form, we will now convert G' into a balanced grammar. (A CFG is *balanced* if every nonterminal is balanced in the sense that the parentheses balance in all derivable strings; for a formal definition see [12] or [9].) Balanced grammars have the useful property that in every production that contains a left parenthesis (< in our case), the matching right parenthesis (</) appears in the same production. Again we resort to Knuth: in [12], Knuth shows how a completely qualified CFG that has a balanced language can be converted to a balanced grammar – however, under the assumption that the language has *bounded associates*. Our grammars generally do not have this property (one can easily write a servlet that results in any desirable grammar), so we need to modify Knuth's algorithm to accommodate for a more general setting. Although $\mathcal{L}(G')$ is balanced, there may in fact not exist a balanced grammar G'' with $\mathcal{L}(G') = \mathcal{L}(G'')$, as observed in [12]. Hence we resort to approximation (using a local variant of [14]): the grammar G'' that we produce has the property that it is balanced and $\mathcal{L}(G') \subseteq \mathcal{L}(G'')$. Surprisingly, the loss of precision incurred by this approximation is limited to the degree that it does not affect precision of our well-formedness and validity analyses. A detailed explanation of this rather technical algorithm is given in the technical report [9] along with proofs of soundness and relative completeness.

Example. For the example grammar shown in Section 2, notice that $\mathcal{L}(R_{12})$ and $\mathcal{L}(R_{15})$ are not balanced: the former has an excess of < symbols (for the `html` and `body` start tags), and the latter has a converse excess of </ symbols. Our algorithm straightens this and outputs a grammar where every production that contains a < symbol also contains the matching </ symbol. In this simple example, no approximations are necessary.

3.2   Step 2: Transforming to Tag-Form

The symbols <, >, and " are essential for our further transformation to tag-form since they function as context delimiters in XML documents in the sense that they delimit the *tag*, *element content*, and *attribute value* contexts, respectively. Given a balanced grammar $G = (V, \Sigma, S, P)$ we will in the following classify nonterminals and symbols occurring on right-hand sides of productions in P according to their possible contexts. If such classification can be uniquely determined, we will use the contexts to extract a grammar on tag-form for $\mathcal{L}(G)$, otherwise we have evidence that some strings in $\mathcal{L}(G)$ are not well-formed.

Let $\mathcal{C}$ be a lattice with values $\bot$, tag, content, attrval, and error ordered by

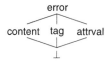

and define a function $\delta : \mathcal{C} \times \Sigma \to \mathcal{C}$ by

$$\delta(c, \sigma) = \begin{cases} c & \text{if } \sigma \notin \{<, >, "\} \text{ or } c = \bot \\ \text{tag} & \text{if } (\sigma = < \text{ and } c = \text{content}) \text{ or } (\sigma = " \text{ and } c = \text{attrval}) \\ \text{attrval} & \text{if } (\sigma = " \text{ and } c = \text{tag}) \text{ or } (\sigma = > \text{ and } c = \text{attrval}) \\ \text{content} & \text{if } \sigma = > \text{ and } (c = \text{tag or } c = \text{content}) \\ \text{error} & \text{otherwise} \end{cases}$$

Intuitively, δ determines transitions on $\mathcal{C}$ according to the context delimiters $\{<, >, "\}$ and is the identity function on all other symbols.

We may now define a constraint system on the grammar G expressed as a function $\Delta : \mathcal{C} \times U^* \to \mathcal{C}$ defined by the following rules:

$$\Delta(\text{content}, s) \sqsupseteq \text{content} \quad \text{for all } s \in S$$

$$\Delta_G(c, A) \sqsupseteq \Delta_G(c, \theta) \quad \text{for all } A \to \theta \in P$$

$$\Delta(c, x) \sqsupseteq \begin{cases} c & \text{when } x = \epsilon \\ \Delta(\delta(c, \sigma), y) & \text{when } x = \sigma y \text{ where } \sigma \in \Sigma, y \in U^* \\ \Delta(\Delta(c, \theta), y) & \text{when } x = Ay \text{ where } A \in V, y \in U^* \text{ and } A \to \theta \in P \end{cases}$$

The constraint system will always have a unique least solution Δ_G, which can be found using a standard fixed-point algorithm. (This is the case because a finite subset of U^* containing all nonterminals and all prefixes of right-hand sides of productions in P is enough to fulfill the constraints.) Furthermore, if $\Delta_G(\text{content}, s) = \text{error}$ for some $s \in S$ then $\mathcal{L}(G)$ contains a non-well-formed string. In that case, we can issue a precise warning message by producing a derivation starting from s and using productions $A \to \theta$ with $\Delta_G(c, \theta) = \text{error}$.

Assume now that $\Delta_G(\text{content}, s) \neq \text{error}$ for all $s \in S$. The balanced grammar G can then be converted as follows into an equivalent grammar on tag-form.

First, we will ensure that nonterminals occur in unique contexts in all derivations. For every $A \in V$ and $c \in \{\text{content, tag, attrval}\}$ where $\Delta_G(c, A) \neq \bot$, create an annotated nonterminal A_c with the same productions as A. Then make A_c a start nonterminal if $A \in S$ and replace every production $B_{c_1} \to \alpha A \omega$ where $\Delta_G(c_1, \alpha) = c_2$ with a production $B_{c_1} \to \alpha A_{c_2} \omega$. All unannotated nonterminals and productions are now unreachable and can be removed.

Now that the grammar is balanced with respect to < and </ and each nonterminal is used in only one context in any derivation, it is straightforward to bring the grammar on tag-form (except for the attribute nonterminals) by repeatedly applying Transformation 1 and Transformation 2 from [12] to eliminate all nonterminals $A \in V$ where $\Delta_G(c, A) \neq c$. We can handle attribute nonterminals similarly by considering a few more context delimiters (whitespace and =). Due to the limited space, we omit the tedious details.

Example. The extracted CFG for the example program in Section 2 has a balanced language and our transformation results in a grammar on tag-form. After applying some basic simplification rules to make it more readable, we obtain the following grammar with C_1 being the only start nonterminal (assuming that we consider $S = \{N_1, N_6\}$ in the original grammar):

$C_1 \rightarrow$ < html A_1 > C_2 C_4 </ html > $C_8 \rightarrow$ < h3 > X_1 </ h3 >
$C_2 \rightarrow$ < head > C_3 </ head > $C_9 \rightarrow C_5 \mid C_{13}$ X_3
$C_3 \rightarrow$ < title > X_1 </ title > $C_{10} \rightarrow$ < hr A_2 ></ hr >
$C_4 \rightarrow$ < body > C_{10} C_{11} C_{10} C_8 C_9 C_{10} </ body > $C_{11} \rightarrow$ < div A_3 > C_{12} </ div >
$C_5 \rightarrow$ < form A_4 A_5 > C_6 C_7 </ form > $C_{12} \rightarrow$ < small > X_2 </ small >
$C_6 \rightarrow$ < input A_6 A_7 > </ input > $C_{13} \rightarrow$ < b > Phone: </ b >
$C_7 \rightarrow$ < input A_8 A_9 > </ input >

$A_1 \rightarrow$ ␣xmlns="http://www.w3.org/1999/xhtml" $A_6 \rightarrow$ ␣type="text"
$A_2 \rightarrow$ ␣size="1" $A_7 \rightarrow$ ␣name="NAME"
$A_3 \rightarrow$ ␣align="right" $A_8 \rightarrow$ ␣type="submit"
$A_4 \rightarrow$ ␣action=" V_1 " $A_9 \rightarrow$ ␣value="lookup"
$A_5 \rightarrow$ ␣method="POST"

$X_1 \rightarrow$ Enter␣name $\mid \mathcal{L}_{\text{CDATA}}$ $V_1 \rightarrow$ contextpath/show
$X_2 \rightarrow$ Session␣initiated␣[$\mathcal{L}_{\text{DATE}}$]
$X_3 \rightarrow \mathcal{L}_{\text{phone}}$

$\mathcal{L}_{\text{CDATA}}$ is the set of all strings that can be returned from misc.encodeXML, $\mathcal{L}_{\text{DATE}}$ are the legal date string values, $\mathcal{L}_{\text{phone}}$ contains the possible output of the method directory.phone, and contextpath denotes the application context path as obtained by getContextPath. These regular languages are obtained by the preliminary string analysis.

3.3   Step 3: Checking Well-Formedness

The previous steps have checked a number of necessary conditions for well-formedness. Now that we have the grammar on tag-form, we can easily check the remaining properties:

– All start productions must be on element form. (In other words, there is always exactly one root element.)
– For every production $C_1 \rightarrow$ < T_1 A > C_2 </ T_2 > on element form, both $\mathcal{L}(T_1)$ and $\mathcal{L}(T_2)$ must be singleton languages and equal. (Otherwise, one could derive a string where a start tag does not match its end tag.)

– For every production $C_1 \rightarrow$ < T_1 A > C_2 </ T_2 > on element form, the attributes corresponding to A must have disjoint names. More precisely, whenever $A \Rightarrow^+ \alpha A_1 \phi A_2 \omega$ where $\alpha, \phi, \omega \in U^*$ and $A_i \rightarrow W_i\ T_i' =$ " V_i " for $i = 1, 2$, we check that $\mathcal{L}(T_1') \cap \mathcal{L}(T_2') = \emptyset$. If the sub-grammars of T_1' and T_2' are linear, this check is straightforward; otherwise, since the property is generally undecidable we sacrifice completeness and issue a warning.

The only way sub-grammars that correspond to attribute names can be nonlinear is if the program being analyzed uses a recursive method to build individual attribute names in a contrived way where a part of a name is written to the output stream *before* the recursive call and another part is written *after* the call. With the exception of this pathological case, the checks described above are passed if and only if $\mathcal{L}(G)$ contains only well-formed XML documents. Our running example passes the well-formedness check.

4 Checking Validity Using XML Graphs

An *XML graph* is a finite structure that represents a potentially infinite set of XML trees, as defined in [10,8] (where XML graphs are called *summary graphs*). We here give a brief description of a variant of the formalism, tailored to our present setting.

An XML graph contains finite sets of nodes of various kinds: element nodes ($\mathcal{N}_\mathcal{E}$), attribute nodes ($\mathcal{N}_\mathcal{A}$), text nodes ($\mathcal{N}_\mathcal{T}$), sequence nodes ($\mathcal{N}_\mathcal{S}$), and choice nodes ($\mathcal{N}_\mathcal{C}$). (The definition of summary graphs used in earlier papers also involves gap nodes, which we do not need here.) Let $\mathcal{N} = \mathcal{N}_\mathcal{E} \cup \mathcal{N}_\mathcal{A} \cup \mathcal{N}_\mathcal{T} \cup \mathcal{N}_\mathcal{S} \cup \mathcal{N}_\mathcal{C}$. The graph has a set of root nodes $\mathcal{R} \subseteq \mathcal{N}$. The map *contents* : $\mathcal{N}_\mathcal{E} \cup \mathcal{N}_\mathcal{A} \rightarrow \mathcal{N}$ connects element nodes and attribute nodes with descriptions of their contents. For sequence nodes it returns sequences of nodes, *contents* : $\mathcal{N}_\mathcal{S} \rightarrow \mathcal{N}^*$, and for choice nodes it returns sets of nodes, *contents* : $\mathcal{N}_\mathcal{C} \rightarrow 2^\mathcal{N}$. The map *val* : $\mathcal{N}_\mathcal{T} \cup \mathcal{N}_\mathcal{A} \cup \mathcal{N}_\mathcal{E} \rightarrow REG$, where REG are all regular string languages over the Unicode alphabet, assigns a set of strings to each text node, element node, and attribute node, in the latter two cases representing their possible names.

An XML graph may be viewed as a generalized XML tree that permits choices, loops, and regular sets of possible attribute/element names and text values. The *language* $\mathcal{L}(\chi)$ of an XML graph χ is intuitively the set of XML trees that can be obtained by unfolding it, starting from a root node.

As an example, consider the set of all ul lists with one or more li items that each contain a string from some regular language L. It can be described by an XML graph with six nodes $\mathcal{N} = \{e_1, e_2, s_1, s_2, c, t\}$, roots $\mathcal{R} = \{e_1\}$, and maps *contents* $= \{e_1 \mapsto s_1,\ e_2 \mapsto t,\ s_1 \mapsto e_2\,c,\ s_2 \mapsto \epsilon,\ c \mapsto \{s_1, s_2\}\}$ and *val* $= \{e_1 \mapsto \{\text{ul}\},\ e_2 \mapsto \{\text{li}\},\ t \mapsto L\}$. This is illustrated as follows:

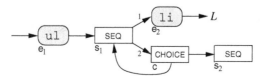

The rounded boxes represent the element nodes e_1 and e_2, the SEQ boxes represent the sequence nodes s_1 and s_2 (edges out of s_1 are ordered according to their indices), and the CHOICE box represents the choice node c. The text node t is represented by its associated language L.

From the XACT project, we have an algorithm that can check for a given XML graph χ and a schema S, written in either DTD or XML Schema, whether or not every XML tree in $\mathcal{L}(\chi)$ is valid according to S. (See [8] for a description of the algorithm and [11] for an implementation.) Hence, our only remaining task in order to be able to validate the output of the servlets is to convert the balanced grammar on tag-form that we produced and checked for well-formedness in Section 3 into an XML graph. Fortunately, this is straightforward to accomplish, as explained in the following.

Starting from the start nonterminals S and their productions, each production $p \in P$ is converted to an XML graph node n_p according to its form. Also, each nonterminal A is converted to a choice node n_A with $contents(n_A) = \{n_p \mid p \text{ is a production of } A\}$:

Element Form. For a production $p = C_1 \rightarrow \texttt{<} T_1 A \texttt{>} C_2 \texttt{</} T_2 \texttt{>}$, n_p becomes an element node. We know from the well-formedness check that $\mathcal{L}(T_1) = \mathcal{L}(T_2)$ is some singleton language $\{s\}$, so we set $name(n_p) = \{s\}$. To capture the attributes and contents, a sequence node n_q is also added, and we set $contents(n_p) = n_q$ and $contents(n_q) = n_A n_{C_2}$.

Text Form. For a production $p = C \rightarrow X$, the sub-grammar starting from X is converted to an equivalent sub-graph rooted by n_p, using only sequence nodes, choice nodes, and text nodes. We omit the details.

Attribute Form. For a production $p = A \rightarrow W\ T \texttt{ = " } V \texttt{ "}$, n_p becomes an attribute node. As in the previous case, the sub-grammar rooted by V is converted to an equivalent sub-graph rooted by a node n_V, and we let $contents(n_p) = n_V$. From the well-formedness check, we know that the sub-grammar of T is linear, so its language is regular and we set $name(n_p)$ accordingly.

Content or Attribute Sequence Form. For a production $p = C \rightarrow C_1 C_2$, n_p becomes a sequence node with $contents(n_p) = n_{C_1} n_{C_2}$. Productions on attribute sequence form are converted similarly.

Empty Form. For a production $p = A \rightarrow \epsilon$, n_p becomes a sequence node with $contents(n_p) = \epsilon$.

The root nodes $\mathcal{R}$ are the nodes that correspond to the start nonterminals.

For the example program from Section 1, we obtain the XML graph shown in Figure 2 (slightly simplified by combining nested sequence nodes). Note that since the program has no recursive methods, there are no loops in the graph. Running the XACT validator on this XML graph and the schema for XHTML gives the result "Valid!", meaning that the program is guaranteed to output only valid XHTML documents.

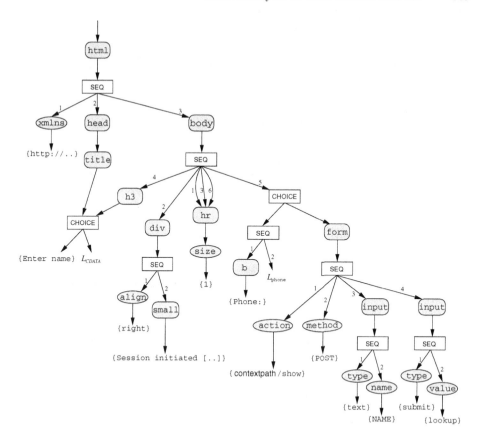

Fig. 2. XML graph for the example program. (We depict element nodes as rounded boxes, attribute nodes as ellipses, and sequence and choice nodes as SEQ and CHOICE boxes, respectively. Edges out of sequence nodes are ordered according to the indices.)

5   Analyzing Inter-servlet Control Flow

Servlet/JSP applications are typically structured as collections of dynamic pages that are connected via a deployment descriptor, `web.xml`, together with links (`<a href="...">`) and forms (`<form action="...">`) appearing in generated XHTML documents. Since links and forms are intertwined with general page layout and various kinds of data, it is often a challenging task to recognize and apprehend the complete control flow of applications consisting of more than a few servlets or JSP pages. We will now briefly describe how to further benefit from the XML graphs to obtain an *inter-servlet* control flow graph for an application.

The goal is to produce a graph with nodes corresponding to the `doGet` and `doPost` methods of each servlet class and edges corresponding to the possible control flow via links or forms in the generated documents. The challenge in producing such a graph is associating a set of possible servlet classes to the links and forms appearing in generated documents by using the URL mappings of the deployment descriptor.

Given an XML graph corresponding to the output of a servlet method we recognize the links and forms by searching (that is, unfolding according to the *contents* map, starting from the roots) for element nodes named a or form, and further, searching for their attribute nodes with names href and action, respectively. From each of the attribute values, we can extract a regular language of all possible target URLs and compare with the mappings described by the deployment descriptor to get the corresponding set of servlet classes. This set forms the inter-servlet flow edges out of the method. By applying the process to all servlet methods we obtain an inter-servlet control flow graph, which is guaranteed to be sound because the XML graphs represent sound approximations of the possible XHTML output.

The inter-servlet control flow graph for our running example is like the one in Figure 1, however extended with an inter-servlet flow edge from the exit node n_5 of the Entry.doGet method to the entry node n_6 of the Show.doPost method.

The inter-servlet control flow graph provides a whole-program view of the Web application. This is useful for visualizing the flow to the programmer and for checking reachability properties of the application workflow. It also serves as the foundation for a number of interesting derived analyses. One such analysis is consistency checking of form fields (as explained in detail in the JWIG paper [5]), which guarantees that all request parameters expected by a servlet exist as form fields in the XHTML output of every immediately preceeding servlet in the flow graph. A related analysis is consistency checking of session state, which can guarantee that every use of a session state variable has been preceeded by a definition. Clearly, such analyses are only feasible if the inter-servlet control flow is known, and, as sketched above, the XML graphs are a key to obtain precise knowledge of this flow.

6   Implementation Considerations and Conclusion

We have presented an approach for analyzing servlet/JSP applications to detect XML well-formedness and validity errors in the output being generated and outlined how to obtain and apply knowledge of the inter-servlet control flow. The front-end, which constructs a CFG for the program being analyzed, is sound; the back-end, which constructs an XML graph from the CFG and analyzes well-formedness and validity is both sound and complete relative to the CFG (under the assumption that certain well-defined contrived patterns do not occur in the program).

We have chosen an approach of imposing as few restrictions as possible on the programs being analyzed. An alternative approach, which might of course lead to a simpler analysis, would be to restrict the class of programs that the analysis can handle or sacrifice soundness. The trade-off we have chosen investigates the possibilities in the end of this design spectrum that is most flexible seen from the programmer's point of view.

Only a complete implementation and experiments on real applications can tell whether the precision and performance are sufficient for practical use. However, we have reasons to believe that this is the case. Regarding the front-end, it is our experience from the JWIG, XACT, and string analysis projects [5,10,6] that the extraction of flow graphs from Java programs works well in practice – regarding both precision and performance – and the extraction of CFGs from flow graphs is both precise and efficient. Similarly, the analysis of XML graphs in the back-end has also shown to work well in practice. The only remaining question is whether the grammar manipulations can be done efficiently, but our preliminary experiments indicate that this is the case. We are presently implementing the grammar manipulations and connecting the components of the analysis system, which will hopefully give more confidence to the practical feasibility of the approach.

Acknowledgments. We thank Aske Simon Christensen for inspiring discussions about various aspects of the program analysis.

References

1. Alfred V. Aho, Ravi Sethi, and Jeffrey D. Ullman. *Compilers: Principles, Techniques, and Tools.* Addison-Wesley, 1986.
2. Assaf Arkin et al. Web Services Business Process Execution Language Version 2.0, December 2005. OASIS, Committee Draft.
3. Jean Berstel and Luc Boasson. Formal properties of XML grammars and languages. *Acta Informatica*, 38(9):649–671, 2002. Springer-Verlag.
4. Anne Brüggemann-Klein and Derick Wood. Balanced context-free grammars, hedge grammars and pushdown caterpillar automata. In *Proc. Extreme Markup Languages*, 2004.
5. Aske Simon Christensen, Anders Møller, and Michael I. Schwartzbach. Extending Java for high-level Web service construction. *ACM Transactions on Programming Languages and Systems*, 25(6):814–875, 2003.
6. Aske Simon Christensen, Anders Møller, and Michael I. Schwartzbach. Precise analysis of string expressions. In *Proc. 10th International Static Analysis Symposium, SAS '03*, volume 2694 of *LNCS*, pages 1–18. Springer-Verlag, June 2003.
7. M. H. Jansen-Vullers, Wil M. P. van der Aalst, and Michael Rosemann. Mining configurable enterprise information systems. *Data & Knowledge Engineering*, 56(3):195–244, 2006.
8. Christian Kirkegaard and Anders Møller. Type checking with XML Schema in XACT. Technical Report RS-05-31, BRICS, 2005. Presented at Programming Language Technologies for XML, PLAN-X '06.
9. Christian Kirkegaard and Anders Møller. Static analysis for Java Servlets and JSP. Technical Report RS-06-10, BRICS, 2006.
10. Christian Kirkegaard, Anders Møller, and Michael I. Schwartzbach. Static analysis of XML transformations in Java. *IEEE Transactions on Software Engineering*, 30(3):181–192, March 2004.
11. Christian Kirkegaard and Anders Møller. dk.brics.schematools, 2006. `http://www.brics.dk/schematools/`.

12. Donald E. Knuth. A characterization of parenthesis languages. *Information and Control*, 11:269–289, 1967.
13. Yasuhiko Minamide. Static approximation of dynamically generated Web pages. In *Proc. 14th International Conference on World Wide Web, WWW '05*, pages 432–441. ACM, May 2005.
14. Mehryar Mohri and Mark-Jan Nederhof. *Robustness in Language and Speech Technology*, chapter 9: Regular Approximation of Context-Free Grammars through Transformation. Kluwer Academic Publishers, 2001.
15. Sun Microsystems. Java Servlet Specification, Version 2.4, 2003. Available from `http://java.sun.com/products/servlet/`.
16. Sun Microsystems. JavaServer Pages Specification, Version 2.0, 2003. Available from `http://java.sun.com/products/jsp/`.
17. Raja Vallee-Rai, Laurie Hendren, Vijay Sundaresan, Patrick Lam, Etienne Gagnon, and Phong Co. Soot – a Java optimization framework. In *Proc. IBM Centre for Advanced Studies Conference, CASCON '99*. IBM, November 1999.
18. Wil M. P. van der Aalst, Lachlan Aldred, Marlon Dumas, and Arthur H. M. ter Hofstede. Design and implementation of the YAWL system. In *Proc. 16th International Conference on Advanced Information Systems Engineering, CAiSE '04*, volume 3084 of *LNCS*. Springer-Verlag, June 2004.

Cryptographically-Masked Flows

Aslan Askarov, Daniel Hedin, and Andrei Sabelfeld

Department of Computer Science and Engineering
Chalmers University of Technology
412 96 Göteborg, Sweden

Abstract. Cryptographic operations are essential for many security-critical systems. Reasoning about information flow in such systems is challenging because typical (noninterference-based) information-flow definitions allow no flow from secret to public data. Unfortunately, this implies that programs with encryption are ruled out because encrypted output depends on secret inputs: the plaintext and the key. However, it is desirable to allow flows arising from encryption with secret keys provided that the underlying cryptographic algorithm is strong enough. In this paper we conservatively extend the noninterference definition to allow safe encryption, decryption, and key generation. To illustrate the usefulness of this approach, we propose (and implement) a type system that guarantees noninterference for a small imperative language with primitive cryptographic operations. The type system prevents dangerous program behavior (e.g., giving away a secret key or confusing keys and non-keys), which we exemplify with secure implementations of cryptographic protocols. Because the model is based on a standard noninterference property, it allows us to develop some natural extensions. In particular, we consider public-key cryptography and integrity, which accommodate reasoning about primitives that are vulnerable to chosen-ciphertext attacks.

1   Introduction

Cryptographic operations are ubiquitous in security-critical systems. Reasoning about information flow in such systems is challenging because typical information-flow definitions allow no flow from secret to public data. The latter requirement underlies *noninterference* [11,16], which demands that public outputs are unchanged as secret inputs are varied. While traditional noninterference breaks in the presence of cryptographic operations, the challenge is to distinguish between breaking noninterference because of legitimate use of sufficiently strong encryption and breaking noninterference due to an unintended leak.

A common approach to handling cryptographic primitives in information-flow aware systems is by allowing *declassification* of encryption results. The intention of declassification is that the result of encryption can be released to the attacker. Declassification, however, is a versatile mechanism: different declassification dimensions correspond to different reasons why information is released [29,4]. Attempts at framing cryptographically-masked flows into different dimensions have been made although, as we discuss, not always with satisfactory results.

In this paper, we introduce cryptographic primitives into an information-flow setting while preserving a form of noninterference property. This is achieved by building in

K. Yi (Ed.): SAS 2006, LNCS 4134, pp. 353–369, 2006.

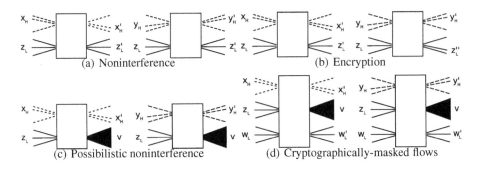

Fig. 1. From noninterference to cryptographically-masked flows

the model a basic assumption that attackers may not distinguish between ciphertexts and that decryption using the wrong key fails. Although this assumption is stronger than some probabilistic and computational cryptographic models (which allow some information to leak when comparing ciphertexts), we argue that it can still be reasonable, and that it opens up possibilities for tracking information flow in the presence of cryptographic primitives in expressive programming languages.

The intuition behind our approach is sketched below and illustrated in Figure 1, where dashed and solid lines correspond to secret and public values, respectively. Fixing some public (low) input x_L and varying secret (high) input from x_H to y_H may not reflect on a public output z'_L of a system that satisfies noninterference (illustrated in Figure 1(a)). Suppose the system in question involves encryption, such as in the program $z = \mathrm{enc}(k, x)$ for some secret key k. Clearly, noninterference is broken: variation in the secret input from x_H to y_H may cause variation in the public output from z'_L to z''_L (illustrated in Figure 1(b)).

However, noninterference can be recovered if the result of encryption is possibly *any* value v. This means that variation of the high input from x_H to y_H does not affect the public output—any value v is a possible public output in both cases. This form of noninterference is known as *possibilistic noninterference* [24] (illustrated in Figure 1(c)). Overall, although low outputs might depend on low inputs and ciphertexts, no observation about possible low outputs may reveal information about changes in high inputs (illustrated in Figure 1(d)).

This paper makes a case for possibilistic noninterference as a natural model for cryptographically-masked flows. Further, we have designed and implemented a security type system that provably enforces possibilistic noninterference for an imperative language with primitive cryptographic operations and communication channels. The type system prevents dangerous program behavior (e.g., giving away a secret key or confusing keys or non-keys), which we exemplify with secure implementations of cryptographic protocols. Because the model is based on a standard noninterference property, it allows us to develop some natural extensions. In particular, we consider public-key cryptography and integrity, which accommodates reasoning about primitives that are vulnerable to chosen-ciphertext attacks.

sec. levels	$\sigma ::= \text{L} \mid \text{H}$	basic types	$t ::= \text{int} \mid \text{enc}_\gamma \, \tau$
key levels	$\gamma ::= \text{P} \mid \text{S}$	prim. types	$\tau ::= t \, \sigma \mid \text{key} \, \gamma \mid (\tau_1, \tau_2)$
global decls.	$gd ::= \text{global} \, x \, \gamma \mid ch \, \tau$	local decls.	$ld ::= x \, \tau$

expressions $e ::= n \mid x \mid e_1 \, op \, e_2 \mid \text{enc}_\gamma \, (e_1, e_2) \mid \text{dec}_\gamma \, (e_1, e_2) \mid \text{newkey} \, \gamma \mid (e_1, e_2)$
$\qquad\qquad \mid \text{fst}(e) \mid \text{snd}(e)$

statements $c ::= \text{skip} \mid x := e \mid \text{if } e \text{ then } b_1 \text{ else } b_2 \mid \text{while } e \text{ do } b \mid \text{out}(ch, e)$
$\qquad\qquad \mid \text{in}(x, ch)$

block $b ::= \{ld_1; \ldots ld_n; c_1; \ldots; c_m\}$

actor $actor ::= A \, b$ $\qquad\qquad$ program $prog ::= gd_1; \ldots gd_n; actor_1 \ldots actor_m$

Fig. 2. Syntax

2   Language

We explore how to model cryptographic flows in a small imperative language equipped with primitive encryption functions, dynamic key generation, and channels for communication. This section introduces the syntax and semantics of the language. For space reasons we are forced to omit the standard features of the language. The complete rules can be, however, found in the full version of this paper [3].

Syntax. The syntax of the language is defined in Figure 2. Let $x \in VarName$ range over the set of variable names and $ch \in ChanName$ range over the set of channel names. A *program* consists of a sequence of *global declarations* followed by a sequence of *actors*. A global declaration is either a declaration of a *global key* or the declaration of a channel. Global keys are declared by associating a variable name with a *key level*. Values and keys have corresponding *security levels*. Values are either *public (low)* L or *secret (high)* H. The key levels declare the maximum value security level the key can safely encrypt. In particular, a key of level S may safely encrypt public and secret values, whereas a key of level P may only safely encrypt public values. Let $KeyLvl = \{\text{S}, \text{P}\}$ be the set of key levels. Global keys are assumed to have appropriate values at the beginning of the execution of a program and correspond to initial shared secrets between the actors of the program. A *channel* is declared by associating a channel name with the type of the messages that will be sent over the channel. Let A range over the set of *actor names*. An actor is defined by naming a *block*, representing the code of the actor. A block is simply a sequence of variable declarations followed by a sequence of commands. Variables are local to the block in which they are declared. The commands include the standard commands of an imperative language and commands for sending on and receiving from a given channel. Apart from expressions for generating new keys and for encryption and decryption, expressions are standard: integers, variables, total binary operators, pair formation, and projection.

Semantics. The semantics of the system is defined as a big-step operational semantics. The actors of a program run concurrently and interact with each other by sending and receiving messages on the declared channels. We refrain from modeling the semantics for the entire system and instead provide semantics for isolated actors. Thus we deliberately ignore information flows via races and other flows that may arise in concurrent systems (cf. [27]). First we define the values and environments, which are used in the following definition of the semantics of expressions and commands. Let $n \in \mathbb{Z}$ range over the *integers* and $k \in Key = Key_P \cup Key_S$ range over *keys*, where Key_P and Key_S are disjoint. The *values* are built up by the *ordinary values*, integers, keys and *pairs* of values, together with the *encrypted values* $u \in U = U_P \cup U_S$.

$$\text{values} \in Value \quad v ::= n \mid k \mid (v_1, v_2) \mid u$$

The system is parameterized over two *symmetric encryption schemes*—one for each key level γ—represented by triples $SE_\gamma = (\mathcal{K}_\gamma, \mathcal{E}_\gamma, \mathcal{D}_\gamma)$, where

- $\mathcal{K}_\gamma$ is a *key generation* algorithm that on each invocation generates a new key.
- $\mathcal{E}_\gamma$ is a *probabilistic* encryption algorithm that takes a key $k \in Key_\gamma$, a value $v \in Value$ and returns a ciphertext $u \in U_\gamma$.
- $\mathcal{D}_\gamma$ is a deterministic decryption algorithm that takes a key $k \in Key_\gamma$, a ciphertext $u \in U_\gamma$ and returns a value $v \in Value$ or fails. Decryption should satisfy $\mathcal{D}_\gamma(k, \mathcal{E}_\gamma(k, v)) = v$.

The reason for the use of different encryption schemes for different security levels is to lay the ground for an extension of the system into a *multi-level* system, i.e. a system with more than two security levels. In such a system we would have one encryption schema at each security level, trusted to encrypt values up to and including the security level. We shall assume that the keys sets Key_P and Key_S of the two different encryption schemes are distinct; let pk range over Key_P and sk over Key_S.

Input and output is modeled in terms of streams of values with the cons operation "$\cdot$" and the distinguished empty stream ϵ. The *full environment* E consists of four components: (i) the variable environment M, which is a stack of mappings from variable names to lifted values (values joined with a special value for undefined $Value^\bullet = Value \cup \{\bullet\}$); (ii) the key-stream environment G, which maps an encryption scheme level to the *stream of keys* generated by successive use of the key generator (let ks range over streams of keys); (iii) the input environment I and (iv) the output environment O, which map channel names to streams of values.

Semantics of Expressions. The evaluation of expressions has the form $\langle (M, G), e \rangle \Downarrow \langle G', v \rangle$: evaluating an expression in a given variable and key-stream environment yields a value and a possibly updated key-stream environment. The semantics of integers, variables, total binary operators, pair formation, and projection are entirely standard.

Figure 3 presents the rules specific to the treatment of cryptography; the rest of the rules can be found in [3]. Key generation (S-NEWKEY) takes the level of the key to be generated and returns the topmost element in the key stream associated to that level in the key-stream environment. Encryption (S-ENC) and decryption (S-DEC) both use the encryption schemes SE_γ introduced above.

Semantics of Commands. Commands are state transformers of the form $\langle E, c \rangle \Downarrow E'$: the command c yields the new environment E' when run in the environment E. The

$$(\text{S-NEWKEY})\frac{G(\gamma) = k \cdot ks}{\langle (M, G), \texttt{newkey } \gamma \rangle \Downarrow \langle G[\gamma \mapsto ks], k \rangle}$$

$$(\text{S-ENC})\frac{\langle (M, G), e_1 \rangle \Downarrow \langle G', k \rangle \quad \langle (M, G'), e_2 \rangle \Downarrow \langle G'', v \rangle \quad k \in Key_\gamma}{\langle (M, G), \texttt{enc}_\gamma (e_1, e_2) \rangle \Downarrow \langle G'', u \rangle}$$

$$(\text{S-DEC})\frac{\langle (M, G), e_1 \rangle \Downarrow \langle G', k \rangle \quad \langle (M, G'), e_2 \rangle \Downarrow \langle G'', u \rangle \quad k \in Key_\gamma}{\langle (M, G), \texttt{dec}_\gamma (e_1, e_2) \rangle \Downarrow \langle G'', v \rangle}$$

Fig. 3. Semantics of Expressions

semantics of the commands is entirely standard for a while language with channels—everything specific to encryption is in the expressions. For space reasons the semantics of the commands is not presented here but can be found in [3].

3   Security

This section states the assumptions our semantic model makes on the underlying encryption schema and shows how these assumptions lead up to a natural formulation of possibilistic noninterference. The section concludes by investigating the relation between our assumptions and common cryptographic attacker models.

Encryption Model. As was mentioned above, this paper only considers *probabilistic encryption schemes*. A probabilistic encryption scheme is a triple $(\mathcal{K}, \mathcal{E}, \mathcal{D})$ where the encryption algorithm is a function from a key, a plaintext, and some initial *random data*, referred to as the *initial vector*. Such an algorithm will produce a set of possible ciphertexts for each plaintext-key pair, one ciphertext for each initial vector.

To be able to formulate and prove possibilistic noninterference for our system we need to demand two properties of the underlying encryption schemes. The first property is the assumption that an adversary can learn nothing about the plaintext or the key by observing the ciphertext. This property, known as Shannon's *perfect secrecy* [30], is used to justify our *indistinguishability* relation on ciphertexts.

The second property is an *authenticity property* needed in the treatment of decryption. More precisely we are assuming that decryption using the *wrong* key fails:

$$\mathcal{D}(k, \mathcal{E}(k', v)) = \bot \text{ if } k \neq k'$$

Insufficiency of Standard Noninterference. The prevailing notion when defining confidentiality in the analysis of information flows is noninterference. Noninterference is typically formalized as the preservation of a *low-equivalence* relation under the execution of a program: if a program is run in two low-equivalent environments then the resulting environments should be low-equivalent. For ordinary values like integers low-equivalence demands that public values are equal. However, from the assumption that an adversary can learn nothing about the plaintext from observing the ciphertext it is secure to treat all ciphertexts of the same length[1] as low-equivalent. However appealing this may be, such a treatment leads the ability of masking implicit flows in ciphertexts. Consider the program on Listing 1 for some public channel ch and encryption with secret key k:

If all encrypted values are considered equal then we cannot distinguish between the first and the second output value, even though it is clear that the equality/inequality of the first and the second value reflects the secret value h.

```
l := enc(k, a);
out(ch, l);
if (h) then l := enc(k, b) else skip;
out(ch, l);
```

Listing 1. Occlusion

Possibilistic Noninterference. To address this problem we use a variant of noninterference known as possibilistic noninterference, which allows us to create a notion of low-equivalence that disallows the above example without disallowing intuitively secure uses. Before we formalize our notion of possibilistic noninterference, let us lift the evaluation relation to a set of results as follows:

$$\langle E, c \rangle \Downarrow \hat{E} \text{ iff } \hat{E} = \{ E' \mid \langle E, c \rangle \Downarrow E' \}$$

With this we can formulate our notion of possibilistic noninterference. Let $E_1 \sim_\Sigma E_2$ denote that the environments E_1 and E_2 are low-equivalent w.r.t the environment type Σ. A pair of commands, c_1 and c_2 are noninterfering if

$$NI(c_1, c_2)_\Sigma \equiv \forall E_1, E_2 . E_1 \sim_\Sigma E_2 \land$$
$$\langle E_1, c_1 \rangle \Downarrow \hat{E}_1 \land \hat{E}_1 \neq \emptyset \land \langle E_2, c_2 \rangle \Downarrow \hat{E}_2 \land \hat{E}_2 \neq \emptyset \Longrightarrow$$
$$\forall E_1' \in \hat{E}_1 \exists E_2' \in \hat{E}_2 . E_1' \sim_\Sigma E_2'$$

That is, two commands are considered *equivalent* if, for every pair of low-equivalent environments *in which the commands terminate* it holds that there exists the *possibility* that each environment produced by the first command when run in the first environment can be produced by the second command when run in the second environment.

By only considering environments for which the commands terminate, we ignore the issue with crashes. This is equivalent to saying that normal and abnormal termination cannot be distinguished by the attacker.

Adequacy of the Model. The choice of possibilistic noninterference does not automatically solve the above problem—using the full low-equivalence relation on ciphertexts would lead to the same danger of masking insecure flows. Instead the low-equivalence relation has to be crafted carefully to avoid masked insecure flows and at the same time allow secure usage of encryption primitives. We will now show how this can be done for probabilistic encryption schemes. Consider first what happens in the above example. Let two low-equivalent environments E_1 and E_2 s.t. h is *true* in the first and *false* in the second. The result of running the *if* statement of the example above in the second

---

[1] We do not assume that encryption hides the length of messages.

environment E_2 is the singleton set $\hat{E}_2 = \{E_2\}$. However, the result of running it in the first environment is the set of environments $\hat{E}_1 = \{E_1[l = c] \mid encrypt(b) = c\}$, where each c is obtained by encrypting b under the same key but with different initial vectors. The demand of possibilistic noninterference is that for each environment in $\hat{E}_1$ there should exists a low-equivalent environment in $\hat{E}_2$. This is only the case if all ciphertexts $\{c \mid encrypt(b) = c\}$ are low-equivalent. Thus, any low-equivalence relation that does not consider the different ciphertexts originating from one plaintext and one key to be the equivalent will prevent this kind of masking. However, we must make sure that each ciphertext produced by one plaintext and key has a low-equivalent ciphertext for each other choice of plaintext and key.

Fortunately, for probabilistic encryption schemes we can easily form a low-equivalence relation $\doteq$ with these properties by regarding ciphertexts *with the same random initial vector* to be equivalent:

$$\forall k_1, k_2, v_1, v_2 \;.\; \mathcal{E}(k_1, v_1, iv) \doteq \mathcal{E}(k_2, v_2, iv)$$

where iv ranges over initial vectors. This relation has the following properties: (i) different ciphertexts produced by one plaintext and one key will have different initial vectors and will not be low-equivalent, and (ii) since each plaintext and key will produce ciphertexts using all initial vectors, for each ciphertext produced by one plaintext and key there will be exactly one low-equivalent ciphertext for every other choice of plaintext and key.

Relation to Computational Adversary Models. The perfect secrecy and authenticity demands on the encryption schemes are fairly strong. However, there are schemes for which the probability of breaking these assumptions is provably negligible.

The first demand that the ciphertexts should give no information about the plaintexts is commonly relaxed to the notion of *semantic security under chosen plaintext attack* (SEM-CPA) by assuming that the adversary has *limited computational power*. Semantic security states that "*Whatever is efficiently computable about the cleartext given the cyphertext, is also efficiently computable without the cyphertext*" [17]. [2]

In the same way we may allow a relaxation of the demand of authenticity, which can be implemented by combining *Message Authentication Code* (MAC) with a SEM-CPA encryption scheme to form a new scheme that is both secure (SEM-CPA) and authenticity preserving (INT-PTXT)[6]. A scheme is INT-PTXT if the chance that an adversary can produce ciphertexts C s.t. $M = \mathcal{D}_k(C) \neq \perp$ and M was never a parameter of $\mathcal{E}_k(\cdot)$ is negligible. To see that the probability of a successful decryption using the wrong key is negligible under an INT-PTXT scheme consider the following. If a ciphertext $C = \mathcal{E}_k(M)$ decrypts successfully using another key than was used to construct the message i.e. $M' = \mathcal{D}_{k'}(C)$ for $k' \neq k$ then the scheme cannot be INT-PTXT, since M' was never a parameter of $\mathcal{E}_{k'}(\cdot)$.

On Semantic Security. We believe that it is possible to prove a general result that if a program with SEM-CPA + INT-PTXT encryption primitives is secure w.r.t. possibilistic noninterference then it is also semantically secure. This result is likely to involve

---

[2] There is another frequently used notion of security under a computationally limited adversary, IND-CPA. IND-CPA has been shown to be equivalent to SEM-CPA [17,6].

restrictions on *key cycles*, which are a known problem when reconciling the formal and computational views of cryptography [2], or demanding that the underlying schema is secure in the presence of such cycles (cf. *KDM security* [7]).

With such a result at hand, we shall be able to capitalize on the modularity of our approach. For a given language and type system, as soon as we can prove that all well-typed programs are noninterfering, we automatically get semantic security. This opens up possibilities for reasoning about expressive languages and type systems, where all we have to worry about are noninterference proofs (which are typically simpler than proofs of computational soundness).

4   Types

The syntax of the types is defined in Figure 2. A *primitive type* is either a *security annotated basic type*, a pair of primitive types or a *key type*. The security annotation assigns a security level to the basic type expressing whether it is *secret* or *public*. The types of encrypted values are *structural* in the sense that the type reflects the original type of the encrypted values as well as the level of the key that was used in the encryption. For instance, enc_S (int H) L is the type of a secret integer that has been encrypted with a secret key once and enc_S (enc_S (int H) L) L is the type of an integer that has been encrypted with a secret key twice. The type of the variable environment Ω is a map from variables to primitive types, the type of the input environment and the output environment alike Θ is a map from channel names to primitive types, and the key-stream environment defines its own type (in the domain of the environment). The type of the entire environment, Σ, is the pair of a variable type environment and a channel type environment.

Well-Formed Values. Well-formedness defines the meaning of the types ignoring the security annotations. The well-formedness is entirely standard and is omitted for space reasons.

Low-Equivalence. In Figure 4 we formalize the low-equivalence relation. For complex types, i.e., pairs and environments, low-equivalence is defined structurally by demanding the parts of the complex type to be low-equivalent w.r.t. the corresponding type. Any values are low-equivalent w.r.t. a secret type. Integers are low-equivalent w.r.t. a public integer type if they are equal. Low-equivalence for keys is slightly different since keys are not annotated with a security level—only a key level—whose meaning is defined by well-formed values as different sets. Even though it is semantically meaningful to add a security level to key types—the values of keys can be indirectly affected by computation—we have chosen not to. Instead, a public key is considered to be of low security and a secret key of high security. Thus, public keys are low-equivalent if they are equal, and any two secret keys are low-equivalent.

The most interesting rule is the rule defining low-equivalence w.r.t. a public encryption type (LE-ENC-L1) and (LE-ENC-L2). These two rules define the difference in meaning between encryption with a secret and a public key. First, in both rules, the encrypted values must be low-equivalent w.r.t. the low-equivalence relation of encrypted values. Second, there must exist a pair of low-equivalent keys w.r.t. the key type of the encryption type that decrypt the encrypted value to two values. This is where the rules differ.

$$\text{(LE-KEY-L)} \frac{}{pk^{\bullet} \sim_{\text{key P}} pk^{\bullet}} \qquad \text{(LE-PAIR)} \frac{v_{11} \sim_{\tau_1} v_{21} \qquad v_{12} \sim_{\tau_2} v_{22}}{(v_{11}, v_{12}) \sim_{(\tau_1, \tau_2)} (v_{21}, v_{22})}$$

$$\text{(LE-KEY-H)} \frac{}{sk_1^{\bullet} \sim_{\text{key S}} sk_2^{\bullet}} \qquad \text{(LE-MEM)} \frac{\forall x \in \text{dom}\,(\Omega) \qquad M_1(x) \sim_{\Omega(x)} M_2(x)}{M_1 \sim_{\Omega} M_2}$$

$$\text{(LE-INT-L)} \frac{}{n^{\bullet} \sim_{\text{int L}} n^{\bullet}}$$

$$\text{(LE-INT-H)} \frac{}{n_1^{\bullet} \sim_{\text{int H}} n_2^{\bullet}} \qquad \text{(LE-INENV)} \frac{\forall ch \in dom(\Theta) . \, I_1(ch) \sim_{\Theta(ch)} I_2(ch)}{I_1 \sim_{\Theta} I_2}$$

$$\text{(LE-ENC-L3)} \frac{}{\bullet \sim_{\text{encp } \tau \text{ L}} \bullet} \qquad \text{(LE-OUTENV)} \frac{\forall ch \in dom(\Theta) . \\ O_1(ch) \sim_{\Theta(ch)} O_2(ch)}{O_1 \sim_{\Theta} O_2}$$

$$\text{(LE-ENC-H)} \frac{}{u_1^{\bullet} \sim_{\text{enc}_{\gamma} \tau \text{ H}} u_2^{\bullet}} \qquad \text{(LE-KGEN)} \frac{G_1(\text{S}) \sim G_2(\text{S}) \qquad G_1(\text{P}) \sim G_2(\text{P})}{G_1 \sim G_2}$$

$$\text{(LE-KGENP)} \frac{pk_1 \sim_{\text{key P}} pk_2 \\ K_1 \sim_{\text{P}} K_2}{pk_1 \cdot K_1 \sim_{\text{P}} pk_2 \cdot K_2} \qquad \text{(LE-KGENS)} \frac{sk_1 \sim_{\text{key S}} sk_2 \\ K_1 \sim_{\text{S}} K_2}{sk_1 \cdot K_1 \sim_{\text{S}} sk_2 \cdot K_2}$$

$$\text{(LE-ENC-L1)} \frac{\exists v_i, k_i . \, v_i = \mathcal{D}_{\gamma}(k_i, u_i) \qquad i = 1, 2 \qquad k_1 \sim_{\text{key S}} k_2 \qquad v_1 \sim_{\tau} v_2 \\ u_1 \doteq u_2}{u_1 \sim_{\text{encs } \tau \text{ L}} u_2}$$

$$\text{(LE-ENC-L2)} \frac{\exists v_i, k_i . \, v_i = \mathcal{D}_{\gamma}(k_i, u_i) \qquad k_1 \sim_{\text{key P}} k_2 \qquad v_1 \sim_{tolow(\tau)} v_2 \\ u_1 \doteq u_2}{u_1 \sim_{\text{encp } \tau \text{ L}} u_2}$$

Fig. 4. Low-equivalence

Since ciphertexts created by public keys can be decrypted by anyone with access to the public keys, we have to demand that the inside of the encrypted value contains only public values. This is done in the (LE-ENC-L2) rule, which demands that the inside is not only low-equivalent w.r.t. its type τ, but low-equivalent w.r.t. $tolow(\tau)$, which is defined as follows:

$$tolow(t\, \sigma) = t\ \text{L} \quad tolow(\text{key P}) = \text{key P} \quad tolow((\tau_1, \tau_2)) = (tolow(\tau_1), tolow(\tau_2))$$

The (LE-ENC-L1) rule can be seen as encoding the power of the attackers. For encryption with secret keys the demand is only that the resulting values should be low-equivalent w.r.t. the primitive type, τ, of the encryption type. This way, we demand low-equivalence inside encrypted values and make certain that that the result of decrypting low-equivalent encrypted values will result in low-equivalent values and that secret values are not stored inside encrypted values that are created by public keys.

Subtyping. The subtyping is entirely standard; it allows public information to be seen as secret with the exception of invariant subtyping for keys. The subtyping relation for primitive types, $<:$, and the subtyping relation for security levels, $\sqsubseteq$, defines the corresponding join operators. The subtyping relation can be found in [3].

$$(\text{T-NEWKEY})\frac{pc \sqsubseteq \mathit{lvl}(\text{key }\gamma)}{\Omega, pc \vdash \text{newkey } \gamma : \text{key }\gamma} \qquad (\text{T-ENC1})\frac{\begin{array}{c}\Omega, pc \vdash e_1 : \text{key S}\\ \Omega, pc \vdash e_2 : \tau\end{array}}{\Omega, pc \vdash \text{enc}_\text{S} (e_1, e_2) : \text{enc}_\text{S} \tau \text{ L}}$$

$$(\text{T-ENC2})\frac{\begin{array}{c}\Omega, pc \vdash e_1 : \text{key P}\\ \Omega, pc \vdash e_2 : \tau \quad \mathit{lvl}(\tau) = \sigma\end{array}}{\Omega, pc \vdash \text{enc}_\text{P} (e_1, e_2) : \text{enc}_\text{P} \tau \sigma} \qquad (\text{T-DEC})\frac{\begin{array}{c}\Omega, pc \vdash e_1 : \text{key }\gamma\\ \Omega, pc \vdash e_2 : \text{enc}_\gamma \tau \sigma\end{array}}{\Omega, pc \vdash \text{dec}_\gamma (e_1, e_2) : \tau^\sigma}$$

Fig. 5. Type Rules of Expressions

Expression Type Rules. The type rules for expressions are of the form $\Omega, pc \vdash e : \tau$. Figure 5 defines typing rules for non-standard expressions, while the rest of the rules can be found in [3]. The generation of a new key with the requested security level results in a key with that security level if the requested level is not below the context type. The reason for this is that we assume that the public-key stream is publicly observable. Encryption with secret keys will always result in public encrypted values. Encryption with public keys is possible on any value but produces a result that is as secret as the original value. Both the type rule for key generation and the type rule for public encryption makes use of function $\mathit{lvl}(\cdot)$ that computes the security level of the given value:

$$\mathit{lvl}(t\,\sigma) = \sigma \quad \mathit{lvl}((\tau_1, \tau_2)) = \mathit{lvl}(\tau_1) \sqcup \mathit{lvl}(\tau_2) \quad \mathit{lvl}(\text{key P}) = \text{L} \quad \mathit{lvl}(\text{key S}) = \text{H}$$

Decryption is allowed only if the key level of the key used for decryption matches the key level of the encrypted value. The result of the decryption is tainted by the security level of the encrypted values. The taint function is defined as follows:

$$(t\,\sigma)^{\sigma'} = t\,(\sigma \sqcup \sigma') \quad (\tau_1, \tau_2)^\sigma = (\tau_1^\sigma, \tau_2^\sigma) \quad (\text{key P})^\text{L} = \text{key P} \quad (\text{key S})^\sigma = \text{key S}$$

Command Type Rules. As with expressions most of the rules are standard for a security type system (cf. [34]). As is standard, following Denning's original approach to analyzing programs for secure information flow [13], in order to prevent implicit flows the notion of *security context* is defined. The security context of a program point is defined to be the least upper bound of the security levels of the conditional expressions of the enclosing conditionals. The context affects the the commands with side-effects, i.e., variable assignment, input, and output. A block of local declarations followed by a sequence of statements is checked by first adding the declared variables to the variable environment and then checking all statements in the new type environment. The type rule for sequences of statements (T-SEQ) checks all statements of the sequence. *If* and *while* are the two constructs that can lead to indirect flows since they affect the control flow. Thus, the body of the *if* and the *while* are checked in the context of the security level of the control expression. This way, when a branch is depending on a secret the body of that branch is prevented from causing any low side effects. The type rules of commands can be found in [3].

5   Soundness

The main soundness theorem of the paper states that well-typed programs are noninterfering. Typically, for typed programming languages, the soundness is phrased in terms of *progress*, i.e. well-typed programs can always be evaluated in well-formed environments, and *preservation*, i.e. after this step has been made the resulting environment is well formed. It may be interesting to note that the way we have avoided to model error makes this system not satisfy progress: decryption with the wrong key or computing with an uninitialized variable will prevent evaluation. The well known solution is to model failure in the semantics. To keep the presentation cleaner we refrain from this.

The soundness theorem states that well-typed programs are noninterfering. Section 3 lifts the evaluation relation of commands to sets and formulates noninterference for commands. Before giving the formulation of the soundness theorem we must lift the codomain of the evaluation relation of expressions to sets and formulate noninterference for expressions:

$$\langle (M, G), e \rangle \Downarrow \langle G', \hat{v} \rangle \text{ iff } \hat{v} = \{ v \mid \langle (M, G), e \rangle \Downarrow \langle G', v \rangle \}$$

With this we can define noninterference for expressions, which is equivalent to the noninterference of statements defined above. Put simply, if two expressions e_1 and e_2 are run in low-equivalent key-stream and variable environments, yielding pairs of new key-stream environments and results, then these results should be low-equivalent:

$$NI(e_1, e_2)_{\Omega, \tau} \equiv \forall M_1, M_2, G_1, G_2 \, . \, M_1 \sim_\Omega M_2 \wedge G_1 \sim G_2 \wedge$$
$$\langle (M_i, G_i), e_i \rangle \Downarrow \langle G_i', \hat{v}_i \rangle \wedge \hat{v}_i \neq \emptyset \Longrightarrow$$
$$G_1' \sim G_2' \wedge \forall v_1 \in \hat{v}_1 \, \exists v_2 \in \hat{v}_2 \, . \, v_1 \sim_\tau v_2$$

We arrive at the soundness theorems for expressions and commands, both proved by induction on type derivation [3].

Theorem 1. *Soundness for expressions* $\Omega, pc \vdash e : \tau \Longrightarrow NI(e, e)_{\Omega, \tau}$

Theorem 2. *Soundness for commands* $\Sigma, pc \vdash c \Longrightarrow NI(c, c)_\Sigma$

6   Extensions

In this section we consider two extensions: integrity and public-key cryptography.

Integrity. Confidentiality classifies information into public and secret, i.e., information that may or may not be given to the world, respectively. Dually, integrity classifies information into *untrusted* (or *low-integrity*) and *trusted* (or *high-integrity*), i.e., whether the information may or may not have been *affected* by the world.

Tracking the integrity of data enables us to explore some additional dimensions of cryptography: weaknesses of the encryption algorithms and the effect of encryption on integrity. Consider for example, a primitive that is vulnerable to chosen ciphertext attacks. With integrity controls, it is natural to express the restriction that untrusted encrypted values may not be decrypted.

In the presence of integrity the security levels for values are pairs of the form (σ, ι), where σ is a confidentiality level, and ι is a corresponding integrity level. The following tables define two functions—$\mathtt{safe}_\mathcal{E}(\alpha, (\sigma, \iota))$ and $\mathtt{safe}_\mathcal{D}(\alpha, (\sigma, \iota))$—that indicate if it is safe to encrypt (decrypt) a plaintext (ciphertext) of security level (σ, ι) with an encryption scheme that has property α. Here α ranges over standard notions [5]—IND-CCA (indistinguishable under chosen-ciphertext attacks) and IND-CPA (indistinguishable under chosen-plaintext attacks).

	(H,H)	(L,L)	(H,L)	(L,H)
IND-CCA	safe	safe	safe	safe
IND-CPA	safe	safe	safe	safe

$$\mathtt{safe}_\mathcal{E}(\alpha, (\sigma, \iota))$$

	(H,H)	(L,L)	(H,L)	(L,H)
IND-CCA	safe	safe	safe	safe
IND-CPA	safe	-	-	safe

$$\mathtt{safe}_\mathcal{D}(\alpha, (\sigma, \iota))$$

In this way we can provide different type rules for different assumptions on the vulnerability properties of the encryption and decryption algorithms:

$$(\text{T-ENC*})\ \frac{\Omega, pc \vdash e_1 : \mathtt{key}\ \mathsf{S} \quad \Omega, pc \vdash e_2 : \tau \quad lvl(\tau) = (\sigma, \iota) \quad \mathtt{safe}_\mathcal{E}(\alpha, (\sigma, \iota))}{\Omega, pc \vdash \mathtt{enc}^\alpha_\mathsf{S}(e_1, e_2) : \mathtt{enc}_\mathsf{S}\ \tau\ (\mathsf{L}, \mathsf{H})}$$

$$(\text{T-DEC*})\ \frac{\Omega, pc \vdash e_1 : \mathtt{key}\ \gamma \quad \mathtt{safe}_\mathcal{D}(\alpha, (\sigma, \iota)) \quad \Omega, pc \vdash e_2 : \mathtt{enc}_\gamma\ \tau\ (\sigma, \iota)}{\Omega, pc \vdash \mathtt{dec}^\alpha_\gamma(e_1, e_2) : \tau^{(\sigma, \iota)}}$$

A Note on the Integrity of Keys. The current model allows very limited interaction with keys apart from encryption. Since the values of keys cannot be programmatically inspected, the power of the attacker is limited to choice between secure keys. Thus, the model cannot in its present form distinguish between encryption with high and low-integrity keys w.r.t. *confidentiality*. The intuition is clear: since the attacker can only choose between secure keys, that choice will give different but safe encrypted values.

Public-Key Cryptography. Even though the present system deals only with symmetric-key cryptography, there is nothing in the model that prevents modeling public-key cryptography. The set of secret keys would contain the *private* keys and the set of public keys would contain the *public* keys, where the private keys and the public keys are dual. In this system values encrypted with public keys would be considered public, since only actors with access to the private keys would be able to decrypt them.

However, public-key cryptography is most interesting in the presence of integrity. In the same way we can model that encryption of secrets using secret keys results in public values, we can model that encryption raises the integrity of the encrypted value to the integrity of the key, which corresponds to signing.

7   Programming with Encryption: Examples

We have implemented a prototype of the type system and mechanically type-checked two applications: secure backup and a Wide-Mouthed-Frog protocol implementation. In both examples the type system prevents dangerous insecurities such as sending sensitive unencrypted data over a public channel or not using a secret key for encryption. This section discusses some interesting fragments of these implementations.

Secure Data Backup. In the secure backup scenario a low-confidentiality channel is used for sending sensitive information to the remote storage. Listing 2 presents the code for the backup operation. Here and below we slightly simplify the syntax with respect to Figure 2 for the sake of readability.

Here, the global declarations contain secret key K and low channel backup. The type of the latter says that only encrypted high integers may be sent over this channel.

Lines 5 and 7 declare and initialize a high integer variable data. Line 6 declares the variable ctxt of type enc secret (int high) low. On line 8 the value of variable data is encrypted with

```
1 global K secret;
2 backup enc secret (int high) low;
3
4 actor Backup {
5    data int high;
6    ctxt enc secret (int high) low;
7    data := ...
8    ctxt := encrypt(K, data);
9    out backup ctxt;
10 }
```

Listing 2. Backup code

secret key K and the resulting ciphertext is assigned to the variable ctxt. Since type of ctxt matches the type of the backup channel it might be sent over this channel. This is done by the out command on line 9.

When recovering data, an actor reads the data from the public channel and decrypts it. Assuming the same global declarations Listing 3 presents the recovery code. Here, line 4 reads data from the backup channel. It's decrypted using the key K on line 5.

```
1 actor Restore {
2    data int high;
3    ctxt enc secret (int high) low;
4    in ctxt backup;
5    data := decrypt(K, ctxt);
6 }
```

Listing 3. Recovery code

An example of an easy-to-overlook error is to have the following line in place of line 9 in the body of actor Backup: out backup data;. This is an insecurity that the type system rejects. Generally, in the secure backup example the type system ensures that secret data is encrypted before it is sent over the backup channel, thus preventing accidental leaks.

Wide-Mouthed-Frog Protocol. The Wide-Mouthed-Frog protocol [8] is a simple key exchange protocol with trusted server and timestamps. In this protocol secret keys K_{AS} and K_{BS} are shared between server S and principals A and B, respectively. Principal A generates a fresh session key K_{AB}, which is transferred to B in two messages:

$$1. \ A \rightarrow S : A, \{T_A, B, K_{AB}\}K_{AS}$$
$$2. \ S \rightarrow B : \{T_S, A, K_{AB}\}K_{BS}$$

The first message consist of A's name and a tuple encrypted with the shared key K_{AS}. This tuple contains three elements—a timestamp T_A, the name of principal B, and a generated key K_{AB}. Upon receipt of this message, S decrypts it, checks the timestamp, replaces T_A with its own timestamp T_S, encrypts it with key K_{BS}, and forwards the resulting message to B. Principal B then checks whether the second message is timely.

Obviously, there is more to implementation of the protocol than expressed by the two-step description. Our type system guarantees that implementations do not introduce information-flow leaks in the protocol. Listing 4 presents the implementation of this protocol for principal A. The full version of this paper [3] contains the implementation for the server S and principal B.)

This program declares two channels: chanS for communicating with the server, and chanAB for sending messages to B, once the key has been exchanged. The type of the channel chanS corresponds to the first message in the protocol—a pair consisting of a low integer and an encryption with secret key of a three-element tuple (expressed by nested pairs). Since the level of the key used for encrypting this tuple is secret, it is safe to label the result of encryption

```
1  global Kas secret;
2  chanS <int low, enc secret
3    (<int low, <int low, key secret>>) low>;
4  chanAB enc secret (int high) low;
5  actor A {
6    idA int low; idB int low; tsA int low;
7    messageToB int high;
8    Kab key secret;
9    // ... initialization
10   Kab := newkey (secret);
11   out chanS <idA,
12       encrypt(Kas, <tsA,<idB, Kab>>)>;
13   out chanAB encrypt (Kab, messageToB);
14 }
```

Listing 4. WMF Implementation

as low. The body of the actor declaration defines low-confidentiality variables idA and idB that stand for the names of the principals; variable tsA stores the current timestamp; the high-confidentiality variable messageToB contains the information that A wants to send to B.

The new key is generated on line 10. Line 12 constructs the first message of the protocol and sends it to the server. Line 13 uses the newly generated key and sends the secret message to the principal B.

In this example, the type system prevents non-secret session keys in the key establishment protocol. As in the previous example, it also guarantees that secret information may not leave the system unless it is encrypted with a secret key.

8   Related Work

As mentioned in the introduction, declassification models are sometimes used to justify cryptographic primitives in languages with information-flow control. Declassification mechanisms facilitate information release. A recent classification of declassification [29] suggests that information release policies represent aspects of *what* is declassified, by *whom*, *when* and *where* in the system. These correspond to dimensions of information release. The relation of our model to declassification is somewhat subtle, because masking does not actually model information release. Hence, none of the release dimensions is directly suitable for cryptographically-masked flows.

Furthermore, attempts at framing cryptographically-masked flows into different dimensions do not always lead to satisfactory results. For example, releasing the difference between two values of a secret whenever the results of its encryption are different can be a deceptive policy when assumptions about the underlying cryptographic primitives are not explicitly stated. If the underlying encryption function is bijective (assuming the key is fixed) then releasing the result of encryption is equivalent to releasing the secret itself. This phenomenon applies to typical policies from the *what* dimension, such as delimited release [28].

Another example of releasing the secret itself, together with the result of a cryptographic primitive applied to the secret, can be found in [9]. The password checker example is based on matching the hash of the password with the hash of a user query.

The password has a label $H \overset{cert}{\leadsto} L$, which means that the level of the password is eventually declassified from high to low. This, however, allows the password itself to be released to the attacker in cleartext.

Nevertheless, declassification is meaningful in the context of cryptographic computation when the attacker is capable of learning some information from ciphertext. Temporal policies express *when*, at earliest, the attacker might learn the secret. Volpano and Smith's relative secrecy [33,32] guarantees that the attacker cannot learn the secret in polynomial time in the size of the secret. Approaches by Laud [20,21], Laud and Vene [22], provide computational guarantees for a simple imperative language but with the assumption that keys can be statically distinguished. Mitchell et al. [23,25] reason about security with respect to polynomial-time attackers for a form of the π calculus.

A source of our inspiration is Abadi's secrecy model for symmetric-key cryptographic protocols [1]. This model assumes that an attacker is unable to decrypt ciphertexts encrypted with secret keys. Compared to [1], we end up with simpler typing rules. For example, because of the probabilistic encryption assumption, we do not need to deal with explicit confounders. In addition, our approach accommodates natural extensions with integrity and public-key cryptography. Another source of inspiration is a logical relations technique by Sumii and Pierce that facilitates manual security proofs for cryptographic protocols [31]. This technique is not accompanied by static enforcement mechanisms (such as a type system), however.

Gordon and Jeffrey [18] extend Abadi's work to multiple security levels that may be dynamically created and may become compromised. This and other work within Gordon and Jeffrey's Cryptyc project, however, relies on trace-based properties (such as correspondence) that are weaker than noninterference. Dam and Giambiagi's work on *admissibility* [12,15] focuses on protocol implementation, with the goal that information leaks in the implementation must adhere to those declared in protocol specification.

Duggan's and Chothia et al.'s cryptographic types [14,10] help enforce security for a distributed programming language. This is realized through a combination of static and dynamic checks, leading to access-control guarantees (albeit without information-flow guarantees) for secrecy and integrity. Myers et al.'s qualified robustness [26] is based on a possibilistic treatment of *endorsement*, operation dual to declassification.

Hicks et al. [19] define a notion of *noninterference modulo trusted functions*, which requires parts of programs free of cryptographic functions to be in a certain sense indistinguishable. The cryptographic functions are trusted to release information if their security labels satisfy trust constraints. It is a worthwhile direction for future work to formally investigate the relation to *noninterference modulo trusted functions*. We do not expect it to be straightforward because the definition of the indistinguishability relation from [19] involves two-level semantics.

9   Conclusions and Future Work

We have developed an approach to tracking information flow in the presence of cryptographic operations, based on possibilistic noninterference. We have argued that a possibilistic treatment of cryptographic operations leads to a natural model of attackers that may not distinguish between ciphertexts. This model has a close connection to probabilistic encryption and, we believe, it naturally connects to computational adversary models (cf. Section 3).

Our case for possibilistic noninterference is driven by the possibility of capitalizing on the available machinery for reasoning about noninterference in programming languages. We have demonstrated that possibilistic noninterference can be provably and straightforwardly enforced via a security-type system for a language that includes cryptographic primitives and message passing. The type system is amenable to extensions, including integrity and public-key cryptography, which makes it attractive for developing secure implementations of non-trivial cryptographic protocols. We plan to explore a semantic justification of these extensions, crystallizing guarantees provided by the typing rules, and to consider cases studies in which it is critical to achieve these guarantees.

Acknowledgments. We wish to thank Martín Abadi and Peeter Laud for helpful comments. This work was supported, in part, by the Swedish Research Council and, in part, by the Information Society Technologies programme of the European Commission, Future and Emerging Technologies under the IST-2005-015905 MOBIUS project.

References

1. M. Abadi. Secrecy by typing in security protocols. *J. ACM*, 46(5):749–786, September 1999.
2. M. Abadi and P. Rogaway. Reconciling two views of cryptography (the computational soundness of formal encryption). *J. of Cryptology*, 15(2):103–127, 2002.
3. A. Askarov, D. Hedin, and A. Sabelfeld. Cryptographically-masked flows. Technical report, Chalmers University of Technology, June 2006. Located at `http://www.cs.chalmers.se/~aaskarov/sas06full.pdf`.
4. A. Askarov and A. Sabelfeld. Security-typed languages for implementation of cryptographic protocols: A case study. In *Proc. European Symp. on Research in Computer Security*, volume 3679 of *LNCS*, pages 197–221. Springer-Verlag, September 2005.
5. M. Bellare, A. Desa, D. Pointcheval, and P. Rogaway. Relations among notions of security for public-key encryption schemes. In *Advances in Cryptology- Crypto 98*, volume 1462 of *LNCS*, pages 26–46, January 1998.
6. M. Bellare and C. Namprempre. Authenticated encryption: Relations among notions and analysis of the generic composition paradigm. In *Advances in Cryptology - Asiacrypt 2000*, volume 1976 of *LNCS*, pages 531–545, January 2000.
7. J. Black, P. Rogaway, and T. Shrimpton. Encryption-scheme security in the presence of key-dependent messages. In *Selected Areas in Cryptography*, volume 2595 of *LNCS*, pages 62–75. Springer-Verlag, August 2002.
8. M. Burrows, M. Abadi, and R. Needham. A logic of authentication. *ACM Transactions on Computer Systems*, 8(1):18–36, February 1990.
9. S. Chong and A. C. Myers. Security policies for downgrading. In *ACM Conference on Computer and Communications Security*, pages 198–209, October 2004.
10. T. Chothia, D. Duggan, and J. Vitek. Type-based distributed access control. In *Proc. IEEE Computer Security Foundations Workshop*, pages 170–186, 2003.
11. E. S. Cohen. Information transmission in sequential programs. In R. A. DeMillo, D. P. Dobkin, A. K. Jones, and R. J. Lipton, editors, *Foundations of Secure Computation*, pages 297–335. Academic Press, 1978.
12. M. Dam and P. Giambiagi. Confidentiality for mobile code: The case of a simple payment protocol. In *Proc. IEEE Computer Security Foundations Workshop*, pages 233–244, July 2000.

13. D. E. Denning and P. J. Denning. Certification of programs for secure information flow. *Comm. of the ACM*, 20(7):504–513, July 1977.
14. D. Duggan. Cryptographic types. In *Proc. IEEE Computer Security Foundations Workshop*, pages 238–252, June 2002.
15. P. Giambiagi and M. Dam. On the secure implementation of security protocols. In *Proc. European Symp. on Programming*, volume 2618 of *LNCS*, pages 144–158. Springer-Verlag, April 2003.
16. J. A. Goguen and J. Meseguer. Security policies and security models. In *Proc. IEEE Symp. on Security and Privacy*, pages 11–20, April 1982.
17. S. Goldwasser and S. Micali. Probabilistic encryption. *Journal of Computer and System Sciences*, 28:270–299, 1984.
18. A. Gordon and A. Jeffrey. Secrecy despite compromise: Types, cryptography, and the pi-calculus. In *Proc. CONCUR'05*, number 3653 in LNCS, pages 186–201. Springer-Verlag, August 2005.
19. B. Hicks, D. King, and P. McDaniel. Declassification with cryptographic functions in a security-typed language. Technical Report NAS-TR-0004-2005, Network and Security Center, Department of Computer Science, Pennsylvania State University, May 2005.
20. P. Laud. Semantics and program analysis of computationally secure information flow. In *Proc. European Symp. on Programming*, volume 2028 of *LNCS*, pages 77–91. Springer-Verlag, April 2001.
21. P. Laud. Handling encryption in an analysis for secure information flow. In *Proc. European Symp. on Programming*, volume 2618 of *LNCS*, pages 159–173. Springer-Verlag, April 2003.
22. P. Laud and V. Vene. A type system for computationally secure information flow. In *Proc. Fundamentals of Computation Theory*, volume 3623 of *LNCS*, pages 365–377, August 2005.
23. P. Lincoln, J. C. Mitchell, M. Mitchell, and A. Scedrov. A probabilistic poly-time framework for protocol analysis. In *ACM Conference on Computer and Communications Security*, pages 112–121, November 1998.
24. D. McCullough. Noninterference and the composability of security properties. In *Proc. IEEE Symp. on Security and Privacy*, pages 177–186, May 1988.
25. J. C. Mitchell. Probabilistic polynomial-time process calculus and security protocol analysis. In *Proc. European Symp. on Programming*, volume 2028 of *LNCS*, pages 23–29. Springer-Verlag, April 2001.
26. A. C. Myers, A. Sabelfeld, and S. Zdancewic. Enforcing robust declassification and qualified robustness. *J. Computer Security*, 2006. To appear.
27. A. Sabelfeld and A. C. Myers. Language-based information-flow security. *IEEE J. Selected Areas in Communications*, 21(1):5–19, January 2003.
28. A. Sabelfeld and A. C. Myers. A model for delimited information release. In *Proc. International Symp. on Software Security (ISSS'03)*, volume 3233 of *LNCS*, pages 174–191. Springer-Verlag, October 2004.
29. A. Sabelfeld and D. Sands. Dimensions and principles of declassification. In *Proc. IEEE Computer Security Foundations Workshop*, pages 255–269, June 2005.
30. C. E. Shannon. A mathematical theory of communication. *Bell System Tech. J.*, 27:623–656, 1948.
31. E. Sumii and B. Pierce. Logical relations for encryption. In *Proc. IEEE Computer Security Foundations Workshop*, pages 256–269, June 2001.
32. D. Volpano. Secure introduction of one-way functions. In *Proc. IEEE Computer Security Foundations Workshop*, pages 246–254, July 2000.
33. D. Volpano and G. Smith. Verifying secrets and relative secrecy. In *Proc. ACM Symp. on Principles of Programming Languages*, pages 268–276, January 2000.
34. D. Volpano, G. Smith, and C. Irvine. A sound type system for secure flow analysis. *J. Computer Security*, 4(3):167–187, 1996.

Proving the Properties of Communicating Imperfectly-Clocked Synchronous Systems

Julien Bertrane

École Normale Supérieure, Paris, France
bertrane@di.ens.fr

Abstract. Our work aims at certifying that all the executions of several collaborating synchronous systems in a realistic environment follow a given specification. In order to analyze the numerous executions that may happen while considering a set of synchronous systems whose clocks are non-perfect and that communicate through non-instantaneous channels, we define two new abstract domains. The *Changes counting domain* and the *Integral bounding domain* gap the imprecisions of the previously defined Constraint domain that occur because of these hardware imprecisions. We define a reduced product between these domains that allows a much more precise though sound analysis than the three analyses that may have been defined in each domain.

1 Introduction

The design of critical embedded command systems often relies on the GALS (globally asynchronous, locally synchronous) paradigm. This means that several synchronous subsystems communicate with each other in order to compute the decisions, each one being timed by its own clock. These clocks may however desynchronize the one compared to the others. The reason for this design method is that the propagation of the information inside large systems is too long for it to be made of a single synchronous system. Furthermore, in order to prevent design and hardware errors, it is common to use several redundant units executing on different systems.

The designers have therefore to take this clock skew problem into consideration. Another consequence of such a design is that it implies communications between the synchronous systems, for example through buses. The communication delays between the subsystems cannot be neglected nor considered constant. The two temporal imprecisions caused by this hardware limitations make their analysis very difficult.

We introduce several abstract domains that interact and allow an abstract interpretation based analysis of the code of embedded systems built according to the previous hypotheses. Their goal is to try to prove that the software part of the system is robust enough to satisfy the specifications despite the hardware imprecisions.

Previous Works

The design of data processing systems for critical software is often based on the Lustre and SCADE synchronous programming frameworks. Their theoretical

K. Yi (Ed.): SAS 2006, LNCS 4134, pp. 370–386, 2006.

foundations and properties were presented in [9,11] and [3,2,8]. We try to never choose between their syntax, and any example given may be easily written in both of them. The difficulties resulting from asynchrony and non-instantaneous communications for synchronous systems were also studied in [7]. A way to face these difficulties is presented in [1]: a protocol is defined that ensures the robustness of the system to clock desynchronization. Our studies doesn't aim at proposing robustness techniques but at proving them, even if they are hidden inside a huge amount of code. S. Thompson and A. Mycroft, proposed in [12] several abstractions to study asynchronous circuits that share some characteristics with the changes counting domain we introduce here : both describe signals through their value changes. We make an extensive use of the abstract interpretation theory and tools presented in particular of [6,5,10]. We presented a simpler analysis method in [4].

Sect. 2 presents the characteristics and the limits of the synchronous subsystems that we study and of the hardware they will be run on. We then introduce in Sect. 3 the semantics of the executions of these systems. In Sect. 4, we recall briefly the *Constraint domain*. Sect. 5 extends our abstract model by defining a new abstract domain, the *Changes counting domain* and considering a reduced product with the *Constraint domain*. This extension is continued in Sect. 6 with the definition of a third abstract domain, the *Integral bounding domain*, also interacting thanks to a reduced product with the two former ones. An example of the interaction between these domains is presented in Sect. 7. In Sect. 8, we give some details about an implementation of these domains and about future improvements.

2   Communications Between Non-perfect Systems

The systems we analyze are made of several units written in a synchronous language, either based on the *node* notion like `Lustre` or on a graphical representation like `SCADE`. In our examples, we use graphical descriptions, since it is easy to include the numerical bounds of the limitations of the hardware in them. In this work, we only consider boolean values and boolean operators.

First, the synchronous systems execute on non-perfect clocks. In order to model their imprecision, each system is connected to a time interval containing the delay between two consecutive ticks. In our example, systems are boxes containing a small box providing this interval. The two effects of a unit (buffering of inputs and computation of an output emitted at the next tick) may be considered separately, as we did in [4]. The buffering and periodic reading is computed by an operator called `DISCR` (depicted as | | | in [4]). The computation and the release of its result is made by an operator called `SHIFT`.

These systems are connected through buses. The transfer of an information along a bus in non-instantaneous. Buses are thus timed by an interval specifying the minimum and the maximum duration of this communication. Of course, a value doesn't necessarily arrive in a system exactly at the time it gets used. Therefore, we assume that these systems are plugged on buffers that receive the

372   J. Bertrane

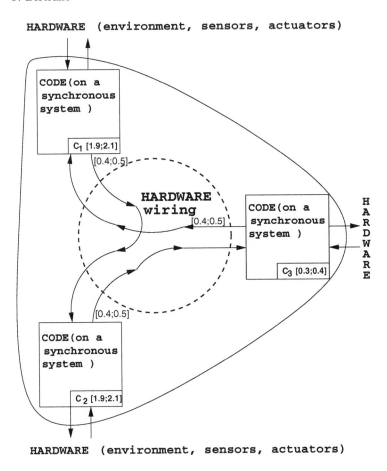

Fig. 1. Three synchronous systems, with bounds on their clock imprecisions and their communication delays

values transmitted by the bus. If a new value arrives in a buffer which has still not been read, then the new value replaces the older one. A bus is graphically represented by a wire and its delay interval.

Therefore, a diagram contains informations not only on the software but also on the hardware, as shown on Fig 1. It presents three synchronous systems connected with three clocks C_1, C_2 and C_3. C_1 and C_2 have the same characteristics : for these clocks, the length of a cycle between two ticks belongs to $[1.9; 2.1]$. In the case of C_3, the cycle length is assumed to belong to $[0.3; 0.4]$. The communication buses are denoted by arrows connecting synchronous systems (inside the hardware wiring label). In a real system, we could have more complex wiring, for example each couple of systems may be connected in both sense (emission and reception). In that case, arrows may split to send the same information to several systems. The characteristics of all the buses in this example are the same : the communication lasts between 0.4 and 0.5 time units.

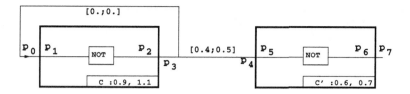

Fig. 2. A couple of communicating imperfectly clocked synchronous systems

3   Concrete Semantics of Communicating Non-perfectly Clocked Synchronous Systems

The concrete semantics of a communicating group of non-perfectly clocked synchronous systems is the precise description of all its possible behaviors. Indeed, because of the hardware imprecision, we cannot define **the** behaviour for a system, since it is not unique, even for a given input : we don't even know the precise time of each clock tick, but only an approximation of this time. We first define an equivalent to the classical notion of variable, since our representation does not provide names for each point of a program :

Definition 1 (Control point). *A control point is any input or output of an operator or of a synchronous system. The set of control points is denoted by P.*

We may now define informally the concrete semantics :

Definition 2 (Concrete semantics). *The concrete semantics of a communicating group of non-perfectly clocked synchronous systems S is the set of all its possible executions. It belongs to $\mathcal{P}(P \to (\mathbb{R}^+ \to \mathbb{B}))$, where $\mathbb{R}^+$ is the time (after the beginning of the execution).*

Since this set is not easy to handle, we immediately abstract it in the canonical way into an element of $P \to \mathcal{P}(\mathbb{R}^+ \to \mathbb{B})$. The function $[\![S]\!] \in P \to \mathcal{P}(\mathbb{R}^+ \to \mathbb{B})$ maps each control point p_i to the set $[\![S]\!](p_i)$ of behaviors possible at point p_i. Each of these behaviors is described by a **signal** : a function v connecting each time t to the value $v(t) \in \mathbb{B}$ at control point p_i at the time t.

Now, we can incrementally build (see Fig. 3) the semantics (as soon as the parameters C, C' and the communication delays are chosen) of the system presented on Fig. 2. On this figure, t stands for *true*, f for *false*, and we let $C_0 = 0$, C_1, C_2, $C'_0 = 0$, C'_1, C'_2 as well as vertical dashed lines denote the first clocks ticks. The arrows show which already built part allows to build a new segment of the signals. For example, in the first step of the building of this solution, we use the initialization convention which expresses that before time $t = 0$, the signals are set to false. During the second step, we discover that between $C_0 = 0$ and C_1, the signal at p_3 is set to false, since p_3 is simply the result of the previous cycle at point p_2, which was false. The same occurs for p_6 and p_7. The signal at p_4 is the delayed version of the one at p_3. And each step extends the previous one.

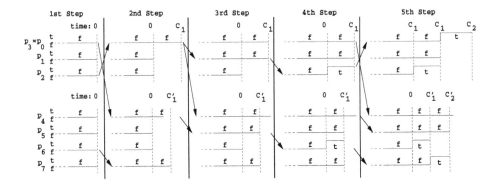

Fig. 3. The semantics of the diagram on Fig. 2

Studying this concrete semantics is very difficult because we cannot even describe **one** behavior at **one** control point, since it lasts an infinite time. *A fortiori*, describing infinitely many of them seems impossible, as well as manipulating them. We therefore make use of the abstract interpretation framework and define several abstract domains that are able of manipulating this "infinite" elements or sets, and prove their properties.

4   Constraint Domain

We defined in [4] an abstract domain based on the notion of temporal constraints. It allows the proof of some temporal properties and it is our first abstract domain, with only a few modifications. The two basic elements are :

- A constraint denoted by $\exists[a;b] : x$, meaning that any signal takes the value x at least once during the interval $[a;b]$.
- A constraint denoted by $\forall\langle a;b\rangle : x$, meaning that any signal takes the value x during the whole interval $[a;b]$.

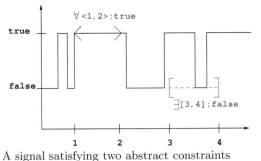

A signal satisfying two abstract constraints

These constraints and the formula built with them using the conjunction and disjunction operators may express many temporal properties. This abstract domain is denoted by $\mathcal{C}$. The connection between this abstract domain and the concrete semantics is maintained by a **concretization** function γ that connects any abstract formula to all the signals that satisfy it. In order to perform an analysis, we defined in [4] abstract operators that spread any information obtained in a control point to its neighbors, remaining in this abstract domain. For each operator OP, we defined in [4] a backward abstract operator $\overleftarrow{\Psi}^{\#}_{\text{OP}}$. They are very intuitive : for example, $\overleftarrow{\Psi}^{\#}_{\text{AND}}(\forall\langle a;b\rangle : \texttt{True}) = (\forall\langle a;b\rangle : \texttt{True}, \forall\langle a;b\rangle : \texttt{True})$. The result is a couple of constraints since the AND operator has two inputs, and we are reasoning backwards. On the other hand, $\overleftarrow{\Psi}^{\#}_{\text{AND}}$ cannot deal precisely with the constraint $\forall\langle a;b\rangle : \texttt{False}$, which would require a non-countable infinity of disjunctions, and it doesn't gain in that case any information, returning top ($\top$), i.e. the absence of constraint.

We now also connect any time-independent (i.e. logical) operator with a trivial forward abstract operator $\overrightarrow{\Psi}^{\#}$ that simply mimics the execution of the operator :
$\overrightarrow{\Psi}^{\#}_{\text{AND}}(\forall\langle 1;3\rangle : \texttt{True}, \forall\langle 2;4\rangle : \texttt{True}) = \forall\langle 2;3\rangle : \texttt{True}$.

Spreading abstract information from one control point to the other ones, we prove abstract properties of the communicating non-perfectly clocked synchronous systems. The abstract interpretation theory provides a simple way to prove that this propagation of the information is sound. For any gate performing a transformation Ψ, the abstract counterpart $\Psi^{\#}$ must satisfy :

$$\Psi \circ \gamma \subseteq \gamma \circ \Psi^{\#}.$$

All of the abstract operators we defined in [4] satisfy this condition.

Constraints Borders. We define four functions connecting a constraint to a real :

$$\texttt{right\_border} : \begin{cases} \forall\langle a;b\rangle : \texttt{False} \mapsto b \\ \exists[a;b] : \texttt{False} \mapsto b \end{cases}$$

$$\texttt{left\_border} : \begin{cases} \forall\langle a;b\rangle : \texttt{False} \mapsto a \\ \exists[a;b] : \texttt{False} \mapsto a \end{cases}$$

$$\texttt{right\_influence\_border} : \begin{cases} \forall\langle a;b\rangle : \texttt{False} \mapsto b \\ \exists[a;b] : \texttt{False} \mapsto a \end{cases}$$

$$\texttt{left\_influence\_border} : \begin{cases} \forall\langle a;b\rangle : \texttt{False} \mapsto a \\ \exists[a;b] : \texttt{False} \mapsto b \end{cases}$$

right_border and left_border simply give the borders of the constraints. right_influence_border(c), where c is a constraint, gives the latest (i.e. the bigest) time after which we have for sure thanks to c an information on any signal satisfying c. In case of a $\forall\langle a;b\rangle : u$ constraint, we know the signal value at any point inside $[a;b]$, so that the result is b. On the other hand, a $\exists[a;b] : u$ constraint only says that after a, we will have one information about the signal. Similarly, left_influence_border gives the earliest time before which we have an information on the signal.

In order to prevent the loss of information which leads among others the result of $\overleftarrow{\Psi}^{\#}_{\text{AND}}(\forall\langle a;b\rangle : \texttt{False})$ to be defined as $\top$, we introduce a new abstract domain which interacts with the Constraint domain and prevents this imprecision.

5   Changes Counting Domain

Goals of the Changes Counting Domain. Synchronous programs are often used in embedded systems, that they control through *actuators*, after having com-

puted reactualized orders depending on what they received from *sensors*. Most
of these sensors, however, work **in real time**, i.e. they deliver a value at any
time. For example, the temperature is usually measured by a resistance varying
continuously with the temperature. Of course, engineers take this into consideration and discretize the signal, and as a consequence stabilize it. We try to take
advantage of this kind of properties by creating a new abstract domain that
interacts with our Constraint domain.

Definition of the Changes Counting Domain. In fact we define two abstract domains, but they are close enough to share most of the code of their abstract
transfer functions. The **Changes counting** domain, denoted by $\mathcal{N}$ simply describes, at each control point, the maximal number of changes that may happen :

- either during a particular interval $[a; b]$: it is the Local Changes counting
  domain
- or during any interval of given width (after time $t = 0$, starting point of the
  execution) : it is the Global Changes counting domain.

The only difference is in fact that the global version adds a universal quantifier
to its condition.

Definition 3 (Local Changes Counting Domain). *The set of Local Changes
counting is* $(\mathbb{N} \cup \{+\infty\}) \times \mathbb{R}^+ \times (\mathbb{R}^+ \cup \{+\infty\})$. *The* top *element, denoted by* $\top$
is $(+\infty, 0, +\infty)$. *The* bottom *element, denoted by* $\bot$ *is* $(+\infty, 0, 0)$.

Definition 4 (Global Changes Counting Domain). *The set of Global Cha-
nges counting is* $(\mathbb{N} \cup \{+\infty\}) \times (\mathbb{R}^+ \cup \{+\infty\})$. *The* top *element, denoted by* $\top$
is $(+\infty, +\infty)$. *The* bottom *element, denoted by* $\bot$ *is* $(+\infty, 0)$.

In the following, we consider the Global Changes counting domain only. All the
statements can be easily adapted to the Local Changes counting domain by
considering **one** interval instead of **all** of the ones with a particular width. The
meaning of an element $(n, \delta)_{\mathcal{N}} \in \mathcal{N}$ connected to a control point p_1, where S_1
denotes set of signals in the concrete semantics, is :

$$\forall v \in S_1, \forall x \in \mathbb{R}^+, \not\exists x_0, ..., x_{n+1} \in [x; x + \delta], \text{ such that}$$

$$x_0 < x_1 < ... < x_n < x_{n+1}$$
$$v(x_0) \neq v(x_1) \wedge v(x_1) \neq v(x_2) \wedge ... \wedge v(x_n) \neq v(x_{n+1}).$$

This prevents v from changing its value more than n times during $[x; x+\delta]$. This
automatically defines a *concretization function* γ as the following set :

$$\gamma(n, \delta) \triangleq \left\{ v : \mathbb{R}^+ \mapsto \mathbb{B}, \left| \begin{array}{l} \forall x \in \mathbb{R}^+, \not\exists x_0, ..., x_{n+1} \in [x; x + \delta], \\ x_0 < x_1 < ... < x_n < x_{n+1} \\ v(x_0) \neq v(x_1) \wedge ... \wedge v(x_n) \neq v(x_{n+1}) \end{array} \right. \right\}$$

This function relates the concrete and the abstract domain. It automatically defines a pre-order $\leqslant_\mathcal{N}$ on $\mathcal{N} : \forall n_1, n_2 \in \mathcal{N}, n_1 \leqslant_\mathcal{N} n_2 \iff \gamma(n_1) \subseteq \gamma(n_2)$. In fact, we consider the abstract elements modulo $\leqslant_\mathcal{N} \cap \geqslant_\mathcal{N}$ so that $\leqslant_\mathcal{N}$ is an order.

Applications of This Domain. This domain is useful in three types of context :

- It may simply be a direct consequence of the property that we try to prove (or its negation). It is interesting in that case to rewrite it in the Changes counting domain.
- Some operators (like the discretization previously considered) may induce a stability that may be converted into a Changes counting domain element.
- An input may be by physical construction (hardware property) stable and this property may be translated into a Changes counting domain element.

*Transfer Function Inside the **Changes counting** Domain.* If the width (called δ above) of any abstract element of the Changes counting domain was the same for each abstract element of this domain, the transfer functions would be really easy to define. Considering for example the AND gate connecting two input control points p_1 and p_2 to an output control point p_3, if we know that :

- any signal in the semantics connected to point p_1 changes its value at most n_1 times during any interval of width δ,
- any signal in the semantics connected to point p_2 changes its value at most n_2 times during any interval of width δ,

clearly, any signal in the semantics connected to point p_3 changes its value at most $n_1 + n_2$ times during any interval of width δ. In that simplified case, this allows a simple definition of an **abstract forward transfer function** for the AND operator.

But, if we try to compute the result of the abstract forward transfer function $\Psi_{\mathrm{AND}}^{\#}$ on the couple of abstract elements $(5, 2.1)_\mathcal{N}, (3, 4.7)_\mathcal{N}$, one for each input of the AND gate, we cannot use the same argument.

However, as pictured on Fig. 4, if the signal at the second input control point cannot change its value more than three times during 4.7 time units, it also cannot change its value more than three times during 2.1 time units, and therefore satisfies the abstract element $(3, 2.1)_\mathcal{N}$. As a consequence :

$$\overrightarrow{\Psi}_{\mathrm{AND}}^{\#}{}_\mathcal{N}((5, 2.1), (3, 4.7)) \leqslant_\mathcal{N} \overrightarrow{\Psi}_{\mathrm{AND}}^{\#}{}_\mathcal{N}((5, 2.1), (3, 2.1))$$

and this allows the same type of computation as the one above : the output control point satisfies the abstract element $(8, 2.1)_\mathcal{N}$. This is done automatically by a *reframing* function :

Definition 5. *A **reframing** function takes **two** abstract elements containing a notion of interval, and returns two new abstract elements whose interval widths*

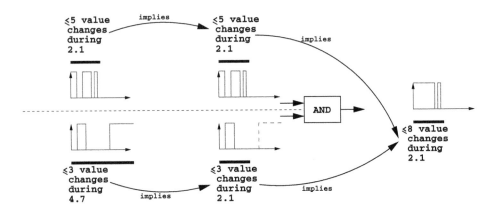

Fig. 4. Computing the abstract operator AND in the changes counting domain

are equal, and that are consequences of the two input elements. We call φ_0 the basic reframing function that returns its input elements, only modified in that the interval width is the shortest of its two input interval widths.

For instance, $\varphi_0((5, 2.1), (3, 4.7)) \triangleq ((5, 2.1), (3, 2.1))$. Trickier reframing functions may easily be defined for the Changes counting domain elements.

Transfer Functions of Time-Independent Operators. All the time-independent operators OP are connected to an abstract forward transfer function $\Psi_{\texttt{OP\#}}$ defined by :

$$\Psi_{\texttt{OP\#},\varphi}((n_1, \delta_1), (n_2, \delta_2)) \triangleq (\tilde{n}_1 + \tilde{n}_2, \tilde{\delta}_1)$$

where φ is a reframing function and $\varphi((n_1, \delta_1), (n_2, \delta_2)) = ((\tilde{n}_1, \tilde{\delta}_1), (\tilde{n}_2, \tilde{\delta}_1))$. This abstract function is clearly sound, since the result of a time-independent operator may change only if one of its inputs changes.

Transfer Function of Time-Dependent Operators. This case is much more difficult. We consider for instance the operator $\texttt{DISCR}_{[\mu,\nu]}$ which models the periodic reading of an input buffer (according to an imprecise clock whose cycles last between μ and ν time units; $\mu, \nu \in \mathbb{R}_*^+$). First, we may deduce stability information without even looking at the input, since this operator performs a discretization. We know that the output signal may not change its value more than once during any interval $[x; x + \mu], x \in \mathbb{R}^+$, which generates the abstract element $(1, \mu)_\mathcal{N}$.

But this may not be precise enough. Another argument can be considered. We assume that we already know that during any interval $[x; x + \delta]$, any input signal may change its value at most n times :$(n, \delta)_\mathcal{N}$. Let us consider any interval $[y; y + \eta]$ at the control point after the discretization. It is included in at most

$j = \left\lceil \frac{\eta}{\mu} \right\rceil + 1$ consecutive cycles[1] of the discretizer, which cover an interval $[z, z + hws\rho]$, with $\rho \leqslant \left\lceil \frac{\eta}{\mu} \right\rceil * \nu + \nu$.

Now, $[z, z + \rho]$ is of width ρ, and during these j cycles, only $\left\lceil \frac{\rho}{\delta} \right\rceil * n$ value changes may occur at the input control point. Since the operator is only discretizing the input signal, it doesn't add any value change, and therefore at most $\left\lceil \frac{\rho}{\delta} \right\rceil * n$ value changes may occur during the j cycles, and a fortiori during $[y; y + \eta]$. Since $\rho \leqslant \left\lceil \frac{\eta}{\mu} \right\rceil * \nu + \nu$,

we know that $\left\lceil \frac{\rho}{\delta} \right\rceil * n \leqslant \left\lceil \frac{\left\lceil \frac{\eta}{\mu} \right\rceil * \nu + \nu}{\delta} \right\rceil * n$, and we

may soundly define :

$$\overrightarrow{\Psi}^{\#}_{\text{DISCR}[\mu,\nu]\eta}(n, \delta) \triangleq \left(\left\lceil \frac{\left\lceil \frac{\eta}{\mu} \right\rceil * \nu + \nu}{\delta} \right\rceil * n, \eta \right)$$

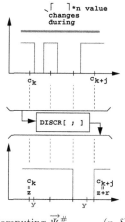

Computing $\overrightarrow{\Psi}^{\#}_{\text{DISCR}[\mu,\nu]\eta}(n, \delta)$

We introduced a η parameter in the computation of the abstract operator that will necessarily also be a parameter of our analysis. The operator and the analysis are sound for any η. When an analysis is not successful, modifying this parameter is a way to refine it.

*Reduced Product Between the **Constraints** Domain and the **Changes Counting** Domain.* It is clear that any signal that may not change its value more than once in 2 time units, and that also satisfies the constrains $\forall\langle 0; 0 \rangle$: True and $\forall\langle 2; 2 \rangle$: True is always equal to True between 0 and 2. Indeed, if it was equal to *False* at some point t between 0 and 2, then it would change its value at least twice during the $[0; 2]$ interval (once between 0 and t, and once between t and 2).

We now generalize informally to a more realistic yet simple example the reduced product : we study how the conjunction $(c_1 \wedge c_2)_C$ of two constraints and the abstract element $(1, stab)_N$ may be reduced.

We define a function ρ connecting any pair (c_1, c_2) of constraints and any real *stab* that satisfies the following conditions :

- the intervals of the two constraints are disjoint
- the values of the constraints are equal. We call b this value.
- in case c_1 is before c_2 (which makes sense when the first condition is satisfied), left_influence_border(c_2) − right_influence_border(c_1) < *stab*, and conversely in the other case.

to a new constraint : $\forall\langle$right_border(c_1); left_border(c_2)$\rangle$: b.

---

[1] $\lceil v \rceil$ denotes the smallest integer greater or equal to v.

For example, we consider on
the figure on the right that the
following abstract elements are
satisfied :

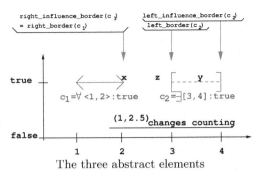

- $c_1 = \forall\langle 1; 2\rangle : true$
- $c_2 = \exists[3; 4] : true$
- $(1, 2.5)_\mathcal{N}$, i.e. one value
  change at most during any interval of width 2.5

The three abstract elements

This transformation is sound for the same reason as the one proving the
$\forall\langle 0; 0\rangle$: True $\wedge$ $\forall\langle 2; 2\rangle$: True $\wedge$ $(1, 2.)_\mathcal{N}$ case. For instance, if we assume that
a signal s_p at a control point p satisfies the constraints c_1 and c_2, the changes
counting condition $(1, stab)$, that the three previous conditions are satisfied and
that c_1 is before c_2, then we know that :

- at a point x after right_influence_border(c_1) and before right_border(c_1),
  the signal takes the value b
- at a point y after left_border(c_2) and before left_influence_border(c_2),
  the signal takes the value b

If at some point z between x and y, the signal takes the value $\neg b$, then $(1, stab)_\mathcal{N}$
is not satisfied, since the width of $[x; y]$ is smaller than the width of

$$[\texttt{right\_influence\_border}(c_1); \texttt{left\_influence\_border}(c_2)]$$

which is smaller than $stab$: the signals changes its value once between x and z
and once between z and y. As a consequence, the signal must take the value b
at point z, and therefore at any point between x and y and a fortiori during the
whole interval $[\texttt{right\_border}(c_1); \texttt{left\_border}(c_2)]$.

This argument is generalized to any finite set of constraints. The ρ function
is applied to all the pairs present in the constraint set, and the result is soundly
added to this set of abstract elements. It may also be generalized to the case
where the changes counting abstract element is $(n, stab)_\mathcal{N}$ instead of $(1, stab)_\mathcal{N}$.

6   Integral Bounding

Origin and Goals of This Domain. We assume that a system contains two control
points p_1 and p_2 clocked by different desynchronized clocks C_1 and C_2. Comparing the values $v_1(t)$ and $v_2(t)$ of the semantics restricted to these control points
at a time t is needed in order to set interesting properties and to prove them.
However, which time t should we consider ? It would be necessary to consider
any n-th tick $C_1(n)$ and $C_2(n)$. But we often don't even know their interleaving.
However, one thing that vary continuously with a slight move of a clock tick is
the integral of the value. We consider the boolean signals are converted into 0

or 1 integer signals. Since the semantics is defined step by step, following the clocks, the signals may vary only finitely many times during an interval of finite width, and there is no risk of undefined integral.

Definition of the Integral Bounding Domain. As for the changes counting domain, this domain may be split into a **local** and a **global** version. We present the more complex global one, from which it is easy to extract the local version. The basic element of the **Integral bounding** domain, denoted by $\mathcal{I}$, is the *Integral bound.*

Definition 6 (Integral bound). *The set of Integral bounds is* $\mathbb{R}^+ \times \mathbb{R}^+ \times \mathbb{R}^+$. *The* top *element, denoted by* $\top$ *is* $(+\infty, 0, +\infty)$. *The* bottom *element, denoted by* $\bot$ *is* $(1, 1, 0)$.

The meaning of an element (δ, α, β) at a control point p_1, where S_1 denotes the set of signals in the concrete semantics, is :

$$\forall v \in S_1, \forall x \in \mathbb{R}^+, \alpha \leqslant \int_x^{x+\delta} \texttt{int\_of\_bool}(v(t))dt \leqslant \beta,$$

where $\texttt{int\_of\_bool} : \begin{cases} True \mapsto 1 \\ False \mapsto 0 \end{cases}$. We may therefore define a *concretization function* γ as the following set :

$$\gamma(\delta, \alpha, \beta) \triangleq \left\{ v : \mathbb{R}^+ \mapsto \mathbb{B}, \forall x \in \mathbb{R}^+, \alpha \leqslant \int_x^{x+\delta} \texttt{int\_of\_bool}(v(t))dt \leqslant \beta \right\}.$$

It automatically defines a pre-order on $\mathcal{I}$: $\forall i_1, i_2 \in \mathcal{I}, i_1 \leqslant_{\mathcal{I}} i_2 \iff \gamma(i_1) \subseteq \gamma(i_2)$ In fact, we consider the equivalence classes of elements of this abstract domain according the equivalence relation $\leqslant_{\mathcal{I}} \cap \geqslant_{\mathcal{I}}$. On these classes, $\leqslant_{\mathcal{I}}$ is an order.

The Integral bounding domain transfer functions that propagate the information available at one control point to the other ones according to the syntax are all constant equal to $\top$, which is clearly sound. A reason for this deliberate loss of precision is that the Integral bounding domain is always used in reduced products, that will be described in the next sections.

Reduced Product Between the **Integral Bounding** *Domain and the* **Changes Counting Domain.** In the ideal case, we are in presence of two already proven properties of any signal v in the semantics for a particular control point p_1 and for any $x \in \mathbb{R}^+$:

- v satisfies a changes counting condition : the value $v(t)$ at time t doesn't change more than n times during any interval $[x; x + \delta]$
- v satisfies an integral bounding condition : $\alpha \leqslant \int_x^{x+\delta} v(t)dt \leqslant \beta$.

This is optimal in that the width of both types of the intervals (δ) is the same. If this isn't the case, we may reuse a *reframe* function defined before. Now, if we consider $[x; x + \delta[$ as the union $\bigcup_j [x + \frac{j}{k} \times \delta; x + \frac{j+1}{k} \times \delta[$, and we try to dispatch the n value changes inside these k intervals, we discover that there

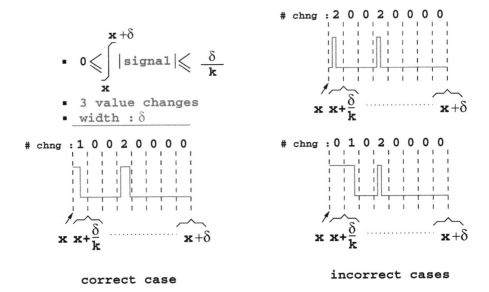

Fig. 5. Three cases that may happen while dispatching the n value changes in the intervals, the two on the right are discarded, because they do not satisfy the conditions, respectively the changes counting condition and the integral bounding one

is a finite disjunction of cases, and that we have some information about the constraints on each of these cases. Some must be discarded, since in any case, they won't satisfy the Integral bounding condition. Three cases are presented on Fig. 5.

*Reduced Product Between the **Integral Bounding** Domain and the **Constraint Domain**.* We consider here a control point where the following local integral bounding condition is satisfied :

$$0 \leqslant \int_x^{x+4} v(t)dt \leqslant 3.$$

We also assume that at this control point, the constraints $\forall\langle x; x+1\rangle :$ **True** and $\forall\langle x+3; x+4\rangle :$ **True** hold. Since

$$\int_x^{x+4} v(t)dt = \int_x^{x+1} v(t)dt + \int_{x+1}^{x+3} v(t)dt + \int_{x+3}^{x+4} v(t)dt = 2 + \int_{x+1}^{x+3} v(t)dt,$$

it is clear that we may safely replace the integral bounding condition by a new more precise one :

$$0 \leqslant \int_{x+1}^{x+3} v(t)dt \leqslant 1.$$

Having, as in this example, the interval of a Constraint included in the interval of a local integral bounding is exceptional. But in the case of a global integral bounding condition, we may "choose" any starting point : the condition is valid for each of them. An interesting choice made by the analyzer for this starting or ending point would be the borders of the Constraint elements already accumulated at the considered control point.

*The Reduced Product Between the **Integral Bounding**, the **Constraint** and the **Changes Counting** Domain.* A reduced product is obtained from the three basic domains by considering all the optimizations described earlier and combining them. We propose an example in the next section.

7   Analyzing Imperfectly-Clocked Synchronous Systems

We present here the simulation of an analysis build on top of the three presented domains of an academic example. We analyze a simple system which could easily be build for example in SCADE. A graphical representation of this system is presented on Fig. 6. The classical PRE operator is initiated with the false value, as a p4=false->PRE p2 in Lustre. We assume the entrance signal is quite stable : it may not change its value more than once in any interval of width 100 time units.

The stability at point p_1 is translated into the abstract element $(1, 100)_\mathcal{N}$. Following the abstract operator for the changes counting domain defined in Sect. 5, we get a condition for the signals at points p_2 and p_3 :

$$\Psi^{\#}_{\text{DISCR}[39,41]116}(1, 100)_\mathcal{N} = \left(\left\lceil \frac{\left\lceil \frac{116}{39} \right\rceil * 41 + 41}{100} \right\rceil * n, 116\right) = (2, 116)_\mathcal{N}.$$

As a consequence, at points p_2, p_3, and p_4 the signals satisfy the condition $(2, 116)_\mathcal{N}$ and a fortiori $(2, 100)_\mathcal{N}$. At point p_5, the abstract operator for the logical gate XOR computes the abstract element $(4, 116)_\mathcal{N}$. Imagine we try to prove that for a signal v at point p_5, $\int_x^{x+100} v(t)dt < 95$. We propose a proof by contradiction. We therefore assume $(100, 95, 100)_\mathcal{I}$ is satisfied at point p_5 and try to prove that we converge into $\perp$.

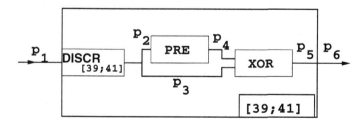

Fig. 6. A example of system where the cooperation between the three abstract domains is needed

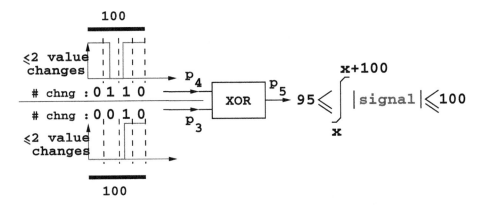

Fig. 7. One possibility of repartition of the value changes

The analyzer will distribute, as in the Sect. presenting the reduced product between the integral bounding domain and the changes counting domain, the possible changes (at most four) into subintervals of $[x; x + 100]$. We consider a case with three value changes. Let us assume that $[x; x + 100]$ is divided into four subintervals (i.e. $k = 4$). The analyzer will then distribute these changes to the inputs, since a change in the result of a XOR operator necessarily comes from a change in one of its inputs. One of the possibilities is presented on Fig 7. However, it is soon discarded. Indeed, it implies (among others) the abstract constraint $\forall \langle 75; 100 \rangle$: true for points p_4 and p_2. Hence, $\overrightarrow{\Psi}_{\text{XOR}}^{\#}(\forall \langle 75; 100 \rangle$: True, $\forall \langle 75; 100 \rangle$: True$) = \forall \langle 75; 100 \rangle$: False for the point p_5, which is detected as incompatible with the $95 \leqslant \int_x^{x+100} signal(t)dt \leqslant 100$ condition by the reduced product between the Integral bounding domain and the Constraint domain. The interaction of the three abstract domains gaps thus their local weaknesses.

This is a much simplified view of what our analyzer does, even in that simple case. But step by step, our analyzer discards the impossible cases. If it fails, it will perform a refinement, either by dividing each interval again, or by changing the parameters of the abstract operators. If all the cases get discarded, this means that a sound abstract overapproximation of the concrete semantics is empty, and thus that this concrete semantics is empty, which puts a end to this proof by contradiction.

8   Implementation and Future Improvements

This domains were implemented and combined into a prototype of analyzer written in ocaml. The principle is the same as in the above example. We consider the intersection A of an overapproximation of the semantics and of the negation of the wanted property. We iterate the abstract operators in order to get a precise abstract representation $A^{\#}$ of A. If the analyzer proves that $A^{\#} = \bot$, the property is proved, since its negation does not intersect with the semantics of the system. Otherwise, either the analyzer is not precise enough, or the property is false and a counter-example may be found in the concretization of $A^{\#}$.

Instead of reals, which are omnipresent in our domains, we used the `float` type. This may cause rounding errors during the analysis that we would not detect. We would like to take them into consideration, as explained in [5]. We would also like to prove the robustness of some systems to errors in the communication or in the execution. Communication errors could of course be simulated by removing the bus link and setting at its arrival the value to ⊤, but there are few chances that a system would still satisfy any interesting specification in that case. A more interesting approach would introduce probabilities for an information to be lost in the communication, and it would require a probability for the system to recover from this error. A modified version of the integral bounding domain could undertake this feature.

9   Conclusion

The computerized commands of an embedded system are usually made of several communicating synchronous systems, each one with its own clock. During a real execution, the clocks tick imperfectly and the communication delays between the systems are non-constant. We proposed a realistic model that allows the specification of the allowed clock skew between several clocks as well as the variable communication delays. In this model, there may be a non-coutable infinity of different executions of a the synchronous subsystems. We introduced two new abstract domains that can express and handle temporal properties despite of these hardware imperfections. The result of the reduced product of them with a previously defined abstract domain is able of both expressing and proving many of the interesting temporal properties in such an environment. It is the basis of a working prototype of static analyzer.

References

1. A. Benveniste, P. Caspi, P. Le Guernic, H. Marchand, J.-P. Talpin, and S. Tripakis. A protocol for loosely time-triggered architectures. *LNCS, Proceedings of the Second International Conference on Embedded Software, p. : 252 - 265*, 2002.
2. G. Berry. *The Constructive Semantics of Pure Esterel.* 1999.
3. G. Berry. *Proof, language, and interaction: essays in honour of Robin Milner, Pages: 425 - 454: The foundations of Esterel.* MIT Press, 2000.
4. J. Bertrane. Static analysis by abstract interpretation of the quasi-synchronous composition of synchronous programs. *VMCAI*, 2005.
5. B. Blanchet, P. Cousot, R. Cousot, J. Feret, L. Mauborgne, A. Miné, D. Monniaux, and X. Rival. Design and implementation of a special-purpose static program analyzer for safety-critical real-time embedded software. *The Essence of Computation: Complexity, Analysis, Transformation. Essays Dedicated to Neil D. Jones, LNCS 2566, 85-108. Springer*, 2002.

6. B. Blanchet, P. Cousot, R. Cousot, J. Feret, L. Mauborgne, A. Miné, D. Monniaux, and X. Rival. A static analyzer for large safety-critical software. *Proc. ACM SIGPLAN 2003 Conf. PLDI, 196-207, San Diego, CA, USA,* . *ACM Press,* 7-14 juin 2003.

7. P. Caspi. Embedded control: From asynchrony to synchrony and back. *1st International Workshop on Embedded Software, EMSOFT2001, Lake Tahoe, Volume 2211 in LNCS,* October 2001.

8. P. Caspi, A. Curic, A. Maignan, C. Sofronis, S. Tripakis, and P. Niebert. From simulink to scade/lustre to tta: a layered approach for distributed embedded applications. *Proceedings of the 2003 ACM SIGPLAN conference on Language, compiler, and tool for embedded systems,* 2003.

9. P. Caspi, D. Pilaud, N. Halbwachs, and J. Plaice. Lustre: A declarative language for programming synchronous systems. *Proceedings of the 14th ACM symposium on Principles of programming languages, POPL'87,* 1987.

10. P. Cousot and R. Cousot. Abstract interpretation and application to logic programs. *Journal of Logic Programming, 13(2–3):103—179,* 1992.

11. N. Halbwachs. *Synchronous programming of reactive systems.* Dordrecht Boston , Kluwer Academic Publishers, 1993.

12. S. Thompson and A. Mycroft. Abstract interpretation of asynchronous circuits. *SAS, Verona, Italy,* August 2004.

Parametric and Termination-Sensitive Control Dependence
(Extended Abstract)

Feng Chen and Grigore Roşu

Department of Computer Science
University of Illinois at Urbana - Champaign, USA
{fengchen, grosu}@uiuc.edu

Abstract. A parametric approach to control dependence is presented, where the parameter is any prefix-invariant property on paths in the control-flow graph (CFG). Existing control dependencies, both direct and indirect, can be obtained as instances of the parametric framework for particular properties on paths. A novel control dependence relation, called termination-sensitive control dependence, is obtained also as an instance of the parametric framework. This control dependence is sensitive to the termination information of loops, which can be given via annotations. If all loops are annotated as terminating then it becomes the classic control dependence, while if all loops are annotated as non-terminating then it becomes the weak control dependence; since in practice some loops are terminating and others are not, termination-sensitive control dependence is expected to improve the precision of analysis tools using it. The unifying formal framework for direct and indirect control dependence suggests also, in a natural way, a unifying terminology for the various notions of control dependence, which is also proposed in this paper. Finally, a worst-case $O(n^2)$ algorithm to compute the indirect termination-sensitive control dependence for languages that allow only "structured" jumps (i.e., ones that do not jump into the middle of a different block), such as Java and C#, is given, avoiding the $O(n^3)$ complexity of the trivial algorithm calculating the transitive closure of the direct dependence.

1 Introduction

Control dependence plays a fundamental role in program analysis: in program slicing [13,18], in compiler optimization [12,1], in total program correctness [15], and in security (of information flows) [11]. Intuitively, a statement S control-depends on a choice statement C iff the choice made at C determines whether S is executed or not. Because of the significance and broad range of applications of control dependence, related definitions and algorithms have been extensively investigated: [12] gives an efficient algorithm to compute (direct) control dependence; [15] introduces strong control dependence (also called the range of the control statement in [19]) as well as weak control dependence; [4] defines a generalized control dependence to capture both classic and weak direct control dependencies, together with their corresponding algorithms.

Although all these notions of control dependence are related, there is no adequate unifying framework for all of them, not even a uniform or consistent terminology. This

K. Yi (Ed.): SAS 2006, LNCS 4134, pp. 387–404, 2006.

often results in confusion and difficulty in understanding existing work, and may slow future developments, in particular defining new, or domain-specific control dependence relations. For example, the strong control dependence in [15] is the transitive closure of the control dependence in [12], contradicting common practice in formal terminology, since the former is actually weaker than the latter as a binary relation; the generalized control dependence in [4] addresses only the *direct* control dependencies (classic and weak), but omits the word "direct" in definitions and proofs, and also proposes the terminology "loop control dependence" for (direct) weak control dependence; [15] claims that strong control dependence is included in weak control dependence, which appears quite intuitive, but it is non-trivial to prove rigorously. A rigorous development of a unifying framework for the various control dependences, like the one proposed in this paper, would enhance understanding and clarify terminology in this area.

A first important step in this direction is made by [4], which defines a generalized control dependence that is parametrized by a property on paths and captures both classic and weak direct control dependences. A linear time algorithm [4] detects all statements that directly depend on a choice statement. However, the parametric approach in [4] covers only *direct* control dependence. The first contribution of our work, *parametric control dependence* (Section 3), consists of an extension of the work in [4] that also includes *indirect* control dependencies, as well as *comparisons* of different concrete instances of it. Our compact prefix-invariance property of the parameter is equivalent to the intersection of all the constraints on the parameter required by the results in [4], modulo the fact that we do not add a self-looping edge to the terminal node of the CFG to capture weak control dependence; in fact, we need to apply no transformations on CFGs in order to capture particular control dependencies as special cases. We also develop a rigorous mathematical theory in Section 3, capturing formally many results about different control dependence relations (Corollaries 1, 2 and 3).

The second contribution of this paper consists of defining a new control dependence relation that we call *termination-sensitive control dependence*, because it is sensitive to the termination information of loops, which can be given as annotations. If all loops are annotated as terminating then the termination-sensitive control dependence becomes the classic control dependence, while if all loops are annotated as non-terminating then it becomes the weak control dependence. If some loops are annotated as terminating while others not, then the termination-sensitive dependence strictly includes the classic control dependence and is strictly included in the weak one. Thus, one can regard it as a "knob" allowing one to tune the precision anywhere in between the two most widely accepted, but rather extreme control dependence relations. Since in practice some loops are terminating and others are not, termination-sensitive control dependence is expected to improve the precision of analysis tools using it. We introduce this termination-sensitive control dependence and derive all its properties as a formal instance of the parametric control dependence in the first part of the paper; it is in fact this new control dependence together with the lack of foundational and algorithmic support for *indirect* variants of control dependence of the generic control dependence in [4] that motivated our parametric approach to control dependence presented in Section 3.

The third contribution of our paper, Section 5, consists of an $O(n^2)$ algorithm to compute all *control scopes* for all the (branch) statements in a program of size n, in the context of higher level programming languages, such as Java and C#; statement S is in the control scope of C if and only if S termination-sensitive *indirectly* control-depends on C (control scope will be defined in Section 5). Since our control scopes become precisely the transitive closures of the classic and weak *direct* control dependencies when the loops are all annotated as terminating and as non-terminating, respectively, this generic algorithm seamlessly yields special instance algorithms to calculate the *indirect* versions of these dependencies, namely the complete strong and weak control dependencies, in $O(n^2)$ complexity. These results appear to be new even in the widely accepted, but in our view restricted, framework of strong and weak control dependence.

Section 2 revisits control dependence notions and presents them in a uniform light, as instances of the forthcoming parametric control dependence. Section 3 presents our parametric version of control dependence; a result relating the control dependence relations associated to different path properties allows us to compare the various instances of control dependence, in particular to show that the termination-sensitive (indirect) control dependence, discussed in Section 4, includes the standard control dependence but is included by the weak control dependence. Section 5 discusses the $O(|V|^2)$ algorithm to compute the entire termination-sensitive indirect control dependence. Due to space limitations, the interested reader is referred to [8] for detailed proofs.

Motivation. Even though *direct* variants of control dependence tend to suffice in program slicing efforts, there are many applications that need *indirect* control dependence. For example, in [19], the (indirect) control dependence is used to define and reason about information flow in security, and in [15], (indirect) weak control dependence is used to prove total correctness of programs. A less standard application domain is that of runtime analysis or multithreaded systems, described in more detail below.

Our main motivation for the termination-sensitive control dependence came from efforts in debugging multithreaded systems, namely in improving the accuracy and the coverage of predictive runtime analysis [7]. Since we refer back to it later in the paper, we explain this runtime analysis on a very simple example. Assume the running threads and events in Figure 1, where e_1 causally precedes, or "happens-before", e_2 (e.g., e_1 writes a shared variable and e_2 reads it right afterwards), and the statement generating e_3' is in the control scope of the statement generating e_2, while the statement generating e_3 is not in the control scope of e_2. Then we say that e_3' *is dependent upon* e_1, but that e_3 is *not* dependent upon e_1, despite the fact that e_1 obviously happened before e_3.

The intuition here is that e_3 would happen anyway, with or without e_1 happening. Because of its combined static/dynamic flavor, we call this new dependence relation on events the *hybrid dependence*. Interestingly, if the events in the scope of e_2 are not relevant for the property to check, then any permutation/linearization of relevant events consistent with the intra-thread total order and the hybrid dependence corresponds to some valid execution of the multithreaded system. Therefore, if any of these permutations violate the property, then the system can do

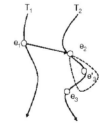

Fig. 1. Predictive Analysis

so in a different execution. In particular, without any other dependencies but those in Figure 1, the property "e_1 must happen before e_3" can be violated by the program generating this execution, even though the particular observed run does not! Indeed, there is no evidence in the observed run that e_1 should precede e_3, since e_3 happens anyway.

The control scope of a statement is determined statically, as the set of statements that control depend on it. Unfortunately, classic control dependence does not consider non-terminating loops, thus leading to false positives in the runtime analysis, while weak control dependence makes the worst case assumption (all loops are not terminating), resulting in over-restrictive dependence among events and thus false negatives. Termination-sensitive control dependence takes the termination information of loops into account in order to build a more precise control dependence relation.

2   Control Dependence Revisited

Here we discuss some of the major known results on control dependence, introducing at the same time a uniform notation and terminology. Some of the results in this section are mentioned in other works as "folklore"; however, we were not able to find them proved formally in the literature. We will show that all these results follow as corollaries of the general results in the next section. The structure of the results in this section anticipates the structure of those for parametric control dependence in the next section.

Preliminaries. A *directed graph* G is a pair $\langle V, E \rangle$, where $E \subseteq V \times V$. The elements of V are called *nodes* and those of E are called *edges*. A *finite path* of G is a finite sequence of nodes $u_1 u_2 ... u_{m+1}$ such that $(u_i, u_{i+1}) \in E$ for all $0 < i \le m$, where $m > 0$ is its *length*. If $u = u_1$ and $v = u_{m+1}$ then we call this path a $u - v$ *path*. For any node u, we let λ_u be the empty path from u to itself; its length is 0. An *infinite path* is an infinite sequence $u_1 u_2 ...$ such that $(u_i, u_{i+1}) \in E$ for all $i > 0$. A u–*path* is a (finite or infinite) path starting with u. We let $Paths(G)$ be the set of all paths of G, finite or infinite. For a path π either infinite or finite in length greater than or equal to $k \ge 0$, we let $\pi|_k$ be the path containing the first k edges of π, i.e., $u_1 u_2 ... u_{k+1}$. We also define the concatenation of paths: if $\alpha = u_1 u_2 ... u_m$ finite and $\pi = u_m u_{m+1} ...$ finite or infinite, then $\alpha \pi$ is the finite or infinite path $u_1 u_2 ... u_m u_{m+1} ...$. A *property* of paths in a graph G is a set $\mathcal{P} \subseteq Paths(G)$. For any $\pi \in Paths(G)$, we say that $\mathcal{P}(\pi)$ holds, or simply $\mathcal{P}(\pi)$, iff $\pi \in \mathcal{P}$.

Definition 1. *[12] A **control flow graph** CFG = $\langle V, E, START, END \rangle$ is a directed graph $\langle V, E \rangle$ together with an **entry node**, START, from which every other node is reachable, and an **exit node**, END, reachable from any other node. We make the standard assumption that nodes in V except END can have either one or two successors. Let $V_C \subseteq V$ denote the set of nodes with two successors and call them **choice nodes**.*

Nodes in V correspond to statements in the program, edges in E indicate possible flows of control in the program, and choice nodes correspond to choice statements, such as conditionals, e.g., C_1 in Figure 2 (A). Conditionals can also be parts of loops, e.g., C_1 and C_2 in Figure 2 (C). Due to the assumption on the number of successors, $|E| = O(|V|)$. In this paper, we tend to use letters at the beginning of the Greek alphabet, such as α, β, γ, etc., for $u - v$ paths, and letters π, π' and so on, for infinite or $u - END$ paths, though this convention is not strictly obeyed. From here on we fix a CFG.

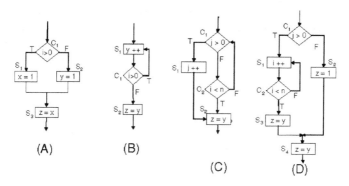

Fig. 2. Some control flow graphs

2.1   Classic Control Dependence

Definition 2. *([12,11]) Node u is **post-dominated** by node v, written $u \diamondsuit\!\!\rightarrow v$, iff all u – END paths contain v. Let **PostDom**(u) be the set of post-dominators of u except u.*

The notation $u \diamondsuit\!\!\rightarrow v$ symbolizes that no matter how we leave u (the first two edges of the diamond), we eventually converge (the other two edges of the diamond) and reach (the arrow) v. In Figure 2 (A), $C_1 \diamondsuit\!\!\rightarrow S_3$, while S_1 and S_2 do *not* post-dominate C_1; in Figure 2 (B), $C_1 \diamondsuit\!\!\rightarrow S_2$, while S_1 is *not* a post-dominator of C_1 – however, there is no guarantee that S_2 will be reached once C_1 is reached, because of the potentially infinite loop through C_1. In our context of predictive runtime analysis, this reflects a serious limitation of the classic notion of control dependence; we will discuss this issue shortly.

Lemma 1. *The post-dominance relation, $\diamondsuit\!\!\rightarrow$, is a partial order on the nodes of CFG.*

The following properties of post-dominance are immediate corollaries of our parametric control dependence framework in Section 3:

Corollary 1. *The following hold: (1) If $v_1 \neq v_2 \in PostDom(u)$ then either $v_1 \diamondsuit\!\!\rightarrow v_2$ or $v_2 \diamondsuit\!\!\rightarrow v_1$, i.e., $\langle PostDom(u), \diamondsuit\!\!\rightarrow\rangle$ is a total order; and (2) For any u, if $PostDom(u) \neq \emptyset$ then PostDom(u) has a unique first element w.r.t. $\diamondsuit\!\!\rightarrow$.*

Definition 3. *Let ipd(u) be the first element of $\langle PostDom(u), \diamondsuit\!\!\rightarrow\rangle$, called the **immediate post-dominator** of u; let $u \diamondsuit\!\!\rightarrow v$ iff v = ipd(u).*

The immediate post-dominator is the post-dominator that appears first on *any u – END* path. For example, in Figure 2 (A), $C_1 \diamondsuit\!\!\rightarrow S_3$ since S_3 appears before any other post-dominators of C_1 on any path from C_1 to *END*; in Figure 2 (B), $C_1 \diamondsuit\!\!\rightarrow S_2$.

Proposition 1. *$\diamondsuit\!\!\rightarrow$ is an inverted tree rooted at END.*

One can encode $\diamondsuit\!\!\rightarrow$ as a *post-dominance tree* [14,12] with *END* at its root. Using post-dominance, *direct* control dependence can be defined as in [12]:

Definition 4. *Node v is **directly control dependent** on node u, written $u \overset{dcd}{\leadsto} v$, iff (1) there exists a u – v path α such that v post-dominates every node in α different from u; and (2) u is **not** post-dominated by v.*

For example, in Figure 2 (A), S_1 and S_2 are directly control dependent on C_1 but S_3 is not; while in Figure 2 (B), S_1 is directly control dependent on C_1 but S_2 is not. In Figure 2 (C), S_1 is directly control dependent on C_1 but not on C_2 (because S_1 does not post-dominate C_1). Note that direct control dependence is *not* a partial order on nodes: in Figure 2 (C), C_1 and C_2 are directly control dependent on each other.

The notion of *direct* control dependence has been widely used in program analysis, e.g., in program slicing [13,18] and compiler construction [12], where it was called just "control dependence". However, this relation only captures the *direct* dependence among statements; it does *not* capture *indirect* dependence. Recall, e.g., that in Figure 2 (C), S_1 does *not* directly control depend on C_2; however, note that once C_2 is reached, *the execution of S_1 depends on the control decision made at C_2!* Therefore, S_1 *control depends* on C_2 by all means, suggesting that the terminology proposed in [12] for control dependence is, perhaps, not the most appropriate one. We will shortly see that S_1 is in the *transitive closure* of the direct control dependence on C_2; for some reason, this transitive closure of direct control dependence was misleadingly called "strong control dependence" in [15]. We will call it simply "control dependence" in what follows, because we think it captures best the *dependence* of some statements on the *control* decision made by others. As an example of an application where (indirect) control dependence is needed in the context of information flow, see [11]. Another use of it appears in the context of debugging multithreaded systems (see the discussion in Section 1 on predictive runtime analysis regarding the sample execution trace in Figure 1); e.g., in Figure 2 (C), if $C_1C_2C_1S_1S_2$ is an execution, the analysis needs to know that S_1 also depends on the choice made at C_2 to *not* exit the loop, which is caused by an indirect control dependence in the CFG.

In fact, even before direct control dependence was introduced in [12], Dennings already discussed the indirect influence of control statements on the program flow in [11]. It was also called the *range* of branches in [19], which is nothing but the transitive closure of direct control dependence, as informally mentioned in [12,16] without proof. Podgurski and Clarke [15] called it "strong control dependence", to emphasize that it was stronger than their "weak" control dependence, still without proving that it was the transitive closure of the direct control dependence, thus leading to a slightly inconsistent terminology: for a relation R (control dependence in their case) "strong R" ended up strictly including R. For reasons explained above, we prefer to drop the adjective "strong" and call it just control dependence:

Definition 5. *Node v is **control dependent** on u, written $u \overset{cd}{\leadsto} v$, iff there exists some $u - v$ path that does* not *contain $ipd(u)$, the immediate post-dominator of u.*

For example, in Figure 2 (C), $C_2 \overset{cd}{\leadsto} S_1$. One can prove the following properties of control dependence, all of which follow from our parametric framework:

Corollary 2. *(Follows by Theorem 1 and Proposition 4) For $\overset{dcd}{\leadsto}$ and $\overset{cd}{\leadsto}$, the following hold:*

1. $\overset{cd}{\leadsto} = \overset{dcd^+}{\leadsto}$ *(one cannot replace $\overset{dcd^+}{\leadsto}$ by $\overset{dcd^*}{\leadsto}$ because $\overset{cd}{\leadsto}$ needs not be reflexive);*
2. *If $u \overset{cd}{\leadsto} v$ then $PostDom(u) \subseteq PostDom(v)$; in particular, $ipd(v) \diamond\!\!\rightarrow ipd(u)$;*
3. $u \overset{cd}{\leadsto} v$ *iff there exists some $u - v$ path α such that $\alpha \cap PostDom(u) = \emptyset$.*

Therefore, control dependence is nothing but the transitive closure of the direct control dependence, so it is a relation *weaker* than the direct control dependence.

2.2 Weak Control Dependence

Although control dependence now also captures "indirect" dependence, it still has another important limitation: it is insensitive to (non-terminating) loops; e.g., in Figure 2 (C), S_2 is *not* control dependent on C_1 (the former is the post-dominator of the latter). This may lead, e.g., to incorrect runtime analysis of multi-threaded systems. Reconsider the execution in Figure 1. Suppose it is generated by the program in Figure 2 (C). More specifically, suppose that e_1 is a write on the shared variable j, e_2 is the following read on j generated by C_1, e_3' is the write on j generated by S_1, and e_3 is the write on z generated by S_2. One may think that e_3 is *not* control dependent on e_2 by definition, that is, that e_3 will happen regardless of e_2. However, since the loop is potentially non-terminating, S_2 may *never be executed* at runtime. Thus, the observed existence of e_3 is a consequence of a fortunate control choice made by C_1 when e_2 took place. Therefore, e_3 *should be control dependent* on e_2. Podgurski and Clarke [15] introduced strong post-dominance to handle control dependence in the presence of loops:

Definition 6. *Node u is **strongly post-dominated** by v, written $u \overset{s}{\diamond\!\!\!\rightarrow} v$, iff (1) $u \diamond\!\!\!\rightarrow v$ and (2) there is some integer $k \geq 1$ s.t. every u–path of length larger than or equal to k passes through v. Node v is a **proper strong post-dominator** of u iff $u \overset{s}{\diamond\!\!\!\rightarrow} v$ and $u \neq v$.*

In other words, u is strongly post-dominated by v iff u is post-dominated by v and there is no infinite u–path that does *not* pass through v; e.g, in Figure 2 (B), S_2 does not strongly post-dominate C_1, because there is an infinite path from C_1 that will not pass through S_2, while in Figure 2 (D), S_1 is strongly post-dominated by C_2 but C_2 is not strongly post-dominated by S_3. There may be no proper strong post-dominators for some nodes; e.g., in Figure 2 (C), neither C_1 nor C_2 have proper strong post-dominators, since they can choose to either stay in the loop forever or jump out of it. Based on strong post-dominance, weak control dependence is defined in [15] as follows:

Definition 7. *Node v is **directly weakly control dependent** on u, written $u \overset{dwcd}{\leadsto} v$, iff u has successors u' and u'' s.t. $u' \overset{s}{\diamond\!\!\!\rightarrow} v$ but u'' is not strongly post-dominated by v; **weak control dependence**, written $\overset{wcd}{\leadsto}$, is the transitive closure of $\overset{dwcd}{\leadsto}$.*

In Figure 2 (D), $C_1 \overset{dwcd}{\leadsto} S_4$ because $S_2 \overset{s}{\diamond\!\!\!\rightarrow} S_4$ but not $S_1 \overset{s}{\diamond\!\!\!\rightarrow} S_4$. Weak control dependence is a generalization of control dependence, that is, every control dependence is a weak control dependence. This was informally mentioned in [15], but it is not straightforward to prove it rigorously using their original definitions. However, it will follow as a corollary of our parametric framework, as shown at the end of Section 3. What makes this result even more interesting is that *direct* weak control dependence is *not* a generalization of *direct* control dependence. E.g., in Figure 2 (D), S_3 is directly control dependent but not directly weak control dependent on C_1, while it is directly weak control dependent but not directly control dependent on C_2. Weak control dependence is not a partial order either: e.g., in Figure 2 (C), both $C_1 \overset{dwcd}{\rightsquigarrow} C_2$ and $C_2 \overset{dwcd}{\rightsquigarrow} C_1$. The (direct) weak control dependence makes the worst-case assumption that all loops are non-terminating, which is very rarely the case in practice. In fact, most loops *terminate*.

3   Parametric Control Dependence

We next propose a parametric framework to define and reason about control dependence, which incorporates both direct control dependence and direct weak control dependence, as well as their indirect variants, as special cases. This framework can be easily instantiated to define other control dependence relations, such as the termination-sensitive control dependence discussed in Section 4. It is fair to say that here we do *not* intend to generalize *all* approaches to control dependence. For example, we believe that the nice recent work in [16] on extending control dependence to work with CFGs with more than one or with no end nodes could also be cast as an instance of a parametric framework, but it is not trivial and we do not attempt to explicitly capture that here. Also, we believe that the symbolic approach in [3] which interprets CFGs as Kripke structures and then calculating post-dominators by efficient fair CTL model-checking queries, can be also extended to well-presentable properties on paths, like our "parameters" below, but again, we do not intend to investigate this interesting problem here.

Definition 8. *A set $\mathcal{P} \subseteq Paths(CFG)$ is a **prefix-invariant property** on paths iff (1) $\mathcal{P}(\lambda_{END})$; and (2) $\mathcal{P}(\alpha\pi) \Leftrightarrow \mathcal{P}(\pi)$ for any $\alpha\pi \in Paths(CFG)$ (α is finite). A $u \overset{\mathcal{P}}{-}$**path** is any u–path in $\mathcal{P}$. Node u is $\mathcal{P}$-**post-dominated** by node v, written $u \overset{\mathcal{P}}{\diamond\!\!\rightarrow} v$, iff all $u \overset{\mathcal{P}}{-}$paths contain v. $\mathbf{PostDom}_{\mathcal{P}}(u)$ is the set of $\mathcal{P}$-post-dominators of u different from u.*

From now on in this section, we fix a prefix-invariant property $\mathcal{P}$. One can show that $\mathcal{P}$ contains all $u - END$ paths, that is, $\mathcal{P}(\alpha)$ holds for any $u - END$ path α. By Definition 1 (*END* is reachable from any u), there exists at least one finite $u \overset{\mathcal{P}}{-}$path. Note that for some nodes u, $PostDom_{\mathcal{P}}(u)$ can be empty. For example, as shown after Definition 6, some nodes may not have strong post-dominators, which will be shown shortly to be a special case of $\mathcal{P}$-post-dominators for a well chosen property $\mathcal{P}$.

Proposition 2. *For $\overset{\mathcal{P}}{\diamond\!\!\rightarrow}$, the following hold:*

1. $\overset{\mathcal{P}}{\diamond\!\!\rightarrow} \subseteq \diamond\!\!\rightarrow$, *that is, $u \overset{\mathcal{P}}{\diamond\!\!\rightarrow} v$ implies $u \diamond\!\!\rightarrow v$;*
2. $\overset{\mathcal{P}}{\diamond\!\!\rightarrow}$ *is a partial order;*
3. *If $u \overset{\mathcal{P}}{\diamond\!\!\rightarrow} v$ and there is a $u - u'$ path that does not contain v, then $u' \overset{\mathcal{P}}{\diamond\!\!\rightarrow} v$;*
4. *If $v_1 \neq v_2 \in PostDom_{\mathcal{P}}(u)$, then either $v_1 \overset{\mathcal{P}}{\diamond\!\!\rightarrow} v_2$ or $v_2 \overset{\mathcal{P}}{\diamond\!\!\rightarrow} v_1$; in other words, $\langle PostDom_{\mathcal{P}}(u), \overset{\mathcal{P}}{\diamond\!\!\rightarrow}\rangle$ is a total order;*
5. *If $PostDom_{\mathcal{P}}(u) \neq \emptyset$ then $PostDom_{\mathcal{P}}(u)$ has a unique first element w.r.t. $\overset{\mathcal{P}}{\diamond\!\!\rightarrow}$;*

6. $\overset{\mathcal{P}}{\diamond\!\!\rightarrow}$ is a forest of inverted trees, where $u \overset{\mathcal{P}}{\diamond\!\!\rightarrow} v$ iff $v = ipd_{\mathcal{P}}(u)$, where $ipd_{\mathcal{P}}(u)$ is the first element of $\langle PostDom_{\mathcal{P}}(u), \overset{\mathcal{P}}{\diamond\!\!\rightarrow} \rangle$, called the **immediate $\mathcal{P}$-post-dominator** of u.

One can show that post-dominance and strong post-dominance are two special cases of $\mathcal{P}$-post-dominance by choosing appropriate parameters $\mathcal{P}$: let $\mathcal{P}_{\perp}$ denote the set of all finite paths ending with END and let $\mathcal{P}_{\perp\infty}$ be the union of $\mathcal{P}_{\perp}$ with all infinite paths.

Proposition 3. Both $\mathcal{P}_{\perp}$ and $\mathcal{P}_{\perp\infty}$ are prefix-invariant, and $\diamond\!\!\rightarrow = \overset{\mathcal{P}_{\perp}}{\diamond\!\!\rightarrow}$ and $\overset{s}{\diamond\!\!\rightarrow} = \overset{\mathcal{P}_{\perp\infty}}{\diamond\!\!\rightarrow}$.

We will discuss a third special case of $\mathcal{P}$-post-dominance in Section 4, where additional termination information of loops will be taken into account.

Definition 9. Node v is **directly $\mathcal{P}$-control dependent** on u, written $u \overset{d\mathcal{P}}{\rightsquigarrow} v$, iff: (1) there is a u–v path s.t. v $\mathcal{P}$-post-dominates its nodes except u; (2) v does _not_ $\mathcal{P}$-post-dominate u. Node v is **$\mathcal{P}$-control dependent** on u, written $u \overset{\mathcal{P}}{\rightsquigarrow} v$, iff there exists some u – v path that does not contain $ipd_{\mathcal{P}}(u)$.

Note that $\overset{d\mathcal{P}}{\rightsquigarrow}$ is _not_ a partial order. For example, $\overset{dcd}{\rightsquigarrow}$ and $\overset{dwcd}{\rightsquigarrow}$, which will be shortly shown to be special cases of $\overset{d\mathcal{P}}{\rightsquigarrow}$, are not partial orders. This means that, in the worst case, the time needed to compute the transitive closure of $\overset{d\mathcal{P}}{\rightsquigarrow}$ is $O(|V|^3)$ [10].

Theorem 1. For $\overset{d\mathcal{P}}{\rightsquigarrow}$ and $\overset{\mathcal{P}}{\rightsquigarrow}$, the following hold:

1. $\overset{\mathcal{P}}{\rightsquigarrow} = \overset{d\mathcal{P}}{\rightsquigarrow}^{+}$;
2. If $u \overset{\mathcal{P}}{\rightsquigarrow} v$ then $PostDom_{\mathcal{P}}(u) \subseteq PostDom_{\mathcal{P}}(v)$; in particular, $ipd_{\mathcal{P}}(v) \overset{\mathcal{P}}{\diamond\!\!\rightarrow} ipd_{\mathcal{P}}(u)$;
3. $u \overset{\mathcal{P}}{\rightsquigarrow} v$ iff there exists some u – v path α such that $\alpha \cap PostDom_{\mathcal{P}}(u) = \emptyset$.

One can also show that direct control dependence and direct weak control dependence are two special cases of direct $\mathcal{P}$-control dependence, while control dependence and weak control dependence are two special cases of $\mathcal{P}$-control dependence:

Proposition 4. $\overset{dcd}{\rightsquigarrow} = \overset{d\mathcal{P}_{\perp}}{\rightsquigarrow}$ and $\overset{dwcd}{\rightsquigarrow} = \overset{d\mathcal{P}_{\perp\infty}}{\rightsquigarrow}$, and $\overset{cd}{\rightsquigarrow} = \overset{\mathcal{P}_{\perp}}{\rightsquigarrow}$ and $\overset{wcd}{\rightsquigarrow} = \overset{\mathcal{P}_{\perp\infty}}{\rightsquigarrow}$.

The following proposition will allow us to _compare_ control dependencies, based on just a simple comparison of their corresponding parameters:

Proposition 5. If $\mathcal{P} \subseteq \mathcal{P}'$ are prefix-invariant properties then: (1) $\overset{\mathcal{P}'}{\diamond\!\!\rightarrow} \subseteq \overset{\mathcal{P}}{\diamond\!\!\rightarrow}$; (2) $PostDom_{\mathcal{P}'}(u) \subseteq PostDom_{\mathcal{P}}(u)$; (3) $ipd_{\mathcal{P}}(u) \overset{\mathcal{P}}{\diamond\!\!\rightarrow} ipd_{\mathcal{P}'}(u)$; and (4) $\overset{\mathcal{P}}{\rightsquigarrow} \subseteq \overset{\mathcal{P}'}{\rightsquigarrow}$.

Corollary 3. $\overset{cd}{\rightsquigarrow} \subseteq \overset{\mathcal{P}}{\rightsquigarrow}$ for any prefix-invariant property $\mathcal{P}$; in particular, $\overset{cd}{\rightsquigarrow} \subseteq \overset{wcd}{\rightsquigarrow}$.

Interestingly, the inclusion of the direct versions of the dependences in the corollary above does _not_ hold. For example, it is _not_ the case that $\overset{dcd}{\rightsquigarrow} \subseteq \overset{dwcd}{\rightsquigarrow}$.

4   Termination-Sensitive Control Dependence

Weak control dependence takes loops into account using strong post-dominance, which is more suitable for proving total correctness of programs [15] than classic control dependence. However, weak control dependence unfortunately makes the worst-case assumption about the termination of loops in the program, namely, all loops are assumed to be potentially infinite. Considering the fact that *most loops terminate* in real programs, this assumption is too conservative in practice. Let us look at the example in Figure 2 (D). The loop containing S_1 and C_2 obviously terminates, so S_3 will be eventually executed once C_2 is reached. In other words, the execution of S_3 *does not depend* on the choice made at C_2. However, by Definition 7, $C_2 \overset{wcd}{\leadsto} S_3$. Such over-restrictive assumptions may bring *false positives* to static program analysis, while for our runtime predictive analysis, they may generate over-restrictive control dependences on events, reducing the number of potential permutations of events when investigating possible actual executions, resulting in more *false negatives*, i.e., a reduced coverage.

In this section, we introduce a new control dependence relation, named *termination-sensitive control dependence*, as another instantiation of the parametric control dependence framework presented in Section 3. As indicated by its name, this control dependence takes the termination information of loops into account to improve the precision of program analyses that make use of control dependence. Although termination analysis is an undecidable problem, there exist some effective algorithms to approximately determine termination of programs, e.g., [9,5] (more discussion on these algorithms is out of the scope of this paper). Besides, termination information can also be provided by users (e.g., using special annotations) or detected by heuristics-based criteria (for example, a loop whose condition is $i < n$ and in which i is increased at each iteration will always terminate). Here we only focus on defining a more precise control dependence relation using existing termination information, which is assumed to be correct.

Definition 10. *A termination-sensitive control flow graph* $\langle V, E, START, END, V_\infty \rangle$ *is a CFG* $\langle V, E, START, END \rangle$ *together with a distinguished set of nodes* $V_\infty \subseteq V$.

The nodes in V_∞ can be thought of as nodes that can lead to non-terminating executions. In practice, one would like to annotate as few statements as possible to provide the termination information; if that is the case, then V_∞ can contain precisely the conditions of those loops that may not terminate. Theoretically, one can add to V_∞ *all* the unavoidable statements in such loops, but this is not necessary. Besides, some of these statements can themselves be loops, but ones which terminate. From here on, we fix an arbitrary termination-sensitive CFG and define complete paths as follows:

Definition 11. *A complete path* π *is a path that is either finite and ends with END, or is infinite and* $\inf(\pi) \cap V_\infty \neq \emptyset$, *where* $\inf(\pi)$ *gives those nodes visited infinitely often in* π. *Let* $\mathcal{P}_\top$ *denote the set of complete paths of the termination-sensitive CFG.*

Note that infinite paths generated by "nested" loops in which the outer ones are annotated as "non-terminating" (in V_∞), while the inner ones are "terminating", are considered complete as far as the outer loop is executed infinitely often. One may want to instead annotate the "terminating" nodes as a subset $V_\top \subseteq V$ and then require the complete path to satisfy $inf(\pi) \cap V_\top = \emptyset$; while this is reasonable and fits our parametric setting as well, such an approach would be less precise, because it would exclude common paths as the ones generated by nested loops as above. There is an interesting similarity between termination-sensitive CFGs and Buchi automata [6], where the role of *accepting states* is played by V_∞ and that of *accepted words* by complete paths.

One can show that $\mathcal{P}_\top$ is also a prefix-invariant property on paths. Indeed, for any $u - v$ path α and v–path π, $\alpha\pi$ is a $u - END$ path iff π is a $v - END$ path. Besides, if $\alpha\pi$ is infinite, then since α is finite, $inf(\alpha\pi) = inf(\pi)$. Therefore, $inf(\alpha\pi) \cap V_\infty = inf(\pi) \cap V_\infty$; in particular, $inf(\alpha\pi) \cap V_\infty \neq \emptyset$ iff $inf(\pi) \cap V_\infty \neq \emptyset$. Based on the parametric framework for control dependence introduced in Section 3, we can define corresponding post-dominance and dependence notions: $\mathcal{P}_\top$-post-dominance, immediate $\mathcal{P}_\top$-post-dominance, direct $\mathcal{P}_\top$-control dependence, and $\mathcal{P}_\top$-control dependence. The following results follow immediately from the generic framework in the previous section:

Corollary 4. *For $\overset{\mathcal{P}_\top}{\diamondsuit\!\!\rightarrow}$, the following hold:*

1. $\overset{\mathcal{P}_\top}{\diamondsuit\!\!\rightarrow} \subseteq \diamondsuit\!\!\rightarrow$, *that is, $u \overset{\mathcal{P}_\top}{\diamondsuit\!\!\rightarrow} v$ implies $u \diamondsuit\!\!\rightarrow v$;*
2. $\overset{\mathcal{P}_\top}{\diamondsuit\!\!\rightarrow}$ *is a partial order;*
3. *If $v_1 \neq v_2 \in PostDom_{\mathcal{P}_\top}(u)$, then either $v_1 \overset{\mathcal{P}_\top}{\diamondsuit\!\!\rightarrow} v_2$ or $v_2 \overset{\mathcal{P}_\top}{\diamondsuit\!\!\rightarrow} v_1$; in other words, $\langle PostDom_{\mathcal{P}_\top}(u), \overset{\mathcal{P}_\top}{\diamondsuit\!\!\rightarrow} \rangle$ is a total order;*
4. *If $PostDom_{\mathcal{P}_\top}(u) \neq \emptyset$ then $PostDom_{\mathcal{P}_\top}(u)$ has a unique first element w.r.t. $\overset{\mathcal{P}_\top}{\diamondsuit\!\!\rightarrow}$;*
5. $\overset{\mathcal{P}_\top}{\diamondsuit\!\!\rightarrow}$ *is a forest of inverted trees;*

Corollary 5. *For $\overset{d\mathcal{P}_\top}{\leadsto}$ and $\overset{\mathcal{P}_\top}{\leadsto}$, the following hold:*

1. $\overset{\mathcal{P}_\top}{\leadsto} = \overset{d\mathcal{P}_\top}{\leadsto}{}^+$;
2. *If $u \overset{\mathcal{P}_\top}{\leadsto} v$ then $PostDom_{\mathcal{P}_\top}(u) \subseteq PostDom_{\mathcal{P}_\top}(v)$; in particular, $ipd_{\mathcal{P}_\top}(v) \overset{\mathcal{P}_\top}{\diamondsuit\!\!\rightarrow} ipd_{\mathcal{P}_\top}(u)$;*
3. $u \overset{\mathcal{P}_\top}{\leadsto} v$ *iff there exists some $u - v$ path α such that $\alpha \cap PostDom_{\mathcal{P}_\top}(u) = \emptyset$.*

Now we are ready to define termination-sensitive control dependence and to compare this new control dependence with classical and weak control dependence:

Definition 12. *Let $\overset{tscd}{\leadsto} := \overset{\mathcal{P}_\top}{\leadsto}$ be the **termination-sensitive control dependence**.*

Proposition 6. $\overset{cd}{\leadsto} \subseteq \overset{tscd}{\leadsto} \subseteq \overset{wcd}{\leadsto}$ *(it follows by Proposition 5, since $\mathcal{P}_\perp \subseteq \mathcal{P}_\top \subseteq \mathcal{P}_{\perp\infty}$).*

Note that there are no inclusions between the direct versions of these control dependences, i.e., between $\overset{d\mathcal{P}_\perp}{\leadsto}$ (or $\overset{dcd}{\leadsto}$) and $\overset{d\mathcal{P}_\top}{\leadsto}$ or between $\overset{d\mathcal{P}_\top}{\leadsto}$ and $\overset{d\mathcal{P}_{\perp\infty}}{\leadsto}$ (or $\overset{dwcd}{\leadsto}$). For example, consider the CFG in Figure 2 (D). Suppose that $C_2 \in V_\infty$ (i.e., the loop containing S_1 and C_2 is annotated as "non-terminating"). Then $C_1 \overset{d\mathcal{P}_\perp}{\leadsto} S_3$ but S_3 is not directly $\mathcal{P}_\top$-control dependent on C_1, while $C_2 \overset{d\mathcal{P}_\top}{\leadsto} S_3$ but S_3 is not directly control dependent on C_2. Suppose next that $C_2 \notin V_\infty$. Then $C_1 \overset{d\mathcal{P}_\top}{\leadsto} S_3$ but S_3 is not directly weak control dependent on C_1, while $C_2 \overset{d\mathcal{P}_{\perp\infty}}{\leadsto} S_2$ but S_2 is not directly $\mathcal{P}_\top$-control dependent on C_2.

By Proposition 6, the set V_∞ acts as a "knob" tuning the precision of the control dependence relation. For example, if $V_\infty = \emptyset$ then termination-sensitive control dependence becomes precisely classic control dependence. If $V_\infty = V$ then it becomes weak control dependence. In practice, V_∞ is somewhere in-between $\emptyset$ and V. However, the more nodes are added to V_∞, the more dependences are added, i.e., the weaker the dependence relation becomes. For example, in Figure 2 (C), suppose that $C_2 \notin V_\infty$. Then S_2 is not termination-sensitive control dependent on C_2. But if the user declares that $C_2 \in V_\infty$ despite the actual semantics of the program, we will have $C_2 \overset{tscd}{\rightsquigarrow} S_2$.

Ideally, one would like to pick a V_∞ which would generate a *minimal* set of complete paths $\mathcal{P}_\top$ that includes all the actual execution paths of the program to analyze. Unfortunately, the selection of such an optimal V_∞ is difficult to achieve, because one would need to automatically prove termination of loops, an undecidable problem. A safe approach would be to start with $V_\infty = V$, and then remove from it all the statements which are not loop conditions, then all those loop conditions controlling terminating loops which can be detected by heuristic criteria or declared so by users or code generators.

5 Control Scope

The *control scope* of a conditional statement is the set of statements that control depend on it, where the control dependence is *termination-sensitive* and *indirect*. In other words, S is in the control scope of C iff the execution of S depends upon a fortunate choice made by C. Algorithms to compute direct control dependence [12] and direct weak control dependence [4] are well-known. These algorithms take linear time to detect all the statements that *directly* depend upon a given statement C, and can be used to construct program dependence graphs (PDG) [13], which are widely adopted in program slicing. These linear algorithms to calculate control dependencies are sufficient in applications where high online speed is not crucial and where only the direct dependencies are necessary, such as debugging. However, there are applications that need the transitive versions of the control dependences. For example, in [19], the (indirect) control dependence is used to define and reason about information flow in security, and in [15], (indirect) weak control dependence is used to prove total correctness of programs. Also, in predictive runtime analysis, one prefers to calculate all the dependencies statically and then spend constant time at runtime to check whether the statements generating two events depend upon each other, to reduce the runtime overhead.

From here on, by control dependence we mean *termination-sensitive control dependence*. Statically calculating all the direct dependencies for all the statements can therefore be achieved in $O(|V|^2)$, since the parameter property on paths that leads to our control dependence fits the framework in [4]. However, it is not clear how to effectively calculate *indirect* control dependencies. A blind application of the transitive closure of direct dependence would yield an $O(|V|^3)$ algorithm (since direct control dependence is not a partial order), which can be impractical even on relatively small programs. Without additional information about the program which generates the CFG, there is nothing that one can do to decrease the complexity of calculating control dependence. However, CFGs are typically generated from actual code that is stored as lines of sequences of characters in files. In what follows, we augment the CFG with code references and show that, under some mild and common restrictions, we can calculate the entire control dependence relation in $O(|V|^2)$, which is the same as the complexity of calculating direct control dependence. These results appear to be new even for classic and weak control dependence relations, both special cases of our (termination-sensitive) control dependence. It may seem that $O(|V|^2)$ is still impractical in large applications; however, in the case of predictive runtime analysis or unit testing, we only need to calculate the control scopes for relatively small units, e.g., only intra-procedurally.

The nodes of a CFG generally correspond to either *simple statements* (ones that do not contain sub-statements) or to conditions that are part of *compound statements* (ones that contain sub-statements); these are formalized in Definition 14. We consider two types of compound statements, conditionals and loops; note that although a programming language may also support other kinds of compound statements, e.g., try..catch, such statements are decomposed into simple statements when constructing the CFG, so they need not appear explicitly in the CFG (they appear only implicitly, encoded by corresponding edges). Even though CFGs capture faithfully the control flow of a program, unfortunately, precious structural information about the program, such as where a compound statement starts and where it ends, is generally not reflected in a CFG.

In what follows we augment CFGs with structural information by adding to each node a corresponding unique line, or code reference number, which can be thought of as the position in the program of the statement corresponding to that node. The reference numbers of all nodes are assumed distinct. Since there is a one-to-one correspondence between (simple and compound) statements in the program and nodes in the CFG, we can identify statements with the reference numbers of their corresponding nodes. Since the corresponding node in the CFG of a loop is its condition, the reference number of a statement is not necessarily the line number where that statement starts! E.g., the reference of do..while in Fig. 3 (B) is 3. We next formalize this:

Definition 13. *A sequential CFG (SCFG)* $\langle V, E, START, END, \#, b \rangle$ *is a CFG together with injective maps* $\# : V \to \mathbb{N}$ *and* $b : V_C \to Intervals(\mathbb{N})$ *such that: (1)* $\#(C) \in b(C)$ *for any* $C \in V_C$; *and (2)* $b(C') \subset b(C)$ *for any* $C \neq C' \in V_C$ *with* $\#(C') \in b(C)$.

$\#$ associates to each node (simple statement with out-degree 1 or condition part of a compound —conditional or loop— statement with out-degree 2) a unique number. b returns for each condition the code boundaries of its compound statement, as an interval bounded by the smallest and the largest reference numbers of nodes in the SCFG covered by that statement; some statements *may include but not overlap* other statements.

Fig. 3 shows some SCFGs. Nodes are shown in ascending order of and labeled with their line numbers; conditions are also labeled with their statement boundaries. The computation of the b function is straightforward and can be done at parse time at no additional cost. For example, in Fig. 3 (A), $b(1) = [1, 3]$; in (B), $b(3) = [2, 3]$; and in (C), $b(1) = [1, 6]$. For each SCFG, one can define a function $next : V - V_C - \{END\} \to \mathbb{N}$, which associates to each node $S \in V - V_C - \{END\}$ the number $\#(S')$ where $(S, S') \in E$ is the unique outgoing edge from S. For "jump" statements, including break, continue,

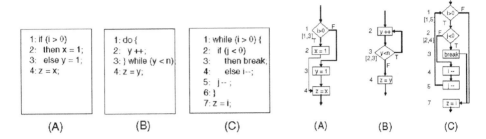

Fig. 3. Sample programs and their SCFGs

return, and exception throwing, *next* is the reference number of the statement that S jumps to; e.g., in Fig. 3 (C), $next(3) = 7$. If S is a simple non-jump statement at the end of a loop body, then $next(S)$ is the reference number of the loop statement; e.g., in (B), $next(2) = 3$, and in (C), $next(5) = 1$. For all other simple statements, the *next* function simply returns the reference number of the next statement in the program; e.g., in (A), $next(2) = next(3) = 4$, and in (C), $next(4) = 5$. We can identify statements in the program with their corresponding nodes in the SCFG. From here on, we call *all* the nodes in an SCFG statements and define the following SCFG terminology:

Definition 14. *Nodes in V_C are called **compound statements** and those in $V - V_C$ are called **simple statements**. If C is compound statement and S is any statement with $\#(S) \in b(C)$ then S is a **sub-statement** of C, or C **contains** S; if additionally there is no proper sub-statement C' of C that properly contains S then S is a **direct sub-statement** of C.*

The requirements of SCFGs are common to all programing languages. Most higher level structured programming languages, such as Java and C#, impose additional restrictions on jump statements; e.g., **continue**, **break**, **return**, exception throwing, can only jump to specific positions determined statically at compile time. We next define a corresponding version of SCFG that captures formally such restrictions on jumps:

Definition 15. *A **structured SCFG (SSCFG)** is an SCFG $\langle V, E, START, END, \#, b \rangle$ s.t.: (1) Each compound statement C has a unique entry point, $entry(C)$, which is the lower bound of $b(C)$; if $\#(S) \notin b(C)$ and $next(S) \in b(C)$ then $next(S) = entry(C)$; and (2) Backward control flows can only be caused by loops: for any $(S, S') \in E$ with $\#(S) > \#(S')$, there is a compound statement C such that $\#(S) \in b(C)$ and $\#(S') = entry(C)$; in this case, we call C a **loop statement**; all compound statements which are not loops are called **conditional statements**. For every loop statement L, we let **next**(L) be the statement following L, i.e., $next(L) := max(\#(S_1), \#(S_2))$ where $(L, S_1), (L, S_2) \in E$.*

We next focus on computing the control scope of compound statements. The *control scope* of a compound statement C is the set of statements that are control-dependent on C. Unfortunately, such statements can be spread all over the program, thus making their precise bookkeeping hard. We show that in the context of an SSCFG, the statements that control depend on a compound statement C are located in a *window*, or an *interval*, of references, say *scope (C)*, which we call *control scope interval*. Note that our use of intervals is *not* related to the concept of (maximal) interval discussed in [2] and used in elimination methods [17]. The control scope intervals may be larger than the control scopes, but we show that the extra statements can be efficiently detected. In other words, *scope (C)* characterizes unambiguously the statements that are control-dependent on *C*.

An immediate observation is that all sub-statements of a compound statement are control dependent on it. Besides, a jump statement from within a compound statement *C* may extend the control scope of *C*. For example, in Fig. 3 (C), the `break` statement extends the scope of the `if` statement to the end of the loop, thus making statement 5 control-depend on the compound statement 2. This can be formalized as follows:

Definition 16. *Given C a compound statement with* $\flat(C) = [b_1, b_2]$, *let* **pre-scope**(C) *be* $\flat(C)$ *when C is a loop statement, and* $[b_1, max(b_2, next(J_1) - 1, ..., next(J_n)) - 1]$ *when C is a conditional statement, where* J_i *for* $i \in [1, n]$ *are the direct substatements of C.*

For example, in Fig. 3 (C), the pre-scope of the loop is [1, 6] while the pre-scope of the `if` statement is [2, 6]. Note that in this definition, the pre-scopes of loop statements do *not* consider the effects of their direct sub-statements (when, e.g., an exception is thrown or a break/continue for an outer loop) because, as we discuss below, the backward edges of loops cause a different situation to handle. Pre-scopes of statements can be calculated at no additional cost at parse time, since the targets of jumps are known statically (we focus on intra-procedure analysis here; exceptions not caught in the analyzed procedure, are assumed to jump to the end of the procedure). Note, however, that the pre-scope of *C* may already

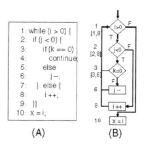

Fig. 4.

contain statements that do *not* control-depend on *C*: e.g., in Fig. 4, the pre-scope of the conditional 3 is [3, 8] (due to the `continue` statement), so 8 is in pre-scope(3); however, 8 does *not* control-depend on 3. To filter out such statements, we next introduce a new relation between statements:

Definition 17. *Statement S' is* **forward-reachable** *from S iff there exists an S − S' path that contains no loop statement L such that L contains both S and S'.*

In Fig. 3 (C), node 3 is reachable but not forward-reachable from 4, and in Fig. 4, statement 8 is reachable but not forward-reachable from statement 3. Although the intuition for forward-reachability is "from *S* one can go forward and reach *S'*", it is *not* always the case that one can find an *S − S'* path with increasing reference numbers: in Fig. 4, statement 10 is forward-reachable from 2, but the path between them always contains 1. Next proposition gives an effective way to compute forward-reachability:

Proposition 7. *Given statements S and S' in an SSCFG G, S' is forward-reachable from S iff S' reachable from S in a graph that replaces each edge* $e = (n_1, n_2)$ *with* $n_1 > n_2$ *in G (i.e., one corresponding to a loop L with entry(L) = n_2), by $(n_1, next(L))$.*

The following allows us now to relate the pre-scopes and control dependence:

Proposition 8. *If #(S) ∈ pre-scope(C) and S forward-reachable from C, then C $\overset{tscd}{\leadsto}$ S.*

Definition 18. *A **control scope interval** of C is one that contains: (1) all nodes that control depend on C; and (2) only forward-reachable nodes that control-depend on C.*

Recall that the control scope of a compound statement C is the set of all statements that control-depend on C, and note that a control scope interval of C can contain statements that are not forward-reachable but still control depend on C.

We next describe an $O(|V|^2)$ algorithm that computes control scope intervals for *all* the compound statements. Theorem 2 (given below) will then provide us an efficient procedure to extract the actual control scopes from our control scope intervals, that is, to filter out all the statements in the control scope interval of each C that do not control-depend on C.

Let us depict prescopes on SSCFGs, like in Fig. 5. The ranges of arrows give the prescopes of the statements; forward arrows represent branch statements and backward arrows represent loop statements. There are two types of overlapped prescopes, shown in Fig. 5 (A) and (B). In the first case, C_2 is forward reachable from C_1. Then the control scope interval of C_1 should contain that of C_2: consider $S_1 \notin pre\text{-}scope(C_1)$ in (A); C_1 may choose the branch with C_2 and then skip S_1, so $C_1 \overset{tscd}{\leadsto} S_1$. In the second case, C_1 and C_2 must have the same control scope intervals: in (B),

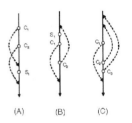

Fig. 5. Prescopes overlap

the execution of S_1 in the second iteration of the loop depends on the choice made at C_1 in the first iteration. When $pre\text{-}scope(C_1)$ overlaps several nested loops, like in (C), then all loops must have the same control scope interval as C_1. Based on these observations, we can derive the following algorithm which is explained in more detail in [8]:

> *(Step 1)* Extend prescopes (Fig. 5 (A)) by a backward traversal of the code/SSCFG: if prescopes of two statements overlap, then extend the prescope of the outer statement accordingly;
> *(Step 2)* Compute equivalence classes of statements that have the same control scope (Fig. 5 (B) and (C)); these are precisely the *connected components* of the graph representing the overlap between loops and other conditionals;
> *(Step 3)* Compute the actual control scope interval of each equivalence class as the *union* of the extended prescopes of all the statements in that class; if the class contains loops in V_∞, then the upper bound of its interval is set to ∞.

Steps 1 and 2 take $O(|V|^2)$ and step 3, which also takes the termination information of loops into account, takes $O(|V|)$. To calculate the actual control scopes, all one needs to do is to remove from control scope intervals those statements that are not control-dependent. The following theorem gives us a simple way to do it:

Theorem 2. *C $\overset{tscd}{\leadsto}$ S iff #(S) is in the control scope interval of C, and S is forward-reachable from C or there is some loop L with $\hat{C} = \hat{L}$ (same equiv class) and S ∈ b(L).*

6 Conclusion

This paper presented three novel contributions to control dependence. First, it introduced *parametric control dependence* as a general framework to define various control dependence relations, both direct and indirect. Second, it defined a new control dependence relation, called *termination-sensitive control dependence*, generalizing both classic and weak control dependence by taking explicit termination information of loops into account. Finally, an $O(|V|^2)$ algorithm was described to compute the (indirect) control dependence of all the statements; this algorithm works only for languages without arbitrary jumps inside blocks, including Java and C# (but not C). It would be interesting to also incorporate the recent work on control dependence in [16] in a parametric framework. Another question is whether one can combine the TSCD analysis with data-flow analysis and extend the algorithm in Section 5 with inter-procedural analysis.

References

1. A. V. Aho, R. Sethi, and J. D. Ullman. *Compilers, principles, techniques, and tools.* Addison-Wesley, 1986.
2. F. E. Allen and J. Cocke. A program data flow analysis procedure. *Commun. ACM,* 19(3):137, 1976.
3. B. Aminof, T. Ball, and O. Kupferman. Reasoning about systems with transition fairness. In *the 11th International Conference on Logic for Programming Artificial Intelligence and Reasoning,* 2004.
4. G. Bilardi and K. Pingali. A framework for generalized control dependence. In *PLDI'96,* 1996.
5. A. R. Bradley, Z. Manna, and H. Sipma. Termination analysis of integer linear loops. In *the 16th International Conference on Concurrency Theory (CONCUR'05),* 2005.
6. J. Büchi. Weak second-order arithmetic and finite automata. *Zeit. Math. Logik und Grundl. Math.,* 6:66–92, 1960.
7. F. Chen and G. Roşu. Predicting concurrency errors at runtime using sliced causality. Technical Report UIUCDCS-R-2005-2660, Dept. of CS at UIUC, 2005.
8. F. Chen and G. Roşu. Parametric and termination-sensitive control dependence. Technical Report UIUCDCS-R-2006-2712, Dept. of CS at UIUC, 2006.
9. M. Colon and H. Sipma. Practical methods for proving program termination. In *CAV'02,* 2002.
10. T. H. Cormen, C. E. Leiserson, and R. L. Rivest. *Introduction to Algorithms.* MIT Press, 1990.
11. D. E. Denning and P. J. Denning. Certification of programs for secure information flow. *Commun. ACM,* 20(7):504–513, 1977.
12. J. Ferrante, K. J. Ottenstein, and J. D. Warren. The program dependence graph and its use in optimization. *ACM Trans. Program. Lang. Syst.,* 9(3):319–349, 1987.
13. S. Horwitz and T. W. Reps. The use of program dependence graphs in software engineering. In *ICSE,* 1992.
14. T. Lengauer and R. E. Tarjan. A fast algorithm for finding dominators in a flowgraph. *ACM Trans. Program. Lang. Syst.,* 1(1):121–141, 1979.
15. A. Podgurski and L. A. Clarke. A formal model of program dependences and its implications for software testing, debugging, and maintenance. *IEEE Transactions on Software Engineering,* 16(9):965–979, 1990.

16. V. Ranganath, T. Amtoft, A. Banerjee, M. B. Dwyer, and J. Hatcliff. A new foundation for control-dependence and slicing for modern program structures. In *The European Symposium on Programming (ESOP'05)*, 2005.

17. B. G. Ryder and M. C. Paull. Elimination algorithms for data flow analysis. *ACM Comput. Surv.*, 18(3):277–316, 1986.

18. F. Tip. A survey of program slicing techniques. Technical Report CS-R9438, Centre for Mathematics and Computer Science, 1994.

19. M. Weiser. Program slicing. In *ICSE'81*, 1981.

Memory Leak Analysis by Contradiction*

Maksim Orlovich and Radu Rugina

Computer Science Department
Cornell University
Ithaca, NY 14853
{maksim, rugina}@cs.cornell.edu

Abstract. We present a novel leak detection algorithm. To prove the absence of a memory leak, the algorithm assumes its presence and runs a backward heap analysis to disprove this assumption. We have implemented this approach in a memory leak analysis tool and used it to analyze several routines that manipulate linked lists and trees. Because of the reverse nature of the algorithm, the analysis can locally reason about the absence of memory leaks. We have also used the tool as a scalable, but unsound leak detector for C programs. The tool has found several bugs in larger programs from the SPEC2000 suite.

1 Introduction

Low-level programming languages such as C and C++ provide manual memory management and require explicit deallocation of program structures by programmers. As a result, memory leaks represent a standard cause of errors in such languages. Memory leaks are difficult to identify, as the only symptom is a slow increase in memory consumption. For long-running applications, this eventually causes to the system running out of memory. In recent years, a number of static memory leak analysis and verification techniques have been developed [1,2,3,4,5].

This paper presents a new static memory leak detection analysis that reasons about the absence of errors by disproving their presence. To show that an assignment in the program is leak-free, the analysis assumes the opposite – that the assignment causes the program to lose the last reference to a heap cell, called the *error cell*. Then, the algorithm performs a backward dataflow analysis, trying to contradict the feasibility of the error cell. If each backward path leads to a contradiction, then the original assumption was wrong. Otherwise, if there is a backward path that validates the feasibility of the error cell, the analysis reports a program trace that leads to the error. The memory leak analysis by contradiction approach has several appealing properties:

- It can be used to reason about the presence or absence of leaks in incomplete programs. It can determine that program fragments are leak-free regardless of their input heap, or identify the inputs under which the program fragment may leak;
- It can be used in interactive tools in a demand-driven fashion, where programmers query particular statements in the program, asking about the possibility of memory leaks at those points.

---

* This work was supported by NSF grant CNS-0406345, DARPA grant FA8750-04-2-0011, and AFOSR grant F9550-06-1-0244 .

K. Yi (Ed.): SAS 2006, LNCS 4134, pp. 405–424, 2006.

To the best of our knowledge, existing approaches to memory leak analysis and detection cannot give such guarantees, or be used in such a way.

We have implemented the proposed algorithm in a prototype analysis tool and used it to analyze memory leaks in standard library functions that manipulate recursive heap structures. The tool can show that most of these programs do not leak memory, regardless of their inputs, or leak only for malformed inputs. We have also used the tool to find errors in larger programs from the SPEC2000 benchmarks suite. In this setting, the tool analyzes each program assignment, and uses a cutoff to limit the amount of backward exploration per assignment. The tool has found several memory leaks in these programs.

The rest of the paper is organized as follows. Section 2 presents the scope of this paper. Section 3 illustrates the main idea with a simple example. We show the reverse heap analysis algorithm in Section 4. Experimental results are presented in Section 5. Finally, we discuss related work in Section 6, and conclude in Section 7.

2   Leak Classification and Analysis Scope

The notion of a memory leak is closely related to the notion of lifetime of heap cells: a cell is being leaked if the program or the run-time system doesn't reclaim its memory when the lifetime has ended. However, there are different ways of defining lifetime. These can be classified into three main categories, based on the following heap cell properties:

1. *Referencing*: the lifetime of a cell ends when it there are no references to that cell (excluding references from dead cells). This notion is used, for instance, by reference-counting garbage collectors.
2. *Reachability*: the lifetime of a cell ends when it is no longer reachable from program variables. This notion is used by tracing and copying garbage collectors.
3. *Liveness*: the lifetime of a cell ends after the last access to that cell. This is the most precise notion of lifetime.

The above three classes are increasingly stronger notions of lifetime; they correspond to three classes of leaks. A system that targets a given class of leaks cannot make guarantees about leaks in the stronger classes. For instance, reference counting approaches do not detect unreachable heap cycles; and reachability-based approaches do not detect cells that are still reachable, but no longer needed (sometimes referred to as "Java memory leaks"). The scope of this work is the analysis of referencing leaks. As some of the existing static analyses [6,4], our technique does not detect unreachable cycles.

The analysis is sound for the imperative language described in Section 4 (essentially a subset of C without pointer arithmetic, unions, and casts), provided that the underlying points-to information is sound. We use our implemented tool in two settings:

- *Verification*. We use the tool to verify the absence of referencing leaks for algorithms written in our language.
- *Bug-finding*. We also use our implementation as a scalable error-detection tool that targets all of the C language. In this setting, the tool makes several unsound assumptions. Despite of being unsound, the tool is useful at identifying potential errors, with a relatively low number of false warnings.

```
1   typedef struct list {
2        int data;
3        struct list *next;
4   } List;
5
6   List *reverse(List *x) {
7        List *y, *t;
8        y = NULL;
9        while (x != NULL) {
10            t = x->next;
11            x->next = y;
12            y = x;
13            x = t;
14        }
15        return y;
16  }
```

Fig. 1. Example program

3   Example

Figure 1 shows a function that performs in-place list reversal. The function takes a linked list x as argument, and returns the reversed list pointed to by y. The function is written using C syntax, but assumes type-safety.

Suppose we want to prove that the assignment y = x at line 12 cannot cause a memory leak. For this, assume by absurd that a leak occurs at this point. That is, assume that the execution of y = x causes the program to loose the last reference to a valid allocated cell at this point, the error cell. We describe this cell using a dataflow fact {y} indicating that y is the sole reference to the cell in question. Starting with this fact, we analyze program statements backward, looking for a contradiction. In this case, the contradiction shows up right away, at the predecessor statement x->next = y at line 11. No program state before line 11 can make it possible to have a heap cell referenced only by y at the next program point. This is because:

- either y did not reference the cell in question before line 11, in which case it won't reference it after the assignment;
- or y did reference the cell in question, in which case there will be two distinct references to the cell after the assignment, one from y and one from x->next. These represent different memory locations because of the type-safety assumption. Hence, y is not the only reference to the cell after line 11;

Each of the two cases yields a contradiction. Hence, the initial assumption is invalid and the assignment y = x cannot cause a memory leak.

Similar analyses can be performed for each of the assignments in this program. The analysis of assignments x->next = y at line 11, and x = t at line 13 are the same as above. The analysis of t = x->next at line 10 requires exploring multiple backward paths, one that wraps around the loop and yields a contradiction at x = t, and one that goes out of the loop and yields a contradiction at the procedure entry point where t's scope begins. Finally, the analysis of y = NULL at line 8 is contradicted right away, as the scope of y begins at that point.

Additionally, the analysis must check that local variables do not leak memory when they go out of scope at the end of the procedure. The analysis models the return statement return y as a sequence: "ret = y; y = NULL; t = NULL;", where ret is a special return variable. Assignment y = NULL is contradicted by ret = y; and t = NULL is contradicted by x = t at line 13, and y = NULL at line 8. The assignment to ret needs not be checked.

Hence, the analysis concludes that reverse is leak-free. Not only the analysis has quickly contradicted each assignment, mostly using one single backward step per assignment, but the analysis has actually determine that reverse doesn't leak memory regardless of its input heap.

In contrast, forward heap analyses (such as [4] or [7]) cannot determine this fact because they would need to exhaustively enumerate all possible heaps at the entry of reverse. Without knowledge about all variables and program structures that might point into the list passed to reverse, enumerating all heaps is not feasible.

4   Backward Memory Leak Analysis

We present the memory leak analysis using a core imperative language consisting of statements and expressions with the following syntax:

$$Statements \; s \in St \quad s ::= *e_0 \leftarrow e_1 \mid * e \leftarrow \texttt{malloc} \mid \texttt{free}(e) \mid \texttt{cond}(e_0 \equiv e_1)$$
$$\texttt{return} \; e \mid \texttt{enter} \mid * e_0 \leftarrow p(e_1, ..., e_k)$$

$$Expressions \; e \in E \quad e ::= n \mid a \mid * e \mid e.f \mid e_0 \oplus e_1$$

where $n \in \mathbb{Z}$ ranges over numeric constants (NULL being represented as constant 0), $a \in A$ ranges over symbolic addresses, $f \in F$ over structure fields, $p \in P$ over procedures, $\oplus$ over arithmetic operators, and $\equiv$ over the comparison operators $=$ and $\neq$. The special statement enter describes the beginning of scope for local variables. The entry node of each procedure the enter statement, and the exit node is the return statement. The condition statement $\texttt{cond}(e_0 \equiv e_1)$ ensures that the program execution proceeds only if the condition succeeds. Condition statements can be used to model if statements and while statements as non-deterministic branches in the control-flow graph, followed by the appropriate cond statements on each of the branches.

Expressions are represented using a small set of primitives. Symbolic addresses a are the addresses of variables (globals, locals, and parameters). We denote by a_x the symbolic address of variable x. The syntax for expressions doesn't contain variables because variables can be expressed as dereferences of their symbolic addresses. For instance, a_x models the C expression &x; $*a_x$ models C expression x; $(*a_x).f$ models &(x->f); and $*((*a_x).f)$ models x->f. With this representation, each memory read is explicit in the form of a dereference $*e$; and each assignment has the form $*e \leftarrow e'$, making the memory write $*e$ explicit. The set $\text{Mem}(e)$ denotes the subexpressions of e that represent memory locations. This set is defined recursively as follows:

$$\text{Mem}(n) = \text{Mem}(a) = \varnothing \qquad \text{Mem}(e.f) = \text{Mem}(e)$$
$$\text{Mem}(*e) = \{*e\} \cup \text{Mem}(e) \qquad \text{Mem}(e_0 \oplus e_1) = \text{Mem}(e_0) \cup \text{Mem}(e_1)$$

To simplify the rest of the presentation, we define expression contexts $\mathcal{E}$ as expressions with holes $[\cdot]$:

$$\mathcal{E} ::= \mathcal{E}.f \mid *\mathcal{E} \mid \mathcal{E} \oplus e \mid e \oplus \mathcal{E} \mid [\cdot]$$

If $\mathcal{E}$ is an expression context and e is an expression, then $\mathcal{E}[e]$ is the expression obtained by filling the hole of the context $\mathcal{E}$ with expression e.

The core language is a subset of C that supports heap structures and pointers to variables or to heap cells. The execution of the program disallows casts between numeric constants and pointers. All structures have the same set of non-overlapping fields, so that an update to a structure field does not affect the values of other fields. Essentially, unions and unsafe pointer casts are not allowed. The language semantics are defined in Appendix A using evaluation relations for expressions and statements. The relation $(e, \sigma) \rightarrow v$ indicates that the evaluation of expression e in store σ yields value v; and the relation $(s, \sigma) \rightarrow \sigma'$ indicates that the evaluation of statement s in store σ yields a new store σ'.

4.1   Aliasing and Disjointness

To resolve pointer aliasing, the leak analysis assumes that an underlying analysis provides: 1) a partitioning of the memory into regions (i.e. different regions model disjoint sets of memory locations); and 2) points-to information between regions. We assume a flow-insensitive points-to interface consisting of a set Rgn of regions, and a function $\text{pt}(e)$ that returns the set of regions that expression e may point into.

Flow-insensitive points-to analyses such as [8,9] can be used to provide the region partitioning and the points-to information, but they require the availability of the entire program. For incomplete programs, the following approaches can be used: 1) type-based points-to information for type-safe languages, with one region for each type and points-to relations according to type declarations; and 2) address-taken points-to information, with one region for each memory location whose address has not been stored in the program, and one region for everything else.

The analysis uses the points-to information to resolve alias queries. An expression e is *disjoint* from a region set rs, written $e \# rs$, if updates in any of the regions in rs do not affect value of e. The analysis answers such queries using the points-to information:

$$e \# rs \quad \text{iff} \quad \forall(*e') \in \text{Mem}(e) \;.\; \text{pt}(e') \cap rs = \varnothing$$

For expression contexts, $\mathcal{E}[e] \# rs$ means that all of the sub-expressions of $\mathcal{E}[e]$ other than e are disjoint from regions in rs: $\mathcal{E}[e] \# rs$ if and only if $\forall(*e') \in \text{Mem}(\mathcal{E}[e]) - \{e\} \;.\; \text{pt}(e') \cap rs = \varnothing$.

4.2   Error Cell Abstraction

The analysis starts from the potential error point, a program assignment, assuming that the assignment has overwritten the last reference to the error cell. The analysis models this cell using a triple of the form (S, H, M), where:

$$ImplicitMiss(e, (S, H, M)) = (e = n) \lor (e = a) \lor (e = \mathcal{E}[*n]) \lor (e = \mathcal{E}[n.f]) \lor$$
$$(e = *e' \land (S \cap \mathsf{pt}(e') = \varnothing))$$

$$Miss(e, (S, H, M)) = e \in M \lor ImplicitMiss(e, (S, H, M))$$

$$Infeasible(S, H, M) = \exists e \in H \ . \ Miss(e, (S, H, M))$$

$$Cleanup(S, H, M) = (S, H, M'), \quad \text{where:}$$
$$M' = \{e \mid e \in M \land \neg ImplicitMiss(e, (S, H, M))\}$$

Fig. 2. Helper functions used by the analysis

- $S \subseteq \mathsf{Rgn}$ is the conservative set of regions that might hold pointers to the error cell;
- H is a set of expressions that point to the error cell; and
- M is a set of expressions that do not reference the cell.

We refer to H as the hit set, and to M as the miss set, similarly to [4]. The partial ordering for this abstraction is such that $(S_1, H_1, M_1) \sqsubseteq (S_2, H_2, M_2)$ if and only if $S_1 \subseteq S_2$, $H_1 \supseteq H_2$, and $M_1 \supseteq M_2$. The join operation is defined accordingly: $(S_1, H_1, M_1) \sqcup (S_2, H_2, M_2) = (S_1 \cup S_2, H_1 \cap H_2, M_1 \cap M_2)$. Two elements of the dataflow lattice have special meaning: the top element $\top$ indicates that the error cell is always feasible; and the bottom element $\bot$ indicates a contradiction, i.e., that the error cell is not feasible.

Figure 2 shows several helper functions that the analysis uses to reasons about dataflow triples. The function *ImplicitMiss* helps the analysis identify new miss expressions, to which we refer as implicit miss expressions. These include:

- *Numeric constants* n. Addresses manufactured from numeric constants cannot reference the cell, because casting integers into pointers is not allowed;
- *Symbolic addresses* a. Leaks can occur only for heap cells, which cannot be referenced by symbolic addresses;
- *Invalid expressions* $\mathcal{E}[*n]$ *and* $\mathcal{E}[n.f]$. These include null pointer dereferences and null field accesses. Evaluating such expressions would cause run-time errors, so they are not valid references to the error cell;
- *Lvalue expressions that represent regions outside of the region set* S. If $S \cap \mathsf{pt}(e) = \varnothing$, then $*e$ is an implicit miss expression.

The function *Infeasible* identifies infeasible dataflow facts: a dataflow fact d is infeasible if there is an expression that hits and misses the error cell. Such facts represent impossible states of the error cell; they are equivalent to the bottom value $\bot$, and correspond to contradictions in our framework.

To keep the dataflow facts as small as possible and avoid redundancy in the abstraction, the analysis uses a function *Cleanup* to remove implicit miss expressions from dataflow triples. This function always yields an abstraction higher up in our lattice (i.e., more conservative dataflow information). Hence, using *Cleanup* after applying a transfer function does not affect the correctness of the analysis.

$$\frac{e \mathbin{\#} w \quad e^{sgn}}{{}^{sgn}e} \quad [\text{Filter1}]$$

$$\frac{e_1 = *e \quad e \mathbin{\#} w \quad e_1^{sgn}}{{}^{sgn}e_1} \quad [\text{Filter4}]$$

$$\frac{e_1 \mathbin{\#} w \quad e_1^{--} \quad e \mathbin{\#} w \quad (*e)^{+}}{{}^{+}(*e)} \quad [\text{Filter2}]$$

$$\frac{\mathcal{E}[*e_0] \mathbin{\#} w \quad \mathcal{E}[*e_0]^{sgn}}{{}^{sgn}\mathcal{E}[e_1]} \quad [\text{Subst1}]$$

$$\frac{e_1 \mathbin{\#} w \quad e_1^{+} \quad e \mathbin{\#} w \quad (*e)^{-}}{{}^{-}(*e)} \quad [\text{Filter3}]$$

$$\frac{e_0 \mathbin{\#} w \quad (*e_0)^{--}}{{}^{-}e_1} \quad [\text{Subst2}]$$

Fig. 3. Analysis rules for an assignment $*e_0 \leftarrow e_1$. The sign *sgn* is either $+$ or $-$. The set $w = \mathsf{pt}(e_0)$ is the conservative set of written regions.

4.3 Intra-procedural Analysis

For each abstraction (S, H, M) that describes the error cell after a statement, the analysis computes an abstraction (S', H', M') that describes the known facts about the error cell before the statement. Hence, the analysis computes an over-approximation of the state before each statement (as opposed to weakest preconditions, which are under-approximations). We refer to the state after the statement as the post-state, and the state before the statement as the pre-state.

The overall analysis uses a worklist algorithm to perform the backward dataflow computation. The analysis is initiated at assignment and a few other program points, as discussed later in Section 4.5. Then, the information is propagated backward. When the analysis reaches a contradiction ($\bot$) on all backward paths, the error is disproved. When the abstraction of the error cell is $\top$, or when the analysis reaches the entry point of a program fragment, the analysis reports a potential violation. The analysis of each statement is presented below.

Analysis assignments: $*e_0 \leftarrow e_1$. Given a dataflow triple (S, H, M) that describes the post-state of the error cell, the analysis computes a new dataflow fact that describes the pre-state of the cell. The transfer function for assignments is:

$$[\![*e_0 \leftarrow e_1]\!](S, H, M) = \begin{cases} \bot & \text{if } Infeasible(S', H', M') \\ Cleanup(S', H', M') & \text{otherwise} \end{cases}$$

$$\text{where} \quad H', M' \text{ are derived using the rules in Figure 3}$$
$$S' = S \cup \mathsf{pt}(e_0)$$

The region set S always grows since the post-state gives no information about the old value of the written location. The analysis must conservatively assume that $*e_0$ might reference the cell in the pre-state (we discuss how to improve this in Section 4.8).

To keep the analysis rules succinct, we write e^{+} and e^{-} for $e \in H$ and $e \in M$ (hit/miss expressions in the post-state); and ${}^{+}e$ and ${}^{-}e$ for $e \in H'$ and $e \in M'$ (hit/miss expressions in the pre-state). We also write e^{--} to denote that $Miss(e, (S, H, M))$. The set w is the set of regions potentially written by the assignment: $w = \mathsf{pt}(e_0)$. Hence, an expression has the same value before and after the statement if it is disjoint from w.

The inference rules in Figure 3 are used to derive hit and miss expressions in the pre-state. If the premises hold in the post-state, then the conclusion holds in the pre-state. Each rule is implemented by iterating over expressions in H and M, matching them against the rightmost expression in the premise. If the rule applies (i.e., all other premises hold), then the expression in the conclusion is added to H' or M'. Our implementation also checks for contradictions as new expressions are generated in the pre-state, returning $\bot$ as soon as the first contradiction occurs.

The first four rules filter out existing expressions from H and M if the assignment might invalidate them. Clearly, each expression disjoint from w will maintain its hit or miss status (rule [FILTER1]). The other filtering rules are less obvious. They attempt to preserve expressions that fail this simple test. Consider rule [FILTER2]. If expression e_1 is disjoint from w and e_1 misses in the post-state, then it also misses it in the pre-state. Hence, the assignment writes a value that doesn't reference the cell. Therefore, each expression $*e$ that hits the cell in the post-state must necessarily be a location different than the one written by the assignment, provided that its address e is not affected by the assignment. Therefore, if all these premises are met, $*e$ has the same value in the pre-state, so it will hit the error cell before the statement. Rule [FILTER3] is symmetric. Rule [FILTER4] indicates that the RHS expression e_1 can be preserved if its address is not changed by the assignment. The reason is that, if e_1 happens to be written, it is updated with its old value.

Rule [SUBST1] derives new hit and miss expressions in the pre-state by substitution. If $e_0 \# w$, then $*e_0$ in the post-state has the same value as e_1 in the pre-state. Hence, if an expression $e = \mathcal{E}[*e_0]$ hits (misses) in the post-state, we can substitute e_1 for $*e_0$ to derive an expression $\mathcal{E}[e_1]$ that hits (misses) in the pre-state. For this to be safe, the expression $\mathcal{E}[*e_0]$ must be disjoint from w. The last rule, [SUBST2] is similar to substitution, but for implicit misses and for a simple context $\mathcal{E} = [\cdot]$.

Example. Consider a triple $(\{r_y\}, \{*a_y\}, \{\})$ describing the error cell in the post-state. Here, a_y is the symbolic address of variable y, and r_y is the region that contains y. Let $x \leftarrow y$ be the assignment to analyze, represented in our formulation as $*a_x \leftarrow *a_y$. Assume that variables x and y belong to different regions, so all necessary disjointness conditions are met. By rule [SUBST2] we get $^-(*a_y)$, because $*a_x$ is an implicit miss in the post-state. By rule [FILTER1], $^+(*a_y)$ also holds. Hence, a contradiction occurs.

Analysis of allocations: $*e_0 \leftarrow$ malloc. The analysis tries to determine if the error cell has been allocated at this site. First, if $(*e_0)^+$ and some expression unaliased to $*e_0$ also references the cell, then a contradiction occurs. Second, if there is evidence that the error cell has not been allocated at this site, it proceeds past this statement, treating the allocation as a nullification $*e_0 \leftarrow 0$. Note that the nullification automatically causes a contradiction when a fields of $*e_0$ hits the error cell in the post-state. Otherwise, if none of the above conditions are met, the analysis conservatively stops and returns $\top$, signaling that the leak might be feasible and the error cell might be allocated at this site. The transfer function is defined as follows:

$$
[\![*e_0 \leftarrow \texttt{malloc}]\!](d) = \begin{cases} \bot & \text{if } \textit{UnaliasedHit} \wedge (*e_0 \in H \wedge e_0 \# w) \\ [\![*e_0 \leftarrow 0]\!](d) & \text{if } \textit{UnaliasedHit} \vee (\textit{Miss}(*e_0, d) \wedge e_0 \# w) \\ \top & \text{otherwise} \end{cases}
$$

where $d = (S, H, M)$, $w = \mathsf{pt}(e_0)$, and $UnaliasedHit = \exists (*e) \in H : \mathsf{pt}(e) \cap w = \varnothing$. Here, $\bot$ indicates a contradiction, and $\top$ indicates a potential leak for a cell allocated at this site.

Analysis of deallocations: $\mathtt{free}(e)$. When the analysis reaches a deallocation $\mathtt{free}(e)$, a contradiction occurs if e references the error cell. In other words, losing the last reference of a cell that has been freed is not an error. Otherwise, the analysis learns that e misses in the pre-state and keeps the rest of the state unchanged. The algorithm is:

$$[\![\mathtt{free}(e)]\!](S, H, M) = \begin{cases} \bot & \text{if } e \in H \\ (S, H, M) & \text{if } Miss(e, (S, H, M)) \\ (S, H, M \cup \{e\}) & \text{otherwise} \end{cases}$$

Analysis of conditions: $\mathtt{cond}(e_0 \equiv e_1)$. For conditions, the analysis knows that the (in)equality has succeeded in the post-state. It uses this information to derive new hit and miss expressions in the pre-state, as indicated by the following rules:

$\mathtt{cond}(e_0 = e_1)$				$\mathtt{cond}(e_0 \neq e_1)$	
$\dfrac{e_0^+}{^+e_1}$	$\dfrac{e_1^+}{^+e_0}$	$\dfrac{e_0^{--}}{^-e_1}$	$\dfrac{e_1^{--}}{^-e_0}$	$\dfrac{e_0^+}{^-e_1}$	$\dfrac{e_1^+}{^-e_0}$

If H' and M' are the new hit and miss expressions derived using the above rules, $M'' = M \cup M'$, and $H'' = H \cup H'$, then the transfer function for conditions is:

$$[\![\mathtt{cond}(e_0 \equiv e_1)]\!](S, H, M) = \begin{cases} \bot & \text{if } Infeasible(S, H'', M'') \\ Cleanup(S, H'', M'') & \text{otherwise} \end{cases}$$

4.4 Inter-procedural Analysis

The inter-procedural analysis follows the general structure of the worklist inter-procedural analysis algorithm proposed by Sharir and Pnueli [10]. Information is propagated from the points after procedure calls to the corresponding procedure exit points, and from procedure entry points to the corresponding points before the call. The analysis uses backward procedure summaries to cache previous analysis results. The entire inter-procedural worklist algorithm is presented in Appendix B.

The analysis uses two functions, *Map* and *Unmap*, to account for the necessary changes in the analysis information when crossing procedure boundaries, such as assignments of actuals to formals, or to model the scopes of local variables. The analysis uses *Map* when moving from the caller into the callee space, and uses *Unmap* when moving back into the caller space. The mapping process is performed right before $\mathtt{return}$, and the unmapping right after $\mathtt{enter}$. Each pair is discussed below.

Analysis for Map and $\mathtt{return}(e)$. For simplicity, consider a procedure p with one formal parameter $\mathtt{formal}$ and one local variable $\mathtt{local}$. Let $\mathtt{ret}$ be a special variable that models the return value. Variables $\mathtt{local}$, $\mathtt{formal}$, and $\mathtt{ret}$ are represented in this section using C-style notation instead of the normalized representation for expressions. Consider a call-site that invokes p with an actual argument e_{act}.

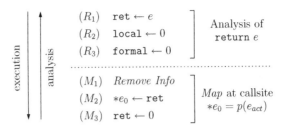

Fig. 4. Analysis for *Map* and `return(e)`

The call-site mapping process and the analysis of the return of p are described in Figure 4. The execution proceeds from top to bottom, and the analysis works in the reverse order. We explain the actions in this diagram in the execution order. Each node `return(e)` is modeled as a sequence that assigns the returned expression to `ret`, and then nullifies all local and formal variables, showing that they go out of scope. The transfer function of `return` is the composition of the transfer functions of these assignments, in reverse order.

The mapping function *Map* takes place at the point right before a call site $*e_0 \leftarrow p(e_{act})$. The mapping process assigns the return variable `ret` to expression $*e_0$ and then nullifies the return variable. The mapping process also removes from H and M all the expressions that involve locals or parameters of the caller, keeping only information relevant to the callee. This is shown by the *Remove Info* step right before the analysis moves into the callee's space.

Analysis for Unmap and `enter`. When the analysis reaches the entry of a procedure, it moves back to the caller space, to the point right before the call. The analysis of the `enter` statement and the unmapping process are described in Figure 5. We use a special operation $scope(s)$ to indicate that symbol s enters its scope. For the analysis, which is reversed, $scope(s)$ indicates that s goes out of scope. The transfer function of $scope(s)$ has two possible outcomes: it yields a contradiction if s occurs in one of the hit expressions; otherwise, it removes all hit and miss expressions that refer to s. The analysis of `enter` is modeled using a $scope$ operation for each of its locals.

The unmap process accounts for the assignments of actuals to formals and for restoring part of the information that *Map* has filtered out. One complication that arises for recursive functions is that expression e_{act} in the caller might refer to variable `formal`. A direct assignment `formal` $\leftarrow e_{act}$ would then talk about two different instances of the same variable `formal`, the one of the caller and the one of the callee. This problem can be solved using a `shadow` variable to perform the assignment in two steps. In execution order, first assign the actual to the shadow, then move to the callee space and assign the shadow to the formal. In between the two `shadow` assignments, the formal enters its scope (and goes out of scope for the analysis). The analysis also restores expressions that *Map* has filtered out, provided that they cannot be modified by the callee. For instance, local variables whose addresses have not been taken can be safely restored. In general, restoring expressions requires knowledge about the locations being modified by the callee, i.e., MOD information.

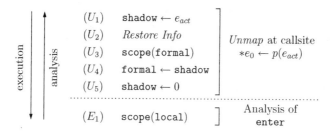

Fig. 5. Analysis for *Unmap* and `enter`

4.5   Leak Probing Points

The last piece that completes the analysis is defining the initialization points. The analysis issues one query for each assignment, to determine if the assignment might leak memory. We refer to each leak query as a *leak probe*. For each assignment $*e_0 \leftarrow e_1$ the analysis builds a dataflow triple $(\mathrm{pt}(e_0), \{*e_0\}, \{e_1\})$ to describe an error cell referenced by e_0, but not by e_1. In many cases, e_1 is an implicit miss and can be omitted from the miss set. The analysis then asks whether this triple might hold at the point right before the assignment.

In addition to assignments, the analysis issues leak probes at the following points:

1. *Allocations*: each $*e_0 \leftarrow$ `malloc` is probed as $*e_0 \leftarrow 0$.
2. *Deallocations*: for each `free`(e), the analysis issues a probe that corresponds to $*(e.f) \leftarrow 0$, for each field f of e. This checks for leaks caused by freeing a cell that holds the last reference to another cell.
3. *Locals and formals*: at return points, it issues a probe for each local variable and formal parameter. These correspond to the nullifications (R_2) and (R_3) in Figure 4. The assignment to `ret` needs not be checked.
4. *Assigned returns*: for each call $*e_0 \leftarrow p(...)$, it issues a probe that corresponds to the assignment (M_2) in Figure 4. Note that this probe will immediately propagate into the callee.
5. *Leaked returns:* Although in our language return values are always assigned, in C function calls are not required to do so. In that case, the assignment (M_2) is missing and the returned value might be leaked. The analysis uses a probe that corresponds to the nullification of `ret` (M_3), to check for leaked returns.

4.6   Formal Framework and Soundness

This section summarize the soundness result for the transfer functions in our analysis. This result states that the abstract semantics of statements are sound with respect to the concrete execution of the program, provided that the points-to information is sound. The definitions below define the notion of soundness for the points-to information, and describe the abstraction function. Then, the soundness theorem is stated. In these definitions, L denotes the set of all memory addresses, including symbolic addresses $a \in A$ and heap addresses.

Definition 1 (Points-to Soundness). *Let* Rgn *be the finite set of memory regions. A points-to abstraction* pt $: E \rightarrow 2^{\mathsf{Rgn}}$ *is a sound approximation of a concrete store* σ, *with witness mapping* $\mu : L \rightarrow$ Rgn *from locations to regions, written* $\sigma \models_\mu$ pt, *if:* $\forall e \in E . (e, \sigma) \rightarrow l \wedge l \in L \Rightarrow \mu(l) \in \mathsf{pt}(e)$.

Definition 2 (Abstraction Function). *Let* σ *be a store,* $l \in L - A$ *a heap location in* σ, $l \in dom(\sigma)$, *and* μ *a mapping from locations to regions. A dataflow fact* d *is a conservative approximation of* l *in* σ *with respect to* μ, *written* $(l, \sigma) \models_\mu d$, *if* $d = \top$, *or* $d = (S, H, M)$ *and:*

1. $\forall e \in H . (e, \sigma) \rightarrow l$
2. $\forall e \in M . (e, \sigma) \rightarrow l \Rightarrow l' \neq l$
3. $\forall l' \in L . \sigma(l') = l \Rightarrow \mu(l') \in S$

Definition 3 (Dataflow Validity). *Let* s *be a statement,* d *and* d' *two dataflow facts, and* pt *the points-to information. The triple* $\{d\}\ s\ \{d'\}$ *is valid relative to* pt, *written* $\models_{\mathsf{pt}} \{d\}\ s\ \{d'\}$, *if for any pre- and post-stores for which* pt *is sound, and for any location that is approximated by* d' *in the post-store, the location is then approximated by* d *in the pre-store:* $\forall l, \sigma, \sigma', \mu . (\sigma' \models_\mu \mathsf{pt} \wedge \sigma \models_\mu \mathsf{pt} \wedge (l, \sigma') \models_\mu d' \wedge (s, \sigma) \rightarrow \sigma') \Rightarrow (l, \sigma) \models_\mu d$.

From this definition, it follows that $\{\top\}\ s\ \{d'\}$ is valid for any d'. Also, $\bot$ can never approximate the error cell: $\forall l, \sigma, \mu . (l, \sigma) \not\models_\mu \bot$. Therefore, $\{\bot\}\ s\ \{d'\}$ is never valid.

Theorem 1 (Transfer Function Soundness). *For any assignment, malloc, free, or condition statement* s, *if* d' *is a dataflow fact after* s, *and* pt *is the points-to information, then the dataflow fact* $d = [\![s]\!](d')$ *that the transfer function computes before* s *is sound relative to the points-to information* pt: $\models_{\mathsf{pt}} \{ [\![s]\!](d') \}\ s\ \{ d' \}$.

Due to lack of space, we omit the proof of the theorem. The proof is presented in [11].

4.7   Termination

The leak detection analysis is guaranteed to terminate, because of three reasons. First, region sets are bounded by the finite set Rgn. Second, hit and miss expressions can only shrink during the analysis. Although the set of expressions in unbounded, these sets have finite size when a node is reached for the first time; after that, they only decrease. Third, the transfer functions are monotonic. It is easy to see that larger hit and miss sets will cause the inference rules to derive more facts in the pre-state.

4.8   Extensions

We propose several extensions that improve the precision of the basic analysis:

- *Diminish the region set increase via points-to information.* As mentioned earlier, the region set S grows during the analysis because the state after an assignment doesn't give information about the old value of the location being written. The analysis conservatively assumes that the old value hit the error cell in the pre-state. This is overly conservative, especially in the case of assignments of integers or other non-pointer values. The analysis can use points-to information to avoid this. If $*e_0$ is the LHS of the assignment being probed, and $*e$ is the LHS of the currently analyzed assignment, the analysis can determine that $^-(*e)$ if $*e$ and $*e_0$ are unaliased: $\mathsf{pt}(e_0) \cap \mathsf{pt}(e) = \varnothing$. In this case, $\mathsf{pt}(e_0)$ is not added to S.

- *Enable region set removal via strong updates.* A second improvement is to augment the abstraction so that the analysis also removes regions from S. For this, we tag each region in S with a program expression $*e$, or with a top value. An expression tag shows that the region contains at most one reference to the cell, and that reference, if present, is $*e$. Top indicates imprecision. When the analysis identifies a region r that contains at most one reference $*e$, and the analysis rules imply $^-(*e)$, then it can safely remove r from S in the pre-state.

- *Separated abstraction*: We propose a variation of the analysis where the analysis computes more than one triple (S, H, M) per program point. Two triples are merged only if their subset of regions that contain the hit expressions $S \cap H$ is the same. Otherwise, the triples are maintained separated. Because of less frequent merges, the analysis becomes more precise.

5 Experiments

We have implemented the algorithms presented in this paper in an analysis system developed in our group, CRYSTAL. All of the C constructs (including arrays, pointer arithmetic, and unions) are translated into an intermediate representation that is very similar to the normalized representation from Section 4. Therefore, the implementation closely follows the formal presentation; at the same time, it handles all of the complexity of C. The leak detector uses the extensions discussed in the previous section. The results were collected on a 3Ghz Pentium 4 machine running Red Hat Enterprise Linux 4.

Heap manipulation benchmarks. We have tested our leak analyzer on several small heap manipulation routines. For this experiments, we only consider programs written in the type-safe subset of C from Section 4. The benchmarks include iterative and recursive versions of standard linked list operations (insert, delete, reverse, merge) for singly-linked and doubly-linked lists; two versions of the Deutsch-Schorr-Waite pointer reversal algorithm, for lists and for trees; and AVL tree manipulations. The singly-linked list manipulations are a representative subset of those from [1] and [12]. The doubly-linked list implementations are part of the Gnome's GLib library [1].

We have experimented with each procedure in isolation, or with small groups of procedures when some of them called others. Warnings were reported when the analysis reached the entry of a procedure that is never called. Recursive functions have been wrapped into non-recursive functions. We use a type-based points-to region partitioning and points-to analysis. All of the programs were analyzed in less than one second.

Figure 6 shows analysis statistics and results for the small benchmarks. The meaning of the two-letter prefix is as follows: s means "singly" and d means "doubly"; i

---

[1] ftp://ftp.gtk.org/pub/gtk

| Program | Probes | | Trace Length | | Abstractions |
	Total	Warn / Leak	Median	Max	per point
si-create	5	0 / 0	2	6	1.0
si-delete	11	0 / 0	10	29	1.4
si-insert	13	1 / 0	2	130	1.8
si-reverse	9	0 / 0	1	6	1.0
si-rotate	6	1 / 1	2	10	1.1
si-merge	16	0 / 0	12	200	1.7
sr-append	11	0 / 0	2	57	2.0
sr-insert	11	2 / 0	13	114	2.7
sr-reverse	11	0 / 0	1	82	1.6
sr-rev-leak	13	1 / 1	1	95	2.8
di-delete	9	2 / 2	6	89	2.7
di-prepend	7	1 / 1	7	15	1.1
di-reverse	7	0 / 0	1	12	1.2
di-merge	19	0 / 0	1	24	1.2
avl-rotate	6	0 / 0	1	2	1.0
avl-balance	6	1 / 0	22	803	1.3
avl-insert	31	2 / 0	2	1627	3.9
dsw-list	14	0 / 0	2	91	2.1
dsw-tree	18	1 / 0	15	1367	8.6

Fig. 6. Experiments on recursive structure manipulations

means "iterative" and r means "recursive". The first group of columns presents the total number of probes, the number of warned probes, and the number of actual errors. The analysis assumes any possible inputs, including malformed inputs. The tool has determined that no leaks occur for about half of the programs. It has found the memory leak in the buggy version of the recursive list reversal program sr-rev-leak from [12]. Some procedures leak memory if the inputs are malformed: si-rotate leaks when its second argument doesn't point to the last element, as the function expects; and di-delete and di-prepend leak if the input doesn't satisfy the doubly-linked list invariant. We consider these warnings legitimate. The remaining ones are false positives and are due to imprecision in the analysis.

The last three columns show analysis statistics: the median and maximum length of reverse traces (measured as applications of transfer functions), and the average number of abstraction triples per program point. The trace statistics indicate that for most of the probes contradictions show up quickly, but there are a few probes that require significantly more work, especially for complex pointer manipulations. The last column shows that the analysis usually creates few (around 2) abstractions per program point.

Larger benchmarks. We have also experimented with this tool on larger programs from the SPEC200 benchmark suite[2]. To make the tool useful for larger programs, we use several heuristics that cut down the amount of backward exploration: there is a limit on

---

[2] We omit gcc because all warnings referred to data allocated via alloca.

Benchmark	Size KLOC	Time (sec)	Probes Total	Aband.	Warn	Bugs
ammp	13.2	6.95s	1550	123	24	20
art	1.2	1.20s	32	16	1	1
bzip2	4.6	3.36s	108	62	2	1
crafty	19.4	27.71s	1493	1174	0	0
equake	1.5	1.50s	55	12	0	0
gap	59.4	108.66s	13517	6685	1	0
gzip	7.7	5.11s	489	173	3	1
mcf	1.9	4.21s	392	64	0	0
mesa	50.2	34.50s	5037	956	2	2
parser	10.9	19.36s	2859	1021	0	0
perlbmk	61.8	340.07s	25151	15801	1	1
twolf	19.7	20.29s	2526	1105	0	0
vortex	52.6	304.59s	9448	7421	26	0
vpr	16.9	15.14s	1216	530	0	0

Fig. 7. Experiments on the SPEC2000 benchmarks

the number of transfer functions per probe (currently 500), and a limit on the size of the region set S (currently 50). When the analysis reaches these limits, it abandons the probe. The analysis also limits the amount of inter-procedural exploration by ignoring callees more than one level deep, but allows tracking the error cell back into the callers. The tool uses type-based points-to information, which is unsound for type-unsafe C programs. Other sources of unsoundness include ignoring library functions other than memory allocators; and the unsound treatment of arrays, where the analysis does not probe assignments of array elements. The analysis cannot reason about array index dependencies, so array element probes would otherwise lead to false warnings.

Figure 7 shows the results. The first column shows the sizes of these programs and the second column the analysis times. The remaining columns show the analysis results: the number of probes explored; the number of probes abandoned because of the cut-off; the number of probes warned; and the number of actual bugs found. Warned probes are those for which the analysis reaches a validating allocation site for the error cell.

Most of the leaks found (e.g., in ammp and perlbmk) are situations where the application doesn't free memory upon returning on error handlers. Interestingly, this happens even for out-of-memory error handlers: the application allocates several buffers and if allocation fails for one, none of the others are freed. In art a function actually forgets to deallocate a local buffer on the normal return path. The main reasons for false warnings are the imprecision of the type-based region approximation; the use of pointer arithmetic; and the fact that programs such as vortex use complex, custom memory management.

Overall, we again find that the length distribution of backward traces is uneven. In most of the cases, the analysis can quickly identify a contradiction, within just a few lines of code. However, a few points generate very long backward traces, along which the analyses loses precision, and therefore becomes unlikely to produce meaningful results. The cutoff helps eliminate such cases from our reports.

6   Related Work

Manevich et al. [13] propose a backward flow analysis with the goal of tracing back null pointer errors, and disprove such errors. Although our analysis is similar in spirit to theirs, the analysis of memory leaks in heap structures is a more challenging problem than that of distinguishing between null and non-null values.

A related line of research has explored demand-driven inter-procedural analyses and frameworks [14,15,16,17]. Given a dataflow fact d at a program point p, a demand-driven flow analysis explores backward program paths starting from p with the goal of determining whether d is part of the forward dataflow solution at p. Our backward analysis is, in fact, a demand-driven analysis, although we are not interested in an answer to a forward analysis (since we don't have one), but rather with respect to the program semantics. Furthermore, to the best of our knowledge, the analysis in this paper is the first reverse, demand-driven heap analysis.

Several static leak detection analyses have been recently proposed. Heine and Lam [3] use a notion of pointer ownership to describe those variables responsible for freeing heap cells, and formulate the analysis as an ownership constraint system. In our previous work [4], we used a shape analysis with local reasoning about single heap cells to detect memory leaks and accesses through dangling pointers. Xie and Aiken [5] reduce the problem of memory leak detection to a Boolean satisfiability problem, and then use a SAT-solver to identify potential errors. Their analysis is path- and context-sensitive, but uses unsound techniques to handle recursion and loops. Dor et al. [1] use TVLA, a shape analysis tool based on 3-valued logic, to prove the absence of memory leaks and other memory errors in several list manipulation programs. Their analysis verifies these programs successfully, but is intra-procedural and cannot be applied to recursive and multi-procedure programs. Of these analyses, [3,4] target referencing leaks; and [1,5] target reachability leaks. We are not aware of analyses that can detect liveness memory leaks. Compared to our work, the above approaches cannot answer memory leak queries in a demand-driven fashion; and cannot reason about the absence of errors for incomplete programs.

Shape analyses [18,7,4] have been proposed with the goal of being able to distinguish, for instance, between cyclic and acyclic heap structures. These are all forward, exhaustive analyses. In contrast, the heap analysis in this paper is a reverse, demand-driven heap analysis.

The leak detection analysis in this paper uses an abstraction similar to the one that we developed in our previous work on shape analysis [4], where the algorithm analyzes a single heap cell at a time. This is a good match to memory leak detection by contradiction, because the analysis needs to reason about one single cell, the error cell. There two main differences between these analyses. First, the leak analysis in this paper is not aimed at computing shapes or precise reference counts. Therefore, the analysis uses a simpler abstraction (without reference counts), and doesn't require bifurcation. Second, the analysis is backwards. Analyzing the state of a heap cell in the reverse direction is non-trivial and less intuitive than the forward analysis.

Finally, dynamic memory leak detector tools such as Purify [19] or SWAT [20] instrument the program and only errors at run-time. Dynamic tools will miss errors that do not happen in that run; in particular, they will miss errors that only occur in rarely executed code fragments.

7   Conclusions

We have presented a new approach to memory leak detection where errors are disproved by contradicting their presence. To determine whether a memory leak can occur at a program point, the analysis uses a reverse inter-procedural flow analysis to disprove its negation. We have used this approach to analyze a set of complex list manipulation routines in isolation. We have also used this approach in an error-detection tool and found several memory leaks in the SPEC benchmarks.

References

1. Dor, N., Rodeh, M., Sagiv, M.: Checking cleanness in linked lists. In: Proceedings of the 8th International Static Analysis Symposium, Santa Barbara, CA (2000)
2. Shaham, R., Kolodner, E.K., Sagiv, M.: Automatic removal of array memory leaks in java. In: Proceedings of the 2000 International Conference on Compiler Construction, Berlin, Germany (2000)
3. Heine, D., Lam, M.: A practical flow-sensitive and context-sensitive C and C++ memory leak detector. In: Proceedings of the SIGPLAN '03 Conference on Program Language Design and Implementation, San Diego, CA (2003)
4. Hackett, B., Rugina, R.: Shape analysis with tracked locations. In: Proceedings of the 32th Annual ACM Symposium on the Principles of Programming Languages, Long Beach, CA (2005)
5. Xie, Y., Aiken, A.: Context- and path-sensitive memory leak detection. In: ACM SIGSOFT Symposium on the Foundations of Software Engineering, Lisbon, Portugal (2005)
6. Heine, D., Lam, M.: A practical flow-sensitive and context-sensitive C and C++ memory leak detector. In: Proceedings of PLDI, San Diego, CA (2003)
7. Sagiv, M., Reps, T., Wilhelm, R.: Parametric shape analysis via 3-valued logic. ACM Transactions on Programming Languages and Systems **24**(3) (2002)
8. Steensgaard, B.: Points-to analysis in almost linear time. In: Proceedings of the 23rd Annual ACM Symposium on the Principles of Programming Languages, St. Petersburg Beach, FL (1996)
9. Andersen, L.O.: Program Analysis and Specialization for the C Programming Language. PhD thesis, DIKU, University of Copenhagen (1994)
10. Sharir, M., Pnueli, A.: Two approaches to interprocedural data flow analysis. In Muchnick, S., Jones, N., eds.: Program Flow Analysis: Theory and Applications. Prentice Hall Inc (1981)
11. Orlovich, M., Rugina, R.: Memory leak analysis by contradiction. Technical report, Cornell University (2006)
12. Rinetzky, N., Sagiv, M.: Interprocedural shape analysis for recursive programs. In: Proceedings of the 2001 International Conference on Compiler Construction, Genova, Italy (2001)
13. Manevich, R., Sridharan, M., Adams, S., Das, M., Yang, Z.: PSE: Explaining program failures via postmortem static analysis. In: Proceedings of the ACM SIGSOFT '99 Symposium on the Foundations of Software Engineering, Newport Beach, CA (2002)
14. Strom, R., Yellin, D.: Extending typestate checking using conditional liveness analysis. IEEE Transactions on Software Engineering **19**(5) (1993) 478–485

15. Duesterwald, E., Gupta, R., Soffa, M.: Demand-driven computation of interprocedural data flow. In: Proceedings of the 22nd Annual ACM Symposium on the Principles of Programming Languages, San Francisco, CA (1995)
16. Horwitz, S., Reps, T., Sagiv, M.: Demand interprocedural dataflow analysis. In: Proceedings of the ACM Symposium on the Foundations of Software Engineering, Washington, DC (1995)
17. Sagiv, S., Reps, T., Horwitz, S.: Precise interprocedural dataflow analysis with applications to constant propagation. Theoretical Computer Science **167**(1&2) (1996) 131–170
18. Ghiya, R., Hendren, L.: Is is a tree, a DAG or a cyclic graph? a shape analysis for heap-directed pointers in C. In: Proceedings of the 23rd Annual ACM Symposium on the Principles of Programming Languages, St. Petersburg Beach, FL (1996)
19. Hastings, R., Joyce, B.: Purify: Fast detection of memory leaks and access errors. In: Proceedings of the 1992 Winter Usenix Conference. (1992)
20. Hauswirth, M., Chilimbi, T.: Low-overhead memory leak detection using adaptive statistical profiling. In: Proceedings of the 11th International Conference on Architectural Support for Programming Languages and Operating Systems, Boston, MA (2004)

A   Language Semantics

The language semantics are defined using the following domains:

$$
\begin{array}{ll}
\text{Numeric constants} \;\; n \in \mathbb{Z} & \text{Locations} \;\; l \in L = A + (C \times F) \\
\text{Symbolic addresses} \;\; a \in A & \text{Values} \;\;\; v \in V = \mathbb{Z} + L \\
\text{Heap cell addresses} \;\; c \in C & \text{Stores} \;\;\; \sigma \in \Sigma = L \to V \\
\text{Structure fields} \;\;\; f \in F &
\end{array}
$$

The following rules define the evaluation of expressions and statements:

$$
\cfrac{}{(n,\sigma) \to n} \quad \cfrac{}{(a,\sigma) \to a} \quad \cfrac{(e,\sigma) \to l \;\; l \in dom(\sigma)}{(*e,\sigma) \to \sigma(l)} \quad \cfrac{(e,\sigma) \to (c,f_1) \;\; c \in C}{(e.f,\sigma) \to (c,f)} \quad \cfrac{(e_0,\sigma) \to v_0 \;\; (e_1,\sigma) \to v_1 \;\; v_0, v_1 \in \mathbb{Z} \;\; v = v_0 \oplus v_1}{(e_0 \oplus e_1,\sigma) \to v}
$$

$$
\cfrac{(e_0,\sigma) \to l \;\; (e_1,\sigma) \to v \;\; l \in dom(\sigma)}{(*e_0 \leftarrow e_1,\sigma) \to \sigma[l \mapsto v]} \qquad \cfrac{(e_0,\sigma) \to v_0 \;\; (e_1,\sigma) \to v_1 \;\; v_0 \equiv v_1}{(\mathtt{cond}(e_0 \equiv e_1),\sigma) \to \sigma}
$$

$$
\cfrac{(e_0,\sigma) \to l \;\; l \in dom(\sigma) \;\; c\,fresh \;\; \sigma' = \sigma[l \mapsto (c,f_1)] \cup \{(c,f) \mapsto 0\}_{f \in F}}{(*e_0 \leftarrow \mathtt{malloc},\sigma) \to \sigma'} \qquad \cfrac{(e,\sigma) \to (c,f_1) \;\; (c,f_1) \in dom(\sigma) \;\; \sigma' = \sigma - \{(c,f) \mapsto \text{-}\}_{f \in F}}{(\mathtt{free}(e),\sigma) \to \sigma'}
$$

B   Demand-Driven Inter-procedural Analysis Algorithm

Figure 8 shows the entire inter-procedural demand-driven dataflow analysis-by-contradiction algorithm. Each procedure in the program is represented using a control-flow graph whose nodes $n \in N$ are program statements. For each CFG node n, $pred(n)$ represents the predecessors of n in the graph. Node n_e^p is the entry node of procedure p, and node n_x^p is the exit (i.e., return) node. Given a dataflow fact d_0 that describes the error cell and a control-flow graph node n_0, the algorithm returns "Success" if it can determine that a leak cannot occur at point n_0; otherwise, it returns "Potential Leak".

LEAKANALYSISBYCONTRADICTION($d_0 \in D, n_0 \in N$)
1   **for** each $n \in N, c \in C, i \in D_i$
2        $R(n)(c)(i) \leftarrow \bot$
3   **for** each $p \in P$
4        $S(p)(none) \leftarrow Callsites(p) \times \{none\}$
5
6    $W \leftarrow \varnothing$
7   INSERT($d_0, none, n_0$)
8
9   **while** $W \neq \varnothing$
10   remove (n, c, i) from W
11       $s \leftarrow R(n)(c)(i)$
12   **switch** n
13   **case** *call* p :
14          $c' \leftarrow i$
15   INSERT($Map(\{\,(i,s)\,\}, n), c', n_x^p$)
16          $S(p)(c') \leftarrow S(p)(c') \cup \{\,(n,c)\,\}$
17   **if** ($R(n_e^p)(c') \neq \bot$)
18   **then for** each $n' \in pred(n)$
19   INSERT($Unmap(R(n_e^p)(c'), n), c, n'$)
20
21   **case** n_e^p :
22   **if** ($Callsites(p) = \varnothing$)
23   **then return** "Potential Leak"
24   **for** each $(n', c') \in S(p)(c)$
25   **for** each $n'' \in pred(n')$
26   INSERT($Unmap(\{\,(i,s)\,\}, n'), c', n''$)
27
28   **case default** :
29          $d \leftarrow [\![n]\!]^{\bullet}(i, s)$
30   **if** ($d = \top$)
31   **then return** "Potential Leak"
32   **for** each $n' \in pred(n)$
33   INSERT(d, c, n')
34
35   **return** "Success" (NoLeak)

INSERT($d \in D, c \in C, n \in N$)
36   **for** each $i \in D_i$
37       $R(n)(c)(i) \leftarrow R(n)(c)(i) \sqcup d(i)$
38   **if** $R(n)(c)(i)$ has changed
39   **then** $W \leftarrow W \cup \{\,(n,c,i)\,\}$

Fig. 8. Inter-Procedural Demand Analysis by Contradiction

Separable Abstractions. The algorithm is formulated to work with *separable dataflow abstractions*. A separable abstraction is a map $D = D_i \rightarrow D_s$, where D_i is a finite set called the *index domain*, and $(D_s, \sqcup, \sqsubseteq, \bot, \top)$ is a lattice called the *secondary domain*.

Dataflow facts $d \in D_i \rightarrow D_s$ are represented using association lists, and compo-nents with bottom secondary values are omitted. For instance, $d = \{(i, s)\}$ stands for $\lambda i'$. if $(i' = i)$ then s else $\perp$. The ordering over D is the pointwise ordering of func-tions. For a lattice element $d \in D$, each pair $(i, d(i))$ is called a *component* of the ab-straction d. Transfer functions are expressed component-wise: $[\![n]\!]^{\bullet} : (D_i \times D_s) \rightarrow D$. A standard (non-separable) dataflow abstraction is represented as a separable abstrac-tion with one single component. The basic leak analysis uses a non-separable abstrac-tion; and one of the extensions in Section 4.8 uses a separable abstraction to avoid merging dataflow facts and improve the analysis precision.

Worklist Algorithm. The analysis uses a worklist algorithm. Each worklist element is a single component (not an entire abstraction) and each procedure context c is an index from D_i. There is an additional context *none*, explained below. The set $C = D_i \cup \{none\}$ denotes all possible contexts. The backward propagation stores dataflow facts in the result function $R : N \rightarrow C \rightarrow D$. For a node n and a context c, the value of $R(n)(c) \in D$ is the dataflow fact computed *after* node n in a context c of the enclosing procedure.

The analysis uses reverse summaries for procedures. The procedure summary for a context c maps a single component with index $i = c$ at procedure exit to a corresponding dataflow fact d at procedure entry. Dataflow facts whose birth-points occur inside of a function are given the special context *none*. Procedure summaries are not stored in a separate data structure; instead, they are implicitly captured in R: the summary or procedure p for a context c is $R(n_e^p)(c)$.

When the analysis reaches a procedure entry point, it propagates the information to all of the callers that have requested a result for the current context c. For this, the algo-rithm uses a *call-site map* $S : P \rightarrow C \rightarrow (N \times C)$. When the analysis of a component reaches the entry of p with context c, it propagates the component to the points indi-cated by $S(p)(c)$. This contains pairs (n', c') of target points and target contexts at those points. The call site map is set up every time a procedure call is encountered (line 16), and used when reaching procedure entries (line 23). For facts with context *none* (born inside procedures), S contains all possible call sites, as indicated by the initialization at lines 6-7.

The analysis uses two functions, *Map* and *Unmap*, to account for the necessary changes in the analysis information when crossing procedure boundaries. Function *Map* is used when moving from the caller into the callee space; function *Unmap* is used for moving back into the caller space. *Map* and *Unmap* each take two arguments: the dataflow fact d to process, and the call-site n where the mapping or unmapping takes place.

Path-Sensitive Dataflow Analysis with Iterative Refinement

Dinakar Dhurjati[1], Manuvir Das[2], and Yue Yang[2]

[1] University of Illinois at Urbana Champaign
{dhurjati@cs.uiuc.edu}
[2] Center for Software Excellence, Microsoft Corporation
{manuvir, jasony@microsoft.com}

Abstract. In this paper, we present a new method for supporting abstraction refinement in path-sensitive dataflow analysis. We show how an adjustable merge criterion can be used as an interface to control the degree of abstraction. In particular, we partition the merge criterion with two sets of predicates — one related to the dataflow facts being propagated and the other related to path feasibility. These tracked predicates are then used to guide merge operations and path feasibility analysis, so that expensive computations are performed only at the right places. Refinement amounts to lazily growing the path predicate set to recover lost precision. We have implemented our refinement technique in ESP, a software validation tool for C/C++ programs. We apply ESP to validate a future version of Windows against critical security properties. Our experience suggests that applying iterative refinement to path-sensitive dataflow analysis is both effective in cutting down spurious errors and scalable enough for solving real world problems.

1 Introduction

In recent years, model checking and dataflow analysis have emerged as competing approaches for compile-time defect detection. Many model checking tools [1,2,3,4,5,6] have enjoyed the benefit of abstraction refinement. The process starts with a coarse (simple) abstract model. Once the model is checked, the feasibility of the resulting abstract counterexample is examined. If feasible, the result reveals a real error; otherwise, the result is a false positive. In the latter case, the abstraction is refined and fed back to the model checker for successive checking.

Although abstraction refinement has proven effective in model checking, similar techniques have not been widely adopted in dataflow analysis [7,8,9,10]. The main difficulties involved in supporting abstraction refinement in dataflow analysis are: (1) How do we control the abstraction? Model checking has an a priori abstract model, which naturally represents the abstraction; in dataflow analysis, the abstraction is computed directly from a source program as dataflow facts by obtaining the least fixed point solution to a set of transfer functions. (2) How do we identify false positives? The abstract counterexample produced by a model checker is a single path. Therefore, the model checking refinement process can

K. Yi (Ed.): SAS 2006, LNCS 4134, pp. 425–442, 2006.

prove its feasibility using theorem proving. In contrast, the abstract trace generated by dataflow analysis is a summary of up to exponentially many (or even infinitely many) execution paths in the original program — rigorously proving its feasibility is very difficult.

In this paper, we address these difficulties. Our first insight is that the merge criterion in dataflow analysis plays a key role in determining path-sensitivity. By extending the *fixed* merge criterion to an *adjustable* one, abstractions can be tuned in response to the characteristics of the paths being analyzed. Our second insight is that in the absence of a single counterexample, the refinement process can be effective if spurious error traces, and the missing predicates that lead to these traces, can be identified heuristically. By combining an adjustable merge criterion with efficient heuristics for finding where precision is lost, the analysis can adaptively adjust its precision in a demand-driven fashion. We apply these refinement techniques to ESP [10,11], a validation tool for large C/C++ programs, with promising results.

Loss of precision in dataflow analysis mainly arises in two situations: (1) when states along different paths are merged at merge points and (2) when dataflow facts are propagated across infeasible paths. Consider ESP as an example, its path-sensitive dataflow analysis incorporates two mechanisms to preserve the precision of path-sensitive analysis: an effective merge algorithm based on *property simulation* [10] and a path feasibility analyzer called SSM (Symbolic State Manager) [12]. However, these mechanisms are "static", in the sense that they are based on a fixed set of rules. Although ESP can preserve precision in common cases, sometimes it is still overly conservative — the merge may be too aggressive or the tracking on simulation states may be too imprecise. As a fixed-precision analysis, ESP is not able to recover precision loss should it arise. The iterative refinement technique described in this paper removes this limitation.

Example. To illustrate how a false positive may be introduced in static analysis, consider the example in Figure 1. The finite state machine in Figure 1(a) encodes a property adapted from the requirement on Windows kernel objects. We intend to validate that a program should not call `UseHandle` on an object that has been previously closed by `CloseHandle`. Figure 1(b) shows a function that processes a handle according to various status values. Albeit simple, this code snippet reflects a common coding practice: Programmers often use internal flags (such as $flag1$ and $flag2$ in this example) to record programming states and later use them to guide control flow. If an analysis does not track enough branch correlations, it may report a violation to the property protocol at L4. In contrast, a more precise analysis reveals that no valid error path can lead to this point because of the guard on $flag1$ at L3. Hence, the warning is a false positive.   □

Contributions. A practical analysis tool is aimed at supporting industrial programs with complex language features. Therefore, it must satisfy several challenging (and sometimes conflicting) goals at once: (1) it should scale to large programs, (2) it should offer enough precision, and (3) it should produce use-

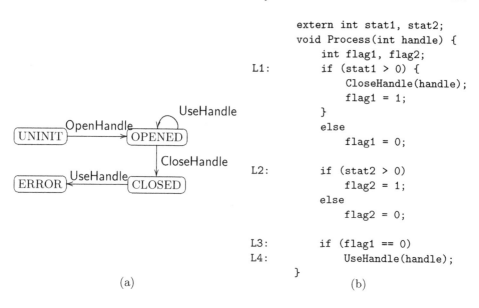

```
                            extern int stat1, stat2;
                            void Process(int handle) {
                              int flag1, flag2;
                        L1:    if (stat1 > 0) {
                                 CloseHandle(handle);
                                 flag1 = 1;
                               }
                               else
                                 flag1 = 0;

                        L2:    if (stat2 > 0)
                                 flag2 = 1;
                               else
                                 flag2 = 0;

                        L3:    if (flag1 == 0)
                        L4:      UseHandle(handle);
                               }
```

(a)   (b)

Fig. 1. Usage of Windows kernel objects. Figure (a) shows the finite state machine of the typestate property. Figure (b) shows a simplified code pattern adapted from the Windows kernel.

ful feedback to help programmers investigate bugs. This paper addresses these tradeoffs and integrates practical techniques to produce useful results. Our contributions can be summarized as follows.

- We show how the merge criterion in dataflow analysis can be extended to support *adaptable abstractions*. In particular, we apply two predicate sets to control precision: one is a fixed set consisting of predicates related to the property of interest, and the other is an adjustable set consisting of predicates related to path feasibility (these predicates are referred to as *path predicates*).
- We apply the following heuristic to quickly recognize potential false positives: Along with an error trace, there often exists a corresponding *good trace* (a path leading to a valid property state) that ends at the same program point. If these "good state" and "error state" co-exist, it is likely that the error state is reached because useful predicates present in the good state have been inadvertently dropped from the error state during the analysis. Therefore, addition of these distinguishing predicates to the tracked path predicate set will help eliminate spurious errors.
- We implement the refinement techniques in ESP. We show experimental evidence that iterative refinement is effective in filtering out false positives and is scalable enough to be applied to large-scale programs.

The remainder of the paper is organized as follows. In Section 2, we review the techniques applied in ESP. In Section 3, we describe our iterative refinement

approach. In Section 4, we discuss experimental results. In Section 5, we review
related work. We conclude in Section 6.

2   Background

ESP checks program properties related to *typestates* [13]: For a value created during program execution, its ordinary type is invariant but its typestate may be
updated by certain operations. ESP allows a user to write a custom specification
encoded in a finite state machine, as illustrated in Figure 1(a), to describe typestate transitions. According to the specification, ESP instruments the source
program with the state-changing events. It then employs an inter-procedural
dataflow analysis algorithm, based on *function summaries* [8], to compute the
typestate behavior at every program point. To obtain path-sensitivity, ESP uses
the combination of property simulation [10] and path simulation [12].

2.1   Property Simulation

In ESP, a symbolic state is divided into the *property state* (typestate according to
the specified protocol) and the *simulation state* (state related to path feasibility).
The property simulation algorithm defines a merge heuristic centered around
the property of interest: At a merge point, if two symbolic states have the same
property state, ESP merges the simulation states. Otherwise, ESP explores the
two paths independently as in a full path-sensitive analysis.

The simulation state is an element in a lattice whose elements are abstractions
of heap and store. Let D be the domain of property states and S be the domain
of simulation states. Given a symbolic state $s \in S$, we denote its property state
by $ps(s)$ and its simulation state by $ss(s)$. The merge criterion for s is characterized by the following grouping function:

$$\alpha_{ps}(s) = \{[\{d\}, \sqcup_{s' \in s[d]} ss(s')] \mid d \in D \wedge s[d] \neq \phi\}$$

where $s[d] = \{s' | s' \in S \ \wedge \ d = ps(s')\}$ and $\sqcup$ is the
least upper bound in the simulation state lattice.

Example. To see the different effects caused by various merge policies, consider
Figure 1(b). Assume that the property state is OPENED when function Process
is entered. A full path-sensitive analysis tracks all paths reaching program point
L3, resulting in four symbolic states at L3:

$[\{\texttt{CLOSED}\}, \{stat1 > 0, flag1 = 1, stat2 > 0, flag2 = 1\}]$
$[\{\texttt{CLOSED}\}, \{stat1 > 0, flag1 = 1, stat2 <= 0, flag2 = 0\}]$
$[\{\texttt{OPENED}\}, \{stat1 <= 0, flag1 = 0, stat2 > 0, flag2 = 1\}]$
$[\{\texttt{OPENED}\}, \{stat1 <= 0, flag1 = 0, stat2 <= 0, flag2 = 0\}]$

ESP, on the other hand, drops the correlation between variables stat2 and flag2
because the branch at L2 does not affect the property state. As a result, only

two symbolic states are kept at L3:

$$[\{\texttt{CLOSED}\}, \{stat1 > 0, flag1 = 1\}]$$
$$[\{\texttt{OPENED}\}, \{stat1 <= 0, flag1 = 0\}]$$

Since the dropped facts are irrelevant to the property of interest, ESP still maintains enough information to conclude that L4 is not reachable if the property state is CLOSED.   □

Property simulation matches the coding practice of a careful programmer: The correlation between a given property state and the program state is usually guarded in the code by branch conditions. ESP makes such implicit correlation explicit. The adjustable merge criterion developed in this paper builds upon this insight by taking additional path predicates into account as well.

2.2   Path Simulation

The symbolic path simulator, referred to as *Simulation State Manager* (SSM) in this paper, manages simulation states and acts as a theorem prover to answer queries about path feasibility. A simulation state mainly consists of two sets of information: (1) the symbolic store (mapping from locations to values) and (2) a set of constraints (or path predicates) imposed on values. These path predicates are implicitly conjuncted. To reason about facts related to path feasibility, SSM applies a decision procedure based on a set of inference rules. The path simulator performs a set of transfer functions on behalf of ESP for instructions such as assignments, branches, procedure calls (into-binding), call returns (back-binding), and merges. These transfer functions update simulation states accordingly and filter out infeasible paths.

Path feasibility analysis is undecidable in general. To guarantee convergence and efficiency, the Simulation State Manager makes conservative assumptions when necessary. While such over approximation is sound (*i.e.*, it will not miss errors), it may introduce imprecision. The refinement technique in this paper allows the analysis to start with a light-weight decision procedure and fine-tune it based on counterexamples.

2.3   Imprecision Due to Property Simulation

Although the ESP merge heuristic is precise in most cases, sometimes it can be too conservative.

Example. In Figure 2(a). The branch at L1 does not change the property state. Therefore, ESP merges the simulation states at L2 and loses the correlation between stat and flag. As a result, a false positive is reported at L4.   □

Our refinement technique would pick up an additional path predicate, say stat > 0, and add it to the merge criterion. This would direct the analysis to track the

```
        extern int stat;                      extern int stat;
        void Process(int handle) {            void Process(int handle) {
            int flag = 0;                         int flag = 0;
L1:         if (stat > 0)                         if ((stat & 0x81) != 0)
                flag = 1;                             return;
            else
                flag = 2;                         CloseHandle(handle);
                                          L1:     flag = stat & 0x1;
L2:         if (stat > 0)
                CloseHandle();            L2:     if (flag != 0) {
                                          L3:         UseHandle(handle);
L3:         if (flag != 1)                        }
L4:             UseHandle();              }
        }
                    (a)                                   (b)
```

Fig. 2. Examples that illustrate the need of refinement. Figure (a) shows a false positive caused by the ESP merge heuristic. Figure (b) shows a false positive caused by the path feasibility analysis.

branch at L1 accurately since the branch arms impose different facts about the predicate. With this additional precision, the analysis can rule out the false error.

Even when an error reported by ESP is a real error, it may still be beneficial to apply refinement to "concretize" the abstract counterexample, *i.e.*, to expand the merged paths at certain branch points so that the trace can be more explicit and meaningful for inspection purposes.

2.4   Imprecision Due to Path Simulation

The Simulation State Manager uses a set of inference rules to implement the underlying decision procedure. By default, it supports a subset of congruence closure and uninterpreted functions. While it is possible to apply a heavy-weight theorem prover that combines many theories, it would significantly hinder the scalability of our analysis. Therefore, when the complexity of certain branch correlations get too complicated, the correlations would be dropped due to the lack of reasoning power in the theorem prover.

Example. In Figure 2(b), the fact $(stat \& 0x81) = 0$ should hold at L1 because the function would have returned otherwise. This fact should imply $flag = 0$ at L2. However, if the theorem prover does not employ inference rules to track bit-wise operations, it might not be able to deduce such information — this would result in a false positive at L3.   □

The above example reflects a coding pattern where operations are controlled by certain bits in a flag. While tracking this is critical for certain code bases and properties, it is not important in general. Therefore, it is beneficial to start an analysis with a light-weight theorem prover and only add precision as needed.

3   Refining Dataflow Analysis

There are three key steps in the dataflow refinement process: (1) identifying "suspicious" error traces that need refinement, (2) selecting a minimal set of dropped branch correlations that may contribute to the precision loss and adding them to the merge criterion, and (3) enforcing the extended merge criterion in the subsequent iteration.

3.1   Identifying False Positives

As previously mentioned, generating one concrete counterexample out of an abstract ESP counterexample may not be scalable. The novelty of our approach is that instead of trying to ascertain that an error trace reported by ESP is a false positive before starting the refinement process, we develop an inexpensive heuristic that can identify false positives with high probability.

Definition. *Corresponding Good State* — Given a candidate error state E, its corresponding good state is defined as a symbolic state G at the same program point as E, such that the property state of G is not ERROR.   □

Heuristic 1. Given a candidate error state E, if there exists a corresponding good state E', E is subject to refinement; otherwise, E is not subject to refinement.   □

Example. At program point L4 in Figure 2(a), the error is indicated by state [CLOSED, $\{stat > 0, flag \neq 1\}$]. There also exists a good state, [OPENED, $\{stat <= 0, flag \neq 1\}$], which correctly keeps track of the correlations. According to heuristic 1, the error at L4 is subject to refinement.   □

This heuristic is based on the following intuition: If at a program point, there only exists an error trace without any good traces, there is no evidence that the program can behave correctly. Hence, the error is likely to be real.

We now formally examine heuristic 1 using a case analysis. For a given candidate error state, there may or may not exist a corresponding good state at the same program point. Among the four possible combinations (as listed below), heuristic 1 directly supports category (1) and (4). For category (2) and (3), while the heuristic cannot properly distinguish whether the error is a false positive, the refinement policy imposed by the heuristic can still be beneficial. This explains why our inexpensive heuristic can be surprisingly effective in practice.

Category 1 [False error, With good state]. Heuristic 1 directly targets this category. A false positive in this group would be properly identified.

Category 2 [Real error, With good state]. These error states would also be profiled as plausible errors needing refinement. Although these errors are not false positives, selecting them for refinement can indeed be helpful for inspection purposes because expanding the abstract trace will make the error message more explicit and meaningful.

Category 3 [False error, Without good state]. It may appear that our heuristic is not suitable for this category because these false errors would not be subject to refinement. This, however, is not a deficiency of the heuristic. This is because ESP is conservative — it reports all (and potentially more) paths that can reach a program point. Therefore, if the error path is infeasible and there is no corresponding good path, it means that there is no feasible path at all that can reach this program point, *i.e.*, the "false error" is part of "dead code". From a software engineering point of view, it may be desirable to reveal these as real errors.

Category 4 [Real error, Without good state]. Heuristic 1 is correct in not identifying these real errors as false positives.

3.2 Selecting New Predicates

After a potential false positive is identified, we need to determine what are the additional predicates that are most likely to improve the precision. One approach is to collect all the path predicates accumulated in the error state. However, most of these predicates are irrelevant and will result in unnecessary overhead in the subsequent analysis. To pinpoint exactly where precision is lost, we develop heuristic 2 based on the insight from heuristic 1 to gather only the relevant predicates in common scenarios.

Heuristic 2. We compare the simulation states between the candidate error state and its corresponding good state. The difference in path predicates suggests why the error path and the good path deviate. Therefore, we select these distinguishing predicates and add them to the merge criterion for the subsequent iteration. ☐

Example. In Figure 2(a), if we compare the predicates between the simulation state of the error state, [CLOSED, $\{stat > 0, flag \neq 1\}$], and the simulation state of the good state, [OPENED, $\{stat <= 0, flag \neq 1\}$], it is clear that $\{stat > 0\}$ is a distinguishing factor. It should therefore be added to the merge criterion. ☐

This method is efficient because it queries the state information that is already available as dataflow facts computed from the previous iteration; it is also effective because it allows path-sensitivity to be incrementally added at exactly the right place.

3.3 Adjusting the Merge Criterion

After additional path predicates are selected, they are added to the merge criterion. At merge points in the subsequent run, incoming states that differ with respect to these selected path predicates will be tracked independently. This section formally describes this process.

Let $P_1, P_2, ..., P_n$ be the set of predicates that need to be added to the merge criterion in any iteration. Let T be a set of tri-values $\{1, 0, *\}$, with the elements denoting **true**, **false** and **don't know**, respectively. To track the predicates $P_1, P_2, ..., P_n$ accurately in the new run, we change the property state component to $D \times T... \times T$ (or $D \times T^n$). For a symbolic state in the new run, $[\{d, t_1, t_2, ..., t_n\}, ss], t_i$ denotes whether predicate P_i is provable from the simulation state ss using a theorem prover. If $\vdash$ denotes provability, t_i can be defined as follows:

$$t_i = 1 \text{ if } ss \vdash P_i$$
$$= 0 \text{ if } ss \vdash \neg P_i$$
$$= * \text{ otherwise}$$

The merge criterion is extended with a tri-value vector denoting the status of each of the predicates that we have decided to track accurately. At merge points, the incoming symbolic states are compared. If there exists a t_i such that its value is different in the two incoming states, the paths are tracked separately; otherwise, the paths are merged. Formally, the grouping function for the merge criterion is modified as follows:

$$\alpha_{ps}(s) = \{[\{d\}, \sqcup_{s' \in s[d]} s(s')] | \ d \in D \times T^n \wedge s[d] \neq \phi \}$$

where $s[d] = \{s' | s' \in ss \wedge d = ps(s')\}$ and $\sqcup$ is the least upper bound in the execution state lattice.

The tri-values are set to $*$ in the initial state for a given run of the dataflow analysis. To obtain the next set of symbolic states after a program statement, we first invoke the same transfer functions as in the original ESP. For each predicate P_i, we then invoke the Simulation State Manager to prove P_i or $\neg P_i$. Depending on the provability, we assign a tri-value to the $(i + 1)^{th}$ location in the property state component. Once we have the new set of symbolic states we use the grouping function, just like in the original ESP algorithm, to merge the symbolic states whose new property states (the original property state and the predicate vector) are the same.

Example: In Figure 2(a), a subsequent run adds the predicate $\{stat > 0\}$ to the property state component. Let p denote the predicate $\{stat > 0\}$. The new ESP run at program point L2 would have two separate symbolic states $[\{\texttt{CLOSED}, p = 1\}, \{stat > 0, flag = 1\}]$ and $[\{\texttt{CLOSED}, p = 0\}, \{stat <= 0, flag = 2\}]$. Since the the property state components are no longer the same, the two symbolic states will be tracked independently. With this additional correlation, the new run will not produce an error state. $\qquad\Box$

New Automata of State-Changing Events. Changing the merge criterion as outlined above could be viewed as using an alternative property state ma-

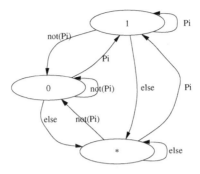

Fig. 3. A tri-value automaton for the ith predicate P_i. Values 1, 0, and * denote **true**, **false** and **don't know**, respectively.

chine for defining state-changing events. This new state machine is the product automaton of the original property automaton with n tri-value automata. The ith tri-value automaton is shown in Figure 3. The product property automaton has $|D| * 3^n$ states, where $|D|$ is the number of states in the original property automaton.

Complexity of the New Merge Algorithm. The original ESP algorithm is polynomial in $|D|$ [10]. The complexity of an ESP run with refined abstraction as described above is exponential in the number of predicates since the size of our new property automaton is exponential in the number of predicates. In practice, however, this is not an issue since only a few predicates matter at any point in the program and most states in the new property state automaton are never reached. Note that we also need to add the cost of $2 * n$ calls to the theorem prover in addition to the cost of the transfer function at each step in the ESP algorithm. We can optimize away most of these queries by using a simple value flow analysis [14] to "slice" the program.

3.4   A More Refined Abstraction Method

The tri-vectors succinctly encode a set of abstract states of the program. However, this is only an approximation (referred to as the *cartesian approximation* in SLAM [15]) to the most precise predicate abstraction. For example, suppose we have added a new predicate $x = 0$. If at the merge points the facts along the two paths are $x < 0$ and $x > 0$ respectively, sometimes it is desirable to keep the fact of $x \neq 0$ after the merge. However, with cartesian approximation, such information is lost.

To regain the precision lost in this situation, we have also implemented an alternative abstraction method based on *distinguishing variables*. Instead of using the tri-value of a predicate to control merging, we project the related variables from the predicate set. At merge points, any incoming states with different facts on the selected variables are tracked separately. In the above example, x would

```
procedure IterativeRefine(P, D)
begin
   for each f ∈ P
      E[f] = φ;
   while true do
      switch ESPRun(P, D, E)
      case SUCCESS:
         output "success"; break;
      case FAILURE(T): //T is a set of ESP error traces
         for each f ∈ P
            E'[f] = φ
         for each t ∈ T
            if (CheckSuspiciousTrace(t)) then
               E' = E' ∪ₚ RelevantPredicates(t)
            if (E' ⊆ E) then
               output T as error; break;
         E = E ∪ₚ E';
end
```

Fig. 4. The iterative refinement algorithm for checking if program P satisfies the property specified in automaton D

be picked out as a controlling factor for merge. Consequently, the incoming paths with $x < 0$ and $x > 0$ are not merged since they affect the value of x.

Essentially this approach enables a mechanism for lazily tracking disjunctions on predicates. Initially, the constraints carried in a simulation state are implicitly conjuncted since it is prohibitive for the Simulation State Manager to eagerly track every disjunction on merge due to the exponential cost. With the variable-based refinement technique, an application is allowed to, and can afford to, have a "deep" analysis when necessary, because it only focuses on a small number of selected variables. Instead of asking the Simulation State Manager to explicitly track the disjunctions, the merge mechanism is used to split the paths along which the disjunctions are tracked independently.

One caveat with this refined abstraction method is that the fixed point computation might not converge when the tracked variable is updated inside a loop. To guarantee termination we unroll such loops for a fixed number of iterations.

3.5   The Iterative Refinement Algorithm

Having discussed the key steps in the refinement process, we now present the iterative refinement algorithm for ESP.

Our analysis starts with the original ESP merge criterion and a set of simple inference rules for reasoning about path feasibility. It then repeats the following process: It first uses heuristic 1 to identify suspicious error traces. It then uses heuristic 2 to collect the missing path predicates. Based on these new predicates, it constructs a new precision policy by adding those selected predicates (or projected variables) to the merge criterion. Finally, it conducts a more thorough analysis along a focused set of paths. During the new iteration, whenever the tracked predicates are involved, paths will be kept separate at merge points and comprehensive inference rules in Simulation State Manager will be enabled in path simulation.

The iterative refinement algorithm for ESP is shown in Figure 4. Given a program P and a property state automaton D, procedure **IterativeRefine** tries to verify if P satisfies D by iteratively calling **ESPRun**. Procedure **ESPRun** takes P, D, and E as input, where E is a map between functions and sets of predicates: For a function f, $E[f]$ represents the predicates that should be tracked accurately when analyzing function f. **ESPRun** performs an analysis similar to the original ESP, except that it uses the new precision policy based on $E[f]$. If **ESPRun** returns success, *i.e.*, it reports no error traces, P satisfies the property specified in D. Otherwise, **ESPRun** returns a set of error traces T. We then apply heuristic 1 to identify suspicious error traces in procedure **CheckSuspiciousTrace**. If we find a suspicious error trace, we use heuristic 2 to generate a set of relevant predicates from the error trace in procedure **RelevantPredicates**. $\cup_p$ can be succinctly described using the following equation: for each f, $(E \cup_p E')[f] = E[f] \cup E'[f]$. Essentially it aggregates the predicates for each function. If there are no new predicates that need to be tracked accurately, we stop and report the remaining errors as real errors. Otherwise we do one more iteration by accurately tracking the predicates in $E \cup_p E'$.

3.6   Incremental Refinement

A more precise analysis applied in a later iteration will explore only a subset of the paths explored by the analysis in previous iterations. In particular, this means that a symbolic state that does not reach the error state in a previous iteration is guaranteed not to reach the error state in subsequent iterations.

We have implemented a form of this optimization in ESP, at all call sites. In a given iteration, we record all of the property states that lead to an error state. In the following iteration, we terminate the analysis for symbolic states at call sites whose property state did not lead to an error state in the previous iteration. This optimization allows us to avoid repeating part of the computation from previous iterations.

4   Results

With the integration of refinement techniques, ESP has been successfully deployed in validating several critical security properties for a future version of Windows. In this section, we summarize our general experience on root cause of false positives and use one of the properties as a case study.

4.1   General Experience

We have studied the root cause of false positives by manually inspecting the error traces from various experiments using the Windows code base. We categorized false positives in several groups: (1) those introduced by the imprecision of our analysis, (2) those introduced by the limitation of our specification method, and (3) those that are "real errors" according to the specification, but the violation to the protocol is by design, e.g., for performance reasons.

The distribution of these categories varies depending on properties being checked, but the first group is usually the most common case. Among this group, we have found that in most cases, the false positives are introduced by lacking reasoning power from the Simulation State Manager. This further confirmed that the ESP merge heuristic is usually precise enough.

The second group of false positives is due to "under specified" properties. This issue arises in practice when specifications are developed based on coarse documentations and program flags are used to track more state transitions than the transitions specified in the property automaton. When these flags are assigned with different values that appear to be "irrelevant" with respect to the specification, the correlations would be lost due to excessive merging. Our refinement method allows ESP to identify the additional branch correlations and track those accurately without requiring refinement of the specifications.

Traces in the third group are "benign". However, they are still worth a careful code review because other invariants are usually required to maintain program correctness.

4.2   Case Study

We have performed a case study by checking a security vulnerability. This vulnerability arises when a program acquires exclusive access to a system resource and then relinquishes the exclusive access by closing its handle but "leaks" the access to the resource through certain API. Checking this kind of property has been difficult with previous tools because it requires precise tracking of value flow in large programs[1].

Scalability: Using two PCs, each with a 3.06GHz Xeon CPU and 2GB of RAM, iterative refinement completed in 765 minutes for ASTs covering 5079 binaries (DLL, SYS, and EXE modules) in a future version of Windows. ESP discovered 83 traces, out of which 47 were confirmed as real bugs and fixed. Being able to perform such an analysis for the whole Windows code base clearly demonstrates the scalability of our approach.

Effectiveness of Heuristic: After those 83 traces were produced, we applied our heuristic again to further classify which of them are likely false positives. We partitioned the traces into two buckets. If at a program point, there only exists an error trace without any good traces, we put it into the high-confidence bucket. If the trace has a corresponding good path, we put it into the low-confidence bucket. The high-confidence bucket contains 38 real bugs and 2 spurious warnings, with a noise ratio of 5%. The low-confidence bucket, on the other hand, contains 9 real bugs and 34 spurious warnings, with a noise ratio of 79%. This

---

[1] We are unable to provide more details about violations of the property because some instances identified by ESP apply to previously shipped products as well.

ranking method allows us to quickly provide the high-confidence bucket to developers and focus on the low-confidence bucket to figure out where the tool needs to be improved. The final spurious traces are mostly due to complex code patterns that are too hard to track. Our existing Simulation State Manager is not powerful enough to handle these cases. Nonetheless, our heuristic has been shown to be highly effective. In our future work, we plan to power up the Simulation State Manager so that the remaining false positives can be further reduced with iterative refinement.

Precision improvement: We also conducted a comparison analysis between using and not using the refinement technique, which has shown that the refinement technique is effective in precision enhancement. As an example, we made two runs on an EXE binary with 11718 LOC and 388 functions, one with refinement and the other without refinement. When refinement is applied, ESP reports 1 real bug and no false positives in 6.9 seconds. When refinement is not used, ESP also reports 3 spurious errors along with the actual bug in 3.2 seconds.

To summarize, these experiments suggested that (1) it is feasible to integrate abstraction refinement to diagnose industrial-sized programs, (2) the heuristic for distinguishing potential false positives is effective, and (3) refinement can improve precision with a modest performance cost.

5   Related Work

The main contribution of this paper is an approach that integrates abstraction refinement, inter-procedural dataflow analysis, and counterexample-based heuristics in a novel way to provide a practical solution for improving software quality. Since our analysis draws on several insights from previous work, there are several categories of related work.

5.1   Path Feasibility Analysis

There is a long line of work on improving path feasibility in dataflow analysis. For example, qualified dataflow analysis [16] uses a given set of assertions on variable values to "qualify" paths under consideration. Bodik et al. [9] mark infeasible paths to improve the accuracy of def-use pair analysis. ESP [10,11], the basis of this paper, uses specification states to distinguish merge policy at merge points and relies on symbolic path simulation to enforce path feasibility. These works all use a pre-defined set of qualifications and do not address refinement issues.

5.2   Demand-Driven Analysis

Our approach is similar to demand-driven analysis [8,17] but addresses different issues. Their algorithms delay the computation of part of the analysis until it is needed; but the analysis is performed with *fixed* precision. Our analysis uses function summaries described in [8] for inter-procedural analysis. In addition, our algorithm delays adding precision to the analysis until it is dictated by evidence.

5.3   Iterative Refinement

Several dataflow algorithms [18,19,20,21] have applied refinement techniques for iteratively adjusting precision. While conceptually similar to our refinement process, these algorithms are domain-specific. For example, Guyer et al. [18] use client-driven refinement for pointer analysis and Plevyak et al. [19] use refinement for inferring concrete types in objet-oriented languages. Trace partitioning discussed in [20,21] focus on deciding which explicit disjunctions to keep during the analysis. In contrast to these analyses, our refinement technique targets more flexible typestate defect detection and can be applied to regain lost facts.

Fischer et al. [22] describe *predicated lattices*, a technique that is close in spirit to our refinement approach. Their framework partitions the program state according to a set of predicates and tracks a lattice element for each partition. Our abstraction mechanism based on the adjustable merge criterion could be viewed as a practical way of implementing predicated lattices. Their work focuses on a general framework and does not address how to pick additional predicates for refinement. In contrast, our particular interest is in combining effective partitioning of predicates with efficient heuristics to recognize important predicates.

5.4   Abstraction Refinement in Model Checking

Abstraction refinement has been an accepted technique in model checking tools, e.g., [1,2,3,4,6,23]. Our approach is different in how program abstraction is represented, selected, and enforced. (1) In model checking, the abstraction is defined by the state space of a given abstract model. In our analysis, the abstraction is done on the fly via selective merging. (2) Model checking techniques use theorem proving to map an abstract counterexample to a concrete program trace to identify false positives. While generating new predicates from the proof of unsatisfiability is more accurate and complete, it is also more expensive. We use an inexpensive but effective heuristic to identify suspicious counterexamples and then check the feasibility during the extra iteration of ESP analysis. (3) Model checking starts with a coarse abstraction and requires an expensive iteration process to reach the ideal abstraction. In contrast, ESP reports very few false positives to begin with. Hence, our seed abstraction is much closer to the desired one, which leads to faster convergence. Studies in [22,24] also show that it is beneficial to use ESP to provide a starting abstraction for the refinement process.

5.5   Counterexample-Based Heuristics

Counterexample-based heuristics are developed in [25,26]. Our heuristic for finding missing predicates is inspired by these works. The main difference is that these works focus on explaining root causes of real errors — they try to pinpoint deviating path segments between error paths and good paths. In contrast, we use the existence of corresponding good traces to quickly identify potential false positives and useful predicates.

5.6   Precise Symbolic Simulation

Several static tools, such as PREfix [27], CMC [28], and Saturn [29], provide precise symbolic simulation but limit exploration of program paths. We offer a complementary approach: instead of truncating the search space, our analysis considers all paths but guides the exploration effort to where it is most productive.

6   Conclusions

A static tool must walk the fine line between precision and scalability. In this paper, we have presented a new approach that allows the dataflow abstraction to be refined incrementally in response to the characteristics of the paths being analyzed. We have used the refinement technique to help validate a future version of the Windows operating system against important security properties. Our experience suggests that the heuristic for finding false positives is highly effective and the refinement method is scalable enough to be of practical use.

Acknowledgments. We thank Stephen Adams, Zhe Yang, Vikram Dhaneshwar, and Hari Hampapuram from the Center for Software Excellence at Microsoft for their infrastructure support and insightful suggestions. Stephen Adams also conducted some experiments. We are also grateful to Tom Ball from Microsoft Research for many valuable discussions.

References

1. Thomas Ball and Sriram Rajamani. The SLAM project: Debugging system software via static analysis. In *Proceedings of the ACM Symposium on Principles of Programming Languages (POPL)*, 2002.
2. Thomas Ball and Sriram K. Rajamani. Automatically validating temporal safety properties of interfaces. In *Proceedings of the 8th international SPIN workshop on Model checking of software*, pages 103–122, New York, NY, USA, 2001. Springer-Verlag New York, Inc.
3. Thomas Henzinger, Ranjit Jhala, Rupak Majumdar, and Gregoire Sutre. Lazy abstraction. In *ACM SIGPLAN 2002 Conference on Programming Language Design and Implementation*, 2002.
4. T. Henzinger, R. Jhala, R. Majumdar, and K. McMillan. Abstractions from proofs. In *Proceedings of the ACM Symposium on Principles of Programming Languages (POPL)*, 2004.
5. Cormac Flanagan. Automatic software model checking using CLP. In *ESOP*, pages 189–203, 2003.
6. Edmund M. Clarke, Orna Grumberg, Somesh Jha, Yuan Lu, and Helmut Veith. Counterexample-guided abstraction refinement for symbolic model checking. *J. ACM*, 50(5):752–794, 2003.
7. P. Cousot and R. Cousot. Abstract interpretation: A unified lattice model for static analysis of programs by construction or approximation of fixpoints. In *Proceedings of the ACM Symposium on Principles of Programming Languages (POPL)*, 1977.

8. Thomas Reps, Susan Horwitz, and Mooly Sagiv. Precise interprocedural data flow analysis via graph reachability. In *Proceedings of the ACM Symposium on Principles of Programming Languages (POPL)*, 1995.

9. Rastislav Bodik, Rajiv Gupta, and Mary Lou Soffa. Refining data flow information using infeasible paths. In *Proceedings of the Sixth European Software Engineering Conference*, 1997.

10. Manuvir Das, Sorin Lerner, and Mark Seigle. ESP: Path-sensitive program verification in polynomial time. In *ACM SIGPLAN 2002 Conference on Programming Language Design and Implementation (PLDI)*, 2002.

11. Nurit Dor, Stephen Adams, Manuvir Das, and Zhe Yang. Software validation via scalable path-sensitive value flow analysis. In *Proceedings of the International Symposium on Software Testing and Analysis (ISSTA)*, 2004.

12. Hari Hampapuram, Yue Yang, and Manuvir Das. Symbolic path simulatin in path-sensitive datflow analysis. In *Proceedings of the 6th ACM SIGPLAN-SIGSOFT Workshop on Program Analysis for Software Tools and Engineering (PASTE)*, 2005.

13. R. Strom and S. Yemini. Typestate: A programming language concept for enhancing software reliability. *IEEE Transactions on Software Engineering*, 12(1):157–171, 1986.

14. Manuvir Das. Unification-based pointer analysis with directional assignments. In *ACM SIGPLAN 2000 Conference on Programming Language Design and Implementation (PLDI)*, 2000.

15. Thomas Ball, Andreas Podelski, and Sriram K. Rajamani. Boolean and Cartesian abstraction for model checking C programs. *Lecture Notes in Computer Science*, 2031, 2001.

16. L. Howard Holley and Barry K. Rosen. Qualified data flow problems. In *Proceedings of the ACM Symposium on Principles of Programming Languages (POPL)*, 1980.

17. Nevin Heintze and Olivier Tardieu. Demand-driven pointer analysis. In *ACM SIGPLAN 2001 Conference on Programming Language Design and Implementation (PLDI)*, 2001.

18. Samuel Z. Guyer and Calvin Lin. Client-driven pointer analysis. In *Proceedings of the International Symposium on Static Analysis (SAS)*, 2003.

19. John Plevyak and Andrew A. Chien. Precise concrete type inference for object-oriented languages. In *Proceedings of the Ninth Conference on Object-Oriented Programming Systems, Languages, and Applications (OOPSLA)*, 1994.

20. Laurent Mauborgne and Xavier Rival. Trace partitioning in abstract interpretation based static analyzers. In M. Sagiv, editor, *European Symposium on Programming (ESOP)*, volume 3444 of *Lecture Notes in Computer Science*, pages 5–20. Springer-Verlag, 2005.

21. Maria Handjieva and Stanislav Tzolovski. Refining static analyses by trace-based partitioning using control flow. In *Proceedings of the 5th International Symposium on Static Analysis (SAS)*, 1998.

22. Jeffrey Fischer, Ranjit Jhala, and Rupak Majumdar. Joining dataflow with predicates. In *Proceedings of the Symposium on the Foundations of Software Engineering (FSE)*, 2005.

23. K. R. M. Leino and F. Logozzo. Loop invariants on demand. In *Proceedings of the 3rd Asian Symposium on Programming Languages and Systems (APLAS)*, 2005.

24. Stephen Adams, Thomas Ball, Manuvir Das, Sorin Lerner, Sriram K. Rajamani, Mark Seigle, and Westley Weimer. Speeding up dataflow analysis using flow-insensitive pointer analysis. In *Proceedings of the 9th International Symposium on Static Analysis (SAS)*, 2002.

25. Thomas Ball, Mayur Naik, and Sriram K. Rajamani. From symptom to cause: Localizing errors in counterexample traces. *SIGPLAN Not.*, 38(1):97–105, 2003.

26. A. Groce and W. Visser. What went wrong: Explaining counterexamples. In *SPIN Workshop on Model Checking of Software*, pages 121–135, May 2003.

27. William R. Bush, Jonathan D. Pincus, and David J. Sielaff. A static analyzer for finding dynamic programming errors. *Software - Practice and Experience*, 30(7):775–802, 2000.

28. Madanlal S. Musuvathi, David Park, Andy Chou, Dawson R Engler, and David L Dill. CMC: A pragmatic approach to model checking real code. In *Proceedings of the Fifth Symposium on Operating Systems Design and Implementation (OSDI)*, 2002.

29. Yichen Xie and Alex Aiken. Scalable error detection using boolean satisfiability. In *Proceedings of the ACM Symposium on Principles of programming Languages (POPL)*, 2005.

Author Index

Lecture Notes in Computer Science

For information about Vols. 1–4033

please contact your bookseller or Springer